Selected Writings on Aesthetics

Selected Writings on Aesthetics

Johann Gottfried Herder

TRANSLATED AND EDITED BY GREGORY MOORE

PRINCETON UNIVERSITY PRESS

PRINCETON AND OXFORD

Copyright © 2006 by Princeton University Press
Published by Princeton University Press, 41 William Street, Princeton,
New Jersey 08540
In the United Kingdom: Princeton University Press, 3 Market Place,
Woodstock, Oxfordshire OX20 1SY

LIBRARY OF CONGRESS CATALOGING-IN-PUBLICATION DATA

Herder, Johann Gottfried, 1744–1803.
    [Selections. English. 2006]
    Selected writings on aesthetics / Johann Gottfried Herder ;
translated and edited by Gregory Moore.
       p.   cm.
    Includes bibliographical references and index.
    ISBN-13: 978-0-691-11595-5 (hardcover : alk. paper)
    ISBN-10: 0-691-11595-8 (hardcover : alk. paper)
    1. Aesthetics. I. Moore, Gregory, 1972– . II. Title.
BH39.H456213 2006
111'.85—dc22   2005029475

British Library Cataloging-in-Publication Data is available

This book has been composed in Sabon

Printed on acid-free paper. ∞

pup.princeton.edu

Printed in the United States of America

10 9 8 7 6 5 4 3 2 1

CONTENTS

Acknowledgments

I thank Barry Nisbet for suggesting me for this project and for his willing and valuable advice throughout; Ian Malcolm at Princeton University Press for his help and patience; Martyn Powell, who commented on an early draft of the introduction; and Dalia Geffen for preparing and improving the manuscript. Most of all I am grateful to Bettina Bildhauer, not only for her encouragement and assistance in rendering some of Herder's occasional stylistic obscurities but for much else besides: I'm sorry.

Note on the Texts

BECAUSE HERDER WROTE widely on aesthetics—and on art and literature more generally—no single volume can pretend to be a comprehensive collection of his work in this area. At most this collection aims to introduce the English-speaking reader to what are, by common scholarly consensus, some of Herder's most important relevant writings, as well as several lesser known but no less interesting texts, and to cover as wide a range of themes as possible. Perhaps the most significant omissions here are the *Fragmente* and *Plastik* (both are already available in translation) and *Kalligone* (Herder's interesting, misguided, and unfortunately very long polemic directed against Kant's *Critique of Judgment*).

The texts are based on two German editions: *Sämtliche Werke*, edited by Bernhard Suphan (Berlin: Weidmann, 1877–1913), and *Werke*, edited by Günter Arnold et al. (Frankfurt am Main: Deutscher Klassiker Verlag, 1985–2000). In compiling my explanatory notes, I drew from the commentaries included in these editions, as well as in two other editions of Herder's writings: *Werke*, edited by Wolfgang Pross, vol. 2 (Munich: Hanser, 1987), and *Kritische Wälder*, edited by Regine Otto, 2 vols. (Berlin and Weimar: Aufbau-Verlag, 1990).

With the exception of the essay "Shakespeare," all texts included in this volume are translated into English for the first time. Several other translations of Herder's writings contain works that bear directly or indirectly on the theme of aesthetics: *Selected Early Works, 1764–1767*, translated by Ernest A. Menze, with Michael Palma (University Park: Pennsylvania State University Press, 1992), includes *Fragmente über die neuere deutsche Literatur* and several shorter writings; the long essay *Plastik* has been translated by Jason Geiger as *Sculpture* (Chicago, IL: University of Chicago Press, 2002); Michael N. Forster's collection *Philosophical Writings* (Cambridge: Cambridge University Press, 2002) includes a fragment on taste and *Essay on the Origin of Language*; F. M. Barnard's *J. G. Herder on Social and Political Culture* (Cambridge: Cambridge University Press, 1969) contains partial translations of *Journal of My Journey in the Year 1769*; there is also the rather antiquated translation by James Marsh of *The Spirit of Hebrew Poetry* (Burlington, VT: Edward Smith, 1833).

H. B. Nisbet's *German Aesthetic and Literary Criticism: Winckelmann, Lessing, Hamann, Herder, Schiller, Goethe* (Cambridge: Cambridge University Press, 1985) includes not only Herder's *Correspondence on Ossian* but also translations of important texts by various contemporaries who profoundly influenced his thought on art and literature. Winckel-mann's major writings (including his *History of Ancient Art*) have been collected as *Essays on the Philosophy and History of Art*, edited by Curtis Bowmann, 3 vols. (Bristol: Thoemmes Press, 2001). Another important contemporary influence was Moses Mendelssohn. His *Philosophische Schriften* (including his *Briefe über die Empfindungen* and *Hauptgrund-sätze der schönen Künste und Wissenschaften*) has been translated by Daniel O. Dahlstrom as *Philosophical Writings* (Cambridge: Cambridge University Press, 1997).

Recommendations for further reading can also be found in the bibliography.

Selected Writings on Aesthetics

Introduction

IN NOTES WRITTEN in 1765 bemoaning the wretched state of German literature, Johann Gottfried Herder took some comfort from the thought that though his country was devoid of "original geniuses in the realm of the ode, the drama, and the epic," he was at least living in "the philosophical century." Those nations lacking poetic inspiration and the political unity necessary for a mature literary tradition ought instead to devote themselves to developing a fuller understanding of the nature of art and the historical and cultural conditions under which it flourishes. Perhaps such a theory would enable writers to discover and mine new seams of poetic creativity. "Not *poetry*," he concluded, "but *aesthetics* should be the field of the Germans."[1]

In some ways this was already true. Despite—or perhaps because of—the painfully felt absence of a native literary culture, German critics were intensely preoccupied with new theoretical approaches to art and literature, and the mid-eighteenth century saw a number of important developments that helped shape an emergent public sphere in the German-speaking world: Johann Christoph Gottsched's attempt to impose a local version of French neoclassicism; the long-running controversy between Gottsched and the Swiss critics Johann Jakob Bodmer and Johann Jakob Breitinger, who championed English literature and criticism, and, combining Addison with Leibniz, opened poetry to the unlimited worlds of the imagination; the birth of modern art history in Johann Joachim Winckelmann's hugely influential interpretations of Greek sculpture; the critical writings of Gotthold Ephraim Lessing, Moses Mendelssohn, and Friedrich Nicolai. And perhaps most significant of all, the very term *aesthetics* was coined in 1735 by Alexander Gottlieb Baumgarten (from the Greek *aisthanesthai*, "to perceive") in his dissertation *Meditationes philosophicae*. Fifteen years later, in the first two volumes of his major work *Aesthetica* (1750–58), he went further and established aesthetics as an independent sphere of philosophical inquiry, cognate with, but separate from, the truths of logic and morality. By the 1760s this newly minted word had already become common currency, and treatises on the subject

---

[1] Herder, *Sämtliche Werke*, ed. Bernhard Suphan (Berlin: Weidmann, 1877–1913), 32:82 (hereafter *SWS*).

were growing so numerous that by 1804 Jean Paul Richter could observe: "There is nothing more abundant in our time than aestheticians."[2]

Herder was certain that although this new discipline could be decisive for the development of German literary politics in the mid-eighteenth century, and for all that he hailed Baumgarten as a new Aristotle, Baumgarten's premature death in 1762 had left his philosophical project incomplete. "O Aesthetics!" Herder exclaims with characteristic exuberance in the *Critical Forests*, his most comprehensive contribution to the subject, "in which cavern of the Muses is sleeping the young man of my philosophical nation destined to raise you to perfection!" Then in his early twenties and an ambitious though obscure clergyman in Riga awakening to the novelty of his own insights, Herder was beginning to think he might be that slumbering youth. Yet those hopes were never realized. Not only were some of his most important and original writings in this area not published during his lifetime, they were in any case soon overshadowed by Kant's *Critique of Judgment* (1790), that work which more than any other shaped the development of modern philosophical aesthetics and took it in a direction never envisaged by either Baumgarten or Herder. In later life, Herder would expend a great deal of energy in his *Metacritique* and *Kalligone* vainly seeking to refute Kant's ideas, but his early work, which shows him assimilating a great deal of contemporary thought and synthesizing it into new constellations, sheds important light on aesthetics at a crucial stage in its evolution. The writings included in this volume, although by no means exhaustive, have been chosen to reflect the extent and diversity of his writings on art and aesthetics, covering as they do such contemporary debates as the nature of aesthetics itself, the debate over classification of the arts, genius, taste and the classical tradition, the relationship between art and morality, and the fable.

Sense and Sensibility

Herder never accepted the critical turn in Kant's philosophy. The Kant he had come to know in 1762, when as a precocious eighteen-year-old he arrived from the East Prussian provinces to study at the University of Königsberg, had yet to begin his *Critique of Pure Reason*. From Kant he learned to esteem philosophical rigor and the analytic method as the only genuine path to truth. If Kant was the very embodiment of the Enlightenment intellectual, then Johann Georg Hamann, another formative influence during Herder's time at Königsberg, represented the other ex-

---

[2] Jean Paul Richter, *Vorschule der Ästhetik*, in *Werke*, ed. Norbert Miller, (Munich: Hanser, 1963), 5:22.

treme. Hamann, a deeply religious thinker who inveighed against the excesses of the eighteenth-century cult of reason, taught that the true source of knowledge was not logic and abstraction but faith and the experiences of the senses, for the outward splendor of the world, nature, and history was a living manifestation of the divine.

Herder spent most of the rest of his life striving to reconcile the opposing poles of Enlightenment thought represented by his early mentors. "A man who desires to be solely head," he once wrote, "is just as much a monster as one who desires to be only heart; the whole, healthy man is both. And that he is both, with each in its place, the heart not in the head and the head not in the heart, is precisely what makes him a human being."[3] Though many *Aufklärer* were prepared to accept the dissociation of the intellect and emotions as the price of progress, Herder most certainly was not. He strove to bridge the growing gap between the affective and rational sides of our nature, keep in check the enlightened despotism of Reason, and unleash the full potential of the human spirit. For this reason—and not only because he saw in Baumgarten's new science a means of regenerating German literature—during the 1760s and 1770s, the period from which the majority of the writings included in this volume are drawn, aesthetics played a particularly significant role in his thinking. For art activates the totality of the organism; it is produced by the cooperation of our sensuous, imaginative, and intellectual faculties, by our interaction with the world around us, and so an analysis of art will inevitably shed light on the complexities of human nature and experience. Aesthetics, Herder realized, signaled the foundation of a new philosophical anthropology.[4]

Herder was one of the few contemporaries who seemed to grasp the revolutionary implications of Baumgarten's enterprise. For aesthetics according to Baumgarten's understanding is not just a philosophy of art but also—indeed, primarily—the "science of sensuous cognition."[5] This was a bold and decisive break with tradition, because since Plato Western thought had been characterized by a profound suspicion and denigration of the senses—especially marked in the rationalist metaphysics of Christian Wolff, which had come to dominate academic philosophy in Germany. Wolff assimilated philosophy to mathematics: the only reliable

[3] *SWS* 9:504.

[4] Ernst Cassirer, *The Philosophy of the Enlightenment* (Boston: Beacon Press, 1966), p. 353.

[5] Baumgarten defines *aesthetics* in the first paragraph of the *Aesthetica* as follows: "Aesthetics (as the theory of the liberal arts, as inferior cognition, as the art of beautiful thinking and as the art of thought analogous to reason) is the science of sensuous cognition." Baumgarten's major work has not been translated into either German or English; however, an abridged version has been produced by Hans Rudolf Schweizer, entitled *Theoretische Ästhetik* (Hamburg: Meiner, 1983).

basis of knowledge was neither empirical evidence nor actual experience, but the calculable and abstract certainty of deductive proof. Establishing an explicit hierarchy among the powers of the human mind, he insisted that only the ideas present to the higher faculties of cognition—reason and the understanding—belonged to the proper domain of philosophy, for they were clear and distinct; that is, they could be analyzed, abstracted, and defined. The impressions that the senses delivered into the mind, however, were either obscure (below the threshold of full consciousness) or "confused"—that is, too concrete, fragmentary, and fleeting to be distinguishable from other objects, and hence an obstacle in the pursuit of stable, abstract truth. Although Baumgarten retained Wolff's distinction between the higher and lower faculties of cognition, for the first time he demanded that the means whereby we acquire and express sensory knowledge be subjected to systematic study. Just as logic is concerned with the operations of reason and the understanding, so a new discipline of aesthetics ought to be concerned with what we apprehend through the senses. Whereas logic arrives at clear and distinct concepts through a process of simplification and abstraction, and hence delivers an impoverished and partial perspective on the world, aesthetics exercises our capacity to grasp reality in all its concrete individuality and complexity. It celebrates the confusion of sensory knowledge, its particularity, vibrancy, and plenitude, precisely those qualities which are necessarily lost in translation from the specific to the general but embodied in exemplary fashion by works of art. Poetry, for example, which for Baumgarten was the paradigmatic form of artistic expression, does not pretend to discover universal laws or principles but lucidly represents individual things, persons, or situations, and the greater the vividness, richness, and inner diversity, the greater the value of the poem. So if logic is the means by which rational cognition is improved and human beings ascend to truth, then aesthetics aims at the perfection of sensuous knowledge; in other words, the creation or discernment of beauty. In short, Baumgarten insisted that sensuous cognition was not unreliable and inferior but possessed an intrinsic value and, in addition to the synthetic operations of pure reason, could constitute an object of serious philosophical inquiry. In fact, he argued, the logician who neglects the senses is a philosopher manqué, an incompletely developed individual unfavorably contrasted with the *felix aestheticus*, who is neither a purely rational nor a sensual being but accommodates within himself the full spectrum of human powers.

Baumgarten's writings were among the many works on poetics and aesthetics that Herder studied intensively during the mid-1760s. From the outset Herder's notes and fragmentary sketches, including a lengthy paragraph-by-paragraph discussion of the first twenty-five sections of the *Aesthetica*, show him moving ambivalently between praise and criticism, teasing out the full implications of Baumgarten's ideas and seeking to move beyond them. One of the most polished pieces from this time is the *Monument to Baumgarten*, among the earliest works included here. In it, Herder recognized Baumgarten's achievement in opening the lower faculties to philosophical scrutiny and, in doing so, shifting the focus of study from the work of art to the psychological processes underpinning the aesthetic experience. That meant that he had put to an end once and for all both the belief that poetry consisted in rhyme or melody and the Aristotelian notion that the primary purpose of poetry was the imitation of nature. As "perfectly sensuous discourse," poetry was a form of expression that stirred the soul with a multitude of vivid and interconnected images. Hence, by studying poetry and discovering the rules of beauty, we learn more about ourselves as human beings than we do about the objective world, about the mysterious alchemy by which dark, unconscious feelings are transmuted into images of perception. If, as Baumgarten claimed, the fundamental principle governing art is not mimesis but the pursuit of sensuous perfection, then it amounts to nothing less than obeying the oracular injunction "Know thyself!"

Nevertheless, Herder viewed Baumgarten as no more than a thinker of the "second rank" who never wholly freed himself from the accepted practices and assumptions of institutional philosophy. As "Wolffian poesy," Baumgarten's aesthetics is still too heavily reliant on a priori deduction and speculation; though it is concerned first and foremost with sensory cognition, paradoxically it remains couched in the arid language and framework of rationalist metaphysics. If aesthetics is, as the derivation of the word suggests, truly the study of feeling, then it must follow Winckelmann's lead, embrace Greek sensuality, and be Hellenized. The aesthetician must not build castles in the air but descend to the level of concrete sensation, to the "ground of the soul," where the most obscure ideas reside, and only then begin to erect general principles. He must replace the nominal definitions of logic with a mode of thinking that enables us to uncover the network of experience that informs our most primitive concepts and to locate the origin of those concepts in the activity of particular senses. He must, finally, be alive not only to human sensibility but also to the manner in which its expressive resources are modified by the environment, history, and culture. These ideas Herder would attempt to put into practice in the *Critical Forests*.

Critical Forests: the *First Grove*

Whereas Baumgarten wrote—already somewhat anachronistically—in a terse Latin, using the technical vocabulary of scholastic philosophy, and in short, syllogistic paragraphs, Herder, who thought it "a weakness of human nature that we wish always to construct a system,"[6] perfected a style that is essayistic, exclamatory, and digressive; he wrote quickly, sometimes clumsily, but always avoiding the appearance of a conventional scholarly work. Not for nothing did he call his first major work *Fragments*; the title of his second, *Critical Forests*, is no less apt. A "sylva" is a collection of occasional poems or miscellanies, "composed, as it were, at a Start; in a kind of Rapture or Transport,"[7] and arranged haphazardly rather than according to some overall plan. Though Herder presumably derived his title from either Martin Opitz or Christian Gryphius, both of whom produced *Poetical Forests* (in 1625 and 1698 respectively), the model for his practice as a critic is partly inspired by the very work to which the *First Grove* is devoted: Lessing's influential essay *Laocoön* (1766), which Lessing himself described as a collection of *"unordered notes."*

Both *Laocoön* and the *First Grove* are chiefly concerned with an issue that exercised a great many seventeenth- and eighteenth-century writers on art: the relation between painting and poetry, and in particular the long-established tendency to equate the poetic and visual arts. This is epitomized in the indiscriminate appeal to Horace's well-worn phrase "ut pictura poesis" (as is poetry so is painting), which was taken to mean, by Addison and later by Bodmer and Breitinger, that the aim of poetry was to excite vivid images in the mind of the reader. Graphic description was therefore the basis of poetry, and accordingly the Swiss critics were lavish in their praise of descriptive poets such as Barthold Heinrich Brockes, Albrecht von Haller, and Ewald Christian von Kleist.

Lessing bridled at this widespread talk of "poetic pictures" and the "descriptive mania" which seized modern versifiers. Though he was by no means the first to distinguish clearly between the separate domains of each art—important influences on his work include James Harris, Denis Diderot, and Moses Mendelssohn—*Laocoön* stands out for the deductive brilliance by which he arrives at the separate rules governing each art form and the unusual severity with which he draws the proper boundaries of poetry and painting. Lessing's point of departure is Winckelmann's celebrated description in *Thoughts on the Imitation of Greek Works* of the statue of the Trojan priest Laocoön and his sons, who is depicted wrestling with serpents sent by the gods to punish his disobedience. The Laocoön group embodies for Winckelmann the "noble simplicity and tranquil grandeur" of the Greek soul, which finds expression in the priest's supposed calm and self-restraint in the face of mortal danger.

---

[6] *SWS* 32:182.

[7] Ephraim Chambers, *Cyclopaedia; or, An Universal Dictionary of Arts and Sciences* (London, 1728).

Lessing accepts Winckelmann's assertion that the pain registered in Laocoön's face is not expressed with the intensity that we would expect. But he does not agree with Winckelmann's reason for claiming so, nor does he think it applies universally to all forms of Greek art. Why does the Laocoön in Virgil's *Aeneid* scream and the statue only sigh? The answer cannot lie, as Winckelmann suggests it does, in the moral superiority of the Greek over the Roman, for the heroes of Sophocles' *Philoctetes* and Homer's *Iliad* all cry out in pain and do not consider it unmanly to do so. Rather, it is a natural consequence of Winckelmann's own insight that beauty was the supreme law governing the visual arts in antiquity. To depict Laocoön with his features contorted in the act of screaming would offend the rule of beauty, for the ugliness of the scream would be frozen forever in the stone. Because the visual arts can represent only a single moment in time, the expression of the statue was toned down to a sigh in order to suggest pain and yet not impair the beauty of the human form. As poets, Virgil, Sophocles, and Homer are free to treat subjects forbidden to painters and sculptors because in poetry, where each moment is fleeting, the representation of actions rather than beauty is the highest law. Although the objective of both arts may be the same— that is, the imitation of reality—their various means for achieving this goal are entirely different. Poetry uses words that succeed one another in time to represent actions; art uses shapes and surfaces, which coexist in space, and thus depicts objects or bodies that also coexist in space. At bottom, poetry and art are distinguished by the types of signs they employ. A natural sign, like the shapes and colors employed by figurative sculpture and painting, resembles the object it represents. An arbitrary sign has no necessary connection, only a conventional one, with its object, and all language consists of tokens based on such contingent agreements. Now, since the aim of all art according to Lessing's mimetic theory is to present the imitated object to the intuitive cognition of the recipient in as direct a manner as possible, it follows that poetry must endeavor by all possible means to transform its arbitrary signs into natural ones. That is, poetry must be as concrete and immediate as possible, dispensing with abstractions, restricting itself to depicting only actions, and refraining from describing bodies. Lessing therefore establishes clear borders separating painting and poetry, which enables him to outlaw any instance of one trespassing on the other's territory: excessively descriptive poetry, for example, or allegorical and historical painting. But such clarity comes at the expense of diminishing their respective domains, and it is this narrowness and simplicity which Herder wants to challenge.

Herder had been fascinated with *Laocoön* since its publication in 1766, when, he confessed to his friend Johann Georg Scheffner, he read it through three times in a single sitting.[8] Two years later, in 1768, Herder saw that Lessing's attempt to derive the essential characteristics of the visual arts and poetry from their differences offered him the opportunity to formulate his own ideas about the nature of poetry and language and to test them against those of Lessing. As a number of critics have observed, the *First Grove* stands in the same relationship to *Laocoön* as Lessing's work stands to Winckelmann. It is, as Herder was at pains to point out in a deferential letter to Lessing, and as the many warm and respectful remarks in the work make clear, neither a critique nor a refutation of his predecessor. He agreed with Lessing that it was possible to establish a classification of the arts based on the various signs they employ to achieve their effect, but he aimed to elaborate and expand the practical and theoretical applications of Lessing's conclusions from the deliberately simplified and one-sided treatment they received in *Laocoön*.

The first eight sections of the *First Grove* are devoted to a minutely detailed examination of the first six chapters of *Laocoön*. Herder returns to the original sources that Lessing cites in support of his arguments, tests his claims, questions his interpretations of his sources, and shows no sign of hurry in wanting to inspect the main theoretical portions of *Laocoön*. It is tempting to dismiss these antiquarian excursions on the tears of Greek heroes, on why Bacchus was represented with horns, on the stature of the Homeric gods, and so on, as hairsplitting, as precisely the kind of schoolmasterly pedantry that Herder was only too ready to condemn in others. But this would be unfair, for these animadversions have a strategic purpose. For a start, this somewhat circuitous and leisurely journey to the heart of *Laocoön*, with Herder sometimes tracing Lessing's steps and arriving at different conclusions, sometimes reaching the same destination by another route, and sometimes getting lost entirely, is precisely in keeping with the ambling and idling character of a critical *sylva*. What is more, the early chapters of Herder's work are designed to reveal a fundamental difference in approach between both men: where Lessing was content to simplify and generalize for the sake of economy, Herder broadens the inquiry, calling attention not only to Lessing's alleged misreadings of sources but marshaling a great deal of additional evidence also. Where Lessing tends to argue deductively, Herder prefers inductively to review the facts before reaching a conclusion and insists on taking into account the historical and cultural determinants of even the most apparently straightforward and incontestable of Lessing's initial assumptions. Is a cry really the natural expression of physical pain, or is pain expressed differently in different societies and in different epochs? And what value was attached

---

[8] Herder, *Briefe*, ed. Wilhelm Dobbek and Günter Arnold (Weimar: Böhlaus Nachfolger, 1977–2004), 1:62.

to such utterances in these various cultures? Was beauty really the supreme law of the ancients? But when? For how long? And under what conditions?

Herder chooses to begin his constructive criticism of Lessing's differentiation of the arts by calling into question his precept that because visual art can represent only a single moment in time, it is barred from representing anything transitory because repeated viewing will cause disgust in the recipient at the object thereby rendered unnatural. By itself this principle is insufficient to explain the modes of representation of the arts, for impermanence belongs to the fundamental nature of the world, and any figure engaged in any action is unnaturally prolonged by art. But if art cannot imitate truthfully, Herder reasons, then its very essence is destroyed and the question of the limits between painting and poetry becomes meaningless. Therefore the reason why painting is restricted to a single moment must lie not in the viewer's subjective response to what it depicts but in the very nature of visual art itself. To clarify Lessing's own train of thought, Herder borrows the distinction between work and energy (*ergon* and *energeia*) first made by Aristotle in the *Nicomachean Ethics* and then taken up and applied to art by James Harris (1709–1780) in his *Three Treatises*, which had appeared in German translation in 1756. For Harris and thus for Herder, an energy is "every *Production*, the *Parts of which exist successively*, and *whose Nature hath its being or Essence in a Transition*." An energetic art operates through time. It does not deliver a completed object that can be surveyed at once; rather, its effect lies precisely in a succession of moments because each moment is effective only as a link in this chain. A "work," on the other hand, is "every *Production*, whose *Parts exist all at once*."[9] Its essence consists not in change, in the succession of its constituent parts, but rather in their coexistence: the totality of the whole can be immediately and instantaneously apprehended at a single glance. In that glance, time is as it were suspended; we are removed from the transience of the world and enfolded in the beautiful illusion created by the artist.

So Herder is able to propose this fundamental distinction: there are those arts which deliver a work (painting and sculpture), and there are "energetic" arts (music, dance, poetry). But this simple division is not sufficiently fine, for it does not bring out the obvious differences between music and poetry, for example, both of which operate energetically and successively. In fact, in one respect music has more in common with painting than it does with poetry, for both music and the visual arts employ natural signs. What is more, these two arts depend for their effect on the

---

[9] Harris, *Three Treatises: The First Concerning Art, the Second Concerning Music, Painting and Poetry, the Third Concerning Happiness* (London, 1744), p. 33.

characteristic distribution of these signs: in music the notes unfold in time, and in painting the colors and shapes coexist in space. So for all their differences, there is nevertheless a basis on which these arts can be fruitfully compared. But the case of poetry is different. It cannot be compared with painting (or music) in terms of the particular configuration of its signs. For unlike music (an art that Lessing chooses to neglect entirely), poetry is more than a simple sequence of sounds: its successive quality is certainly a necessary condition but not a sufficient one of its effect. In fact, what differentiates poetry from the other arts is that its essence is not exhausted by the merely musical and material properties of its signs. Its signs are not natural but arbitrary: words can express abstract meanings precisely because their significance is not determined solely by their sensuous form. The poet, then, by virtue of the arbitrariness of his signs, has more freedom, a greater range of representational possibilities than the artist—a point that Lessing does not fully exploit precisely because he ignores music and simplifies the issue by concentrating solely on poetic and visual art.[10]

But how do the signs of poetry acquire their meaning, and how is this meaning conveyed to the reader or listener if not through their merely spatial or temporal arrangement? Herder's answer is what he calls force, and this force—not time or space, coexistence or succession—constitutes the essence of poetry. Herder never bothers to explain exactly what he means by this term, but it seems that he saw this force as analogous to those operative in the natural world: as one kind of force is responsible for charging a storm cloud with electricity and discharging it through lightning, so another is the mechanism by which words are invested with meaning and that meaning communicated to a reader or listener.

The concept of force allows Herder to reopen the ground for the comparison of painting and poetry which Lessing had declared out of bounds, yet at the same time to retain the contrast between the obviously different ways in which they produce their effect. On the one hand, poetry is different from painting inasmuch as it is an energetic art and does not deliver a work. But it is like painting because, even though its signs are successive, they are able to conjure images of spatial objects before the imagination by virtue of the abstract meaning they contain (and without recourse to the artistic devices that Lessing claims to find in Homer), just as painting delivers a picture to our eyes through colors and figures. The subject of poetry is not confined to actions, as Lessing suggests, a position to which he is forced both by his insistence on mere succession as its

[10] That said, there are other, more important reasons why Lessing does not do so; for example, he does not want to be pushed into defending didactic poetry and so on, which deal in abstractions.

essence and by his excessively narrow and doctrinaire definition of what constitutes poetry. In his desire to exclude the "descriptive mania" of modern poets, he goes too far, banishing the idyll, the ode, the lyric, from the realm of the poetic in favor of the epic, the only genre (along with drama) that might be said to be concerned primarily with actions. By contrast, Herder believes he has arrived at a more moderate and plausible account of the operations of poetry and its relation to the other arts.

So Herder distinguishes three types of arts: the plastic arts, which deliver a work and operate in or through space; the energetic or successive arts, which unfold in time; and poetry, which produces its effect through "force." Like Lessing's, Herder's ulterior motive is to reassert the supremacy of poetry over other arts; but rather than radically delimit the boundaries of the poetic and effectively narrow its domain, Herder suggests that it is superior because it both shares territory with painting and music, and has a realm all to itself. But already by the time he came to write the *Fourth Grove*, Herder realized that this semiotic theory needed to be supplemented by a more nuanced one that foregrounds the relation of the arts to particular senses.

The *Fourth Grove*

Herder's *Fourth Grove* is arguably his most important and fundamental work on aesthetics, a work that, had it ever been published in his lifetime, might, in the opinion of Robert T. Clark, "have changed the entire course of German aesthetics."[11] Regardless of whether this claim is true or not, it is certain than when the work finally appeared in 1846, the current had shifted in philosophical aesthetics, and Herder's attempt, building on the typology of the arts he had sketched in the *First Grove*, to derive the modes of representation particular to each art from the manner in which they are perceived had ceased to have any immediate relevance. As with the earlier *Grove*, Herder developed his ideas through critical dialogue with other thinkers. But the respectful tone with which he had sought to expand Lessing's ideas gives way in the *Fourth Grove* to withering contempt and sarcasm. The objects of his opprobrium are Friedrich Just Riedel (1742–1785), professor of philosophy at Erfurt, and, to a lesser extent, Riedel's mentor Christian Adolf Klotz (1738–1771), professor of rhetoric at Halle and the victim of Herder's abuse in the *Second* and *Third Grove*. The intemperate tenor of Herder's philippics is partly the consequence of the lingering resentment he felt at the underhand behavior of

---

[11] Clark, *Herder: His Life and Thought* (Berkeley: University of California Press, 1955), p. 88.

both men in connection with the second edition of the first collection of *Fragments*: Riedel had quoted from the then unpublished work in his *On the Public*, and, at the beginning of 1769, Klotz reviewed the volume on the basis of a copy obtained from the printer by illicit means. But Herder's opposition to Riedel did not stem just from a personal grudge. Riedel was also the author of *Theory of the Beaux Arts and Belles Lettres* (1767), a work that along with his *On the Public*, was in Herder's view so utterly misconceived that it presented him with an irresistible opportunity to elucidate his own ideas about the proper form that an aesthetics should take.

In Herder's view Riedel's theory represents a particularly egregious example of what he calls an "aesthetics from above." That is, he combines, like Baumgarten, a number of already familiar and untested ideas to construct a system on a purely deductive basis, starting where he ought to have ended up, with the most abstract or general concepts. For example, Riedel argues that beauty—like the good, like truth—is an innate, entirely subjective, and ultimately indefinable notion that is communicated to the mind without the intervention of conscious thought. We are immediately and unreflectively "convinced" of that which is true or false, good or bad, beautiful or ugly, by virtue of certain "inner feelings" or fundamental faculties: the *sensus communis*, conscience, and taste. These, Riedel declares, are the basic categories of the human mind through which we apprehend the world. In the first part of the *Fourth Grove*, Herder is eloquently contemptuous of this naive psychology. There is, he insists, no such thing as immediate conviction; no sensation could be conveyed into the mind without passing through some reflective process. Herder shows, by constructing a developmental history of the mind, that from our earliest childhood the act of perception is always supported by the understanding, always involves judgment; the soul combines, differentiates, and compares the flood of impressions relayed by the senses, and these, over time, congeal and are then overlaid with new judgments, ultimately forming concepts. Habit has obscured these individual operations of our consciousness so that they have become second nature, so that what we take to be a simple, immediate act of cognition is in reality the product of a complex procedure of which we are no longer consciously aware. The task of philosophy—and in this particular instance, aesthetics—as Herder sees it, is precisely to undo the work of habit, to scrape away the sediment that has accreted around our concepts so that we can follow the inferential steps in their gradual evolution.

Another salvo is aimed at Baumgarten himself. Though in the *Fourth Grove* Herder generally speaks warmly of the author of the *Aesthetica*, defending him against his detractors such as Riedel, he censures Baumgarten for including in his definition of aesthetics the phrase the "art of thinking beautifully" (*ars pulchre cogitandi*). This implies that aesthetics should instruct or guide artistic activity by supplying a system of rules for connoisseurs or virtuosi. But that is not the concern of aesthetics. Herder draws a clear line between the theory and the practice of our innate aesthetic powers, between the artist or man of taste and the philosopher, between the production or appreciation of beauty and its systematic study. Aesthetics must remain a rigorously descriptive discipline, a science, and as such it proceeds on the basis of analysis, proofs, and argument rather than through intuition. Where the artist embraces the pleasure of the confused sensation of the beautiful, the philosopher coolly examines this feeling in order to discover the hidden laws of human psychology, takes apart our sensuous concepts, renders them distinct, and resolves beauty into truth.

The second part of the *Fourth Grove* represents Herder's attempt to apply the principles he had defined in the first part of the treatise; though the work does not represent a complete, fully worked out theory of art, Herder intends his argument to exemplify the notion of an "aesthetics from below" in which abstract concepts such as beauty, sublimity, and grandeur are traced back to their origins in our experience. By undertaking what he calls a "physiology of the senses," Herder hopes not only to reveal how each of the three higher senses—sight, hearing, and touch— shapes our perception of the world and of aesthetic objects in particular, but also, by building on the typology he had elaborated in the *First Grove*, to offer yet another means of distinguishing the arts: by relating their different modes of representation to the particular ways in which we perceive them. Only by such a procedure, he believes, can we both recognize and account for the distinctive forms of beauty produced by painting, sculpture, and music.

In the philosophical history of the senses, sight has always seemed self-evidently the most important and refined one, and this was especially true in the age of reason. In his *Essays on the Pleasures of the Imagination* (1709), Joseph Addison was typical in describing sight as "the most perfect and most delightful of all senses."[12] Vision delivers the external world in the most direct and objective way. Enlightenment, one might say, consists in opening one's eyes and believing what one sees rather than placing one's faith in illusion and superstition. Though Herder does acknowledge that vision is the "most philosophical sense," that its objects are the clearest, he sets himself against the dominant visualism of his age. By itself, Herder claims—building on ideas first expressed by Diderot and Condillac and drawing on well-known case studies of blind individuals such as the mathematician Nicolas Saunderson—sight delivers only an incomplete, two-dimensional picture of the world consisting of planes, colors,

---

[12] Addison, *Works* (New York: Putnam, 1856), 6:322.

contours, and degrees of light and shadow. The eye glides off surfaces; we are mere observers without any contact with the objects around us. Only touch furnishes us with ideas of space, extension, and solidity; it is through the hand that we truly grasp the world in all senses of that word, by enabling us to perceive objects in three-dimensional space. Indeed, vision is a relative newcomer. Feeling is the first of our senses to develop, our original mode of perception, and the one that delivers the earliest and most certain knowledge not only of the world but of ourselves as sentient beings. Consciousness of our own existence as subjects is—as it is for Descartes—rooted not in the self-awareness of a disembodied intelligence but in the intuitive immediacy of sensation. As Herder puts it—subtly rewording the Cartesian cogito—in "On the Sense of Touch," an unpublished fragment written around this time, "I feel! I am!"

That we think we see the world in three dimensions is due to the fact that no sense works alone. The mind coordinates and orders them into a system, constantly analyzing, comparing, and synthesizing the impressions they communicate, so that when we learn concepts of distance and volume, for example, we automatically integrate them into our visual, planar representation of the world. Hence we see what originally we could only have felt. Only habit obscures this connection between the senses and encourages us to downplay the role of touch in the formation of our knowledge of the world and denigrate that sense as "coarse." Sight may indeed be a more recent evolution and a refined form of sensory perception, but it is also a secondary, inauthentic feeling, an irresponsible extension of touch forgetful of and unfaithful to its foundation. Where sight is swift, cold, and superficial, touch is slow, thorough, and intimate. Though Herder pleads for a reevaluation of the sense of touch, he does not demand that it be restored to its original rights. His aim—at least in the *Fourth Grove*—is rather more modest: to investigate the significance of this understanding of touch for aesthetics, to return to the hand those aspects of aesthetic perception which the eye has arrogated to itself.

In the *First Grove* Herder followed Lessing in choosing not to distinguish between painting and sculpture; both were lumped together as visual arts dependent for their effect on natural, coexistent signs. But there are obvious differences between the two, and Herder now possesses the theoretical framework to do justice to these differences. What separates sculpture from painting (or any other art of design), he now points out, is that a statue is a three-dimensional body in space, whereas a picture consists of shapes and colors juxtaposed on a flat canvas or panel. In other words, a painting is an object of sight and sculpture an object of touch; each is perceived by and addressed to a different sense, and it is in this that their fundamental difference consists. Thus where painterly beauty consists in the pleasing arrangement of lines and colors on a surface, sculptural beauty resides in graceful form. Yet it is important to recognize that Herder does not mean to suggest that we best appreciate sculptural form by groping the marble with our eyes shut. Rather, the psychology of the aesthetic state here is a complex operation involving both vision and touch, a heightened form of the perceptual processes underpinning our relationships with everyday objects in the world. A painting can be viewed only from a single point of view. A statue, however, is a body inhabiting space; we must walk around it and inspect it from multiple perspectives. Though sight alone must thereby necessarily reduce the statue to a polygon, a grid of planes and angles, the mind imaginatively recuperates the three-dimensionality of the object on the basis of ideas such as mass and extension originally furnished by touch. Herder therefore speaks figuratively of the eye being transformed into a hand as it follows the elliptical line that describes the beautiful roundedness of the corporeal whole, and here his understanding of the connoisseur's relation to plastic art deliberately recalls Winckelmann's erotically charged descriptions in *Description of the Torso in Belvedere in Rome*. The theory of the interaction between sight and feeling also allows him to account for the development of specific techniques in painting and sculpture, such as perspectival painting and colossal statuary.

In addition to sculpture, Herder discusses in some detail another art form he had all but ignored in the *First Grove*: music. Music is related to the third sense on which he bases his systematic aesthetics, hearing, which Herder describes as the most profound of the three main senses. Where the objects of sight lie outside us, arranged side by side, the objects of hearing seem to lie deep within us and appear successively; because of their interiority, they possess the power to move the soul directly. In the several sections that he devotes to the "fine art of hearing," Herder is concerned to construct a new foundation for musical aesthetics, which leads him to polemicize against the dominant acoustical and mathematical paradigms of pioneering musicologists such as Rameau and d'Alembert (for they explain nothing about the subjective nature of musical experience). The true task of aesthetics must be to understand how music affects the psychological state of the listener. Accordingly, Herder insists on a sharp distinction between tone—the simple elements of music—and sound—a larger aggregate of tones. Whether it be a chord produced by simultaneously striking notes in a regular harmonic series or a discordant noise generated by depressing random keys on a piano, sound affects only the sense organs of hearing: the outer ear, the auditory nerves, and so on. Only tone, Herder claims, yields an "inner feeling" and operates directly on the soul. This is because, as he explains, looking forward to the prizewinning *Essay on the Origin of Language* (1771), music originated as a kind of intensified speech, as a language designed to communicate sentiment. As such,

Herder—like Rousseau before him—flatly denies that musical beauty is expressed through harmony or polyphony (since the latter depends on the temporal coexistence of sounds); only melody, which consists of tones in succession, manifests the beautiful in music and must therefore be the basis of a properly scientific understanding of it.

Herder did not intend the *Fourth Grove* to be a complete system; he claimed to be offering only "ideas and lineaments" for a theory of the beautiful. This is especially obvious in the rather perfunctory discussions of art forms other than music, painting, and sculpture, which relate most obviously to a particular sense. Nevertheless, he does not ignore them entirely. Thus, he is able to accommodate dance by describing it, in a phrase borrowed from John Brown, as "music made visible"; but architecture and landscape gardening find no place in his theory and are dismissed as merely mechanical arts. Briefest of all is his treatment of poetry, which nevertheless retains the special status it was granted in the *First Grove*. There, poetry was different from the other arts because the signs it employs bear no natural relationship to the things they signify; here, its uniqueness resides in the fact that it has no relationship to a specific sense and that sense's necessarily limited apprehension of the world. Rather, poetry is the only art addressed directly to the imagination and hence is able to draw on every sense and every other art form, combining tones, images, and feelings in its discourse.

Ultimately, Herder's truly original ideas toward a philosophical aesthetics collapse under the weight of the polemics heaped on the hapless Riedel. At the end of the *Fourth Grove*, Herder regrets his vituperative tone, for it has overwhelmed his original contribution to aesthetics; and in his *Journal of My Travels in 1769*, written shortly after completing the *Fourth Grove*, when he fled the intellectual confines of provincial Riga for France, he complained that he had wasted his recent years on "critical, useless, crude, and wretched forests."[13] Though he acknowledged that the demolition of unsound theoretical edifices such as Riedel's was necessary for the construction of new ones, Herder's frustration and weariness are probably some of the reasons the *Fourth Grove* never saw the light of day during his lifetime. Furthermore, though he certainly recognized the importance of his ideas about the sense of touch, his awareness of the extent of the task facing him, which he recorded in his *Journal*, may have contributed to his reluctance to publish the *Fourth Grove* as it stood. Nevertheless, he continued to work on the ideas developed therein, producing a number of sketches that culminated in the first draft of *Plastic Art* in 1770, finally published, after significant revision, in 1778. When that essay appeared, incorporating significant amounts of material originally

[13] *SWS* 4:363.

used in the *Fourth Grove* (and hence not included here), Herder presumably regarded the earlier polemic as obsolete. But that does not mean that he abandoned the problem of the differentiation of the arts altogether. A later and lighthearted dialogue, *Does Painting or Music Have a Greater Effect?*, returns to the same issue.

Shakespeare and Genius

When Herder arrived in Strassburg in 1770 to undergo what would turn out to be a complicated and painful eye operation, he had, after a year or so spent in Nantes and Paris, grown weary of French culture and literature. Confined to his room, he threw himself into an enthusiastic study of Ossian and Shakespeare and encouraged others to do the same—among them his future wife, Caroline Flachsland, and his new friend Goethe. The rude vigor of Ossianic and Shakespearean poetry, it seemed to Herder, was poles apart from the mannered artfulness of French literature or the anemic German imitations thereof advocated by literary reformers such as Gottsched. Like Homer, like the poets of the Old Testament, these northern European poets were unconstrained by rules or literary conventions and could therefore, Herder realized, serve as models to regenerate German letters.

These intuitions were by no means uncommon in the eighteenth century. Like that of many young Germans, Herder's response to Shakespeare owed a great deal to Edward Young's *Conjectures on Original Composition* (1759), which was published in two separate German translations in 1760. Young's work did much to popularize in Germany the new artistic concept of genius, which had become fundamental to French and especially British critical discourse during the early and mid-eighteenth century. For Young (and for Shaftesbury) the genius was a second Creator, a Promethean figure who imitated not the ancients or other writers but only nature. Rather than be guided by elegance and learning, the genius created intuitively, immediately, and through God-given powers. His activity was not mechanical and artificial but organic and natural: "An *Original* may said to be of a *vegetable* nature; it rises spontaneously from the vital root of Genius; it *grows*, it is not *made*."[14] Inevitably, Shakespeare was for Young—as he was already for Joseph Addison—the prototype of an original genius who had no call for the rules of neoclassicism (which, "like Crutches, are a needful aid to the lame, tho' an impediment to the strong"), and it was as such that through Young's mediation he came to be regarded in Germany, though Wieland's idiosyncratic translations of

---

[14] Edward Young, *Conjectures on Original Composition* (London: Dodsley, 1759), p. 12.

twenty-two Shakespearean dramas into prose between 1762 and 1766 also helped to underscore his apparently wild and exuberant style.

Not until 1773 was Herder, by now court preacher in Bückeburg, able to refine his thoughts on Shakespeare and genius, in an eponymous essay included in *On German Art and Character*, a collection compiled by Herder himself and often described as the manifesto of the Sturm und Drang movement of the 1770s. Herder's *Shakespeare* is a milestone in the history of literary theory, showcasing the historical-genetic approach to cultural artifacts that he developed as a counterweight to the normative injunctions of Enlightenment aesthetics. Herder rejects as flawed the contemporary dispute between Shakespeare's champions (such as Lessing) and detractors (for example, Voltaire) because, regardless of whether they heap praise or mockery on him, both parties take as their starting point and criteria for judging him the very conventions that Shakespeare quite evidently disregards. Instead, Herder wants to show *why* Shakespeare could not be bound by neoclassical rules and hence *why* he can serve as a new, freer model for modern European drama. Herder seeks to account for Shakespeare, to understand him, to enter into emotional dialogue with him, and thereby to "bring him to life for us Germans."

This is possible only on the basis of a proper understanding of the historical and cultural context within which art and genius emerge. Though poetic inspiration is universal, the manner in which it is expressed is not. By comparing Greek tragedy (as typified by Sophocles) and the northern European drama of Shakespeare, Herder shows that each emerged under vastly different environmental conditions and from different antecedents; because each was shaped by different social, political, and material forces, they could not but be different and guided by different rules. Greek tragedy evolved from the preexisting dithyramb and chorus, taking as its subject matter simple mythical events that gradually became more complicated through the introduction of a more intricate plot. The classical unities of time, place, and action, which Aristotle merely "discovered" rather than proclaimed *ex cathedra*, were no arbitrary imposition on the creative artist; they were an entirely natural and necessary product of the simplicity of Greek life and character. To attempt to replicate Sophoclean tragedy, or to apply its rules, in the entirely different milieu of seventeenth- and eighteenth-century France amounted to a refusal to acknowledge the historical and cultural specificity of Greek drama, and as such was not only absurd but harmful. The plays of Voltaire and Corneille are true neither to their own time nor to that of the Greeks from which they purport to derive their legitimacy; they are but an elegant and decorous parody of the originals, mere simulacra lacking the soul, the living spirit of the original. Shakespeare, by contrast, reflects his own historical reality. The greater complexity and diversity of social life in early

modernity are manifested in the sheer variety of events, times, locali-
ties, and characters in his plays, precisely those features which seemed
to men like Gottsched to offend against the proprieties of dramatic art.
Where Sophoclean drama, born of myth, remained abstract and universal, Shakespeare's theater, the roots of which lie in the popular history plays of the Renaissance, discloses his world in all its vibrancy and
individuality.

But although Sophocles and Shakespeare may be outwardly dissimilar,
they have a spiritual kinship that all artistic geniuses share: they are true
not only to nature (as Young argued) but also to the popular culture from
which they emerged (which is Herder's decisive contribution to the concept of genius). Both are mouthpieces of their nation's collective genius,
expressing its thoughts and sentiments, manners and morals; in each case
their art is a development of traditional modes of expression. Though
their purpose is the same, their means are necessarily different. Yet each
dramatic form has its own legitimacy, and—this is the crux of Herder's
argument—so might any other literature that is unfettered and loyal to
its national character. Hence Herder's concluding apostrophe to Goethe,
whose first major success, the Shakespeare-inspired drama *Götz von
Berlichingen*, which is set in medieval Germany, put into practice Herder's
ideas and heralded a new literature rooted in native traditions and forms.

But there is more to it. As the expression of popular culture, the genius
is also part of the very mechanism of the universe. In *Yet Another Philosophy of History*, which was published in 1774, Herder views history as
an apparently aimless process whose plan is inscrutable and known only
to God. He repeatedly compares history to a mighty drama in which props
and players are moved about on a universal stage so that the great dramatist's purpose may be achieved, even if the characters are only dimly aware
of it. In *Shakespeare*, Herder reverses this analogy and suggests that
Shakespeare dramatizes history, but not just in the ordinary sense of writing historical plays. The poet is a creator in miniature, a mediator between
the world and God, whose work is akin to Revelation. By making history
live again, by reconstructing and reproducing its modes of operation, by
re-creating the divine plan on the stage, Shakespeare enables humanity to
glimpse the workings of God in nature.

Taste

When Herder returned to the concept of genius a few years later, he had
grown tired of the excesses of the *Stürmer und Dränger*, and his tone was
altogether cooler and more sober. The essay *On the Causes of Sunken
Taste* was written in 1774 in response to a competition on that subject an-

nounced by the Berlin Academy of Sciences and Letters, and much to the surprise of Herder, who dismissed his work as a "belletristic school exercise,"[15] he was duly awarded the prize in 1775—something of a sensation, for just four years previously his *Essay on the Origin of Language* had been honored by the same academy. Though it was not the first time Herder had concerned himself with the problem of taste—he discusses the problem in *Is the Beauty of the Body a Herald of the Beauty of the Soul?* and in the *Fourth Grove*—this essay shows him wrestling with a question fundamental to eighteenth-century aesthetics: what is the relation between genius and taste?

The modern concept of taste first emerged through the writings of Baltasar Gracián.[16] He and almost every relevant thinker up to the first quarter of the eighteenth century used the term *taste* to designate the means by which one could lead a graceful and exemplary life. For Christian Thomasius, who introduced the term *bon goût* into German in 1687, the man of taste, as opposed to the pedant or *homme galant*, showed discrimination in the affairs of everyday life; he did not slavishly follow fashion or cultivate an air of idiosyncrasy but rather demonstrated decorum, elegance, and self-confidence. Already in the late seventeenth century, French thinkers such as Dominique Bouhours were occasionally linking taste to discussions of art, but in Germany it was not systematically employed as an aesthetic category until 1727, the year in which both Johann Ulrich König's *Inquiry into Good Taste in Poetry and Rhetoric* and Bodmer's *Letters on the Nature of Good Taste* were published. For both writers taste signified a kind of instinctive or intuitive judgment, independent of but nevertheless ultimately in accord with reason, which teaches us to "esteem that which . . . reason would infallibly have approved if it had had the time to examine it sufficiently" and by virtue of which it is thus the "leader and steward of the other noble powers of the human soul."[17] Though taste was inevitably subject to local variations among different peoples, it was nevertheless deemed to be universal, and as such a standard by which the value of works of art could be measured and rules governing the artist deduced. Good taste in art was, naturally enough, reasonable, balanced, measured; and bad or corrupt taste pedantic, emotional, immoderate. These virtues were best embodied by the art of the ancients and the polite literature of the day.

But already by the middle of the century the concept of taste was being challenged. In his *Discours sur les sciences et les arts* (1750), Rousseau

---

[15] Herder to Johann Georg Hamann, 18 June 1776, *Briefe* 3:193.

[16] Franz Schümmer, "Die Entwicklung des Geschmackbegriffs in der Philosophie des 17/18 Jahrhundert," *Archiv für Begriffsgeschichte* 1 (1955): 120–41.

[17] König, *Untersuchung von dem guten Geschmack in der Dicht- und Rede-Kunst. Anhang zu: Des Freyherrn v. Canitz' Gedichte* (Leipzig, 1727), p. 261.

cast doubt on the moral and political value of the cultivation of taste. Taste was also beginning to be seen as derivative, learned, and inferior compared with the natural gifts of genius; this is evident as early as 1757 in Diderot's article on genius in the *Encyclopédie*. Soon Young would echo these sentiments, followed of course by Herder himself. By the 1770s, as the Sturm und Drang movement gathered pace, these ideas had become widespread. The worship of genius meant also a one-sided celebration of "feeling," and the denigration of taste signaled a rejection of the rational culture (*Verstandeskultur*) of French neoclassicism and the Enlightenment. At the very moment when it was about to be swept away and rendered obsolete by the proto-Romantic trends in European thought, we find Herder unexpectedly fighting a rearguard action and attempting, in one of the last major works devoted to the topic in European letters, to salvage the concept of taste, to reclaim it as a means of safeguarding the equilibrium of human powers.

These developments explain why Herder begins his treatise by discussing the relation of taste to genius, reason, and virtue. The antagonisms that his contemporaries claim to find between these categories, he argues, neither exist nor are the causes of the corruption of taste. Or rather, if such oppositions do obtain, they are pathological developments, which is why Herder suggests that a historical approach to the problem is superior to the "psychological" method preferred by his unnamed opponents. Taste, he claims, is no barrier to genius. It is in fact nothing more than the order and harmonious arrangement of the sensuous powers of genius, a necessary restraint that gives direction to unruly creative impulses. If Herder had insisted before on the sovereignty of the self-legislating artist, now he is just as adamant that the intuitive and untutored expression of genius is insufficient to bring forth works of lasting value. The Egyptians possessed genius but not taste—hence their monstrous and unrefined art; only in Greece was genius first harnessed productively by taste. Even Shakespeare, Herder now concedes, was guided by taste and by rules—even if they were his own, not the inherited and stultifying precepts of another age. Similarly, reason as such is not opposed to taste, which breathes life into the brittle and arid structures of the intellect. Only when genius is exercised in conjunction with what Herder calls true reason does that order of our instinctive powers arise which constitutes taste. Only the misuse of reason, only pedantry and irrationality can ever corrupt taste. Finally, taste and virtue overlap but are not identical: taste is the order of our sensuous nature, but virtue is the equilibrium of *all* the powers of the mind. That means that while those states in which the finest taste flourished are not the most virtuous, where morals are thoroughly depraved so too will taste be. Good taste can become the model of virtue, or at least of decency, but there is no more intimate connection between the two.

In the historical section of the treatise Herder adopts the traditional French scheme according to which there were four ages of good taste: Attic Greece, Augustan Rome, the Renaissance, and the reign of Louis XIV, the latter supposedly the apogee of *bon goût*. But Herder makes significant revisions to this view of European history. For a start, he sees the corruption of taste not as an avoidable aberration but as a natural and necessary process: its causes become clear only when one has identified the historical conditions under which it emerged and prospered. When the unique constellation of physical and cultural factors giving rise to a nation's taste ceases to operate, then taste declines. Herder also reevaluates the conventional estimations of the different ages of good taste. Only in Greece was taste an entirely natural phenomenon, a "flower"; only Greek culture developed a national spirit through the participation of the public or people, and not from the patronage of powerful rulers, whose influence Herder generally views with profound suspicion. With the slide into tyranny under the caesars, those literary genres native to Roman culture, which embodied the democratic virtues of the Republic, namely oratory and history, were uprooted before they could bear fruit. Augustan civilization was an ephemeral hothouse flower, an exotic, foreign species transplanted to Rome for the purposes of political spectacle and legitimacy. The Medici and Louis XIV also presided over learned cultures that sacrificed indigenous and popular expression to the cult of imitation, encouraging works that were accessible only to an educated elite and therefore sprang up with the seeds of their decline within them from the start. Typically and unsurprisingly, Voltaire's *siècle de Louis XIV* is for Herder the most precarious rather than most perfect of all the periods under review. His aim, then, is to show that good taste in Europe has, at least since the Hellenic age, always been a superficial and short-lived phenomenon, choked at each turn by the weeds of despotism and luxury. The Greeks prove that political freedom and the flowering of taste go hand in hand.

But Herder does not dismiss outright the mannered and uncouth chapters in the history of taste. The obscure and fustian style of a Persius or Tacitus; the degeneracy of Latin occasioned by the spread of Christianity and the barbarian invasions; the forced imitation of the ancients during the Italian Renaissance—these lapses in and errors of taste may show how far we have traveled from the harmony enjoyed by the ancients, but they are merely staging posts in the historical evolution of humanity. The natural forces that brought forth genius in one land will do so again in another, and once there is genius, taste is sure to follow; Herder holds out the prospect that beneath the rubble of modern ideas, Germany is working toward "an age of *exalted philosophical taste.*" But if an enduring age of taste is ever to come about, we as human beings must act as midwives to Nature's geniuses; we must create the conditions under which taste can thrive. And that is possible only through education. Taste shall be cultivated not only by studying the ancients and the liberal arts but by freeing it from fashion and the dictates of the court. Thus liberated, taste shall help to usher in an age of *Humanität*.

Aesthetic Education

Herder's ideas on the moral and pedagogical dimensions of the experience of beauty can be found scattered throughout his writings in one form or another, and they are developed further in another prizewinning essay, *On the Influence of the Belles Lettres on the Higher Sciences*, which might be seen as a kind of companion piece to the essay on taste. But his conviction that art has a role to play in education should not be interpreted as advocating narrow didacticism. Just as he rejected the "top-down" approach in aesthetics practiced by lazy thinkers such as Riedel, preferring to start from the evidence of the senses rather than nominal definitions and unquestioned general concepts, so he thought that the cultivation of young minds should not be entrusted to grammarians who suffocate their charges with high-flown theories and arid speculation. Instead, Herder demanded that education have as its goal the production of a balanced human being whose sensuous and intellectual powers interoperate in perfect harmony.

In some ways, Herder's ideal here is reminiscent of Baumgarten's *felix aestheticus*, a figure who successfully combines a love of the sensory world with rational cognition. Yet even Baumgarten himself, Herder points out in his early essay on that philosopher, fell short of his own ideal: of the two souls dwelling in Baumgarten's breast, the poet and the Wolffian logician, it was the latter who ultimately triumphed. In his *Journal* of 1769, Herder sketches out some of his thoughts concerning what Schiller would soon call an aesthetic education. Overtaxing the youthful mind with abstractions learned secondhand from dusty schoolbooks and depriving it of a rich variety of sensations induces a state of intellectual torpor and prematurely ages the child. Wherever possible, whether the subject be philosophy, ethics, or theology, concrete concepts should be introduced to the young via their senses, so that children learn to think for themselves and make these ideas their own. Furthermore, *all* of the senses should be put to use; returning to the conclusions he had recently drawn in the *Fourth Grove*, Herder demanded not only that touch be included as a vital aid to learning, but that the body as a whole must not be neglected in education, for without its proper exercise, without the free play of the senses, the soul is left paralyzed and confined. Hence if young minds are to arrive at concepts of truth, they must be exposed to the full gamut of sensory experience: "Many, powerful, vivid, true, individual sensations . . . are the basis of a host of many, powerful, vivid, true, individual ideas, and that is original genius."[18]

Similar ideas are expressed much later in the essay *On the Influence of the Belles Lettres on the Higher Sciences*, the basic argument of which is very simple. Just as images precede concepts and clear cognition precedes distinct cognition, so the higher sciences must be based on the belles lettres, because otherwise they lack a stable, firm foundation. By "belles lettres" Herder did not mean a study of the fashionable literature of the age, which is undemanding and frivolous and produces only aesthetes and dandies who are incapable of any practical activity and wreak havoc in the four traditional faculties of learning. Rather, the belles lettres are a school of the senses, of the imagination, of the passions and inclinations. They serve to cultivate the lower faculties of the soul, bring order to our emotions and fancies, and thereby lay the foundations for independent, abstract thinking in the higher realms of knowledge. A thorough grounding in classical literature and languages is particularly suited to this end. But we should not understand the concept of the belles lettres too narrowly here: geography and natural history are among them, and the canonical authors whom Herder recommends are not only poets. But what they all have in common is that they help to avoid premature and narrow specialization and to place academic disciplines in a meaningful relationship to life. They are *humaniora*: they inspire and nurture in us the feeling of humanity by which we realize ourselves and develop our potential to its fullest extent.

The Fable

In the eighteenth century the fable enjoyed an unprecedented popularity and prestige as a literary genre. In France and then later in Germany (especially during the period 1740–70), the works of serious fabulists such as La Fontaine were not only widely read but were also discussed by some of the foremost critics of the age. What explains the popularity of the fable in the eighteenth century? Part of the reason is certainly the widespread belief that moral instruction was the paramount pedagogical obligation and literature a necessary means of discharging it. So if a firm underlying moral was required of all literary works, then the fable, didactic by nature, fulfilled this requirement more neatly and naturally than any other genre. Those parents unable to afford the private tutors recommended by educational reformers such as Locke and Rousseau, and who took upon

[18] *SWS* 4:454.

themselves the burden of teaching their offspring, were assisted by the many collections of fables aimed specifically at the layman seeking to educate his children. Locke himself, in *Some Thoughts Concerning Education* (1693), declared Aesop's *Fables* to be the best means of stimulating a child's interest in reading and learning, and his ideas, enthusiastically received in France and Germany, were later echoed by Fénelon and Wolff, who also approved the fable as a supremely effective method of inculcating moral truths.[19]

That Herder should be interested in the fable is unsurprising given his profession as cleric and educator, and his conviction that literature ought to be uplifting and edifying was very much of his time. For this reason, though he had moved to Weimar in 1776, Herder could only deplore the nascent ideology of Weimar Classicism and the insistence of Karl Philipp Moritz, Goethe, and others on the autonomy and purposelessness of the artwork. For Herder, the belief that the realm of the aesthetic was hermetically sealed from the concerns of quotidian life signaled a retreat into misguided escapism and empty formalism. Art and literature had urgent moral obligations; as a powerful tool of social and political change they must seek always to communicate with the public. Like many of his contemporaries, Herder regarded the fable as the sine qua non of didactic literature. But his essay *Image, Poetry, and Fable*, first published in the third collection of his *Scattered Leaves* in 1787, is not only an intervention in a live contemporary debate about the nature, meaning, and function of the fable but also one of his most important contributions to a general poetics.

The term *fable* embraces a number of different meanings in seventeenth- and eighteenth-century poetics. It might denote the Aesopian fable proper, or apologue; be used in the Aristotelian sense of the narrative or plot of a dramatic or epic work; or, finally, refer to a myth or legend. This multivalence comes out particularly clearly in the work of one of the most influential theorists of the fable, René Le Bossu. In his 1675 work *Traité de poeme épique*, Le Bossu defined the fable as any "discourse invented in order to form morals by means of instructions disguised under the allegories of an action," a formula that would echo throughout subsequent treatments of the theme by La Motte, Richer, and others. Le Bossu intended *fable* to refer to plot or narrative in the first instance, a two-part framework consisting of both truth (the moral) and fiction (the illustration of that truth through an invented action or story) within which the poetic work is given expression. The difference between the epic and the Aesopian fable proper lies simply in the kind of characters the respective

[19] Thomas Noel, *Theories of the Fable in the Eighteenth Century* (New York: Columbia University Press, 1975).

genre employs to perform the underlying action: whether mythical figures such as gods or men (the epic) or animals with certain human attributes (the Aesopian fable). So for Le Bossu and his successors, the fable—if we ignore the less substantial issues that preoccupied their attention, such as reflections on the length of the fable or the precise function of animal characters—consisted in a mixture of both invention and truth, poetry and morality; its fictionality, its allegorical structure, and its ability to convey a general meaning that served to differentiate it from the specificity of history.

The major break with this tradition was effected by Lessing in his (1759) collection *Fables*, which included five theoretical essays setting out his novel standpoint. Lessing argued that the claim that the fable was allegorical in nature applied only to what he called the complex fable. His preference, however, was for the simple fable, which unfolds only on a single level of meaning, which represents a realistic case history rather than an imaginary or hypothetical situation (and this, he thought, was the truly Aesopian variety). The fable's purpose is to activate the intuitive cognition of a general moral principle. Accordingly, the fable ought to be stripped of all unnecessary poetical effects and attributes, all extraneous ornamentation, and returned to the pristine state that it supposedly enjoyed among the ancients. Ultimately, Lessing viewed the fable as a philosophical instrument, not as a poetic genre; it existed only on the margins of literature, "on the shared border of poetry and morality." The baroque flourishes and discursiveness favored by La Fontaine and his imitators only obscured the moral force of the fable; instead Lessing pleaded for concision and directness (his own fables are rarely longer than a brief paragraph); the fable should be designed to instruct, not to entertain, and hence prose is the appropriate medium for the genre.

Lessing's attempt to reform the fable was controversial; while many of his contemporaries praised the critical perceptions in his essays and applauded his attempts to purify the fable, they were also dismayed by the reactionary tendency of his ideas. The fable, it was felt, had assumed a permanent position among the poetic genres. Most vocal and vigorous in their response to Lessing's puritanical crusade were the Swiss critics Bodmer and Breitinger, whose *Lessing's Unaesopian Fables* (1760) was a mixture of parody and polemic, accusing Lessing of having surrendered any commitment to virtue, religion, and nature.

It is against this general background that we should view Herder's own intervention in the debate about the fable. His definitive treatment of the topic in *Image, Poetry, and Fable* is a belated refutation of Lessing's famous theory. In the preface to his essay, he notes that much of the material dates from his early sketch "Aesop and Lessing," which he had originally intended to appear in the second collection of *Fragments* some twenty years earlier. The theory of the fable, he complains, has not been advanced since Lessing's contribution; subsequent critics had either imitated Lessing or failed to produce an original or coherent theory. Though there are substantial differences between his early and later treatments of the theme, Herder's main criticism of Lessing is the same in both: he takes issue with Lessing's rejection of the allegorical and the poetical essence of the fable. For Herder, the fable does indeed belong on the border between poetry and morality, but if forced to place it in one realm or the other, he would choose poetry: "Its essence is invention; its life, plot; its aim, sensuous understanding. . . . I regard the fable as a source, a miniature, of the great poetic genres, where most of the poetic rules are found in their original simplicity and, to a certain extent, in their original form."[20]

Herder takes up this idea in the later essay, seeking to demonstrate the fable's essentially poetic nature and clarifying its relation to morality and truth. But this time, he prefixes his poetological discussion of the generic characteristics of the fable with wide-ranging psychological and anthropological reflections on the origins of poetry as such in the operations of the mind. He begins by insisting on the inherent creativity involved in cognitive processes: an "image"—the basic stuff of human thought—is the name he gives to any representation of external objects brought to consciousness in the soul; this is achieved by the "inner sense" that imposes order on the chaos of sensations flooding the mind, separating one object from another, by giving each outline and form, by creating unity in diversity. We do not passively perceive images but rather create them; the process of translation by which an object is transformed into an image, and an image into a thought, is inherently allegorical, and allegory is the essence of poetry. Thus, both thought and language, even ordinary discourse, are constructed on a poetical foundation and are subject to the same rules of veracity, vividness, and clarity that govern poetry. But whereas Nietzsche, arguing along similar lines, would later conclude that the inevitable metaphoricity underpinning our perceptual and linguistic habits points to the impossibility of objective truth, Herder is adamant that although we create the images by which we apprehend the world, in doing so we are merely tracing the outlines that God has drawn for us; the truth is still out there.

In the second section, Herder explains how poetry as such arises from the image through the same process of allegorical transference. Just as with a single external object, we do not perceive the object itself but project an image created by our soul, so when we cognize a whole series of objects—in other words, the world as a whole—we project our feelings and values; human knowledge is inescapably anthropomorphic and hence

[20] SWS 2:197–98.

"poetic" in the older sense of that word; that is, fictitious or invented. Because we are ignorant or incapable of understanding the true causes of natural phenomena, we personify and ascribe agency to them. Drawing on the pioneering work of his friend the Göttingen scholar Christian Gottlob Heyne, Herder argues that the earliest form of poetry, as an attempt to come to terms with objective reality, is mythology and religion. But where Heyne assumes that the mythical or poetic form of consciousness, even if it served as the basis of all later knowledge, belongs to the prehistory of human thought, Herder sees myth or poetry not as constitutive of an irrevocably past epoch but as the enduring procedure of the human mind, for the analogical transference of our cognitive and affective structures onto objects is the only way in which human beings perceive the world. Thus even modern physics is an interpretation, a kind of poetics for our senses. That is not to deny that there is a great deal of difference between modern science and primitive religion; the content of human knowledge changes, but the earliest form remains the same. In the same way, the outer trappings of poetry have changed, though the poetic impulse is constant; there is development in poetry, too, from the oral sagas rooted in mythology (*Dichtung*) to the more refined written art of poetry (*Dichtkunst*), which is made possible by the evolution of a greater symbolic language and by borrowing features from other arts, such as meter from the rhythms of dance.

The Aesopian fable is an inevitable and early product of this anthropomorphic mode of thinking. Like all poetry, the fable derives from the natural human urge to form images as a means of creating order out of the chaos of nature. What makes it distinctive, however, is the moral lesson that the poet consciously incorporates in those images which he creates. The fable is, then, according to Herder's definition, "moralized poetry."

The remainder of the essay is devoted to solving some of the traditional problems addressed by theorists of the fable, for example why the fable often employs animals as actors. Herder's answer to this question and others follows directly from the poetological theory he has elaborated in the two preceding sections: for "sensuous man," all aspects of Nature are potential actors, but he feels an especially close bond to the animal world and those species most resembling him and comprehensible to him. Bestial characters are not employed by the fabulist to instill a sense of wonder (as Breitinger argued) or because of their universally recognizable characteristics (as Lessing supposed); instead, the animal fable (as its traditional introductory phrase "once upon a time" implies) expresses a lingering nostalgia for a lost age of unity when human beings felt themselves firmly ensconced in the bosom of Nature. Animals are simply animals, not bloodless abstractions: the fable's effectiveness always rests on concrete analogy or allegory. The fable must be living; it must be relevant and recognizable; it must avoid convoluted and abstruse comparisons. As such, it does not matter who or what the characters are; all that matters is that the result fulfills the general requirements of truth, vividness, and clarity and that the invented narrative enables intuitive cognition of a moral lesson.

In the same way, the lesson that the fable imparts is not a universal moral principle but rather a practical rule of thumb, for a fable always contains more than an abstract injunction whose utility is uncertain; it also includes the concrete situation to which it applies in everyday life. Therefore Lessing's distinction between the simple and complex fable is invalid: all true fables are complex; all fables, as species of poetry, are inescapably based on allegory. Devoid of any connection to the problems we encounter in real life, a fable will be vague, monotonous, and ultimately ineffectual. So while Herder approves of Lessing's suggestion that fables be used in the classroom to develop original thinking, he rejects his restriction of the exercise to abstract thought. Herder demands the cultivation of practical knowledge and thinking, particularly the training of students to transpose and apply the lesson learned from one situation to a parallel one.

For Herder, the fable's poetic nature and its moral content explain its peculiar convincingness; other forms of poetry or rhetoric—such as the comparison and example—may possess a didactic element, but only the fable has an insistent quality that brooks no refusal. This irresistibility stems from its connection with nature, in regard to both means and ends. The fable animates the creatures of nature to serve as actors; it demonstrates to us the "moral laws of Creation itself in their inner necessity." But animated nature speaking to us also gives us a lesson in fundamental unity, which uncivilized humanity felt so strongly that it guided every aspect of life but which modern, alienated man only dimly senses. The fable's ultimate end is not only to communicate a rule of thumb; both the lesson of the fable and the fable itself body forth the moral order of the world in sublime proportions, bringing to intuitive clarity the universal laws of nature and the immutable union of all beings in the realm of Creation. A fable that fails to achieve this sublimity is not a fable at all but a comparison, an example, or simply an amusing story. In Herder's hands, then, the fable is no longer a simple didactic tale, or even the more sophisticated moral poetry of La Fontaine. It is transformed into something approaching divine revelation set in a formula that reflects the mythological golden age of cosmic unity.

This ambitious and widely ranging treatment of a single poetic genre, moving easily from the human to the divine, from the social to the psychological, is typical of Herder's writings on aesthetics as a whole. Few thinkers have reflected so sensitively and productively on the cultural, historical, anthropological, ethical, and theological dimensions of art and the creative process. The importance of aesthetics to the evolution and texture of his own thought, as well as his profound contribution to that discipline, deserves wider recognition.

Is the Beauty of the Body a Herald of the Beauty of the Soul?

"In the countenance dwells the spirit!" This maxim has been in currency since the earliest times; even today it is the basis of our judgments in our daily commerce with others, and only those on whom Nature herself has bestowed a repugnant form seem to doubt it. For that reason we consider their objections biased and stick with the tenet to which we subscribed: "in the countenance dwells the spirit!"

If this rule is universally true, then surely Mother Nature can have given us no better letter of recommendation to our fellow men than a favorable face—but on the other hand wretched are we indeed if an unfavorable physique means that we must not only forgo the consolation of seeking redress in our soul but also arouse the general suspicion that "our *spirit* is worth nothing" or "our heart is bad." Why? Because our body, the dwelling place of the soul, is so unalluring.

Those whose *bodies* have been ennobled by Nature will then triumph; to become acquainted with the most beautiful spirit one must make the acquaintance of the most beautiful body; you will never go astray if you allow yourself to be guided by this visible sign of the spirit, this eloquent witness. But for those who arrived too late when Nature was handing out well-proportioned limbs, there is no choice but to do as the Spartans did with their ugly and feeble infants and throw themselves into the river; let them then go to a hospital or to Charon's skiff or return to their mother's womb to be born again.

Therefore I think it not entirely without purpose to throw some light on this maxim which so often guides our judgments and to gather some observations, deductions, and examples with respect to the question, *is the beauty of the body a herald of the beauty of the soul?* I think this treatise will appeal to many readers: the *beautiful* will read me because they expect a flattering "yes" in answer to this question; the *ugly* will do so because they anticipate consolation and an edifying "no!" But only those who are neither *beautiful* nor *ugly*, or at least who do not make much of either quality, can be my *impartial* judges. To the last category few members of the fair sex are apt to belong, then, if indeed Gellert, that great poet of women, is correct when he says:

dass es beinah kein Mädchen gibt
die nicht den Putz und ihr Gesichtgen liebt.

Nevertheless, I shall submit to the opinion of these partial judgesses with such respect for the name "the fair sex" that I might almost be inclined to underwrite the proposition "the beauty of the body is certainly an infallible herald of the beauty of the soul!" with willing hand and yet more willing heart simply to please them. But unfortunately I recall that a judge and a philosopher ought to be incorrupt and impartial, or at least should pretend to be so; so I shall furrow my brow, adopt a serious expression, and begin my inquiry.

The ancients, especially the ancient Greeks, laid such value on the noble form of the body that their philosophers, among whom I shall single out Socrates and his pupils Plato and Xenophon, declared it to be a symbol of divine qualities and the footprint of the gods. In Plato we find a discussion *about beauty* between Socrates and a young Athenian, Phaedrus, where the proposition that "the beauty of the body is a herald of the beauty of the spirits" is defended with such noble simplicity that Socrates seems to me still an amiable sage.

Let us hear how Plato addresses the question I am treating here: our souls, he says, have been sent from the realm of the gods down to earth, either as reward for the virtue they have practiced in a former life or as punishment for their vices. Their fate in this world is determined accordingly. A beautiful soul is assigned to the womb of a blooming mother; here the soul fashions for itself a *body* from the most delicate blood, and the beauty of this frame shall be its glory, its agreeable *home*, the instrument with which it works with blissful serenity, and the mirror wherein its beauty is revealed. An evil soul, however, is given to the womb of a vicious mother; its body shall be a gloomy dungeon and its countenance the mirror wherein the black disposition of the spirit is reflected.

What Plato claims he may well prove. Yet when I, who unfortunately do not possess sufficient power of memory to recall how my soul came to inhabit my body, lay bare this pretty fable, I discover in it the kernel of the following truth, one that is very much pertinent to my proposition: "In our mother's womb the constitution of our bodies as well as of our spirit is given form." It is here, then, that our explanation must begin.

It is a fact known only too well that in their blood parents pass on their physical and mental constitution through a number of traits. Just as we sometimes think we can recognize almost entire families by their face and temperament when we are acquainted with but three of their members, so it is even better known that children carry the spirit and physical character of their parents mostly in their eyes, in their brow, and in their face.

Just as we therefore raise, preserve, and propagate breeds and races of *noble* and at the same time *beautiful* animals, and particularly by keeping them for the purposes of crossbreeding, so too the *beautiful* and *noble* blood linking human generations might be preserved and passed on. Have there ever existed peoples among whom nobility of the spirit and beauty of the *body* were almost so widespread a mark of their character that it set them apart from other nations? And are there indeed peoples among whom beauty and ugliness are not uncommon because one of these qualities is universal? If I am not mistaken, I have encountered this conceit in Montesquieu, Montaigne and Beaumelle, where it is given new and further turns.

At this juncture I ought to address the questions debated by the philosophers: Does our soul propagate itself at the same time as the body, like a grapevine? How does one part operate on the other? And so on. But since these questions still number among the mysteries and are only obliquely related to my purpose, then should my path touch them, I shall leave it to each of my readers to fill this gap in his thoughts by himself. I, however, shall carry on my way.

In the mother's womb the development of the body and soul both depend on the same things, coincidences, often trifles, and they will therefore inevitably come to resemble each other. The same passion that causes the mother's blood to be in a state of ferment and disorder makes the infant's body unhealthy and imparts to the spirit a character trait that subsequently determines a great deal in his nature. I intend here to refer to individual cases, cases that we now remark upon all too rarely, however, because in our age the common character of our constitution is *frailty*, frailty of body and frailty of soul. The same great passions, which in their utmost degree are productive of monstrosities, cause, in more modest measure, the *irregular* developments that in the soul and in the body almost always run parallel with one another.

If, however, the human body reaches maturity without a tempest of passion and without debilitating congestion of the blood flow, then the soul, which inhabits this unconfined dwelling place and develops accordingly, has the room to extend itself upward and in all directions. And calmly and freely it rouses itself from the slumber of its previous state to experience the first gentle sensations that naturally determine many episodes of its new life.

The ancient Lacedaemonians cast their feeble children away because they reasoned that the children possessed equally feeble souls, just as the sick man is always fainthearted and the generous man healthy, even in his dying moments. Doubtless the Lacedaemonians acted wrongly, even in political terms, but their error can at least be *explained* by their warlike constitution, for they prized physical strength above all else. But when in our feeble age Wegelin[1] seeks to imitate their strength and Rousseau[2] does not show himself to be especially averse to this examination of children, then the comparison is indeed intolerable.

Nevertheless, they are still correct on this point: "Feeble bodies produce feeble souls," and I will not allow anyone to object: Look at this feeble man, this bag of bones and its strong soul; behold this great man whom the wind can blow over. All this I concede and say merely: My friend! Has *Nature* bestowed on this man a feeble body? And has *Art* not exalted his spirit instead of Nature? That is the simplest question; the more difficult one would be this: In what does this man's greatness consist? Is it perhaps precisely a consequence of the feebleness of his spirit? And in what does the feebleness of his body consist? Is it perhaps a consequence of the errors that only the *strong man* could make? Here we speak of *Nature*, and not of *Art*.

In the gallant and charming discourse of polite society one hears and utters nothing but exceptions; one passes judgment on exceptions and on the basis of exceptions in order, with a perpetual, courteous "but on the contrary!" to say and agree on precisely nothing. Whoever does not wish merely to while away the time will infer from the majority of cases in order to alight on what is *general* and *certain*, or at least on what is *probable*.

Behold that man whose strong body testifies to his strong soul: the contours of his body are regular; his physique is well built; there is freedom in his posture and power in his breast; there is lightness in his legs and strength in his shoulders—and thus will his spirit also be, which was formed together with this body. Behold! There is honesty in his brow; there is intelligence between his eyes and health in his cheeks; there is charm in his mouth and a manly fire blazing in his eyes: behold the mirror of his soul.

Behold this woman: her beautiful body is apparently a symbol of the beauty of her soul. The gently inclined profile of her face, the delicate fullness of her figure, and the spirituality pervading her entire being betoken an equally beautiful soul. Behold! It lies in her eyes, on her brow, on her cheeks, her lips. Her lover will say: those are the eyes of Pallas, the forehead of Juno, the lips of Suada, the cheeks of the Graces, the eyebrows of Venus. We would not go quite so far, but even the coldest of men will not deny that her body is suggestive of a beautiful soul.

In this way, then, the beauty of the body is related to the beauty of the soul, for they are twins who develop together.

Hence, wherever Nature cannot bring forth beautiful bodies, beautiful

[1] Wegelin, *Über die Gesetzgebung des Lycurgus.*
[2] Rousseau, *Émile*, bk. 1.

souls are also unknown. That Negroes are the brothers of apes is manifest not only in their lips but also in their bodies as a whole, and even more so in their spirit. Hume says that a genius has never been known to exist among them, and it is sufficiently well known that they believe apes to be men who out of idleness refrain from speaking so that they may avoid work. Thus they themselves recognize their kinship with apes, a kinship, moreover, that physical causes make even closer. In short, the Nature who, when fashioning their bodies, set aside their heads before they were finished,

> when from crude loam their form was first won

was the same Nature who grew vexed when also molding their souls, tossing them away

> when the brain box was scarce yet done.

The same holds true for the frigid zones. In Greenland men and women cannot be told apart because they are equally ugly, and it is known that just as their physical stature is diminutive and misshapen, so is their spirit confined, superstitious, stupid, and small. Only the temperate zones are the workshops of Nature, where the beauty of the body and of the spirit are together brought to maturity, developed and exalted by her hand.

A great man of our time, indeed perhaps the greatest in his knowledge of antiquities and classical beauty, President Winckelmann in Rome,[3] holds Greece and Italy to be the only regions where Nature has cultivated the beautiful in its fullest measure; on this side of the Alps, he claims, there are haphazard and half-finished features even in the most beautiful faces. I shall leave it to the aforementioned abbé to defend this remark aimed against the fair sex of his countrymen, the Germans, for my problem is touched by his beautiful ideal only thus far: if our northern Nature cannot bring the beauty of the body to full perfection, then she cannot also perfect the feeling and refined sense for beauty. We must therefore be compensated for this lack of beauties by an insensitivity and a certain northern severity that might be more of a blessing than a curse: if our feeling for beauty were underdeveloped compared with that of the countries prized by Winckelmann, then we would not notice the absence of beauty.

Up to a certain point, education conforms with our experience that body and spirit develop in parallel. The wet nurse who poisons the blood of an infant often alters its entire growth and gives its spirit a form that can perhaps never be undone. The child, whose face is distorted by prolonged, severe, and bitter shrieks, so that at last this caricatured grimace is stamped permanently on his features, often undergoes an equally re-

---

[3] See Winckelmann's *History of Ancient Art*.

pugnant and irreversible change in his spirit. The person who from child-hood is mollycoddled intolerably and who thereby acquires an effeminate constitution will surely possess an effeminate spirit. The person whose body has developed over many years according to a baroque taste has in all likelihood imparted precisely this taste to his spirit. The *talapoins* and *fakirs* in India, very devout priestly clans, bear their holy imposture just as well in their furrowed brows and downcast eyes as they do in their black and malicious hearts; for them holiness is hereditary, as it is among the *marabouts* of Africa.

The character of our body and soul becomes fixed in our twentieth year, and just as we can thereafter alter our facial features only with difficulty, so it is even harder to give the soul new impetus and to change its consti-tution—unless Nature is defeated by daily effort, exceptional cunning, and unceasing diligence in the pursuit of great ends. Until now I have shown in general terms the real possibility that the beauty of the body can testify to the beauty of the spirit. Now I shall enter into more detail.

The word *beauty* as it is commonly understood is so fluctuating, inde-terminate, and ambiguous that not only nations but also individual men imprint on their imagination an ideal of beauty that perhaps sometimes becomes a pretty *crotchet* of their peculiar constitution but is mostly a composition of those features that made an impression on us as our taste was formed and developed. As Montesquieu has observed,[4] this first, powerful impression accounts for the idiosyncrasy of the lover who takes delight in a little lisping here, in a dimple on the chin there, or here again in a small pockmark on the cheek, because these things coincide with the ideal image that was interwoven in our fancy from the very start.

However, if we examine the taste of everyday life, all judgments can be reduced to the following three kinds: The *lowest* taste is satisfied by mere *heartiness* and judges at most according to *sprightliness* and the color of the cheeks. A more refined taste perceives *regularity* in the finest features. The third kind of taste is alive to *spiritual beauty*, which reveals itself in the eyes, the cheeks, and the attitudes and nuances of the whole body. To what extent do these three stages attest to the beauty of the soul?

Most people are neither beautiful nor ugly, and this large *middling spe-cies* lends *solidity* to the whole race, as it were, and preserves the unbro-ken line of the generations. A good, not ill-constituted man who lives merely to act and seek gratification, who seldom raises his action to the level of conscious reflection and his gratification to the level of fine feel-ing, deems beautiful that which is amenable to these ends. In those na-tions which reckon the other sex merely among those *tolerable* and *use-ful* things that are supposed to inhabit their houses and put them in order,

[4] In *On Taste.*

what is prized most of all is a cheerful durability (as long as it is not actually repugnant) in lieu of all physical charms, and *plain, sound* common sense in lieu of all spiritual beauty. It is said that these two species of beauty ought therefore to form the first couple: neither is *fine* but both are *robust* and *useful*, for that which is fine evaporates or is easily broken.

If this first category of taste admits of more exact definition, then we can say that it finds beauty in *color*, something that may enhance beauty but never constitutes it. Just as a certain *language* holds a *beautiful* maid and a *ruddy-cheeked* maid to be one and the same, so that very tongue will assume *beauty* and *vivacity* of spirit to be identical. A pale complexion is generally a symbol of *innocence* and a red color a sign of *sprightliness*; hence even the black Negro's girl must be at least *nut brown* if he shall think her beautiful, and the *white* god whom he worships, though he believes him to be a stranger and his enemy, is nevertheless always the *good* god.

If, as I have claimed, mere *complexion*—the Frenchman may call it by as many names as he desires, whether *fraîcheur, coloris, incarnate, vermeil*, and so on—does not constitute beauty, then it also hereby forfeits its right "to be a herald of spiritual beauty." A red color often signifies an *unhealthy* sprightliness in body and spirit: a *white lily* often changes into a *yellow* one, and still more often does it belong to those that simply grow there; they toil not, neither do they spin; yet they array themselves in the glory of Solomon.

Because the second degree—that is, a *fine, regular form*—properly constitutes beauty, it can be a good herald inasmuch as it *promises an equally regular spirit*, one that is perhaps placid, like a calm sea on a summer's evening, gentle, incapable of great passion, be it good or ill; in short, it promises a tranquil, balanced, and orderly heart and mind. The reasons for this I gave earlier, but what they promise is admittedly nothing more than a hint, and just as a certain writer calls this regular form, if it be not enlivened by spiritual charms, a *statuesque beauty*, so the regularity of the spirit, which is supposed to accompany it, can likewise be the disposition to all that is beautiful, but often it remains mere disposition. Just as outwardly this regularity is intended only for the eye, so inwardly it also belongs, if not among the mute, then at least among the quiet charms that will never disturb, but seldom enliven, a spiritual pleasure.

Perhaps this is the appropriate juncture to mention that the greatest men have mostly possessed *irregular* features, because the *passion* that elevated them to greatness also caused them to develop early. Conversely, those handsome and suave gentlemen whose minds are filled with the portrait of their bodies are usually born only to convey, nurture, and delight in the thought "My, how beautiful I am!" Julius Caesar may always have carried a picture of Venus with him, whose son he claimed to be; but he will have shown it mostly to ladies. In the Roman senate and in the three hundred battles that made him great, he surely never thought that he was a *beautiful* man—but of course after his triumphs he did so all the more.

The third and highest degree of beauty is the spiritual *charm*, *poise* and *grace* that enliven everything mentioned above and therefore probably have the greatest claim to announce this very charm of the spirit. Those members of both sexes who possess this beauty are thus apt to love the beaux arts and belles lettres, to be made for the pleasures and variety that they offer; and when they now weep at a tragedy or an oratorio and now laugh at a comedy or a lively jest in society, they do so from the same abundance of heart. The same languishing blue eye in which now a sympathetic tear wells up will at another time bathe in *pleasure*; the same fiery eye that is now held in check can also flash with menace; the same sweet lips that now enrapture me can also twist into contempt; and the lovely foot that in the dance rises so lightly, twirls so nimbly, and glides so gently can also, with the same lightness and nimbleness, kick and stamp with displeasure. The same charming features that are now bewitching can at another time mock with the very same grace. And furthermore, just as the gentle can very easily degenerate into the frivolous, so this sweet charm turns unnoticed into a pretty courteousness that in the fine sense we call *coquetry*.

Now let us put all this together: how is the beauty of the body a herald of the beauty of the soul? At most it heralds *that* form of beauty which prophesies health, sprightliness, and fire in a person's thinking, a sensitive and tender heart, and a disposition to moral goodness. But whoever wishes to infer from beauty a *deeper* understanding, a *strong* and *truly virtuous* soul, will draw ten false conclusions for every true one.

Hence the male sex need not grieve inconsolably over the beauty of the body: for men make pretensions not to a *beautiful* soul so much as to a *strong*, *noble*, and *great soul*, which they seek to exalt only through beauty. "If you do not find me beautiful, then I shall compel you to respect me," a man can say, whereas the power over which the *fair* sex disposes is yet more secure, for even the serious-minded man must *love* her for her beautiful *body* and soul. A man who desires to be beautiful like a woman in body and soul is as intolerable as a hen that crows. For a man the following should apply: "Let the nobility of the body manifest the nobility of the soul."

Generally speaking, this latter characteristic can be inferred only with probability and not with certainty. Socrates possessed a constitution that afforded one physiognomist the opportunity to denounce him as the most vicious of men. Socrates' listeners hissed the man down, but their teacher conceded that his opponent was right: "I might have given in to my natural propensities had not philosophy improved me." And of course we have strength and opportunity enough to reform our soul, though not our body.

Yet even a dissembler can, through long practice and effort, imitate the charms of Nature, so that ultimately we are led to draw a false conclusion and ask: This peacock is so beautiful, how beautifully will it sing? This nightingale sings so beautifully, how beautifully will it taste?

If we were to qualify our *proposition*, we might say: "*The beauty of the body* (regularity and grace) is a reliable but not infallible *herald of the beauty of the soul*, if the latter is taken to mean not true greatness and moral goodness but only a slight and perceptible disposition toward them."

I might draw to a close at this point were it not for the fact that I wish to append several conclusions that return what I have said to the familiar language of everyday life.

"To infer from the *face* to the *heart*" is always deceptive and ought never to be heard. Our facial features develop in the years of our youth, when our heart has not yet struck out on its own, and if therefore an unfavorable conformity between heart and face should obtain, then a friend of mankind ought rather to have this excuse ready: "If this man had power over himself, he will have been able to reform his morality; but his face was already molded. Why should the poor wretch awaken an unfavorable prepossession through something that was not in his power to alter?"

To infer from the face to the true *nimbleness*, *greatness*, and *strength* of the spirit is also deceptive. Favorable features can at most only prophesy a *potential* and capacity for this greatness, but whether this *potential* is realized and is raised to perfection is another matter entirely. The *dullard* who wants to amount to something adopts with much effort the self-important air of a scholar, of a clever, spirited, and profound man; and the greatest men are commonly so rough and ready in their *face*, *features*, and *decency* that their beautiful soul does not shine through in a beautiful body.

But our mien can show an inborn and not acquired capacity, an inborn sensibility that has not yet become moral virtue; it can show the nature of our upbringing and the person we would like to be; in short, it can show the character of the soul, particularly in society, if I may use the word *character* only in the light French sense, where it signifies not the whole cast of mind and temperament but only the distinctive qualities of both. Just as the French, especially through their culture of social intercourse, are mindful of catching, as it were, the soul in the nuances of the body, so their language also possesses exceedingly fine words with which to express "how the soul speaks through the body." In German it will be difficult, without resorting to paraphrase, to render with a single stroke the likes of *air sombre, morne, constraint, gauche, soucieux*; a *visage blafard, rébarbatif, refrogné, opilé,* and *rechigné*; a *prude, bellâtre, precieuse, coquette, grimacière, minaudière*; a *petit-soin, musard, bavard, folâtre*.

Our imagination generally discovers more in the features of the face than Nature imputes to them, and mostly as much as we wish to find. If an enamored Petrarch finds so much that is remarkable in the eyes of his Laura that he can fill several books with sonnets; if Winckelmann, borne on the wings of his imagination, apprehends such infinite beauties of spiritual divinity in the statue of Apollo in the Belvedere in Rome that he soars upward to rapture, then we must congratulate the man who can perceive in another's body so much spirit, so much beauty of the soul, and not distract him. Each person judges according to his eyes, and why should I rouse someone from a sweet dream if it gives him so much pleasure?

A Monument to Baumgarten

How the most singular phenomena not only in the realm of the mind but also in the republic of philosophers depend on external causes! The various events and circumstances of life lead our manner of thinking in different directions, and it is the complexion of our schooling in particular—as the first coating applied to the young soul, so to speak—that exerts the greatest influence on the form in which that soul subsequently appears before the world. It was no different with Alexander Gottlieb Baumgarten. His earliest learned education was in the hands of a—philologist: perfect for what else than for Latin and poetry? And how was he taught these subjects in the hands of a philologist? How else than to regard both as blossoms, as fruits, more like a toy than a tool, more like candy dissolving on the tongue than a source of proper nourishment. So that is how the young Baumgarten developed, who thought each day unfulfilled if he had not composed verse in Latin; who could not better digest his cherished Sunday sermon than by forcing it into a Latin meter; and, finally, whose grounding in Latin and philology, his biographer tells us, "had the uncommon benefit of subsequently enabling him, in later life, to deliver his inaugural lecture in Frankfurt in Latin." An uncommon benefit indeed!

Baumgarten's academic studies coincided with the very time when Wolff's philosophy was regarded as a heresy in Germany—motive enough for a mind born to contemplation and hitherto prevented from doing so by theology and word studies. He overcame the obstacle that this infamous name represented; indeed, the very obstacle itself spurred him on, his genius was roused, and Baumgarten the philosopher cultivated himself by reading Wolff's writings.

But of course the lineaments of his earlier education inevitably showed through the new guise that his spirit had adopted. From the methods inculcated into him at the orphanage he retained the tabular form in which he therefore wrapped everything; and from Christgau he retained his teacher's forced Latin style, which strives so assiduously to weave in flowers of speech and also—this is most pertinent here—the taste for Latin poetry.

A Wolffian philosopher and a Christgauian poet conjoined in a single person: certainly a rare and curious phenomenon in those days, when it was believed that no two things were more inimical to each other than taste and philosophical contemplation, when one philosophized about everything known and unknown, save for beauty and the feeling of beauty. In those days, then, there emerged the philosopher who first thought of reconciling both things, which were already united in his own cast of mind, and hence attempted to extend this Wolffian poesy to poetic art.

This gave rise to his *Philosophical Meditations on Some Matters Pertaining to Poetry*, a short academic treatise wherein I nevertheless discern the entire outline of his metapoetics and a work that I may regard *for myself* as the bull's hide that might encompass the entirety of Dido's royal city; that is, of a true philosophical poetics. The firstborn of a mind I always behold with a little shudder of respect for the human soul that conceived it, and that I have not imagined or mistakenly divined the manner of its origin in Baumgarten's soul is confirmed by the preface and the work itself as a whole. I think it an accurate summary of its character when I say it is *an attempt to transplant Wolffian philosophy into the soil so dear to our Baumgarten, the soil of his childhood sweetheart, poetic art*, or to determine the fundamental concepts of the poem with a philosophical exactitude and rigor.

To this end, then, he seeks a philosophical definition of poetic art and turns to psychology and enumerates with philosophical economy the *cognitions* that contribute to the poetic. After cognitions he treats *method*, and after method poetic language, in order everywhere to determine sound concepts and to develop the subsidiary concepts that follow from his main idea that "poetry is perfectly sensuous discourse." This treatise was thus the work of a discerning analyst, who develops the entire nature of poetry, this glorious and fruitful tree, from the germ of his short definition consisting of three words: *oratio, sensitiva, perfecta*.

Though I do not propose to address now the question of the truth and adequacy of his concept of poetry, I shall make this exception: of all the definitions of poetry that have sought to comprehend its essence in a single concept, Baumgarten's is, I think, *the most philosophical*.

Why? Perhaps because it is composed of obscure and—as our suave Latinists will say—barbarous terminology? Perhaps because the words *oratio sensitiva perfecta* are the vaguest and might therefore admit of the longest *definition*? Or because Baumgarten's definition derives from the Wolffian school, by whose hand everything is immediately stamped with the seal of philosophy? For none of these reasons! Rather, it is because this definition *leads me deepest into the soul* and allows me, as it were, to educe the essence of poetry from the nature of the human spirit. Because, second, *these few words do most to adumbrate* what we encounter when we penetrate to the very depths of poetry. Because, furthermore, it *affords the best view over the entire philosophy of the beautiful* and therefore enables poetry to be united with its sisters, the fine arts; and finally, because it leaves least room for *abuse in the practice of poetry.*

1

Baumgarten's account of poetry is drawn from psychology and hence also gives us most cause to trace poetry back to its mother and companion, the human soul. It must be possible—this was Baumgarten's great insight—to apportion to poetry its own domain in the human spirit, in the soul, and to demarcate its boundaries exactly. And in this realm must reside powers that originally produced poetry and powers that are now in turn exercised by it. We must therefore journey into these dark regions to bring back from them, as from an enchanted grotto, word of where this goddess dwells.

In Wolff's language this would be called *the domain of the lower faculties,* of the representations of *sense,* of *extensively clear* concepts; and with characteristic discrimination Baumgarten traveled through these normally mist-shrouded lands in order to find everything that was poetic in the sensitive faculty, in the imagination, in the wits, in the poetic faculty, in judgment, in the power of description, in feeling, and in the passions. Here his psychology has merits that can be recognized only by one who knows how to value discoveries in the human spirit and has perceived the shortcomings of this kind in the psychological systems that preceded Baumgarten. The higher cognitive powers can ultimately be studied through many a theory of psychology and logic because they are always productive of less confused concepts: idea, proposition, and inference; but how cluttered was everything in the sensitive faculty of my soul, in the fancy and in taste, in feeling and in passion! And if my whole feeling for the beautiful and the good lies precisely in this obscure ground, O then let a Montaigne, a Rousseau, a Locke, a Home come and, with all their knowledge of the soul, explain to me and illustrate the Baumgartian psychology. How I would hurry if, laden with experiences of the human spirit, a Plato, a Socrates of our times desired to instruct me according to the precision with which Baumgarten has determined this region of the soul.

The principles of Aristotle, Batteux, and others are far from possessing such psychological richness; they are directed more toward the barren matter of the thing imitated in a poem than the living person who operates upon such an object and are thus concerned less with him who produces an effect than with the isolated effect itself. Even in the hands of an Aristotle and Batteux, then, these principles have not been as fruitful as the highest principle of poetry and the fine arts ought to be. And let us not mention those wretched philosophers who see the essence of poetic art in, for example, verse, rhyme, and melody. But a philosopher of poetry after Baumgarten?

The human soul lies before him, in its *sensuous*—that is, its most effectual and vivid—parts, like an enormous ocean that even in its calmest moments seems full of waves that are lifted up to heaven: there I place you, O philosopher of feeling, as on a high rock jutting out amid the waves. Now gaze down into the dark abyss of the human soul, where the sensations of the brute shade into the sensations of man, and as it were commingle with the soul from afar; gaze down into the abyss of *obscure* thoughts, from which there subsequently arise drives and emotions and pleasure and pain. Place the feeling of beauty where it belongs: between the angel and the animal, between the perfection of the infinite and the sensuous, vegetal gratification of cattle. If you can count, measure, and weigh a thought and feeling, then determine the richness, the sublimity, and the dignity of a knowledge of the human. If you can refract the sunbeam of a thought and sensation, then divide that pregnant, that powerful representation which operates upon my soul now with the most concentrated, now with more diffuse, light and separate it from the false glitter of speech. If you know the workshops of my animal spirits, then show me the spirit of beauty that courses through my veins, fills my heart, lifts my breast, and is mine for the duration; show me beauty instead of conviction and reason and truth. Show me how the impressions in my sense organs become images in my soul, how my imagination pours rapture into my veins and at that very moment weaves a mist around my faculty of reason. Then awaken for me these poetic images, which produce such grand and sweet dreams for my soul, which deceive me with emotions and worlds that magically transport me into other people's natures and feelings. Behold! That lies in the sensuous region of my soul!

Now out of this, create poetry, just as Prometheus created human nature: and remove me to the world of objects that fill my soul with such light and intensity. Show me the power that individual subjects and examples and descriptions and resemblances and fictions can exert on me, so that I learn to look and love and admire. Then from language and expression forge for me the means, the instruments by which I can assail and assuage the soul in so decisive a fashion and melt, illumine, and delight it in sweet joy and even sweeter pain. Do this, O philosopher of feeling, and I shall revere you also as my teacher in matters of taste. You will have the power to hone my discernment and sharpen my wits, to examine my judgment of sensuous understanding and transform it into correct deductions; and all this because you speak from my soul and also reach into my soul to instruct me. Philosopher of beauty, of feeling, and of poetic art, then you shall possess words that grant you omnipotence!

I imagine that through this work I am speaking with men who have the very same feeling of humanity as I do; and which philosophy, dear reader, will be more agreeable to you: the one that roams throughout the world and forgets itself or the companion of your nature and—to speak with a Briton—the homely philosophy of your heart? What theory of the science of the beautiful will be more pleasing than one that knows how to entice forth your sensations and that in colloquy with your heart vies with your self; one where everything that it presents to you it has purloined from your own being? Only to have the *object* before one's eyes is wearying; it demands a unilateral gaze outward and an unflinching eye that neglects no aspect, no refraction of light; it is only for readers who go in search of mere knowledge motivated by a thirst for conquest, and not for those who believe *examining, becoming acquainted* with a thing rather than *knowing* it to be of paramount importance. Such people, who have no attachments and do not cling to a proposition merely for the sake of it, like to read nothing better than their own soul. If experiences are dredged from the bottom of the soul, if sensations are rendered distinct to them, then these persons, who are untroubled by the question as to how these experiences can be accommodated within a system and how these individual sensations will accord with this and that object, will be satisfied by the examination of themselves and necessarily think subjective rather than objective philosophy of greater import.

Hence, even if we admit what cannot indeed be admitted, that the principle of Aristotle and Batteux is just as true and comprehensive as that of Baumgarten, then we cannot say that it is just as adequate and human, for it is preeminently Baumgarten's principle that teaches us to become initiated into the profoundest secrets of our soul and to make a psychological discovery with each rule of beauty. Moses Mendelssohn's eulogium applies perfectly to it:

If the philosopher pursues the traces of the sensations on their obscure paths, new perspectives in psychology must open themselves to him, ones that he would otherwise never have uncovered by rational inferences and by experience. The human soul is as inexhaustible as Nature; mere reflection cannot possibly establish everything about it, and everyday experience is rarely decisive. Those happy moments in which, as it were, we catch Nature in the act never escape us as easily as when we want to observe ourselves. At such moments the soul is much too preoccupied with other concerns to be able to perceive what transpires in it. Hence, one will have to analyze carefully the phenomena in which the impulses of our soul are most moved and compare them with the theory in order to shed a new light on this theory and extend its borders through new discoveries. Yet are there any phenomena that move every impulse of the human soul more than the effects of fine art do?

And so if the highest principle of the fine arts is supposed to draw our attention to nothing but these very impulses and sensations of the soul, then which is better? It is precisely this principle, then, that we have to thank for the *Letters on Sensations*, the *Theory of Sensations*, and the sundry psychological paths to which Baumgarten's aesthetics directs us. This much is settled: by itself the principle "*imitate Nature!*" leads mostly to arid observations. But the principle "*pursue sensuous perfection!*" concentrates, as it were, all the rays of Nature in my soul and is nothing other than the application of the oracular injunction O mortal! Know thyself!

2

If the best principle is that which says the most with the fewest words, then Baumgarten's possesses this quality to the utmost degree and is the seat of the entire art and science of the beautiful. With real joy did I read Baumgarten's attempt to derive the most significant properties of poetry from those three words, and he did this so naturally, so happily that with this definition I thought I had a treasure before me. And yet more certain did the treasure seem to me when I found the main principles of all the beaux arts and belles lettres unfolded by Moses Mendelssohn from this so very simple proposition. Just as the most splendid gemstone appears at its most glorious when mounted in the finest setting, so does a principle when, laden with thoughts and views, its words are measured out with a Spartan hand. That it is always more difficult to suggest a lot with a little than to say nothing with a great deal may be demonstrated by the frequently prattling definitions of our modern philosophers, who conceal themselves behind a multitude of words as behind fig leaves, and who seem to think: well, if one term does not hit the spot, then at least the other will. But behind these fig leaves lurks a nakedness, and if we remove one superfluous, incorrect word after another, then ultimately nothing is left but the word that is to be defined. That is what the definitions in Basedow's philosophy, for instance, are generally like, as well as his more specific definition of poetic art; that is what the definitions of Schlegel and a great many Frenchmen are like: they lose their way in a throng of words that are often out of place.

Seldom has there been a more felicitous mind in this respect than Baumgarten; seldom has there been a philosopher who could think through more correctly, separate more neatly, and express more succinctly the subsidiary concepts of a fundamental idea. The outlines of his philosophical textbooks are, as it were, wholly spirit, which assumed only as much flesh as was necessary to become visible; and I know few other thinkers who might succeed in drawing with a monogram the most intricate concept in all its grandeur and truth. One might think that when Baumgarten was endowed with the power of description, the quantity was carefully measured out, so that he received only as much as was necessary for the utmost correctness. Here even his barbarous language, his modern Latin, his scholastic terminology, lend him such sterling support that I even go willingly to his Latin and would ignore a German translation of his metaphysics, even had it been rendered by his greatest interpreter, Meier. Though his expressions might often be complete *quasimodogenita*, if I could one day conquer the mountain that understanding him and Wolff represents—what a vista of thoughts and definitions would be spread before me!

Let this also apply to his *sensuous discourse*: always barbarous, but also always so pregnant with ideas that in short I would not want another word or paraphrase to take its place. One must know how to orient oneself in the inmost depths of Wolffian terminology, even if one ought to impose limits on this expression: hence, I would not like to exchange it on the basis of its inner content. [Here the manuscript breaks off.]

Well, of course, if we were concerned merely with barbarous terminology squeezing itself through scholastic classifications and the iron bars of paragraphic division; but now? Should the combination of such different centuries, nations, mentalities, and languages not have discovered new perspectives from which to view things more clearly? Not have cast more penetrating glances into the human soul? Not have advanced further toward the goal of general observations? Not at least have cleared old obstacles from the path? Should we not at least, having taken several wrong turns, now walk with greater assurance along the avenue of method? Should we not have traveled from error to truth and, faced with new phenomena, have arrived at new discoveries? In the speculative part of philosophy, especially in psychology and in the house of the scientific, should we not have accomplished a great deal? And if we had achieved none of this, if the philosophical culture of our time were certainly not more exalted than might be shown ten times over, then I shall set upon it brandishing my sword.

So the philosophical culture of our time is *different*. It has grown entwined with different forms of knowledge and been raised together with different sciences; it is viewed from different perspectives, built on different principles, used in conjunction with different aids and instruments, directed toward different ends—in short, it is fashioned according to a different time and way of thinking. Anyone who disputes this speaks as an *exsulant* of our age and of common sense. I can thus briefly and abruptly move to the conclusion that one must also read the Greeks as one's age dictates, in a temple belonging to our century and manner of thinking. It is true that I stand here before good taste as before the altar of Isis, who has been and is and will be; yet she too appears in many forms and among many rites of worship. So, too, does the *voluptas* of fine taste—to speak with Quintilian—always remain the same: among the learned and the unlearned, among different peoples and ages; but all the more does the *ratio artis, quam docti intelligent* acquire its own peculiar form depending on the mentality of a people, of a century, of a language, of a major writer, and through the coincidence of countless minor details. Different paths lead to a different goal, and different refractions of light lend a different color to the science of taste. Therefore take from our age the torch of criticism as we wander among the Greeks; or if you prefer, divert the course of Greek waters so that we may purify and irrigate our *aesthetics*.

It will be *purified* by the simplicity of the Greeks, for although *Baumgarten* gave shape to aesthetics in our land and in our age, it is of course everywhere wrapped in the Latin of the schoolmen. Just as there has long existed in learned education the tradition of immersing young souls in the study of the language before they are able by themselves to relate the concepts to the words—and according to the well-known proverb a jar will long keep the fragrance of what it was once steeped in when new and delicate—so too does Baumgarten's manner of thinking seem to have developed in such an erudite form of language. And thus for aesthetics also, the form was fixed long before it was poured into the cast; the favorite terms of the Wolffian school, its classifications, and its magic formulas, were already wound like the warp and woof in the loom, and now the concepts of the beautiful were passed through it; Gessner's thesaurus provided additional flowers of speech, and with that the fabric was finished— a fabric whose splendor lay in its material and in its artistry: the work of a philosophical master craftsman that none dared to complete, like the painting of Apelles, whose master died leaving it unfinished; the original of *an aesthetics after the Baumgartian manner*, which none of his pupils has matched.

But why necessarily an aesthetics after the Baumgartian manner, if an aesthetics *after the Greek manner* would be better? If, as Lessing claims, it is the prerogative of the ancients never to have done too much or too little in anything, then this applies equally to the philosophy of the Greeks. And if in general we must allow a few beaten tracks to grow over because we would prefer to stroll along the more flowery and fruitful avenues of the ancients, where would we sooner take such a path than in the philosophy of the beautiful?

Well, then! If Baumgarten's aesthetics were returned to the simplicity and moderation that characterize the teaching of Aristotle and Longinus, it would admittedly lose something of its nebulousness and superfluous adjuncts, but it would also gain a great deal of substance and beauty; indeed it would gain everything that it presently lacks.

The first error of his aesthetics, as is known, is that too much is arrived at by a priori deduction and as if plucked from the air; it therefore loses itself in the ether of general propositions, which are often too broad to be fleshed out with details, often too idiosyncratic to accord with one another in the manner that we would want. Only the Greek Muse can lead us out of the ethereal regions of overly subtle reasoning and back down to earth, for the very difference between philosophy and sophistry in Greece was that the former passed judgment over things present to us, was always the neighbor of experience and hence almost always the neighbor of utility and truth. Thus the judgments of Socrates remained either wholly earthbound, whither he had summoned them from the heavens, or, even in the spiritual flights of Plato, at least still within our range of vision, by which I mean within the sphere of observation. Thus even the rules of the infamous Aristotle still adhere fairly closely to the individual facts from which they are picked like flowers, and even his poetry contains—rules. But who of the new breed of philosopher will be satisfied with rules, will desire to infer from them in the first instance and with all his inferences to remain on terra firma? Far beyond our normal range of vision, far beyond the sphere of individual observations, indeed often far beyond usefulness and truth—that is the soaring trajectory of modern abstraction, which often rises up to touch the void before falling exhausted and feebly to the ground. Should there not be examples hereof in Baumgarten's aesthetics also? How much chaff in terminology, definitions, classifications of words, and scholastic subtleties we could rid ourselves of if a Greek hand were to sift through everything, to sift it all in the sieve of usefulness and truth! How often in Baumgarten do we see main propositions arrive from on high, for which we then have to find room on earth!

Let his work be whatever it may be; it is not what its name declares it to be: *aesthetics*, the science of feeling. The original source on which it drew was not indeed Greek feeling, sensation, the inner sentiment of the beautiful, but rather speculation. And where speculation ought to draw near the sea of the human soul (though Baumgarten did not get this far in his plan), where it ought to flow into psychology, well, instead it floats above the sensation of the beautiful, as slick as oil. In the same way, Homer's Titaressus "pours his fair-flowing streams into Peneius; and he does not mingle with the silver eddies of Peneius but flows on over his waters like olive oil." With my induction I do not wish to transform a Baumgartian philosophy derived from strict principles into the sophistical reasoning of a St. Mard based on mere sentiments, for I desire not a French but a Greek aesthetics. And such an aesthetics—how it would fetch everything from the depths of our feeling, how it would draw on sensation and from it extract the glorious spirit. It would philosophize within the human soul like a swimmer half submerged beneath the sea. Home's *Principles of Criticism* (which is more deserving of the name of aesthetics than all of Baumgarten's oeuvre)—these principles, augmented by the psychology of the Germans and then returned to *that* nation which has remained, in its doctrines of the beautiful, whether in art or in letters, most true to the feeling for Nature, then *hellenized* in line with this people's feeling for Nature—now that would be aesthetics!

Critical Forests, or Reflections on the Art and Science of the Beautiful

FIRST GROVE, DEDICATED TO MR. LESSING'S *LAOCOÖN*

Leser, wie gefall ich dir?
Leser, wie gefällst du mir?
—LOGAU

1

MR. LESSING'S *LAOCOÖN*, a work on which the three Graces of the human sciences—the Muses of philosophy, poetry, and fine art—have busied themselves, has been for me, during the critical pestilence currently raging in Germany, one of those propitious phantoms that Democritus prayed we might encounter. I should compare it most fittingly with the statue from which it takes its name, were not the appearance of completion, of the authorial ἐποίησε, the very attitude that this *Laocoön* desires least to adopt. Let this way of speaking with its comparisons of the different arts remain the province of our *beaux-artistes* of style; I shall consider *Laocoön* as a collection of materials, an assemblage of unordered notes—even as this alone it more than merits our consideration.

Our modern critics, a swarm of mice seemingly banished to our fair country by Apollo Smintheus to despoil those few flowery and fruitful meadows that, scattered here and there, still remain among the estates of genius—the majority of these heralds of Apollo have not known how to praise *Laocoön* save at Winckelmann's expense; for what praise gushes more readily from the lips of great men than acclaim at the expense of a third party? Lessing is said to have pointed out many inexcusable errors on Winckelmann's part, to have taught him to philosophize, to have shown him the limits and essence of art, and especially to have revealed that his knowledge of the ancients rests on shaky ground. Would that not be a great achievement indeed? To show Winckelmann, a man who has modeled himself so thoroughly after the ancients; who lives and moves and has his being in Greece; who displays an astonishing appreciation of the art of antiquity; for whom, by his own admission, the study of Homer has daily been his pious morning prayer—to show this man that he has not read Homer, that he does not know the Greeks: why? Because Lessing knows the Greeks, because Lessing has read Homer! Even worse is it to claim that Winckelmann is not a philosopher because he does not philosophize after Lessing's manner, preferring instead to stroll through the Academy of the ancient Greek sages and especially along the banks of the sacred Ilissos. And then, worst of all, to teach Winckelmann the essence of art—oh, you unhappy judges who, deaf and imbecilic like Claudius, pass judgment on the greatest writers of our time as if you were sleeping, as if you were examining schoolchildren on what they know and do not know, what they demonstrate and do not demonstrate, and especially where they have gone wrong compared with this or that fellow.[1]

Even Lessing himself, as is only right and proper, has had to serve enlightened critics as a means of proving to the public how sharp-sighted they are. If to one critic he was the greatest antiquarian of our times, the foremost theorist of art, then to another he was—alas!—a superficial wit; and a third—a devout, critical Christian[2]—thought him a scholastic philosopher, an aesthetician of Baumgarten's school who, in the language of our new theorists of the beautiful and equipped with a few ounces of Baumgartian philosophy, means to bid defiance to the savants of every age. Oh, we must plug our ears as we make our way through these choruses of croaking frogs, just as Ulysses did before the song of the sirens!

For me, *Laocoön* possesses enough beauty on its own terms that it would gain nothing by contrasting it with another work. L.'s criticisms of W. at either end of his treatise are either nothing but *parerga*, as both men will regard them, or at least they do not affect Winckelmann's primary purpose: art. Thus, as an essay on the limits of poetry and painting, *Laocoön* has its own worth and excellence; but to consider it as a polemic, as an examination of Winckelmann's oeuvre, is in my opinion to see things from quite the wrong point of view. And what is more, the genius of a

---

[1] Of these lofty judgments of Winckelmann, I shall cite only one. In Klotz's *Acta litteraria*, vol. 3, p. 319, we hear the following with respect to the *Laocoön*: "Reddiderunt forte virum doctum nimiae laudes securiorem, quibus prima illius opuscula, *multo meliora eo*, quod de allegoria *compilauit*, extulerunt quidam, *quibus si me quoque accensueris, nec miror, nec indignor*. Vtinam ne exemplo Winckelmannus suo aliquando doceat, saepe nocere auctorum *famae et ingeniis praeconum* et amicorum voces, plausus et laudes, minuere *diligentiam*, addere *fastum et fiduciam!*" Unless Mr. Klotz says this based on his own experience, I do not know whether the individual judgments that he has seen fit to pass on Winckelmann and the sundry improvements he has sought to impose on him justify Klotz, of all people, passing such a decisive overall judgment on Winckelmann, and without proofs at that.

[2] Here too I shall cite only one witness: Huch, *Versuch über die Verdienste des Archilochus um die Satire*, 1767; for each of the above characterizations I could call another witness, were it worth the trouble.

Lessing and that of a Winckelmann are so different that I could not bring myself to measure one against the other.

Where Lessing is at his best in the *Laocoön*, there speaks the critic, the arbiter of *poetic* taste, the poet. How Sophocles' Philoctetes suffers and how Homer's heroes may weep and how Virgil's Laocoön may open his mouth, and how physical agonies may be poured out on the stage—how Virgil, Petronius, and Sadolet depict Laocoön, how the poet can imitate the artist and the artist the poet—who speaks here but the critic of the poet? It is he who deals a blow to Chateaubrun's Philoctetes, it is he who shows Spence and Caylus their errors, it is he who classifies Homer's poetic beings and distinguishes poetic from painterly beauty—everywhere it is the critic of the poet; that is his business. And his purpose also. To counteract false poetic taste, to determine the limits of the two arts, so that the one does not encroach on, anticipate, tread too close to the other; that is his purpose. Whatever he may find lying on his path that might bear on the inner essence of art he will of course pick up, but for me Lessing will always be the critic of poetry who feels himself to be a poet.

Winckelmann, however, is a master of Greek art who even in his *History of Ancient Art* is more concerned with furnishing a historical metaphysics of the beautiful derived from the ancients, and from the Greeks in particular, than with history proper. And hence he is even less preoccupied with a critique of artistic taste. The false taste of other ages and nations is never his main object; he censures it only when he encounters it among the neighbors and predecessors of the ancients, for otherwise how often, in accordance with his noble Greek idea, would he have had to brandish his cane and weary his hand by dealing extra blows! And if he does not write as a critic of artistic taste, then how much more removed could he be from the critic of poetry? As an artist he read the poets, as a teacher of art he uses them; and he would have been unable to write as he does if he had read the poets differently, and not as an artist. Winckelmann, before whom, like that Greek artist, Beauty herself appeared (though she was the beauty of art); bewitched by her he thus sought, with fire painted on his mind, glinting in his eye and stirring in his heart, the form she had taken—this external form of artistic beauty, this image of love he sought everywhere. He fancied he saw it even in her mere reflection, supposed he saw it, like Kleist's Amynt of his beloved Lalage, even in her footsteps, even in her likeness on the water, even in the breath of the zephyr, which of course could have come from another Lalage (the beauty of the poet). Thus in his feeling for this *plastic* and not *poetic* beauty did he stand before Virgil's Laocoön as he did before the Laocoön of Polydorus, and that is how Winckelmann must be read, for the limitations of human nature mean that we can see only one thing at a time, we can see only what and how we want to see. With Winckelmann this one thing was *art*. Should I therefore dispute his knowledge of the ancients because he read Homer not as a poet but as an artist, not on account of the poetic nature of his Muse, not like Lessing? Should I put down as a capital crime a mere side glance that he casts in the direction of poetry to elucidate his art, assuming that this side glance did not touch the inner essence of poetry? And because, conversely, Lessing draws everything from the depths of the soul, should I think him a speculative, would-be wit; and if on occasion he went too far with his cheerful conclusions, should I think him nothing but a guesser? Why can we not take two such original thinkers as Winckelmann and Lessing as they are? And in their style of writing, too, they are both accompanied by a Greek Grace; only it is not the same Grace.

Winckelmann's style is like an ancient work of art. Formed in all its parts, each thought obtrudes and stands there, noble, simple, sublime, complete: it *is*. However or wherever that thought may have arisen, whether through effort or of its own accord, in a Greek or in Winckelmann himself—it is enough that through the latter's agency it suddenly stands there and exists, like a Minerva sprung from Jupiter's head. As upon the shore of a sea of ideas, where, at the horizon, one's gaze vanishes into the clouds—thus do I stand on Winckelmann's writings and survey what lies before me. A field filled with warriors who, gathered together from far and wide, at first direct the gaze into the distance, where it lingers; but when finally the eye returns more sublimely from this expanse, it will cleave to each individual warrior and ask him where he has come from, consider who he is, and then, from the testimony of many, it will be able to learn about the career of a single hero.

Lessing's style of writing is that of a poet, that is, of a writer, one who has not made but is making, who does not present a finished train of thought but who thinks out loud; we see his work *as it comes into being*, like the shield of Achilles in Homer. He seems, as it were, to present us with the occasion of each reflection, to take it apart and put it back together again piece by piece; now the mainspring is released, the wheel turns, one idea, one inference entails another, the conclusion draws near, and *there is* the product of his cogitation. Each section is thought through, the τεταγμένον of a completed idea; his book is an unfolding poem, with digressions and episodes, but always unfixed, always in hand, in progress, in development. This difference between the two—Winckelmann the artist who has fashioned a work and Lessing the still-busy poet—extends even to individual images, descriptions, and stylistic flourishes. The former is a sublime master of art; the latter a cheerful companion even in the philosophical passages of his writings, and his book is an entertaining dialogue for our mind.

Thus might we describe both men. And how different! How excellent in their differences! So let us be rid of the spectacles through which we squint at them, peering from one to the other in order to praise through contrast! Whoever cannot read L. and W. as they are shall read neither; he shall read only himself!

2

W. depicts his Laocoön with the same feeling as if he had fashioned the statue himself:

> The pain is revealed in every muscle and sinew of his body, and one can almost feel it oneself in the painful contraction of the abdomen without looking at the face or other parts of the body at all. However, this pain expresses itself without any sign of rage either in his face or in his posture. He does not raise his voice in a terrible scream, which Virgil describes his Laocoön doing; the way in which his mouth is open does not permit it. Rather, he emits the anxious and subdued sigh described by Sadolet. The pain of body and the nobility of soul are distributed and weighed out, as it were, over the entire figure with equal intensity. Laocoön suffers, but he suffers like the Philoctetes of Sophocles; his anguish pierces our very soul, but at the same time we wish that we were able to endure our suffering as well as this great man does.[3]

"Laocoön suffers like the Philoctetes of Sophocles."[4] This comparison serves as Mr. Lessing's point of departure, and his aim is to show that it is baseless, that Sophocles' Philoctetes does not merely sigh anxiously and oppressedly but wails, cries, fills the desert island terribly with wild imprecations so that the theater also echoes with the sounds of despondency, of sorrow and despair. So first, Lessing says, Winckelmann must have misread Sophocles; second, he makes an illicit comparison and then draws an illicit conclusion.

Let the Philoctetes of Sophocles decide: how does he suffer? It is strange that the impression this play has left on me from long ago is the same that Winckelmann believes it makes: namely, the impression of a hero who struggles against the pain that assails him, holds it back with hollow sighs for as long as he can, and finally, when the "oh!" and the dreadful "alas!" overwhelm him, still utters only solitary, stolen sounds of sorrow and conceals the rest within his great soul. Let us open our Sophocles, let us read as if we were watching the drama, and I believe we shall discover what Philoctetes is made of, that same Philoctetes whom Sophocles created and Winckelmann cites.

---

[3] *Reflections on the Painting and Sculpture of the Greeks*, pp. 21, 22.
[4] Lessing in *Laocoön*, p. 3 [1:8].

At the beginning of the third act pain ambushes him, but is this manifested in a howling cry? No, in a sudden silence, in mute dismay, and, as this begins finally to dissipate, in a hollow, contorted ἀᾶ, ἀᾶ that Neoptolemus can barely hear.[5] "What is it?" the latter asks with a start. "A mere nothing, boy; go on," replies Philoctetes, his face full of love, full of the self-restraint of the hero. In this way the scene of dumb anguish continues: the worried, uneasy, questioning Neoptolemus and Philoctetes, who—does not roar and rage; who suppresses his pain and for a good while tries to conceal it even from Neoptolemus; who in the meantime only complains to the gods with a timid ὦ θεοί. And what effect must precisely this scene of silent agony have on the spectator? He sees Philoctetes suffer wordlessly, with only a contorted gesture, with only a suppressed "ah me!"; and who does not feel this oppressed "ah me!" more powerfully than the howling cry of a Mars who, wounded in battle, bellows like ten thousand men or, if you will, ten thousand oxen? At Mars we take fright; with Philoctetes we feel compassion, we sympathize with him and are filled with consternation; like Neoptolemus we are anxious, at a loss, we know not what we should do, how we should help. Upon hearing his sad ἀᾶ we approach him and say: "What ails thee? Wilt thou not tell me? Wilt thou not speak? Why groan aloud and call on God?" And Philoctetes replies with a crooked smile, with an expression in which pain and courage and friendliness commingle: "No, a mere twinge; I think 'tis passing now. I beseech the gods to grant a fair and prosperous voyage." It would require a Greek Garrick to weigh here the correct measures of pain and courage, human sentiment and the heroic soul.

Overwhelmed finally by pain, he succumbs; he erupts—but in sounds of howling despair, of raging cries? Not at all, in a sad ἀπόλωλα, τέκνον· βρύκομαι, τέκνον· παπαῖ, ἀπαππαπαῖ, παπαππαπαππαπαππαπαῖ: these are his drawn-out, plaintive cries. He begs for the hero's cure, for his companion to hack off his foot; he whimpers. Nothing more? No, nothing more! As Neoptolemus says, he broke out only in ἰυγὴν καὶ στόνον, in groans and sighs, and oh! how touching must this be! His lame foot, his grimacing face, his breast heaving as he sighs, his sides sunken with groans, his soft "ah me!" Beyond this the poet does not go, and to forestall any exaggeration of expression, he has Philoctetes drift into unconsciousness with the pain! He has suffered so much, summoned his strength for so long, that he is beside himself.

He regains his senses! He recovers! But the illness returns like a wan-

---

[5] Νεοπτόλεμος ἕρπ', εἰ θέλεις. τί δή ποθ' ὧδ' ἐξ οὐδενὸς
λόγου σιωπᾷς κἀπόπληκτος ὧδ' ἔχει;
Φιλοκτήτης ἀᾶ, ἀᾶ.
Νεοπτνλεμος τί δ' ἔστιν;
Φιλοκτήτης οὐδὲν δεινόν ἀλλ' ἴθ', ὦ τέκνον.

derer who has lost his way; black blood oozes forth, his ἀπαππαπαῖ begins: he pleads, he groans; he curses Ulysses, he rages against the gods, he calls out to Death, but he does all this only in fits and starts, these are only moments! The pain eases, and behold: he uses the moment of recovery to prepare himself for the third seizure. It duly comes, and, because the intensity of dramatic expression can rise no higher, Sophocles has him—has him do everything possible to prevent him from crying out—he raves, he groans, he pleads, he rages, breathlessly he comes to, and——passes out. What an agonizing scene! Perhaps the most intense expression ever demanded by a tragedy, which only a Greek actor could achieve.

But what is the most intense form of expression in this agonizing scene, what is its keynote? A cry? Hardly, for Sophocles seems to take especial care to ensure that a cry is not the keynote. Where are "the laments, the cries, the wild curses with which his anguish filled the camp and interrupted all the sacrifices and sacred rites, which resounded no less terribly through the desert island?"[6] Where are they? On the stage? Yes, but they are merely described,[7] described by his enemy Ulysses, who wishes to justify his decision to maroon and abandon him; the cries are not enacted; it is not as if they were the principal expression of the scene. True, a different poet, an Aeschylus, for example, would have been more inclined to make these cries the keynote of the exchange and perhaps, as he did with his Eumenides, have terrified a pregnant woman so much that she miscarried. In the hands of an exaggerated, modern tragedian, Philoctetes would surely already begin his howling behind the scenes before bursting onto the stage with a deafening, wild cry, rather as, for example, Hudemann's Cain, in the finest and latest coup de théâtre, announces his entrance by throwing his club before him and tumbling headlong after it. But in the wise Sophocles? How has he balanced the tone of fear? How carefully he has prepared us for it! How long he has suppressed it! How often he has interrupted it! How much he has generally moderated it! We might call the whole scene a picture of anguish that shows all the degrees of agony from mute distress to that numbing pain which is so great, as it were, that we no longer feel it; but taken as a whole the picture of subdued and not articulated pain: that is what it indisputably is in Sophocles, from beginning to end.

And hence the brevity of the act, which is short in words but long in performance. If the screaming, the "cries of anguish, moaning, the disjointed ἀᾶ," were of consequence in this regard, as Mr. Lessing thinks,[8] then I know of no sounds that must succeed one another more quickly or

---

[6] Laocoön, p. 3 [1:8].
[7] Sophocles, Philoctetes, act 1, scene 1.
[8] Laocoön, p. 4 [1:8].

cause the spectator more displeasure. But the restraint, the agonized self-mastery, the long, silent struggles with his torment, which are finally ended with a stolen ὦ μοι! μοι!—these are drawn out, they creep, and they are the keynote of the entire scene. Now add the twilit chorus, which sings a lullaby and soothing song to the slumbering Philoctetes in soft, slow breaths and which here does not merely bring the act to a close but appears itself within the act, for the sleeping Philoctetes lies before the spectator; include the chorus, as I say, and it is a long, whole, complete act that fills my soul—not by uttering the cry but by suppressing it. And thus Winckelmann can justly say that Laocoön suffers like Sophocles' Philoctetes. Only Laocoön suffers as a statue, whose sigh lasts forever, forever oppresses his breast; Philoctetes suffers as a tragic character, who must end his protracted sigh with an "ah me!" and greet the returning pain with an "oh!" who may wander up and down a string of distress but does so with sharp, with slowly recurring, with somewhat ascending and descending intermediate tones of subdued anguish. Sophocles was therefore the same wise master in his *Philoctetes* as Polydorus was with his *Laocoön*, and in both we see, taking into account their different subject matter, the same wise intention of seeking the tranquil, most pregnant expression and avoiding exaggeration. And that is precisely what Winckelmann says!

A cry is indeed the natural expression of physical pain,[9] but every art of imitation, and therefore every species of poetry, has its own limits in representing this expression. How various is Homer in the ways in which his warriors, his heroes fall, and how repetitive in what they have in common; but neither this variety nor this repetitiveness makes comprehensible to me Lessing's words "Homer's wounded warriors not infrequently fall to the ground with a cry!"[10] *Very infrequently*, I should say (if my memory of Homer does not deceive me), and *almost not at all*, except when the more specific determination of a character demands it. For all that it is common for a warrior to fall and die *with rattling armor*, as the ground shakes, and so on, as *dark night enfolded his eyes*,[11] it is nevertheless unusual for him to fall and die with a *cry*, with a *howl*; and in that case it is not "the natural expression of physical pain" but a character trait of the wounded hero. So a Phereclus, for example, *howls* when he is wounded;[12] but this Phereclus is a Trojan, an unwarlike artist, a cowardly turntail who is caught as he flees; obviously such a figure can distinguish himself by howling on his knees, but clearly not because "suffering Na-

---

[9] *Laocoön*, p. 4 [1:8].
[10] *Laocoön*, p. 4 [1:8–9].
[11] ἀμφὶ δὲ ὄσσε κελαινὴ νὺξ ἐκάλυψε.
[12] *Iliad* 5.68 ἔριπ᾽ οἰμώξας.

ture must have her due," but in keeping with his character. In keeping with her character Venus *shrieks aloud*,[13] for she is the tender goddess of love; scarcely has her delicate skin been grazed, scarcely does she notice the red ichor, the blood of the gods, than her hands sink; she leaves the field of battle, she weeps before her brother, mother and father, and the whole of heaven: she is inconsolable. Who will now say that Homer characterizes her thus "not because she must be made to represent the tender goddess of sensuality but because suffering Nature must have her due?" If that were true, why would he, with every image, with every word, with very movement, describe the flesh of the tender goddess so precisely?[14] Moreover, why would he let Pallas mock her, as if perchance she had scratched herself during some amorous adventure? Why would even her beloved father, Jupiter, smile at her? Does Jupiter smile and Pallas mock to give suffering Nature her due? And does a scratch to that glistening skin really cause Nature to suffer? Iron Mars screams just as little,[15] but that is for another reason—because he is iron, iron-eating Mars, who rages in the tumult of the battlefield and cries out just as wildly when wounded. Nothing is more certain than when we allow Homer to speak for himself, for if it had ever occurred to him to use the cry as a "natural expression of physical pain" and not with loftier intentions, then the expression "he was wounded and cried out" would be just as common as "he fell and darkness enfolded his eyes."

We have seen, then, that Homer does not use "the predicate of crying out as a general expression of physical pain," does not employ it as an absolute description to "give suffering Nature her due." That this particular man cries out and no other must lie in a more specific determination of his character. And so I think it vague to talk in general terms of how Homer's heroes act and feel;[16] for no hero's feelings are identical with another's, no more than are his words, his gestures, his body, his features; each is *an individual* soul that finds expression in this form and no other.

Still less does "crying aloud" seem to me the important, unchanging characteristic that would have to belong to the unchanging expression of a human emotion, for one man can sigh, another groan, a third cry out, and a Hannibal laugh in his greatest distress. But least of all is it the *necessary* determination of the *hero*, viewed as a human being, such that he would have to be a monster if he did not cry out. If that were the case, Homer would have sung of nothing but monsters. His Agamemnon, lord of men, the most glorious of the Greeks before Troy, is wounded in valiant

---

[13] *Iliad* 5.343 ἢ δὲ μέγα ἰάχουσα.
[14] *Iliad* 5.337 ἀβληχρήν.
[15] *Iliad* 5.859.
[16] *Laocoön*, p. 5 [1:9–10].

battle; he shudders[17]—but he forgets to cry out, to weep; he steels himself and, spear in hand, launches himself yet more keenly at the enemy. Should he be thought incapable of human feeling because he did not cry out like Mars or Lady Venus? Hector, the bravest of the Trojans, is thrown to the ground by the stone wielded by Ajax, and his chest is crushed; the spear drops from his hands, shield and helmet are lost, round about him rings his armor inlaid with bronze—but he forgets to scream.[18] He is comforted, he is given water; he regains his senses, looks up, but then sinks to his knees, spews black blood—and yet there is one thing this monster does not think to do: to cry out and weep over the pain in his chest and the wounds in his flank. It is the same with all the heroes of Homer, who observes their character in this respect also. Unexpectedly and at a critical moment, Menelaus is struck by Pandarus's arrow; his blood flows, Agamemnon shudders, Menelaus likewise;[19] but nothing more! When he sees the arrow in the wound, he pulls it out and leaves it to his brother and comrades to groan at his plight. As is known, Homer has a proper hierarchy of bravery, and it is brought to bear even in this apparently minor detail. Ulysses holds back his pain because he knows his wound is not mortal;[20] Agamemnon and Menelaus may shudder when they are wounded;[21] finally, the wounded Diomedes "*stood*, called upon Sthenelus to draw the arrow from his wound, and as the blood flowed his feelings did not pour out in tears and cries but in fiery prayers directed at the enemy."[22] That is how inhuman Homer's heroes are, and the greater the hero, the greater the inhumanity: his Achilles is even invulnerable to physical harm.

Is it the case, then, that Homer's heroes *must* cry and weep to "remain faithful to human nature in their sensitiveness to pain and injury and in the expression of this feeling by cries or tears"?[23] I would not wish that assertion to be read by an ancient Greek whose heroic soul still wandered the earth invisibly as a blessed demon. What, he would say, what is more natural than for a hero who joins battle to be wounded, to receive a blow; he can therefore take fright when an arrow strikes him unawares; but none of Homer's Greek heroes cries and weeps in battle, not even the Trojans, whom Homer subtly belittles in the details of his description. A Hector, even as death enfolds him, even with his last, dying plea, sheds no tear, utters no cry;[24] Sarpedon claws at the dust as he dies and the more bravely,

---

17 *Iliad* 11.254 ῥίγησέν τ' ἄρ' ἔπειτα ἄναξ ἀνδρῶν Ἀγαμέμνων.
18 *Iliad* 14.418.
19 *Iliad* 4.148.
20 *Iliad* 11.439.
21 *Iliad* 4.148.
22 *Iliad* 5.95ff.
23 *Laocoön*, p. 5 [1:9].
24 *Iliad* 22.330ff.

the more calmly in his pain.[25] Only the cowards tremble and weep and cry out: Phereclus, the cowardly fugitive, and tender Venus and iron-eating Trojan Mars. That is how *my* Homer writes.

So does Lessing's intriguing speculation about the sensitivity of the Greeks, about the contrast between them and both rude barbarians and refined Europeans hold good?[26] Not where the sensitivity to physical pain is concerned, at least not as the character trait of a Homeric hero; and not generally, not as a necessary mark of human feeling. So is there nothing else beyond physical pain that moves us to tears, and to loud, plaintive tears? Without doubt there is, and precisely this sensitivity, if indeed it be a merit of the Greeks, may redound to their greater honor, but to address it would evidently involve a digression from the proposition that Mr. L. believes he has demonstrated:[27] that "crying aloud when in physical pain,[28] especially according to the ancient Greek way of thinking, can quite well consist with nobility of soul"; a strange proposition, which the first chapter no more proves than does an army of weeping heroes, the like of which I do not know in Homer.[29] So as not to go away empty-handed, let us follow Lessing down the path on which he has gone astray.

3

The susceptibility of the Greeks to gentle tears is so familiar to us from any number of testimonies that unlike Mr. Lessing we need not take only a single example; and, moreover, one that is based on mere conjecture and perhaps does not prove what it is meant to prove.[30] Greeks and Trojans gather their dead. Both shed hot tears, but Priam forbids the Trojans to weep. Why does he forbid them to do so? He is afraid, Madame Dacier says, that they would grow too softhearted and take up the battle on the following day with less courage. "But why," asks Mr. Lessing, "why should only Priam fear this? The poet's meaning goes deeper: he wants to tell us that only the civilized Greek can weep and yet be brave at the same time, while the uncivilized Trojan, to be brave, must first stifle all human feel-

---

[25] *Iliad* 16.486.

[26] *Laocoön*, pp. 4–9 [1:9–11].

[27] *Laocoön*, p. 9 [1:11].

[28] That crying aloud, that uttering a brave, titanic cry was not on other occasions peculiar to Homer's heroes I do not deny; but what relevance does it have here?

[29] Drawing on his own special knowledge of Homer, Mr. Klotz was able to parrot Lessing: "clamor et eiulatus ex Graecorum opinione nihil detraxit magnitudini animi. *Homeri heroes clamantes cadunt*: sunt quidem illi heroes Homeri natura mortali maiores, sed numquam tamen, etc." (*Acta litteraria*, vol. 3, p. 286).

[30] *Laocoön*, p. 7 [1:10].

ing." He is too hard on the poor Trojans! Might Priam wish them to hold back their tears not because he is an uncivilized barbarian but because the tears of the Trojans, his children, were more consuming than the tears of the Greeks? The Greeks were the invaders and fought for honor; it was thus easier for them to take courage once more, and that is why Agamemnon had no need to be concerned. The Trojans, however, suffered; they were the besieged who fought not so much for honor as for their security, for their lives;[31] they felt in distress, and half sunk in despair, they knew that it was all because of a thief that they had lost their menfolk and their children, that it was all because of a thief that they were forced to bury their family. Here the feelings of this distressed people were outraged, here hot tears flowed and murmured protestations of innocence poured forth. And Priam did not let them weep! Why? Because he was an uncivilized barbarian and knew his Trojans could not weep and fight at the same time? What if he had restrained them in his role as the father of his ill-fated city and of his misfortune-bringing son? Or so that they might not wail and despair of a fate that lay so close to his own heart? But if this is not the real reason either, then the Trojans are not yet Laplanders or Scythians, for they weep for their kin and Priam fears that they will grow too softhearted, that their tears will eat too deeply into their souls. The very opposite explanation, then! But one can always make whatever one wants out of such interpretations, and a mere allegory—"the poet's meaning goes deeper,"—can ultimately lead us so deeply into that meaning that we lose the ground beneath our feet.

In the poetic art of the Greeks as a whole we find so much evidence of this nation's susceptibility to pain and tears that there is no need to rely on mere conjecture, and in large part their poetry is, as it were, a living imprint of this feeling, of this gentle soul. Let us call this part elegiac poetry, but let no one understand by this name that limping ape which, according to our learned textbooks on poetics, is distinguished solely by meter; rather, I take elegy here to be the poetic art of lament, what Horace called the *versus querimoniae,* wherever it may be found, in epic or ode, tragedy or idyll; for each of these genres can become *elegiac.* In this sense the elegy has its own domain in the human soul; namely, the sensibility to pain and grief. From here we can thus look out over nations and ages and by comparing them find where the Greeks themselves stand also. Let me mark out a few vantage points we might adopt.

1. Not every people has an equally tender heart for mild sorrows. Among some nations even lamentations possess a coarse strength, a heroic roaring that overwhelms them, and such a people will, though it has poets

---

[31] χρειοῖ ἀναγκαίη, πρό τε παίδων καὶ πρὸ γυναικῶν (*Iliad* 8.57).

great in other things, be exceedingly unfamiliar with the language of these gentle tears. Thus the northern Scandinavians, whose heroism steeled them even when they suffered bereavement, barely uttered short sighs and—were silent. When they sang, their song was scarcely the mild tears of elegiac complaint.

King Regner Lodbrog dies;[32] he dies in the most terrible pain. Is his death recounted in elegies? Does his tormented, dying humanity, the breaking heart of the father separated from his sons, have its due? A single gentle tear would have profaned Odin's successor. His death is chronicled in a song of triumph that commemorates his deeds, full of heroic joy, full of vengeance, full of courage, full of divine hope. "We have fought with our swords," his song concludes.

> How eagerly would my sons now rush to war, did they know the distress of their father, whom a multitude of venomous serpents tear! I have given to my children a mother who hath filled their hearts with valor. I am fast approaching to my end. A cruel death awaits me from the viper's bite. A snake dwells in the midst of my heart. I hope that the sword of some of my sons shall yet be stained with the blood of Ella. The valiant youths will wax red with anger, and will not sit in peace. Fifty and one times have I reared the standard in battle. In my youth I learned to dye the sword in blood: my hope was then that no king among men would be more renowned than me. The goddesses of death will now soon call me; I must not mourn my death. Now I end my song. The goddesses invite me away; they whom Odin has sent to me from his hall. I will sit upon a lofty seat, and drink ale joyfully with the goddesses of death. The hours of my life are run out. I will smile when I die.

That is the best example I can find to support Mr. Lessing's observation concerning the hard northern heroism.

Let us take another example from one of the best critical writings of our time.[33] Assbiøn Prude, the heroic Dane, captured by his enemies, his innards churning with slow rage—does he lament, does he sigh? He thinks of his mother, of all the joys of his youth and his manhood; he feels all his anguish, but as a hero: thus does he die. Thus dies the Esquimaux at the stake.[34] Friend and fatherland, children and mother—everything that is most dear to him in the world he hails in his death song; but in order to weep over them, to pay his debt of human feelings? A single gentle tear would dishonor the hero, his clan, his friend, and his fatherland.

---

[32] Mallet's *Geschichte von Dänemark*, pp. 112, 113.

[33] [Gerstenberg,] *Briefe über die Merkwürdigkeiten der Litteratur*, [pt. 1, 1766], p. 112, 113.

[34] [Johann Friedrich Schröter, *Allgemeine] Geschichte [der Länder und Völker] von Amerika*, pt. 1 [1752], p. 404.

Therefore no "ah!" escapes his lips, even amid the most terrible agonies; blistered and burned, he sings his song of torment. He is untied so that he may die an even slower death and—with laughter and mockery smokes his pipe with others; the torments begin anew; he mocks, falls silent; he becomes their teacher in new agonies, sings, and dies in triumph. Thus the Esquimaux!

So where the heart of a people is made of flint, the most intense pain—no matter whether it strikes body or soul—produces nothing but heroic sparks, for how should a flintstone shed a tender, elegiac tear? Valor, this love of one's country and of the glory of one's tribe, the heroic fellowship with a friend who shall be one's avenging angel: the whole development of an uncouth and strong character into the unflinching successor of Odin and other tearless heroes who inspire their people, their republic with the very spirit of bravery—all this served to deaden human sentiment and feeling and tears.

2. Now let this valor, this love of one's country and of the glory of one's tribe, this feeling for friendship and the undissembling openness of the soul—let all these noble and great convictions express themselves without such entrenchment and hardness; then the greatest courage will show itself to be the most sensitive humanity. "In their deeds they are beings of a higher order, in their feelings true men."

And are we to assume that these dual beings of a higher order, these heroes, these *semones*, existed only among the Greeks? And that our ancestors were barbarians and all northern barbarians monsters? Human feeling must dwell in all men; where this feeling is stifled and overwhelmed by raw bravery, it must first be violently stormed by a thousand examples, by a great exemplar living among a nation, by the whole spirit of the people, and by all the impressions education leaves behind from childhood on; ultimately human feeling must be compelled to compete with these examples, to follow this great exemplar who determines the spirit of this nation. And where it is not stifled, there undissembled Nature will reveal herself; the sentiments of humanity will clothe themselves in the raiment of the hero and in turn the hero's soul be unashamed to shed human tears—whichever nation he may belong to!

And what if we discovered such a people even among the northern mountains, in the midst of barbarians, even under the name of a barbarian tribe that was concerned with nothing but warfare? A people as distant from the land of Greece as from its manners, yet which exhibited all the human sensibility that scarcely a Greek has shown—would then this contrast remain quite so clear? "Our northern ancestors were barbarians. To master all pain, to face death's stroke with unflinching eye, to weep neither at the loss of one's dearest friend nor at one's own sins: these are the traits of *old northern heroism*. Not so the Greek!"[35] If I were to interrupt at this point and continue: "Not so the Scot, the Celt, the Irishman! He expressed his pain and grief. He was not ashamed of any human weakness, but it must not prevent him from attaining honor nor from fulfilling his duty." Then I would have said in support of my barbarians everything that Lessing says of his Greeks when he contrasts them with the northern barbarians, and withal I would still not have said quite enough.

I know of no poetic people on earth who combined to such a degree grand and gentle sentiments in a single cast of mind and who possessed so completely in a single soul the heroism of bravery and human feeling than— the ancient Scots, as their recently discovered songs testify. These songs are a reliable witness, for their originality is a proven fact and we know that the life of this nation was spent entirely in deeds, sentiments, and songs, where the songs had no other purpose than immortalizing those very deeds and sentiments. That is not all: every bardic song reveals a people whose entire soul blazed with courage and a solemn love; a people whose manner of thinking was in general lent a certain melancholy color by a heroic seriousness and who transferred that melancholy even to their gentle sentiments. I can find no better name to describe most specimens of Erse poetic art than *solemn laments*; and they have, as far as this aspect of human feeling is concerned, no equal in antiquity, not even in Greek antiquity.

Shilric[36] parts from his beloved Vinvela: afar, afar he goes to the wars of Fingal; he leaves her; she remains alone; perhaps he will fall in battle; but Vinvela shall remember him. I know no work that sings so movingly, in five exchanges of dialogue, by evoking the sweetness of love and the firm resolve of the departing hero, of two such noble and sensitive characters saying their farewells. I shall lift from Lessing his words about the Greeks: "Here the Scot! He expressed his pain and grief. He was not ashamed of any human weakness, but it must not prevent him from attaining honor nor from fulfilling his duty." And yet this Scot was a barbarian hailing from northern peaks.

Shilric grieves for his distant Vinvela;[37] she appears, she speaks, her voice like the breeze in the reeds of the pool: "I heard of your death: I heard and mourned thee, Shilric; I am pale in the tomb." She fleets, she sails away, as gray mist before the wind. Schilric laments her: it is the gentlest, most solemn elegy of love! "Only a Scot," I would say with Lessing's enthusiasm, "only a Scot can weep and yet be brave at the same time!"

---

[35] *Laocoön*, p. 5 [1:9].
[36] *Fragments of Ancient Poetry*, p. 1 [fragment 1].
[37] Ibid., p. 4 [fragment 2].

What can surpass the poem "Comála"?[38] What can surpass its truth and simplicity; sweetness and majesty; strength and tenderness of thought, of sentiment, of expression; its form and content; what can surpass the elegiac love songs of this nation, which delights in nothing but bardic lays full of the tragic exploits and tragic love of heroes? Nothing, not even anything produced by the ancient Greeks! The love of the Greeks, their gentle sentiments and laments seem softer and verbose when I compare them with these barbarians, for whom love dwelled in a proud, heroically proud soul, rose to a gentle fervor, to a sublime heroic tenderness, and in its elegies, too, moves and enchants us by expressing a noble cast of mind. The diluted laments of our modern elegists weary my ear, but in this solemn antiquity there resounds a melancholy love that teaches us that "not only the civilized Greek can weep and yet be brave at the same time," but the barbarian Scot can do it better.

But perhaps all this was true with only one human sentiment while all others were necessarily stifled by bravery? Yet how can one be uttered without simultaneously making room for all? The elegiac voice of the Scots is just as sweet and brave when expressing love of one's *father* and of one's tribe as it is when expressing the *love of women*. We know what importance the glory of the tribe had in ancient times, a sentiment that in our day seems to be have been washed from our souls, save for a foolish pride in one's ancestors. Where do nobler tears flow than when Fingal's son, Ossian,[39] renews the memory of his sons and his father, of their deeds and their deaths—where are there nobler tears than on the cheeks of the old man, who stands "like an ancient oak: but the blast has lopped my branches away; and I tremble at the wings of the north. I moulder alone in my place." That is the lament of brave Ossian, and that is the lament of Armin and gray-hair'd Carryl also—that is the lament of heroes, of fathers of their tribes. All the sentiments of heroes and of men—for example, the love of one's country, of one's tribe, of one's friends, of women, and of humanity—all these sentiments live on in this nation's poems, which are like imprints of their soul.

And hence it was not the Greek alone who could weep and yet be brave at the same time.[40] Hence, not everyone whom we call a barbarian, who lived in a raw climate and was unconversant with the civilization of the Greeks, was the kind of man who "to be brave must first stifle all human feeling." Hence, if the Greeks combined both, it was due not to their national soul, their temperament, their climate, or their cultivation; and hence there must be other causes that either produced or did not produce

---

[38] Ibid., p. 81 ["Comála: A Dramatic Poem," in *Fingal*].
[39] Ibid., pp. 17, 21–22 [fragments 6–8].
[40] *Laocoön*, p. 7 [1:10].

this blend of heroism and human feeling, both in them and in the barbarians. Ought not these reasons lead us on to the question, To what and why were the Greeks so sensitive?

4

1. If there be an age in which the word *fatherland* has not yet become an empty sound, but is

> —ein Silberton dem Ohr,
> Licht dem Verstand und hoher Flug zum Denken,
> dem Herzen groß Gefühl,

then the term *fatherland* must make the poet a hero as much as it makes the hero a poet, and both of them sympathetic sons of their fatherland. The hero will fight for his country, the poet sing on its behalf, and if neither can save it anymore, then both will weep for it. And if poet and hero and son of the fatherland are now united in a single person, then we find ourselves in the *age of patriotic laments*. These complaints will issue not from a learned pen but from an overflowing heart; they will live not only on the page but in the memory, in the soul; the voice of tradition will preserve them and the mouth of the people sing them; they will provoke tears and deeds: they are a national treasure, and the feeling that they celebrate and arouse is a national feeling, the national spirit. It will therefore be a single patriotic sentiment that now blossoms into deeds, now into songs, now into tears for the fatherland, depending on whether patriotism, as it develops, guides the sentiment this way or that and does not choke any of its offshoots. Among the Scandinavians the example of Odin's fortitude stifled one form of expression, the tears of the hero, and strengthened another: heroic exploits.

But let now a new spirit of the age succeed this one; let the whole world become the land of the wise man or of the good and agreeable fool. Gradually the bonds that tied the heart of the native-born to his soil will weaken; the misfortune or the sense of separation from his fatherland will thus no longer weigh on his soul quite so heavily, and so the noble tear shed for the fatherland has dried, a tear that did not shame but rather honored the hero and the sage. At worst it will make way for the selfish or lascivious tear shed by an Ovid as he babbles sadly or by Bussy-Rabutin in his senseless complaint for a lustful court. And thus one source of this heroic feeling has dried up: "the cultivation and education of men for their fatherland."

2. If each race, each family, undivided and united as a whole, still forms a tree, where the branches and fruit redound to the honor of the trunk

and where the trunk itself suffers injury if they are severed, then how significant are the delicate brushstrokes with which Homer portrays his heroes as they fall: "He fell, in the bloom of youth; it was not the father who counseled him to war! He is descended from a noble race; but he was the last of the line—he came from a distant land; but never will he return there—the sons of the wealthy fell; the father accumulated everything for strangers to enjoy." To this world, then, belong Priam's heroic laments for his Hector, for the glory of his race, for the walls of Troy; to this world belong Ossian's laments for his deceased sons; Hector's moving embrace of his little Astyanax; the laments of Electra and of other tragic heroines, the poignant passing of the Orientals *to their fathers*, and so on—a vein of feeling that runs through the best poems and stories, not only of the Greeks but of all the peoples *in whom this unity of the generations, this family feeling has dwelled.*

But now stifle this feeling; go beyond the natural requirements of the unspoiled human soul and of the simpler way of life; turn marriage into an economic exchange, a social convention, and married couples into nothing but people who trouble and amuse each other; raise the sons in such a way that suckled at the breasts of a stranger, a nursemaid, they are already no longer brothers and will grow further apart the older they become; join together people who were distant even on their wedding day and place in their arms children who share only their name—all this will of course deaden a nerve of feeling. The honorific name "Achilles was a son of Peleus" is gradually extinguished, the yearning of Ulysses for his Penelope and his rocky Ithaca we think extravagant; the sentimental pride of the Orientals in the dignity of their family is in our estimation ridiculous, and the laments of a Haller, Klopstock, Canitz, or Öder seem to many good husbands as poetic as an invocation to the Muse.

There was a time (it has not yet passed among the savages!) when there existed friends such as we otherwise scarcely encounter today: two inseparable companions in fortune and misfortune, bound together by the most sacred laws, who, by competing to fulfill the most exacting duties, were exemplars for their native city and the object of their country's admiration. Because this feeling for friendship was instilled in them by their upbringing, they often sealed it with their death and their blood; they never abandoned their friend, even in mortal danger, which the courage of that time was bound to confront more often than our modern licentiousness must; the slightest disloyalty toward their friend drew upon them the mockery of their tribe and the abomination of the city; they were bound by every law to avenge his death, and the last words of the one—who was perhaps captured, perhaps slain—were—addressed to his friend, to his companion in life. There was once a Hercules and Ioláüs, an Aeneas and Achates, an Orestes and a Pylades, a Theseus and Pirithoüs, a David and Jonathan: hence for the *hero* a wellspring of amicable feeling, which for the mere citizen and associate has all but dried up. There once flowed, when death or misfortune separated those friends whom life could not part, such noble hero's tears that Achilles wept for his Patroclus, just as Pylades wept for his Orestes and David for his Jonathan.

Now let the world in which such amity flourished disappear; the modern mode of life shall no longer make necessary two such companions in life and death; the solemnity of these fellowships shall diminish, men's disposition to work and ways of life become more various and inconstant, as it were; the condition of citizens and fellow citizens more peaceful, each a god in his own world—then where shall we still find an army of lovers, of male sweethearts, a Boeotian ιερος λοχος? A friend will yet be a companion and something desirable, only he will not be what he was in the world of heroes and friendly alliances, no matter, incidentally, whether this world existed in Greece or Scotland or America. If a new fountain of hero's tears is stopped, then this most touching image of two friends is now at the very least a curio and no longer, as in past times, a spectacle performed before the world. And in the same degree as Achilles, as a *hero*, would necessarily be different in our day and age, so the "Achilles weeping for his Patroclus, driven almost mad by grief and rage," must seem alien to us also.

If there exists a time and place where beauty still owes more to Nature than to finery and rouge, where love is not yet gallantry and the male gift of pleasing is rather more than courtesy, there sentiment, language, and even the tear of love shall also have dignity and not dishonor even the eye of a hero. Of course, the hero will not elegize, like Polyphemus, the cyclops of Theocritus; but the Philoctetes of Chateaubrun and the lovesick Greek heroes of the French stage are even less likely to do so. True sentiment and manly virtue have their dignity and majesty without borrowing them from monstrous metaphors, from gallant puns, or from decorous sighs, and in this respect also let the language of love of the ancient heroes—the Scots, for instance—stand as an example. They act like heroes and feel like human beings.

But since, of course, no feeling lays claim to the realm of fancy as its proper domain more readily than does love, so there is none that can more easily fall away from dignity and truth and sink into fantasy and frivolity. Hence, for various reasons, there can only ever be but a thin line separating a hero's tears of love and contempt. Of all the human frailties of which a hero must not feel ashamed, this is the most delicate; and this is proven by the large troupe of lovesick heroes parading in novels and the theater. Here, however, the Greek poets had a considerable, insufficiently unrecognized advantage: namely, access to a national realm of love, which, full of exceedingly poetic fancies, must have freed them from many an embarrassment. The erotic adventures of their gods and goddesses; the whole retinue of Venus, of the Graces, and of Cupid; and a hundred beautiful and entertaining anecdotes drawn from the mythology of love lent their language of love a sweetness and dignity that our age imitates only too often but ends up becoming—ridiculous. If in our elegies and odes Cupid flutters about with his darts, if an entire nomenclature of amatory expressions has been borrowed from the Greeks and Romans and poured out even in letters exchanged between men, then our modern trifles lose the dignity, well, not of a hero's soul, but only of common sense and are reduced to banal nonsense. Or if, finally, even the gothic tone of love typical of the Middle Ages of the knights and giants flows together with the sweet decorousness of our age, then it is transformed into the heartbreaking *parenthyrsus*, the lachrymose gallantry with which truly a Greek hero, for all his sensibility for the frailties of human nature, was no more familiar than was wise Socrates with the monasticism of the Capuchins.

Generally speaking, when the scenery of human life was more perspicuous, when the affairs of the world may not yet have been so entangled and refined but were all the more creditable to humanity, when usefulness and ability and virtue were not yet accounted so crookedly but were human, in those days a feeling of humanity drew souls ever more closely together, and the tombs of the great and good of the land demanded the hero's tears. The life of the hero was simpler and more transparent, and his virtues and merits therefore closer to the heart also; for a hero, a statesman, a man of merit, of wisdom, a man such as the ancient world demanded and cultivated, could sooner lure forth a *human* tear than, for example, a tactically minded general, a minister, an officer of the law, a *literator* of the modern world, if that is all he is; for with the loss of all their abilities and virtues, only the fewest such men are *human* in the full sense of that word, and what is better able to excite human feelings than——human nature? Where are the names without deeds, the ranks without real merit, the endeavors and offices of our age without spirit and life, the religions without human virtue—where are all the sundry learned, wealthy, noble, pious fools of our civic and polished and Most Christian world? Are they worth a *human* tear?

Finally, since the true use of human life and happiness was perhaps better known, though not through sermons and morals, and life was enjoyed more and lived more humanely, then the bitter blows of existence were naturally more affecting. The death of a young man cut down in the prime of his years like a young and beautiful poplar tree—such an incident is the occasion in Homer for images that can cause a tender tear of humanity to well up even in the hero's eye, because they are—human. And I would scarcely think highly of the youth whom these Homeric images did not move. An equally delicate sentiment is raised by the death of a man who has lived only half his life, who, like Homer's Protesilaus, for example, left behind half-finished palaces of splendor, half-completed designs of manly pride, who has acquired aptitudes and skills to no avail, whom Diana has in vain taught to hunt and Pallas to fight: poignant images of a human world into which Homer transports us so readily and wherein of course those heroes must live, who are "in their deeds gods and in their feelings men."

I cannot pursue this matter to its conclusion here. Taking only the details I have already adduced, we apprehend an age in which heroes, regardless of how high they are raised above human nature, nevertheless remain faithful to it in their feeling of sorrow and in the expression of this sentiment by tears, more faithful than we, in whom this gentle feeling is either stifled or recast as a womanish lasciviousness. I therefore return myself to this world when I desire to feel Homer's heroes and the Greek tragedies with all my soul, but I would not wish to limit this feeling to Greece alone. For wherever this aforementioned age of humanity obtains, we find also this balance between bravery and sentiment; and this, I think, is always the age between barbarism and the state of docile civility and polite appearance in which we now live. In such a time notions of fatherland, honor, family, friend, and humanity all become extinct, after a certain fashion; and so feeling and its expression, the tear, are extinguished also.

But can the sensation of physical pain change? A blow is still a blow, a wound still a wound, a box on the ear still a box on the ear, and will always be such for as long as the world exists. Thus the case of pain is different from the foregoing feelings, and our soft and flaccid state has rather infinitely increased our sensitivity to pain, often to the level of effeminacy. Accordingly, if a Greek Theseus, Hercules, or Philoctetes feels pain, a wound, once, then a sybarite of our age must feel it sevenfold, and if "the cry is supposed to be the natural expression of physical pain and the due of suffering Nature, a character trait of Greek heroes," then it follows that where the Greek screamed once our contemporary, with a feeling seven times more intense, could and should have to cry seven times more loudly in order to be a Homeric hero.

How can it have come to pass that "we more refined Europeans of a wiser, later age know better how to govern our mouths and our eyes, and have thus denied ourselves so cruelly the privilege of suffering Nature"? If we have lost the feelings for fatherland, friend, family, and humanity, and hence also the tender feeling of pain at their loss, and have covered over this loss, this lack of feelings, with courtesy and propriety—that would explain it. Yet now there is supposed to dwell in us a greater degree of sensitivity to physical pain, and yet suffering Nature demands less, infinitely less of us? And furthermore, what was honorable or at least permissible for the Greek heroes, who felt pain less keenly, is supposed to be a disgrace for us weaklings and forbidden by propriety, which is supposed to give at least the appearance of strength? And forbidden because it is a sign of weakness?

And this was ever among the Greeks a character trait of Homeric heroes? Then I do not know my Homer and I do not know my Greeks. When in the assembly an Agamemnon weeps over the loss of the Greeks,[41] for which he was to blame because of his quarrel with Achilles, then I love his royal tears; they flow on behalf of children, and in their outpouring, which Homer can compare with a stream, they relieve his sad, fatherly heart; but this Agamemnon would not cry out and howl when he is wounded. When Achilles, publicly insulted by Agamemnon, feels his honor slighted and weeps before his mother, Thetis,[42] I gladly see his glory-loving tears; I weep with him, with the young hero; but when wounded, he does not weep or cry out; otherwise he is no longer Achilles. He may howl and moan and grieve for his friend Patroclus;[43] I feel his tears and his noble heart; I would not admire him if he were not a stoic hero; thus does Agamemnon sigh over his wounded brother[44] and Priam over his slain son—these are sorrows of the soul and noble tears with which, indeed, the screams and the weeping over a wound cannot compare. None of Homer's heroes cries and weeps over such a thing, and would it be worth changing everything in Homer to make Lessing's proposition true: "High as Homer raises his heroes above human nature in other respects, he still has them remain faithful to it in their sensitiveness to pain and injury, and in the expression of this by cries or tears"?[45] I would that Mr. Lessing had not written these words.

5

But Philoctetes? Mr. Lessing has devoted a long section to defending Sophocles for admitting physical pain to the stage and letting a hero cry out in this pain.[46] His defense as a whole issues from the perspective of the dramatist and betrays, in the fine manner in which it is elaborated, the author of the *Dramaturgy*; it is a pity, however, that it is built entirely on false premises; in the case of Sophocles' Philoctetes, he supposes the scream to be the *keynote* of his expression of pain and thus the *principal*

---

[41] *Iliad* 9.14 [13–22].
[42] *Iliad* 1.349, 357, 360ff.
[43] *Iliad* 28.22–35; 23:12–23.
[44] *Iliad* 4.148.
[45] *Laocoön*, p. 5 [1:9].
[46] *Laocoön*, pp. 31–49 [4].

means of arousing sympathy, which it is not. And it is a pity, too, that it is drawn up merely as dramaturgy, as an outline for a drama; I think it better to give oneself over to the impressions of the performance, not to justify Sophocles from the point of view of the dramatist but, like a Greek spectator, to attend to undissembled impressions——

And which impressions are these, generally speaking? If there is one Greek play that is written to be performed and not read, then it is *Philoctetes*, for the whole effect of the tragedy derives from the vitality of its performance. So let us turn our eyes and mind toward the Athenian stage. The scene opens: we see an untrod shore, a desert, sea-girt isle—how did these travelers end up here?[47] What will take place in this desolate wilderness? Here, we are told, is Philoctetes, the famous son of Poeas: Wretched, lonely man! Robbed of all human company, banished here to perpetual solitude. How will he pass his days? And he is sick, afflicted with the festering sore on his foot! Now he is even more pitiful, this hermit! Who will care for you here, provide for you, wash and dress your wound? And how did you get here? Oh, you were marooned—without mercy, without assistance—and because of a crime, because of your obstinacy? No, because of your lamentable shrieks! Oh, the monsters! What can this sick, wretched man do but weep and cry out? And that they did not even grant him relief, did not bear this little discomfort, but marooned him! Who marooned him? The Greeks, his people, his companions—but perhaps just one wicked man was to blame? No, he was put ashore on the orders of the Greek generals, by Ulysses himself. And this same Ulysses can tell us this, and so coldly, can break off his account so indifferently, because he has hatched new plots against him—oh, what malice! Who would not want to take the side of a poor, lonely, abandoned, afflicted man, pitied by no one, against this treacherous rogue, the instrument of his misfortune?

Now the dwelling place of the wretch hoves closer into view—it is an uninhabited cave! Are there yet household furniture and food within? Trodden leaves—a miserable couch fit for animals! Here must lie the hero without whom Troy cannot be conquered: a cup hewn from a log, some tinder—these are the only treasures of the king! And ye gods! Here there are pus-covered rags, testament to his affliction! He is abroad—but how far can the wretch hobble? Doubtless he was compelled to—in quest of food, perhaps! Or of a soothing herb! If only he could find it! If only we could glimpse him! Meanwhile the scene of betrayal begins,[48] as Ulysses succeeds in persuading Neoptolemus—this kindhearted, honorable man, the son of honorable Achilles—to take a stranger, a wretch hostage by

[47] Sophocles, *Philoctetes*, act 1.
[48] Scene 2 [50–134].

cunning, by lies and intrigues. I know that the Greeks, especially Sophocles, may hate those immoral monsters no more than he may hate those who are moral, and that on his stage he presents nothing but men, neither angels nor devils; but Ulysses as he appears here is not merely the sly, crafty Ulysses of Homer; he is a seducer who brazenly divulges the principles of his perfidy, which cast aside all virtue, and fie upon the scoundrel who dresses his wickedness in *principles*. Sophocles thus prefers to face the condemnation of the moralizing pedants who demand that every utterance on the stage be wrapped in a Pythagorean maxim; he would rather paint his Ulysses blacker than he usually depicts characters—in order to win us over to poor Philoctetes, whom Ulysses has double-crossed and means to double-cross again.

The chorus and Neoptolemus now seek to implant this sympathy for Philoctetes more deeply within us;[49] they reiterate the foregoing descriptions of distress, multiply them with their conjectures as to his condition, and——from afar a groaning is heard! That it is a groaning and not a shriek is demonstrated by the conduct of Neoptolemus, who, disconcerted also by the nature of his commission, cannot tell from whence it comes. The lamentation draws nearer, it becomes a whimpering, a deep, plaintive cry—only now is it audible! They are not mistaken: Philoctetes must be approaching and oh! As the shepherd arrives to the sound of a reed pipe, so Philoctetes is accompanied by the sound of moaning—he enters! Or rather, he shuffles along in order—

Will he now throw himself onto the stage with a bellow? Will he start to bawl so that Peter Quince might say "Let him roar again; let him roar again"? If only the critics could be persuaded that there is no bellowing, of which there is so little trace in the Greek! During a long act Philoctetes speaks with the stranger without thinking of screaming;[50] even the far-resounding groans we heard previously Sophocles has left offstage. Wise Sophocles! How can I think Philoctetes effeminate, how can I find his lamentation contemptible when he uttered it only because he thought himself alone, when he at once concealed his moans from the strangers and can always take refuge in conversation? The sufferer is a hero.

And Sophocles takes great care with this character. Philoctetes must first make himself a friend of our soul before our body can sympathize with him,[51] and how concerned is the poor man with the strangers? That they might deceive him is the furthest thought from his mind; the kindhearted fellow takes them for castaways, for people deserving his commiseration—this friend of mankind! He sees their Greek dress, a painful re-

[49] Scene 3 [135–220].
[50] Act 2 [221–538].
[51] Act 2, scene 1.

minder for him of his treacherous countrymen; but all this he has put behind him. How he hopes that they are Greeks; how he longs to hear a
Greek voice again! This is an honest Greek who can arouse the interest of
Greeks. He hears them speak Greek; in his joy, poor Philoctetes forgets
his bitter grief. He makes the acquaintance of the son of Achilles, the son
of his dear friend; he becomes more open; he tells Neoptolemus his story,
movingly, as if Penia herself had appeared. He is a friend to his friends; to
fallen Achilles he offers his tears of friendship; he forgets his own woes
and heaves a sigh over a dead hero who is more fortunate than he. He is
a friend to his friends; the son of Achilles sees Philoctetes pity him, even
as he betrays him. He grieves over the death of the heroes and—yet more
noble—he grieves simply because they were good men; the villains he
curses! How much has Philoctetes now awakened our interest in him, as
a friend of mankind, as a Greek in body and soul, as a hero. And this hero
shall rot here, on a desert island, far from the contest with other heroes?
It is an absence keenly felt, for where these heroes perform great deeds,
where they die garlanded with laurels, he must bemoan a wound that is
truly no hero's wound. He, a Greek to his very core, must squander his
life far from his country, far from his loving father, who perhaps already
walks among the shades: he, an honest man who has been betrayed——
O Neoptolemus, you wish to abandon him! Oh, if only Philoctetes
pleaded with him! But now he does so, and urgently: he lays siege to his
heart from so many sides that the entreaty of the chorus, "O pity him!"
becomes our protest also. We grow annoyed with Neoptolemus when his
revulsion at Philoctetes' malady causes him to demur and love him when
he——promises him that he will not betray him after all! See how
Philoctetes implores him, how he thanks him, how he then invites him
into his cave and—

Now the disguised merchant captain approaches.[52] Philoctetes hears
that he is to go to Troy; Ulysses has publicly promised to show him to the
Greek army, and—he does not think the merchant worthy of his reply. A
single heroic expression of astonishment—"Gods! This wretch, this traitor has sworn to bring me to the Greek camp?"—betrays the whole heroic
soul of Philoctetes; he continues talking,[53] he wants to board the ship; this
honest soul believes Neoptolemus, entrusts him with his weapons, surren-
ders himself to his care. How I feel for Philoctetes! But for Philoctetes the
screamer? I feel nothing yet! I feel for Philoctetes the hero, the Greek, the
nobleman—and the most wretched man made even more wretched by
what his enemies plan for him. As yet we imaginatively sympathize merely
with his soul, and only now comes the rare scene in which his bout of sick-

[52] Act 2, scene 2 [539–627].
[53] Scene 3.

ness is depicted. The chorus anticipates it with a song about the exceedingly pitiable fate of Philoctetes,[54] and then the seizure arrives.[55] I have already described it and need not repeat that description here. I am vexed when, on the one hand, the scene is made into nothing but a hue and cry and, on the other, it is thought by the commendable French—by Brumoy,[56] for example—to be a bolt, something inserted to fill up the five acts. What silence must have reigned on the stage in Athens as this act unfolded!

The manifestations of physical pain are over and I need go no further. I shall therefore turn back from the Athenian stage and return to where I left Lessing—yet how different are our ideas about the impression that this drama ought to make. Only one of us can be right, which means the other simply could not exercise his imagination sufficiently in order not to read but to see. I shall be on my guard to ensure that this does not apply to me.

Mr. Lessing makes "the idea of physical pain" the principal idea of the play,[57] and he seeks out the refined means by which the poet was able to strengthen and enlarge this idea.[58] I must confess that if *this* were the principal idea of the tragedy, then several of the means cited by Mr. Lessing would have had little effect on me. The impression of physical pain is far too confused and, as it were, physical to leave room for the questions,[59] Where is the pain? Is it internal or external? What does the wound look like? What poison is at work in it? If the representation of physical pain were so feeble that it needed to be strengthened by such matters, then the effect of the theater is lost; in that case it is better if I go as a surgeon to inspect the wound personally. No! The idea of pain is theatrical, and I therefore have no need of theatrical reinforcement—if pain is the principal idea of the play, then I wish to become acquainted with it from afar, from the grimaces, from the sounds of distress; it is almost a matter of indifference to me why a man should be crying and gesticulating, whether over a lame foot or a wound deep in his breast. The critic loses everything when he retreats from the theatrical illusion and, to strengthen it, to make it more plausible, supplies us with the certificate of a surgeon—tells us what kind of malady it is, that it is a real wound, a poison that can cause this much pain. Irrespective of whether Sophocles actually gave thought to such matters, it is enough that I should require them to strengthen my idea of pain. And in that case I bid farewell to the theater! For I find myself in a hospital.

So, theatrical pity! And how can I be moved to pity if the principal idea

[54] Scene 3.

[55] Scene 3.

[56] [Brumoy,] *Théâtre des Grecs* [1730], 2:89.

[57] *Laocoön*, pp. 3, 4, 31, 32 [1:8; 4:24, 25].

[58] *Laocoön*, pp. 33–49 [4].

[59] *Laocoön*, pp. 33, 34 [4:25].

of the play is physical pain? What, then, are the chief means of exciting sympathy? I cannot think of any apart from the usual utterances, cries, tears, and convulsions; these Mr. Lessing also adduces, and he takes great trouble[60] to explain why these expressions of pain do not offend propriety and in what their decisive effect consists.[61] Good! But if whimpering, crying out, and the most terrible convulsions are the means, the principal means, of planting in me the idea of physical pain and striking my heart, then what can be the best effect of this blow? With physical pain I cannot but sympathize physically: that is, sympathy causes a similarly painful tension to be produced in my fibers; I suffer the pain in my own body. And would this compassion be agreeable? Anything but; the cry of distress, the convulsion passes through my every limb with a shudder; I feel it myself; the same spasmodic movements manifest themselves in me, as if I were a string tuned to the same pitch. Whether the whimpering man gripped by a seizure is Philoctetes does not concern me: he is an animal, just as I am; he is a human being: human pain agitates my nervous system, just as it does when I see a dying animal, a man with the death rattle, a creature in torment who feels as I do. And how is this impression in the slightest degree pleasurable, agreeable? It is excruciating; even the appearance of it, even its enactment are quite excruciating. In the moment that we receive this impression, there can be no thought of artistic illusion, of the pleasures of the imagination: Nature, my animal being suffers within me, for I see and hear an animal of my species suffer.

And would one not require a gladiator's soul to endure a play in which this idea, this feeling of physical pain, were the principal idea, the principal feeling? I know of no third possibility beyond these two: I am either deceived or I am not. In the first case, even if it is only for a moment that I mistake the actor for a quivering, screaming man in torment, woe is me! My nerves twitch! The artistic deceiver who, for my gratification, wanted to give the appearance of hanging himself—I cannot watch him for a single moment longer as soon as the illusion is lifted, as soon as he really chokes. I cannot watch the tightrope dancer for a single moment longer as soon as I see him plunge and fall on the sword lying below, as soon as I see him lying on the ground with a mutilated foot. The sight of Philoctetes becomes unbearable to my eyes as soon as I think that he is the suffering Philoctetes. Only the soul of a gladiator can wish to study this illusion of physical pain, rather like that statue of the dying gladiator, in order to descry how much soul still remained in him. Only a monster, according to the legend of Michelangelo, could crucify a person merely to observe how he dies.

[60] *Laocoön*, pp. 3, 32, 34 [1:8; 4:25, 26].
[61] *Laocoön*, pp. 41–49 [4:30–32].

Mr. L. may say that "nothing is more deceptive than the laying down of general laws for our emotions."[62] Here the law lies in my immediate feeling itself, namely in that feeling which is farthest removed from general principles, that feeling with which I am endowed as an animal capable of sympathy. As soon as the suffering body of Philoctetes becomes the focus of my attention, it remains the case that the "closer the actor approaches nature, or reality, the more our eyes and ears must be offended."[63] An ocean of disagreeable emotions will wash over me without admixture of a single agreeable drop. The representation of the artistic deception? It is disturbed by the very illusion; I have nothing before me but the spectacle of a man wracked by convulsions, in sympathy with whom I too very nearly feel palpitations, of a whimpering man whose "ah!" cuts through my heart. It is no longer a tragedy but a cruel pantomime, a sight to cultivate the souls of gladiators: I look for the exit.

Now let us suppose the second case, namely that the Greek actor with all his σκενοποιια and declamation cannot bring the screams and the grimaces of pain to the point of illusion (something that Mr. Lessing does not venture to affirm);[64] assuming, then, that I remain a sober spectator, I cannot conceive of a more repulsive pantomime than aped convulsions, howling cries, and, if the illusion is to be complete, the foul stench of a wound. Then the theatrical mummer of Philoctetes would scarcely be able to say to the spectator what the true Philoctetes said to Neoptolemus: "But though mad'st light of all the sores to eye and ear and nostrils that my malady inflicts."[65] With a repulsive and unfortunately not illusory pantomime this is unavoidable.

I open the Letters Concerning Recent Literature and find that their foremost writer in matters of rigorous philosophy shares my opinion in a similar case.[66] He inquires as to "why the imitation of disgust can never please us" and cites as reasons: "because this disagreeable sensation affects only our lower senses, taste, smell, and touch: the obscurest senses which do not have the slightest share in the works of the fine arts; because, secondly, the sensation of disgust becomes disagreeable not through the representation of reality, as with other disagreeable impressions, but immediately through intuition; and because, finally, in this sensation the soul does not recognize any obvious mixture of pleasure." He therefore excludes the disgusting entirely from the realm of imitation in the fine arts and excludes the highest degree of the horrible from pantomimic representation in tragedy, "partly because illusion in this instance would be dif-

---

[62] Laocoön, p. 42 [4:28].
[63] Laocoön, p. 32 [4:24].
[64] Laocoön, p. 49 [4:32].
[65] Sophocles, Philoctetes, act 4, scene 1 [874–75].
[66] Letters Concerning Recent Literature, pt. 5, letters 82–84.

ficult and partly because pantomime ought to remain, on the tragic stage, within its limits as an auxiliary art." I wish the philosopher D. would pronounce on the matter in hand, for more than one of these reasons speaks against the physical pain of Philoctetes as the stuff of tragedy. Its illusion can arouse only the most obscure sense, animal sympathy; this sensation belongs always to Nature and never to imitation; it has nothing agreeable about it; it is scarcely capable of illusion; it turns the tragic stage into a pantomime, which the more perfect it were, the more it would divert the spectator. So physical pain cannot be the principal idea of a tragedy at all.

And yet in Sophocles' *Philoctetes*, a masterpiece of the theater, it is! "How many things," Mr. Lessing says, "would seem incontestable in theory had not genius succeeded in proving the opposite by fact!"[67] Hardly, I think. What is truly incontestable in theory, and does not merely seem so, will never be refuted by a genius, particularly if the theory lay in our unaffected emotions. I regret the trouble that Mr. Lessing takes to vindicate Sophocles and to refute the Englishman Smith; neither requires such effort; and if he did, if Sophocles were bent on achieving his tragic purpose through expressions of physical pain, then L., for all the good things that he does say, would not have said very much at all.

But Sophocles, the tragic genius, felt that too much spoke against the realization of this purpose and trod an entirely different path, one that could not fail him and that Mr. L. seems to have glimpsed out of the corner of his eye. I ought to recapitulate some of its outlines, which I sketched earlier.

1. The first idea of Philoctetes is of an abandoned, afflicted, wretched hermit who has been betrayed, a Robinson Crusoe, whose pitiable cave we are shown; this situation Mr. L. examines with his customary strength.
2. The wretch is to suffer a new blow dealt by the cunning of his old foe: here our sympathy for him grows, and the contrast between Ulysses and Neoptolemus gives the whole scene humanity.
3. The chorus and Neoptolemus press the barbs of compassion more deeply into our heart: they sing of his misery in full measure. How eager we are now to set eyes on the man who plays out an extraordinary scene on this desert island and for whom new misfortune lies in wait. Throughout this act Philoctetes is yet to be seen; still less is the representation of his physical pain the principal idea. In this act Sophocles has three concerns: to prepare us for Philoctetes long before he enters; to relate the most difficult and untheatrical elements of the story rather than show them through action; and to win our hearts and minds so that we learn to tolerate his appearance. And as if he had not already done enough to prepare us for his entrance, the wild man must be announced by a murmured complaint from afar, which draws near and—

[67] *Laocoön*, p. 33 [4:25].

1. Now at the sight of the strangers, the sighs are gone, completely gone. Why? Why does Sophocles leave them offstage? He must not only secure Philoctetes against all contempt; he must also ensure that our first glimpse of him is of nothing but a suffering *hero*. I do not know why L. does not pursue our *first impression* of the hero; from afar we barely heard him whimper; now we see him endure his agonies. There stands and speaks, amid stifled pain, this friend of mankind, this Greek, this hero—why did Mr. L. not develop more the interest that Philoctetes arouses as a Greek, as a sympathetic friend of the strangers, as the admirer of Greek heroes? One can hardly sympathize with him more than we are already inclined to do.

2. And he shows another side of his greatness. The erstwhile supplicant hears Ulysses' new betrayal; how is the pleading wretch suddenly transformed into a hero?

3. Into a hero who before his enemies still remains unhumbled and proud: the hallmark of Greek greatness is "love for one's friends, unflagging hatred of one's enemies"![68] And who else but an honest man can so generously entrust his arrows and his life to Neoptolemus? Such a man is not merely secured against contempt from all sides; he has our heart.

4. The chorus prepares us for the scene of misery and clearly adopts a tone of respect for a hero who suffers, who has suffered for so long, and who does not cry out. How little, how little, then, is the chief trait of Sophocles' Philoctetes on the stage that which L. is wont to characterize as the horrible; he is still the great, suffering hero, and he is so throughout two long scenes!

And the idea of his wretchedness and of Neoptolemus's promise begins almost to disappear; can his pain have been exaggerated, can it have diminished in nine years? Would we not otherwise see him suffer ourselves? If there is nothing more than what we have seen, then—and now the fit comes. It is simply a fit, and I do not know why Mr. L. praises the choice of a *wound*,[69] which could bring no advantage save extending a horrible wail of lamentation over five acts! Sophocles knew better and chose—a short seizure. He placed it in the middle of the play so that it stands out: it arrives suddenly; the poison, as a punishment of the gods, will make a greater impression if it is not merely a creeping affliction: it comes in waves so that it does not weary the spectator by its duration; it veers into delirium to turn the attention of the spectator away from the pantomime and toward the suffering soul; the fit is long suppressed by Philoctetes and is accompanied only as he talks by isolated sounds of complaint; it ends in tranquil sleep, and this gives us time to consider what Philoctetes has endured. There

[68] *Laocoön*, p. 43 [4:29].
[69] *Laocoön*, p. 33 [4:25].

is no greater misunderstanding of the entire scene than to take it merely for the pantomime of physical pain, and there is no greater misunderstanding of the play as a whole than to assume Philoctetes is there to shriek and howl over a wound. The fit has passed, and afterward there is no more sign of pain than before——but I do not care to write a commentary on Sophocles. Let he who wishes to judge read for himself!

So that is why W. can compare his Laocoön with Philoctetes! That is why the scream can never, and least of all in Homer, have been the character trait of a hero! That is why a scream is never the principal means by which Philoctetes arouses sympathy and why physical pain is never the principal idea of a drama! That is why a play certainly has its own *beautiful nature*, as it were, and clear limits separating it from other forms of poetry. That it why we can justly call it a series of *poetic pictures of action*! Who better to teach us about this material than—the author of *Laocoön* and of the *Dramaturgy* himself, were he to pronounce upon the extent of pantomime in tragedy, the individual *beautiful nature* of drama, and the particular limits between painting and drama?

6

The great Winckelmann has shown us the beautiful nature of the Greeks so masterfully that no one but the ignorant and unfeeling will deny that "among the ancients beauty was the supreme law of the plastic arts." Nevertheless, I think the original source and some of its streams still lie undiscovered: *why* did the Greeks attain such heights in the depiction of the beautiful that they surpassed all other nations? Mr. Lessing adds a supplement here,[70] for he presents the Greek, in opposition to the artistic taste of our age, as an artist who confined art to narrow limits and restricted it to the imitation of beautiful bodies only: "The Greek artist represented only the beautiful."

Only the beautiful? Well, dear reader, I have read the wise animadversions and qualifications that have been most learnedly advanced against this proposition of Lessing's, but one must first understand L. before one confutes him. Does he mean to say that the Greeks depicted nothing ugly? I think not, and I wish I could magic away his words "The Greeks never depicted a Fury."[71] For if his proposition went that far, then Mr. Klotz would have occasion in every one of his future writings to adduce an example to prove that the ancients also depicted Furies, Medusas, and so on—which in fact anyone who has strolled through a museum will know.

[70] *Laocoön*, pp. 9–22 [2].
[71] *Laocoön*, p. 16 [2:15].

Or did the ancients have a law according to which ugly figures had to be depicted beautifully because anything that is represented in art must be beautiful? I know that Lessing has been understood in this way and dear old Medusa has been cited as an objection, but this is not the gist of Lessing's meaning either.

This is how I understand him: it went against the prevailing taste of the Greeks for an artist to model and depict *excellence* in order that he might show his worth solely by *imitation*, that he might prove himself solely by capturing a *resemblance*. Rather, Greek taste made the *beautiful* the main object so that the artist need not boast merely of passable skills as a craftsman. And this interpretation naturally entails the following specifications.

> To judge of a *prevailing* taste one should not take into account every single example, for Pauson, Pyreicus, and other Rhyparographers, as long as they do not attract followers and cannot yet battle for supremacy with others, do not hinder the portrayers of beauty.
>
> To judge of a prevailing taste one must not accept the words of a lawgiver,[72] of a political philosopher, as proof of what is current, for they say only what there ought to be, not what there is.
>
> The best witnesses to a prevailing taste are the *public works of art*, the prescriptions of the authorities; and since Mr. Lessing has considered these points excellently, one teaches him nothing new when one says: "Greek artists represented only the beautiful"—"Contradictory testimonies of writers and the examples of artists *lead me* to confine this observation to far narrower limits and to *restrict* it to public monuments only."[73] I think that these monuments were Mr. L.'s original source, and he perhaps seeks prescriptions even where there are none.[74]
>
> To judge of a prevailing taste one should not take works of art adorning temples, where religion was the primary purpose or where religious taste could not be changed. Mr. L. makes this qualification himself,[75] and I confess that it moderates his proposition to such a degree that it says as much or as little as he wants it to.
>
> Finally, to judge of a prevailing taste one ought not to take all ages equally, but only those in which taste appears already fully formed, in which it appears uncorrupted by any *cacozelia*: in one instance no law has yet been passed, in another it has fallen into abeyance for a while but is nonetheless still a law of the land. And after these specifications, L. can indeed establish that "among the ancients beauty was the supreme law of the plastic arts."

---

[72] *Laocoön*, p. 11 [2:13, 14]. Nota bene where Mr. L. cites the name of Aristotle.
[73] Klotz, *Geschichte der Münzen* [1767], pp. 41, 42.
[74] *Laocoön*, p. 12 [2:13]. The law of the Thebans εις το χειρον seems dubious to me.
[75] *Laocoön*, p. 103 [9:55].

But among which ancients? Since when? For how long? Which bylaws, which corollary laws? And where does one get the authority for claiming that beauty became the supreme law for the Greeks above all other nations? These are also important questions, and to the last even W. scarcely does justice.

Mr. L. encounters two situations that are relevant here: "That among the ancients even the arts were subject to the civil code and what influence the plastic arts exert on the character of a nation."[76] But both situations he could discuss only in passing. It ought to be possible to derive from their causes how, with the Greeks, the laws of art were not merely *permitted*, which is as far as Mr. L. goes, but rather how they were *necessary*—how for the Greeks art and poetry and music were part of the fabric of the state to a much larger extent than they are today; how, therefore, the state could not exist without them, as its mainsprings at that time, and they could not exist without the state—how therefore the influence of the nation on art and of art on the nation was not merely physical and psychological but also in large part political—how among the Greeks, therefore, there were so many causes—and not only their national character, but also their education, their way of life, the level of their culture, religion and state—which could and indeed were bound to furnish the representation of beauty with a wider range of impressions. It is an important problem,[77] the solution of which requires more than a little superficial knowledge of the Greeks. Thus, our vulgar Graeculis—who, following fashionable taste, like nothing better than to talk of the art and beauty of the Greeks—have so little entertained a notion on this subject that they believe they have explained everything when they prattle about nothing but a certain fine, beautiful feeling of the Greeks for art and beauty, of a feeling that the Greeks possessed and the Romans did not and that today lives again in our modern German Greeks. All of Klotz's writings are full of this sweet babble,[78] for with a certain unnameable feeling, of course, with a sixth sense for beauty, one can find whatever one wants without needing to wrack one's brain. A philosophical mind like Lessing's could not be satisfied with such a *qualitas occulta*, and could even a halfway philosophical mind settle for that with a smile?

But let us not stray too far from Laocoön. If among the Greeks beauty was the supreme law of art, violent postures and hideous contortions were

---

[76] *Laocoön*, pp. 12–15 [2:14].

[77] Prof. Heyne's *Programma, quo proluduntur nonnulla ad quaestionem de caussis fabularum seu mythorum veterum physicis* [1764] has given me more satisfaction than the entire philosophy of Banier; and in general this worthy connoisseur of the ancients has learned the most important lesson from his Greeks: tranquil grandeur, calm fullness, even in delivery and expression.

[78] See Klotz, *Geschichte der Münzen*, pp. 106, 107.

to be either avoided or toned down, and of this L. gives the best example. Nevertheless, he has met with opposition, and one of his opponents,[79] finding now a stone that seems to speak for Lessing and now one that seems to speak against him, is also, in his intermittent fever, now for, now against Lessing's proposition, so that the well-disposed reader ultimately has no idea where he stands. Is there a firmer thread that we might take hold of here?

First, then, the gods of the ancient Greeks were unquestionably depicted in the interests of beauty; their gods and goddesses were not, like the Egyptian gods, allegorical monsters; nor, like the Persian and Indian gods, were they almost entirely without image; nor, like the Etruscan gods, sad and unseemly figures; rather, their form pleased the eye. In the whole nature of things, the Greeks could find no better representation of divinity, as the epitome of perfection, than the human form; and in turn, though this is something we shall need to demonstrate, none of the deities was characterized in such a way that they *might always have to be depicted as ugly* in order to be what they were meant to be. Greek conceptions of the gods were determined by poets, and these poets were poets of beauty.

For instance, the Greeks had a Jupiter, who was of course not always μειλίχιος, but often the Wrathful, the Terrible also; and the poet could describe him as such depending on his intentions. But what of the artist? Who would want *always* to behold a wrathful Jupiter? For, after all, his anger passes with the thunderstorm. So what is more natural than that the artist, with an eye on the *eternal* aspect of his work of art, should prefer the appearance of beautiful grandeur and endow Jupiter's countenance only with majestic solemnity? Now, there may very well have existed depictions of the wrathful god, particularly in the earlier periods of Greek religion, but what does this matter? The fundamental idea associated with Jupiter, even when he hurls his thunderbolts, still remains—majestic solemnity, beautiful grandeur; that is his abiding form; his anger is a transient one.

When Venus grieves for Adonis, Moschus has her fly into a terrible rage; Juno, too, can quarrel like a queen and Apollo be consumed by brave fury—but is this rage, this quarrelsome face, this furious countenance, really their unchanging demeanor, a necessary trait of their character? No! It is transitory, it is a passing cloud. Now the artist sets out to depict Venus, Apollo, Juno; he will take, if he wants to avoid betraying his folly or idiosyncrasy, the mien peculiar to Venus, Apollo, and Juno, the one with which they would manifest themselves if they sat before him as models, and *this is*—a beautiful form.

---

[79] Compare Klotz's *Acta litteraria* with his *Geschichte der Münzen* and his work on polished gemstones [*Über den Nutzen und Gebrauch der alten geschnittenen Steine*, 1768].

Yet in Greek mythology there were always figures in whom ugliness was a character trait also: for example, Gorgons, Bacchantae, Titans, fauns, Furies, and so on. Let us consider Medusa first, for Pallas decorated her mighty shield with her head. Is Medusa a figure who must necessarily be depicted as ugly, who has but a single known form, one that is terrible in the highest degree? Those who talk so much about the heavenly form of Medusa as an I-don't-know-why and a paradox[80] ought to know that this was Medusa's original form, that she was once an enchanting woman whom Neptune ravished and who was thereupon transformed by the virginal Minerva.[81] Now the artist came to depict her: two forms lay before him, and he chose—the beautiful one before her transformation; but to characterize her as Medusa he wove snakes into her hair.

Is there any other explanation of these snakes that I might appeal to apart from "the peculiar feeling of the Greeks and Romans for serpents"?[82] A peculiar appetite indeed, but one that explains nothing here. A beautiful Medusa without snakes would no longer be recognizable, would no longer be Medusa—she would be merely a beautiful face; for this reason, and not because of some appetite for snakes, the artist was obliged to use this attribute. And why not? If he conceals the snakes in her hair, they can serve as an ornament; and are they ugly? Terrible, but not ugly; but this terribleness, if toned down and contrasted with a beautiful countenance, is agreeable; it raises in us the idea of the extraordinary, of the power of the goddess Minerva; it is therefore required as a character trait and fit for a multifaceted impression: it exalts beauty. Therefore Medusa need not necessarily be an image of ugliness.

And the Furies just as little. The *Venerable Ones*—that is what the Athenians called them and that is how the artists could depict them: "On the images neither of these nor of any of the underworld deities which stand in the Aeropagus," Pausanias says, "is there anything terrible."[83] And if not in the forms of the Furies, the proper goddesses of vengeance and torment; if not in the forms of the gods of the underworld; if not even in the Aeropagus, the most solemn site in Athens—then where and in what forms *might* the abominable be the dominant character?

I therefore venture to say that all the figures of Greek myth who were supposed to appear as principal figures, individually, in accordance with their intrinsic and abiding character, were never *obliged* to possess the re-

---

[80] Klotz, *Geschichte der Münzen*, pp. 46, 47.

[81] Pausanias tells her story in a manner even more fitting for art; see *Description of Greece*, Corinth, chap. 21.

[82] Klotz, *Geschichte der Münzen*, p. 47: "It is true that our feeling in this regard is just as different from the feeling of the Greeks and Romans as it is from the sentiment of cannibals."

[83] Pausanias, *Description of Greece*, vol. 1, *Attica*, chap. 28, 6.

pugnant and the horrible as necessary attributes of their form. This applies even to Sleep and Death, who were shown as boys resting in the arms of Night,[84] and even to the infernal gods—what a beautiful range of representations was available to the artist, whose religion at least did not compel him to offend taste and upset sensibilities. There were no loathsome images as in the Scandinavian and other northern religions, no grotesqueries as in the mythologies of the heathen lands of the east, no Grim Reaper personifying death, and no monster depicting the Devil as with the idols of our vulgar masses. Of all the peoples of the world, the Greeks have possessed, as far as the sensuous and plastic part of their religion is concerned, the most excellent mythology, and in this I do not except even their religious colonies.

Second, their religion nevertheless contained abundant representations, situations, and stories that must undoubtedly have furnished the artist with repugnant forms, if not as the main idea then at least as secondary ideas. How now? As secondary ideas, to be sure. A mythology that furnished nothing but forms in blissful repose the poet would certainly have found lifeless and monotonous, and the poetry that it brought forth would not have been Greek. It sufficed that these were secondary ideas, subordinate concepts, unfixed and temporary representations. With these the poet felt perfectly at home, and the artist, too, was not at all uncomfortable.

A Jupiter, for example, who has the Titans under the wheels of his chariot, can and ought to hurl his thunderbolts at them as monsters, as disagreeable forms, but these forms are not the main object in view; their horribleness is subordinated to Jupiter and thus serves to increase his majesty; therefore it does not violate the supreme law of art. A beautiful Bacchus among frenzied Maenads and exuberant, trumpet-blowing Bacchantae, among fauns and satyrs, will appear all the more lovely and beautiful. The terrible Medusa emblazoned on the cuirass of Pallas will enhance the manly beauty of the goddess still further, for here Medusa is not the principal figure but rather an ornament on her clothing. The same goes for Perseus with his Gorgon and for lame Vulcan in the hall of the gods; the same goes also for Cerberus beneath the feet of majestic Pluto— how many sheets of paper might have been spared the objections scrawled on them if one had stopped to consider that in a composition a secondary figure may be exempted from the supreme law without injury to the whole.

---

[84] *Laocoön*, p. 121 [11:n1]. Lessing's explanation of the διεστραμμένους seems to run counter to linguistic usage; and if it were a matter of supposition, I could just as easily say they slept with their feet crossed; that is, with one foot over the other in order to show up the relationship between Sleep and Death, and so on.

Third, what I have said regarding the Greek gods also applies to their heroes. Neither their demigods nor human heroes number monasticism, rapturous piety, penitential contortion, or self-abasing humility among their chief traits. By himself, then, on his own terms, the hero leaves room for noble beauty, particularly if he is to appear as the principal character in his abiding form. But throw obstacles in his path, and his soul will be agitated by anger, by distress, by sorrow; true, he will not make a Stoic philosopher, but will his sensitive and human nature be allowed to contradict his higher nature?

Take the depiction of Agamemnon at the sacrifice of Iphigenia. Timanthes concealed his face; but why? Pliny says that he so exhausted himself in depicting sorrowful faces that he despaired of his ability to give a still more sorrowful one to the father.[85] Mr. L. has Pliny say this and——thus justly refutes the reason he adduces,[86] for it is true that the "intensity of the emotions intensifies the corresponding expression in the face; the highest degree will cause the most extreme expression, and nothing in art is easier to express than this." That would mean Pliny was wrong, and even more wrong was the writer who,[87] without controverting the reason cited by L., believes Pliny simply because the latter is *idoneus auctor*. But what if Pliny said no such thing?

The passage in Pliny is as follows: "Timanthes cum moestos pinxisset omnes, praecipue patruum, et tristitiae omnen imaginem consumpsisset, patris ipsius vultum velavit, *quem digne non poterat ostendere*." What does Pliny say? That Timanthes so exhausted himself in depicting sorrowful faces that he despaired of his ability to give a *still more sorrowful one* to the father? No, rather that a more *sorrowful* face would have been unworthy of him, that he could not have shown him thus as *dignified*. I shall follow Valerius Maximus's description of the painting by Timanthes: Calchas appears sad, Ulysses deeply troubled, Ajax crying out, Menelaus loudly wailing.[88] And how does Agamemnon appear? Impassive, beside himself, benumbed, the features of his face fixed like iron or—raving; for that, I believe, is how the highest degree of emotion expresses itself. Would Agamemnon appear dignified here? Is the sight of his glassy-eyed stare worthy of a father? Hardly! And loudly wailing Menelaus, moaning Ajax, deeply troubled Ulysses, sad Calachas, would seem more moved than the impassive father himself. So he should appear raving? A hero raving in vain, Agamemnon gnashing his teeth is an undignified sight. If mortals were to slay his child, he would save her; he would wrest the sacrificial

---

[85] [Pliny *Natural History*] 35.15.
[86] *Laocoön*, pp. 18, 19 [2:16].
[87] Klotz, *Acta litteraria* 3:291.
[88] Valerius Maximus, [*Factorum ac dictorum memorabilium libri IX*], bk. 8, chap. 11.

dagger from Calchas's hands and not render himself useless by crying out, by giving himself over to his futile sorrow. But if the gods demand the sacrifice, if the welfare of the Greeks requires it, if its necessity has now been accepted, then, O king, steel yourself; and if your paternal heart is breaking, then—avert your eyes, cover your face; thus do you appear worthy of your status as a father and a king and a sensitive Greek and a patriotic hero.

Worthy also of the painter's art? But whether the foregoing was his only and main motivation; whether the nice reasoning that Mr. L. attributes to Timanthes, "that he knew the limits of his art, that he might have preferred to soften the ugliness and the distortions in Agamemnon's face; but since that was not possible he therefore veiled him; that this concealment is a sacrifice that the artist made to beauty";[89] whether Timanthes really reasoned in this manner I do not know. At least the sacrifice could not have been very hard for him, for he brought only the offerings of others. More than one poet had already *veiled* Agamemnon in his drama,[90] and so there was no need for Timanthes to indulge in his own subtle ratiocination on the subject. It would have been impudent if he had wished to uncover what the poet had veiled, particularly as it was so appropriate to his art. But why did the poet veil Agamemnon? For the sake of a future Timanthes perhaps? To avoid a figure that could not be *painted*? To make a sacrifice to art? To art, yes, though hardly to the brush of Timanthes, but rather to drama, his own art, and to the Grace who watches over it! It is not as if she demanded a stoic hero at the sacrifice of his child; the Greek Grace is not that inhuman. It is not as if she would refuse to tolerate a sad, sighing father; why not, if the situation demanded it? But here the highest note of a father's pain and of the most terrible grief should be struck by a hero, a hero who at the same time was a king, who would thereby save the Greeks, who had promised them the sacrifice—should he therefore break his word, not love his people, yet also not wish to express his melancholy? He has her sacrificed, he does not rush about in vain like a keener; he averts his eyes and weeps a father's tears: thus does he appear—worthy of his status as a king and a father, and consequently worthy also of the dramatic Grace. Only because this Grace could permit another character, a Clytemnestra, a Hecuba, and other heroes, to behave still more plausibly in ways that in this situation she denied to Agamemnon do we see that in Euripides, too, this concealment is rather a sacrifice for his hero *in this particular situation* than for the hero in general or for the Grace of dramatic art in general, and that here the Grace of another art certainly steps aside.

[89] *Laocoön*, p. 19 [2:16].
[90] For example, Euripides in his *Iphigenia*, and so on.

Be that as it may, the painting of Timanthes, even with its screaming Ajax,[91] still speaks *for* Mr. Lessing, and so do the raving Ajax, the terrible Medea, the suffering Hercules, and the moaning Laocoön as well; and there are always ten examples to a single contrary one which confirm his proposition "How much Greek artists avoided the ugly and how carefully they sought beauty, even in the most difficult cases." But are we to believe that with the extension of art beyond the boundaries of the beautiful in modern times there has been a desire to alter *its essence* and to confer on it a new supreme law, "truth and expression"?[92] Or might not this conveyance beyond the boundaries of the beautiful in our age be merely "a feature of the taste prevailing in this and that school," and thus a *cacozelia* in which the Greeks, with their Pauson and Pyreicus, were not lacking either? The question will be answered more fully in what follows. "If we wish to compare the painter and poet in particular instances (and thus the art of two different ages), we must first know whether they both enjoyed complete freedom; whether, that is, they could work toward producing the greatest possible effect in their respective arts without external constraint."[93] And who has here breathed clearer air?

7

"Religion often represented just such an external constraint on the classical artist."[94] Lessing's first example here is Bacchus depicted with horns, an example that also seems to have led him to this exceedingly true exception. A horned Bacchus! "Indeed, such natural horns are a degradation of the human form and can be becoming only to beings who are given a kind of intermediate form between man and animal." No one could show greater consideration in removing the horns from his friend's brow than Mr. L. with his beautiful Bacchus.

To begin with, he declares them to be mere ornament for the brow.[95] And why? Because the poet says:

tibi cum sine cornibus adstas
Virgineum caput est—

"Thus he could show himself without horns," Mr. L. says, "and the horns

[91] Mr. L. is free to believe Valerius; it does not matter. For the screaming Ajax is not the main focus of attention in the painting and nor is it the center, the nub of his proposition, which is intended to apply to the composition as a whole and not to a secondary figure.
[92] *Lacooön*, pp. 10, 23 [2:12, 3:19].
[93] *Lacooön*, p. 102 [9:55].
[94] *Laocoön*, p. 103 [9:55].
[95] *Laocoön*, p. 95 [8:50].

were but an ornament for the brow that he could put on and take off at will." What, does this last "thus" follow from the passage in Ovid, from this solemn invocation? Was Bacchus not a god? A god who, like other gods, showed himself in more than one form, who could appear now in virginal beauty, now in the terrible din of battle, now as a beautiful youth, like the pirates of Homer? And did Bacchus not only have this in common with other gods; did he not also have the *peculiar distinction* of being the god of a thousand forms, μυριομορφος, and thus possess the innumerable epithets that Orpheus, the epigrammatists, Nonnus et al. bestowed on him? Does it follow from the passage in Ovid that Bacchus——could thereby become διμορφος, πολυμορφος, μυριομορφος, if he——took off his horns as an old maid might lay aside her false teeth and breasts? Faint praise! His horns may seem a mere ornament for the brow and a crown of patience made of real gold—but to a pious Christian bridegroom and not to the Bacchus of myth.

So perhaps it is not Bacchus who stands there with horns sprouting forth, but rather a faun; for "indeed, such natural horns are a degradation of the human form and can be becoming only to beings who are given a kind of intermediate form between man and animal."[96] With such becoming conclusions! As if Bacchus were not often enough given such names, and even less becoming ones, as if he were not often enough called κεραος, δικεραος, χρυσοκεραος, ταυρωπος, ταυρομετωπος, ταυροκεραος, κερασφορος; that is, horned, two-horned, golden-horned, bull-horned. In fine, the horns were, in certain interpretations, *essential* to him and were part of his sacred allegory, in which form the Greeks had inherited him from other nations who esteemed allegory higher than the beauty of the human form.

But to say that Bacchus necessarily appeared with horns in *all* his temples is a step too far,[97] and it brings Mr. L. no advantage save allowing him afterward to practice his talent for guessing what might have become of all these statues of the horned Bacchus, since none are extant today.[98] I think it enough to say that the Bacchus whom the poets declare to be polymorphous also had "*many forms*" among the artists and in his temples; that in accordance with the older allegorizing mythology, the horns must have been very *symbolic* of Bacchus and therefore often seemed to the work master, also, who was employed in the service of religion, a necessary attribute of the god; that in the better days, when the Greeks themselves sacrificed much of their sacred allegory for the sake of beauty, the *simply beautiful* statues of Bacchus without horns, and in particular the

---

[96] *Laocoön*, p. 104 [9:55].
[97] *Laocoön*, p. 103 [9:55].
[98] *Lacooön*, p. 104 [9:55].

works of art devoted to him, also became the best. And thus all contradictions resolve themselves.

Generally speaking, the question of how religion in its *different forms at different times* influenced art and poetry ought to be raised more often. In the most ancient times, when the foreign ideas inherited from abroad were still current, the images of the gods were admittedly often undignified and Jupiter himself was not averse to appearing as either sex, with a labrys, and in the form of a dung beetle. But soon the clouds of this allegorical mentality, the legacy of the Egyptians and Orientals, were dispersed in the clear Greek air; the vain mysteries and symbols in mythology, philosophy, poetry, and art were taken by the Greeks from their sealed chambers and brought to the open marketplace, and beauty began to emerge as the supreme law of both poetry and art, though in different and distinctive ways. Homer, the son of a heavenly genius, became the father of beautiful poets and beautiful artists, and happy is the land where the spirit of the age—manifested in religion and manners and learning and culture—imposes as few constraints on the sensuousness of poetry and even greater sensuousness of art as did Greece in its heyday. I am surprised that in his writings W. did not have cause to remark more on this sloughing off of foreign, antiquated, and allegorical notions and demonstrate how this process might be turned to account, for one of the knottiest problems in the history of art is "how the Greeks transformed so many foreign and oppressive ideas into their own beautiful nature!"

The surest path would start from here, if we wished now to pass unharmed through meaning and beauty, allegory and beauty in both art and poetry; but I would have to delve too deeply into the difference between the poetic and plastic arts. So let us return to our prolegomena.

8

If beauty is the supreme law of the plastic arts, then of course Laocoön must not scream but only sigh oppressedly; for if even Sophocles found a bellowing Philoctetes making his dramatic entrance as absurd as Lessing finds the stoical Philoctetes, then how much more must the artist, for whom a sigh and an open-mouthed scream lasts forever.

Without wishing to establish, through a handful of suppositions, who imitated whom, whether the artist imitated the poet or the poet the artist, I shall make only one observation that did not occur to Mr. Lessing at this juncture:[99] besides Pisander,[100] whom Lessing mentions only as a doubt-

---

[99] *Laocoön*, pp. 50–67 [5].
[100] *Lacooön*, p. 51 [5:34].

ful source for Virgil, there were other Greeks from whom Virgil could have drawn the particular subject matter, the story of Laocoön. Mr. L. himself remarks that a *Laocoön* was among the lost plays of Sophocles,[101] and Servius believes that Virgil derived the story of Laocoön from the Greek of Euphormio—these suppositions can at least take us further than the empty name of a Pisander or a Quintus Calaber, who did not deserve to be cited by Mr. Lessing even as half an authority.[102] For what does his tale of Titans have to do with our Virgil or Laocoön?

Quintus Calaber is a late writer, a poet prone to exaggeration, a rum fellow—more we do not need to know in order to dispute his admission as a witness in this matter. In his treatment of Laocoön he invents so much that the poetic fable scarcely remains a fable; it becomes an extravagant tale of giants. Why must the earth tremble beneath the feet of the warning Trojan? If Troy is to fall through Minerva's cunning, what good is all the power of Jupiter, Neptune, and Pluto? Why must his innocent eyes be put out? Why must he go mad? Perhaps so that he may now continue, blindly and obdurately, in his counsel and thus appear as a defiant Titan against the gods? So that he may now merit through this persistent counsel the new punishment of the serpents? What good is it first of all to turn the well-meaning patriot into a Titan, a crazed criminal, and then afterward even—let innocents suffer on his behalf? Laocoön himself suffers no injury from the serpents; his poor, innocent children are seized and torn to shreds—what a strange, abhorrent scene, lacking judgment and purpose, structure and poetic understanding!

I shall stick with Virgil and the artist, then. Virgil may have drawn from Pisander, from Euphormio, or from some other source, but he does so as a poet, as an epic poet, as the Homer of the Romans. He therefore clothed this tale in epic dress as well, pouring it into a kind of neo-Homeric cast, and in such a form does it appear before our eyes. We have a writer who took pains to compare Virgil with the Greeks and to gloss him from that perspective;[103] it is a pity, however, that in his comparison he has eyes only for mere words, images, and individual bits and pieces. To explain the manner of Virgil's poetry in the light of Homer and other Greeks did not occur to him; otherwise in this version of the story of Laocoön, too, we would glimpse a poet who wished to draw from Homer. Perhaps my conjectures as to which passage from Homer Virgil imitated may be to our purpose.

Aeneas, in the middle of recounting the fall of Troy, comes to the tale of Laocoön, and behold!

---

[101] *Lacooön*, p. 8 [1:11].
[102] *Lacooön*, p. 52 [5:34].
[103] Fulvius Ursinus, *Virgilius collatione scriptorum graecorum illustratus opera et industria* (Antwerp, 1567).

Hic aliud maius miseris multoque tremendum
obiicitur magis atque improvida pectora turbat.
Laocoön——[104]

Who, at the beginning of this scene with the serpent, does not immediately think of the Homeric Nestor, who also introduces such a scene with a similar ενθ' εφανη μευα σημα?[105] The events of the two episodes are different, but the manner of the story is exactly the same. In Homer the loquacious old man recounts how, before their departure, the Greeks brought a sacrifice to the immortals around a spring, whereupon near a poplar tree a great portent appeared; a red-flecked terrible serpent, sent by Jupiter himself, suddenly darted forth from the foot of the altar and slithered up the tree, where the tender brood of a sparrow was nested on the topmost bough, cowering beneath the leaves—eight in all, and the mother that bore them was the ninth. Without mercy the serpent choked the twittering young, but as the mother flitted around her beloved brood, wailing, the serpent coiled himself around her wing, caught her, and choked her as she screamed—and so on. I believe Virgil had Homer in mind, as he couched Laocoön in the epic mode; but he enhanced the epic quality so that from Homer's simple tale a fully painted picture emerged— yet I would rather have Homer's simple tale back.

In Homer all the Greeks are already expectant: camped around a spring, preoccupied with the offering to the immortals, and thus minded to heed a sign from heaven as soon as it should appear. In Virgil everyone is unsettled, distracted, attending to the Greek traitor and not to Laocoön's sacrifice; the serpents appear, and what a sound, what a splashing noise they must make in the sea before they are seen: "Two serpents leaning into the sea in great coils and making side by side for the shore. Breasting the waves, they held high their blood-stained crests, and the rest of their bodies plowed the waves behind them, their backs winding, coil upon measureless coil, through the sounding foam of the sea. Now they were on land. Their eyes were blazing and flecked with blood. They hissed as they licked their lips with quivering tongues." What a terribly long preparation, so epic, so painterly that—I do not know why a single Greek waits for their arrival! How much Virgil devotes to the incidentals of a picture, which Homer furnished with a single word! And the whole description is overladen with consummate details—very nearly a sure sign that the poet worked from another's hand, that his writing was not fired by his own imagination. Otherwise, why would he linger for so long on the serpents' shoreward swimming and for even longer on their winding and coiling? These are the main focus of his attention; again and again

---

[104] Virgil *Aeneid* 2.199 [198–200].
[105] Homer *Iliad* 2.308–26.

they appear before his eyes, and he never trembles more than when he thinks of the immeasurable coils, the serpents twining around their victims, their postures. Virgil must have imitated either a work of art or—what is more likely in my opinion—Homer's description. The imitator always betrays himself when he scribbles with too much artifice and finishes off incidentals with the utmost care. For this very reason, I venture to say that Virgil's description fills the ear more than it does the soul. With all the splashing of the serpents, it does nothing more than divert and benumb us; with all the entwining around Laocoön, which is presented here with such precision, our eye turns from Laocoön to the serpents; we forget to attend to his face and his soul, which speaks through it. Ultimately his soul does manifest itself—but in a deafening cry, in the bellowing of a wounded bull fleeing from the altar:

> clamores horrendos ad sidera tollit——

It is admittedly an "excellent feature for the hearing," as I gladly concede to Mr. Lessing,[106] but for the soul it is an empty sound. The poet has become so entangled in the convolutions of his serpents that he forgets one thing, but this thing is unfortunately the most important: Laocoön himself, his fear, and his state of mind. These features Homer does not forget, even when describing his young brood of sparrows and their poor mother, and he paints for us not a picture for the eye and even less an "excellent feature for the hearing," but rather a picture in the soul. I do not know why Mr. L. lingers for so long on the secondary features, the "coilings of the serpents," and so on,[107] which merit boundless praise with the artist and sculptor but certainly not with the poet. Indeed, if only Virgil had followed the example of an artist! But would that not be contrary to the purpose of Lessing's entire work?

And where he is too lenient on Virgil he is too harsh on Petronius,[108] as most of his criticisms might be seen to apply more surely to Virgil vis-à-vis Homer than Petronius vis-à-vis Virgil. I am familiar with the forced manner of Petronius's verse and freely admit that no spark of poetic genius flashes forth from his description of Laocoön; but need therefore the picture he describes, need the whole gallery of pictures at Naples have existed only in his imagination? Why? Because a novelist may not be a historian? May not! Of course he may not be; but does that mean he is not, could not be a historian? Particularly the bad novelists. What their imagination leaves incomplete they supplement with interpolated history; they furnish us with semihistorical novels or novelistic semihistory—like the

---

[106] *Laocoön*, p. 30 [4:23].
[107] *Laocoön*, pp. 59–66 [5:36–39].
[108] *Laocoön*, pp. 54, 55 [5:n6].

Abbé Terrasson, who wrote his *Séthos* with Diodorus of Sicily to hand—and others give us a novel replete with geography or true history. Should Petronius not also declare himself a member of this category? In all probability, yes; and the wide variety of judgments that critics have always passed on Petronius stems from this mixture of truth and invention, history and fantasy. His imagination is playful, barren, forced, and its offspring have the character of their mother; but his judgment, the historical features on the corrupted taste of the age which he often inserts into his work are fine, laudable. I think it therefore very likely that Petronius, who passionately desired to be a poet, may well have meant to burnish his description of Laocoön by imitating an actual painting, that the painting of Laocoön may well have existed somewhere other than in his imagination. And if it did exist? Well, then the critical blows that Mr. L. deals to Petronius land on the wrong person this time, and his secret means of exposing the style of an imitator fails him. If Petronius had described a painting, what is more likely than that his eye lingered on subordinate ideas, that he might also exaggerate them? If he thought he could hear in the picture, so to speak, the sound of the serpents, if he encountered a painting of Laocoön's children, suffering and frightened to death, then for him, the versifier of an artistic scene, the imitator of the painting, these figures were eye-catching enough to compete with the brush, to embellish in the best manner possible what are subordinate ideas for the imagination but in the painting main ideas for the eye. By contrast, the size of the serpents—with whose description Virgil was so taken—was not the chief concern of Petronius; it could not be in the painting, where the size had only, as it were, to be inferred from the noise made in the waves. Petronius's description as a whole is an aggregation of *visible* ideas, so why not an imitation of an actual picture? And in that case it is not so obviously an example of the schoolboyish imitation of another poet and even less obviously the best example with universal validity. As slavish as it is, in comparison a Quintus Calaber is not yet exactly the *better* poet and student of Nature;[109] and as infinitely inferior to Virgil as it is, it must be said that in his description, too, Virgil is not entirely a poet; he is an imitator of Homer and demonstrates this by so boundlessly enlarging and embellishing incidentals that we lose sight of the whole.

What would follow from this? This: although Virgil worked from Homer, he always altered his story *after his own fashion*, regardless of whether he drew it from Pisander, Euphormio, or Sophocles, and therefore the artist beside him could have drawn from the very same source and yet depart from Virgil in the manner in which he *represented it*, even if he too merely followed the Greek letter.

[109] *Lacooön*, p. 57 [5:n6].

Let us assume, then, Virgil had the lost *Laocoön* of Sophocles before him. Which idea must the Sophoclean Muse have imparted to him? Sophocles, such a wise poet of the stage, the first, as it were, to establish morality and propriety on it, who was perhaps alone in striking the right balance in this respect; Sophocles, who with his Philoctetes knew how to transform the agonies of the body into agonies of the soul—how will he have depicted his Laocoön? With a terrible scream as his main attribute? An excellent means of moving the eardrum, but not our heart. He will certainly have sought better routes to our heart, and hence he will have also measured Laocoön's pains and cries with the same scales of poetic genius with which he measures those of Philoctetes. Now allow that a wise Greek artist borrowed this subject from a wise Greek poet; allow that he made use of the manner of the theatrical description and learned from Sophocles' *Laocoön*, just as Timanthes learned the prudent veiling of Agamemnon from Euripides; in that case, I believe I can see the scales of expression hovering at precisely the point at which they hovered with the artist's Laocoön. The quantity of the sigh is measured out.

> The pain is revealed in every muscle and sinew of his body, and one can almost feel it oneself in the painful contraction of the abdomen without looking at the face or other parts of the body at all. However, this pain expresses itself without any sign of rage either in his face or in his posture. He does not raise his voice in a terrible scream, which Virgil describes his Laocoön doing; the way in which his mouth is open does not permit it. Rather, he emits the anxious and subdued sigh described by Sadolet. The pain of body and the nobility of soul are distributed and weighed out, as it were, over the entire figure with equal intensity. Laocoön suffers, but he suffers like the Philoctetes of Sophocles; his anguish pierces our very soul, but at the same time we wish that we were able to endure our suffering as well as this great man does.

I know nothing more worthy than these words, and thus the Roman poet, the imitator of Homer, does not come into play at all.

I realize that hitherto I have merely tidied up those critical materials which Mr. L. used as a foundation for his *Laocoön* but which he could have easily omitted without injury to the main substance of his book. It is time to lead my readers away from the critical debris and take them closer to the main substance.

9

L. seeks to grasp the first difference between poetry and the plastic arts in the *moment* to which art must confine its imitative effort by virtue of its material limitations.[110] Hence this moment can never be chosen too significantly, and that alone is significant and fruitful which gives free rein to the imagination. Now, all critics who have reflected on the limits of the arts have alighted on this idea, but the use that Mr. L. makes of it is all his own. If, namely, art is confined to a moment, and if this moment endures, then art shall not choose the climax of an emotion, for the imagination can conceive of nothing beyond the utmost; art expresses nothing transitory because this transience is perpetuated by art.

By contrast, nothing compels the poet to compress his picture into a single moment. He may, if he so chooses, take up each action at its origin and pursue it through all possible variations to its *end*. Each variation that would cost the artist a separate work costs the poet but a single pen stroke, and so on. This characteristic of poetry is, as I say, by itself well known, but Mr. L. makes this well-known characteristic practicable.

So art chooses nothing fleeting for the single moment that it takes as its subject,[111] but is there anything in Nature that is not transitory, that is wholly permanent? We live in a world of appearances, where one phenomenon follows upon another and one moment is annihilated by the next; everything in the world is bound to the wings of time, and movement, change, activity, are the very soul of Nature. In metaphysical terms, then—but here we do not wish to speak metaphysically but rather sensuously; and in sensuous terms, that is, as the world appears to our eyes, are there not sufficient constant, enduring objects that art ought therefore to imitate? Indeed, there are, and to a certain extent all bodies are such objects and precisely insofar as they are bodies. Though they may unfold in time and their states may vary, though they are rapidly changed by each moment of their existence, *our eyes* do not perceive these moments. The artist can therefore furnish the appearances of bodies: he depicts bodies, he imitates *immutable* Nature.

But what if this immutable Nature were also at the same time dead Nature? What if a body's permanence attested precisely to its soullessness? Then if this immutable permanence were made the aim of art without restriction—how could this principle not deprive art of *its best expression*? Imagine, dear reader, a soulful expression through a body you desired, and it is fleeting. The more it characterizes a human passion, then the more it describes a changing state of human nature, and the more it "assumes such an unnatural appearance that it makes a weaker impression, the more often we look at it, until it finally fills us with disgust or horror." Though the imagination may have free scope, though it may have room to soar, it must nevertheless ultimately encounter a limit and unwillingly

[110] *Lacooön*, p. 24 [3:19].
[111] *Lacooön*, p. 25 [3:20].

return; indeed, the more swiftly it travels, the more pregnant is the chosen moment, and the sooner it reaches its goal. Just as I can say to a laughing La Mettrie when he is still laughing the third or fourth time I see him
"You are a fool!" so in the end I shall also be able to say to Myron's cow:
"Now move along, you, what are you standing there for?" And though I
may have reason to find a constantly screaming Laocoön ultimately intolerable, only a little later I should find just as much reason to be weary
of a sighing Laocoön because he is still sighing. And then the standing
Laocoön because he is still standing; and then a rose by Huysum because
it is still in bloom and not yet wilted; and finally every imitation of Nature by art shall vex me. In Nature *everything* is ephemeral: the passion
of the soul and the sensation of the body, the operations of the soul and
the movements of the body, every state of mutable, finite Nature. Now, if
art has at its disposal only one moment in which *everything* shall be comprehended, then it must bestow an unnatural permanence on every changing state of Nature. And with that, art ceases to imitate Nature.

Nothing is more dangerous than transforming a delicacy of our taste
into a universal principle and making it into a law; one good aspect
thereby results in ten precarious ones. Mr. L. wished to exclude the highest degree of emotion from a statue's form: all well and good. His reason
for doing so was that this passion would be transitory: not so good![112]
Then, finally, he raised this reason into a principle: art must express nothing that can be thought of as transitory; and this assumption is the most
misleading. For art is thereby rendered dead and soulless; it is plunged
into that idle repose which only the monks of the Middle Ages could find
pleasing; it forfeits all the soul of its expression.

And what might be the alleged reason for administering such a cruel
critical physic? Because the prolongation of a transitory phenomenon in
art, whether agreeable or otherwise, gives it such an unnatural appearance that *the more often we look at it*[113]—I cannot continue! The more
often we look at it! Who will reckon on this? Who will deny himself a
pleasure in youth because *eventually* it must grow feebler the *more often*
we enjoy it? Who will wrangle with himself, quarrel with his feelings instead of surrendering himself serenely to the agreeable moment without a
thought for the future? Without summoning ghosts of our prospective
selves to chase away our joys? All sensuous joys are meant only *for the
first glance*, and so too are the phenomena of fine art. "La Mettrie, who
had himself portrayed in painting and engraving as a second Democritus,
seems to be laughing only the first few times we look at him. Look at him
often and the philosopher turns into a fool. His laugh becomes a grin."

[112] *Lacooön*, p. 25 [3:19–20].
[113] *Lacooön*, p. 25 [3:20].

That may well be! But what if this laughing Democritus had wished to be depicted only for our first glance? What then? If his laughter were already contemptible and loathsome at first glance, if the philosopher thereby became a fool at once and his Democritean expression a grin, then of course it is unfortunate for him and for the artist. The laughter ought indeed to have been omitted, not on account of its permanence but because it is a contemptible and loathsome sight. If this was not the case, if you think the philosopher a fool only after frequent visits, then, my delicate friend, imagine you have not yet seen him or—avoid him. But do not for that reason deny us our first glimpse of him, let alone make a law that from this day forth no philosopher shall be painted laughing. Why? Because laughter is said to be a transitory phenomenon. Yet every state of the world is more or less transitory. Sulzer had himself engraved with a bowed head, with his chin resting on a finger and with a profound, philosophical expression on his face.[114] Following Mr. Lessing's principle, one would have to address his image accordingly: "Philosopher, will you have finished your aesthetics soon? Do your bowed head and raised finger not ache? Sighing Laocoön, for how long will you sigh? Will your bosom be oppressed, your abdomen contracted each time that I see you? With you a transitory moment, a sigh, is unnaturally prolonged." Jupiter hurling the thunderbolt and Diana hunting, Hercules carrying Atlas on his back and every figure depicted performing the slightest action and movement, indeed in any bodily state whatsoever, is then unnaturally prolonged, for none endures forever. Thus, if the opinion in question ever became a principle, the essence of art would be destroyed.

Nor can it therefore be a reason why art should not express the climax of an emotion; it is not delicacy of taste but rather squeamishness.

Every work of plastic art is, if we accept the classification of Aristotle, a *work* and not an energy: it is all there at once in all of its parts; its essence consists not in change or succession but in coexistence. If an artist has made it perfectly so as to be grasped entirely and exactly in the first glance, which has to deliver a complete idea, then its purpose has been achieved, the effect endures forever: it is a *work*. It is there all at once, and that is how it shall be viewed; the first glance shall be permanent, exhaustive, eternal, and only human frailty, the carelessness of our senses, and the disagreeableness of prolonged effort make necessary, where works demand to be examined more deeply, perhaps the second, perhaps the hundredth viewing. Yet each occasion is but a single glance. What I have seen I do not need to see again, and what becomes abhorrent to me not through the utter *singularity of the glance* but rather through change, *through* repeated viewing, lies not in art but rather in my jaded taste. Now, can this

---

[114] [Sulzer,] *Sammlung vermischter Schriften*, vol. 5 [1762].

weariness form a principle of art? Can it yield even a single sound reason for another proposition?

So I shall dispense with Mr. L.'s insistence on this principle as a principle, as a law, and think it sufficient to say that the climax of an emotion is abhorrent to our first glance and places too great a constraint, as it were, on the imagination; consequently, it ought to be avoided in art, at least as its main aspect. If the effect produced by art is a *work*, designed for a single but, as it were, eternal viewing, then this single glance must contain, to the highest degree possible, as much that is beautiful for the eye and as much that is significant and fruitful for the imagination. Hence issue those infinite and immeasurable qualities that this plastic art possesses before all other fine arts: namely, a supreme ideal of beauty for the eye and the tranquil repose of Greek expression for the fancy; both are the means of holding us in the arms of eternal rapture and compelling us to linger in the depths of a long, happy glance.

"Why is it," a philosopher of beauty asks,[115] "that there exists only in painting and sculpture, and not in poetry, an ideal beauty, an *aliquid immensum infinitumque*, which artists imagine as they picture the outline of their work?" I do not think that he has resolved this question on behalf of art when he remarks that "ideal beauty is most difficult to attain in the fine arts." For the question remains the same: "Why, then, must such a difficult goal be attained?" For no other reason, I believe, than that art delivers only *works*, which represent a single moment and are designed to be apprehended in a single pregnant glance; these works must therefore make their moment so agreeable, so beautiful, that nothing exceeds it, that the soul, sunk in contemplation of the same, as it were, comes to a rest and loses the sense of time passing. *Those* beaux arts and belles lettres, however, which produce their effect through time and change, which have energy as their essence, are not obliged to deliver a single moment; they need never devour our soul in this momentary climax, for otherwise the agreeableness that is due to succession, to the combination and alternation of these moments, is disturbed, and every moment is thus employed merely as a link in a chain and in no other way. If one of these moments, states, and actions becomes an island, an isolated climax, the essence of energetic art is lost. By the same token, if the character of the single, everlasting moment represented by plastic art is not such that it could grant an eternal glance, then its essence is not realized either. With bodies this single, eternal sight is perfect beauty; and to the extent that the soul is supposed to operate through the body, beauty consists in noble Greek tranquillity. This tranquillity lies midway between lifeless inactivity and passionate, exaggerated movement; the imagination can continue

---

[115] *Letters Concerning Recent Literature*, pt. 4 [letter 66], p. 285.

to hover between both extremes and therefore derives the longest pleasure from this glance of the soul. Lifeless inactivity severs our thread of ideas with a single snip; the figure is dead; who wishes to rouse it? Exaggerated expression, by contrast, again curtails the flight of fancy, for who can conceive of something greater than the utmost? But the tranquil repose of Greek expression rocks our soul between both extremes, and beholding it we imagine at the same time the calm depths of the sea from which this gentle wave of emotion and passion rose and rippled the surface. And then at the same time, what if the wave rose higher? What if this zephyr's breath became a raging storm of passion? How the surf would tower and expression swell! What a wide sphere of thoughts resides, therefore, in the glance directed at the gentle repose of Greek expression!

I believe I have discovered, in the essence of art, the solution to two problems. *Why* is beauty the supreme law in plastic art? Because art achieves its effect *through the coexistence of its parts*, because its effect is therefore encompassed *within a single moment* and creates its work for *a single eternal glance*. This single glance therefore delivers the utmost degree of that which holds us fast in its arms forever—*beauty*. Nevertheless, physical beauty alone does not yet satisfy us; just as a soul looks out on the world through our eyes, so a soul shines forth in the beautiful form presented to us. In what state do we find this soul? Without doubt in that state which is able to arrest my glance forever and occasion in me the most sustained contemplation. And which is that? It is not a state of idle repose, which gives me nothing to reflect on; it is not exaggerated expression, which clips the wings of my imagination. It is, rather, the first stirring of a movement, the dawning of the day, which allows us to see across to both extremes and thus alone grants us an eternal glance.

In this way the concepts underlying the distinction readily admit of generalization, and we no longer speak of sculpture and poetry, but rather of arts that either deliver *works* or operate through an uninterrupted *energy*. What is true of poetry in this respect will also be true of music and dance, for these two arts likewise aim not at *a single glance* but at a succession of moments, the combination of which constitutes their very effect; they are therefore governed by quite distinct laws. But it does not mean that I have explained the Roman poet of Laocoön when I mention that his words *clamores horrendos ad sidera tollit* do not present a grimacing, screaming mouth and thus an ugly image;[116] for of course Virgil was not addressing the eye, and still less did this feature of his picture become an *eternal sight* in the artistic sense. But what if his entire description, which I regard as a picture *for my soul*, showed me no other inner state of Laocoön than the one expressed in this scream; does this feature not remain

[116] *Laocoön*, p. 30 [4:23].

the principal figure in the poet's picture also? Whenever I call to mind Virgil's Laocoön, do I not think of a man crying out? For in *his* pain he did not reveal his soul in any other way. Now the point of view changes. We must explain in terms of the essence of poetry, in terms of the poet's energetic purpose, the question as to whether this feature of Laocoön, this *single* utterance of his feelings, ought to become the principal figure, an enduring impression in my imagination. It is not enough that the *clamores horrendos ad sidera tollit* is an excellent feature for the hearing; (if I understand a feature for the hearing) the poet must also be concerned to make it Laocoön's main feature in my fancy. If he does not, then the poet, even though I do not immediately demand from him a beautiful image, has spoiled the whole impression he intended to make on me.

It is not my intention to explore this in Virgil. I have vindicated Winckelmann, who (perhaps only historically) can say: "The Laocoön of the artist does not cry out like the Laocoön of Virgil." I have examined the reason that Mr. L. adduces for the difference between both arts and traced it back to the *singularity of the glance* in which plastic art and no other art manifests itself. I wish that Mr. L. had made Aristotle's distinction between *work* and *energy* the basis of his entire work; for in the end all of the individual distinctions he mentions amount anyway to this primary distinction.

10

How can the poet imitate the artist and the artist the poet? I believe that the distinction Mr. L. makes in respect of the different kinds of imitation is already implicit in our language,[117] and with a single word it thus makes everything immediately clear in the analysis also. *Einen nachahmen* means, as I think, to imitate the subject, the work of the other; *einem nachahmen*, though, is to borrow the other's style and manner of treating the same or similar subject.

To get to the bottom of this distinction, Mr. L. seeks out an opponent with whom he may do battle, and this opponent is Spence.[118] True, Spence was erudite, brimming with allusions and analogies; a mere word, a solitary feature of a picture, was all he needed to discern an allusion and an imitation, and I readily concede that his work is seldom much more than an index of parallel passages of the poets (and unfortunately only the Roman poets) and artists (and indeed mostly Greek artists). However, Mr. L. plays a mean trick on him when in the main body of his text he cites *useful*

---

[117] *Lacooön*, pp. 78, 79 [7:45].
[118] *Lacooön*, p. 80 [7:46].

elucidations that accrued to the ancient writings from the comparison with works of art, and then in his footnotes he refutes almost every one of these useful elucidations. Irrespective of whether useful elucidations in Spence are of this kind or these are indeed the only ones, I am grateful for Spence.

And I am not certain whether Mr. L. is entirely justified in all his objections to these elucidations. Juvenal speaks of a soldier's helmet, where among other metaphors he also writes:

> nudam effigiem clypeo fulgentis et hasta
> pendentisque Dei perituro ostenderet hosti.

Addison thought he could best explain the attitude of the *Dei pendentis* by referring to pictorial representations in which Mars *floats down* to Rhea and thus, as it were, *hovers* above her. Now, I myself am not well disposed toward the explanation of Addison and Spence either, but what does Mr. L. have against it? That it would be a *hysteron proteron* for Juvenal to speak of the she-wolf and the young boys and only afterward of the event to which they owed their existence.[119] What does a hysteron proteron matter in a poet, especially in a satirical poet? But this is not how I care to talk, for that would mean not explaining the poet but rather salvaging an explanation that we have adapted to fit him. Show me first where this hysteron proteron is! "In the earliest days of the Republic, the soldier broke up the costliest goblets, masterpieces of Greek artists, in order to place a she-wolf, a little Romulus and Remus, and a hovering Mars upon his helmet." That is what Juvenal means, so where is the hysteron proteron? The Roman soldier is a collective noun, a *nomen collectivum*, and his helmet stands for all Roman helmets; this helmet could be placed on the head of one soldier, that helmet on another; and the she-wolf and the two little ones on the rock as well as the hovering Mars would in themselves be an emblem of Rome's origin and of the uncouth soldier who took such pride in his city's divine origin. Then Juvenal might have cited several examples that, drawn from *one story*, are arrayed together so that they serve as the *emblem of one thing* but indeed by themselves are not meant to constitute a whole. But why as the emblem of one thing? "Consider whether a love scene would be a suitable emblem for the helmet of a Roman soldier."[120] Why not? It was no longer the image of a love scene alone but the image of the divine origin of the Romans, of the origin of which the soldier, as a Roman, was proud. It depicted not the catching of Rhea unawares but the hour that gave life to the founder of Rome, and thus it was not at all unsuitable as an image for the helmet of a *Roman*, who did not detest his Mars in this hovering attitude either

[119] *Lacooön*, p. 83 [7:n3].
[120] *Lacooön*, p. 83 [7:n3].

and was not unpleased to be his descendant, for this was what made him a Roman.

I have said that Juvenal's images could have been individually represented on the helmets of the soldiers; but why would it be a hysteron proteron if they had also been arranged beside one another on a single helmet, only divided into different groups, of which the poet mentions several? If there is space for more symbols of Rome's origin, then let the artist inscribe them; it does not run counter to my sense or to Juvenal's.

But does Mars really *hover*, Mr. L. continues, does he really?[121] And his brooding skepticism indeed goes a long way. Might Spence have observed correctly, might he have faithfully reproduced the original, and might he also——have had the coin in his possession? "It is harsh," I am bound to repeat after Mr. L., "it is harsh to question a man's veracity, even in a trifling matter"—particularly as there are other well-known coins of this type.

His doubts persist and turn into outright denial. "A body hovering without a visible cause for its exemption from the law of gravity is an incongruity of which no example can be found in ancient works of art."[122] Well, that is going too far! In the present instance Mars is anything but a hovering body, a body hovering without visible cause, an incongruity, a body that offends the eye, that breaks the laws of motion, of gravity, of bodily equilibrium—where is our Mars in any of these things? He is a body descending toward the earth precisely in accordance with the laws of motion and gravity and equilibrium, or, in Shakespeare's fine phrase about Mercury, kissing the hill with his feet. On a work of such modest dimensions no one will think that Mars has floated down from heaven, that he has fallen through the air, that he is suspended in the air without wings or wires, or whatever the reason may be that he is still so happily embarked on his descent—no one will think this, for we see Mars only at the moment when he is about to alight on the ground. It is the drop back to earth after a gentle leap, and we do not need to be a god to perform such an act or to picture to ourselves a god who obeys completely different laws of motion, gravity, and equilibrium; anyone can imitate the gentle attitude of Mars, and the artist chose it without incongruity. The aforementioned general proposition scarcely belongs here and, in the scope that Mr. L. gives it, admits of qualification. To offend what our eyes deem probable a body must very evidently not hover but lie suspended, and lie suspended in the boundless air; and how rare is this on a coin, on a cut gemstone, and indeed how rare in paintings also, where the probability of the eyes is always redressed without theorems of motion. So what—as-

---

[121] *Laocoön*, p. 84 [7:n3].
[122] *Lacooön*, pp. 84, 85 [7:n3].

suming one wanted to reckon such matters more precisely—is really the point of the tiny wings on Mercury's feet when he takes a mighty leap—as depicted, for example, in one of the Farnese frescoes by Carracci? Do they make his swoop down seem more likely than a Mars who hovers above the earth? And then Homer's divine horses, which, between earth and starry heaven, spring at a single bound as far as the shepherd can see as he looks out from the peak of the highest mountain and gazes over the black ocean—what would be the point of giving them a pair of little wings also (which incidentally Homer does not give them), of conceiving them in terms of mechanics? But now let Apollo, Diana, Luna, Juno, Minerva, and any other Olympians who wished to accompany them swing forth in their air chariot; if the artist shows them only in a position near or above the earth as they descend, then we gladly forget the vastness of the air, which moreover we cannot see here in its full extent. We have no need of a wire that would affix the descending figure to a star; we have no need of the Cacklogallinians' carriage, which in Swift's journey to the moon spent the night on the first cloud they encountered.

I find even less satisfying Lessing's amended reading of this passage: it is more far-fetched and metaphysical than all the previous readings.[123] In short, should Spence not still be a repository for the elucidation of the ancients, especially if a better mind were to avail himself of Spence's compilations of parallel passages? But it is true that he would be left with Spence's crotchety insistence that wherever the slightest similarity exists the poets must have copied a work of art. Mr. L. refutes this insistence in several examples;[124] and with some it might have been possible to demonstrate *from the internal structure* of the poetic descriptions also that they flowed from the poet's fancy and not from the work of the artist, because otherwise the poet would have been *obliged* to imagine them differently.

11

Few critical observations are more useful than when L. disputes with Spence about the different ways in which gods, spiritual beings, and moral beings appear to the artist and the poet;[125] then again, within and without the walls of Troy all goes wrong, by which I mean in both poetry and art.

Gods and spiritual beings: "To the artist they are personified abstractions that must always retain the same characteristics if they are to be rec-

---

[123] *Lacooön*, p. 87 [7:n3].
[124] *Lacooön*, pp. 90, 91 [7:nn4, 5, 8].
[125] *Lacooön*, pp. 113–18 [10].

ognized; to the poet they are real, acting beings."[126] I do not know whether this distinction is as firm and essential to both arts as Lessing claims here—and I think that an "I do not know" of this nature, which touches on nothing less than the use of mythology as a whole in all the beaux arts and belles lettres, does indeed merit a little care and attention.

Are the gods and spiritual beings, therefore, nothing but personified abstractions for the artist? It is true that as long as an individual figure is meant to be nothing more than a recognizable image of a heavenly being, then the attributes linked to its general character are the object in view. Now let this figure enter into action in a painting, for example; suppose also that this action does not issue from its character: the instant this happens, historical mythology takes the place of emblematic mythology, and the figure is no longer recognizable by what it *is* but rather by *what it does*. This, Mr. L. concedes; only he thinks that the actions must not be contradictory to its character; and from the example he gives I see that he is very discerning in his examination of this contradiction. Venus presenting her son, Cupid, with her divine armor is, he opines, a subject that certainly can be depicted by the artist, for here she would still be distinguishable as a goddess of love; the artist can bestow on her all the charm and beauty that are properly hers as the goddess of love; in fact, she becomes even more recognizable as such through this action. But a wrathful, scornful Venus would not be recognizable at all.[127] But if we develop this distinction, I find I cannot agree with Mr. Lessing.

Gods and spiritual beings are admittedly personified abstractions and types for the artist as long as he depicts them singly, in a manner that befits them, or, at the very most, performing an unchanging action; but then they are abstractions only out of necessity, by compulsion, *in order that they are recognizable*. Venus, Juno, and Minerva have *this* form of beauty *and no other*; it is not as if this were always an intrinsic trait of their abstract nature; it is sufficient that it is an *external attribute* of this deity, beloved of poets and fixed by them at some point in the past. I am not knowledgeable enough about the abstract concept of love to judge whether each small detail present in the form of Venus belongs only to her and no other divine beauty because it is a necessary characteristic of the abstraction of love. Whether, for example, the υγρον of her eyes and the smile creasing her cheeks and the dimple on her chin were as essential to this concept as the majestic breast of Juno and the slender waist of Diana and the innocent face of Hebe might be precisely antagonistic to it. I have never studied mythology as an index of general concepts in this fashion and have found myself in some embarrassment each time I have seen how others prefer to regard it as such.

---

[126] *Lacooön*, pp. 99, 100 [8:52].
[127] *Laocoön*, pp. 100, 101 [8:53, 54].

This much is certain: poets, and only poets, invented and defined mythology and certainly not, I wager, as a gallery of abstract ideas that they happened to embody in figures. What remains of the most poetic stories of Homer if, following Damm's teaching, I wish to view his gods merely as acting abstractions? They are heavenly *individuals* who indeed establish a character through their actions but who are not there to exemplify this or that idea: this is an important distinction. Venus may always be the goddess of love, but not everything that she does in Homer is done to personify the idea of love; Vulcan may be whatever he may be, but when he pours the gods their goblets of nectar, he is nothing more than—their cupbearer.

My conclusion, therefore, is as follows: for the poet, gods and spiritual beings are "not merely real, acting beings who, in addition to their *general character, possess other qualities and feelings*, which, *as circumstances demand*, may stand out more prominently than the former," as Mr. L. says.[128] Rather, *these other qualities and feelings*—in short, a certain individuality peculiar to these beings—are their true nature; and the *general character*, which is perhaps derived from this individuality, is only a later, imperfect concept that always remained of *secondary importance*; indeed it was often ignored by poets.

Now I shall reason further. If, therefore, in the mythology and pneumatology of the most ancient poets, the individual or historically acting part preserves its predominance over the part that acts according to type, and these very poets were indeed the original creators and fathers of this mythology and pneumatology, then plastic art, to the extent that it deals with mythological subjects, is merely their handmaiden. Plastic art borrows its creatures and representations insofar as it is able to use and express them.

So with each single figure—and hence we are speaking mostly of the works of sculptors, who carve forms that stand alone—*the insufficiency, the limits*, but not *the essence* of art demand that the persons be depicted according to type rather than as individuals, for otherwise we lose them in the throng of historical personages and they are in danger of becoming unrecognizable.

But as soon as the limits of his art permit the artist to follow the poet, then the latter, to whom mythology properly belongs, immediately reasserts his rights and the disposition of the work of art becomes poetic, in accordance with the origin of mythological ideas. The artist restricted himself to the abstract idea merely to avoid the unrecognizable; necessity and insufficiency were his law; but if this law, this fear is lifted, if he may hope to make a figure recognizable by means other than uniformly rep-

[128] *Lacooön*, p. 99 [8:52].

resenting its character, if *the essence* of his art does not preclude this alternative means of distinguishing a figure, if thereby he even achieves an end that he could not otherwise accomplish through the abstract idea, then he enjoys the same rights as the poet. All mythology is properly a realm of *poetic* ideas, and when the artist gives it form he too becomes a poet.

And on what does the artist's unrestricted exercise of his privileges depend? On *action*. If the artist—a painter, for example—can invest his work with *action*, if he can group several persons together, who represent a poetic or historical situation, if he can represent them in a recognizable and beautiful manner—oh, he shall surely forget the internal and external characteristics of his gods, which were necessary only as long as he depicted them singly. He can even let his action *visibly* contradict the abstract character; he can even paint a Venus furious at her Cupid, for though she may not at this moment remain *Love* as such, she nevertheless remains what she originally is: *the goddess of love*, the mother of Cupid. If the artist can bring Venus and the slain Adonis into painterly action, then, with the poet, we exclaim to Venus: "Sleep no more, Cypris, beneath thy purple coverlet, but awake to thy misery; put on the sable robe and fall to beating thy breast, and tell it to the world: The beauteous Adonis is dead." And all the same we wish to see Adonis as the poet sees him: "The beauteous Adonis lieth low in the hills, his thigh pierced with the tusk. He breathes a last sigh: black blood drips down his flesh that is whiter than the snow, and the eyes beneath his brow wax dim; the rose departs from his lip, Adonis lies dying." Does Adonis perchance die as the idea of connubial love and happiness and beauty? Does Venus grieve in order to show the idea of love in masquerade? Is she recognizable to every unimpaired mythological eye *because* she appears here as the abstract idea of love? No, the subject of the painting is poetic, historical; so are the artist's figures not also? Each time that he can make them thus—good! I then forget the abstract idea that in a single figure he was compelled to represent only by necessity. Cupid, who torments Psyche; and Jupiter, who abducts Ganymede; and Diana, who visits Endymion; and Venus, who weeps over her grazed skin—I promise the artist that in this moment I seek no personified abstractions: in Jupiter no chief of the gods, in Diana's face no virginal purity, in Venus no languishing, amorous glances, and in Cupid no playful seducer. All of these beings belong to the poet, and the artist leaves them to him whenever he can.

I do not know how narrow the Epic cycle would necessarily become for the artist if Mr. Lessing prohibited him from using historical and poetic scenes, permitted him to seek only personified abstractions in mythology, and forbade every little action that might contradict the abstract idea of the character (an idol of our modern mythologists!). Then we should have to bid farewell to an art rich in action! As far as mythology is concerned, it would be nothing but a gallery of uniform ideas and abstract characters!

> When the poet personifies abstractions, he characterizes them sufficiently by their names and the actions he has them perform. The artist lacks these means and must therefore add to his personified abstractions symbols by which they may be recognized. Necessity invented these for the artist, but why should the poet have forced on him what the artist had to accept of necessity, a necessity that he has no part of? Let it therefore be a law unto him not to make the necessities of painting into a part of his wealth and adorn his beings with the symbols of art. He shall let his beings act and also avail himself of poetic attributes.[129]

And so on. How gladly, how unweariedly one hears Mr. L. speak when he—but I do not wish to lavish praise on him. Should all this not also apply to those artistic compositions that we considered earlier? In the realm of the poet, the painter finds personified abstractions that in his picture, too, he characterizes sufficiently by the actions he has them perform. The artist *of a single figure* lacks these means; he must therefore endow his personified abstractions with symbols by which they may be recognized. But did necessity invent his symbols? Why should the artist *with action* have forced on him what the artist *without action* had to accept of necessity, a necessity that he has no part of? Let it therefore be a law unto him not to make what are the *necessities* of his art into a part of his wealth and to heap symbols on his beings, not to adorn them like puppets where they appear as higher individuals, and least of all to make this the leading theme of his art: "To me the figures of mythology are nothing but personified abstractions that must always retain the same characteristics if they are to be recognized." If we assume this principle, what becomes of the art that is supposed to deliver compositions? A masquerade of symbolic and allegorical puppets!

Hence there are considerable differences even between the arts of design, with one or the other approaching more closely to the poetic. Sculpture lies farthest from it; but painting, particularly in its composition, and particularly in the composition of poetic beings, which are originally creatures of the imagination and not of observation, comes much closer to poetry. There is drama among its figures; it positions all of them with the simple intention of representing an action; thus, it omits as far as is possible anything that is not part of the action or that might even contradict it. If in every artistic composition every mythological figure were laden with all the appurtenances that are proper to it but that have no connection with this action; if the historical and poetic painter should treat the

---

[129] *Lacooön*, pp. 115, 116 [10:60].

figure only as a personified abstraction that must always retain the same characteristics, what a confusing and distracting train of symbolic signs and typical predicates! If, in a painted composition, Venus should never appear as anything but *Love itself* (and not simply as the goddess of love) and each time be characterized as *Love itself*, and all the other participating figures likewise, each after their fashion—well, let us be rid of the masquerade ball. In the composition of a poetic subject the painter was here a poet; his figures shall be recognized by their *actions*; the attributes with which he endows them ought to refer to this action; those that do not belong to this depiction he shall omit, as long as the figure can still be recognized; he shall sacrifice as little as possible to the insufficiency, the necessity of his art, and least of all should he make this insufficiency, this law of necessity into his general, fundamental rule: to the artist gods and spiritual beings are personified abstractions, "which must always retain the same characteristics."[130] I take the opposite view: the artist, too, should characterize gods and spiritual beings through their actions, wherever this is possible; and only where it is not possible should they be recognizable as personified abstractions by the symbols attached to them. So at bottom the same law, the same freedom.

12

For poetry there can be no more necessary precept than this:[131] the poet must not make the necessities of painting into a part of his wealth; he must not adorn the creatures of his imagination in painterly fashion; he shall let them act, and the attributes by which he represents them must also be actions, must be poetic and not picturesque. Thus, the ancient poets poeticize, the modern ones paint.

Horace stands out in the finest age of Roman poetry as a lover of moral beings, of personified abstractions. This poetic personification is one of the principal traits of his genius and has greatly embellished his odes. Since, generally speaking, these moral persons, endowed with few yet vivid attributes, enter swiftly, suddenly, right in the middle of the action of his odes, so we love the agreeable sylphs and the beautiful sylphides, who rush past us so aptly. How sweet is his image of the smiling Venus, about whom hover Mirth and Desire.

—Erycina ridens
quam Jocus circumvolat et Cupido—

---

[130] *Lacooön*, p. 99 [8:52].
[131] *Lacooön*, p. 116 [10:60].

What an image! When *Fear* and *Care* also follow their master onboard the galley, also sit behind the horseman, also flit at night about the ceilings of the rich; when *Death* with foot impartial knocks at the cottages of the poor and the palaces of the powerful; when *Fortuna*—

I come now to the Horatian ode that is the richest of all in such poetic personification and where the personified abstractions have given the commentators many a troublesome quarter of an hour. *Fortune, Necessity, Hope, Fidelity*, and so on, are all grouped together as moral persons in this ode, and the whole poem is dedicated to a personified abstraction. The reader will have guessed that I am referring to the "Ode to Fortuna."[132] As usual, Baxter seeks in it his beloved *dilogia*,[133] and Gesner goes perhaps too far in the opposite direction by declaring it to be a treatise on the subject of *Fortune*.[134] But let us read the ode without preconceived opinions.

At the outset Horace does not invoke *Fortune* as an abstraction in order to write a treatise on the subject, as Gesner thinks; he invokes, rather, the *goddess of fortune* and above all the deity worshiped as such at Antium. The ode as a whole thus immediately steps out of the light of a *general concept* and becomes a family heirloom of Rome, of the city of *Anzio*, an altarpiece in the temple of this civic goddess. If only a citizen of Anzio were alive today to explain to us this ode from his native city. And how he would ridicule us for the upright *locus communis* that in this ode we impute to Fortune in general because we do not have the honor of being acquainted with the individual goddess to whom the ode is dedicated.

So what are the attributes of this goddess? "She can raise us up or humble us." Expressed in such a way, this attribute would surely be nothing but locus communis; yet in Horace's mode of expression it becomes typically Roman. This Fortune in Antium is a Roman goddess: she concerns herself with the revolutions of the state, which perhaps Horace even then foresaw, and she bestows and overturns triumphs. Just as the African Jupiter does not correspond exactly with the Roman Jupiter and the Madonna in Loretto is not wholly the Madonna in Parma, so this particular Fortuna is not identical with every other representation of the goddess; she is peculiar to Antium and takes the part of Rome.

"Thee the poor peasant entreats with anxious prayer and whoever braves the Carpathian sea." I do not know why on this point Baxter journeys as far as the moon to seek a *sortem fortunae* there; and to my mind Gesner's explanation that the sea storms arise from unknown causes, that they cannot be foreseen and are thus to be ascribed to Fortune, and so on,

---

[132] Bk. 1, ode 35.
[133] *Horatius*, ed. Baxter, p. 49.
[134] *Eclogae Horatii*, ed. Gesner, p. 71.

is too general; finally, Klotz's explanation that Fortune is depicted on coins with sheaves of wheat, ships' anchors, and God knows what else is for me and for Horace also even more learned.[135] Presumably Horace— the simpleton!—was here thinking of nothing but that *Antium*, the dwelling place of Fortuna, counts countrymen among its populace and lies near the sea; hence the Temple of Fortune is visited by both peasants and mariners.

"Thee the wild Dacian fears, and the roving Scythian, cities, tribes, and martial Latium, and mothers of barbarian kings, and tyrants clad in purple." Nothing could be easier to explain than these lines taken by themselves. They show, namely, the goddess of fortune taking the side of Rome; before her the enemies, the rebels, and the tyrants of Rome must tremble; but now the following is added:

> iniuriosio ne pede proruas
> stantem columnam; neu populas frequens
> ad arma cessantes ad arma
> concitet imperiumque frangat.

No simpler and more pleasant words have ever been spoken than those describing this *standing pillar*: Baxter was emphatic that it referred to Augustus, without considering whether the enemies, the rebellious vassals of Rome, would be so fearful of the downfall of Augustus.[136] Gesner, in keeping with his notion that this ode represented the locus communis de Fortuna, understood it as "each person, upon whom others rest as upon a pillar," without telling us how this general proposition reconciles Dacians and Scythians, barbarians and tyrants. I myself see in this standing pillar—well, nothing more than a standing pillar: perhaps a pillar in Anzio that inscribed with the name of Rome stood before Fortuna, as indeed it was generally the custom to place such columns before statues of Fortune, Peace, or Safety.[137] Now the image of her displeasure occurred to Horace: what if she stretched out her foot and overturned the pillar? Then for the poet this collapse would be a symbol, an omen of the fall of Rome. The thronging populace would call the peaceable to arms and smash to pieces the empire, this immense world pillar. The ode as a whole leads one to suppose that Horace saw this storm prefigured in many a breaking wave in his own day, or, to use his image, that Fortuna seemed even then to stir her immense toe with the aim of toppling the pillar. Why, though, do Dacians and Scythians, barbarians and tyrants, fear this—and

[135] [Klotz,] *Vindiciae [Quintii] Horatii [Flacci. Accedit Commentarius in carmina Poetae]* [1764], p. 152.

[136] *Horatius*, p. 50.

[137] Addison's *Dialogue upon the Usefulness of Ancient Medals* [1726], p. 47.

not Romans or patriots? Horace does not say that that the former fear *this*, the overturning of the pillar, but that they fear and shrink from the goddess of fortune; she who watches over Rome and before whom Rome's pillar stands, but who with one kick can also send it crashing down—this all-powerful goddess the Scythians and barbarians fear and shrink from (for what sacrifice can they bring her other than their fear?) and await the moment of her decision, which in those days seemed to be drawing near.

Up to this point, the ode has been a national treasure of Rome and a family heirloom of Antium; now it grows more symbolic:

> —te semper anteit serva (saeva) Necessitas
> clavos trabales et cuneos manu
> gestans ahena; nec servus
> uncus abest, liquidumque plumbum.

Ever since there have been arbiters of taste, more than one has found this image of Horace wanting. Sanadon was the first to venture to suggest that in view of its detail this picture would be more beautiful on a canvas than in a heroic ode. I cannot say whether Sanadon's feelings in this matter were correct and refined, although I have just read these mocking words directed at him: "Quod haec imago non placuit bono Sanadonio, sui ingenii homo est, delicatus mehercle! et venustulus!" I cannot say whether this *sui ingenii homo delicatus mehercle et venustulus* would be satisfied with the following powerful refutation: "Neque enim intellexisse videtur, quam divina sint: ahena manus, severus uncus."[138] I, who am not refined enough to glimpse the divine in an *ahena manus*, in a *severus uncus*, share Sanadon's feelings and think that any man who reads the ode from beginning to end in a single sitting will find himself arrested by this image, halting before it as if before a painted canvas, and no one wants that in an ode.

These implements may well all be *attirail patibulare* or means of fastening or symbols of Fortuna's supreme power; the brazen hand and *severus uncus* may well be as divine as they seem to Mr. Klotz; nevertheless the passage remains one of the most frigid in Horace.

Or is it because "they are attributes intended for the eye and not the ear. All concepts that we acquire through the eyes would require a much greater effort and produce less clarity were they to be conveyed through the ear"?[139] Lessing's reason, or at least the manner in which he expresses it, is no more satisfying than that of Sanadon or Klotz; for if a concept that we originally acquire through the eyes is not intended for the hearing because it cannot be seen with the ear, then poetry would be deprived

---

[138] Klotz, *Vindiciae Horatii*, p. 154.
[139] *Laocoön*, p. 118 [10:n6].

of its entire share of sensuous, visible objects; and what would it be left with? Thus, the attributes do not render the passage frigid because nails, clamps, and molten lead can be seen but not heard; for who, when he hears *uncus, plumbum, clavos*, will not immediately see *uncus, plumbum, clavos*, in his imagination? Who, when he perceives these objects through the ear, will need to make an effort to picture them in his mind as clearly as if he saw them? It is surely not the attributes themselves, then, that make Horace's passage frigid, but rather the *composition of these attributes to form a picture. Necessitas* precedes Fortuna—fine! And now we expect to discover why she is striding forth, what she wishes to accomplish? She carries wedges and nails—fine! Why does she carry them? *Nor are the clamp and molten lead wanting*—here the reader grows impatient: why do I need to know all this—*what she lacks or does not lack*, what she has or does not have? So I do not get to hear what she intends or is supposed to do with all these items? I stand before a lifeless picture. The question of what she is meant to do with these objects is answered by Mr. Klotz: "With them she is supposed to demonstrate the power of Fortune, of the goddess whom nothing can resist, before whom everything must yield, the goddess with the unalterable will. How beautifully everything fits together! The picture must please everyone who has poetic spirit."[140] If Mr. Klotz had said *who has painterly spirit*—then that would have been fine! But poetic spirit? I could not say in what way the effect produced by this picture might be poetic. The poet has a different brush with which to characterize the goddess whom nothing can resist, before whom everything must yield, who has an unalterable will; he has no need to place in her hand a lump of lead and iron and have her tramp along as she carries it. The least action, indeed the mere phrase "she is the goddess whom nothing can resist, before whom everything must yield," is better than a figure roaming about with deadly weapons. In short, it is not the nature of the attributes themselves, the fact that they are intended for the eye; it is not even the heaping of the attributes as such in which the error of this image consists. Rather, it is their composition to create a mere symbol, a symbol that achieves nothing, that with its prosaic *nec abest* simply stands there, so that none of its ornaments shall be missing, so that it shall parade as a perfect symbol in a picture—this offends the reader, particularly in a Horatian ode. He hails the symbol, as it were, entreating it either to take part in the action of the ode or to remove itself to a canvas, a wall, a painting of Fortuna.

And how did Horace arrive at this dead figure? In all likelihood he copied it from just such a painting, copied the features that one might have encountered in the temple at Antium. So what would be a perplexing error

---

[140] [Klotz,] *Vindiciae Horatii*, pp. 154, 155.

in a Horatian ode to Fortune's locus communis can at least be excused in an ode to Fortuna of Anzio. It immortalized a painting, a beautiful symbolic painting that might have been a treasure of the temple, to which this ode, as a treasure, also belonged. Here one should criticize Horace not as a poet per se but as a poet for Anzio.

I believe that with this insight I am able to illuminate and explain the following, so thoroughly misunderstood moral beings:

> te Spes et albo rara Fides colit
> velata panno—

Spence is wrong to see a thin-dressed figure in this passage;[141] but he is right that the figure is a painterly one, as the epithet "white-robed" makes clear, and the reason for the phrase "white-robed" I do not, like the scholiast, need to seek in the ancient custom of the priests of Fides, who performed sacrifices with their heads covered by a white veil. The answer lies closer to hand: What dress would be more appropriate in a painting of Fidelity than the clothing of innocence? But if the figure is drawn originally from a painting—then how futile is Bentley's puzzling over the question of why Hope and Fidelity are the designated companions of Fortune? If this painting of Fortuna resided in Anzio, then how rich and beautiful would its poetic rendering be!

Now Horace begins to add an allegorical dimension to this rich interpretation: *Hope* and *Fidelity* are mentioned as companions of Fortune— as companions? "Thus will they ever accompany her! Even if she should change her dress, even if she should forsake the houses of the great in a hostile mood. It is only the faithless rabble and the perjured harlot who turn away; only treacherous friends scatter as soon as they have drained our wine jars; *Hope* and *Fidelity* are not like that." I see no more contradiction here than those which may always attend upon an edifying allegorical interpretation,[142] and especially of a figure whose name is ambiguous.

And with this allegory Horace prepares the ground so that he can commend his *Augustus* and the Roman Empire to the protection of the goddess of fortune—a subject with which his ode closes. I find, then, no abstraction—Fortune—treated in it, as one might think if one were to look up the title in a dictionary; it is the goddess of fortune who dwells in Anzio, a goddess of fortune who takes the part of Rome, who even *in the circumstances then prevailing* shall take Rome into her care. It is from Antium, from Rome, and from those bygone days that the personified ideas

---

141 [Spence, *Polymetis*, 1747,] dialogue 10.
142 Bentley has found the most glaring contradiction. See the discussion of this ode in his edition of Horace.

of this ode must therefore take their light, or else one is looking squint-eyed. Nor does Mr. Klotz, in his elucidations based on gemstones and coins,[143] appear to have had the ultimate aim of accounting for the *poetic structure* of this Horatian ode, though that would be perfectly feasible. Generally speaking, if the use of personified beings were to be explained by the example of a lyric poet, then the foremost poet for such a purpose is—Horace, *he* who loves these beautiful apparitions uncommonly and introduces them very much with their individual characters; let a connoisseur of Horace show us this side of him!

But the epic poet also has need of personified ideas, which we are apt to call machines—how should he fashion them? As symbolic beings of the artist, as allegories? Or as acting subjects? If there is one species of poet who must distinguish himself from the artist, it is the epic poet, particularly where his machines are concerned—I wish this thought had occurred to Mr. L.!

I know that some poets have represented passions, virtues and vices, and a whole host of moral beings as personified machines; but I also know how frigid, how superfluous these machines have seemed, often through the entire length of a poem, simply because they appeared as personified abstractions, because they lacked individuality. To paint a real abstraction as a person, to endow it with external form, to express it poetically, is not practicable without symbols, for colors and forms do not reside in the kernel, in the essence of an abstract concept. When, for line after line, the poet has symbolically painted Innocence, Envy, Physics, and so on, he runs the risk that we afterward ask: what did the thing look like? All the individually characteristic features have been forgotten; how can I assemble them so that I have a complete picture before me? The poet's task was akin to the labor of the Danaides: always to draw new features, which in each moment, however, trickle away, and now here I stand with my leaky bucket and have—nothing.

Now this personified abstraction shall act as a machine; and of course it shall do so only in keeping with *its nature*, acting as Innocence, Envy, and Anger must act. Thus I see every move they make in advance; every speech they make I can already guess from their name; I need only this name, only the idea itself, and everything else becomes mere poetic garb, a rhetorical flourish. The whole entity is created from a concept and enshrouded in a word. Can it therefore move me? Excite epic admiration in me? Grant me an unfamiliar and grand spectacle? A being created by a word that anyone can parrot, that anyone can work out in advance is—tinsel.

---

[143] [Klotz,] *Vindiciae Horatii* [pp. 151–55].

No, Homer's machines are not abstract concepts; they are subjects who act of their own accord; they are well-rounded individuals. I cannot guess from some arbitrary idea how Jupiter and Juno and Minerva will behave in this or that situation, as if they were the mere outer clothing of this idea. All his gods are fictitious persons, but *persons* nonetheless, with a quite definite way of thinking, with strengths and weaknesses, with faults and virtues, with everything that appertains to a living being. Not only do they show me their thoughts, words, actions; I see also from the nature, the coherence of these thoughts, words, actions, that they flow from the innermost depths of an individual; the poet enchants me so that for as long as I read I believe such a being exists. You gentleman allegorists, you baptizers of machines, you sculptors of ideas in epic poetry—this is what you do not do! You paint, you delineate; and that is also how I read you: as painters, as delineators, but not as poets, not as a second Prometheus, not as creators of immortal gods and mortal men.

Even the minor creatures of the imagination, which cross the path of Homer's poem only once, as it were—Terror, Rout, and Strife, who rages incessantly—seem *more like individuals* than allegories; Strife, for example, as the sister and comrade of man-slaying Mars, is by his side, in the thick of battle.[144] All this mutes the allegorical quality of the noble idea that "she first rears her crest only a little, but then her head is fixed in the heavens while her feet tread on the earth." We still see a person more than we do a concept merely represented as a person.

Homer has no room for personified abstractions, for allegorical machines viewed as such. Only in the speeches of his heroes does he allow *prayers* and so forth to be allegorized,[145] which therefore issued from their mouths and not properly from his hand, which were therefore meant to be spoken and thought but not given poetic form, not seen in the poem itself, so to speak. But even here he seeks wherever he can to invest them with the luster of a living being; he weaves them into the genealogy of the gods; he adds historical contours; he does not color the allegorical with predicates but *hints* at it in names, in historical contours, in poetic attributes. That is how little Homer's main object is to allegorize, and least of all to allegorize for artists.

Here one might consult Winckelmann's work on allegory; however, I shall abide with two other companions as I continue my journey through the question of how the artist can imitate the poet, and in particular the Greek artist imitate Homer. These companions are *Caylus* and *Lessing*.

[144] *Iliad* 4.440–42; 9.2.

[145] For example, Agamemnon's speech on the goddess Ate, *Iliad* 19.78–144; Phoenix's speech on Prayers, 9:499–514.

13

I believe I have now arrived at the best part of Lessing's work,[146] the part that qualifies the prescriptions of Comte de Caylus, that distinguishes between Homer's manner of representation and that of an artist, and that is a model of practical discrimination. Every reader who appreciates Lessing must have read with amazement the confusing contradictions that[147]——but I think I may assume an acquaintance with the author's own reply to these criticisms.[148]

Let me therefore enter into more detail. "Homer treats of two kinds of beings, visible and invisible. This distinction cannot be made in painting, where everything is visible and visible in but one way."[149]

"The means that painting uses to convey to us that this or that object must be thought of as invisible is a thin cloud."[150]

"It appears that this cloud was borrowed from Homer himself."[151]

"Who can fail to see that concealment by cloud or night is, for the poet, nothing more than *a poetic expression* for rendering a thing invisible? For that reason it has always been a source of surprise to me to see this poetic expression *actually used* and a real cloud introduced into the painting."[152]

I am satisfied with the distinction that Mr. L. makes here; only the grounds for his distinction do I find questionable.

What purpose does the cloud serve for poet and painter? *Concealment.* So where it cannot *conceal*, it is no longer a cloud and may be omitted. That is the case with the painter. The cloud is supposed to conceal and yet does not conceal; the enshrouded hero is still visible; he stands behind a screen and calls to us: "I am invisible; you are not meant to see me; I am not at home." This reasoning, I think, is correct.

But the claim that the cloud is borrowed from the poet, that for him it is nothing but a poetic expression, whereas for the artist it is an actual cloud and thus a poetic expression realized in surprising fashion, seems rather more dubious.

Homer's mist is a poetic mist; but does that mean it is a poetic expression, an artistic turn of phrase that means "to render invisible"?[153] When Achilles makes three further thrusts with his spear at Hector, who has

---

[146] *Laocoön,* pp. 119–49, [11–15].
[147] Klotz, *Geschnittene Steine,* now and again.
[148] *Hamburgische neue Zeitung,* 1768, no. 97.
[149] *Laocoön,* p. 130 [12:66].
[150] *Lacooön,* p. 137 [12:68].
[151] *Lacooön,* p. 137 [12:68].
[152] *Lacooön,* pp. 137, 138 [12:68].
[153] *Lacooön,* p. 137 [12:68].

been concealed in the cloud and swiftly borne away, does this mean, "in the language of poetry, only that Achilles was so enraged that he made the three additional thrusts before realizing that his enemy was no longer before him"? I must say that I am not familiar, nor would I like to be, with "such poetic phraseology." Homer, the enemy of all artificial figures that are nothing more than dressing, nothing more than poetic ornament (and, following Mr. Lessing's explanation, what is this cloud, this poetic expression, other than just such a *flower of speech*?); Homer becomes, on this reading, one of our modern sober-minded poets, poets who think prosaically and speak poetically, whose *gradus ad Parnassum* is the conjuring box by which they transform their prosy thoughts into poetic diction, into poetic metaphors. We might say that such poets write a schoolboyish commentary in which everything is prosified: "He was covered by a cloud, *that is to say*: he was removed from the sight of the enemy; Achilles made three thrusts into the thick mist, *that is to say*: he was so enraged that he did not yet realize that his enemy was gone." But what would remain if we read Homer after this fashion, if with a "that is to say" we also rendered his gods, their heaven, their attributes, and so on, into prose and turned everything into hollow poetic phrases?

No, Homer knows nothing of empty metaphorical expressions. In his work, the mist in which the gods enshroud mortals is real mist, a veiling cloud that is an integral part of the wonder of his fiction, of his epic μῦθος, of his gods. As long as he holds me spellbound in this poetic world, wherein gods and heroes do battle; as long as his Minerva guides me through these marvelous and terrible scenes and has sharpened my eyesight so that I discern not only men in combat but also warring and wounded gods, then I shall see this mist with just as much faith as I see the god himself who weaves it around his favorite. The god and his cloud are equally poetic; if I prosify the one, then a grammatical "that is to say" must follow the other, and in that case I shall lose the whole *mythical* aspect of Homer's creation. I find myself no longer in the epic engagement depicted by a poet but rather in a historical battle: I read and study the tactics of the clashing armies; I see the action unfold on a human scale.

It is precisely within such human limits that Mr. L. seems to see, or at least he claims to. "Achilles did not see an actual mist, and the power of the gods to render invisible did not lie in any mist—but in their ability to bear the object away swiftly. It was only to show that this abduction took place too quickly for the human eye to follow the disappearing body that the poet first conceals it in a mist or cloud. And it was not because a cloud appeared in place of the abducted body but because we think of that which is wrapped in mist as being invisible."[154] What distinctions! What

---

[154] *Lacooön*, pp. 138, 139 [12:69].

amphibolia! "Achilles did not see an actual mist." Indeed! The poetic hero saw it and made three further thrusts with his spear into the mist. "The power of the gods to render invisible lay in their ability to bear the object away swiftly." How strange! If I already can and do imagine gods acting in the world and a miraculous abduction, am I not being overly scrupulous in seeking to reduce the significance of the mist? "Only because the abduction took place quickly does the poet conceal it in a mist; it was not because a cloud appeared, but because we think of that which is wrapped in mist as being invisible." I see, and for this reason Achilles thrusts three times into the mist, not because he saw a mist but because he thought of that which was wrapped in the mist as invisible! Oh, this Homeric Don Quixote! Oh, this Cervantean Homer!

"Neptune blinds Achilles; actually, however, Achilles' eyes are no more blinded than——" The things people would have us believe! Neptune sheds a mist over the eyes of Achilles, he snatches Aeneas away, brings him to safety, warns him not to fight Achilles, leaves him—then he must *return to scatter the mist from Achilles' eyes,*[155] and Achilles—had no mist before his eyes? Homer *just says* that his eyes were blinded?——The light returns to Achilles' eyes, he groans, he starts back at the marvel; he sees his spear lying on the ground but not the man at whom he hurled it; and in agitation he speaks to himself, to his proud heart, and supposes it to be the work of the gods. "What?" a Homeric orthodoxian will say. "Is it not a punishable blasphemy to doubt the existence of the mist of the gods when one witnesses such an obvious miracle of bedazzlement, such an awe-inspiring scene? Those who believe in the Homeric gods must also believe in the cloud that is their handiwork!"

Mr. Lessing must be otherwise acquainted with the cloud dogmatics of the Greek gods than I, for he proceeds to make claims that run counter to the beautiful visibility of Homeric phenomena. "Invisibility," he claims, "is the natural condition of his gods; no blindfolding, no interruption of the rays of light are needed to prevent them from being seen; but an enlightenment, an increased power of mortal vision is required if they are intended to be seen. Homer also has divinities conceal themselves in a cloud now and then, but it is only when they do not want to be seen by their fellow gods."[156] The following will show that as far as his cloud theory of the Greek gods is concerned Mr. L.——is a heretic.

"Invisibility is the natural condition of his gods." Might I ask how it is possible, then, that the gods can be seen *against their will*, that they can be caught *unawares* if they wish to remain unobserved? It was an article of faith among the Greeks that nothing was more dangerous than to be

---

[155] *Iliad* 20.l.341, 342ff.
[156] *Laocoön*, pp. 140, 141 [12:70].

taken by surprise by such a sight,[157] a fate that befell many an unfortunate and unsuspecting mortal. Pallas, the most chaste of the goddesses, whose purity was such that she scarcely dared to see herself unclothed, who indeed of all the goddesses was least inclined to that *false* modesty of concealing oneself and yet desiring to be seen; this virginal Pallas, then, chooses the most secluded and secret spot to lay down her Gorgon shield; she bathes herself, and an equally virtuous Tiresias takes her by surprise, sees her *against his will*, and is blinded. However, to compensate the innocent to some degree, Pallas does not restore his sight to him—for her maidenly modesty cannot permit this—but bestows on him the power of prophecy. How could Pallas be surprised both against her will and that of Tiresias if invisibility were "the natural condition of the gods"?

As with Pallas, so with the chaste Diana when she bathed herself. Calydon glimpsed her, likewise against his will and the will of the goddess, and was turned to stone. It was the same story with Jupiter, when in moments of sweetest pleasure he once forgot his cloud. As he slept with Rhea, his slumber was disturbed by Heliacmon, against the will of Jupiter and that of his beloved bedfellow and that of the river god who caught him unawares—how is this possible if invisibility were "the natural condition of the gods"?

I shall not enumerate such occasions when the gods and goddesses were disturbed in their sleep. This time my Muse is not like the sister of Amor, who

> —wie die Mädchen alle tun,
> Verliebte gern beschleichet.

Instead, I shall cite from the *Greek Anthology* an epigram with its innocent jocularity,[158] its naive playfulness: "Let no one against his will see one of the Naiads naked in my waters, or Venus with the Graces; for according to Homer's dictum to see the gods manifestly is dangerous, and who would dispute Homer?" To grasp the playfulness that lies concealed in this epigram, observe the double meaning that inheres in the phrase "to see manifestly." The epigrammatist means *naked*; Homer means "without foreign garb, as the gods are." A passage from Homer shall thus confirm my view, and this notion seems even to have become axiomatic in Greek mythology.

Juno, who desires to come to the aid of Achilles, delivers the maxim that if Achilles were to see a god come against him in battle,[159] he *would have* to take fright, for "dangerous are the gods when they appear in man-

---

[157] Callimachus, *Hymni in Palladis, Dianam*, and so on.
[158] *Greek Anthology*, bk. 9, epigram 625.
[159] *Iliad* 20.131. χαλεποὶ δὲ θεοὶ φαίνεσθαι ἐναργεῖς.

ifest form" (that is, when they do not appear in human guise). So how is invisibility their natural condition?

Homer seems to proceed according to this axiom whenever he speaks of the gods. When the gods are *among themselves*, they are visible to one another; but if they should be at work among mortals, they adjust the nature of their appearance depending on whether they wish to preserve their incognito or not. When Phoebus Apollo descends from heaven,[160] he does so in his divine form: quiver and bow are slung over his shoulders; the arrows rattle on the shoulders of the angry god as he moves. Down from the peaks of Olympus he strode, and his coming was *like the night*, until he could sit down far from the ships and let fly his plague-bringing arrows. Why must he steal past the Greeks like the night—that is, wrapped in darkness—and assume his divine form when he is out of sight of the ships and of mortals? Why, if the Homeric gods are already invisible to human eyes, if no interruption of the rays of light is needed to *prevent* them from being seen, but rather an increased power of vision is required if they are *intended* to be seen? If I wish to avoid once more taking refuge in sacred allegory, then I am bound to conclude that the cloud is wholly without purpose.

And how often Homer makes use of this supposedly purposeless cloud! Thetis rises from the sea enveloped in a mist, she sits down before her son and reveals herself to him.[161] In a cloud she mounts up to Olympus to petition Jupiter; Jupiter sheds a thick mist around himself when he sits on Ida to survey the battle and wishes to remain unseen.[162] In Homer a cloud is more than once the raiment that the gods assume when they appear without intervening in human affairs, when they appear in their immortal form. Their body may only be *like* a body and the ichor that flows in their veins only *like* blood—that is, not as coarse and earthly as a human body—but nevertheless they have *blood* that can be spilled, a *body* that can be wounded, as is evident in a number of passages.[163] Thus, Venus is wounded by Diomedes, even though he immediately recognizes her as a goddess;[164] and to console her, Dione,[165] the mother of the goddess, tells her what the Olympians since time immemorial have had to suffer at the hands of men: so suffered Mars, bound by two of his brave enemies, held prisoner for thirteen months before being spirited away by Mercury in the nick of time; so suffered Juno, so suffered Pluto——but there is no need to recount the myths, which all demonstrate at the very least that ac-

---

[160] *Iliad* 1. 47 (νυκτὶ ἐοικώς).
[161] *Iliad* 1. 359 (ἠΰτ᾽ ὀμίχλη).
[162] *Iliad* 8.50.
[163] *Iliad* 5.340–42.
[164] *Iliad* 5.330, 331.
[165] Ibid., 381.

cording to Homer's theory of the gods this proposition is pitched too high: "Invisibility is the natural condition of the gods; an increased power of mortal vision is required if they are intended to be seen, but no interruption of the rays of light to prevent them from being seen." But in that case is it not impossible for a god to be recognized, trussed, and wounded against his will? If a god, by his very nature, does not merely elude human vision; if this vision must furthermore be miraculously enhanced so that a mortal may behold him, then is it not nonsensical if the god, again by his very nature, is vulnerable, is conquerable by the hero? To my questions one might reply: to recognize a god or goddess, Diomedes' eyes had first to be opened by another deity, Minerva. But I am speaking here only of a *god's inherent vulnerability*[166] and conclude as follows: a vulnerable body must also be a body that is not by nature invisible; if the nature of that body precluded my eye from catching sight of it, then how, *by the nature of divine flesh*, could my hand catch hold of a god?

But why did Minerva have to dispel the mist from the eyes of Diomedes so that he could discern both gods and men in battle?[167] I could say quite simply: because, in poetic terms, he had mist before his eyes; but I mean to explain Homer prosaically. When Homer's gods act directly on and with men, for example, when they quarrel, fight, drive horses, in short, perform human deeds, then as a rule they also take on the form of mere mortals. In each case Homer uses the phrase "in the likeness of this or that hero."[168] And of course the god was unrecognizable in this instance, for he was in human guise; the heroes only *inferred* that a god must be at work from the superhuman exploits and the quite marvelous feats that this figure accomplished. They were afraid, then, to encounter a god disguised in this way because their maxim was "That man endures not for long who fights with the immortals." With the characteristic honesty of the Greeks, one hero asks another to be open and say whether he is a god or a mortal so that he may know whom he faces. And with divine candor the god reveals himself when he is forced into a corner so that men shall steer clear of him. In brief, because the battle that Homer describes is full of incognito gods come down from heaven, because the poet deliberately assumes that all heroes and combatants are aware of this, then of course Minerva is required to enable men to recognize these incarnated beings. But she *enhances the vision of Diomedes* not so that he might discern immortals, for the immortals here resembled men, but to allow him to *rec-*

---

[166] Gods can also be wounded by other gods; Jupiter warns Juno and Minerva that if they do not turn back, he shall inflict a wound on them that will not heal for *ten years. Iliad* 8.404, 415 [400–408].

[167] *Iliad* 5.116–30.

[168] Neptune: εἰσάμενος Κάλχαντι (*Iliad* 13.45); Minerva: Δηϊφόβῳ ἐϊκυῖα (*Iliad* 22.227), ἣ δ᾽ ἀνδρὶ ἰκέλη Λαοδόκῳ (*Iliad* 4.86, 87).

ognize that this or that murderous figure is something more than he took it for, that this warrior is no mortal but a god come down from heaven,[169] and so on. In fine, the gods appear here in an obstructive vehicle, as it were, and in this vehicle they may become *recognizable* but not visible.

But now let the vehicle fall away, let them be simply gods: the wound, the pain remains with them; it does not vanish with the human form in which they were incarnated. Mars cries out—he leaves the battle and ascends toward heaven; he discards the form of Acamas and behold! He wraps the mantle of a cloud around himself; among the clouds he went to Olympus.[170] And now, returning to his divine form, does he still feel the pain that a mortal could inflict on him? Does he leave the wound behind with the semblance of Acamas? No, it belongs to Mars; Paeëon, the heavenly physician, must heal his hurt; by its very nature, then, his divine body was thus vulnerable; so how was it not visible by its very nature? Or was it indeed invisible?

No! My Homer is too sensuous a poet to be concerned anywhere in his poem with such immaterial gods and with such subtle allegories on the meaning of this or that particular cloud. The inherent invisibility of the gods might have pleased a Persian epic poet, but in an epic poem a Greek eye desires to glimpse beautiful bodies and heavenly forms even among the divinities; it wishes to behold them in this beautiful visibility, which *lies in their very nature*, and not to rely on a miracle or the exceptional grace of the poet for enlightenment, for an increased power of mortal vision to look on them. For such an eye were the Greek gods created. But if the poet requires them to go unseen, then he cloaks them in a cloud, he sheds mist over our eyes. Furthermore, the cloud in which they appear embraces many other exalted subsidiary concepts: the concept of the divinity and sublimity that is proper to a celestial being; if the cloud is lustrous, then it suggests the magnificent throne of a heavenly regent; if dark, it suggests the raiment of the wrathful and furious Jupiter; if fragrant, it heralds the arrival of a fair, delightful goddess. All these subsidiary ideas reside already in our sensuous understanding; they have furnished the poets of every age with the most magnificent images. And Homer is meant to have neglected this noble use of the cloud, is meant not to have grasped it? He alone is meant to have turned it into the mere *hocus-pocus* of a poetic expression, to avoid straightforwardly expressing an abduction or the intrinsic invisibility of the gods? I say again: this Homer I do not recognize.

It is true that in later times, when the Homeric mythology was reduced to its quintessence and from it a few drops of metaphysical spirit were dis-

---

[169] *Iliad* 5.127–30.
[170] Iliad 5.867.

tilled, there was only too much sophistry concerning the intrinsic invisibility of the gods, their mystical appearances, the unearthly nature of their epiphanies, and so on. Such theophanies, such refined metaphysical speculation about the nature of the gods have their proper place in the circle of the later Platonists and Pythagoreans and in the sacred chants of their mysteries. But I believe we are discussing Homer here, not Jamblichus.

In fine, I am satisfied with the reason that if the painter cannot render a figure invisible with his own cloud, then he ought not to ape the poet's cloud either; and what use is heaping further allegories and interpretations about the poet so that he loses his way among them? To my mind the most beautiful visibility and youth are due to the Greek gods as a predicate of their being; and to picture to oneself an Apollo, a Bacchus, a Jupiter, to imagine invisibility as the natural condition of the gods without these qualities—no Greek soul, no Greek poet or artist can do that; even wise Epicurus cannot. If we discard the concept of beautiful visibility, then the nature of the gods, the vividness of their history and deeds, the precisely determined gradations of their ideal forms, the alluring character of their intercourse with the children of mortals, the whole power of mythology—all this is lost. I no longer see the beautiful and sensuous Greek gods; I see mere phantoms who desire to be visible! This hypothesis destroys my highest mythological and poetic and artistic rapture! I am not enamored of this new heretical idea; I shall keep to the ancient Greek orthodoxy.

14

"Nor can the painter imitate the size of the Homeric gods!" And what Mr. L. says on this point[171] boils down to these three reasons: in painting it is not the wonder of poetic invention that prevails but rather the habit of seeing, the intuitive truth of the eye; second, since painting works within space, proportion and disproportion are of greater account for the artist than they are for the poet, whose imagination operates in all possible and actual worlds, not merely betwixt heaven and earth, and least of all is it confined by the four sides of a canvas; third, where the poet could express size through power, strength, and swiftness, the painter is at some disadvantage, since he who works for *space* cannot very well make *strength*, and he who works for *a single glance* cannot very well make swift movement the focus of his activity. We might throw an exceedingly philosophical mantle around these reasons were it worth the cost of making it.

[171] *Laocoön*, pp. 131–36 [12].

I am only too happy to remain with Homer, especially when Mr. L. fancies himself his commentator. "Size, strength, and swiftness," says Mr. L., are

> qualities that Homer always has in store for his gods in a higher and more extraordinary degree than that bestowed on his finest heroes. No one who has read Homer even cursorily will question this assertion in regard to strength and speed. But possibly he has forgotten momentarily the examples that make it clear that the poet also attributed *superhuman* size to his gods. Even the commentators on Homer, ancient as well as modern, do not seem to have paid sufficient attention to the extraordinary size of the poet's gods. This may be gathered from the modifications they feel compelled to make in their explanations of the great size of Minerva's helmet.[172]

Mr. L. refers here to the Clarke-Ernesti edition of Homer, and it is thus a simple matter to identify those commentators, ancient as well as modern, who did not pay sufficient attention to the extraordinary size of Homer's gods. They are Eustatius; Clarke, who cites and thus endorses Eustatius; and Ernesti, who wants Homer's description of Minerva's helmet to be understood as referring to its solidity rather than its size.[173] What? Is superhuman size a characteristic of the Homeric gods? Is it a character trait as equally obvious, recognizable, and necessary as swiftness and strength? And then to crown it all, were the ancient masters of sculpture indebted to Homer, as Mr. L. thinks they are, for the colossal size that they often bestow on their statues?

It is perfectly obvious that if a poet endows his gods with a strength greater than that of heroes and Titans, then he will not have confined this strength in the body of a pygmy, for that would run counter to all poetic and human probability. It would be quite contrary to the intuitiveness of the poet's mode of representation to depict anthropomorphous gods possessed of both immeasurable strength and a form not exceeding normal human dimensions. In esoteric mysteries such gods would be welcome, because the more knots and contradictions one has tied, the more opportunity one has to demonstrate one's facility in unraveling them; but in the realm of manifest poetry such beings are like Micromegas.

So the stature of the body must not completely contradict the degree of its strength even in the manner in which it appears to our senses! But now let us continue: where no superhuman strength is expressed, there is no need for superhuman size, regardless of whether we are dealing with divinities. Indeed, if superhuman strength is not characteristic of this or that deity, then to invest the god with a gargantuan stature would create an in-

---

[172] *Laocoön*, p. 135 [12:68; n3].
[173] *Iliad* 5.744 [724–44], ed. Clarke-Ernesti.

tolerable contradiction in the intuitive character of poetry. I think my conclusions are plausible, and now they shall achieve certainty. Let Homer be my witness: his Jupiter, his Neptune, his Minerva, may very well be as big as can be, but not a Juno who is possessed of queenly beauty. Her appearance may be so imposing that Homer calls her "ox-eyed" and her figure as sublime as befits the woman who lies in Jupiter's arms;[174] she may, when she trembles with anger on her heavenly throne, make high Olympus quake[175]—what notions of her majesty and grandeur! But these ideas, strictly speaking, cannot be conveyed to me first and foremost by her physical stature; my eye must not fix on her size as if it were the most important aspect before me; otherwise I lose sight of the queen of the gods, the fairest of all goddesses: I see a giantess. Where, then, does the long-limbed goddess find room in heaven? How vast must the bridal chamber be, which Vulcan fashioned for her?[176] How huge the key and the bolt to this chamber, which no other god can open?[177] How many hundred-weights of ambrosia does she need to cleanse her body?[178] How many tons of oil to anoint it? How big must her comb, her belt, her jewelry be? Where will she find room atop Mount Ida to hold Jupiter in her sweet embrace?[179] When he clasps her in his arms and presses her to his royal breast, will Ida and the earth shake? I shall not continue; I think that is quite enough! The sweetness and grandeur of Homer's picture of her dressing, adornment, and embrace vanish if we imagine her immeasurable form.[180] As soon as even a single recognizable feature of Juno's gigantic stature becomes the main object in view, the limits of beauty recede into the distance or—if you prefer—the limits of supreme perfection attainable by the female form. My eye succumbs when it must apprehend the monstrous, and the admiration that I now feel is transformed into a kind of terrible self-awareness and horror and revulsion. So has Homer not done well "to attribute *superhuman* size to his goddess in not quite so obvious a fashion"?

These vast dimensions would produce an even worse effect in the case of Venus. If she is for Homer the laughter-loving goddess,[181] what would become of the sweet laughter on the face of a giantess? She may only mean to draw her mouth into a smile, and her lips may only gently quiver; yet

---

[174] βοῶπις πότνια Ἥρη.

[175] *Iliad* 8.198, 199.

[176] *Iliad* 14.163–68.

[177] *Ibid* 14.168.

[178] ἀμβροσίῃ μὲν πρῶτον ἀπὸ χροὸς ἱμερόεντος λύματα πάντα κάθηρεν, ἀλείψατο δὲ λίπ᾽ ἐλαίῳ (*Iliad*. 14.171–72).

[179] *Iliad* 14.312–53.

[180] *Iliad* 14.153–86.

[181] φιλομειδὴς Ἀφροδίτη [*Iliad* 3.424].

her creased mouth shall seem to me a contortion, the joyfulness that announces itself on her lips becomes a grimace, and the laughter that erupts a monstrous roaring and cackling. How incongruous does this immense form seem to me when she cries out, laments, weeps, and disturbs all of heaven when the skin of her finger is cut!

In short, if *size* and *strength* do not *constitute the chief traits of a deity's character, then his superhuman nature need not be in view either.* But if *the deity's character is not compatible with size and strength at all*—for example, the supreme perfection of the female figure in Juno or the most charming beauty in the daughter of Dion—then *they ought to be removed from our sight.* Our eyes, as human eyes, can determine the ideal of the noble as well as delightful beauty of an apparently human body only according to human dimensions. The difference is that in painting these dimensions remain within the limits of art, yet in poetry they can be raised to the highest level of human fancy; nevertheless, this highest level continues to be *perspicuous* for the fancy; it does not surpass human dimensions. If this intuitiveness, this wholeness is lost, and the stature of Juno and Venus is allowed, even in a single contour, to exceed the proportions within which I imagine physical perfection and beauty to be possible, then the poet has spoiled his impression. Once their characteristics have been agreed on, the gods may not be endowed willy-nilly with superhuman size; if the fancy demands that physical beauty must remain within human dimensions, then so too must Venus and Juno.

Now we turn to the deities whose character and individuality demand the expression of *tremendous strength*: Minerva; Neptune, the great Enfolder of the Earth; and then Jupiter, the mightiest of all the gods. And I repeat once more: *let not their physical size contradict their actions; but that does not mean that strength may be inferred from size in Homer!*

Homer does not paint us a picture of a single god; nor does he paint their "superhuman size." He shows us their nature through their actions, through their movements.

The great Jupiter! But is he great in Homer because, as with that angel in the Koran, one brow was separated from the other by a seven-day journey? In that case Jupiter would seem monstrous but not great: so Homer knows a better way. Jupiter bows his dark brow to Thetis in assent, the ambrosial locks shake on the king's immortal head, and Olympus quakes[182]—that is great Jupiter! Not how long but how powerful are his brow and locks; not how vast but how imperious is the head of the immortal king; that is what the poet concentrates on. That is Jupiter, supreme in might! Zeus, the sacker of cities.

On one occasion this Jupiter wishes to demonstrate the extent of his

[182] *Iliad* 1.528–30.

overwhelming power before all the other gods; and so he measures himself against them—but on the basis of physical size, length of arms, strength of sinews? What an unworthy, monstrous spectacle that would be! Jupiter has a better proposal for his gods and goddesses: all the Olympians are to lay hold of a chain of gold that shall hang down from heaven and pull with all their might; and yet they would not be able to drag Jupiter to the earth out of heaven. "But," he continues, "whenever I was really minded to pull with all my heart, then with the earth itself I would draw it up and with the sea as well; and the rope I would then bind around a peak of Olympus and all those things would hang in space. By so much do I surpass gods and surpass men."[183] We could not find a more sublime and simple image of the supremacy of the god most high, but we would look in vain for an image of this god's immensity before other gods and before men.

Thus Neptune's size is inferred and implied through his steps rather than explicitly described,[184] for to measure his whole form according to these steps would be monstrous and not Homeric. Rather, in this instance, too, the wise poet has established a scale marking the expression of size through strength and of strength through movement, a scale that is arranged according to the rank of his gods so that he can mete out to them with the greatest economy of expression the dignity that the greatest strength expresses. Just as the supreme god shows his size *with a nod of his brow*, so the next most august deity, Neptune, shows his size one notch lower on the scale, *in his stride*.[185] Similarly, Minerva's stature is measured by her strength when she picks up a huge stone and with it knocks Mars to the ground.[186] Perhaps, though, Mr. L. attaches greater significance to this stone than Homer intended it to possess. "It was a large, black, rough stone, which the united strength of men had rolled there for a landmark in times past." Now, whether Homer wished this stone to serve as a precise standard of measurement so that if one of his heroes was twice as strong as the men of his own day but that these again were half as strong as the heroes of an even more remote age, then the stone can be reckoned as equal to the strength of four times the number of men who laid it—that I do not know. Perhaps Homer just meant to say it was an ancient boundary mark.

I believe it is also open to question whether the size of Minerva's hel-

---

[183] *Iliad* 8.17–27.

[184] What an image Jupiter presents when he sits atop Ida holding his golden scales! The scale containing the fates of the Greeks sinks toward the earth, and that of the Trojans is raised aloft toward heaven—how strong is the arm of the god who weighs them! (*Iliad* 8.69–75). It is such images that Homer delivers, and not yardsticks!

[185] *Iliad* 13.10–45.

[186] *Iliad* 21.403–6.

met should be calculated according to extent or weight. "Around her shoulders he flung the tasseled aegis, fraught with terror, all around which Rout is set as crown, and on it is Strife, on it Valor, and on it Assault, that makes the blood run cold, and on it is the Gorgon head of the terrible monster, terrible and awful, a portent of Zeus who bears the aegis. And on her head she set the helmet with two ridges and with bosses four, made of gold, and

ἑκατὸν πολείων πρυλέεσσ᾽ ἀραρυῖαν.[187]

What is the significance of those last words, "which was sufficient for foot soldiers from a hundred cities"? Ernesti claims that it means the helmet "could withstand the assault of an army raised from a hundred cities and not just one"; the scholiast suggests: "The images of infantrymen from a hundred cities could be engraved on it"; this explanation then accords with the description of the terrible aegis. Or, as others have claimed, "To lift or carry the helmet the foot soldiers of a hundred cities would scarcely suffice." This last explanation is, I think, the most in keeping with Homer's tone, for it delivers the most powerful image of the inherent might of the goddess, which is here subtly and sublimely expressed in the carrying of a helmet. But whichever explanation is correct, none has been devised to modify the passage, but only to explain Homer's meaning; and of all the explanations, it seems to me that the one that Mr. L. accepts, though it be ancient, is the least likely: "Under which as many troops could hide as a hundred cities could bring into the field."[188] When has there ever existed a helmet whose purpose was to see how many warriors could fit beneath it? How shall the heroes stand if they are to be measured with the helmet as though by the bushel? How might this childish or fanciful image have occurred to Homer, who apparently has the soldiers of a hundred cities crawl beneath the helmet so that all can take part in a game of blindman's buff? And so on. In fine, Homer does not explicitly provide us with the dimensions of Minerva's physical stature but leaves it to us to infer her size—or rather, if the explanation that I think most appropriate should be correct, her inner strength—from her helmet: "And on her head she set the helmet, to lift which would require the combined strength of soldiers from a hundred cities"—what a subtle image of her divine strength!

Man-slaying Mars, rude and monstrous in all he does, in his onslaught and in his battle cry—why should he not be so when he also tumbles to the ground? And so Homer permits himself the following image: just as Mars shrieks like ten thousand warriors, so he can also cover seven hides

---

[187] *Iliad* 5.737 [744].
[188] *Laocoön*, p. 135 [12:n3].

of land when thrown to the ground:[189] a gigantic fellow! But after all, it is Mars! Would Homer let any other god cry out and stretch in his fall as he does Mars? Would such an unusual posture befit queenly Juno or comely Venus, indeed? Moreover, Homer measures his colossus as he lies; he did not dare compel us to gaze up at the monstrous sight of this god standing upright. Moreover, it is only when gods fight against gods that Homer summons all his powers to describe a clash of giants, which is so very different from a human contest. Arrayed with men in battle order, as leaders of mortal armies, the "superhuman size" of the gods vanishes completely from view. When Mars and Minerva lead an army into battle, as depicted on the shield of Achilles, they can be distinguished by clothes fashioned of gold, by their beauty, by their fair and lofty stature in their armor, for after all, they are supposed to represent gods on the shield—they can stand out in the comely form they have assumed and the people at their feet can be somewhat smaller,[190] but a Mars who stretches over seven hides is inconceivable here. I do not know why Mr. L. cites a passage that does so little to prove his assertion.[191] In this instance, Homer modifies the size of the gods who mingle among men, just as Clarke and Ernesti did not wish to modify Minerva's size in the previous example; and anyway, the image on the shield is irrelevant here.

It is time that I drew this discussion to a close. In Homer size, strength, and swiftness are not predicates of equal weight which distinguish his gods from his finest heroes.[192] No one who has read Homer even cursorily will agree to this assertion, even in regard to strength and speed. Diomedes overpowers the unwarlike Venus, and Diomedes was not yet Achilles. He overpowers Mars, and here I shall let Dione speak on my behalf.[193]

The *individual character* of the Homeric gods and goddesses is thus the main object in view, to which their size and strength must also conform. Here is no question of a general theorem; here character comes before divinity.

Thus, in Homer there are goddesses who are *inferior* in strength to heroes; there are goddesses who *must* be *equal* in size to men; and there are gods who may not quite surpass human dimensions. Let Venus bear witness in the first case, in the second Juno, Venus, and perhaps every goddess, and in the third Apollo.

Further: size is never the poet's main object, from which we are to infer

---

[189] *Iliad* 21.407.
[190] *Iliad* 18.516–19.
[191] *Laocoön*, p. 136 [12:67].
[192] *Laocoön*, p. 135 [12:68].
[193] *Iliad* 5.381–415.

the strength of the deity; rather, size is mentioned only so as not to contradict the image of power and majesty.

Thus, if these latter qualities can be recognized through other characteristics, then all the better for the poet; and what is a better mark of majesty than the might expressed through one's deeds, the swiftness of one's movement?

Thus, Homer allows size to be inferred from strength, but never vice versa. From the bowed head of Zeus, from the stride of Neptune, from the throw of Minerva, we deduce the size of these gods, but not the other way around.

Just as he prefers to remain in his creation between heaven and earth,[194] so he never likes to overstretch the fancy with respect to the dimensions of size. Where a characteristic was necessary, it was included and modified.

Modified especially when gods appear among men, for if we are to picture a skirmish between gods[195] and a heaven populated by gods, then a little overstretching is necessary to grasp the wondrous μῶρον of his gods. Who can depict what he has never seen, what he encounters merely by enhancing the human?

And here, too, I do not think it axiomatic that "the poet also attributed *superhuman* size to his gods." For Homer gives even the infinite itself human dimensions, and for this reason, and for a thousand others, he is my poet.

Finally, were the sculptors indebted to Homer for the colossal size that they sometimes bestowed on their statues?[196] This question reminds me of the one we might ask an Indian: On what does the earth rest? On an elephant! And on what does the elephant rest? To whom exactly might Homer be indebted for the colossal size that here and there he bestows on this or that god? It seems to me that we might discover the origin of this and many other Homeric ideas in Egypt, especially in places where *the most ancient* tales of the gods, where a tradition of mythological anecdotes prevails, those Homeric ideas that do not conform to the ideal of beauty according to which he otherwise depicts his gods but instead tend toward extravagant immensity. I have a mind to read several pamphlets dealing with a few specimens of this claim,[197] pamphlets that appear too valuable to be allowed simply to vanish from sight among other writings of this nature, particularly as the task as a whole—the question, What did Homer borrow from the Egyptians? How did he transform the ancient

---

[194] *Iliad* 8.13–16.
[195] *Iliad* 21.385–408.
[196] *Laocoön*, p. 136 [12:n3].
[197] Harles, *De Jove Homeri* [1763], and so on.

myths of an earlier time into the beauties of his art?—seems to me vast and as yet unexplored.

15

Several pictures that Mr. L. cites from Homer have yet to be translated;[198] he presents them only indirectly and by adumbrating individual features—but even so they still contain so much life that I do not despair that one day a brilliant mind shall translate Homer into our language. I read Homer—thank goodness!—in *his* language; but I would like nevertheless to experience the delight of reading him in my own tongue, if a Meinhard had even once attempted such a task. This worthy man possessed so much talent for rendering the poetry of a foreign language into German prose, or, if you prefer, for deftly raising German prose to the simple nobility possessed by the poetic idiom of a foreign tongue that it seemed as if the Muse of our fatherland had chosen him to become the mouthpiece of other nations. That, I believe, is his great merit; and how he would have multiplied his achievements by translating Homer! I must anyway become a Greek when I read Homer, whatever the language in which I do so; why not, then, in my mother tongue? Secretly I must read him in *my native tongue* even now; secretly the reader's soul translates him wherever it can, even when it hears him in Greek. And I, sensuous reader that I am, cannot even imagine a truly profitable and vivid reading of Homer without this covert translation of ideas. Only when I translate him for myself do I read him as if I heard him: he sings to me in Greek, and just as swiftly, harmoniously, and nobly do my German thoughts seek to fly after him; then and only then can I give myself and others a vivid and definite account of Homer; only then can I feel him with all my soul. In every other instance, I believe, one reads him as if one were a commentator, a scholiast, a classical scholar, or a student of languages, and this reading is indeterminate and lifeless. It is one thing, Winckelmann says, to understand Homer and quite another to be able to explain him; and in my soul this is accomplished by means of a translation, by means of a rapid transformation in my way of thinking and in my language.

Moreover, German is far superior to French and English as a translator of Homer; perhaps it alone can steer a middle course between the paraphrase and pedantry that distinguish most Latin versions; and let us call this middle course by an old German word whose heavy use has become abhorrent and ridiculous to us through so much bad practice: *Germanization* [*Verdeutschung*]. Of course I shall always study my Homer

---

[198] *Laocoön*, pp. 143, 150 [13:72–73; 15:76].

in the original, even if Meinhard had translated him; but I would not be ashamed to have the translation lying close to hand so that I might glance within it, compete with it each time I encountered a powerful image that I wished to feel in its totality in my mother tongue—that is how I read Homer.

It is not necessity, then, that makes me wish we had Meinhard's Homer; it is *patriotism*, a feeling for the true method of reading him, a feeling for my mother tongue, as opposed to the sundry sweet Latin translations of Hector and Andromache, for example,[199] a feeling, finally, opposed to the insignificant reasons that have been adduced in an attempt to frighten off a translator of genius from taking on Homer.[200] If Pope had shared this opinion, what would have become of the English Homer? And will any sensible Englishman who can read Homer in the Greek no longer desire to read him—because Pope has rendered him into English?

If my speaking fair of Homer does not quite belong here, then I hope it has deserved a place elsewhere. And so I shall continue. "It is impossible," writes Mr. L., "to translate this musical picture that the words of the poet present into another language."[201] And in another passage, in which he develops the progressive manner of Homer in splendid fashion, Mr. L. does not overlook the advantage that Homer's language gave him: "It not only allows him the greatest possible freedom in the accumulation and combination of epithets, but it finds such a happy arrangement for these accumulated adjectives that the awkward suspension of their noun disappears. Modern languages are lacking entirely in one or more of these advantages. Our language does not enjoy this advantage. Or should I say, it does enjoy it but can seldom make use of it without ambiguity."[202] These remarks have revived an old thought in me, a thought I have always entertained when reading Homer and with which they share several features.

Homer sang before literary prose existed; thus he knows no closed periods. That is *not* to say there is not a single point in Homer; these he has, dear reader, and if he does not have enough, then by all means scribble a few more in his text. I am speaking not of marks of punctuation, in which our grammarians believe the essence of the period to consist, but rather of the arrangement of many individual features to create a single picture, one that begins *from the spot* at which the subject strikes our eye, leads us on feature by feature, but *interweaves* these features, inverts them in such a way that the meaning of the whole is suspended, the meaning is

---

[199] Klotz, *Epistolae Homericae* [1764], *variis locis.*
[200] Riedel's *Life of Meinhard* [*Denkmahl des Herrn J. N. Meinhard*, 1768], pp. 60, 61.
[201] Laocoön, p. 143 [13:72].
[202] *Laocoön*, p. 181 [18:93–94].

not complete until we have reached the end. And this trick of prose periods, I claim, Homer does not possess. In his poetry feature after feature falls asunder, as it were; with each epithet he marches on; he knows no interweaving, no artificial suspension of meaning. "The Greek combines the subject and the first predicate and leaves the others. He says 'round wheels, brazen, eight-spoked.' And so we know immediately what he is speaking of. In conformity with the natural order of thought, we first become acquainted with the thing itself and then with its accidents. Our language does not enjoy this advantage."[203] It is an advantage enjoyed by no modern language originally fashioned for prose.

And if Homer's manner consists in this *progressive quality*, and his language (which he bequeathed to his rhapsodists) and only *his* language has this progressive quality as its manner, as the law governing its composition, then how would it be with a translation? In a translation produced according to the new manner of construction that in some former time became a law of our modern languages, Homer will lose *his manner*, the essence of his poetry, that quality which marches on with every feature: he will be prosified. The prose will touch not the colors, the figures of his pictures, but rather the way they are arranged, their composition and manner—and it is here, I think, that he loses most! Such a loss makes itself felt in his mode of expression throughout his work; it is the greatest loss, for it obstructs the path of his Muse.

I shall take Homer's image of Apollo descending and say: here the poet is as far above the prosaist writing in a modern language as life itself is above the picture. Armed with bow and quiver, the enraged Apollo strides down from the peaks of Olympus. Not only do I see him descending, I also hear him. At every step the arrows rattle on the shoulders of the angry god. He strides on, like the night. Now he sits opposite the ships and lets the first arrow fly at the mules and dogs. Dreadful is the clang of the silver bow. Then, with more poisonous dart, he smites the men; and everywhere the pyres of the dead burn incessantly. "It is impossible," says Mr. L., whose words I have here drawn on in large measure, "to translate this musical picture that the words of the poet present into another language." And it is just as impossible, I should continue, for a modern language to follow step by step the progressive quality of this picture, which marches on with each feature. Each new word produces a new picture.

Now let us hear Homer in a modern language—perhaps even in Pope himself, who certainly understood the manner of Homer's language like no other poet before or since. He must overturn the words; he must paraphrase.[204] A single word in Homer he makes into a clause; a progressive

---

[203] *Laocoön*, p. 182 [18:94].
[204] *The Iliad*, translated by Pope [1715–1720], bk. 1, pp. 61–72.

feature stands alone, like a definition. Here he anticipates a detail, there he explains it—in short, the progressive manner of Homer is lost. Homer's image is a fully realized portrait, a historical picture, motionless, but rendered with poetic pigments. Homer's poetry, even in Pope's language, is poetic, beautifully consonant prose.

To demonstrate the difficulty of translating Homer, let me draw attention to another peculiarity I have discerned in his manner, which causes it to diverge even further from modern languages. This peculiarity involves the poet recurring to an existing principal feature that now serves as the thread that *draws* the picture *along* and binds its individual details together to create a whole. Some examples may serve to illustrate my point. Apollo strides down from Olympus, angry at heart, quiver and bow on his shoulder—is the picture completed? No, it rolls on; but to keep the details he has already furnished before our eyes, Homer seems merely to develop the ensuing details from those that went before. Quiver and bow on his shoulder? Yes, the arrows *rattled* on the shoulder. *Angry at heart* Apollo descends? Yes, they rattled on the shoulder of the *angry god*. *Down* he *strode*—he *came*? Thus they rattled as he *moved*. Now Homer has returned to his point of departure: he stepped forward and at the same time stepped back; he has renewed every fleeting detail; and still we have the whole picture before our eyes. In this very way he continues to develop his image. The last detail reminded us of the steps of the striding god and is now elaborated: his *coming* was like the night. Why has Apollo thrown night around his shoulders? If the poet does not have the time to explain, he allows the reason to be inferred; it would be out of place here to ponder those things which now, shrouded by night, he sweeps past; he does not allow himself to be distracted from the image of the marching god. Now Apollo has left behind the ships; he sits down apart from them and lets fly an arrow—if he *finds his target*, then the picture is at an end; but it cannot yet be at an end. For that would mean that the image of the rattling bow is lost; so now it is gathered up once more—*dreadful was the clang of the silver bow*; the first arrow strikes home, then another, smiting animals, dogs, men; funeral pyres burn: thus for nine days did the missiles of the god range through the army——now the picture is finished: the god, the bow, the arrow, their effect—everything lies before our eyes, no detail is lost, no color has faded in the wake of a word rushing past; the poet retrieved and reiterated each detail at precisely the right moment, and the image rolls onward, round and round in a circle.

This is not how our descriptive poets proceed; they paint with each word, and with each word the color too is lost, the detail gone; at the end we have only the final word, nothing more. Not so the First Poet; he interweaves recurring details, which the second time around imprint, impress the image more deeply on the soul and leave behind a sting, as Eupolis, the comedy writer, said of Pericles, the greatest orator of Greece. The arrangement of his pictures resembles the speech of Ulysses, whose words fluttered like snowflakes on a winter's day; that is, as Pliny says, *crebre, assidue, large*. He leaves no stone unturned in striking his target, and his arrows, like those of Philoctetes, *return whence they came*.

As he steps out in front of the throng, Menelaus catches sight of the thieves who robbed him of his honor and his bride, and is glad "just as a lion is glad when he comes upon a great carcase." That might well have been the end of it, but for Homer the image has not been engraved deeply enough into our soul. What precisely is meant by "when he comes upon a great carcase"? Homer continues: *having found a horned stag or a wild goat*. Perhaps now the image of Menelaus's joy has receded from view, so Homer develops the picture further: *he is hungry, greedily he devours it*. And to leave behind as the final sting in the soul his greedy devouring, the thrill of the chase, Homer summons behind him a loudly advancing hunt: swift dogs, vigorous youths pursue him. Now the picture is complete; I see the hungry lion, the prey, the chase; I see what animal he hunts, his joy, and his greedy hunger, which allows him to forget the danger. So was Menelaus glad, and so on.[205] His picture is a circle where one detail flows into the next, where what went before returns and elaborates what follows.

I should have to enumerate every one of Homer's pictures, every one of his similes if I wished to adduce every example, for they all follow the same pattern. New details do not always trickle into the description; the earlier ones recur, add more color, the dance of the figures turns back in on itself and suddenly breaks off. The scene alternates between action and feeling, movement and repose, and often the word that shall renew the action, that shall link the earlier details together, stands out because it comes at the beginning of a line and thus props up the discourse. Every one of Homer's pictures is musical: the tone reverberates in our ears for a little while; if it should begin to fade, the same string is struck and the tone rings out once more, this time with greater force; and all the different tones combine to create the harmony of the picture. In this way, Homer overcomes the principal drawback of his art: that its effect vanishes, as it were, with each passing moment. In this way, he enables each detail of his picture to endure.

I have furnished a few examples of Homer's refined artistry in the composition of pictures and discussed them from the point of view of language in order to show that I can see difficulties that a translation might throw up, of which many of those who have an awful lot to say about the translation of Homer remain ignorant. However, even these difficulties are not

[205] *Iliad* 3.21–26.

enough to drive me to despair. Here too the genius will find counsel: he will take apart and renew details, allow an image to fade away and bring it back before our eyes once more; at the very least he shall seek to emulate Homer. I wish that Mr. L. would elucidate this circularity in Homer's pictures. Homer does not describe; but when he must do so, he employs the aforementioned device to deliver, by means of tones that fade yet recur in each moment, a single, whole impression. This energy of his manner might best be understood in musical terms.

16

Generally speaking, we should not think that a philosopher who undertakes to elucidate the distinction between poetry and one of the fine arts intends thereby to provide an exhaustive definition of the essence of poetry. Mr. L. shows what poetry is not in contrast to painting; but to gain a complete understanding of the essence of poetry as a whole one would have to compare it with, and philosophically distinguish it from, *all* its sister arts and letters: for example, music, dance, and rhetoric.

"Painting produces its effect in space through figures and colors, poetry does so through articulated sounds in time. Bodies are the true subjects of the former, actions of the latter." Thus does Mr. L. conclude his inquiry. Now let a philosophically minded musician take up the thread and ask, To what extent are poetry and music subject to common rules, since the province of both is succession of time? How does the former go to work when it sings of *action*? The rhetorician might continue: Any form of discourse can depict *action*, so what makes poetry distinctive? How do the various genres and kinds of poetry represent action differently? If one were finally to unite these theories, one would have the essence of poetry.

Even with the one-sided nature of the comparison that we have before us, however, I still feel that we are lacking some essential quality of poetry to perform the calculation. I shall take up Lessing's argument from the point at which he promises to trace the matter from first principles. He reasons thus:

If it is true that in its imitations painting uses completely different means or signs than does poetry, namely figures and colors in space rather than articulated sounds in time, and if these signs must indisputably bear a suitable relation to the thing signified, then signs existing in space can express only objects whose wholes or parts coexist, while signs that follow one another can express only objects whose wholes or parts are consecutive.

Objects or parts of objects that exist in space are called *bodies*. Accordingly, bodies with their visible properties are the true subjects of poetry.

Objects or parts of objects that follow one another are called *actions*. Accordingly, actions are the true subjects of poetry.[206]

Perhaps the whole chain of reasoning would be sound if it started from a fixed point; but now let us try to find it. "If it is true that in its imitations painting uses completely different means or signs than does poetry"—quite true!

"The former, namely figures and colors in space rather than articulated sounds in time"—already the terms of comparison are no longer quite so definite! For the articulated sounds are not to poetry what colors and figures are to painting!

"If these signs must indisputably bear a suitable relation to the thing signified"—at this point any comparison between the two breaks down. The articulated sounds in poetry do not bear exactly the same relation to the things they signify as the figures and colors in painting do to their objects. Can two so very different things yield up a common term, a first principle by which we might distinguish, by which we might uncover the essence of both arts?

The signs of painting are *natural*: the connection of the signs to the thing signified is grounded in the properties of the very thing they signify. The signs of poetry are *arbitrary*: the articulated sounds have nothing in common with the thing that they are designed to express but are rather *accepted* as signs only by a universal convention. They are therefore of a completely different nature, and the *tertium comparationis* recedes from view.

Painting produces its effect entirely in space, upon objects arranged side by side, through signs that show the thing *naturally*. Poetry, however, does not work *through succession* in quite the same manner as painting does through space. What rests *on the succession* of its articulated sounds is not the same as that which rests on the coexistence of the parts in painting. The successive quality of the signs of poetry is nothing but a *conditio sine qua non* and thus merely represents an element of restriction placed on it, but the coexistence of the signs of painting is the very essence of the art and the basis of painterly beauty. Though it is true that poetry operates through consecutive sounds—that is, words—the consecutiveness of the sounds, the succession of the words is not the focal point of its effect.

To make this distinction clearer, let us compare two arts that produce their effect by natural means, namely painting and music. Here I can say painting operates wholly *through space*, just as music does *through the succession of time*. What the coexistence of colors and figures is to the for-

[206] *Laocoön*, p. 153 [16:78].

mer—that is, the basis of beauty—the succession of tones is to the latter—that is, the basis of melody. Just as pleasure—the effect of painting—is grounded on the sight of what is coexistent, so the effect of music is achieved by what is successive, by the combination and variation of tones. Therefore, I can conclude, just as painting can awaken in us, merely by means of an illusion, the idea of passing time, so this secondary effect must never become its principal concern: that is, to operate, as painting, through colors and yet in the succession of time; otherwise the essence of the art is lost. The color clavichord is a testament to this. In contrast, music, which works wholly through the succession of time, must never make the depiction of objects in space its main object, as inexperienced bunglers do. Painting must never take leave of coexistence, and music must never depart from succession, for both are the *natural* means of their effect.

But with poetry the scene has shifted. Here, what is natural in the signs—for example, sounds, musicality, the succession of tones—contributes little or nothing to the effect of poetry; the meaning, which lies in the words by dint of an arbitrary agreement, or the soul that inheres in the articulated sounds is everything. The succession of tones cannot be reckoned as essential to poetry as the coexistence of colors is to painting, "for these signs do not bear the same relation to the thing signified at all."[207]

The ground is shaking: and what of the edifice? Before we turn to look at it, let us first lay our foundations by other means. Painting operates in *space* and by means of an artful representation of space. Music and all energetic arts operate not just *in* but also *through* time, through an artful succession of tones. Would it not be possible to reduce the essence of poetry as well to such a primary concept, since it achieves its effect on the soul through arbitrary signs, through the meaning of words? We shall call the means of this effect *force*; and thus, as *space*, *time*, and *force* are the primary concepts of metaphysics, as the mathematical sciences can all be traced back to one of these, so we shall also say in the theory of the belles lettres: those arts which deliver *works* operate in space; the arts that operate through energy, in the succession of time; the belles lettres, or rather the only branch of the belles lettres, poetry, operates through *force*. Through *force*, which inhabits words; through force, which, though it passes through the ear, affects the soul directly. This *force*, not coexistence or succession, is the essence of poetry.

Now the question arises, Which objects can this poetic force better bring before the soul, objects of space, coexisting objects, or objects of time, successive objects? And again in more concrete terms, In which medium does the poetic force operate more freely, in space or in time?

It operates *in space*, and it does so by rendering its language sensuous.

---

[207] *Laocoön*, p. 153 [16:78].

With any sign, it is not the sign itself but rather the meaning thereof that must be perceived; the soul must perceive not the vehicle of the force, the words, but rather the force itself, the *meaning*: this is the first sort of intuitive cognition. But poetry also presents every object, as it were, visibly before the soul; that is, it gathers together as many characteristics as it requires to form the impression all at once, to lead the object before the eyes of the imagination, and to deceive the latter with the spectacle: this is the second sort of intuitive cognition. The first sort can be achieved by any vivid form of language that is not quibbling or philosophy, and the second can be achieved by poetry alone and constitutes its essence, namely *sensuously perfect discourse*. One can thus say that the first essential aspect of poetry is really a *kind of painting, sensuous representation*.

It operates *in time*, for it is *language*. This is not *primarily* the case, inasmuch as language is a *natural* mode of expression—of the passions and emotions, for example—for this marks merely the outer limits of poetry; but it is *especially* the case because, first, it affects the soul through the rapidity, the coming and going of its representations and because, second, it produces its energetic effect partly through the alternation of different elements and partly through the whole that it constructs in the sequence of time. The former it shares with another species of discourse, but the latter, through which it is capable of a succession and a melody of representations, so to speak, and of a single whole whose parts express themselves little by little, whose perfection thus energizes—this makes poetry a music of the soul, as the Greeks called it. And this second kind of succession Mr. L. did not touch on at all.

Neither of the two aspects alone constitutes the whole essence of poetry. Not its energy or its musicality, for this cannot obtain without the sensuousness of its representations, which it *paints before* the soul. But not its painterly quality, either, for poetry operates energetically, and it is precisely through succession that it constructs the concept of the sensuously perfect *whole* in the soul. Only if both aspects are considered together can I say that the essence of poetry is force, which operates *out of space* (the objects to which it gives sensuous expression) and *in time* (through a succession of many parts forming one poetic whole); in short, then, it is sensuously perfect discourse.

Having made these initial assumptions, let us now return to Mr. Lessing. For him *actions* are the chief subject of poetry, but only *he* can derive this concept from his concept of succession. I gladly confess that I cannot.

"Objects or parts of objects that follow one another are called actions."[208] What? Suppose I let as many things as I like follow upon one another, and each is a body, a lifeless aspect; none is yet action merely by

---

[208] *Laocoön*, p. 154 [16:78].

virtue of its succession. I see time fleet away, each moment chasing the next—but do I see action? Different scenes from Nature pass before my eyes, singly, dead, one after the other; do I see action? Pater Castel's color clavichord will never deliver actions by playing a succession of colors, even were they waving or serpentine lines; a melodic chain of tones will never be a chain of actions. I thus dispute the claim that objects or parts of objects that follow one another may therefore generally be called *actions*; and likewise I dispute the claim that because poetry yields succession, it has actions for its subject.

The concept of succession is only half of the idea of an action; it must be *a succession through force*: thus arises an action. I imagine a being active in the succession of time; I imagine changes that follow one upon another through the force of a substance: thus arises the force of an *action*. And if actions are the subject of poetry, then I wager that this subject can never be defined with the barren concept of succession: *force* is the center of its sphere.

And this is the force that cleaves to the interior of words, the magic power that affects my soul through the fancy and memory; it is the essence of poetry. The reader will see that we have arrived back where we began: namely, that poetry produces its effect through arbitrary signs; that the force of poetry lies wholly in this arbitrariness, in the meaning of the words, but not *in the succession of tones and words*, not in the sounds, insofar as they are natural sounds.

Mr. L., however, deduces everything from this succession of sounds and words; only belatedly does it occur to him that the signs of poetry might be *arbitrary*,[209] but even then he does not consider the real meaning of the objection "poetry operates through arbitrary signs."

For how does he reply to this objection? He argues that in the verbal description of bodies illusion, the principal object of poetry, is lost; that therefore language in general can depict bodies but poetry, the sensuously most perfect form of language, cannot." Now we appear to be on the right track. Precisely because poetry cannot be *painterly enough* in depicting bodily objects, it must not depict them. But not because it is *not painting*; not because it depicts with successive sounds; not because space is the province of the painter and mere succession of time the domain of the poet—none of these, as far as I can see, is the reason. The successiveness of the sounds is, as I have said, of little consequence to the poet; he does not produce his effect through them as natural signs. But if his *force* should desert him, if he cannot, independently of his sounds, *deceive* the soul with the images he presents, then the poet is lost, and he is nothing but a painter of words, an interpreter of symbols in terms of symbols. But

---

[209] *Laocoön*, p. 165 [17:85].

we are not yet on the right track, as Lessing's own example may serve to show.[210] If it is Haller's ultimate purpose in his poem *The Alps* to teach us to recognize in verse form the gentian and its blue brother and the herbs that resemble it and those which do not, then he has certainly lost sight of the purpose of the poet—that is, to deceive me—and I, as reader, have lost sight of my purpose—that is, to be deceived. This alone, then, is the reason why poetry must not describe bodies. But if I now turn from Haller's poem to a botanical textbook, how will I learn to distinguish gentian and its brothers there? How else than through successive sounds, through language? The botanist will take me from one part to the other; he will make clear to me the combination of these parts; he will seek to count out to my imagination what the eye of course takes in at a single glance, surveying both the plant's individual parts and the totality; he will do everything that Mr. L. says the poet ought not to do. Will he be intelligible to me? That is not the question, if I understand Lessing rightly: the poet must become clear to me, he must deceive me in a certain fashion. If he is unable to do this, if I perceive only the parts distinctly but do not grasp the whole intuitively, then all the rules that Mr. L. lays down for the poet I can prescribe just as well to the author of a botanical textbook. I shall say to him very gravely:[211] "How do we arrive at a distinct conception of an object in space, of a plant? We first look at its parts singly, then the combination of parts, and finally the totality. Our senses perform these various operations with such astonishing rapidity that they seem to us but a single operation, and this rapidity is absolutely necessary. Now let us assume that the author of a textbook on botany takes us from one part of the object to the other in the most beautiful order; let us assume that he knows how to make the combination of these parts ever so clear to us; how much time would he use in doing this? That which the eye takes in at a single glance, he counts out to us with perceptible slowness, and it often happens that when we arrive at the end of his description we have already forgotten the first features. And yet we are supposed to form a notion of the whole from these features. To the eye, parts once seen remain continually present; it can run over them again and again. For the ear, however, the parts once heard are lost unless they remain in the memory. And if they do remain there, what trouble and effort it costs to renew all their impressions in the same order and with the same vividness; to review them in the mind all at once with only moderate rapidity, to arrive at an approximate idea of the whole! It may be very nice to recite such descriptions, holding the flower in one's hands; but by themselves they say little or nothing."

[210] *Laocoön*, p. 168 [17:88].
[211] *Laocoön*, pp. 166, 167 [17:85–88].

Thus does Mr. L. speak to the poet, and why should I not likewise speak to the botanist, who means to instruct me solely through words? I see no difference between their two cases: there is precisely the same object, a body, and precisely the same means to describe it, language, and precisely the same hindrance to this means—the successive quality of language, of words. Hence, the lesson must apply just as well to the botanist as to every delineator who uses words.

Hence, the reason that Mr. L. adduces—namely that "succession hinders the description of bodies"—must, because it is true of all forms of language, because in such a case all forms of language aim not to make a *definitum* intelligible as a word, but rather to render it intuitive as a thing—this reason must really lie *without* the province of poetry.

Hence, within the province of poetry there can be no proper law either, at least no supreme law; rather, only a subordinate notion remains, from which little or nothing can be deduced. My whole chain of reasoning starts from this twofold premise: First, the successive nature of the sounds in poetry is not the *principal*, not the *natural*, means by which it produces its effect; that means is rather the force that arbitrarily attaches to these sounds and operates on the soul according to laws other than the succession of sounds. Second, the successiveness of sounds is actually characteristic not of *poetry alone* but rather of *all language*, and thus it does little to help define or distinguish it in its inner essence. So if Mr. L. makes succession the basis of the difference between poetry and painting in his book, can we really expect him to have determined their limits with the utmost exactitude?

17

To arrive at a more fruitful path than the one with which this barren subordinate notion presents us, Mr. L. makes a leap I shall not imitate: "poetry depicts by means of successive sounds; consequently, it depicts successions; consequently, it has successions and nothing but successions for its subject. Successions are actions: consequently"[212]—and consequently Mr. L. has found what he was looking for. But where did he find it? The concept of action he found in succession; and he concluded that it depicts only progressive objects because it depicts by means of successive sounds— what has become of the nexus here? If we assume that the succession of sounds in poetry is analogous to the coexistence of colors in painting, then what relation is there between the succession of the sounds and the succession of objects that it depicts? To what extent do they keep pace with

[212] *Laocoön*, pp. 153, 154 [15:77, 16:78].

one another? How can we even think of comparing them? And to what extent is the one less deducible from the other? And if poetry does indeed depict successions, why must these successions be actions? And so on. The demarcation of the limits of poetry and painting according to such an outline can scarcely be exact.

It is scarcely exact from the point of view of painting, "whose essence is the depiction of bodies," for I am at least aware of progressive actions in painting, of which Mr. L. gives an example:[213] drapery that in its folds unites two different moments in one.

It is even less exact from the point of view of poetry, where little or nothing follows from the successiveness of the sounds. It does not follow that poetry ought not to depict bodies, for if no successive sounds can raise concepts of coexisting objects, I fail to see how language as such, merely audible language, could effect *intuitive* cognition, for *images*, I would say, are not audible. I do not see how language as such could awaken pictorial concepts *in juxtaposition*, for the successive sounds themselves do not hang together. Finally, I also do not see how a whole—for example, an ode, a proof, a tragedy—could emerge in the soul *from many partial concepts*, for the entire succession of sounds does not constitute such a whole: "For the ear the parts once heard are lost." Everything or nothing, then, can be inferred from the succession of sounds.

Still less do "the unsuitableness and unpoetic nature of all descriptive poetry"[214] follow from *this*.

Still less does it follow from *this* that the essence of poetry is progression,[215] that poetry must use one single property of a body, that harmony is the rule governing descriptive epithets.[216]

Indeed, it does not even follow that "only on these principles can the grand style of Homer be defined and explained." I reject much of what Mr. Lessing claims and all of his reasons for doing so, but nevertheless I do not reject everything that only *he* builds on these foundations. May I begin with Homer?

"Homer represents nothing put progressive actions. He depicts bodies and single objects only when they contribute toward those actions, and then only by a single trait. Even when Homer is forced by peculiar circumstances to fix our attention longer on a single object, he places this single object by means of countless artistic devices in a series of moments, in each of which it has a different appearance."[217] Fine! Capital! There we have the true style of Homer! But whether Homer opted for this man-

---

[213] *Laocoön*, pp. 178, 179 [18:91–92].
[214] *Laocoön*, pp. 174, 175 [18:89–90].
[215] *Laocoön*, pp. 154, 155 [16:79].
[216] *Laocoön*, p. 155 [16:79].
[217] *Laocoön*, p. 155 [16:79–80].

ner because he wished *to describe by means of successive sounds*,[218] because he despaired of depicting corporeal objects in any other way, because he was concerned that even if he took us from one part of the object to the other in the most beautiful order, that even if he knew how to
make the combination of these parts ever so clear to us,[219] then to the eye
the parts once seen would remain continually present but for the ear the
parts once heard, and consequently the labors of the poet also, would be
lost—whether this is why Homer set his objects in a series of moments
has never occurred to me.

When he has Hebe *put together* Juno's chariot piece by piece before our
eyes,[220] does the poet resist the temptation of depicting what is coexistent by means of successive sounds? I see wheels and axle, the seat, the
pole, the traces, and the straps, not as these parts are when fitted together,
but as they are *slowly assembled* by Hebe. First the wheels, and not just
the wheels but their parts, the brazen spokes and the golden rims and the
tires of bronze and the silver hub, and so on, are slowly counted out to
me; only then do the axles come, and then the seat; everything is broken
down into its parts, and by the time it is the turn of the last piece, I have
surely forgotten the first. The chariot stands assembled, I defy the fancy
that could now intuitively form a picture of the chariot all at once in a
single glance and yet in all its parts: for example, the brazen spokes and
the golden rims and the tires of bronze, and so on! I scarcely see, then,
what Homer has done to weaken, as it were, the effect of successive
sounds, to render present what is coexistent *by means of countless artistic devices*. If the great object aimed at here is the clear concept of the coexistent in all its parts, then "what trouble and effort it costs to renew all
these impressions in the same order and with the same vividness; to review them in the mind all at once with only moderate rapidity, to arrive
at an approximate idea of the whole." If the poet was working toward
this idea of the whole by dismantling it before our eyes in order subsequently to present it complete in all its parts, then I say he has labored
just as futilely as Brockes when he describes plants for us. Here Hebe's
action, the *assembly* of the chariot, does not come into consideration at
all; the focus is on the trick of putting together *successive parts* of a whole
that is intended to be shown and thought all at once. Both Brockes and
Homer are alike in this intention; indeed, Homer takes even more time
because he also describes the action of assembling. "But it is not only
where Homer combines further aims with his descriptions that he dis-
perses the image of his object over a kind of history of it; he does this also

---

[218] *Laocoön*, p. 153 [16:78].
[219] *Laocoön*, p. 167 [17:86].
[220] *Iliad* 5.722–31.

where his sole object is to show us the picture, in order that its parts, which in nature we find side by side, may follow one another in his description *just as naturally*, and *keep pace, as it were, with the flow of the narrative*. For example, he wishes to show us the bow of Pandarus"[221]— but how can Mr. L. find in Homer's description a parallel between the successiveness of the sounds and the coexistence of the parts, and between the parts of the object and the parts of the narrative? If Homer wishes to paint for us the bow of Pandarus and begins by taking us on the ibex hunt, from which animal's horns the bow was fashioned, and now shows us the rocks where Pandarus slew it and now measures out the length of the horns, now gives them out to an artisan and allows us to watch his every labor, who can say that Homer let the successive quality of his description approximate, so to speak, the coexistent nature of the object and let the parts of the bow keep pace with the flow of the narrative? Instead of their supposedly converging through this Homeric device, I see them scattered farther afield; they lie hidden among many extraneous features (hunt, ibex, place of ambush, spot where the ibex was wounded, where it was felled, workshop of the artisan), and had it been the purpose of Homer's history of the bow to show me intuitively and *at once* all the parts of the bow, then he certainly chose the worst possible means. My imagination at least has abandoned itself to the story of how the bow of Pandarus was fashioned; but thereafter to picture the bow in all its parts *at once*, to omit now the extraneous features of the story— what an effort! What a task to separate them all!

> Homer describes the shield of Achilles in more than a hundred splendid verses, its material, its form, all the figures which filled its enormous surface, so exactly and in such detail that it was not difficult for modern artists to make a drawing of it exact in every part. Homer does not paint the shield as finished and complete, but as a shield *that is being made*. Thus, here too he has made use of that admirable artistic device: transforming what is coexistent in his subject into what is consecutive, and thereby making the living picture of an action out of the tedious painting of a physical object.[222]

A fine observation! And rightly contrasted with Virgil! But did Homer really seize on the *making* of the shield in order, as it were, to deliver the impression of coexistence by means of what is consecutive? Does Homer let "the various parts and properties in space follow one another in such rapid succession *that we believe we hear them all at once*"? Was it his purpose in describing the making of the shield to transform space into time and to present us, through temporal succession, with the sight of a single

---

[221] *Laocoön*, pp. 163, 164 [16:83].
[222] *Laocoön*, pp. 183, 184 [18:94–95].

bodily whole, which we could otherwise grasp only through space?[223] If the answer to these questions is yes, then I must confess that my memory is too feeble to realize his purpose. Perhaps there are ten pictures on the shield, perhaps fewer; perhaps I even saw them being forged: then I marvel at the work, but not with the believing wonder of the eyewitness who has the whole shield before his eyes, for whom the consecutive has been transformed into the coexistent. Only in the mind of the divine master can the shield, with all its adornments, have ever formed a painterly whole. I, however, am obliged to pass once more around the shield if I wish to see again the adornment that vanishes with each successive epithet; and yet where are the adornments if I am to arrange them into a whole shield? *Seeing the shield come into being* is of no consequence here; nor can it be, unless its purpose is to distract me further. The *successive* nature of the process is and remains the difficulty.

Let us assume that Homer's language is as excellent as can be—every word delivers a picture—there is no suspension of the nouns—it progresses as swiftly as Diana on her way.[224] But should this swift progression be designed, as it were, to diminish, to destroy the obstacle of space in order thereby to produce the illusory appearance of a *spatial* object, of a body in space—well, that no language can accomplish. *For that purpose* Homer will hardly have remained so faithful to his progressive style, *for that purpose* he will certainly not have given only a single characteristic to each object, and least of all will he have chosen to show, *for that purpose*, the consecutive development of an object "to allow its parts to keep pace with the flow of the narrative." That no language *can* accomplish; still less does the language of the poet, and least of all the First Poet, *desire* to do so. His manner shows that he does not proceed progressively in order to furnish us—regardless of what it may represent—with *a picture of the whole* through succession; rather he marches *through the parts* precisely because he has no interest whatsoever in the picture of the whole.

I sincerely hope I have not misconstrued Mr. L.'s position. On the matter itself we are in agreement; only his reasoning gives me trouble. If someone should think the difference between us trifling, that is of no consequence to me; but to others it will seem substantial.

Homer always renders actions progressively because he *must do so*, because all these component actions are segments of the whole action that he depicts, because he is an epic poet. I *do not need*, therefore, to become acquainted with the chariot of Juno and the scepter of Agamemnon and the bow of Pandarus *more closely* than is necessary for these objects, woven into the action, to produce their intended effect on my soul. That

---

[223] *Laocoön*, p. 166 [17:86].
[224] *Laocoön*, pp. 180, 181 [18:93].

is why I hear the history of the bow: not so that it can take the place of a painting but so that it implants in me in advance an idea of its strength, of the might of its arms, and hence of the power of its string, its arrow, its shot. When Pandarus takes the bow, fits an arrow to the string, draws it back—and shoots!—woe the Menelaus whom such an arrow will strike, for we know how mighty it is. Thus, Mr. L. is wrong to say that in the story of the bow Homer's concern was his picture and nothing but his picture. Far from it; Homer's interest lay in the strength, in the power of the bow. The strength, and not the form, of the bow is an essential part of the poem; this property and no other is meant here to operate energetically, so that when afterward Pandarus lets fly his arrow, when afterward the string twangs, the arrow strikes home, we feel the arrow all the more. In consequence of this energy, which is a poem's main goal, Homer permits himself to turn away from the battle, to wander over to the hunt, and to relate the history of the bow; I see no other way of representing this concept in all its potency than through narrative. Through a picture we can only really apprehend form; from form we must infer size and from size strength; through a story we apprehend this last quality immediately— and if the energetic artist, the poet, is interested only in this strength, why should he burden himself with other labors? Let the painter paint a picture, let him paint form; the poet, however, effects strength, energy. Homer, too, effects it from the beginning to the end of his description, but not, to be sure, when I read him according to Mr. L.'s interpretation of Pandarus's shot. There we hear only a successive but not an energetic picture (a poet's main object!), where the illusion arises not in a painterly fashion, through the accumulation of successive sounds, but *energetically*, in each sound, so that we shall *start with fright* when a bow such as this finally strikes its target.

The same is true of the scepter of Agamemnon: I do not regard the story at all as an "artistic device, by means of which the poet causes us to linger over a single object without entering into a tiring description of its parts."[225] His scepter is an ancient, royal scepter of divine origin! The idea is meant to move us; any other artifices and allegories are of no concern to me.

Homer describes the chariot of Juno.[226] Why? Evidently because without the poet I cannot see it, because I must first become acquainted with it so that I may know a heavenly chariot. Why is it assembled before my eyes? Evidently because the best way to become acquainted with a heavenly chariot is to see it initially lying in parts and then put together. Thus, this chariot of the gods is assembled to depict its excellence, the intrinsic value of its every part, its artful construction, but not to gather these parts

---

[225] *Laocoön*, pp. 159–63 [16:80–83].
[226] *Iliad* 5.722–31.

successively, for we cannot see them coexisting. The assembling of the parts is no artistic device, no quid pro quo in order thereby to present us with an image of the whole; the poet's purpose is not to gather together the entire spectacle; the energy of the narrative lies in the very act of *assembling*; that is all. With each new part, if its concept is rendered sensuously perfect in our soul, we are meant to exclaim: "Splendid! divine! regal!" The whole with its parts was not my picture; I leave that to a coachman. The chariot is assembled, the energy therefore completed, and I exclaim once more: "Splendid! divine! regal!" And let Juno and Minerva drive the horses.

The shield of Achilles *comes into being* in Vulcan's hands.[227] why? Evidently because it must come into being! Achilles has need of armor, Thetis implores Vulcan to fashion some, he promises to do so, rises, and sets to work—why should he not work? The gods appear as actors throughout Homer's poem, their scenes alternating with those of mortals. Now it is night, the action is suspended; Vulcan we have not seen since he appeared as the lame cupbearer of the gods; Achilles has lost his armor when Patroclus was slain; now Thetis goes to Vulcan, now Vulcan can forge the metal: the shield comes into being. The whole scene is part of the action of the poem, part of the movement of the epic; it is not a device that obtrudes from Homer's poem; it is not a peculiarity of his style. It is here, indeed, in the development, in the fashioning of the shield that the entire force of the energy, the poet's sole object, lies. With each adornment that Vulcan engraves, I admire the skillful god; with each description of its extent and surface, I recognize the *power* of the shield, which is *in the process of being wrought* for Achilles, and which the reader, caught up in the action, awaits as anxiously as Thetis.

In fine, I know no successions in Homer that function solely as artistic devices, as artistic devices born of necessity, that exist for the sake of a picture, of a description; rather, they are the essence of his poem, they are the body of epic action. In each feature revealed in the unfolding of these successions there must reside energy, Homer's object. Every other hypothesis involving devices and expressions to avoid what is coexistent in the description of physical objects causes me to depart from Homer's manner. I know that this is a serious reproach, I know that there is no greater impediment to a poet's force than failing to read him in accordance with his style; for this reason alone I shall not retract my criticism. Anyone who claims to see in the assembly of Juno's chariot, in the story of the bow and the scepter, and in the fashioning of the shield nothing more than an artifice to circumvent the description of a body has no idea what poetic action is. Homer's energy is wasted on him. If Homer requires a description of a body, then he provides

---

[227] *Iliad* 18.478–608.

it, even if that body is a Thersites; he knows of no artistic devices, no poetic trickery and deceit; progression is the very soul of the epic.

18

Now, Homer is not the only poet; soon after him came Tyrtaeus, Anacreon, Pindar, Aeschylus, and so on. His επος, his progressive narrative, was transformed gradually into a μελος, into something rather more like song, and then into an ειδος, into a picture; these genres nevertheless remain poetry. Thus, a singer (μελοποιος) and a lyrical painter (ειδοποιος), Anacreon and Pindar respectively, stand opposed to the narrative poet (εποποιος), Homer.

Homer composes his poem as a narrative: "It happened! There was!" In Homer, then, everything can be action and must rush to action. This is the direction in which the energy of his Muse strives; wondrous, heart-stirring *events* are his world; he has it in his power to utter the words of divine creation: "There was!" Anacreon oscillates between song and narrative; his narrative becomes a short song, his short song an επος of the god of love. His expression can thus be "There was!" or "I want!" or "Thou shalt!"—it is enough that his μελος resounds with delight and joy: the energy, the Muse of his every song is a feeling of gladness.

Pindar intends a large lyrical painting, a labyrinthine ode that shall become, through apparent digressions, through secondary figures rendered in different shadings, an energetic whole where no part exists for itself, where each shall appear ordered in terms of the totality: an ειδος, a poetic picture, where already the artist, not the art, is everywhere visible. "I sing!"

How shall we compare them? The ideal whole of Homer, Anacreon, and Pindar—how different they are! How dissimilar are the goals they pursue! The one wishes to do naught but invent: he narrates, he enchants, the whole at which he aims is the event, he is a poet of past times. The other does not wish to speak: from him bursts forth a song of joy, his whole is the expression of a sweet feeling. The third speaks with his own voice so that we hear him: the odic whole is an edifice built with symmetry and high art. If each can achieve his end in his own way, can represent his whole to me in its entirety, can deceive me *by this intuition*—what more can I ask for?

According to a long-accepted and in itself harmless hypothesis, the whole of every genre of poetry may be viewed as a form of painting, building, or work of art, where all parts are supposed to cooperate to realize their main object, the whole. In all genres, that main object is poetic illusion, but each has a different means of achieving it. The lofty, wondrous illusion in which the epic enfolds me is not the trifling, sweet sentiment that the Anacreontic song imparts to me; nor is it the tragic emotion into which tragedy transports me. Yet each works toward *its* illusion, after *its own* fashion, using *its own* means to represent something with the utmost intuitiveness. Whether this something is epic action or tragic action or a single Anacreontic sensation or a perfect whole of Pindaric pictures or—whatever it may be, it must always be judged within its limits, according to its means and purpose.

So a Pindaric ode should not be judged as an epic poem lacking a progressive quality; a song should not be judged as a picture in want of an outline; a didactic poem should not be judged as a fable, nor a fable as descriptive poetry. If we agree not to quarrel over the meaning of the word *poetry* or *poem*, then every established genre of poetry has its own ideal—one may have a loftier, weightier, grander ideal than another, but each has its own nonetheless. I must refrain from applying the laws of one genre to another or even to poetic art as a whole.

So if Homer "represents nothing but progressive actions," if "he depicts bodies and single objects only when they contribute toward these actions, and then only by a single trait,"[228] then in doing so he may well conform to *his* epic ideal. Perhaps, though, an Ossian, a Milton, a Klopstock, are guided by a different ideal, according to which they do not progress with each feature and their Muse chooses a different course? Perhaps, then, this progressive quality is merely *Homer's* epic *manner* and not even the manner of *epic poetry* in general? The critic may utter a timid "perhaps" in answer to these questions, but the genius settles them with the resounding voice of the example.

If Homer's practice leads me to the observation that "Homer represents nothing but progressive actions," then there is even less justification in immediately subjoining the main proposition: "*Poetry* represents nothing but progressive actions; consequently actions are the true subjects of poetry." If I notice that Homer "depicts bodies and single objects only when they contribute toward these actions, and then only by a single trait,"[229] then I may not straightaway seal that remark with the conclusion: "Consequently *poetry* also depicts bodies, but only by suggestion through actions; consequently *poetry*, in its progressive imitations, can use only a

---

[228] *Laocoön*, p. 155 [16:79].

[229] All bodies that are meant to produce an effect in Homer's poem are depicted with *as many* traits as are required to do so. Homer rarely limits himself to a single one. Even if he is concerned only with a stone, an implement, a bow, and so on, he takes time to mention as many properties of the body as are needed to energize in the epic manner. If he depicts a thing with only a single feature, then this is usually general and insignificant in this particular instance; they are the customary epithets he bestows on all sorts of things and which often recur in his poetry.

single property of a body," and everything else that is supposed to follow from this with regard to the rule that insists on the harmony of descriptive adjectives and on economy in the description of physical objects——and so on. That these principles do not flow from a main property of poetry—for example, from the successiveness of its sounds, whence Mr. L. derives them—has been proven. That these principles, even if they did guide Homer's practice in the way in which Mr. L. believes them to, do not flow from the successive nature of poetry in general either, but rather from its more specific *epic* purpose, has also been demonstrated. Now, why should Homer's epic style dictate style, principles, and laws to all poetry without restriction, as Mr. L. seems to suggest it should?

I tremble before the bloodbath that is bound to be occasioned among poets both ancient and modern by the propositions "actions are the true subjects of poetry; poetry depicts bodies, but only by suggestion through actions, and only by a single trait,"[230] and so on. Mr. L. should not have confessed that Homer's practice led him to his conclusions, for if we examine each proposition individually, then scarcely—scarcely is Homer the only poet left standing. Poets from Tyrtaeus to Gleim and from Gleim back to Anacreon, from Ossian to Milton and from Klopstock to Virgil are swept away, leaving behind a gaping hole. Not to mention the didactic, descriptive, and pastoral poets.

Mr. L. has declared himself against some of these, and his principles compel him to declare himself against even more. "The detailed depictions of physical objects (without the above-mentioned Homeric device for transforming what is coexistent in them into what is really consecutive)"—I mentioned above that Homer knows nothing of such artifices, and anyway what could an artifice contribute toward so great a purpose?—"have always been recognized by the best critics as being pieces of pedantic trifling, to which little or no genius can be attributed."[231] Those whom he cites as the best critics are Horace, Pope, Kleist, and Marmontel. To my mind, however, their support of Mr. L. is not as clear-cut as he thinks. In the passage that he quotes, Horace reproves as poetasters not those who paint a grove, an altar, a brook, and so on, but rather those who *paint in the wrong place*:

> Inceptis gravibus plerumque et magna professis
> purpureus, late qui splendeat, unus et alter
> adsuitur pannus, cum lucus et ara Diane etc.
> aut flumen Rhenum, aut pluvius describitur arcus.
> sed nunc non erat his locus—[232]

[230] *Laocoön*, pp. 154, 155 [16:78–79].
[231] *Laocoön*, pp. 173, 174 [17:89].
[232] [Horace] *De arte poetica* 14–19.

Pope called a *purely descriptive* poem a banquet of nothing but sauces; but by that he did not mean to suggest that "every detailed depiction of physical objects" appearing without the Homeric device was a piece of pedantic trifling devoid of genius. Kleist, it seems to me, wanted to introduce a kind of plot into his *Spring* (a plan is already present in the poem inasmuch as it is not a host of pictures, which he seems to have drawn at random from the infinite realm of rejuvenated Nature, but rather, as one critical work has argued, a stroll that depicts the objects in the natural order in which they presented themselves to his eye); Kleist wanted, I say, to introduce a plot but not throw out every detailed depiction of physical objects as a piece of pedantic trifling. And finally, Marmontel may indeed desire that the eclogue contain more morality and fewer physical descriptions, but whether the eclogue thereby becomes a succession of feelings sparingly interlaced with images and therefore also "a series of progressive actions in which all bodies shall be depicted only by a single feature" I do not know; but if not, then according to Mr. L. it is not poetry.

Action, passion, feeling! I also love these qualities above all things in poems; I also hate nothing more than the mania for dead and idle description, particularly when it takes up pages, folios, poems; but not with the deadly hatred that demands the prohibition of every single detailed picture, even if it could represent things as coexisting; not with the deadly hatred that allows each body to participate in the action with only a single epithet; and not because poetry must employ successive sounds in its descriptions or because Homer does or does not do this and that——that is not why I hate it.

If I have learned *anything* from Homer it is that poetry operates energetically: never with the intention of delivering (albeit successively) a work, image, picture, down to every last detail, but rather that the whole force must be experienced and felt while the energy endures. I have learned from Homer that poetry never produces its effect on the ear, through sounds, or on the memory, depending on how long I can retain a feature from the succession; but rather on the fancy, and it must therefore be considered from this perspective and no other. That is how I set poetry against painting, and I regret that Mr. L. did not pay heed to this focal point of poetry's essence, its "effect on our soul, its energy."

19

Painting operates not only out of space, that is, with bodies for its subject, but also in space, through a body's properties, which it arranges according to its end in view. Thus, it is not just true that a subject of painting must possess visibility and form; rather, visibility and form are also those very properties of bodies through which it achieves its effect. But if poetry does not operate through space—that is, through coexisting objects, through colors and figures—it does not yet follow that it cannot operate *out of space*; that is, that it cannot depict bodies from the perspective of visibility and form. This does not follow from the means of its effect, for it operates through the mind and not through the successive sounds of words.

Painting affects the eye through colors and figures; poetry the lower faculties of the soul, especially the fancy, through the meaning of words. Now, since an action of the fancy can always be called an intuition, then poetry, insofar as it renders a concept, an image intuitive, may rightly be called a painter for the imagination, and every whole of a single poem is the whole of a single work of art.

Whereas painting brings forth *a work*, which is not yet anything while it is being made but everything after it is done, everything in the whole of a single glance, poetry is *energetic*; that is, the soul must already feel everything while poetry operates and not begin to feel only after the energy has ended and not wish to feel through a recapitulation of the succession. So if I have not felt anything at any point during a description of beauty, then a last look will grant me nothing.

Painting aims to deceive the eye, poetry the fancy—but again, not after the manner of a work, so that I recognize the thing in the description. Rather, with each representation I see the object *according to the poet's purpose* in showing it to me. In every genre of poetry the nature of the illusion is therefore different; but with paintings there are only two kinds of illusion: illusory beauty and illusory truth. The work of the artist and the energy of the poet must therefore be judged according to one of these aims.

The artist thus operates with shapes for the whole of a single glance, in order to deceive the eye; the poet with the force exerted by the words *as* they unfold in succession, in order to deceive the soul with the most perfect illusion. If anyone can therefore compare color and word, succession of time and a single moment, form and force—well, let him compare.

Some of the ways in which this task might be accomplished have been prescribed by a discerning Englishman, who has furnished, after the manner of Shaftesbury, one discourse on art and another on music, painting, and poetry.[233] It is a pity, though, that in the latter treatise, instead of simply elaborating the *difference* between these three arts, he indulges the empty fancy of seeking to determine which art is *superior* to the others. A mere order of rank between completely different things leads to a

---

[233] James Harris, *Three Treatises, the first concerning art, the second concerning music, painting and poetry, the third concerning happiness* (1744).

schoolboyish contest of the kind that painting, music, poetry, and dramatic art were obliged to enter solemnly into a number of years ago, under the supervision of a master of philosophy.[234]

Let us see in what Harris considers the difference to consist. First, he makes the very clear division between arts that deliver a *work* and those which operate through *energy*. The former are those which produce their effect by means of coexisting parts, like a sculpture or a painting; the latter are those which operate successively, for example, dance and music. The focal point of Lessing's work, where all rays of light converge, was thus already given by Aristotle. If the agency of an art is *energy*, then the perfection of such an art can be perceived only *while it endures*; if it is a *work*, then perfection will be visible not during the energy that produces it but only afterward.

Painting, music, and *poetry* are alike in being *mimetic* or *imitative* but differ in the *media* by which they imitate; *painting* by *figure* and *color, music* by *sound* and *motion*—painting and music by a *natural* medium, poetry by an *artificial* and *arbitrary* medium. The author of *Philosophical Writings* has analyzed this difference most thoroughly.

Every art has its *subject.* The fittest subjects of *painting* are all such things and incidents as are peculiarly characterized by figure and color; the human body; all powers of the soul that are expressed by the body; all actions and incidents whose wholeness depends on a short and self-evident succession of incidents; actions whose incidents are all along similar during that succession; all actions concurring in the same point of time; all actions that are known universally rather than actions known to but a few. We see that viewed from this perspective, Lessing's *Laocoön* is incomplete, for generally speaking he has written more on behalf of the poet than of the painter.

The *subjects of music* are all such things and incidents as are most eminently characterized by motion and sound; these include all species of motions, sounds, voices, passions expressed through sounds, and so on.

The *subjects of poetry* are those belonging to both previous arts. First, insofar as they are imitated by *natural* means. Here it was easy to adjudge that poetry must be inferior to painting, for everything pointed to the conclusion that words are no colors and the mouth no paintbrush. This too I find astonishing: how here poetry may be said to be *equal* to music in its natural sounds. In short, the comparison has miscarried. By *words significant* as by *arbitrarily agreed signs*: this ought really to be the point of Lessing's comparison.

In the proper subjects of painting (that is, those which are character-

---

[234] *Wettstreit der Malerei, Musik, Poesie und Schauspielkunst: Reden—gehalten unter der Aufsicht Wolfgang Ludwig Gräfenhahns, der Weltweisheit Magisters* (Bayreuth, 1746).

ized by certain colors, figures, and postures, whose comprehension depends not on a succession of events—or at least on a short and self-evident succession—which admits a large variety of such circumstances as all concur in the same individual point of time)—in all these subjects the poet is inferior to the painter, for *first*, the former imitates by arbitrary signs, the latter through the medium of Nature; here the latter shows all the circumstances in the same point of time as they appear in Nature, and the former does so only partly, by entering into some degree of detail and thereby becoming tedious or obscure.

There are also subjects that are peculiar to poetry: all actions whose whole is of so lengthened a duration that no point of time can be given fit for painting; also manners, passions, sentiments, and character as such, which are best exhibited by the medium of language. Here painting is wholly inferior to poetry, brooks no comparison——

Harris subsequently goes on to explore the limits of poetry and music, whither I shall not follow him. Here I wish poetic art could have another Lessing. Harris considers more closely the moral and mental effects of poetry: another untouched string that I too shall not pluck. I meant only to draw the attention of my readers to a writer who treats the same subject as Lessing, who in some instances goes further than Lessing, and who is discerning enough to exhaust his subject briefly and succinctly—if only, instead of the empty controversy concerning a hierarchy of the arts, he had concentrated on their differences, then their limits, and finally their laws.

20

I do not mean to suggest that where the main aim of his book is concerned Mr. L. is not justified vis-à-vis Caylus and his apes in the distinction he draws; but his reasons for making this distinction, and especially the main reason, are not always right. He seems to me still only halfway there, as when he claims that poetry ought to deliver *a work by means of succession* and not operate energetically *in the succession* itself.

The poet, for example, who intended to paint beauty for us, be it Constantinus Manasses or Ariosto, did not set out to do so only to ask afterward: "What did Helen or Alcina look like?"[235] Nor did he mean to give us in his description a complete picture, and so on. Rather, he leads us through the parts, so as to render each of them beautifully intuitive, so that if we had forgotten all the parts, we would know this much on the evidence of our eyes: Helena and Alcina were enchanting. If by doing so Ariosto had no effect on Mr. Lessing, perhaps he would make an impression

[235] *Laocoön*, p. 204 [20:105].

on those of his countrymen who are accustomed to appreciating beauty part by part in a real Alcina or a statue of Venus; or *if* Ariosto himself were to see an Alcina, would he perhaps——But by and large there is little that can be concluded from a comparison here. Homer does not describe his Helen.[236] Why? Because she does not concern him, because from the beginning to the end of his poem he has no time for the question, What did she look like? Rather, the question is always, What happened here? Helen appears, the elders see her; of course they had to feel and say what they felt and said, but Homer does not let them do so "to show us Helen's beauty by its effect." Ariosto, however, the Homer of Italy, who inherited everything from the Greek Homer save this constant progression of the action; Ariosto, whose manner throughout his poem is based not only on the words "it came to pass" but also "it was" and "what was it like?"; either Ariosto should not have asked such questions or he was obliged to take us *through the parts*. But not so that we afterward gather and assemble the parts; not so that the fancy shall afterward endeavor to picture the whole of a single work of art; Ariosto intended to achieve his purpose in the description itself, by taking us through the parts. Was he successful? On that question each reader may make up his own mind; it is sufficient that Ariosto meant to realize his object *during the energy*.

If the poet prefers to show beauty in its effect, in motion—that is, as charm—it is not so that this dynamic beauty corresponds to the dynamic verse. It does not mean that every feature of the description that is form or figure and not effect or movement therefore becomes unpoetic.[237] Rather, I generalize the proposition only as follows: Every description of beauty must operate energetically, that is, according to the poet's intention and during each feature that it delivers. It is within these terms of reference that Ariosto may wish to defend himself; but Lessing's injunction that the poet ought to show physical beauty only by its effect, only in motion,[238] sweeps too much away.

Too much even in Homer. If he did not wish to depict Juno physically, but only by an epithet, is there a more effective or charming feature than "white-elbowed Juno" (if I may be permitted this awful word!)? But I could not really say whether this feature is the one by means of which she participates in the action, which through her body describes action, and so on. The same goes for his fair-kneed Briseis and flashing-eyed Pallas and broad-shouldered Ajax and swift-footed Achilles and fair-haired Helen—where are effect, motion, charm, and action here? This is always a fine appeal to the poets: "Paint for us the pleasure, the affection, the love

---

[236] *Laocoön*, pp. 202, 215 [20:105, 21:111].
[237] *Laocoön*, p. 217 [21:112].
[238] *Laocoön*, p. 215 [21:111].

and delight that beauty brings" (if the energy of your poem demands this!) "and you have painted beauty itself"[239] (insofar as you are obliged to paint it according to the foregoing parentheses). But not the other way around: "Poets, do not depict physical beauty if you cannot depict it entirely by charm, by the effect it produces; let no part of the whole escape you: do not depict beauty according to its external aspect." This way around I have little confidence in the proposition.

Who can deny that in some genres of erotic poetry physical beauty *must* be described? And in that case who must not also concede that some parts of this physical beauty *cannot* be described in terms of charm, of motion? Assuming that Ariosto had meant to, had wanted to furnish a picture of his Alcina, how could he then describe her nose, throat, teeth, and arms by their *effect*? Mr. L. asks what a nose might be that Envy knows not how to improve,[240] and I ask what a nose is that appears as charm, as beautiful motion. Either Ariosto had to omit such parts—and since he had already begun his description, the omission would have seemed to an Italian like that satire on the beautiful but big-nosed girl, who praised every part of her face to the skies and was about to describe her nose when suddenly she stopped, powerless to continue—or he had to depict in terms of their external appearance those features which could not be rendered intuitive by any other means, and was thus compelled to linger all the more on other charming spiritual features. I think this combination too much to the taste of the Italians for them to let this criticism of Lessing's deprive them of these and similar descriptions, with which their poets abound. The reason Ariosto is said to be mistaken with his depiction is even less sound: "What kind of picture do these vague formulae suggest? In the mouth of a drawing master who wanted to call the attention of his pupils to the beauties of the academic model they might possibly mean something; one look at this model and they see the brow, nose, hand, etc. But in the poem I see nothing."[241] As if the poet had also to illustrate by means of an engraving the figures whom he describes? Who has never seen nose, hand, and brow? For whom is it an effort to imagine the fitting bounds of a brow, the finely chiseled nose, and the slenderness of a dainty hand each time the poet mentions them? Here I do not feel annoyance, as Mr. L. does, at the futility of my best efforts to see such a thing *individually*; and then afterward to assemble every feature, to imagine all in one and one in all, to imagine Alcina with every one of these parts as a whole, distinctly, like a drawing master—oh, the poet does not demand this effort of me! He led me from one part to another, showed me the beauty in

---

[239] *Laocoön*, p. 215 [21:111].
[240] *Laocoön*, p. 210 [20:108].
[241] *Laocoön*, p. 210 [20:108].

each; that is where his Muse energized, and why not? For she did not undertake to furnish an academic model of beauty that we were supposed to take in all at once and in all its parts.

And if poetic art shall abstain from depicting a beautiful figure because its parts coexist, then Homer ought also to have abstained from depicting an ugly figure, a Thersites, because his misshapen parts likewise coexist and must also be imagined as coexisting if a picture of ugliness is to arise. Lessing has wrapped Homer in his tissue of critical rules and now wants to enlist him to prove a point when he can scarcely work himself free. "The poet's use of ugliness becomes possible for the very reason that in his description it is reduced to a less offensive manifestation of physical imperfection and ceases, as it were, to be ugly in its effect."[242] It seems to me that Mr. L. lunges and misses in his attempt to overcome the embarrassment. If the question were, How can the Greek poet depict an ugly person when the Greek artist did not care to? then this reply may well be valid: the figure does not appear before our eyes all at once; in the poet's description it is less repulsive; it ceases to be ugly in its effect on our sight. But what does that signify here? A physical form is being depicted, successively depicted, for after all its parts and misshapen parts exist together, for after all they must be conceived in connection with one another if the concept of ugliness is to arise. Let us therefore rid ourselves of Thersites, not, as L.'s principles demand, because he is ugly but because he is a body, because he must be depicted as a physical object and yet successively.

"But the poet can use him! He uses him to——"[243] and can he thus use forms, physical descriptions? And if he can use them, is he permitted them? So what are we quarreling about? If he can use ugly forms, then how much more readily can he use beautiful ones? And if he is permitted the former, then how much more readily does he obtain permission for the latter? So if the poet imbues physical objects with energy, he can also describe them—what more do we want? The power of the bow has abated; it lies limp on the ground! By making this concession, Mr. L. has refuted the greater part of his book.

21

And to what end does Homer use Thersites? The question turns Homeric once more, and in questions relating to Homer I rarely give the same answer as Mr. L. "Homer makes Thersites ugly in order to make him ridiculous. It is not merely through his ugliness that he becomes so, but with-

---

[242] *Laocoön*, p. 232 [23:121].
[243] *Laocoön*, p. 232 [23:121].

out it he would not be ridiculous."[244] On this assertion Mr. L. bases a part of his theory of the ridiculous, which I wish had been elaborated elsewhere and erected on a different foundation.

In my reading of Homer the leading feature of Thersites is not ridiculousness but ugliness; he is not a laughable fellow but a maliciously snarling one, the *blackest soul of all those gathered before Troy*.[245] The other Greeks sit quietly; only Thersites keeps chattering.[246] He begins to utter abuse, not in sport, but with the bitterest bile; he reviles the kings, and certainly not in the manner of a court jester, but as an enemy, a deadly enemy. How coarsely and severely does he rail at Agamemnon for his greed, his cowardice, his injustice![247] And all this in front of the army, slanderous and mendacious, in the most insolent tone, as a judge of kings! And as if he were speaking in the name of all Greeks,[248] as if they had all put him up to it! And in the very same breath he berates the whole nation, disparages all Greeks as cowards and worthless wretches, speaks in a tone that would suggest he had done more than anyone else, had to care for them all, could command them all, pass judgment on them all![249] And still this is not enough! He even feels compelled to defame a man who is absent, the bravest of all Greeks, Achilles, and defames him with the most awful lie, namely that Achilles has no heart.[250] Oh, what a despicable, ugly fellow! From the Greek point of view there was no more despicable wretch to be found before the gates of Troy.

And if he said all this out of brash impertinence? But Homer knows him better: Thersites had long been in the habit of setting himself so vulgarly against the kings in order—to raise a laugh among the Greeks, to find favor with them[251]—and now the fellow becomes even more spiteful, even more ugly. According to Greek notions of honor there can be no uglier soul.

For this reason he is hated by all the Greeks;[252] for this reason, too, they break into merry laughter despite their troubled hearts when Ulysses takes pity on Agamemnon and with his staff induces Thersites to be silent;[253] for this reason the Greeks cry as one: "This deed is far the best

---

[244] *Laocoön*, p. 233 [23:121, 122].

[245] Ulysses describes him as follows:

οὐ γὰρ ἐγὼ σέο φημὶ χερειότερον βροτὸν ἄλλον
ἔμμεναι, ὅσσοι ἅμ' Ἀτρεΐδῃς ὑπὸ Ἴλιον ἦλθον. (*Iliad* 2.248–49)

[246] *Iliad* 2.212.

[247] *Iliad* 2.221–42.

[248] *Iliad* 2.227. ἅς τοι Ἀχαιοὶ δίδομεν κ.τ.λ.

[249] *Iliad* 2.235.

[250] *Iliad* 2.241.

[251] *Iliad* 2.215–16. ὅ τι οἱ εἴσαιτο γελοίϊον Ἀργείοισιν ἔμμεναι.

[252] *Iliad* 2.222, 223.

[253] *Iliad* 2.270–77.

that Ulysses has performed, since he has made this scurrilous babbler cease from his harangues."

Thus does Homer depict him with each feature, thus does Thersites reveal himself with each word, thus does Ulysses treat him with eye and mouth and hand. He casts an angry glance at him,[254] speaks to and deals with him *en canaille*; and that is how Thersites himself subsequently behaves: he cowers and weeps—the most contemptible, the ugliest soul before Troy! According to the Greek point of view, the worth of a man, of a soldier, of a hero, was based on noble pride in himself, on respect for those who earned glory, on a manly love of truth, on respect for the people, on ready obedience to his superiors, on honor—and in every sense Thersites was the ideal of an ugly soul.

And from a Greek point of view such an ugly soul must also inhabit the ugliest body; and that is how Homer depicts him: "No baser mortal and ugly beyond all men who came to Troy."[255]

Now, where does it say that Homer makes Thersites ugly to make him ridiculous? He most assuredly does not want to present him as a buffoon; it is merely a misconstrual of the Greek expression that has led Mr. L. and others to this erroneous conclusion.[256] "He was so vile," says Homer, "that he forgot his duty, quarreled with the kings, invited a beating, merely in order to raise a laugh among the Greeks." What a despicable soul! A soul who thinks all others as ill-humored and revoltingly snarling as himself, who fancies everyone is amused by his malice. That is how I explain Homer, and I find this feature of Thersites—like the description of his speeches, his actions as a whole—spiteful and ugly. That is how Ulysses takes him: he chides his maliciousness, abominates his cowardice, punishes his defiance; that is how the Greeks take him: they hate him, listen to him grudgingly, and are glad when his back is made to bleed; that is how he stands out and that is how he is dealt with.

I fail to see, then, that γελοιον is Thersites' dominant characteristic, let alone that ugliness was necessary to make him so, as Mr. L. theorizes.[257] An ugly body and an ugly soul—this is not the kind of contrast that produces the ridiculous! From the Greek point of view, no two things belong together more, and Homer also gives him the ugly body precisely to reinforce the indignation directed against him, to render his ugly soul visible before our eyes, to make the fellow thoroughly contemptible. The ridiculous is so little the principal color in Thersites that even the features that have

---

[254] *Iliad* 2.245. ὑπόδρα ἰδών.

[255] αἴσχιστος δὲ ἀνὴρ ὑπὸ Ἴλιον ἦλθε· (*Iliad* 2.216). οὐ χερειότερον βροτὸν ἄλλον (*Iliad* 2.248).

[256] τι οἱ εἴσαιτο γελοίϊον Ἀργείοισιν ἔμμεναι (*Iliad* 2.215–16 ["whatever he thought would raise a laugh among the Argives"].

[257] *Laocoön*, pp. 233, 234 [23:121, 122].

customarily been seen to point to it—his chatter,[258] his great clamor,[259] his vulgar language,[260] his desire to amuse the Greeks[261]—depict not a buffoon but, from the Greek point of view, an utterly worthless wretch. Even when the Greeks laugh at him it is *Schadenfreude*, it is laughter born of hatred, not innocent joy at an amusing buffoon who is innocently ridiculous. If Thersites were such a man, were he also stupid, ugly in body, but not malicious—well, then I could never forgive Ulysses for treating him as he did. Spare the ugly man who thinks himself beautiful, the fool who thinks himself clever, the coward who thinks himself brave—spare him the bloody welt on his back! Put down your staff, O Ulysses, and if, shrewd man that you are, you know yourself, then say to the *merely ridiculous* one who mocks you what Uncle Tobias Shandy said to the fly: "Go, poor devil, why should I hurt thee? This world surely is wide enough to hold both thee and me." If not, do you desire to thrash a man who is ugly and ridiculous simply because he is ugly and ridiculous? Well, well, Ulysses——

But Homer's Thersites is not laughable; he got what he deserved. We agree with the Greeks in Homer and say: "Never has Ulysses acted more nobly than now!" We are delighted that he is given a sound thrashing. So where is the harmless (the οὐ φθαρτικον) that Aristotle considers indispensable to the ridiculous? It is true that his malicious calumny does not harm Ulysses and Agamemnon, but his own back does not come out of it so well, for who will think a bloody, welt-covered back a οὐ φθαρτικον τι, or a good undergarment? Even to the Greeks a beating, a simple beating, could not seem a ridiculous spectacle if their gloating hatred toward Thersites prevented them from declaring of the punishment: "Not too much!" or "He deserved much more!" The first element of the ridiculous, the *harmless*, is thus rather dubious; and the other, *the contrast of perfections* and *imperfections*, falls down because the principal impression with Thersites is of *imperfection*, of *ugliness* itself. Even he who can become a Greek will see Thersites in this light.

Homer does not make a single person in his poetic universe the epitome of supreme perfection or imperfection, and so in this instance also he tones down *somewhat* the excessive color of the ugly, so that Thersites does not stand out too conspicuously from the remaining figures of his poem. Though he possesses no obvious good qualities, there is a little goodness in him, for he esteems himself; for however vexatious his eloquence, his cleverness, and his honesty may be, he mistrusts his own ugliness; so the otherwise wholly despicable and hateful figure yet becomes somewhat tol-

---

[258] ἀμετροεπὴς *Iliad* 2.212 ["unmeasured in words"].

[259] ἐκολῴα [ibid.] ["to brawl, scold"].

[260] ἔπεα ἄκοσμά οὐ κατὰ κόσμον [*Iliad* 2.213, 214] ["words without order"].

[261] τι οἱ εἴσαιτο γελοΐϊον Ἀργείοισιν [*Iliad* 2.215].

erable, and this points toward the ridiculous. But this ridiculousness is so very much a subsidiary trait, so very much an inessential part of his character, that it intrudes, as an extraneous feature, only temporarily, only retrospectively. Homer allows his ugliness to shade into something harmless in order to moderate his *absolute ugliness*, his *absolute despicableness*, but not the other way around: "Homer makes Thersites ugly in order to make him ridiculous. It is not merely through his ugliness that he becomes so, but without it he would not be ridiculous," and so on. What fine distinctions! But it is a pity that Homer is as innocent of them as I am. His Thersites is quite ugly, but he comes to a ridiculous end. Nevertheless, if we assume that Thersites were the man whom Mr. L. takes him to be, then his observations are in general consistent and correct.

But this selfsame ridiculous Thersites unwittingly presented the occasion for another book, one that runs to 284 pages and wherein *salva venia* he is the main character. Mr. Klotz has decided that Thersites is sufficiently worthy of his attention to devote to him the greater part of a small volume entitled *Epistolae Homericae* (perhaps a second Riccius), in which Mr. Klotz's design is solemnly to banish him, to exile him, to consign him to the flames—in short, to expunge him from Homer. I have said that the *Homeric Letters* is written *about Thersites*, for aside from the fact that he furnishes Klotz with the most substance—that is, the greatest opportunity to prate—I would, if I were the author of the letters, be most thankful to my reader if he allowed the remaining material to steal past without inspecting it more closely.

So after an introduction of eighteen pages, in which, as is his wont, he says nothing more than "I am in the countryside and reading," Mr. Klotz makes the exceedingly novel observation that a great mind also has its faults,[262] that Homer himself at times slumbers, that we need to identify those passages in which he slumbers, that *he*——and now, after all this heightened expectation, comes the great example:

> That Homer slumbers, *I believe*, becomes clear in those sections where he— *whether it be* that in doing so he is accommodating himself to the morals of his age, which were not yet sufficiently refined and had in their simplicity something peasantlike and coarse, or *because it is difficult to hold back what we think will raise laugher in our readers*, or because of a lapse in his judgment— in short, where he stoops to include that which, *I believe*, does *not at all* befit the dignity and gravity of the epic poem. But by occasionally wishing to make his readers laugh in the most inappropriate place, Homer, *I think*, sullies his divine poem *with not insignificant* stains, which cause it *not inconsiderable* disfigurement and awaken vexation in the reader. This becomes clear in Book II.[263]

[262] Klotz, *Epistolae Homericae*, p. 24.
[263] Ibid., p. 24.

Although I quote my serious author with great respect, like a Sorbonist, and would gladly convey his style intact, which was woven

—for Scull,
That's empty, when the Moon is full,

with all its joints and hinges, I think I can nevertheless leap over the few pages in which he cites Homer's description of Thersites.[264] What Homer said is old hat, but what Klotz says about what he said is new.

> *Now, I do not wish to deny* that Homer has gathered together all the qualities that can make a man appear ugly and *ridiculous*; and I can also *easily understand* why Claudius Belurgerius (see Nicii Erythraei *Pinacotheca*, p. 205, and Vincentii Paravicini *Singularia de viris eruditione claris*, cent. III, n. 12, p. 150) delights so much in this picture of Thersites, which is painted by the hand of a skilled artist. But we ought always to consider Quintilian's words: "Nihil potest placere, quod non decet," or in other words: nothing can please that is not decent. If Thersites were to appear perhaps in a satire or some other humorous poem, then he would amuse *me* not a little and *I* would gladly *bestow* praise on his wit and invention.
> Sed nunc non erat his locus, etc. etc.

With the permission of Messrs. Christoph Adolf Klotz and Claudius Belurgerius, I shall here omit a long passage from Horace and examples from Virgil, Tasso, and God knows where else,[265] which demonstrate the erudition of the gentleman epistolarian and which *by themselves* are the perfect confirmation of the maxim that much can come at the wrong time. Let us stick with Thersites.

> Just as it is inappropriate to awaken tragedies in a laughing matter, so it is inappropriate to laugh in a serious matter; *who would* think that proper? Here *we do not mean* to laugh, *we* are full of the anticipation which the poet himself instills in us, wondering how the episode will conclude. We see the whole army agitated, hurrying to the place of assembly; we desire to know whether the Greeks will take up their weapons again or return home; and behold! We encounter that hideous countenance (in Greek μορμολυκειον!), which seizes us by the coattails and holds us back as we attempt to flee. *We resist, we are indignant at him* who has sent this monster to us, and where *we did not merely wish to be* serious but were also compelled to be so, we unfortunately laugh.

With all due respect to Mr. Klotz's seriousness and his coattails, I would like to ask just a couple of little questions: Is Homer singing to us wearing the peruke of a burgomaster or scholiast? Does his Thersites appear

---

[264] Ibid., pp. 25, 26.
[265] Ibid., pp. 28–30.

as a buffoon, as a figure of fun? If not, if he steps forward at this critical juncture as a speaker in the name of the entire Greek *canaille*, to express what was weighing on the minds of men such as him in the Greek army, then certainly Homer can find no better time than this, and the shading in which Thersites appears is so much in accord with the epic tone that I cannot imagine him having any other. He cannot be uglier, for otherwise he would deserve to be struck down at that moment; he cannot be more temperate, for otherwise he would remain silent and there would be no herald to voice the concerns of the rabble. Therefore I need not worry about my coattails and improper laughter! Our earnest Homerist, however, who sees Thersites quite differently—namely as a worthless monkey face, as a monster who pushes himself to the fore and invites laughter— and who is so very afraid of him, continues:

> *If,* on the contrary, *we throw away* the man, if we *cut away* all the verses, let us see whether *we shall not keep a straight face.* I shall say it once more: Homer's Thersites does not please and shall never please me, even if Medea were to rejuvenate him. We wish to chase the man away; or if he resisted and dared revile *us* as he did the Greek generals, then we shall wring his neck. Nevertheless, we do not doubt that *he* too will find his champions, that there will be *some* people who do not wish a hand to be laid upon the good little boy. For there are people who have no intercourse, no acquaintance with the Muses and with Philosophia, who have studied the sciences as if they were learning a trade, who shriek . . .

Dear, oh dear! This reproachful and exceedingly grave tone is carried through eleven pages. And how should I now find the courage to rescue Homer's Thersites, who has been condemned without reason or justification? Oh dear, so I too am one of those who have no intercourse with those old maids, the Muses, and the venerable Lady Philosophia, for I would have thought that Thersites had received quite enough punishment. Full of grave respect, then, I shall put my hand over my mouth and, with due deference, return this ancient poet to the *his temporibus* greatest connoisseur of Homer in Germany so that he may read him again more carefully. For, on the evidence of this or that judgment that he has passed on Homer here and there, many readers have correctly presumed that Mr. Klotz's knowledge of him is based only on the most fleeting perusal of his work; and, as he himself tells us with the most charming candor, Mr. Klotz did indeed once set out with his roommate to leaf through Homer's entire oeuvre in twenty-four days so that he might know something of the design of the work and procure for himself a *copiam vocabulorum.*[266] Now,

---

[266] "Hortabur vero idem (Baumeisterus) me inprimis ad studium graecarum litterarum, quarum in me erat *levis cognitio.* Hinc una cum Neomanno, aequali et familiari meo, divina

that would suggest, of course, that he did not read *Homer in Homer's sense*, and it appears that much of Homer has eluded him as he quick-stepped through the work; by the same token, however, there is a great deal that only *he* seems to have noticed. I can give more instances of these faults at some future time; but for now I shall return to the example of Thersites. As I see it, he is not there to be ridiculous, to tear our coattails, to raise an inappropriate, improper laugh among us. Nor is he there to be merely ugly so that the men before Troy may not all be beautiful. Nor is he in the wrong place so that one would have to wring his neck. He is part of the action of the poem and is the mouthpiece of the Greek rabble, who shall speak out *at this moment* or not at all. He is not ridiculous but ugly, and it is only to moderate this ugliness somewhat that Homer points to a single redeeming feature: instead of putting him to death for his lèse-majesté, he punishes him lightly; instead of making him wholly contempt-ible, he ultimately reconciles him with Agamemnon by means of a sub-sidiary trait. To give him any other character means to judge him on the basis of the Latin translation, and to disclose this in the *Homeric Letters* is[267]—but I prefer to return to my dear Lessing, in whom I find every-where more plausible justifications.

22

And let us now consider him as a psychologist. "The poet uses ugliness to produce the mixed feelings of the ridiculous and the terrible."[268]

Let me begin by observing that though these two species of mixed feel-ing, the ridiculous and the terrible, may be quite different in and of them-selves, the one can be quickly transformed into the other. If we recognize the terrible as harmless, it becomes ridiculous precisely because we thought it terrible; and if we recognize the ridiculous as harmful, it becomes terri-ble precisely because we thought it *only* ridiculous. Perhaps both feelings, on account of their related nature, will use the ugly for the same reason? Let us investigate.

Homeri carmina non tam legi, quam deuoraui, ut intra viginti circiter quatuor dierum spa-tium omnia perlegeremus. Fuit enim tum nobis illud tantum modo propositum, ut formam *aliquam* magni operis et *speciem* animo informaremus atque *verborum nobis compararemus copiam.*" In preface to the *Elegies,* p. 8.

[267] It is true that the Latin translation speaks of *verbis scurrilibus,* of the *non prout de-cebat,* of the *quodcunque videtur ridiculum Argius;* and of course one can therefore trans-late Thersites into Latin phrases in the following manner: hic homo *scurram agere, risum reliquorum Graecorum* captare solebat, *dedecet* carminis gravitatem, and so on. That is all perfectly correct according to the Latin translation, but who wishes to read Homer in Latin?

[268] *Laocoön,* pp. 232, 233 [23:121].

Not everything that is *ridiculous* may be ugly. Among the great multitude of harmless contrasts between perfections and imperfections, there is one that is called *ugly-beautiful* and that expresses itself in several ways; for example, to be ugly and think oneself beautiful; to be ugly and yet be recognized as beautiful; to be ugly and desire to become beautiful by prettifying oneself; and so on. But this peculiar class of ridiculous contrasts is not the only such category. The weak-strong, small-large, significant-insignificant, are each creatures as ridiculous as the ugly-beautiful.

Similarly, not all that is *terrible* need be ugly. If a being inspires *terror* in us on account of its higher nature, its superior power,[269] then the terrible may not be associated either (in the object) with the appearance of the ugly or (in our soul) with the feelings of the ugly. For example, a storm or, to speak metaphorically, a thunderbolt-throwing Jupiter can be dreadful and terrible but without distortion of his face, without an ugly form. A roaring lion, for example, can be a terrible and frightful sight, even if I think myself out of harm's way, but it is by no means an ugly one.

It thus follows that to produce the mixed feelings of the ridiculous or the terrible ugliness need not be introduced as an essential ingredient on every occasion. It can therefore be left to a particular art to decide whether it can use what it *need* not use, whether it is *inclined* to use *here and there* what it *does not absolutely have* to use. I shall continue.

Among the harmless contrasts that constitute the ridiculous, we have in particular the contrast of the ugly-beautiful; so ugliness can in fact be an essential ingredient required to *produce* the ridiculous. In terrible objects ugliness of form is not properly a component at all of the idea of the harmful, of the terrifying itself. The two feelings of terror and aversion in relation to the ugly are of a quite distinct nature; consequently, the ugly can never really work as an essential ingredient of the terrible, can therefore never *produce* it. Hence the use of each cannot be treated in parallel.

Where the ugly applies to the ridiculous, it is an essential part of the contrast, it is indispensable. Where it can be omitted, it must be omitted. Thus, Mr. L. is correct to describe as a monk's silly whim the notion that the wise and honest Aesop, represented in the ugly form of Thersites, should become ridiculous through the contrast between his ugly form and his beautiful soul.

If the ugly applies to the terrible, then it applies merely as a subsidiary idea; it is not part of the feeling of terror. It must therefore be *added* to the mixture as an extra ingredient so that it does not weaken the principal feeling, so that *terror* does not become *aversion* if it is not intended as such.

Where an object is supposed to become *ridiculous* through the inclu-

---

[269] Most Homeric gods are terrible, but are they therefore ugly?

sion of the ingredient of the ugly, it can, as long as it remains within the bounds of probability and a balance is preserved in the contrast, never be *too ugly*. But where the ugly accompanies the terrible, the former certainly can, if it is too strong and treated as the main ingredient, assuredly inhibit the latter. To perceive an object as quite ugly, so that the idea of aversion, of revulsion overwhelms every other notion, certainly does not mean to experience it as quite frightful. The feeling of the terrible manifests itself as a shudder of fear: the blood drains from your face, you grow pale, a cold shiver runs down your body; but Nature soon gathers herself for her defense, the blood returns more vigorously to its previous course, the cheeks flush, the fire spreads again, the fear is past. Terror has been transformed into anger. Thus was the feeling of the terrible conceived, born, and allowed to pass away. But how very different it is with the feeling of the ugly: that discordance, that repulsive appearance which we call ugly communicates discordance and repulsion to my nervous organization also, it brings the strings of sensation into unpleasant contact with one another, it grates my nature. Hence the feeling of the ugly passes through my body in a quite different manner from the feeling of the terrible; they do not belong together.

And even if they are shaken together, they hardly mix. The *cruel* Richard III awakens *terror* in me,[270] the Richard who is *ugly* in body and soul arouses *abhorrence*. The ugliness of his body can indeed enhance the ugliness of his soul and the abhorrence I feel toward him, but it has nothing to do with my terror or with the frightfulness of his character. When I hear the *abhorrent* soul of *Edmund* speak from within a well-proportioned body,[271] I can deplore the beautiful frame that must house such a black soul; I can love it, even though I hate its inhabitant; the abhorrence I feel toward the soul is thus not strengthened or, I should rather say, weakened by the body. But the *terror* aroused by Edmund's black, frightful machinations is something quite different; despite his beautiful body, we feel it work in full measure. Edmund the villain is repugnant to me; Edmund the villain bent on harm is terrible.

So if I concede to Mr. Lessing that "harmful ugliness is always terrible,"[272] then Mr. L. must concede to me that this is so not because of its ugliness but simply because of its harmfulness; that the poet can therefore never *produce* the feeling of the terrible through the ugly; that properly speaking he can never *intensify* that feeling; in short, that the terrible and the ugly are two completely different kinds of objects, that fear and abhorrence are two completely different kinds of feeling. Perhaps Mr. L.

---

[270] *Laocoön*, p. 238 [23:124].
[271] *Laocoön*, p. 237 [23:124].
[272] *Laocoön*, p. 236 [23:124].

meant to say: "Our abhorrence toward another's ugly soul is intensified by our abhorrence toward his ugly body; the poet can thus avail himself of the physical forms of the ugly to intensify *abhorrence*." In that case he is right; but he has not mentioned the existence of any close alliance of these feelings, for abhorrence remains abhorrence, regardless of whether the ugly or the abhorrent resides in the body or in the soul.

I have called the feeling awakened by the ugliness of forms *abhorrence*; Mr. Lessing prefers to label it *disgust*,[273] and in doing so he departs from Mr. Mendelssohn, who claims to locate disgust only in the lower senses of taste, smell, and touch but not in the objects of sight and scarcely at all in those of hearing.[274] Linguistic usage in matters of touch seems to support the latter philosopher only, but with the following distinctions, if I am not mistaken.

Strictly speaking, disgust seems to pertain only to the sense of taste. It is caused not only by excessive sweetness but also by every disagreeable contact with our nerves of taste.[275] Hence the great variety of taste experienced by different tongues, according as their fibers are attuned in this way and no other, according as their fibers can be touched agreeably or disagreeably in this way and no other. Here disgust is thus a principal component of distaste, which proceeds not from prolonged monotonous impressions on our nerves of taste, as Mr. Mendelssohn believes, but rather, as I think, from every contact of the nerves of taste that is disagreeable to our nature. Certain kinds of taste are universally disgusting, others are disgusting only to the peculiar constitution of an individual nature; that is, according to the particular tension of the fibers in this individual subject. Certain kinds of disgust are innate, when the instruments of taste are originally fashioned in this way and no other; others are acquired and have become second nature through a long association of ideas. Some things are disgusting as we taste them, others only after we have tasted them, depending on whether the unpleasant contact occurred quickly or slowly, and so on. The disgusting that preoccupies the eye in objects of taste is nothing but the repetition of previous sensations, but such a strong repetition that it excites sensations itself, which are then mixed together with the original impressions. In objects of taste, then, the eye does not directly experience disgust.

Taste and smell are united in our nature by a secret bond of organization: the strength of one is usually accompanied by the strength of the other, and the loss of one usually entails the loss of the other. Initially, then,

---

[273] *Laocoön*, p. 247 [25:131].
[274] *Letters Concerning Recent Literature*, pt. 5 [letter 82], p. 107 [101].
[275] *Letters Concerning Recent Literature*, ibid.

disgust pertains to *smell* and arises through a disagreeable emotion of the olfactory nerves; but may I say that disgust pertains to smell only by virtue of a bond with taste based on their similar organization? I almost believe that a disgusting odor even causes nausea, that is, a disagreeable contact with the organs of taste. Disgust thus expresses itself through taste; it pertains to smell only to the extent that smell is a sense allied with taste; every other disagreeable odor—for example, an odor that is too strong, too intoxicating—is not disgusting.

Disgust does not properly pertain to *touch.* "An oversoftness of bodies that do not offer sufficient resistance to the nerves that touch them"[276]— for example, the palpating of velvet, fine hairs, and so on—can be no more *disgusting* in the proper sense than so-called tickling; it is *disagreeableness*, a heterogeneous feeling, a more heterogeneous contact than I would like, and namely *disagreeableness* caused by *excessive gentleness*. Now, there is another kind of disagreeableness, the feeling of a heterogeneous tension of the nerves caused by the *excessively vehement*, the *excessively violent*. It is like the piercing screech in our ear when a pencil is scraped against a slate; we feel our whole nervous organization disagreeably agitated, we want to jump out of our skin, but we are not nauseous. The object is disagreeable to our ear, but it is not disgusting.

Disgust pertains even less to *hearing* as such, for an "unbroken succession of perfect consonance"[277] can awaken *weariness*, but properly only that kind of disgust where taste were the principal sense and felt the sweetness of the sounds only insofar as it had similarities with the sweetness of taste. Only this kind of taste would *feel* in excessive consonance a similarity with excessive sweetness also, and hence *feel* disgust toward sounds; no other! I purposely say feel, obscurely feel, for it is not a question here of thinking clearly.

Finally, *disgusting* objects for the eye. Mr. L. believes that a "mole on the face, a harelip, a flat nose with prominent nostrils, a complete lack of eyebrows might well be called such; that in these instances we feel something much more closely akin to disgust; that the more delicate our temperaments, the more we feel in our bodies those sensations that precede nausea."[278] I have no desire to quarrel over names in such uncertain matters concerning the obscurest feeling; nevertheless, it seems to me that the most delicate temperament, in a state of the highest sensitivity—for example, a pregnant woman—would sooner call such objects disagreeable than disgusting, sooner recoil from them and swoon than feel nausea; that

---

[276] *Letters Concerning Recent Literature*, ibid. [p. 100].
[277] *Letters Concerning Recent Literature*, p. 101.
[278] *Laocoön*, pp. 247, 248 [25:131].

we should therefore always denominate the unpleasant sensation a disagreeable feeling or an abhorrent sight rather than disgust. Let us assume, however, that such a sight can excite sensations that precede nausea; does Mr. L. not thereby give nausea as the surest effect of disgust? And since nausea properly pertains only to the sense of taste, then the eye, if it felt disgust, must experience it only by way of an association of ideas of taste. And about the delicacy of temperament I have no wish to argue.

It is enough for me that disgust properly pertains only to taste and to smell as a sense allied with taste. The coarse feeling of the remaining senses perceives disagreeableness and not disgust—unless in this or that individual it forms a close bond, as it were, with taste and smell through either his physical organization or the association of concepts that has become second nature to him. There are those, namely, in whom taste, and consequently also smell, are the most dominant of the lower senses and are able to set the tone for all the sensuous feelings. With them a revolting sight, a disagreeable sound, a disagreeable feeling, approach more closely to disgust; that is, excite sensations that usually precede nausea. But this peculiarity in the disposition of the nervous organization does not change the fact that even in such people the immediate disageeableness of touch, sight, and hearing should be distinct from the mediate disageeableness of those senses experienced with the assistance of a foreign sense, taste. The disgusting can intrude more or less, depending on the disposition of the organization, into every disagreeable sensuous feeling. But that does not mean that every sensuous feeling, every disageeableness is disgust.

So if disgust pertains preeminently to taste, and to the other senses only insofar as they are allied with taste or can substitute for it, then:

> First, the answer given to the question, "Why is disgust not beautiful in the beaux arts and belles lettres?"[279] to the effect that disgust pertains only to the obscure senses, is not universally valid, for disgust does not pertain to the obscurest sense of all, touch.

> Still less is the repugnance that ugliness arouses completely of the same nature as disgust, as Mr. L. opines,[280] for ugliness manifests itself only to the eye, disgust properly only to taste.

> Least of all, then, can the disgusting bear exactly the same relation to imitative art as does the ugly.[281] Let us examine in turn each of the three imitations of the ridiculous, the ugly, and the disgusting.

---

[279] [Mendelssohn,] *Letters Concerning Recent Literature*, pt. 5, ibid. [letter 82, p. 101].
[280] *Laocoön*, p. 247 [25:131].
[281] *Laocoön*, p. 248 [25:132].

23

The ugly can be used in poetry to awaken the ridiculous, namely the apparently beautiful; and, as I have said, poetry is then restricted in the arrangement of its forms only by the demands of plausibility and equilibrium in the contrast. But is the ugly an ingredient of the ridiculous in painting? If the painter can contrast his ugly with his would-be beautiful in such a manner that the ridiculous shines forth, then all is well and good. But since this is rare, since painting, even in Hogarth's most ingenious compositions, always depicts ugly forms more clearly than it represents a ridiculous contrast by means of ugly forms, it remains too corporeal to be able to follow the poet of the ridiculous. The poet hits upon the spirit of the ridiculous by way of the ugly; the artist is left clinging to the ugly body—and the main object is invisible. The poet lifts my soul and brings willing laughter to my lips; the artist titillates me *with ugliness* and I am expected to laugh!

What does the ugly contribute to the terrible? Nothing! Nothing in either poetry or painting. If the poet desires to excite *abhorrence*, however, then an already abhorrent, malicious, fierce soul will express itself through ugly contortions of the body. If this abhorrence is to be intensified, then the poet shall give the soul a wholly ugly body; for how else, indeed, can the dwelling place appear which it has built for itself, in which it worked for so long? If abhorrence is to break off into sympathy, if the poet wishes to show, from a distance, a soul that might be improved, then he shall tone down its abhorrence, at least, by allowing rays of its good nature to shine through, by not depicting an ugly body. Here the painter encounters the limits of his art, for how seldom, indeed, does painting wish to awaken abhorrence, the highest degree of abhorrence? And if only abhorrence, and not the feeling of terror, can be achieved through the ugly, does not the artist come away empty-handed?

Finally, the disgusting—and here I disagree with Mr. L. entirely. The lizard that interrupted Socrates is not in itself a disgusting object, and the disgusting features that Aristophanes adds to it are a concession to the Greek rabble, which they are welcome to keep. All Hottentot tales, as soon as they rely on disgust for their principal effect, seem to me the offspring of British tomfoolery and *malicious* humor. Where Hesiod's depiction of Sadness is concerned, I feel the same way as Longinus, for whatever reason it may be. I have no desire to see the running nose; I have no desire to see what really arouses disgust. Disgust as such is not at all capable of amalgamation with any pleasant feeling; and if the horrible is nothing more than the terrible that has been made disgusting, then whatever admixture of disgust present in the horrible is always unpleasant, always disagreeable.

But one must be careful to think nothing disgusting that might convey only a subordinate notion of disgust by a long association of ideas, which, without being an object of taste and smell, could merely be called disagreeable; finally, one must not deem disgusting in an artistic imitation anything that is scarcely so in Nature herself, for in Nature no unpleasant feeling is confined to a narrower sphere than true disgust.

But I have almost completely forgotten how to find my way back out of my critical grove. How I have strayed about! How manifold were the vistas that presented themselves to me! How many right and wrong thoughts must I have entertained as I dreamily went on my way! So be it! Lessing's *Laocoön* has furnished me with material to ponder: Homer and the human soul were the source from which I drew my thoughts. "Although my reasoning may not be so compelling as Lessing's, my examples will at least smack more of the source."[282]

Incidentally, let every word and phrase that seems to be written *against* Mr. L. be banished from this book. I have reflected *on* his material, and wherever I was obliged to depart from it, in particular under the guidance of the ancients, I spoke candidly and wished to speak in the form of an open letter, if only the variety and content of the material had permitted it. If my doubts and disagreements enable the readers of *Laocoön* to study the work once more, as carefully as I have done, and to emend it on the basis of my doubts or to emend my doubts on the basis of *Laocoön*, then I have done a greater service to *Laocoön* than if I had expressed mere cold praise, after which every reader, as well as the author and owner, must yawn. My book itself: how worthy an object of contemplation has *Laocoön* seemed to me! Be a token of my esteem for its author, for I have no words of praise to offer.

24

The remaining chapters of *Laocoön* are concerned with several errors arising in Winckelmann's writings;[283] I wish, though, that Mr. L. had devoted his attention to the substance of Winckelmann's work and to the whole edifice of his history, which is still beset by a number of difficulties.

Because *for years* I paid daily homage to the ancients, the firstborn of the human spirit, and because I think Winckelmann an honorary Greek who has risen from the ashes of that people to enlighten our century, I cannot but read Winckelmann in the same manner that I read a Homer, a Plato, and a Bacon and in the same manner that he himself contemplates his *Apollo Belvedere*.

[282] Lessing, preface to *Laocoön*.
[283] *Laocoön*, pp. 261–98 [26–29].

Nevertheless, after reading him seven times, my own doubts have inevitably found their way onto paper, doubts that, particularly where they concern the historical edifice he builds from the raw materials of Greek literature, might call on the ancients themselves as witnesses, as guarantors. Since I have had the good fortune of having received from Winckelmann an encouraging nod of approval, I was concerned with turning his works over in my mind once more and then of going before him, adopting the dignified tone in which his spirit expresses itself. How uplifting would have been the idea of finding favor with him, the Greek of our age, of contributing in some measure to the perfection of his immortal works!

But alas! Winckelmann is no more! Cruelly torn by a murderer's hand from the world, from Rome, and from his native Germany! O divine one, if you should still roam the earth like a blessed demon, then behold the dismay that struck me when I received the news of your loss, the incredulous disquiet with which I insisted that you still lived, and finally the tears of melancholy with which I mourned your death! How many a *littérateur* and scholar of antiquity could and perhaps should have died in his place, that the world might one day have something more to show than misleading traces of his genius!

Conclusion

I have followed Mr. L.'s path, and if his *Laocoön* is rather a collection of "unordered notes for a book than a book itself,"[284] then what are my *Critical Forests*? They were written as chance dictated and more in keeping with my reading than through any systematic development of general principles. They show, however, that we can go astray unsystematically, too, that we can just as easily take a false step not only when we deduce anything we want in the most beautiful order from a few postulated definitions, but also when we do so from several torn-out passages in the most beautiful disorder. I am anyway too much of a German not to desire, if I were granted a wish, more order and system in my *Critical Forests*; and even more fervently do I wish that this work enjoyed "the prerogative of the ancients never to have done too much or too little in anything."[285] In the material that *Laocoön* treats, I have now prepared the ground; the future will show what can be erected on it.

For the time being I ask only *one thing*: that the title of my book be not made the object of amusing quibbles, in which many of the wits among

---

[284] Preface to *Laocoön*.
[285] Preface to *Laocoön*.

our critics are not found wanting. In more than one language the word *forests* or *silvae* suggests the idea of assembled materials without plan and order; I only hope that my readers shall endure the journey along the somewhat dusty and secluded path of this first part, so that once they have reached its end, they may command clearer views.

Critical Forests

FOURTH GROVE, ON RIEDEL'S
THEORY OF THE BEAUX ARTS

> Unus erat toto naturae vultus in orbe
> quem dixere Chaos!
> OVID, *Metamorphoses*

I

1

LIKE ALL GOOD THINGS, the fundamental concepts of our new fashionable philosophy come in threes. Here they are in Mr. Riedel's words:

> Man has three ultimate ends, which are subordinated to his spiritual perfection: the true, the good, and the beautiful.
>
> For each Nature has endowed man with a special fundamental faculty [*Grundkraft*]: for the true the *sensus communis*, for the good the conscience, and for the beautiful taste.
>
> The *sensus communis* is the inner feeling of the soul by means of which, without rational inferences, it is immediately convinced of the truth or falsity of a thing. The conscience is the feeling by which the soul is immediately convinced of what is good and evil, and taste the feeling by which the soul is immediately convinced of the beautiful, wherever it is found.

Immediately convinced? If these words have any meaning at all, they imply that we are convinced *without inferences, without judgments*, merely through a *simple sensation*. And of what could a simple sensation convince us? Of nothing more than a particularity, an isolated concept. To combine or to separate two concepts would already be judging; to combine two judgments to arrive at a third would already be inferring: and here we are not supposed to infer or to judge, but rather to feel immediately. Hence what a simple sensation, an immediate feeling raises in me can be nothing but that: a simple sensation, a single feeling. Here language must repeat words each time that ideas renew themselves; and if I were convinced by a thousand things, I would have a thousand isolated concepts, a thousand single feelings, a motley chaos of sensations and impressions.

Let us pursue our analysis. All these disparate impressions—if that is all they are—of what kind and how clear would they be? They would be the most obscure feelings, of course. To cognize a thing with even the least degree of clarity means that one has already distinguished it; but there is never distinction without judgment, and a judgment is no longer an immediate feeling. And then to cognize something distinctly even requires a clear knowledge of its subordinate concepts as such, as the distinguishing marks of the whole, and consequently involves the activity of the inner workings of reason. And Mr. Riedel's inner feeling is supposed to produce conviction wholly without rational inferences; hence it must be the most obscure kind of idea, or else no chaos is ever obscure.

Perhaps the best and only use of logic in its present form is that through the analysis of concepts, it can at least make error evident, if not teach us to avoid it altogether. Let us therefore subject Mr. Riedel's fundamental concepts to further analysis. We saw that they could entail only single sensations, that these sensations had to be of the obscurest kind; let us take one more step, and behold! We have before us the obvious contradiction, the manifest error. Precisely these sensations are supposed to teach us to cognize abstractions? And such complex, fine, intricate abstractions as the true, good, and beautiful? And they are supposed to *convince* us of the latter? That is, to assure us of them rationally, with reasons, distinguishing marks, and grounds? What, and all this without judgment, without inferences? All this a blind, obscure feeling shall accomplish? To convince us immediately of truth and falsehood, good and evil, the beautiful and the ugly, through some obscure prompting, without rational inferences—and yet still convince us? Anyone who fails to see the obvious contradiction in combining such concepts must be blind. Mr. Riedel is even more confused than were he to claim that the coarse feeling of our eyes—which also functions without light, in the greatest darkness, for example, which announces itself when a branch or a blow strikes the eye—is precisely what we call sight and that therefore we have no need of light to see. Mr. R. errs just as flagrantly with respect to the mind's eye, to the inner sense of cognition and feeling.

All this follows from the evolution of Riedel's concepts themselves; let us now take a closer look at experience. Properly speaking, there is nothing in the world of which I am immediately convinced by an inner feeling other than that I exist, that I feel. This truth alone is inwardly cognized without inferences, and the skeptic who would wish momentarily to deny this—that is, who demanded that the immediate conviction produced by a feeling be proven through judgments and inferences—would be by some measure a greater fool than even the most resolute egoist and idealist. He desires that the ego be proven through rational inferences, though the ego itself must have made these same rational inferences; he does not doubt rational inferences and yet doubts the basis of sensation whereupon these rational inferences rest and that they can only modify. He is—if such a person could ever exist—a fool. This inner feeling, then, is humanity's original and true sensus communis; it is acquired immediately, and without inferences and judgment.

The conviction that something exists outside us is of a different nature, and its difference is as difficult to characterize as that between inner and outer. Yet it is still conviction and still feeling. Seen correctly, the dispute with the idealists is only ever a dispute about words, that *what lies outside us* does not lie *within us*; therefore even if the means of representing bodies were nothing more than that, were but convenient formulas peculiar to our natures, they possess, insofar as they are indispensable hypotheses, *outer* certainty. They can never have any other kind so long as I must cognize sense through sense, body through body, outward object through outward object, and therefore so long as I require ideas of the external world for my organs and for their harmonious interaction. It remains, then, an outer feeling and as such an original and true sensus communis of humanity that cannot be acquired through inference and judgment.

But come now! Now I use my organs successively and variously: behold a throng of insular concepts without order, without connection, without bridges, and without dams. They must be arranged; they must be combined—oho! Now my inner feeling no longer operates alone. I learn to combine and to separate; behold: a reflective operation of the soul. I judge. To feel something outside me through my organs of sense was mere feeling; the least differentiation in that something was already judgment; the least distinct differentiation in what we have just called judgment is a doubly reflective operation of the soul and thus already inference, already ratiocination. As long as I am not willfully capricious and scorn names and designations that have been accepted for thousands of years; as long as I am not willfully blind and mix and muddle up operations of the soul that are as different from one another as the simple ray of sunlight is from a beam that has been once and twice refracted, then I do not yet see here the slightest objection against the truth.

However, I see precisely here the basis of the contrary error. And if I can see it, if I can not only demonstrate that it is an error but also show whence it comes, then I have refuted it twice over, so to speak. I have become a philosopher not merely *against* but also *of* that error; not only is its misshapen body made manifest, but so too is the manner in which this deformity came into being.

Let us assume, then, nothing but the distinction between sensation, judgment, and deduction; let us return to our childhood and ask how we obtained our first concepts of bodies—of their solidity, color, and shape, for example. Did we obtain them immediately through a single feeling? No, through nothing less than a plurality of single feelings, through long juxtaposition of the same, through comparison and judgment; only in this way did we learn these concepts and achieve conviction. The concept of magnitude, of breadth, of distance, appears to be sensation, immediate feeling; that it is not, however, is demonstrated by our frequent errors and the smallest experiments with reflection. They show that all these ideas are judgments, late-formed judgments, conclusions resulting from many initially incorrect deductions, many of which are often still found wanting. And if these are the simplest, most sensuous concepts of bodies, which seem to lie so close to the immediate sensation experienced by our organs; if these were formed not through an immediate feeling but through many comparisons and deductions, then what about the most general and finest abstractions? If already I cannot properly see the breadth, magnitude, and distance of a body but must judge, infer these concepts, then how can I say that I do not judge, do not infer ideas such as truth and falsity, good and evil, beauty and false taste, but instead immediately feel them, in the same way that I feel that I think, that I exist? What a disordered mind! What a torrent of concepts!

But of course from our earliest childhood we have grown accustomed to thinking and to all the different modes of thinking and to all of these different modes of thinking working in harmony, so that, as with all habits, it ultimately becomes difficult to observe and distinguish the subsidiary actions that we habitually perform. From the first moment of our lives we have thought, judged, inferred, and all this often alternately, concertedly, simultaneously; everything has therefore become entangled in a knot; or rather, the various fibers have been woven together so tightly into a single thread that if we do not take it apart with care, then the eye really can take it for a simple filament. We judge, we infer rapidly and habitually, and we believe we are still receiving immediate sensations; we omit intermediary steps, and the inference seems a simple judgment; we obscure the connection between the concepts, and the judgment seems an immediate sensation. Our earliest concepts of the color, figure, and breadth of bodies were learned simply by protractedly juxtapositioning single sensations; but it was precisely through this process that they became familiar to us: the intermediary terms linking them grew obscure, they were left as simple, immediate sensation, and it is as such that we put them to use, heedless in our application of them, through ready, hasty, unremarking force of habit. But should the philosopher, the deliberate, inquiring anatomist of the soul, take them as such? If the soul of a Newton, in delivering his mathematical revelations, can at once overlook individual steps, can discard a number of intermediary premises with his customary inner strength and view it all as immediate inference, where his commentator must here and there insert a link in the chain of reasoning to show how it all hangs together, where the pupil must laboriously climb every rung so that he may mount the entire ladder—what, are the intermediary concepts that are overshadowed in the soul of Newton destroyed, negated, abolished by this eclipse, by the fiery manner in which he overlooks the whole? Or are they not rather still present in the chain, showing themselves to be indispensable to the eye of the solitary, inquiring commentator, of the slowly learning pupil? And if the soul of a child (which in its own sphere is as great as the soul of Newton!) seems, through long habituation, ultimately to judge, to infer habitually, without always being conscious that it is distinguishing, does that mean that the distinction as such ceases to be? And does it cease to be for the philosopher, who wishes precisely to enumerate, to differentiate the fundamental faculties and operations of the soul? I think we see the source of the indeterminacy clearly enough.

Perhaps, though, Mr. R. was not concerned with determinacy; perhaps, lost in beautiful confusion, he intended his explanations to say nothing more than this: we cannot always be distinctly conscious of our judgments and inferences; without this consciousness we cognize, feel, and choose truth, beauty, and righteousness with greater vividness because, filled with the object, we forget, as it were, the means of our agency and, unconscious of the formal aspect of our knowledge, embrace its content all the more vividly. Perhaps he wanted to say that Nature has acted benignly, that she leaves the middle rank of humanity in a wonted state of mind, standing on this intermediate level between obscure and distinct ideas; that this intermediate and vivid level is the very horizon that we commonly call the sensus communis in matters of knowledge, the conscience in matters of right and wrong, and taste where objects of beauty are concerned; that these terms mean nothing more than a habitual application of our judgment to objects of various kinds. But why am I fantasizing about what Mr. Riedel wanted to say since he *means* to say the very opposite: for precisely these three habitual applications of a single power of the mind he makes into—and this is his purpose, his great merit, his corrective to philosophy—into *fundamental faculties of the soul*.

And so what was previously merely logical indeterminacy now becomes veritable psychological nonsense. The three monstrous ideas—an immediate feeling that without rational inferences nevertheless convinces us, and convinces us, indeed, of the finest abstractions of the human mind, of truth, beauty, and the good—these creatures born of a perplexing process of reflection are transformed into fundamental faculties, prime, irreducible fundamental faculties coexisting on the even ground of the soul. Coexist? The sensus communis, taste, and conscience coexist as fundamental faculties? So each operates independently as a fundamental faculty? So the sensus communis is possible without taste, and conscience without the sensus communis? So there might be creatures possessed of taste but not understanding, and understanding but not conscience? Creatures who have a feeling for good and evil, or beauty and ugliness, without being capable of a sentiment of truth? Oh, what a psychologist he is! He can conceive taste and conscience without the sensus communis. He can discover in neither of them anything that requires explanation by the latter. He can explain, order, perhaps even create them as fundamental faculties without it—oh, what a psychologist!

One's mind adopts, as it were unnoticed, a gloomy, somber expression when, having seen psychology in the simplicity and exactitude and fine precision to which it was brought by Leibniz's pupils and in which Mendelssohn and Sulzer have cleared up so many paradoxes, especially in the area of obscure and confused ideas; when, after viewing the noble simplicity of this great edifice, it must suddenly enter the Crusian-Riedelian maze, where fundamental faculties have grown over, wildly entwining themselves with other fundamental faculties, where the most complex and intricate capacities of the soul have become basic sensations from which everything follows that one wants and does not want, where the human soul becomes a chaotic abyss of immediate inner feelings, and philosophy a sentimental, obfuscating windbag—O windbag, you are no longer philosophy, you who murder all philosophy!

2

Who murders all philosophy? And on each one of his fundamental faculties, Mr. R. erects a distinct, new philosophy, each of which is meant to be as detached a building as the faculty that serves as its foundation—the philosophy of the mind, of the heart, of taste. We shall approach these edifices and examine their supporting columns; but let us be on our guard so that when they collapse they do not come crashing down on us.

The essence of philosophy is to entice forth, so to speak, ideas that lie within us, to illuminate into distinctness the truths that we knew only obscurely, to develop proofs that we did not grasp clearly in all their intermediary steps. All this requires judgments and inferences, judgments that start from the comparison of two ideas and are developed through a series of inferences until the relation of these ideas to each other becomes evident. Herein lies the essence and formative power of all philosophy: that through it I can see manifestly, certainly truths I did not see before at all, or at least not as clearly, not as distinctly; that through it I can form judgments of taste with a certainty and distinguish beauties in a light in which they had not appeared to me before; that through it I can view the origin, form, and consequences of the essence of good and evil in a manner that I simply had not glimpsed before. Such is the plastic power of philosophy; see how far it surpasses Riedel's fundamental faculties. An immediate feeling without rational inferences cannot be illuminated, cannot be developed; and if it could, what purpose would this long and pointless detour serve? Is it an immediate feeling for truth, beauty, and goodness that impels me, without developed concepts and rational inferences, toward these three so lofty goals of the human soul? Whither can one travel farther, whither in the world can one travel higher than to be convinced of that which is true, good, and beautiful? "The sensus communis imparts to each person as much truth as he needs in order to live and not mistake the good." As much as he needs? To live? And not to mistake the good? Let me complete the intolerable indeterminacy of these words. As I ponder the ideas they contain, I realize how much I owe to my inner feeling: thanks be to the thinker for his idiosyncrasies! I have not only the touchstone, I have the fountain of all truth; I have all truth within me; I have an inner light, an immediate feeling back to which all the philosopher's mediate stuff shall be traced in roundabout fashion: my thanks. With the philosophy of the heart it is no different: if my feeling guides me rightly, then what use is a system? If it leads me directly to the good, then why should it merit philosophical attention? If I have an inner light that warms me, agitates me, burns within me, then what use is the phantasmagoria of abstract concepts and frigid inferences that glitter before my eyes and are nothing but feeble reflections of my inner light? And to crown it all, the philosophy of taste? Read Riedel's *Letters on the Public* and you will find therein its sentence of banishment solemnly declared. Thus all philosophy must come to an end: farewell, philosophy, you idle prattler! We are now in the realm of irrational instincts, in the abysses of immediate inclinations and obscure enthusiasms! Leave us, philosophy, you who dwell on high peaks so that you may illumine the world; leave us in our native country, where we feel so comfortable, in Plato's dark cave.

And if I were unfortunate enough to be a creature who did not have these feelings, or if they at least were not in tune with those of my fellow creatures, then what in the world would this misused word *conviction* signify? We cannot even picture its barest outline: the true, the beautiful, and the good are *qualitas occulta*; he who feels them is welcome to feel them; he who does not—who can help, who can convince him? Not the philosopher, that otherwise mighty ruler over the most independent region of our soul, reason and freedom. He has lost the magic wand with which he sways, convulses, and transforms human souls; his philosophy is incapable of rational inferences, and therefore incapable of proofs, and therefore incapable of ineluctable conviction. You feel that way and I feel this way—we go our separate ways. C. feels so many foreign spirits at work in his soul, feels with each what kind of spirit it is, feels in how many ways it can operate—he feels it! *What cannot but be felt as true is true*—yes, for all I care *it is true*—we go our separate ways. Klotz exclaims to himself: Privy Councillor Klotz, you write so beautifully, oh so very beautifully! So originally, splendidly, rigorously, divinely—I feel it! *What cannot but be felt as beautiful is beautiful*—fine, for all I care it is beautiful! There is no more disagreement! And you, philosopher of virtue and of religion, you who wish to call me back, to tear me away from vice and misery—alas, the voice with which you admonish me and urge my improvement cries itself hoarse; my moral feeling is tuned to a different pitch, look here! The sympathy for vice that resides in my breast carries me away without any rational inferences; so how can it be changed through rational inferences? Virtue is an immediate feeling, but in me it is vice; I am acting in accordance with the mechanics of my heart.————We need only reveal consequences such as these to reject and abominate the premise from which they resulted, and we need only reflect a little on a philosophy containing such fundamental faculties and highest principles to deny it entry to the soul forthwith, just as Plato barred the corrupting poets.

With regard to particular maxims, teachings, and proofs I readily admit that there is still room for improvement in Wolffian philosophy, and indeed much in it has with good reason already been modified. I readily admit that the spirit of philosophy must never become a mechanical repetition and redemonstration of doctrines and hypotheses; but if our great anti-Wolffian thinkers reject every aspect of this philosophy, even its principles, if they do not even spare the first axioms of reason and desire to imbue everything—principles, method, reason itself—with a partisan spirit, then just look at what they replace it with, only to return to the principles of Wolffian philosophy. To me, Baumgarten's psychology has ever seemed a rich treasure chamber of the human soul and a commentary on it that was able to combine, in the sphere of sound understanding, the poetic intuition of a Klopstock with the calm observation and serene introspection of a Montaigne, and, finally, in the higher realms of human thought, with the acute vision of a second Leibniz—such a commentary would be a book of the human soul, a plan for a humane education, and the gateway to an encyclopedia for all the arts and letters. Such order and precision in determining the faculties of the soul, such a wealth of psychological prospects, such an all-encompassing, inexhaustible nature does the human soul possess and Baumgarten allow us to survey: is this not temptation enough for the inquirer himself to descend, in accordance with such a plan, in accordance with such prospects, to the depths of his heart, to seek new experiences, and to trace them back to those same depths? Then what rigorous fundamental concepts he will find! How finely they will be developed, taking into account every modification of every faculty of the soul! With what simplicity, order, wealth, and beauty

will the edifice of the human soul be erected, and on a single, even, firm foundation. I know no philosopher whose ability to formulate definitions of such perfect brevity and concision surpasses that of Aristotle and Baumgarten; indeed, if I had never appreciated this gift, I should have to learn to esteem it in Riedel. Many of Home's observations, which our Germans accepted as new, I long ago encountered in Baumgarten in more exact language. And much of what our modern aestheticians boast about for page after page is often expressed by Baumgarten in a single word, in a modest definition. And if you are not petty enough to be offended by his belittling term "*lower* faculties of the soul," you will discover that he is the foremost philosopher of modern times who has brought a philosophical and often poetic torch to illumine these regions of the soul.——
I consider it an honor to scatter, with conviction, grains of incense before this man's shade at a time when critics see fit to portray him as an imbecilic, unfeeling demonstrator and think it a great merit to slander his philosophy. Whoever has read even a few of our fashionable modern books will not need to ask me, as the Spartan asked the eulogist of Hercules, "But who blames him?"—for everyone blames him who does not understand him.

Let us look instead at Riedel's philosophical method. Here his first principle shall be "What everyone must think true is true!" This principle is not only not a principle but rather an outright confession that his philosophy has no principles and can tolerate none. The rule "What must please everyone is beautiful!" is not the fundamental rule of a philosophy; it implies only that the philosophy of the beautiful has no fundamental rules and that therefore there is no such thing as a philosophy of the beautiful. In his aesthetics, then, the beautiful and the ugly are two immediate feelings, two irreducible sensations. From these immediate feelings everything else supposedly follows, after the manner of the magic lantern of the Theosophists; with them one is supposed to think philosophically and at the same time so very beautifully that one may read for oneself a true rarity in Riedel's comparison of philosophers and aestheticians in the introduction to his *Theory*. With these immediate feelings one is supposed to write so beautifully and feel so fervently that one is not meant to seek truth in beauty, and no one attracts more mockery than that poor fool the thinker. That is Riedel's philosophy of taste, a product of mere feeling and founded on that excellent, supreme principle: "What cannot but be felt as beautiful is beautiful!" Help yourself, anyone who wants to!

3

In the *Letters to and on the Public*, whose content and delivery are indeed *beneath* the dignity of the public *to* and *about* whom he writes, Mr. R.

wished to expound further his idea of aesthetics, or rather, to demonstrate that he has not the slightest notion of it at all. He distinguishes three paths of aesthetics, which he is fond of calling the Aristotelian, Baumgartian, and Homean paths, where the Greek derived his laws from the work of the master; the German, the wretched and arid Baumgarten, derived his from definition; and the Briton derived his from sensation; and on none of these three paths can our fourth great originator find aesthetics. On none of them? And are all three paths—I shall not inquire whether they can be ascribed exclusively to the three men in question—mutually exclusive? When, like a second Aristotle, I analyze the work of a great artist, can I not at the same time attend, with Homean intensity, to the sensation it arouses in me and then go on to gather, with Baumgarten's precision, differentiation, and logicalness, the terms with which to formulate a definition? Is it not the same soul and the same operation of the soul that assumes a masterwork and then perceives its artistry, assumes a sensation of the beautiful that it awakens, and now analyzes that very sensation, assumes—no, does not assume but rather gathers a definition of beauty objectively from the work of art and subjectively from sensation? Is this not all a single function of a single soul? So why then mischievously separate these paths and then mischievously slander them? For without all three together an aesthetics can never come into being.

An aesthetics can certainly not come into being without the *Aristotelian* path, as I shall call it to oblige Mr. R.; and to oblige aesthetics I cry out to the Aristotles of our age: just as Aristotle analyzed his Homer and Sophocles, so you, savants of our times, analyze the artworks of your own great originals, poets and artists, artists and poets. A Winckelmann analyzes his Apollo, like Mengs his Raphael; a Hagedorn his landscape painters, like Hogarth his wavy lines and caricatures. An Addison analyzes his Milton, and Home his Shakespeare; Cesarotti his Ossian, and a better Meier our own Klopstock. A Scamozzi and Vignola analyze their buildings; a Rameau and Nichelmann their music, Noverre his dances, and Diderot painting and dramatic expression. Each man analyzes his own work of art and gathers the traces where the beautiful manifests itself; they all work for aesthetics, but each in his own field. And it is bad enough that in elaborating his whole theory of the beaux arts and belles lettres, Riedel did not think once of such fields and such labors.

So he does something better; he condemns and disparages such labors, and alas! I find myself compelled to venture into the meager details of his reasons for doing so. Thus must we often waste our time and effort by refuting an opponent, by saying a great deal so that he can say nothing at all. "This rule," says Mr. R., "the poet perhaps had in mind and yet perhaps he did not." Perhaps and yet perhaps not? If this rule truly resides in his work, if it is present, an element of the beautiful that produces an effect, then all well and good, the poet indeed had it in mind; it is part of his work. Whether he thought of it distinctly or indistinctly—what bearing does this have on my observation? The greater the poet he was, the less he vitiated himself by working with distinct, debilitating, wearying rules; and when the greatest of all was inspired by the Muse, he was conscious of no law. A Sophocles was not thinking of Aristotle's rules, but does not all of Aristotle lie within him? "The rules that the theorist finds as he turns the pages of *The Iliad*—for whom else are these rules meant?" For no one else! Not for Milton, not for Klopstock, not for Schönaich, and, should Mr. R. want to become a second Butler, not for him either! They are not meant for any genius who can open new avenues, who can take wing and fly where none have flown before—and however else this kabbalah of the mind puts it. They are meant to be not rules but rather observations; they are a philosophy that illuminates, elaborates, one that is designed for philosophers, not for poetlings, not for sovereign geniuses. Why should the fact that dismembered animals cannot multiply prevent the anatomist from dissecting any? "But such rules go into too much detail!" Do they go into detail so that they can be applied? That was not the reason why the rules were sought. Does the detail fail to furnish an ideal of the work? But there the blame lies with the artist, and this is precisely what the analyzer shows. Does the detail fail to deliver a philosophical account of beauty? But there the blame lies with the aesthetician; he has not correctly observed, abstracted, ordered. Does that resolve the matter? "How easy it is to view an author's flaws as beauties and to make them into rules." Admittedly, it is easy, very easy, and without citing, with all my respect for the Swiss, the truly philosophical Breitinger—and, moreover, in an example where he is more justified than Riedel—I ask only, What follows from this error into which we all too easily fall? That because he sees flaws as beauties the philosopher neglects his eyes? Or that he uses them better? That in his exactitude he is on his way to becoming a second Aristotle? Oh, if only Riedel had become one in his *Theory of the Beaux Arts*; what a different book we would have!

Such a forthright judge of others do I have before me, and against Baumgarten he is more than forthright; he is malicious. Yet Riedel, who followed Baumgarten in all the errors of his method, without possessing a single one of his virtues, ought to have been the very last person to lay hands on Baumgarten. "As if," he says, "beauty admitted of definition like truth!" To which I reply: as if it were absurd to claim this? As if the beauty that I have felt, whose phenomena I analyze both in the object itself and in my sensation, could not approach to the distinctness of truth? As if it were not the purpose of aesthetics to render beauty distinct? As if aesthetics should not therefore seek properly to define beauty, this phenomenon of truth? Without fear of uttering an absurdity, I think that it should! "As if an ode were to be treated like a *sorites* and an epic poem like a disputation!" Not by the odist and epic poet, that much is certain. The philosopher, however, does not treat them like a disputation when he "infers rules through a series of irrefutable deductions from the concepts he has posited;" he deserves no ridicule, then, for he infers propositions through which we know beauty. "But where is the general concept of beauty? Beauty is an αρριτον that is perceived rather than taught." Mr. R.'s objection is undigested drivel. Viewed as sensation, beauty is indeed an αρριτον: in the moment of the confused, sweet feeling, of the gentle intoxication it is inexpressible. It is inexpressible if what we wish to determine precisely is how this sensation is connected so powerfully to this object. But the idea that this inexpressible moment should not be illuminated by another person, one who wishes to think rather than to feel; that the inexpressible impression of an object on the senses and the fancy should not be developed to a certain degree; that beauty and the underlying causes of pleasure should not be sought out in an object, such as a building, a poem, a painting—whom will the doubter persuade of this? Only one who has not yet made or read an analysis of a beautiful work of art. But "from arbitrary concepts there follow only arbitrary rules;" so from unarbitrary concepts abstracted from essential components of beauty there must follow true propositions, no? "But perhaps these definitions are then formulated too slavishly and merely abstracted from existing works of art?" Indeed! Then we would have an aesthetics concerned only with all the works of art that already exist; and do we have such an aesthetics? Have we philosophically generalized even the smallest part of it? And if the aesthetics that we already possess were formed so slavishly, were so imperfect, so indeterminate, so repetitive, so misapplied, and had passed into law in all the wrong places—then of course it deserves correction, perfection; but mockery? The whole method deserves nothing but mockery? All its accomplishments merit nothing but mockery? Methinks the Muse of the philosophy of the beautiful rewards scoffers only with contempt.

I do not see how the *Homean* manner of thinking is opposed to the others. Home, too, analyzed works of art, such as his Shakespeare and Ossian; Home, too, began his deductions from a posited concept, just as Baumgarten did. And without combining all three paths, which in reality are but a single path, no aesthetics is truly possible. Aesthetics chooses the method of philosophy, that is, rigorous analysis; it examines as many products of beauty of every kind as it can, attends to the whole, undivided impression; it returns from the depth of this impression to the object itself; it observes its parts both individually and working in harmony; it does not compromise on a merely beautiful half-understood idea; it brings the sum of the ideas rendered distinct under general concepts, and these in turn under their own general concepts; finally, perhaps, there is a general concept in which the universe of all beauty in both arts and letters is reflected. O Aesthetics! The most fruitful, the most beautiful, and in many cases the newest of the abstract sciences, in all the arts of beauty geniuses and artists, philosophers and poets have strewn flowers at your feet—in which cavern of the Muses is sleeping the young man of my philosophical nation who shall bring you to completion! Behold! He will build, and he will immortalize himself by winning the wreath of your perfection; meanwhile I shall burrow beneath Riedelian rubble to clear his way!

4

To circumvent at once the frivolous objections raised against aesthetics as a whole and which spring from a deficient grasp of the concept, I shall now move on to the philosopher who would be too insignificant if he had merely invented the name of aesthetics and not also revolved in his mind its scientific framework. Though Baumgarten is ordinarily an aesthetician most scrupulous in his choice of words, the introduction to his *Aesthetica* shall present us with the best opportunity to demonstrate the difference between a philosophy *of* taste and a philosophy derived *from* taste.

He calls his work a *Theory of the Beaux Arts and Belles Lettres*; and without doubt this is the most appropriate name, one to which, as Mendelssohn and Sulzer have shown, he ought by and large to have been more faithful. He calls it *aesthetics*, the *science of the feeling of the beautiful* or, in the language of Wolff, of *sensuous cognition*; an even more apt expression! Accordingly, it is a philosophy that must possess all the attributes of science and of inquiry, analysis, proofs, and method. But he also calls his aesthetics *the art of thinking beautifully*, and that is quite a different matter: a "je ne sais quoi" of skill and practical instruction in how to apply the powers of genius and taste, or, in his terminology, in how to employ the faculty of sensuous cognition beautifully; and that is precisely what aesthetics, in its primary sense, is not.

Let us take as the object of investigation the powers of our soul to feel the beautiful and the products of beauty they have brought forth: behold a great philosophy, a theory of the feeling of the senses, a logic of the imagination and of poetry, an investigator of wit and discernment, of sensuous judgment and memory; an analyzer of the beautiful wherever it is found, whether in arts and letters, in bodies and souls—this is aesthetics and, if you will, the philosophy *of taste*. The *art of taste* has beauty itself for its object and, ill matched with aesthetics, even wants to think beautifully, judge beautifully, infer beautifully, instead of merely making correct inferences, sharp distinctions, thinking truthfully. The one is *ars pulcre cogitandi*, the other *scientia de pulcro et pulcris philosophice cogitans*;

the one can educate only connoisseurs of taste, whereas the other shall educate philosophers of taste. Mixing both concepts together, therefore, naturally results in a monstrosity of aesthetics, and if Meier adds to his definition that it also "improves" sensuous cognition, then we know even less.

I shall continue to speak in Baumgarten's terminology. As is known, he distinguishes between a natural and an artificial aesthetics, which, though they seem to differ from each other only by degree, are perhaps essentially distinct, even if they presuppose each other. That natural ability to perceive the beautiful, that genius which through practice has become second nature—how does it operate? It does so within the bounds of the habitual, in confused ideas that are yet all the more vivid; in short, as a facility of the beautiful. Here neither poet nor any other blazing genius is conscious of the rules, of the subsidiary concepts of the beautiful, or of effortful reflection; at work is his imagination, his fiery glance that takes in the whole, a thousand powers that rise up within him in unison—and how unfortunate when a rule disturbs him! A natural aesthetics of this kind can neither be furnished by rules nor be replaced, and to mix together two such infinitely dissimilar things betrays a complete lack of understanding.

Artificial aesthetics, or the *science* of the beautiful, *presupposes* the former, but it does not *continue* along the same path at all; indeed, its business is the very opposite. It dissolves, as far as it is able to do so, precisely that which was habitual, that which was beautiful nature, and, as it were, destroys it in the same moment. It is precisely that beautiful confusion—which, if it is not the mother, is at least the inseparable companion of all pleasure—that artificial aesthetics dissolves and seeks to illuminate with distinct ideas: truth takes the place of beauty. It is no longer the body, the thought, the work of art, that produces its effect in confused intuition; dissolved into the elements of beauty, it shall now appear as truth: that which had previously affected me confusedly should now be uttered distinctly—how different are these two ends of the human mind! They cancel each other out almost in the moment of their energy.

So let us not confuse two quite different things so that we criticize one kind of aesthetics from the point of view of the other. If the one aesthetics is sensuous judgment, a nature trained to discern perfection and imperfection in objects of beauty, to enjoy beauty sensuously and hence vividly and hence penetratingly and hence delightedly, then it always remains *sensuous* judgment, confused sensation, and indeed should remain so. Souls of this kind we call geniuses, beautiful souls, men of taste, according to the degree to which they possess this power. Their aesthetics is Nature; it is conviction in matters of beauty. But what about the other type, the properly scientific aesthetics? It fixes its attention on the previous sensation, tears parts from parts, abstracts parts from the whole, which is no longer a beautiful whole; in that moment it is a rent and mutilated beauty. Then it goes through the individual parts, reflects, places them all side by side to restore to itself the previous impression, and compares. The more exactly it reflects, the more sharply it compares, the more distinct does the concept of beauty become; and thus a distinct concept of beauty is no longer a contradiction in terms but simply the complete opposite of the confused sensation of beauty. And thus many empty criticisms that have been hurled in the direction of aesthetics are rendered null and void.

I wish to follow Baumgarten even in these criticisms. Since he did not observe the exact distinction that I assumed from the outset, some of his answers must seem more wearisome than will seem necessary to us. "Is, for instance, aesthetics beneath the dignity, beneath the scope of the philosopher?" Not at all! Indeed, it is the most rigorous philosophy concerned with a worthy and very significant conspectus of the human soul and of the imitations of Nature; it is even a part, a significant part of anthropology, of the knowledge of humankind. I have no need, then, of Baumgarten's polite excuses to the effect that "the philosopher is after all a man who can lose face;" I see in him nothing but the worthy philosopher of humanity. "But confusion is the mother of error." I shall strike out all three of Baumgarten's replies, which rest on a muddled conception of aesthetics. Aesthetics neither loves confused ideas, whether as *conditio sine qua non* or as the dawning of truth, nor seeks to guard against errors—that is the work of more derivative theories; nor does it wish to improve and lift confusion so that in the future beauty may be felt no longer confusedly but distinctly, which would be a contradiction in terms. Aesthetics does none of these things! And how indeed would the last of these be possible without disadvantage to human pleasure? Instead, my brief reply is this: aesthetics as such does not love confused concepts at all; it takes them as its object precisely in order to render them distinct; one cannot therefore also say: "Distinct cognition is better!" for how indeterminate and, from the point of view of humanity, how wrong would that be? And how little it would apply to aesthetics, which loves precisely this better, distinct cognition. There is no more truth in the reproach that "if the analogue of reason is developed, it may bring disadvantage to reason itself," for here the former is not developed and the latter not neglected, as we thought in our confusion: the former is but the object on which the latter practices. An even weaker objection against aesthetics is that it is not science but art, that the aesthetician is born and not made; this is an obvious misunderstanding of the primary concept. Our aesthetics is a science and aspires in no way to cultivate men of genius and taste; it aims only to cultivate philosophers, if aesthetics is taken in the correct sense and is not, as Meier has it, a science that—God help us!—writes beautifully and confusedly what others have said distinctly; for as such it certainly forfeits purpose, dignity, and exactitude.

My more exact determination of the concept has rescued aesthetics from criticism and—just as useful!—must strip it of false uses and wilting laurels. No one shall now be able to claim of aesthetics that it "aims to accommodate scientific knowledge to the common power of comprehension," for it desires in no way to be a whoremongerer of philosophical truths for the dear *captus*, dressed in God knows what false frippery. There is nothing that aesthetics could less wish to be; as philosophy, rigorous, exact philosophy, it has no aim but scientific knowledge without yielding to the common power of comprehension. No one shall claim of aesthetics "that it affords an improvement in cognition beyond the boundaries of the distinct," since it is still rather uncertain whether logic *improves* the so-called higher faculties, and it is at least not the primary aim of aesthetics to provide a new beautiful nature or a feeling that we did not have before. It acquaints us with faculties of the soul with which logic did not acquaint us. True, in individual theories its observations may subsequently give rise to practical rules of thumb, but was that its chief work? Still less does aesthetics lay claim to the laurel crown because "it gives us an advantage over others in carrying out our daily business," for what does it mean to be better than others in attending to one's affairs? How great a range of phenomena does a philosophical knowledge of the beautiful, a psychological elaboration of several faculties of the soul encompass? Finally, least plausible of all are Meier's tautologies to the effect that aesthetics "improves the lower faculties of the soul," especially that it "improves the greater part of human society," "improves taste," "provides the serious sciences with beautiful material," and "promotes the dissemination of the truths native to all branches of learning," and so on— nothing but practical uses that according to Meier's language upset the horizon of aesthetics exceedingly. Serving these ends, aesthetics becomes what, in large part, it already is in Mr. Meier's hands: one part is regurgitated logic and the other a false aesthetic splendor of metaphorical names, similes, examples, and pet maxims; and under this title, what have we Germans gained with our newly coined term *aesthetics*?

5

We have determined, then, the concept of aesthetics, and since I was writing about the concept of a science, I inevitably had to accommodate myself to somewhat petty and frosty distinctions, criticisms, and applications. Now we shall determine the principle or—in the words of Mr. Riedel—the fundamental feeling of the beautiful somewhat more precisely; and here more than ever I am compelled to beg the reader's pardon for availing myself of brief but more convenient scholastic expressions. When one sees the contradictions in which the author of the *Theory* and the *Letters on the Public* has ensnared himself with his claims about the fundamental faculty of the beautiful and the way in which it differs in the judgment of different persons, one will prefer to choose a somewhat thorny yet safer path in order to cut through the middle of such contradictions, rather than hobble along on the wrong path with fine words.

Are all men born with a capacity to perceive the beautiful? In a broad sense, yes! For they are all capable of sensuous representations. We are, so to speak, brutish spirits; our sensuous powers seem, if I may put it this way, to occupy a greater area of our soul than do the few higher faculties; they develop earlier; they operate with greater intensity; they belong perhaps more to the visible determination of our existence than do the others; since here we cannot yet bear fruit, they are the flowers of our perfection. The whole ground of our soul consists of obscure ideas, the most vivid and most numerous ideas, the throng from which the soul prepares its more refined ones; these obscure ideas are the most powerful mainsprings of our life, make the greatest contribution to our happiness and unhappiness. If we imagine the integral parts of the human soul in physical terms, it possesses, if I may be permitted to express myself in this way, a greater mass of powers specific to a sensuous being than to a pure spirit: the soul has therefore been endowed with a human body; it is a human being.

As a human being it has developed, in accordance with its mass of internal powers and within the bounds of its existence, a number of organs with which to perceive surrounding objects and, as it were, to intromit them for its own enjoyment. Even the number of these organs and the vast wealth of impressions flowing into them demonstrate, as it were, how great the mass of the sensuous is within the human soul. We are too little acquainted with the animals; their species are too multifarious and our philosophical knowledge of them too human for us to fathom how far they diverge from us in the ratio of these sensuous powers. And for our purposes the question is of little consequence.

If no two human souls are wholly alike, then perhaps in their natures, too, there may be an infinitely varied and modified combination of powers, all of which can yet possess an equal degree of reality as an aggregate. This internal diversity would then be subsequently expressed through the body—which develops in harmony with the soul—and over an individual's lifetime; for with this person the body rules over the soul, with that one the soul over the body, with one person *this* sense is dominant, with another *that* faculty. So the infinite combinations and inner diversity that Creation has inscribed in the structure of all living beings is possible in aesthetic nature also.

Let us start somewhere in the middle and return to the time when man first became a phenomenon of our world, when he emerged from a state of having been merely a thinking and perceiving vegetable and began to develop into an animal. Still he appears to be endowed with no sentiment other than the obscure idea of his ego, so obscure that only a vegetable can feel it. Yet in this idea the concepts of the entire universe lie contained; from it, all of man's ideas evolve; all sentiments sprout forth from this vegetal feeling, just as in visible Nature the seed carries within it the tree and every leaf is an image of the whole.

Now the embryo has grown into an infant who still experiences everything within himself; even that which he feels outside him lies in his interior. With every sensation he is roused as if from a profound dream to be reminded, as through a violent impetus, more vividly of an idea that his situation in the universe now occasions in him. Thus the infant's powers develop by suffering external influences; but the internal activity of development is his goal, his inward, obscure pleasure, and a constant perfection his essence.

With repeated, identical sensations the infant forms his first judgment: that they are the *same* sensation. This judgment is obscure and must be so, for it shall endure for a lifetime and remain a permanent basis in the soul. It must therefore have the strength and consistency, as it were, of an inner feeling; and so it is preserved as sensation. In the manner of its origin it was already a judgment, a result of combining several concepts; but because the judgment emerged through habit, and the habit of immediately applying that judgment preserved it, the form of its origin grew obscure and only the content remained; it became sensation. In this way the soul of the infant develops; the recurring images produce an abundance of such comparisons and judgments, and thus do we secure the feeling that there is *truth outside us.*

When we reflect on how many secret connections and distinctions, judgments and inferences an infant must make in order to store within himself the first ideas of external bodies, ideas of *figure, form, magnitude, distance,* we cannot help but be amazed. The infant human soul has accomplished and developed, erred and found more than has the philosopher in an entire lifetime of abstractions. But if we take a different view and observe how felicitous it is that the effortful form of all these judgments and inferences has retreated into the gloom of the first dawn; how felicitous it is that the nature of the mechanism lingered in the shadows of oblivion and only the effect of the activity, the product of the operation remains—remains as simple sensation, yet is all the more vivid, strong, unweakened, immediate—then who cannot fail to feel even greater astonishment? How much wisdom might we reckon in this obscure mechanism of the soul? How monstrous and feeble would be the soul that acted distinctly here! And how much in the entire constitution of the soul might be explained by these so very complex operations taking place in the dream-filled dawn of our lives! The sum of all these sensations becomes the basis of all objective certainty and the first visible index of our soul's wealth of ideas.

The soul continues to develop. Since its storehouse of sensuous impressions, as we shall call it, already contains the ideas of the one and the more-than-one, and these are imprinted on it; since the concept of order and sensuous truth is already obscurely present in the soul, what if, during its unceasing activity of obtaining, comparing, and ordering ideas, the soul glimpses, glimpses intuitively, in this or that thing the ground of a third? Behold: that is the root of the concept of the *good*, evidently formed by the most complex mode of reasoning. It teaches an individual to distinguish *this* and *that*, what pleasure this or that concordance gave *him*, gave him more than once; and in this way it teaches him to recognize his *good*; and in this way he gets the concepts of *order, conformity, perfection*, and also, since beauty is nothing but sensuous perfection, the concept of *beauty*. All these ideas are developments of our internal faculty of thought in the earliest stage of our existence, but because the form of their development is obscure, they remain, as sensations, lying on the ground of our soul and cleave so tightly to our ego that we hold them to be innate feelings. This belief alters nothing in practice; we can always build on these ideas as if they were innate feelings; they always remain the trunk of our concepts: strong, powerful, succinct, secure, of the innermost certainty and conviction, as if they were fundamental faculties. But it is a different matter altogether, is it not, if the analyzing philosopher meant to view them in this way simply because their origin is obscure and confused? As if it were not his foremost duty to bring light and order to this confusion?

Our childhood is an obscure dream of ideas such as can only ever follow the vegetal feeling; yet in this obscure dream the soul operates with all its powers. Whatever it apprehends it keenly absorbs to the point of completely incorporating it into its ego, rendering it into the lifeblood of its faculty; gradually the soul raises itself from its slumber, and all its life it will carry around these dream ideas apprehended at an early age, will use them all, and, in a manner of speaking, be constituted of them. But will the soul recall, distinctly recall, its origin? How could it? Now and again a desultory idea may sensuously occur to it, but only a late one, from the last moments of this dawn; and this image that the soul recollects, consciously or unconsciously, from its childhood will convulse it to its core; the soul will recoil as before an abyss or as if it had seen its double, so to speak. But all such images are only tiny individual fragments, which perhaps not all souls possess, at least not in all ages of life; which

appear only rarely and when we are immersed most deeply within ourselves; which are chased away and made impossible by nothing more than
lighthearted distractions; which might explain an astonishing amount
about the human soul that still awaits explanation—it is only the remnants of these images that fleetingly rear up before us like sleep on tear-
stained eyelids and quickly leave us again. That long, true, powerful, first
dream is lost to us and had to be lost! Only a god and the genius of my
childhood—if he could peer into my soul—know this dream!

Our soul continues to stir, and as it does so our various faculties seem
to separate from one another. If the soul perceives that its present state is
no longer identical with its previous one, if it grows used to distinguishing the present from the previous sensation that remained behind as
residue, then behold: the soul leaves the state in which everything was to
it mere sensation; it gets accustomed to recognizing one thing before another by virtue of its "inner clarity;" it finds itself on the obscure path
leading toward *fancy* and *memory*. How often must it glide along this
path! How much practice is necessary to accustom the mind's eye to the
differences, degrees, and nuances of clarity possessed by the past and present! A child will still frequently confuse this distinction, for only through
much practice does he achieve certainty; but this certainty lasts forever,
and with that the first mighty, eternal forms of memory and fancy have
emerged. The closer both still cling to their mother, sensation, the more
obscure yet stronger they are. A child's first fancies become fiery, eternal
images; they lend his entire soul form and color, and the philosopher who
knew and could survey the blazing, indelible words in which these fancies
were written would glimpse therein the first letters spelling out the infant's
whole manner of thinking. Certain waking dreams that we experience in
later life, when the soul is not yet spent—obscure recollections, as if we
had already seen, experienced, and enjoyed the novel, rare, beautiful, or
surprising qualities of a particular place, person, area, beauty, and so
forth—are without doubt the patchwork of these earliest fancies. Such
obscure ideas lie within us in their thousands; they constitute what is rare,
peculiar, and often singular in our concepts and forms of beauty and pleasure; they often inspire aversion and inclination in us, without our knowledge or desire; they rise up in us, as mainsprings waking from a long slumber and, with sympathy and as it were recollection, make us suddenly love
this person and hate that one; they often bristle against truth, a later acquisition, and brighter yet feebler conviction, against reason and will and
habit; they are the obscure ground within us that all too often modifies
and shades the images and colors of our soul that are later laid down on
it. Sulzer has explained several paradoxes from this profundity of the
mind; perhaps with these few observations I have helped to shine some
rays of sunshine into this darkness and at least shall rouse another psy-

chologist to let in yet more light. Often a child cannot distinguish between dreams and waking images; he dreams while he is awake and often assumes a mere dream to have actually happened; this sleep permeated with images continues; the soul is still, as it were, entirely fancy, which clings closely to sensation.

These grow increasingly separate from each other the more *discernment* and its pendant, *wit*, develop; *wit* and *discernment* are the forerunners and preludes of *judgment*; and *judgment* is formed just as sensuously as its precursors. The form it assumed as it developed is obliterated; only the finished judgment remains and becomes ability, habit, second nature. And if now our soul has practiced long enough to pass judgment on the perfection and imperfection of things; if judgment has become as familiar, as evident, as vivid as a sensation, then behold: *taste* has emerged, the "habitual ability to judge the sensuous perfection and imperfection of things as swiftly as if one perceived them immediately." How lengthy, then, was the process whereby our powers were unfolded and combined, misapplied and practiced, whereby that which our sentimental philosophers call the fundamental feeling of the beautiful first *evolved*!

6

A false principle necessarily results in dubious, contradictory conclusions, and Mr. R. has therefore fallen prey to opinions that are so diametrically opposed to one another that I do not know how one man who aspires to be a philosopher can hold both at the same time; how he can devise a theory in which taste is paraded as an innate fundamental faculty, as universal, as certain, as sufficient as human nature itself; and how the same man can write letters in which taste is denied all universal certainty and beauty all objective rules, in which he can claim that since beauty must be merely felt, there exist no external, certain grounds for determining it, that taste is as varied as human sensibility, and hence two downright contradictory judgments about beauty and ugliness can be true at the same time. Oh, for a philosopher with determinate principles and consistent conclusions! I would like to have seen the look on Mendelssohn's face when this polygraph, who does not himself know what he is writing, appeared before him, adopting the most self-important attitude, and wickedly demonstrated to him in a long, wearisome letter that beauty—must be felt. As if Mendelssohn were the foolish demonstrator and Baumgarten another who lacked feeling, who needed to have such an assertion proven to him and in just such a fashion.

Is the feeling of beauty inborn in us? Yes, for all I care! But only as aesthetic nature, which has the capacities and organs to perceive sensuous perfection; which delights in developing these capacities, in using these organs, and in enriching itself with ideas of this kind. Everything lies within this feeling, but as in a seed waiting to germinate, as in a box containing another capacity, like a smaller box; but everything evolves from a single fundamental faculty of the soul to obtain ideas and in doing so, through this unfolding of its activity, to feel itself become ever more perfect and to take pleasure in doing so. How beautiful the human soul thereby becomes! Unity in its foundation, thousandfold diversity in its development, perfection in the totality! Not a trace of the three ready-made fundamental feelings prepared by Nature; everything is formed from a single one and raised to the most manifold perfection.

And what might these three fundamental feelings enable us to conceive in the way of determinate ideas? "The sensus communis shall teach each person as much truth as he requires in order to live." As much? How much is "as much?" Where is the *non plus ultra*? And why do its supporting columns stand precisely where they are and nowhere else? Do I not see that a nation possesses its sensus communis, "the swift feeling of apprehension," merely in proportion to the stage of its development, merely within its own world? Is the sensus communis of the Greenlander and the Hottentot the same as ours with respect to its objects and application? And is the sensus communis of the yeoman the same as the scholar's? Cannot whole compartments of the soul remain empty when they are not being used and whole capacities stay sleeping if they are not roused? Does our sensus communis possess truths that it has not learned, does it possess more truths than it has had opportunity to learn? Does it possess a single truth more? No? And so where is the inner feeling of the soul that teaches each person as much truth as he requires? I cannot find it within me. Instead I find an ever-active power to acquire knowledge; and where this power has been able to operate, where I have had opportunity to gather a number of concepts, to form judgments, to make inferences—there too is my sensus communis: it errs where these judgments erred; it infers erroneously where the inferences on which it built were drawn erroneously; it is even lacking where this storehouse of habitual judgments and inferences is lacking—I therefore see no inner, immediate, universal, infallible teacher of truth. I see an ability to apply the powers of cognition according to the degree that they have been developed.

Is it any different with the conscience? Where is the inner feeling of the soul that is supposed to be grounded in our moral judgment? Of course, the highest principle of moral judgment is as sacred, as determinate, and as certain as reason is reason; but the formation of this judgment, its greater or lesser applicability to this or that case, the stronger or weaker recollection of this or that ground of morality—does this not modify the conscience in as many different ways as there are moral subjects? Where is now the inner, immediate teacher of Nature who amounts to nothing more than an ability to act in accordance with moral principles? These principles may cloak and wrap themselves in layers of individual impressions and sensations, but they nonetheless always remain principles, with the difference that one acts in conformity with them as if they were immediate sensations. They are formed as moral judgments; only when the form of the judgment grew obscure did they become analogous to an immediate feeling through facility and force of habit. That is what conscience is, and there is no other way of settling the dispute about its originality, universality, diversity, and so on, than by attending to the roots of its development and growth.

This is even more apparent with taste. To assume a complete identity, or even a uniformity or similarity, of taste runs counter to appearances, according to which men show the greatest variety in their judgments about beauty. How can this diversity of sentiment, which Mr. R. himself concedes and exaggerates with a multitude of doubts, be explained by his fundamental feelings without abolishing all objective certainty, without abolishing all conviction, rules, and philosophy, without taste becoming the most idiosyncratic, constantly self-contradicting fool? It cannot be done! And is any philosophy still possible in that instance? But if we look to experience and Nature, then it turns out that the contradiction is not so glaring, everything can be accounted for, and I see the ground and order of everything. If taste is nothing but judgment about certain classes of objects, then it is formed as judgment; taste is completely lacking in matters where this judgment could not be formed; taste errs completely in matters where this judgment was wrongly formed; it is crude or weak, strong or refined, depending on that which guided the judgment. Taste is therefore not a fundamental faculty, a universal fundamental faculty of the soul; it is a habitual application of our judgment to objects of beauty. Let us trace its genesis.

As I demonstrated earlier, all human beings possess an aesthetic nature to a greater or lesser degree. This initial assumption implies that when the soul's sensuous powers are first unfolded within this or that relation, this power will also achieve superiority over that power, one will also overshadow another, so that the soul will also tend to develop in one particular direction. If this configuration between evolving mental powers becomes fixed, if the soul acquires the habit of operating according to and within this arrangement, then it is certain that it will be more sensitive to one sphere than to another. And thus one reason for the infinite diversity of judgments about grace and beauty lies already in the diverse development of diverse faculties of the soul in diverse relations to one another.

There are base natures for whom the coarser senses alone are a source of pleasure because these have attained superiority over the others and become, as it were, the dominant feeling; these are natures, then, for whom touch is their finest philosopher and taste the most delightful music. But there are also higher natures who can possess their more refined senses in as much variety as modifications and permutations of their number and qualities allow. A soul made entirely for music can be, as it were, quite heterogeneous to a genius made entirely for the visual arts: the one is nothing but eye, the other nothing but ear; one lives only to see beauty, the other only to hear melody. They are thus creatures belonging to quite distinct species; how could they inwardly understand each other? Would it not be a splendid contest to hear both of them, feeling and existing exclusively in their principal sense, philosophize about grace and beauty? To the one, painting would seem too cold, too superficial, not penetrating enough, too unmelodic, too far removed from tones; to the other, music would appear too fleeting, too confused, too indistinct, too remote from the image that can be apprehended in an eternal glance. Tone and color, eye and ear—who can commensurate them? And where creatures lack a common organ of sensation, as it were, who can unite them? But does this disunity abolish the laws of beauty and grace as such? Can anyone prove that there are no certain rules whatsoever relating to these qualities in the objects themselves? Can anyone prove that everything in Nature is a chaos of individual, disharmonious temperaments that cannot be accorded? What a conclusion to draw! As if the acoustician and the optician do not inwardly enjoy their own world of feeling, so to speak, and if both were also philosophers, each could not analyze his dominant sense in an eminently philosophical and truthful fashion. And precisely the more inward and differentiated the feelings, and the more true and universal are the rules of the beautiful deduced in both arts, the more they will meet at the rear and, ultimately, like the colors of the sunbeam, flow together and form a unity, which one may call beauty, grace, or whatnot. If you wish to see my example verified, then slacken the string somewhat, seek those specimens in Nature who are born exclusively for one art or the other, and listen to their judgment.

The sensibility of human nature is not exactly identical in every region of the earth. A different tissue into which the strings of sensation are woven; a different world of objects and sounds that initially rouse one dormant string or another by setting it in motion; different powers that tune one string or another to a different pitch, thereby setting its tone forever, so to speak—in short, there is a quite different arrangement of our faculty of perception, and yet it still lies in the hands of Nature. How much can she vary a human being? After the initial experience of pleasure and its habitual recurrence, the organ and fancy acquire impetus and direction; the first impressions in the soft wax of our infant soul furnish our judgment with color and form. Imagine two men standing side by side with the same natural disposition; since childhood, the eye of one has been cultivated with Chinese beauties, the eye of the other with Greek beauties; one has attuned his ear to African ape music, the other to the sweet melodies of Italy—what two very different people! Will one not cover his ears when he hears the other's music? Will one not avert his eyes from the beauty prized by the other? Can they ever be reconciled in their taste if their characters are already fully formed and their soul has already closed like a flower at night? No! But is Nature to blame for this? Nature, in whom there lies no certainty regarding what is beautiful; Nature, who scatters a thousand different seeds of a thousand different fundamental tastes? I think not! We shall all still find beautiful the song of the nightingale and the unadorned charms of Nature; if this or that individual diverges in his taste, the ground for this divergence will still be discoverable; notwithstanding all aberrations and idiosyncrasies, therefore, natural rules of the beautiful will still stand firm, even if they were misapplied in the most unfortunate manner; beauty and grace, then, are not yet vague and empty words. As soon as an instance of variant taste can be explained, the principal rule is redefined and consolidated through that very variation.

Nations, centuries, epochs, men—not all attain the same degree of aesthetic development, and ultimately this fact sets the seal on the diversity of their taste. Does the wild, fiery nature of peoples, of times when children tear out their hair standing around the bed of their dying father; where a mother bares her bosom and swears an oath to her son, by the breasts that suckled him; where a friend scatters his shorn hair upon the corpse of his companion, carries him on his shoulders to the funeral pyre, gathers his ashes and puts them in an urn, which he visits often to wet with his tears; where widows, with disheveled hair tear their faces with their nails when Death has robbed them of their husbands; where the chieftains of a tribe scrape their bowed heads in the dust in public displays of grief, in a fit of pain beat their breast and rip their clothes; where a father holds his newborn son in his arms, raises him heavenward, and prays to the gods on his behalf; where the first action of a child who had left his parents and who after a long absence sees them once more is to embrace their knees and, thus prostrated, to await their blessing; where the feasts are sacrifices that begin and end with libations to the gods; where the people speaks to its rulers and the rulers hear the voice of the people and answer it; where we see a person before the altar with a fillet tied about his brow and a priestess, extending her arms over him, calling to heaven and performing the sacred rites; where Pythians, foaming at the mouth, impelled by the presence of a god, sit on their tripod with wild, crazed eyes and fill the rocky cave with their prophetic howling; where the bloodthirsty gods cannot be appeased, except by the spilling of human blood; where Bacchantic women armed with thyrsus staffs stray through the grove and instill terror and horror into the uninitiated who encounters them; where other women shamelessly bare themselves and throw themselves into the arms of the first man who offers himself to them, and so on. Ages, manners, and peoples such as these—though they have the same natural disposition, do they possess the same measure of cultivation, the same judgment of taste as our soft and artificial world of polished nations? The music of a rude and warlike people which inspired enthusiasm and frenzy, which summoned them to battle and to death, which roused dithyrambs and the songs of Tyrtaeus—is this music the same as the soft and sensual pleasure of Lydian flutes, which merely sighs and coos, which warms its listeners with dreams of love and wine and melts the troubled heart at the breast of Phryne? Or is it even the same as our battlefield ruled by artificial confusion and harmonically frigid tactics among the tones? The Greek, the Gothic, the Moorish taste in architecture and sculpture, in mythology and poetry—is it the same? And is this taste not to be explained by the times, manners, and peoples? And does it not in each case have a first principle that has just not been understood well enough, just not felt with the same intensity, just not applied in the right proportion? And does not even this Proteus of taste, which transforms itself under every new sky, in every foreign clime wherein it draws breath, does not this *diversity of taste* itself prove, by the causes of its transformation, that beauty is one, just like perfection, just like truth?

There is thus an ideal of beauty for every art, for every branch of letters, for good taste in general; and it can be found in all peoples and ages and subjects and productions. Admittedly, it is difficult to find. In some ages it is cloaked with a mist whose tendrils twist into different shapes, but in others the fog hangs cold and heavy at its feet while the head of this object of devotion gleams in the clear, bright sky. Admittedly, there are peoples who introduce their national character into their representation of the ideal and stamp its image with their own individual features; but it is also possible to wean oneself from this idiosyncrasy that is both inherited and acquired, to extricate oneself from the irregularities of excessive singularity and ultimately, unguided by the taste of a particular nation or age or individual, to savor the beautiful wherever it manifests itself, in all ages and in all peoples and in all arts and in all varieties of taste, to taste and experience it in its purity, freed everywhere from all foreign elements. Happy he who savors it thus! He has been initiated into the mysteries of all the Muses and of all ages and of all memories and of all works; the sphere of his taste is infinite, like the history of humanity; its circumference touches all centuries and productions, and he and beauty stand in the center. That is he, and any other who is attached only to local and national beauties or even only to the excellencies of his club, who has only his household gods, his Klotz, and whose visit he honors as if it were

Apollo dropping by is a philosopher of cabals. But the idols of his public fall, and guild philosopher of a single day—where are you now?

7

Mr. Riedel has called his theory "an extract of the works of various writers," and that is an ample description of what it is; but an epitomator who has no desire to think for himself must possess certain cardinal virtues that I wish Mr. R. had not been wanting: *succinctness; a simple and orderly arrangement; finally, an acquaintance with those who have labored before him*. Mr. R. has none of these.

Not succinctness. Often, after he has verbosely and repetitively assumed so many facts, observations, and definitions of others, he finally introduces his own definition, which is worse than every preceding trifle. In nothing is Mr. R. more hapless than in his attempts at definition, and with the most exhaustively studied topics at that; wherever he turns up the most data—for instance, in his investigation of beauty, of grandeur, of the sublime, and so on—he is at his most confused and indeterminate. And what use is a philosophy, an academic textbook, or a theory of the fine arts in which I cannot find a single determinate concept? It is a disgrace to philosophy, a corrupter of the youth who are meant to model themselves thereafter; it represents the degeneracy of the century.

Fluency and lightness in the arrangement of the extracts is something I miss even more. Each section is a heap of rubble, thrown together as the pieces came to hand and where I am obliged constantly to climb up and down, as over an old wall in some enchanted castle. And it is no different with the arrangement of the sections and with the book as a whole. With the analysis of such abstract materials as those that are to be theoretically treated here, I lose everything when I lose the thread of the argument, which should lead me ever onward along a path, take me ever closer to the goal, ever deeper into the idea. Even with a difficult subject matter, the author is able to carry me along; the nearer the goal and the harder the Olympic runners work to reach it, the more joyfully one hastens toward the idea, which, shedding its vestments, appears ever more naked before us. But I find none of this in Riedel; I see no thread, no argument, no progressive development, none of the things that make Socratic dialogues, Shaftesbury's and Harris's inquiries, and Lessing's essays on the fable and on painting so diverting, so unwearying. If I must do nothing but climb up and down, go forth and return, wrap up and unwrap—who can endure the infernal labors of Sisyphus and the Danaides, condemned to mockery with bottomless barrels that always draw water yet always remain empty!

Finally, an epitomator ought at least to know the foremost writers whom he should turn to his account. Leaving aside the English, French, and Italians, the learned R. is not even acquainted with the leading German writer on aesthetics; and he is ignorant not only of this man's several treatises published by the Academy but also of his major work. I am speaking of Sulzer's theory of sensations, which Riedel, without in the least penetrating into this author's excellent plan for an aesthetics, cites only once, in the wrong place, among a throng of other writers (whom he has no more read than he has Sulzer), and only very carelessly. How disgraceful it is in a theory of the belles lettres to disregard a Sulzer and instead show more familiarity with the writings of Messrs. Klotz and Dusch, whose contributions to aesthetics are not so very great indeed.

II

1

Do we have a general term in German to describe the quality of all sensible objects by means of which they cause delight? I do not know. Neither our language nor any other was devised by a philosopher, who might have ordered the ethereal nature of abstract concepts into words by beginning from the top and working his way down, so to speak. The inventors of names started from below and moved upward: they observed and named each object individually; we must therefore climb after them, then gather, then review what we have found.

Objects of *sight* are the clearest, the most distinct: they stand before us; they are discrete and ranged alongside one another; they remain our objects for as long we desire them to. Since they are thus the easiest, the clearest, or however else you might care to put it, to cognize; since their parts are more susceptible to decomposition than any other impression, their unity and diversity, which give us pleasure, are the most visible—and hence there follows the concept of "beautiful, beauty!" It follows in accordance with its etymology, for "seeing" [*schauen*], "appearance" [*Schein*], "beautiful" [*schön*], and "beauty" [*Schönheit*] are the related offspring of language. It follows if we pay due attention to its characteristic usage, for the concept is found in its most native sense with all things that present themselves pleasurably to the eye. According to this original meaning, the concept of beauty is a "phenomenon" and thus to be treated, as it were, as an agreeable illusion, as a charming deception. It is properly a concept of surfaces, since really we know bodies, pleasing forms, and agreeably solid shapes only with the aid of touch and cannot immediately see with sight alone volume, angles, and forms; only planes, figures, colors. So, because sight concerns itself with the superficial; because what lies outside us is so remote and has but a weak effect upon us, striking us only with the fine rays of sunlight without affecting us more intimately and inwardly; finally, because of the great number and variety of colors and objects with which it at once overwhelms and ceaselessly diverts us—because of these three attributes, sight is the coldest of the senses. But for this very reason it is also the most artificial, the most philosophical sense: it is attained only with great effort and practice, as those who are cured of blindness testify; it is based on many habitual and complex activities; it operates by nothing but constant comparison, measurement, and inference. To enable us to carry out all these refined cognitive processes, therefore, sight must, even as it works, provide us with the detachment and ease without which it cannot function. Behold! That is a brief characterization of sight and its daughter, visible beauty, which, supported by examples and multiplied by observations, would deliver the foundations for a rich and very agreeable aesthetics of vision, which we do not yet possess.

Because, then, the agreeable objects of this sense are, so to speak, external to us and not so deep within us as those of other organs; because its parts are arrayed alongside one another and therefore most capable of deliberate and pleasant decomposition or, to put it more precisely, contemplation [*Beschauung*]; because its distinctions feel colder and hence can also be expressed more distinctly and with greater differentiation in language; finally, because the operation of the imagination, which is as deficient in names for its workings as our whole psychology is lacking in proper terms, is always most analogous to that of the sense of contemplation [*Beschauen*], of intuition [*Anschauung*]—for all these reasons the language of sight has been seized upon to describe the relation of everything that has a pleasurable effect on the soul. It is sight, then, that allegorizes the images, the representations, the conceits of the soul, and in almost all languages beauty has become the principal term and the most general concept in all the fine arts of pleasure and delight. *Beauty is the key word in all aesthetics.*[1]

---

[1] Mr. R. has used this occasion to point out a deep-seated error on the part of the two great philosophers of the beautiful, Home and Mendelssohn; that the former defines the concept of beauty too narrowly and the latter too broadly: the former because he attributes beauty only to sight, the latter because he calls it the basis of all our natural drives. Mr. R. knows better, more precisely, more fruitfully what beauty is, namely—listen to the great philosopher!—what can please us and even please us when we do not possess it. Mr. Riedel is welcome to keep his novel, very convenient, and very pertinent determination of disinterest in the perception of beauty; but will he allow me to to stick with my own opinion, which is that Home and Mendelssohn are right? Is the concept of beauty not originally and properly a visual concept, as Home avers, and should Home not have determined it according to its origin and properties? Is not the obscure concept of pleasure operative in everything that we choose and seek out? And according to this broad and abstract description, according to this *sensu complexo* of beauty, is not Mr. Mendelssohn's proposition a psychological truth? And is the one or the other's assertion anything more than a secondary consideration that even were it false does not disturb or confuse their principles? Why not let children wield the rod so that if they reach no higher, they may thrash the ankles of great men?

A theory of vision, an aesthetic optics and phenomenology are thus the first gateway to a future edifice of the philosophy of the beautiful. What use is it, what use will it ever be to define beauty from above and to chatter in general and confused terms about beautiful cognition, beautiful speech, beautiful sounds, and so on, as many do, when one ought rather to seek unity and diversity in the sense in which they manifest themselves most clearly, distinctly, and least confusedly, in lines, surfaces, and figures? Here every observation would be, as it were, a phenomenon, visible experience; here many a thing would be represented as in the clear light of day, as on a surface, as in lines and figures, things which, if perceived through an alien sense, appear askew and if sought in the soul extremely obscure. Such a theory would teach us to *see* the beautiful before we apply it to the most reflective objects of the imagination, where we often speak of it like the blind man of color and mirrors, and like our vulgar critics and librarians in Germany and France do when they analyze the finest beauties of thought in the vaguest language of familiar jargon. Here, then, the aesthetics of vision awaits its Newton.

Our language is even poorer in proper expressions for the delight we take in the objects of *hearing*; it must take refuge in borrowed, foreign words, such as *beautiful* or *sweet* sounds, and thus speaks in metaphors. The reasons for this poverty are evident. The effects of that which agreeably enters our ear lie, as it were, deeper *within our* soul, whereas the objects of the eye lie serenely *before us*. The former are produced *in one another*, so to speak, through vibrations that give rise to other vibrations; they are thus not as *discrete*, not as distinct. They are produced through tones and waves of sound that convulse, that gently benumb us, whereas rays of light fall silently like golden beams on our organs of sight without disturbing and unsettling us. The former succeed one another, relieve one another, vanish, and are no more; the latter endure and allow themselves to be unhurriedly grasped and apprehended once more. Our language for expressing the beauties of hearing is therefore not as rich as that for the beauties of sight. I do not mean to say that it could not be richer. If sight did not ceaselessly distract us; if sight and hearing were not, after a certain fashion, adversaries who are rarely found together in equal measure; if hearing, precisely because of its inwardness and successiveness, were not more difficult to develop than sight, which effortlessly takes wing and can always return to find the same world unchanged; then those who are blind from birth show how many fine nuances, unknown to us, might be distinguished in hearing, nuances that today belong only to sight and that could be difficult to articulate, even for the blind, and barely made comprehensible to people who do not share with them the profound sensibility necessary for the experience. Even today Italian has a greater stock of expressions for sweet sound [*Wohllaut*] than other, less musical nations unpossessed of so much fervent feeling, and especially more than the French, who scarcely know anything more than the *jolie* of their *chansons* and *petits airs*. If, like the Greeks, for example, we were to view music more as the music of the soul and also feel poetry as deeply as we do music, which for the Greeks had a wider range of signification and was, as it were, the supreme epitome of the fine arts, then our philosophy, which is still so deficient in general principles and observations pertaining to the beautiful in music, would also have much to gain. Perhaps the fundamental concept of this philosophy of tones would be *melody*, which, however, I distinguish from harmony, euphony, and so on; and if this philosophy sought in melody everything that is agreeable, delightful, and often enchanting in this art, then perhaps it, and it alone, might seek out *those* properties of the delightful which penetrate most deeply into the soul and move it most potently. And such a theory is, as it were, the second gateway to an aesthetics, one that we lack even more than the first.

The third sense is the least examined and ought perhaps to be the first to be investigated: *touch*. We have banished it among the coarser senses; we develop it the least because sight and hearing, lighter senses and closer to the soul, hold us back from it and spare us the effort of obtaining ideas through it. We have excluded touch or feeling from the arts of beauty and condemned it for delivering us nothing but misunderstood metaphors; yet aesthetics, in keeping with its name, ought precisely to be the philosophy of feeling. I have said that this sense, in the form in which we currently possess, cultivate, and apply it, has but little work to do in the sphere of the fine arts; but might I also venture that for us it is not everything it could be, and so in the realm of the beautiful, too, not all that it might one day be?

I thus start from the undeniable experience that it is not sight that furnishes us with concepts of forms and bodies, as is commonly supposed and even the most philosophical *treatise on the principles of the fine arts* has taken for granted. I assume that sight can show us nothing but surfaces, colors, and images and that we can receive concepts of anything that has volume, sphericality, and solid form only through touch and long, repeated feeling of objects. This is demonstrated by all those who are born blind and those who have been cured of blindness. For the former, bodies and forms constituted, as it were, the entirety of their external sensible world, just as simple sounds constituted the entirety of their inner sensible world. The man blind from birth whom Diderot observed taught his son to read using letters *in relief*; he could conceive the mirror only as a device for projecting *bodies in relief*; he failed to understand why this projected relief could not be felt and therefore concluded that it was a deception, that there would have to be a second device to reveal the deception created by the first. He could imagine his eyes only as organs on which the *air* made the same impression as a *stick* makes *on the hand*; thus, he did not envy others their sight because he could form no concepts of surfaces and of their reflection. His only wish was to have *longer arms* so that he might feel distant objects. It was natural, therefore, that he would develop his sense of touch to such a degree of refinement and correctness that it caused astonishment when put to the test. For him, touch was a balance for judging weight, the yardstick for measuring distance, and the source of that which he called beautiful, wherein he discerned a thousand pleasures that we cannot perceive through sight and hearing combined. Touch was everything to him in the external world. But as can be seen in every example, it furnished him with no concepts but form and body; anything possessed of these qualities he grasped a thousand times more exactly, finely, and profoundly than we who use sight as a more convenient stick in place of touch and thereby neglect the latter by overrelying on the former. But surfaces he could not grasp.

The blind Saunderson grasped them just as little. He used adding machines to count instead of numbers; he represented surfaces and figures to himself by means of special devices; lines and polygons had to be turned into bodies so that he could feel them. We know that he left behind devices whose use for others is negligible but which for him were indispensable for studying the area of surfaces. What the sighted, who only ever see bodies as projected reliefs, find most difficult to grasp in geometry, that is, solid bodies, was for him child's play to demonstrate. What the sighted find simplest, the representation of figures on a surface, gave him greater trouble, and his explanation was more trying for those who expected to form concepts of such things without the benefit of vision. It was the same with his optics; plane figures were for him only ancillary concepts that he posited; bodies were his objects, and even the rays of the sun had to be transformed into a body so that he could grasp them.

That sight and touch are as distinct as surface and body, image and form, we perceive most clearly in the case of the man born blind who was cured by Cheselden. Though he suffered from cataracts, he had still been able to discern day from night and, in a strong light, distinguish black, white, and scarlet. But he could do so only through feeling, only by taking them as bodies that moved on his closed eyes. When his eyes were opened, he could not recognize the colors as surfaces, the colors that previously he had distinguished as bodies. When his eyes were opened, he did not see space; all objects lay jumbled in his eyes. He could not separate even the most diverse objects from one another and recognized none of the things that he had previously known through touch. He could discover, then, absolutely no identity between body and surface, between shape and figure. Though he was taught how to discern such correspondences, he forgot them; he knew nothing. He could not grasp that the picture he beheld, that the surfaces before him marked with figures and color were the same bodies he had previously felt; and when he had persuaded himself that this was indeed the case, he was still uncertain whether his new or his old sense deceived him, with the former teaching him nothing but surfaces, the latter nothing but bodies. A thousand other strange uncertainties about space, magnitude, the comparison of two-dimensional spaces, and so on show us that there exist quite definite borders between sight and touch, as between surface and body, figure and shape; that as *touch knows nothing of surface, of color, so sight knows nothing at all of form or shape.* I could demonstrate this proposition by appealing to optics and logic were not these three examples of blind men more eloquent than three such demonstrations.

What follows from this? A great deal. Touch may not be that crude a sense after all, since it is properly *the organ of all sensation of other bodies*, and hence has a world of fine, rich concepts subject to it. Sight is related to touch as surface is to body, and it is only by a habitual abbreviation that we see bodies as surfaces and fancy that we recognize through sight what in childhood we properly learned, and learned very slowly, only by way of touch. In this way and in this way alone did we learn the concepts of space, solidity, and motion, just as we also learned the concepts of magnitude, figure, and surface through many experiments with sight. But because both senses operated together and conjointly, the abbreviated form of all bodies was projected onto the retina of the eye as a figure, and it is this abbreviation that we habitually make use of: we believe that we see bodies and feel surfaces, whereas nothing could be more absurd.

Only errors spring from this illogical and unscientific muddling, and it is precisely these errors that have given rise to the many objections to the truth of sensuous representations. You see the stick lying broken in the water; you reach out for it but grasp nothing; you see that it was only the reflection of the stick itself. You were mistaken, but at fault was not your sense but rather your judgment, which you customarily employ with your senses and which now confounds the objects. Your eye can perceive nothing but surfaces; you saw the surface of the water, and that was sensuous truth. You saw the stick reflected on the surface: you saw rightly, for as an image it was sensuous truth. But you reached out for it; to do that you were wrong, for who would reach out to touch an image on a surface? Touch is meant only for bodies, but did you know through touch that a stick was lying in the water when you wanted to take hold of it? No! And thus it was not your senses but rather your judgment that deceived you, your judgment that due to a muddling caused by long-ingrained habit was overhasty and substituted sight where only touch could be the organ of the concept. Precisely this fact is the root of all those frequently arising misunderstandings over breadth, magnitude, figure, and shape.

I do not desire to lay down new rules setting out how the sense of touch, which has been so very abbreviated and displaced by sight, might be restored to its old rights so that we arrive more slowly but surely at the concept of bodily truth. On this matter Rousseau has already spoken, I believe, and anyway here is not the proper place for such a discussion. I am interested only in the application of touch to aesthetics, a significant portion of which would thereby be quite transformed. *Namely, the beauty of a form, of a body, is not a visual but a tactile concept; thus every one of these beauties must originally be sought in the sense of touch.* The eye is neither their source nor therefore their judge; it is too rapid, too gentle, too superficial for that, and a theory of form and shape derived from the eye is no more appropriate than a theory of music derived from taste; no more appropriate than if the man born blind whom we mentioned earlier were to say: "Now I understand the color scarlet; it is like the sound of a trumpet."

The beauty of bodies, as forms, is thus tactile; all aesthetic terms that describe such beauty, regardless of the context in which they are used, derive from touch: rough, gentle, soft, tender, full, in motion—all these and countless others derive from touch. The whole essence of sculpture is not, as all and sundry have hitherto erroneously assumed and as I shall prove otherwise, visual; or at least it is visual only to a small degree, insofar as a statue possesses surfaces. In itself, however, sculpture—as the fine art of bodies—is above all tangible. When recognized through this sense, it avoids all false taste and judgments, and, slowly and deliberately, to be sure, but therefore all the more certainly, it approaches to the truth. This, then, is the third gateway to the beautiful: *touch or feeling.* And the third work I wish could be written is a philosophy of feeling that is no mere metaphor, as Baumgarten's *Aesthetica* would have remained, even had it been brought to completion, and which would possess nothing in common with what I am proposing.

Human nature possesses two further senses, but these have a smaller share in the sensation of the beautiful. In general I object to how every other theory places them *alongside* the intended three main senses, since after all they are really two related modifications of touch rather than two entirely new feelings, like eye and ear. As such modifications of touch, they furnish us with several names and metaphors that are to our purpose, but because they are not themselves new feelings, they do not have their own fine arts as objects. *Taste*, as we know, has become an important term that expresses nothing more than a light, invigorating feeling. This *gusto* first became current among the Spanish; the Italians and French quickly adopted it, with the English, Germans, and others following suit. Eventually it was even translated back into Latin, though in the greatest age of that language at least it was not in general use as a primary designation.

And precisely because taste can be chewed over and dissected so much, it has indeed been much analyzed, particularly in France. Nevertheless, I do not think it the must fruitful concept or the most fruitful sense from which to develop an aesthetics. What it borrows from the sweet, invigorating, intoxicating, piquant qualities of grace is either mere modifications of touch or, where taste is concerned, unfruitful metaphors. And then the terms we have to describe pleasant and unpleasant smells, which even when describing beauty ought to be added only in moderation—what place do they have in characterizing the universally beautiful?

2

So there are three main senses, at least as far as aesthetics is concerned, though it has been customary to concede to it only two, the eye and the ear. Each of these three senses has it own first concepts, which it delivers itself, and those which are merely appropriated from the others: a feeling is modified as it passes through all the senses, with each contributing something to its new form, and thus only belatedly and finally do complex concepts transfer themselves from the senses to the soul, as different streams flow into one great ocean. Thus arise the concepts of truth and of beauty: they are the work of many and various organs, and, since each of these organs has its own world, they involve the plundering, so to speak, of many such worlds. The imagination takes and creates and forms and compounds, but all its materials were obtained through intermediaries and are but a great chaos.

It is quite clear, then, that we cannot possibly start back to front and speak of the most abstract concepts of the imagination, of beauty, grandeur, sublimity, and so on, without first investigating the most insignificant impressions from which these so very general, so all-encompassing ideas first arose. Each one of these concepts must be a confused chaos if its jumbled impressions are not traced back to each sense, if each concept is not assigned its peculiar origin and meaning, if order is not brought to all in turn, and especially if the proportion is not weighed in which they contribute to this or that primary concept lying obscurely within us. And the very method that I am decrying—has it not been almost the only one hitherto? Here definition starts from above, from beauty and sublimity; one thus begins at the point where one ought to end up, with beauty. If the concept of beauty is to be more than the parroting of the long-familiar words "the object that is pleasing must be sensuous, must possess no imperfection, must delight us in a manner that is satisfying," if the concept of beauty shall be fruitful and yield more than flimsy and wretched general propositions, then, my undemanding philosopher, it must be more than a device emblazoned on your title page. Beauty is a difficult, ponderous concept; it must be abstracted from many individual facts and descriptions, all of which cannot be collected, polished, ordered, and refined enough if we are to deliver from them an analysis of beauty in general; and yet precisely such an analysis is the end product of all individual phenomena.

I went blind straining to see even the merest hint of any of this in Riedel's theory. What in my scheme is the ultimate, most difficult concept, the sum of all sensations of this kind, namely beauty, he demonstrates at the very outset and from it draws a mixture of consectaries that he is welcome to keep. What in my view ought to have been his work's principal aim—that is, to collect, to order, to trace back to their origin the phenomena and data of the beautiful—there is nothing of the kind in Riedel's book. What in my view ought to be the only method employed in aesthetics—analysis, the rigorous analysis of concepts—is the very thing he derides most of all and for which he substitutes nothing more than his ἀρριτον of a Quaker feeling. He has a number of general, abstract concepts—who knows from where?—from Gerard and Mendelssohn and Home and Winckelmann, which he throws together in a motley chaos, alongside whatever else he can find in other writers. The true philosopher has no such general concepts except where they appear to him in an organ of sense; there he sets out after them, pursues them through all the fine nerve branches until they are communicated to other senses and finally to the soul. This physiology of the senses and of sensuous concepts, which to a wise man is everything—object, main end in view, and method— means nothing to Riedel. Where there is *beauty*, there is diversity, and also unity, grandeur, importance, harmony, Nature, naïveté, simplicity, similitude, contrast, truth, probability, rotundity, imitation, illusion, design, color, comparisons, figures, tropes, succinctness, a train of thought; and serious, absurd, ridiculous, comic, whimsical, gentle, frivolous representations; interest, sentiment, pathos, propriety, dignity, morals, costume, decency, taste, genius, enthusiasm, and invention—oh, my hand grows weary! So much for the structure, the plan, and the methodical ordering of Riedel's theory of all the beaux arts and belles lettres! Oh, chaos! Chaos! Chaos!

Is it not deplorable that the most useful things in the world, language and instruction, can at the same time also be the most pernicious? If, without the direction of others, we had to find all our own concepts with their names and distinctions; if each and every one of us had to invent his own language and means of expression—what an effort that would be! What a long, endless journey! The human race would then dissolve into nothing but individual beings, every link would be broken in the long chain of ideas and traditions that extends from the first man to the last, through all nations, ages, and centuries; each subject would be left to his own devices, to his toil and solitary striving, and all humanity would be stuck in an eternal childhood. Each would suffer for the discovery of a handful of truths, suffer all his life, then die without having made use of them himself or been able to bequeath them to others. We would be worse off than the animals, whose instinct endows them with all the arts and skills they require and who have Nature herself, who gave them form, for a teacher. So Mother Nature cared for us in a different way: she gave us language, an instrument whereby we can immediately touch the soul of another person, immediately implant in him knowledge that he did not himself discover but that others did on his behalf. In this way language not only made it easier for each person to travel his own arduous and winding path to knowledge and wisdom but also established an eternal bond that unites the human race into one vast whole. Now no member was alone; no idea in the great chain of human souls has ever been thought in vain; each idea has influenced others; it ordered itself into a sequence, propagated itself throughout centuries and ages, while others have caused good and evil and contributed to the decline or ascent of the human soul. So instruction and language contain a great repository of ideas that is at our disposal, that others discovered and expressed for us, and that we *learn* with a thousand times less effort. But behold! Once this so very estimable aid to the acquisition of knowledge has been secured, there immediately begins a falling off, a decline. Through words we now learn concepts that we had no need to seek out ourselves and that we therefore do not submit to scrutiny; we learn knowledge that we had no need to gather for ourselves and that we therefore snatch up, use, and apply without understanding. And how this debases the human soul! Every new word learned makes it more difficult for the soul to understand the thing to which it refers. Every inherited concept deadens a nerve by which the soul might have discovered it for itself, benumbs our power to understand the concept as inwardly as if we had discovered it by ourselves.

With all sensuous things, we have the eyes and organs that yet prevent this dulling of the soul; we have the opportunity to acquaint ourselves both with the thing itself and its name at the same time, and therefore not to grasp the sign without the concept of the signified, the husk without the kernel. But with abstract ideas? With invention proper? Here the danger is even greater. How effortlessly, in the first case, we assume the outcome of a lengthy operation of the human mind, without ourselves running through the operation that originally produced it. Thus we come by corollaries without grasping their inner logic, problems without understanding their solution, maxims without inferring them from their premises, words without knowing the things to which they refer. In the second case, we learn a whole series of names from books, without discovering them in and with the things themselves, which they are supposed to denominate. We know words and think we know the things that they signify: we embrace the shadow instead of the body that casts it.

Acolytes of knowledge! And so your soul nods off; its every limb grows heavy when it settles into the habit of relying on the words and inventions of others. The man who invented the word that you learn so casually had an entirely different notion of it than you do: he saw the concept; he desired to express it; he struggled with language, he spoke; necessity drove him to articulate what he saw. How different it is for you who know the concept merely by the word that describes it, you who believe you have the former because you hold the latter and employ it with a partial idea. At that moment you are not bathed in the same inner light as he is; you possess merely an arbitrary coin that you have adopted through convention and that others accept from you through the same convention, whereas he who minted the coin knew its intrinsic value. So do not stir yet from this peaceful slumber; carry on dreaming the words of others without onerously wresting your ideas from reality: sleep. I wish you luck with your petrified and lethargic soul, which will soon turn into naught but a great mouth, with not even a single compartment of the brain remaining with which to think.

And that is the woeful state in which the entire realm of scholarship finds itself today. There is much to learn that others have thought on our behalf, and ultimately we learn nothing but *to learn*. From our youth onward every effort is made to lull us into this cosy sleep of the mind; we are spared the trouble of *having* to invent something, and so throughout our lives we shall never be *able* to do so. Everything is done *ad captum*; we abbreviate, excerpt, make things easy, and so our *captus* will naturally remain as one wanted it: the *stunted image of the minds from whom we learned*. We made a real effort not to think *ad captum ipsorum* like them but *ad captum nostrum*; we thus diminished and infantilized their works—hence the childish stature that compared to them we retain throughout our lives. You there, sleeping boy, you learned everything from books, from dictionaries, even; are the words that you read and learn to understand through study the living things you ought to see? Natural history, philosophy, politics, fine arts from books—why, when you have read through Montesquieu and understand and know him, do you think like he thought, he who observed the different realms and forms of government or brought them to life by the power of his imagination, who oversaw them? And you who learn his principles by rote: Do you thereby think as he thought? Are you now Montesquieu?

Today is—alas!—the age of the beautiful. The rage for discussing the fine arts has gripped Germany in particular, just as the citizens of Abdera were seized by a mania for tragedy. And how do we learn the concepts of the beautiful? How else but from books? To read half a theory, to understand a quarter of the words and grasp none of the meaning is more than enough these days to make one a connoisseur of the art in question, for there are others who have even picked up their phrases from book reviews and not from a theory at all. Such people have on their lips a whole host of words whose object they have never seen but which, in accordance with the conventions of literary commerce, they nevertheless pass on to others, just as they received these same words from another party. Oh, this is the final stage in the decline of thought! Wretched, enervated gourmand of the beautiful! The words that you know and learned from your Pernety; the torrent of verbiage including *simplicity* and *grace* and *perspective* and *contrast* and *attitude* and *costume* and the rest of the nonsense that our Klotzes and Meusels carry around in their pockets—do all these words mean the same to you at the moment that you blather them as they did when the artists infused their works with these qualities? As they did to those who contemplated and were moved by the work of art, who captured from it the living words and, as it were, invented them? Do they mean the same to you? Does the word *grace* mean the same to you as it meant, obscurely, in the soul of Correggio when he imbued his paintings with it; as it was to Winckelmann and Hagedorn when they derived it from their ideals—does the word mean the same to you, you dead, bookish soul? It would be an act of high treason against all the Muses and arts if, by prattling about the manly manner of Michelangelo, you wished to measure yourself against him, for he learned his manner from the ancients, he endowed his own works with it!

Riedel's entire theory is a blurred silhouette of such learned and bookish ideas; I except not one of its articles or concepts. *Beauty* and *diversity* and *unity* and *grandeur* and *harmony* and *Nature* and *simplicity* and *similitude*—and all the rest that the book follows through the tumult— they are all words without ideas, shadows without bodies. Nothing has been abstracted from Nature or from art. Nothing has been intuitively cognized. Nothing has been ordered according to its organ of sense, its art, its class of objects. The whole lot is perfunctory and thrown together in the most abominable, awful muddle. It never occurred to him to ask of a single concept: Where did it originate? From where was it abstracted? In which instances is it meant literally and when figuratively? How might or might not one concept entail another? There is none of this! He talks about grace by borrowing from Winckelmann, about naïveté by borrowing from Mendelssohn, and about beauty by borrowing from Baumgarten. But he never borrows from Nature. In every chapter he dreams of words without objects and throws together concepts and chapters that one cannot help but be astonished to see in a theory of the fine arts and in its first, general part at that. Harmony is placed beside Nature; simplicity beside similitude; probability beside rotundity; design beside illusion; tropes beside succinctness; the train of thoughts beside the ridiculous, comic, whimsical, frivolous; the frivolous beside interest and sentiment and pathos and propriety and dignity and morals and costume; decency beside taste and genius beside enthusiasm—as if each one applied to all the fine arts, without distinction, with the same claim to originality, and in that order? As if none had a homeland, its own distinctive features, its proper domain, its gradations, its derivation? As if a theory of the beautiful in all the arts did not depend on all this! And yet not a word about any of these things. Just a chaos of chapters, definitions, and words. And *therefore not one true, original aesthetic concept in the whole book*. Oh, what an excellent theory of the fine arts! Young men: read, learn, listen, and you will be corrupted forever!

3

Why am I lingering over this copyist of general concepts? Let me return to my inquiry into the senses of the beautiful. We saw that there were three: the sense of sight, which perceives *external things alongside one another*; hearing, which perceives *things in succession*; and *touch*, which perceives things *in depth*. External things that are ranged alongside one another are called *surfaces*; things in succession in their simplest form are *tones*; things in depth are solid *bodies*. Thus we have distinct senses for *surfaces*, for *tones*, for *bodies*, and for beauty in *surfaces*, in *tones*, in *bodies*. Three particular classes of *objects*, like the three categories of space.

Now, if there existed arts that imitated Nature in these three categories, each of which gathered the different aspects of the beautiful and represented it, like a microcosm, to the sense proper to that species of object, then we would have three arts of beauty. *One* whose principal object is beauty insofar as it is contained by *space*, insofar as it is reflected on surfaces: this is *painting*, the fine art for *sight*. One whose object is the delight that affects us successively, in simple lines of tones, as it were: this is *music*, the fine art for *hearing*. Finally, one that beautifully represents entire bodies, insofar as they have form and mass: this is *sculpture*, the fine art for *touch*. I shall pause for a moment so that I may elaborate the substance and truth of this distinction.

A theory of sculpture that treats the art in question as wholly and originally an object of sight and derives its only and essential rules from that premise is anything but a philosophical theory. Its fundamental concept is flawed, and must it not therefore yield foreign and false rules? As a theory, must it not be subject to errors and contradictions? Yes, as assuredly as surface is not body and sight not touch. Let us suppose a body of which we had no concept through touch, or even suppose that we had no concept of any body through touch. Now let it become an object of sight. Let sight, but without the assistance of touch, make every effort to assure itself of and acquaint itself with this body; will it ever guess a single property of its solidity? No! And so will it discover all of them? No! And so will it ever obtain a true concept of this body as a body? Never, and hence if the theory of an art of bodies also takes them simply as objects of sight, it cannot be much of a theory at all.

What do we see of a body through the eye? Nothing but surface. This surface may be an elevation or the projection of an outline, but it has only two dimensions: length and breadth! We can no more *see* the third dimension, volume, than the painter can paint a dog sitting behind a closed door. That we often—and with familiar things always—think that we can is due to the precipitateness of our judgment, which, through the old habit of using sight and touch in tandem, mixes them up and, where both together do not suffice, draws on assumptions based on similar cases, combines these with the sensations of both sight and touch, and therefore sees where originally it only felt, sees where it only inferred, only surmised. Were it not so difficult to abstract from this eternal habit, I could assume as an axiom of our fundamental experience what is perhaps now only axiomatic for those who are familiar with the effects of light: namely, the eye, as eye, sees only the surfaces of bodies.

It is no different with a body in sculpture. The eye can approach a statue from whichever side it chooses, but it has only one point of view from which to inspect one part of the statue, as a surface, and so it must change that point of view as often as it desires to look on a different part of the statue, a different surface. As is known, this is one of the greatest difficulties of sculpture relative to painting. Painting is directed toward a single point of view, from and for which it invents, arranges, draws, colors *everything*; for sculpture, however, there are as many points of view as there are radii in the circle that I can draw around the statue and from each of which I can behold it. From no single point do I survey the work in its entirety; I must walk around it in order to have seen it; each point shows me only a tiny surface, and when I have described the whole circumcircle, I have perceived nothing more than a polygon composed of many small sides and angles. All these small sides must first be assembled by the imagination before we can conceive of the totality as a body. And this bodily whole, is it then a product of my eye? Or of my soul? Is the effect, which it shall achieve only as a whole, a visual sensation? Or a sensation of my soul? In this art, therefore, the effect of the whole is completely lost on the unmediated eye. So there is definitely no sculpture for the eye! Not physically, and not aesthetically. Not physically, because the eye cannot see a body as a body; not aesthetically, because when the bodily whole vanishes from sculpture, the very essence of its art and its characteristic effect disappears with it. The first of these claims has been proven. Now I shall demonstrate the second.

The essence of sculpture is beautiful form: not color, not mere proportion of the parts viewed as surfaces, but modeled form [*Bildung*]. It is the beautiful elliptical line that constantly varies its course, that is never violently broken, never rudely contorted, never abruptly cut off, but that rolls over the body with beauty and splendor, shaping it with a constant unity in diversity, with a gentle flow, in a single creative breath. This form possessed by the entire figure and by all of its constituent parts, this form with which the ancients so inimitably endowed their statuary; which the Michelangelos observed so profoundly in these works; which the Winckelmanns and Webbs praised so rapturously and for which the rabble, lacking sensitivity, has so little feeling; this form of beauty, I say, this essence of the sculptor's art, without which it is nothing—can it be properly grasped by sight? No more than a statue as such can be shown on the flat plane of an engraving and still remain a rounded statue. The eye, which apprehends only one side of the statue's aspect, according to the viewpoint that it adopts, transforms this side into a surface, as it were; as the eye moves on, it transforms another side in the same manner, and between these two planes arises an angle. The gentle, undulating form of the body that knew nothing of angles or corners is thus transformed into a complex polygon composed of angled surfaces, but is it not thereby destroyed in its properly rounded, ever-curving line of beauty? And strictly speaking, is not thereby the very essence of this art also lost? What we have before us is no longer a work of sculpture that delights us with its solid beauty as such but rather a complex mesh of surfaces and mirrors that will have done well if it did not manifestly contradict that beauty.

We can see my claims confirmed if we analyze the operations of the eye itself when it perceives the statue: these are directed toward taking the place of touch and seeing the object as if one were feeling or grasping it. Consider the viewer sunk deep in silent contemplation of the *Apollo Belvedere*. He seems to stand in a fixed position, but nothing could be further from the truth. He adopts as many viewpoints as he can, changing his perspective from one moment to the next so that he avoids sharply defined surfaces. To this end he gently glides only around the contours of the body, changes his position, moves from one spot to another and then back again; he follows the line that unfolds and runs back on itself, the line that forms bodies and here, with its gentle declivities, forms the beauty of the body standing before him. He tries his hardest to destroy every recess, every caesura, every superficiality, and, as far as possible, to restore to the many-angled polygon, to which his eye has reduced the body, its beautiful ellipse, which had been blown into being only for his touch. What, so was he not in each moment compelled to destroy, as it were, the constitution of the object that is the very essence of the ocular representation, that is, surface, color, angle? And was he not obliged in each moment to rely on a sense—his eye—that only imperfectly replaced touch? And was therefore the sense that he used anything but a truncation of the original sense, an abbreviated form of the operations of touch? And so he demonstrates in the very act of seeing that to experience the effect of sculpture, which is achieved only through bodies, he wanted only to feel, and feel he did.

Now suppose that he did indeed experience this effect; suppose that by inspecting the work from a thousand different viewpoints and by, as it were, visually feeling his way around the statue, his imagination was now able to conceive the entirety of the beautiful form so perfectly corporeally that the little that was merely surface vanished and the imagination really represented the polygon in all its elliptical solidity. The illusion was complete; what was merely a composite of small, flat surfaces has become a beautiful, tangible body. Look, now the fancy is agitated and talks——as if it did nothing but feel. It speaks of gentle fullness, of that softness

> das alter Griechen leichte Hand,
> von Grazien geführt, mit hartem Stein verband,

of splendid curves, of beautiful rotundity, of rounded elevation, of the marble that stirs and as it were comes alive under the feeling hand. Why does the imagination speak of so many feelings? And why, if they are not exaggerated, are these feelings no metaphors? Because they are experiences. The eye that gathered them was no longer an eye that perceived pictures on a surface; it became a hand, the ray of light became a finger, and the imagination became a kind of immediate touching: the properties that we observe are so many feelings.

And this is the very reason why the enthusiasm of the lover of sculpture exceeds that of the lovers of other arts. When the connoisseur of painting describes a picture, he has before him a surface. He decomposes its figures in terms of their arrangement and presence; he depicts what he sees before him. But now let the lover of the *Apollo Belvedere*, the *Belvedere Torso*, and *Niobe* describe these works; he must depict not a surface but a body, which he feels; or rather, not depict it but make it tangible to others. Then his feeling imagination takes the place of the colder, analyzing eye; then it will always feel Hercules in his whole body and this body in all his deeds. In the mighty contours of his body it feels the strength of this conqueror of giants and in the gentle features of these contours the nimble fighter who defeated Achelous; it feels the great, magnificent breast against which Geryon was crushed, the strong, steadfast flanks that marched to the edge of the earth, the arms that throttled the Nemean lion, the untiring legs, and the whole body that enjoyed immortality in the arms of Eternal Youth. Here the feeling imagination has no limits, knows no bounds. It has put out its eyes, as it were, so that it does not merely depict a dead surface; it sees nothing of what lies before it but instead gropes its way as if in the dark, is enraptured by the body that it touches, travels with it through heaven and hell and to the ends of the earth, then feels anew and gives voice to everything whereof its feeling reminds it. Dead eyes of the painter! Do not begrudge the imagination if it does not, like you, merely analyze and paint and daub and observe. Do you know anything more inexhaustible and profound than the sense of touch? Anything more exhilarating than the solidity of its beautiful object? Anything more vivid than the imagination filled with its sensations? As surface is related to body, so your depiction of this is related to a description of that!

No law of painting can become a law of sculpture without qualification and no little amendment, as if surface could attain the solidity of a body. The essence of painting lies in the enlivening of a surface, and its ideal aims precisely at the combination of a number of figures that—down to every brushstroke that renders their attitude and arrangement and lights and colors—constitute a single, indivisible, two-dimensional world of living appearance. Everything in painting is ordered, executed, and viewed from this prevailing point of view: one stands as before a panel or table (*tavola, tableau*, and so on). The supreme law of sculpture could not be more different. Even the most numerous group of statues does not constitute a whole in the same way that a painted group of figures does. Each statue occupies its own ground, the tangible sphere of its effect and beauty radiates from it alone, and therefore, in accordance with the highest law of sculpture, it must be treated as an individual work. When André Bardon means to reproach the ancients for the picturesque economy with which they arranged their groups of statues, his criticism originates in a viewpoint that is foreign to sculpture. If he had stopped to think, he would not have sought his painterly concepts—such as *quantité des belles figures, surabondance d'objets, oeconomie pittoresque, pensées poëtiques, bien desordre*, and so on—indiscriminately in sculpture, where all these things are of a quite distinct nature. The meaning, the allegory, and the narrative that are introduced into the composition of a single picture are subject to laws different from those permitted and required by the expression of a group of statues: the contrast between the groups and figures, and even more so the effect of light and shadow, is of a different character in the two arts. The painter has everything on a surface before him and can mix, arrange, and expunge colors for as long as he needs to accomplish his illusion, which lies in the painting as a whole. The sculptor, who from each of his blocks carves out bodily truth as a single whole and offers it up to be felt from all sides, is a different kind of creator. A painted figure is nothing in itself; it is everything in relation to the whole of the surface perceived by the eye. A body belonging to sculpture gains little by its relation to the whole; it is everything in itself and for the feeling hand—what a difference that is!

The contour of painting ever seems to me like the outline of a figure on a surface; that is why it is guided by laws governing its precision, taste, and expression. The gentle curvature of the same, which, as it were, gives relief to a body and also allows us to see behind what we are seeing, is in painting merely a beautiful illusion, the purpose of which is to soften the hardness. In sculpture it is the highest truth. Thus the position of the figures in painting is determined only by the single side that they present to the viewer and by the composition of the picture as a whole. In sculpture the figure stands alone and must submit to being felt from all sides. What a different set of laws! In painting the expression of individual figures is dictated solely by the whole to which they belong. In sculpture expression is subject to the material that through the former is to be beautifully presented in the most tangible manner; it is therefore, as it were, a product of dividing the thought by the bodily mass. The recent dispute over whether art ought to express only beautiful bodies would surely have been conducted with less heat and greater precision if the participants had distinguished between one fine art and another and made it clear at the outset which they were discussing. The ugly and disgusting statue that I touch with my thoughts and feel ceaselessly in this distorted and unnatural form becomes repulsive to me. Instead of finding beauty I encounter physical flaws that send a cold shiver down my spine; in the moment that I experience this distorting blemish, I feel a disharmonious vibration of my tactile nerves and, as it were, a kind of inner annihilation of my nature. I am filled with dread, as if I were lost in the darkness. And when with horror I touch Saint Bartholomew all over, who, half flayed and in his death agonies, cries out to me "Non me Praxiteles sed Marcus finxit Agrati," I push him away: *no Praxiteles would have wanted to make you* and, as it were, feel and carve your broken form from the stone! It is clear how incomparably freer painting is in this regard, for it is not required to model a body and present it, as a *solitary* object, as a whole, to the slow, intimate sense of touch; it need only depict one figure scattered among others, among light and colors, and for the hasty eye. How many distinctions there are to be made between these fine arts! And how much they would help, in the writings of Winckelmann, Caylus, Webb, Hagedorn, Lessing, and others, to define more clearly and then resolve the favorite issue of our day.

They will also help to explain why color, which on a painted surface possesses such magical power, has no effect whatsoever when applied to the forms of sculpture. In one passage in his confused book, Mr. R. addresses this question and means to resolve it. But what can a man resolve who has never once considered the distinctions between the various arts? To the question why a marble statue cannot be clothed with colors without suffering harm, he replies, first, that the similarity would be too great; second, that from a distance one would mistake the statue for a real person, then, drawing near it, one would discover the deception and feel nothing but astonishment at what the deception had caused; third, that the idea of similarity would degenerate into an idea of identity, and so on. This muddled mind believes that he is only adducing one reason and ends up offering three: three reasons that all contradict one another; three reasons that explain nothing. "The similarity would be too great!" As if similarity between a work of art and Nature, as long as it did not infringe any other law governing that art form, could ever be *too* great or even a crime! "The similarity degenerates into identity!" As if this were a danger for anyone save for children or fools! But if identity means nothing more than illusion, is that not the goal of art? "But from a distance we would mistake such a statue for a living, breathing human being and approach it!" Might we not also mistake it for a ghost and recite our Hail Marys? If the distance is so great that the eye cannot yet distinguish anything, then the statue is not yet *within its range of effect*. Let the eye draw nearer, let it *seek a standpoint*, and, despite the riot of color, it will never dream it is gazing at a real person. Otherwise, if you mistake Phidias's statue of Jupiter for a bell tower, then the fault lies not with the art but with your defective spectacles; and these can explain nothing in aesthetics. Only laws derived from the essence of sculpture can furnish an explanation here. Through bodies, sculpture imitates forms to be enjoyed by the sense of touch; therefore, everything that is not form, that is not meant for feeling—whether a painted eyeball, a tincture of colors, and so on—is alien to it. It is mere color, which either cannot be felt (and then sculpture has no need of it), or is tangible, is itself body, and thus gets in the way of touching the form; hence color is at odds with sculpture. When applied to a surface, where all the figures are separate, color illumines, guides, and enchants sight; but here, on a body, where everything must be felt as one, color will of necessity obscure touch and weaken the pure effect of the art. "Why would the artist Myron's cow not give us greater pleasure if it were covered in hair?" asks Riedel. What a question! And what an answer when he suggests that "it would then look too much like a cow." A cow that is too like a cow—that is nonsense. But a cow that is covered in real hair and yet is still an artistic image—there lies the contradiction. Sculpture can work only in tangible surfaces, but in this case there are none. The work is no longer a statue but a stuffed scarecrow. Sculpture creates forms for beautiful feeling, but what can we feel on this bag of hair? Artists, you must always give the lion its mane, just as Myron naturally gave his cow hair; but do so through surfaces, through art, and for feeling. Then you need not worry, like our prattling theorist, about excessive similarity, for you are working for beautiful feeling and the sweet illusion of imagination.

I can see a wide range of phenomena that might be explained with this single principle of *beautiful feeling* in sculpture. If we traced sculpture back to this simple origin, we would see that all its laws issue thence, that all instances of false taste in sculpture arose when it was treated as if it were painting or a partly mosaic work, decorated with, for example, golden eyes, silver rings, and so on; and when it was made to compete with all the figures in painting, in all their postures, modes of expression, and colors. It would turn out that the confusion and excesses that have plagued the criticism of these very different arts arose when they were treated as if they were one and the same; even Winckelmann, for example, often mixed them up with each other and with the midway point between the two, the relief. The question of the contest between the two arts would be resolved with far greater philosophical rigor than was managed by the majority of artists who wrote so many strange letters on the subject in the sixteenth century. Both painting and sculpture would appear in a light that would reveal their distinct origin, essence, effect, genius, and rules, and this would satisfy the philosopher, amuse the connoisseur, instruct the art lover, and not only safeguard the artist from false taste but enrapture his true feeling as well.

I shall not mention the many specific problems that this principle would illuminate, extending from some of the qualities and excellencies in the history of the art of the ancients all the way, after many detours and individual rarities, down to the history of the moderns. The wise simplicity of the ancients and the blissful tranquillity, precise contour, and wet drapery with which they endowed their statues is obviously accounted for by this feeling, which, as it were, gropes its way in the dark so that it will not be distracted by sight and here abandon itself to all the outpourings of the imagination. Here nothing ugly, ecstatic, or distorted can ever be the principal expression of a work. For when, in its unlit chamber, the intimate sense of touch encounters such malformations, it recoils with horror; and neither the exaggerated nor the ugly gives the imagination—which should follow only touch—the free and graceful scope to operate. Here blissful tranquillity is the principal condition, for it alone leaves room for the beauty that forever delights touch and cradles the imagination in gentle dreams. Here the contour is as fine as the end of a hair, for it is precisely in tangible perfection, which a line can more or less obliterate, that the pleasure of sculpture lies. Here wet drapery is effective, for otherwise I feel nothing but clothing, oppressive and solid clothing; and the beautiful form of the body, the essence of sculpture, is lost. All these phenomena, which otherwise have been explained so unreliably and often applied so falsely, follow here from one principle: the nature of beautiful feeling.

I know of no theory of sculpture that with philosophical rigor and attention to experience has developed the full implications of this principle. All such theories chase in droves after sight, which here, however, operates only at a distance, as an abbreviated form of touch and, as Descartes already assumed in his optics, with the aid of rays of light that are like rods. In everyday life we might be perfectly willing to tolerate this abbreviation, for it is commodious, nimble, swift, and—most important of all—becoming; who will wish to feel when he can see? But for philosophy and the true theory of art an improper elision can only imperfectly replace the true organ; both demand their own truth. The eye is a thousand times more acute and discerning than touch, but only when it comes to color, surfaces, and the relations of surfaces to one another, which have no place in sculpture. When it comes to form and shape, it is blind. Here the fine feeling of an Albani judges better than a thousand ocular perceptions of a sighted ponderer. Here no artist works better than he who forms his work, withdrawn, sunk as if in living feeling. I have collected many other observations on this theory of touch and found that it sheds so much light on this art—indeed, I have discovered a new logic for the lover and a new way for the artist to emulate the ancients in the perfection of such works—that I would pass the sweetest hours if I could gather these observations under the watchful eyes of an artist and bring them to philosophical perfection. But things are so different in an age of literature, such as ours is starting to become. Out of patriotism for true philosophy and good taste, we are obliged to refute writings that are pernicious and corrupting, and if these have achieved fame—oh dear!—then we must go so far as to analyze and dismantle them completely to ensure that they do no damage. And to think that we spend the best years of our intellectual life engaged in such labors, years in which we might ourselves have achieved something useful, instead of merely neutralizing what is harmful!

4

Between sculpture and painting, that is, between body and surface, we find various forms of relief, ranging from the high relief to the illusion that painting accomplishes when, as it were, it projects figures and colors beyond the surface of the picture. These intermediary genres partake, in keeping with their character, of the laws of one or the other art, depending on whichever they are closest to. I am speaking, then, of painting. If I should repeat myself in the course of my reflections, then let the reader disregard in a theoretical treatise what in a merely belletristic discourse would indeed be a fault.

The blind man to whom Cheselden restored his sight saw all objects as lying like a vast painted panel immediately upon his eyes. Children see in just this way, and so would we if through long experience we had not, so to speak, moved this surface farther back from the eye and framed concepts of the different distances of things. We thus do not obtain these immediately through sight; every object is painted on the retina, albeit in different sizes. The wide sky that meets the earth on the horizon, the distant forest, the nearby meadow and the water before us—they are all originally one surface. Behold the original raw material for painting! Painting imitates the great tableau of Nature in miniature and, like Nature, also presents sky, earth, sea, trees, and human beings on one surface. This representation of things *according to their external appearance on a single plane*, their outline as they appear *together with other objects on one flat continuum*—this is the first concept of painting.

We are immediately confronted with an essential difference between painting and sculpture. The latter also imitates things, but only substantial bodies, and it shows them standing alone, never insofar as they are contained within the great *expansum* of Nature and, as it were, within a continuum of other things. It can give form to shepherds and shepherdesses, but it cannot represent them together with their entire pastoral landscape, beneath their beautiful sky, on their soft grass, near their rumbling waterfall, in their shaded arbor—it cannot reproduce the unbroken continuum of the pastoral scene. Painting, however, can portray everything; and precisely this everything is its essence. It does not, like sculpture, present a thing in isolation; rather, it shows nothing but the external appearance of that thing within the expansum of visible entities. Painting depicts the shepherd and shepherdess not according to their discrete bodily existence but insofar as the pastoral world contains them. Here the green shade of their arbor; there the chorus of nymphs who listen to their songs and the grove through which these echo; above them Dawn, in her rose-tinted robe, who gazes down at them from heaven; beside them the rose laden with silvery dew and the dainty lily glowing in the sunrise; and in the pond before them the image of the garden and the blossoming trees, around which swarms of butterflies with party-colored wings chase one another—precisely this everything, here appearing as the great continuum of the pastoral world, is the unchanging tableau of painting. What sculpture, which represents bodies only as bodies, cannot show at all, the expansum of things, is its essence and vast empire.

Can one art model itself on another without forfeiting its fundamental qualities? No! Everything that can be felt immediately through the contours of a body is the proper domain of sculpture; here dwells that invisible perfection that manifests itself in the material, taking only as much as it requires to make itself tangible; here dwells that archetype of meaning and gentle expression and shapeliness. All this has been imparted to the dead stone in order that it simply reside there. Painting would exceed its limits altogether were it to apply to a single one of its figures the full force of these demands, which pertain only to the corporeality of stone. It can no more meet these demands than sculpture can attain to the essence of painting, which furnishes only the outlines and appearances of objects insofar as they are contained in the expansum of Nature. The brook

——wenn Zephyrs Fittich drauf
der Bäume Blüten weht,
die Silberflut, auf ihre Decke stolz,
Rauscht froh dahin und hauchet Duft——

—this brook is picturesque, but can sculpture give it form? The tree shedding its leaves and covering Petrarch's Laura with them is a beautiful image for painting, but can sculpture give it form? All the phenomena that arise in the continuum of the visible—the night, lightning, air, light, flame, and so on—are picturesque. Sculpture can imitate none of them, and even if it could, it must never intend to; it must never intend to give form to anything that does not contain the sphere of its dignity and expression wholly within itself, within its tangible self. *Spatial phenomena as such are the subject of paintings; tangible, beautiful bodies belong to sculpture.*

From my single concept adduced above, I can draw a further conclusion: for precisely it makes *composition or rather juxtaposition essential to painting.* Since to the eye things appear not really behind but rather alongside one another, already this means that painting must depict, from the single viewpoint that it adopts, a number of objects whose wholes or at least parts are arrayed *beside one another.* If all the laws of composition, distribution, disposition, and so on, that govern painting derive from this primary concept, as is evidently the case, and if this concept is not essential to sculpture, then the severity of these laws will be alien to it. Do not, therefore, look for a picturesque distribution in groups of statues, for sculpture does not depict or *juxtapose* objects on a plane. It creates in depth and it creates form. Conversely, do not separate a figure from the whole in painting, for by itself it is nothing; only in its relation to the whole is it everything.

The color clavichord is accordingly an absurdity. All objects of sight originally appear *alongside* one another; this allows the eye, which is always bedazzled at first, the time and space to sift through and observe them. To begin with, the eye only *gapes*; but if it is to enjoy fine art, it must *see*, and to that end Nature paints her beauties alongside one another. And now someone appears who wants to turn things upside down, to turn *coexistence* into *succession*, eye into ear. What? If he does not give the eye time to observe, if the eye has only a moment to gape at something, then all refined pleasure—indeed, ultimately all pleasure—is forfeit and we are left with a painful, perpetual numbness. The eye is designed for peace and tranquillity; it is the coldest and most philosophical of the senses. It demands that objects be presented before it; these appear only alongside one another, and that is how they are to be observed also. If the eye can view them in this way, if the color clavichord gives it time to do so, then this whole invention is nothing but a play on words; it is a succession of images, nothing more. If the eye cannot view them in this way, then what the clavichord produces is not a beautiful and agreeable art but the art of an inane and painful gaping.

For the very same reason, the acclaimed portrait by Van Loo, in which all the allegorical virtues are executed in such a way that seen through a glass they combine to form the head of his king, has no real merit as a painting. It is fine flattery of the king; it is a good optical conceit, but it is not a painterly one. Within the limits of painting, I can view the original allegorical picture and the final portrait only one at a time; how one image emerges from the other is an optical illusion, not a new painterly virtue. But such corrections follow step by step, and the reader can make them himself.

Third, *light renders visible the great tableau of images that lies before the eye; hence a mass of light also, so to speak, constitutes the whole disposition [Haltung] of the painterly surface*—and which some indeed call modeling. We are not yet talking of colors, of individual instances of light and shade, of specific effects of aerial perspective; we are speaking only of the chiaroscuro, of the diffusion of that clear-obscure which gives all things light, color, and existence. This follows from the first concept associated with the sense organ of painting, whereas sculpture knows nothing of it. The modeling of sculpture conforms solely to the laws of bodies; thereupon rests a statue's position, its posture, its proportion, and so on. The modeling of painting lies on the continuum of its surface and conforms to laws of light and space: hereupon rest transparency and transition, appearance and reflection, position and counterposition, all the rules of composition, insofar as they depend on lighting. Up to this point painting and engraving still coincide with each other, and the former, which has no colors, must imitate all the magic of color by working with the mass of light alone. That it is able to do so to a degree follows from what I have just said; it has, so to speak, *wholly* in its hands that body which, divided and refracted in Nature, yields colors: *light*. To a certain extent, therefore, it can replace color with light, which is the source of color.

But now painting parts company with engraving. *The ray of light, refracted and modified upon a surface, produces colors; colors are therefore the magic dust with which the paintbrush dazzles the eyes.* This is where the fine detail of that brush's distinctive features begins. If many have spoken so perfunctorily of coloring, then they have mostly had in mind the dead application of color, which really dazzles only the physical eye and not the imagination. True coloring assists in the expression of the picture's meaning, in its composition; it is the flower of perfection to which even the cartoon, even the rolling contour aspire. It helps, as it were, to complete all these concepts and stamps the ultimate seal of truth on its appearances in space, for it is by means of color that we see these most clearly, most distinctly, and with the greatest differentiation and no longer doubt their presence. So just as the hand of our imagination can ascend no higher than when it feels all the attributes of its thoughts and of its ideal of beauty given bodily form in stone, so the mind's eye is also satisfied, as it were, when, after examining all the objects arrayed on the single plane of painting, its design, composition, modeling, and so on, it finally loses itself in the *confirmation of all these things through color.* Then the beautiful illusion of the phenomenon is complete.

One thing still remains. *Sight does not properly see distance, extent; for sight, all phenomena lie on one plane; and the same is unquestionably true of the painting of the ancients.* Just as we have eventually learned, through touch and movement, to estimate magnitude, extent, and distance, and just as sight has grown so accustomed to these relations that it immediately perceives them together with the objects themselves, so painting has had to emulate this visual prejudice, giving rise to the last, most artificial technique: *perspective in its various forms.* I am amazed that in their dispute over whether the ancients possessed knowledge of perspective, many moderns appeal without distinction to its excellency in their statuary, as if everything in this art came after perspective. As if the beautiful *forms* of sculpture meant *for touch* could not have risen to such a degree of perfection without being able to represent *distance for the eye?* Touch is, as it were, the first, surest, and truest sense to develop; already in the embryo it is in the earliest stages of its evolution, and only over time are the other senses unfurled from it. The eye follows behind at quite some distance, but how much farther behind lags the eye's ability to judge distance and extent accurately? What is true of the history of human nature is also true of the history of the arts among the nations. The fashioning of forms for touch existed long before the depiction of figures for sight. And how much later did the representation of distances as such develop? And by diverging from their actual dimensions? That is quite another matter!

On the surface, then, one should not appeal to sculpture. As soon as one finds, however, that its artists have abandoned the immediacy of the sense of touch and also fashioned their statues to be displayed in elevated positions and at a distance, does one not also see significant steps being taken in the optics of the art? To create a statue that on the ground, at eye level, is entirely lacking in shape and proportion and yet has shape and proportion when enthroned on high—this art demands a far more advanced knowledge of optics than the simpler measuring of a few distances on a surface. In the latter case, Nature conveys distance by the different sizes of the objects before us; now, if painting has become her imitator, then it need not take any radically new step to reproduce these sizes consistently; thus the first attempt at perspective is made, unconsciously and quite spontaneously. But what a mighty leap it was for sculpture to leave behind bodily truth, proportion, and form—the attributes of touch, its principal sense—and to work toward the illusion of another, alien, fleeting sense. How much consummate artistry was required to give the figure depth and projection, height and symmetry for a distant, lower point of view? And since the ancients knew how to do this and applied it to their statues, are we to believe that they, for whom all arts went hand in hand, were ignorant of the more simple beginnings of painterly perspective? It seems to me that the history of the human spirit's progress both in art and in Nature heaves into view here also. May I sketch a few stages in this development?

The eye's ability to perceive perspective was first exercised on bodies that appeared behind bodies; it is here that we learn to recognize extent, magnitude, and dimension, and here also that perspectival art was first practiced. Those long rows of columns that cause temples apparently to vanish into the distance; those great architectural profiles that stand out as the lightest, straightest, freest, and most sharply defined and that demonstrate proportion and congruity or disproportion and incongruity at their most simple; those arrangements which so readily and easily convey ideas of columns that are near, beautiful, or distant; those arches with their light and their opening, indeed those simple columns which seem to grow thinner the higher they reach—these were without a doubt the first experiments made in this art, just as the tapering of treetops, the curving line (wherever it is found in Nature, whether in caves and forests, in grottos and arbors) that narrows when seen from afar, and finally the long rows of people and avenues shrinking into the distance; just as these were the first models of perspective provided by Nature. Thus it was in buildings that perspectival art could first attain a degree of perfection, even if these were originally only arbors, huts, avenues, and the adornment of caves or grottos. The adornment was simple, keeping close to Nature and to necessity, the mother of all invention.

This art progressed and reached its pinnacle in the design of temples and in scene painting. Since in the latter instance it availed itself of everything in order to afford the eye a great and lavish spectacle, it is absurd to imagine here a wild jumble of objects lacking every notion of order and beauty. Thus far, all antiquity bears witness to these developments, and the progress of human reason, which was obliged not to strike out on its own but merely to follow the examples of Nature, is a guarantor. Once one species of perspectival art achieved perfection, it soon had to drag the others along after it, even if they followed at some distance.

Let us first of all consider sculpture from the point of view of history; but after investigating how this art emerged from touch, was originally directed toward touch without the mediation of other senses, can we say what power tore it from the fine instruments of touch and represented it to the eye, first naturally and then perspectively? It is the same power that as we grew up taught us to substitute the eye for feeling; namely, the habit of making everything as easy as possible for ourselves. This habit, the offspring of our innate love of repose, abridged the tactile sense, so laborious and slow in our interactions with all bodies, and awarded its office to the eye that feels from afar. The very same habit was at work in art also; it took the statue out of the hands of the artist who molds and gives it form, out of the hands of the connoisseur who feels his way around it, and proffered it to the eye. This step brought a fundamental change in sculpture and pointed the way to perspective.

To the man who is cured of blindness, who previously had known everything through touch, the objects he sees must, once the initial befuddlement has passed, when everything lay before his eyes like a vast painted panel, seem smaller and slighter than they appeared to him before. When he was blind, he was able, through feeling, to discern more parts and qualities inherent in these objects; he experienced them in their fullness and completeness; now, after the initially overwhelming clarity of the dazzling light has passed, he sees in them, in contrast to what he perceived through touch, nothing more than an incomplete, meager surface, nothing more than an insubstantial image, into which their abundant form has dwindled. The blind man whose vision was restored by Cheselden was astonished to discover that he did not see in his friends what he had previously felt, and that the people and things he loved most were not the most beautiful to the eye. We can no longer appreciate this difference because by long-ingrained force of habit, touch and sight have been coupled, equated, and compensated with each other. Yet the contrast between the two must originally have been as manifest as the relation of a whole, complete feeling to the more distinct though incomparably weaker and, as it were, pettier sensation of a visual image; as manifest, then, as the relation of a solid body to a plane surface, of the *Apollo Belvedere* to an Apollo depicted in an engraving.

So what had to be done to replace this original, stronger sensation, to give the eye, too, a share in the profound impression that the deep pleasure of touch had previously felt so inexpressibly? The phenomenon had to be stripped of the petty quality that it now possessed before the eye and that it had formerly lacked in its completeness; the mass of the object had to be augmented and enhanced so that it conveyed an impression with the same force that previously manifested itself through touch. *And thus sculpture became colossal.* There is no more profound or natural explanation of this first, early step toward superhuman dimensions. The *Jupiter* of Phidias was to have the same effect on the eye as it would originally have had on touch. To achieve this equation of two organs, touch proper and surrogate touch, the mass of the statue was increased so that it became almost a colossus. As such, it would of course seem vast and incomprehensible to touch and thus to the sense of sight beyond the limits of beauty; but it was made not for this sense but for another; for another that would receive the same powerful impression that it had for touch; for another that delivered impressions only of image and surface, hence for which no impression could be augmented save by enhancing the image and figure. And how could this enhancement occur other than by increasing the mass that its image, its figure projects to the perceiving sense? The statue thus became colossal.

This observation applies equally to the totality of these representations of the great gods and heroes as well as to their individual parts. The essence of this evolving art is thereby able to explain the *Jupiter* of Phidias as intimately as it can the dimensions of its counterpart in Homer; and the disproportionately long legs of *Apollo Belvedere*, which according to Hogarth contribute so much to the impression of its grandeur, corroborate what I have been saying on a smaller scale. I shall pass over the remaining peculiarities that follow from individual examples of outsize sculpture and shall point out only how different painting is with respect to the colossal. Painting, which never has to take the place of an original feeling, which does not have to represent a body directly—that is, as a body—but rather depicts it only as it is reflected in a continuum, cannot make the same use of the colossal that sculpture does. Suppose that a painter wished to paint a colossus in a continuum so that its different size would stand out against smaller figures; well, this difference in their relative sizes is just as visible on a smaller panel as on the most enormous one. A Hercules bound by little Amors has, if his proportions are correctly observed, exactly the same significance in a miniature as on a surface measuring a hide; so what use is vastness of scale? It is fruitless daubing.

But it becomes more than fruitless if we recapitulate our original observation that the essence of painting is the representation of a surface as surface, with all the visible objects that this continuum superficially contains. No human eye can survey a colossal surface, a colossal space, and the colossal objects within it; our eye therefore lingers only on parts of this space: it cannot grasp the whole; the effect is lost. The picture is no longer a picture; it is an assemblage of painted fragments. It is as if the whole did not exist. This is not true of the colossi of sculpture; there the eye is no longer eye; it is a touching that like its original sense, as it were, gradually gropes its way around the statue and in this state of exalted wonderment desires to feel for itself the grand impression that touch would have enjoyed with smaller, more natural proportions. The same reason that accounts for the colossal in one art rules it out in another. Let us change the scene and take a detour through Egypt.

5

Why are most ancient Egyptian works, including their sculpture, not just colossal, like a statue by Phidias, but supercolossal, truly gigantic? Possessed of this magnitude, are they not more than mere surrogates? Are they not rather an overextension, as it were, of the sense of touch, so that even where it operates through the eye it is overwhelmed by the works and loses itself in immeasurable darkness? The reason given earlier is therefore not by itself sufficient, and those which are otherwise adduced explain still less. If, as their misshapen figures suggest, the Egyptians knew nothing of beauty, did they also have no notion of true magnitude? Is this the reason why their statuary was monstrous not only in form but also in height? If they loved works that were durable and imperishable, were not their buildings, their temples, their pyramids, their obelisks, enough to express these qualities? Why also their statues, which consequently vanished into the clouds and, by striving for eternality, became unrecognizable? Indeed, how could they be everlasting, since such height, combined with such weight and erected on such a small base, had to accelerate their collapse? So did the Egyptians act against themselves and their aim of giving their works immortality for no good reason? I think not; and what is more, I believe the Egyptians can explain a great leap forward in the development of the human spirit.

If we do not perceive the magnitude of phenomena immediately but instead only suppose and infer it according to the angle that they paint on our eye, then, without sufficient experience of what is only appearance, we are liable in our earliest judgments to make mistakes about size—which must run into the gigantic. When a child learns to see, all shapes seem to be fixed on the eye; as they begin to recede, what can they be but—enormous colored images? Cheselden's blind man was made to see; he too learned to separate the images from the eye and saw———enormous shapes. We wander in a twilit world, as it were, midway between the pitch-dark night of blindness and the daylight of vision; we can see, but not clearly, not distinctly. We can neither distinguish qualities and colors nor measure distances and intervening spaces—what do we see? We mistake a nearby tree for a distant apparition coming closer, for a terrible monster. These errors are made by our organs of sight and also, as we shall see, by our imagination, by our soul.

What are the first shapes that impress themselves on the soul of a child? Gigantic figures, supernatural monsters. The perceiving imagination of a minor knows as yet no measure of truth, which emerges only through a long chain of judgments. These first impressions, then, must of necessity still lie in the imagination, since it knows not how to order and range them under the appropriate point of view; the imagination is overwhelmed by them as if by colossal deformities, and if their effect is protracted, it grows accustomed to them as the measure of truth; hence children's predilection for the marvelous and the fabulous, which often loses itself in grotesqueries and a ludicrous immensity. Hence also their attachment for the most part to what is astonishing and supernatural in religion and history. Hence their favorite pastimes are fables, witches' stories, and poems. Parents, educators, teachers! These are the limits of the human mind, but do not let them become its template! The gigantic, the colossal is inevitable when the eye is first opened, but the eye should not model itself thereon and take the measure of these forms as the eternal yardstick of all phenomena in life. Physically, the eye weans itself from the monstrous of its own accord; touch and the other senses intervene and help to lift the magic veil; the images recede, find their limits, and attain the measure of truth. But in education let experience be a schoolmistress of truth instead of touch and let Pallas remove the mist from our eyes and dispel the too-near dazzling illusion.

It is obvious how difficult this might be since we cannot always assure ourselves by the immediate judgment of experience of all those things that strike the eye as colossal when we encounter them in stories and in lessons. Some souls, at least as far as some classes of objects are concerned, remain for the rest of their lives like Swift's moon, where phantoms and gigantic figures forever roam. And for all the good the initial jolt of these overstrong impressions does in rousing our soul, in setting its everlasting tone, they nevertheless become just as great a hindrance if in the years of our second education we does not correct and order them down to every detail.

The same is true of the childhood of entire nations, as is shown by the histories of all peoples and their progress in all the arts and sciences. The first notions of religion and the interpretation of Nature; the first ideals of poetry and music; the first laws governing statecraft and conduct; finally, the first beginnings of philosophy and fine art—all these are exaggerations. They are the initially dazzling panel of colored figures that struck the eye; some nations learned to separate them, others allowed them to congeal; and these latter peoples never attained to knowledge of the truth.

So after the Egyptians came to present statues not just to the sense of touch but also to the eye with the aim of conveying the impression of scale, then naturally and in accordance with the analogy of all beginnings, they became exaggerated and colossal. The Egyptians were not the only people to take this step, but fortunately for others it did not remain the highest and ultimate stage in their art. The Greeks went further and found the measure of beauty; the Egyptians, however, this hard and lawful people, at once imposed rule and habit on the form of their experiments. Enamored of the buildings of the boundless, they also endowed their art with this quality; now, as it became law and habit, so the childhood of this people was without end. Their art was like a religion, which, founded in the age of wonder and exaggeration and therefore at the dawn of the world, becomes canon too soon and forever more unalterable and thought to be infallible. It will thus never be amended and will always remain a dream of the dawn. The man who in the twilight gloom took trees to be apparitions—if you do not allow him to assure himself otherwise, if you even command him by law or based on the most reliable testimony to believe that they were indeed ghosts—will always believe them to be such. How necessary it is, therefore, always to inquire and never to desist until one has not only the semblance but also the measure of truth.

In art it was the Greeks who found the measure of truth, and now we turn back to seek the step that took them from colossal statuary to perspective in sculpture. Once a people has discovered the route to fashioning statues that surpass the proportions of touch and are intended only for the eye, then the way is clear to make them for a number of points of view that the eye might adopt. And since the architectural adornment of the stage, as we have seen, had advanced so far, we have arrived directly at the perspectival relief, which leads in turn to sculpture proper, which the Greeks, as we know, likewise used as adornment. And if they were acquainted with perspective in sculpture, would painting have remained ignorant of it? Where it is easier to depict than in sculpture? So we see that if we wish to deny that the Greeks were familiar with perspective, we must as least distinguish its different forms and decide which one it is to be.

More than this is not my purpose here, since I meant to investigate only the laws of painting as they are dictated by its nature. And how much more might be said here with respect to determining the *original visual beauty proper to painting* and the extent to which its sister arts have no claim to it. A little French book entitled *Physics of Beauty and Its Charms*, whose author, I believe, is called Morelly, and which I have also seen in a dreadful old German translation, has made the first attempts to explore the phenomena of touch and sight; but I do not now have it to hand, except in the form of an extract that I made while reading it. It is regularity and symmetry that, according to the book, give rise to beauty, whose effect as charm the author analyzes to some extent. But *a physical and mathematical optics of the beautiful* in general, such as I desire, his little book is certainly not. A truly great *science of beautiful semblance* still lies unborn in the womb of the undiscovered future; it will be founded as much on mathematics and physics as the aesthetics of thought rests on logic and language. I do not haphazardly prophesy its existence because Baumgarten and Boden, for instance, have written of aesthetic and poetic light and shade; whoever is familiar with the works of these authors will know that they treat only of a borrowed and figurative concept. But I am not talking of any metaphor; rather, because—properly speaking—visible beauty is nothing but appearance, there must therefore be an entire science, a great science devoted to this appearance, an aesthetic phenomenology that awaits a second Lambert.

It seems to me that we Germans might be closest to it, because, apart from the exactness of our analyses, to which we have accommodated even our language and style, we have theories of the individual arts of visible beauty that are the envy of our neighbors. If, as Winckelmann says, no one has written about the beautiful with any feeling for it since Plato, then his own writings were composed not after a fleeting glance but rather as he felt, as it were, the pictorial beauties in the living embrace of his hands. His first work, *Reflections on the Painting and Sculpture of the Ancient Greeks*, was formed with the richest unction and in the dawn of his awakening feeling; this and his *Essay on the Capacity for the Sentiment for the Beautiful in Art* and *the essentials of his history of art* are a goldmine that will enrich all aesthetics. If he speaks too generally, then one need only limit his judgment to the art of visible beauty and to his own point of view, which is principally sculpture, in order to love it; and the same also goes perhaps for the Platonic part of the original work by Mengs. But I would have the most to say if I wished to list the contributions to the general aesthetics of the beautiful contained in Hagedorn's *Reflections on Painting*. The *poetic theory of painting; the richest, most painterly philosophy*—but nowadays it is fashionable to talk generally of writings on art and fairly drip with nothing but Hagedorns, de Piles, Félibiens, Lairesses, Hogarths, and Bardons. Even with the most painterly ideas of his treatise, Riedel did not understand this poetic theory of painting, this rich, painterly philosophy, which is a treasure for Germany, and Klotz, for all his citations of the same, is not worthy of reading it.

6

How different is the palace of the *aesthetics of hearing* from the *philosophy of visible beauty*? No less different than are eye and ear, sound and color, time and space. The beauty of the eye is colder, more in front of us, more susceptible to decomposition, and it abides eternally, waiting to be found. The pleasure of music lies hidden deep within us, and its effect is intoxication; it vanishes, leaving behind no more trace of its existence than the ship on the sea and the arrow in the air and the thought in the soul. So can you, O philosopher, turn your inner feeling outside yourself and analyze the indivisible tone like a color? Can you feel and at the same time think and catch the fleeting moment and fix it to eternity? Then speak! Then create a science that yet lies unborn in the womb of sensation!

So we do not have a science of music? Who would suspect that? The Eulers and d'Alemberts and Diderots and Mersennes and Gravesandes and Sauveurs have brought the physics and mathematics of music to a degree of perfection that only the optics of colors has been able to attain. They have computed the varying number of a string's vibrations according to its length, strength, and weight, and on this basis they have calculated tones and hence the relations of tones and hence harmony and hence the rules of composition right up to the level of algebra. In areas concerning what we might call the physical quality and mathematical quantity of tone, acoustics has very nearly been perfected. Conversely, who is not familiar with the excellent *practical guides* to the arts of hearing that Germans in particular have, in their own way, raised almost to the same exalted heights? Is there a music lover and connoisseur who does not recognize Quantz's *Flute*, Bach's *Piano*, Mozart's *Violin School*, and Agricola's *Art of Singing* as masterly theories of these instruments, the likes of which our neighbors scarcely possess? Both ends of musical science, the most abstract part above and the practical part below, are therefore perfect. But is there nothing in between? I think there is indeed! And it is in this vast and empty middle ground that we shall find the as-yet-undeveloped portion we were seeking.

Physics and mathematics—how do they distinguish and determine tones? By the vibrations of a string in a given time, according to its tautness, thickness, and length. And what is calculated from these relations in the tone itself? Nothing but more relations—high pitch and low, loudness and softness, consonant and dissonant intervals, the synchronous and the consecutive, and so on—nothing but relations that in the natural sciences, where they belong, may suffice to recognize the tone and derive conclusions from that knowledge but that, as we will see, are absolutely meaningless for the aesthetics of melody. They explain nothing *of the simple tone, nothing of the energy it exerts on the hearing, nothing of the charm it possesses both in isolation and in succession; these relations explain none of this.* Thus they furnish not one iota toward the establishment of the *philosophy of tonal beauty*.

They explain, I say, nothing *of tone*. For how does physics understand tone? As a sound arising from the vibrations of a body, which it explains externally, as the effect of a body in relation to so many other bodies, to the string, to the air, to the percussion of the tympanum in the ear; in other words, to so many physical objects. It provides a physical explanation. Do I thereby know anything of the tone of the aesthetic feeling itself? No. In the body that produces it, in the swirling air that carries it, in the outer ear that receives and refines it, the tone is sound, a wave of disturbed air, a body. But do I know how it becomes that simple thing, that audible point, as it were, which I sense deep within me, which I call tone and distinguish so distinctly from sound? And is this simple and sensible tone an object of physics? No, no more than is the mathematical point. Physics cannot investigate, explain, or make use of tone. It knows nothing of it.

And mathematics does just as little. It understands tone as the difference between the vibrations of a body in space and time—and thus understands tone as a *quantity*, as an abstract whole composed of parts. Do I thereby learn anything of its quality? No. The first vibration of the string already produces the whole tone that affects the ear, and all subsequent vibrations do nothing but sustain it, nothing but renew it each moment through a repeated pulse of the air. What, the succession of these pulses, the quantity of these homogeneous renewals of the initial vibration—that is the tone? Can this succession explain anything of the tone's originality, interiority, and simplicity? Do I know what a body is when someone says to me: "It travels through this much space in this much time?" And do I know what a tone is if I know that it vibrates so many times a second? Every sensation in every organ is generated by repeated pulses: of the light on the eye, of odors in the nose, vibrations of the air in the ear; but do these repeated pulses ever explain the original sensation of a sense organ? Do they not count in all senses as if they were a single continuous percussion? And if I am acquainted with this continuation only by its abstract concept, do I know anything more than a quantity? I am acquainted with the sensation only as a whole composed of parts and know how these parts relate to one another; I know, for example, how in a ray of light, red and green are variously refracted, how in a sound the vibrations of one string compare with another. What I know, then, is an abstract relation of successive moments. But do I thereby know one whit of the simple, original moment with which all subsequent ones are homogeneous? I know as little of the first as I do of the last. I recognize succession but no simple, inner moment of that succession. Abstracting from relations, the mathematician knows no more *what tone is* than the physicist.

Still less are they both troubled by the question of how tone *affects us* as tone. Not the physicist, who recognizes it merely as sound. He follows it from the string through the air, from the air to the ear, through the auditory canal to the auditory nerve, but always as a sound. How shall he know, then, how the nerve is struck by what is no longer sound but only simple tone? How it affects the soul and moves it? When does the physicist investigate what is no longer body but, as it were, a mathematical point? And how can he investigate its effects? And its various agreeable and disagreeable effects that we feel within us? That the mathematician, who knows the tone only as a relation, is just as incapable is even more manifest. Let us for the present ascribe to the relations of tones in harmony and harmonic melody as much efficacy on the soul as one might wish; then think of this efficacy as a mathematical authority that sits in the center of the brain and does nothing but count and compute relations, taking the same fervent delight in this activity as Newton did in working out new equations. If we assume this, then I believe I can demonstrate irrefutably that *relation cannot be the original source of pleasure in tones and can explain nothing of the first feeling of their effect.* The proof is simple and the conclusions significant.

The *ear as ear no more feels a relation* than the eye immediately sees distance and smell feels a surface. Let a tone, that refined and as it were simplified pulse of air, enter the ear; what relations does it feel in the tone? None! And yet in the first moment it feels, abstracted from all subsequent tones, the original, simple power of a single, immediate sensation. And yet can such a tone, without being succeeded by and combined with others, convulse us so deeply, stir us so profoundly, move us so violently that this single first moment of sensation, this simple musical accent has a greater inner mass than the sum of all the sensations arising from all the relations, from all the harmonies of an extended piece? Those who have an ardent feeling for music: you will confirm this experience, or else you are not really made for it at all—but what kind of *relation* inheres in this simple moment of sensation?

A *relation of the overtones*, says Rameau, which we hear resonate after the fundamental tone, particularly when a coarse string is set in motion, and which make up his greater perfect chord. As is known, Rameau built his entire harmonics and his commentator, d'Alembert, his whole system of music on this observation. Now, we are not concerned here with the question of which principle *could* be used to explain and tease out all the main laws of music, nor whether Rameau's is the foremost principle, which I very much doubt. But one thing is certain: Rameau's theory does not explain the effect of music on the soul at all; despite its author's wishes, there is nothing it makes less comprehensible to us than these various effects; in fine, on this view, it is no principle at all. Even if there resided in that principle all the proportion that Rameau claims to find and d'Alembert does not, then this proportion would explain nothing of the first moment of sensation. The harmonic tones are resonances [*Nachklänge*], and what do they contribute toward the first intonation of pleasure or displeasure? Further, how might we account for the fact that individual tones accompanied by the same resonances are not *all* pleasant? That not *everyone* finds them pleasant? That not everyone finds them pleasant *to the same degree*? That they are not pleasant *in the same way*? That some tones with the same harmonic resonances can be completely disagreeable from the instant that their initial tone [*Anton*] rings out? And anyway, what can a mere relation explain in the sensation, a relation that is only a late, frigid consequence of that sensation and entirely distinct therefrom? The first moment of sensation is as indivisible as the tone that it produced. What do later resonances matter here?

Perhaps, then, it is the *vividness* of the moment that explains the plea-sure—if, that is, the sensation is not too strong and therefore deafening and therefore disagreeable; and also not too weak but involves the proper degree of interest and is therefore pleasurable. This method of explana-tion is a branch of Sulzer's theory of agreeable sensations, which in this instance, however (and indeed this is true of this particular philosopher's theory as a whole), explains not so much the nature as the limits of sen-sation and thus explains everything only negatively. It does not say why, for example, abstracted from loudness or softness—which is something else entirely—the essence of a tone (insofar as the French call this timbre) is agreeable or disagreeable. Why two equally vivid tones convulse us in the most contrasting fashion. Why with respect to its *nature* a tone can make the most contrasting impression on two people possessed of an equally *strong* sensibility. Why, even with an agreed definition of *pleasure*, the same tone can arouse two different yet agreeable sensations in two dif-ferent people. Does Sulzer's argument explain anything of this? Does it explain anything of the *nature* of sensation? No more than *measure* can ever explain *nature*, or *quantity* and *quality* ever be identical.

So after such unsuccessful attempts to discover why a tone is pleasing or not, would it not be better to drop the question entirely? To declare it fruitless, inexplicable, a reef on which so many have foundered and al-ways will? This is exactly what d'Alembert does with a cold, resolute ex-pression, and as a mathematician he has every right to do so. In mathe-matics, the discovery of this reason will never be of consequence because it uses and computes only the quantity of tones and their relations to one another. For the mathematician as such, the question will always remain a reef as well, for as soon as it is certain *that the ear, as ear, cannot per-ceive relations* and *yet the basis of all music resides in the first moment of sensation, in simple melody,* then it must indisputably follow that *no prin-ciple* at all *can explain the true, first, original pleasure experienced by the ear in terms of relations and proportions.* And if the whole force of music *can properly consist in nothing but such individual first moments,* just as a body can consist in nothing but monads; if it is true that *an aggregate of tones cannot be known and explained if its component parts are not knowable and explicable*, then the inevitable consequence will always be that *the essence, the quality, and the effect* of music cannot be explained *according to relations and proportions*. And whoever *conceives tone merely as relation*, whoever has become so blithely insensible as to *be able to envisage it as nothing but* is right to believe and follow Monsieur d'Alembert.

This is precisely the case with the *physicist* proper. Even without my having in hand a metaphysical hypothesis with which to destroy physics, it is obvious that all the external grooves of the ear and even the tympanum cannot properly be the instrument of *sensation*. They are there to purify, to amplify, to modify the sound; they are the microcosm that simply prepares and as it were forges tone from what was hitherto mere noise, mere undulations of the air. Their function in the ear is equivalent to that performed in the eye by those membranes and fluids which refract the image and re-create it as a smaller world but do not retain and explain it. So what the physicist can explain with these instruments of hearing is nothing but what he finds present in the wider, external world on a larger scale: body and sound. With them he can explain loudness and softness, slowness and quickness, but still only as sound, as body. As soon as a simple line—the tone—emerges from the body, from the sound, it eludes the physicist and vanishes deep into the soul; and so he can no more explain what we want explained—that is, the profundity, quality, variety, and pleasure of tone—than the mystery of sight or of any other sense has hitherto been elucidated by a scientist as such. Here it is a matter of an internal, simple, and effective feeling: the physicist knows only of external, complex phenomena and of motions by their consequences.

So let us not think that mathematical and physical acoustics are what we are looking for! If they contain experiences and calculations that serve our purpose, then all well and good; and though we must never reach a conclusion without them, it is certainly just as imperative that we do not stop there. Rather, we ought to carry the experiences further, into the interior of our sensation, and if the latter shall be made eloquent, know how to disremember the calculations. Let us expect to accomplish only preliminary work and also reconcile ourselves to the fact that the pioneer may always have ventured to overstep the boundaries and thus strayed into error. The undiscovered country that we seek is no idle metaphysical chatter; it is an inner physics of the mind, a fertile and profitable territory in the psychology of the beautiful, a vantage point from where we shall be able to survey a multitude of new regions, once observations and correct inferences have led us there. I shall start from two simple propositions.

Sound and tone are identical in their physical origin, for both arise through the vibration of elastic bodies. Every instrument that is agitated as a whole produces a sound [*Schall*], loud and mixed, in which all tones lie dormant; thus the piano or lute will reply to the sound [*Laut*] that strikes them just as indistinctly with the whole polytonality that lies within them, with a sound [*Schall*]. Let a single clear tone ring out near this instrument, and it will answer with nothing but this tone. Let two tones ring out, and two will answer, and so on, until many tones are mixed together and we have the confused sound once more. Thus there is nothing to stop us from viewing sound as a *mass of many tones*, as *a body composed of many bodies*. That is my *first* observation, which is corroborated by physical experiments.

Let us now apply it to aesthetics. It is well known that certain simple tones, independently of their pitch, loudness, or duration but *according to their intrinsic nature*, make different impressions on us. One strikes us, as it were, more smoothly and brightly, another more roughly and obscurely. One seems to rouse and lift our nerves, the other to depress and benumb them. One causes them to contract in astonishment, another to melt in gentle languor——this we know from experience; let it also be our principle. But if now a man was wanting a sensibility sufficiently refined to distinguish the quite different impressions made by individual tones, a difference on which everything here rests, and if for that reason he meant to deny that this difference even exists, there is still one way of enlightening him. You who can form no notion of the loudness or pitch of tones: pay heed to the sound of a flute and reed, lute and violin, trumpet and cor-de-nuit, and ask yourself whether—even with all the tones mixed together so that there can be no talk of loudness and pitch—it still has *the same nature* and, as it were, *one specific mass of sonority* [*Klang*]. Whether each of these whole sounds affects you in the same way. And if not, if there are bodies in which true sound and echo lie; others in which a groaning and whining reside; still others in which a sighing love god of yearning and complaint is confined—if one instrument howls after the sound of the whole, the second shrieks, the third rings, the fourth forms a quiet wave of sound, the fifth a thunderclap of tones; if, further, each of these sounds has its own relation to our sensibility—with this one we feel nothing, with that one we start up, with another we shiver and tremble, this one lulls us to sleep and that one incites us to bravery and anger, still another arouses pity, compassion, love, this one is piercing, this one screeches as it enters the ear, this one flows gently into us—where can I find the words to describe all this? Who is so deaf that he could not feel this variety of sounds? And if he can, then he must also concede *the diversity of individual tones*, which can be essentially different even where they possess the same pitch, the same degree of loudness, and are thus no more comparable than hard and soft, smooth and rough, empty and full, and so on. If he admits the variety of whole sounds, and *sound is nothing but an obscure aggregate of tones*, then he must acknowledge that this variety must also obtain among the tones, and obtain properly and originally among them because they are the essence of sound. Is there a power in aggregate bodies that does not issue from the powers of their simple parts? Do sounds, as sounds, possess a distinct quality and power that do not emanate from the various powers of their constituent tones?

Sound is therefore a corporeal mass of tones; tones are its simple, effective moments. And what else follows from this? Initially I shall stick more to securing my mode of reasoning than drawing specific conclusions. This is what follows: a race of people, a nation, or an epoch that does not possess sufficient refinement to investigate the first moments of melody must, if it recognizes them, of course keep to sounds; but it *must also not confuse what is merely aggregation in the sounds with the essence of the simple moments.* I have given an example of the former, but it is even more necessary to illustrate the latter. Rameau takes a coarse string and strikes it; the string is still so thick and inelastic that it generates overtones that follow the fundamental tone. The string is therefore the intermediary between sound and tone; it does not produce a mass of tones so confused as to make its musical sound [*Laut*] a noise, but neither is it fine or taut enough for the sound to be a simple silvery tone. What follows from this? For Rameau and d'Alembert a great deal. For my attempt to explain the first moment of melody, nothing, because in this instance there is no pure first moment. Rameau's fundamental harmony is an obscure concept combining many such first moments; it thus takes a compound to be the simple essence of music and the mere residue of sound to be its original element. All bodies bring forth *in sound* all the tones that they are able to produce, just as the entire length of a stretched cord will quiver when struck. That our ear picks up only those tones which are harmonious with it, just as the piano answers only the tone that is harmonious with it; that the ear lets pass the inharmonious or too fleeting intermediate tones and instead flings itself with greater attentiveness on the more distant tones homogenous with it—what is this but the question once more, Why in a sound, in a mass of tones, are some harmonious and others not? And is this experience therefore the underlying principle of all music? On the contrary, there is no principle more one-sided. It takes harmony for a fundamental concept or—and this amounts to the same thing—the combination of parts that form sound for the essential moment of tone. Therefore it can extend no further than to rules for the combination of sounds—that is, to harmony—and therefore it seeks and finds nothing more than relations and therefore knows nothing of the essence of music, of the original tone, or of melody. It is born of the semiobscurity that is sound, and because it took this for the essence of music, it can reach only to semiobscure sounds, to harmonies. Let us therefore consolidate our second observation: *sound and tone are not identical; the former is only an obscure form of composition; the latter is the essence of music.* And equipped with these two principles, let us set off to find our way out of the confusions of mathematics and physics.

7

Sound is a corporeal mass of tones, in which the latter are its essential elements. In the same degree as the masses can be different *in nature*, therefore, the elements must also be *different* with respect to the nature of their sensation. All elastic bodies resound, but not all are sensible in the same way. Therefore there must be as many different classes among the moments of individual tones as there were in their totalities—and different classes arranged not by pitch, as Euler has enumerated them, nor by loudness, however these might be counted out, but by the *sensibility of their constitution and nature.* This constitution is in the first place *disagreeable* and *agreeable*, and then below these two main categories there are as many subcategories as there are disagreeable and agreeable feelings. Each of these feelings must be aroused by a tone or combination of tones, and ultimately there must be as many kinds of tones and sounds as are required to awaken every sensation within us. These conclusions follow naturally from one another, and if the aesthetician of hearing will make the effort to compare ear and eye, tone and color, sound and stream of light, a tonal sensation and visual impression, then at every step he will find confirmation in the analogy with the clearer sense.

I assume, then, this inward tonal variety. How can it be explained? Not, as I say, in terms of pitch or loudness, for abstracted from these it still finds expression, if not in tones, then in their aggregate sounds. Relation and proportion as such are even less fitted to explain it, for these can obtain only with the quantity of the whole, not with the quality of an individual moment, as we shall presently see. Nor can it be explained by a mere change in our state of mind, for with certain tones and sounds the tonal variety persists even in the most contrasting mental states. Whence might it arise? Sound is an aggregate of tones. Just as a specific tone always answers the reverberation of a piano, and the others—at least for us—lie dormant and inaudible; just as when a coarse string quivers and passes through every interval of tones we hear only those that are harmonious, so, when applied to the ear, this analogy must also yield the reason for the *diverse sensibility of tones.*

If we go past the grooves of the ear and the tympanum, organs that exist only to refine sound, we encounter a string music of auditory fibers, which, differing in their number, in their position, in their relation to one another, and in their length, await, as it were, the modified sound. Why was one nerve not sufficient? Why are not all fibers equal in strength? Why are they arranged in different rows and at different distances? Given how they are currently positioned, can each tone strike each fiber in the same measure, in the same relation, and in the same way? We would not need to be acquainted with the structure of the ear and the motion of sound to make that claim, and so we find ourselves on the threshold of the explanation. In the variety of the nerve branches of the ear must lie also the essential and specific variety of the tones and masses of tones—that is, the sounds—insofar as this is, with respect to quality, the basis of musically agreeable and disagreeable sound. The more strongly and profoundly this different quality is experienced in the ear rather than in the eye, the more clearly must the proof be found in the auditory fibers rather than in the nerves of the eye—which after all are also viewed as strings on which the play of colors is performed.

Sound, as body, or its element, *tone*, as line, therefore strikes its string as the ear plays. In this direction or that one? Homogeneously or not? Thereupon rests the *disagreeableness* or, so to speak, the *smoothness* of the tone. That tone is *disagreeable* which causes its nerve to quiver in so uncongenial a direction that all fibers are brought into an unnatural emotion vis-à-vis one another, as if the nerve were about to snap. Then there arises a piercing, grating feeling, or however else we might experience it. It seems to me that all these disagreeable feelings might be expressed through irregular lines, each after its own fashion, which the *mathematics of intensive quantities* might attempt to investigate further. But this vast and difficult science has delivered little more than a first principle.

That tone is *agreeable* which touches and flows through the nervous fibers homogeneously and thus harmoniously; obviously, there are thus two main varieties of this agreeableness. Either a homogeneous *tension* is produced in the nerve and the fibers are at once braced more tightly, or the nerve is *relaxed* and the fibers gradually melt as if in gentle languor. The former is identical to the feeling that in the soul we call *the sublime*; the latter is the *feeling of the beautiful*, or pleasure. Behold: hence issues the main division in music between *hard* and *soft* sounds, tones, and keys—and this demonstrates the analogy between the entire general sensibility of body and soul, in the way that all inclinations and passions are revealed therein.

A British empirical philosopher pursues both these feelings deep into our nature, right down to the tissue of fibers that immediately surrounds the soul, as it were, and who everywhere traces the sublime to a feeling of *tension* and the beautiful to a gentle *relaxation* of the nerves. I am speaking of Burke, author of the *Philosophical Enquiry into the Origin of Our Ideas of the Sublime and the Beautiful*, a treatise that Mendelssohn brought to our attention and Lessing has long promised to translate. Burke can keep his coupling of these two feelings with self-preservation and the social passions; he can keep his *qualitates occultas* of concepts that from a more intellectual viewpoint can admittedly no more be rectified; he can keep everything that is system. But the actual observations contained in his treatise are real discoveries, where now and then, as if through an inner shudder, as if through a profound awareness, one feels their truth. They are discoveries in an exceedingly obscure region that from a distance seems to ordinary eyes an enchanted, cloud-wrapped isle but, when one sails through the mists, is transformed into a lush and luxuriant landscape, a Madeira. It is a pity, though, that Burke was unable to pursue his observations on the feeling of beauty in general through to the thinner threads of finer and more specific feelings! It is a pity that he was not musician enough and in general lacked sufficient artistic experience to make the same observations about these reflective powers! It is a pity, finally, that it is almost impossible, without danger of its becoming a Quaker sensation, to evaluate the *weight* of every impression, every *kind* of nervous vibration, every *communication* and *propagation* of the feelings, which rush, so to speak, from nerve to nerve, and to analyze the intertwining of a multitude of fibers to form a single main category of feeling. How many new and fine observations that would yield, each one a product of the operation of the beautiful and a fertile truth of aesthetics! How many would we have even if we followed Burke's path through the *sense of hearing*? Now he mostly observes only the *clearer* qualities of things that admit of *observation*, of *decomposition*; now he is mostly concerned with a *general* feeling, without properly fathoming its specific varieties; now his objects of experience are mostly drawn from great and unrefined Nature—darkness and brightness, power and privation, smallness, vastness, infinity, light and color, bitterness and smell, sound and loudness, and the cries of animals—these are now his dearest and most abundant objects and not the more polished imitations of the arts. The Briton has thus gathered his laurel crown in the deep and wild groves of Nature; he sought it on precipitous peaks. Yet there are still garlands of flowers to be picked from the flatter regions of beautified Nature————more exact and circumspect Germans! Still they await their favorites, and still there hangs a wreath for the philosopher of melody! Burke confessed that he did not possess enough of an ear to analyze the beautiful in music, and therefore he did not venture to approach the task. Let he who is without hearing follow Burke's modest example; but let the sensitive connoisseur follow his lead on the path where he has blazed a trail——

After taking these first steps toward an explanation of the varieties of charm in tones, one would be on the threshold of apportioning to each species of feeling its own domain of the soul, from where it spreads out into this or that sensation. Here is the road to a *pathetics of all simple mu-*

sical accents, which would examine how certain sensations of the soul recur with certain tones and certain excitations of the brain; how there might therefore exist certain sounds for certain states of mind; and, generally speaking, a material soul whose external sensitive tissue might not entirely elude investigation. What views we would command from here, what views of the many limits and shared borders of the passions, as well as those of sounds and tones! We would see how Dryden's Timotheus passes from emotion to emotion, plunges his Alexander into one sea and then another and, as if his tones were the thread of Ariadne, picks his way through all the labyrinths of sensation and through every smaller aberration in every such labyrinth. If Nature did not know a more direct route to the human soul than through the ear by way of speech and no more direct route to passion than through the ear by way of sounds, tones, and accents—Muse of music, what powers of inspiration are in your hands to unriddle the physiology of the human soul!

In the history of both nations and of the human spirit throughout the ages there are obscurities that cannot be understood by history alone, that are often ridiculed uncomprehendingly, and that can be illuminated only by a certain knowledge of psychology. That is the case with the music of those peoples who associated their tones with certain ideas and their accents with certain subjects; who possessed their song of war and of concord, their tone of anger and of love, their melodies of wisdom and of vice. In this music we would admittedly find many exaggerations: exaggerations among the Egyptians, who raised every such fine thread linking tone and idea into a law; exaggerations among the Pythagoreans, who explained the world in terms of such relations; exaggerations among the Platonists, who made them the basis of political romances; exaggerations among the commentators who admired, exaggerated, and understood nothing; exaggerations among the readers, who laugh and laugh and understand nothing. But in a pragmatic history of music we would seek to understand before we judge, and perhaps say: Look! *a rude and simple people, but one that feels more deeply.* We perceive only sound, where they perceived the element of sound; that is, tone.

We perceive only sound, where they perceived tone. The man born blind has an incomparably deeper feeling for the first moments of melody than the man who sees and is ceaselessly distracted, whom a thousand external superficial images divert from his internal sensibility for tone. The blind man has turned away from such things; he therefore naturally and always enjoys the undisturbed peace that we must snatch on a summer's night so that we might feel more profoundly the sweet sound of a lute or a Benda violin. The blind man, sunk forever in his undisturbed tranquillity, withdrawn wholly into his feeling self, and, I mean this quite seriously, all ears—what does a man free of distraction not perceive in the powerful sweetness of a single tone? Or in the fair voice of his maiden, which for him

——den Himmel öffnet und ins ganze Herz
Ruh und Vergnügen singt.

Does he here calculate relations and proportions? Or harmonies and intervals? How cold, how wretched! In a simple initial tone [*Anton*], which convulses him to his very core and carries him away, he perhaps feels a million times more than we feel in the colorful confusion of an entire piece of music. And it was the same for the more simple, inward, less distracted ancients also. Accustomed since childhood to the true accents of Nature, open since childhood to deeper impressions instead of fugitive images, they felt, where we, who are everywhere distracted, whose feeling is enfeebled by abstractions and a thousand other things, feel nothing. Our first auditory nerve has thus grown more insensible: they heard the element—tone—where we hear only sound, the aggregate of tones.

They heard tone where we hear only sound. Those peoples whose language is still close to song, who utter not dull, confused sounds so much as tones that are already simplified and easily differentiated, who sustain these tones longer and accentuate them more melodiously—singing nations of this kind are naturally closer to the elements of musical feeling than others who utter only reverberating bodies of syllables and sounds [*Lauten*]. The organs of speech and hearing of the former are constituted in such a way that what some peoples merely articulate as an obscure noise, in which all the tones still lie dormant, is with them purified five times like the heavenly kiss of Venus. It is thus no longer, like the clang of iron or the murmuring of a bell, obscurely present, scarcely comprehensible as sound; it has become a silvery tone whose pitch can be musically determined and whose expression can be sweetly appreciated. Where one people delivers words clad in bronze, another, equipped with finer organs of speech, gives forth silver waves, which, forged into darts by its finer instruments of hearing, strike the soul with tones like simple points. These, then, are no metaphors such as those describing the recitative of the ancient Greeks, who possessed, as it were, two dimensions of speech more than we have, harmonics and rhythmics—no metaphors, even if they felt tones more deeply than we do. Even today the half-sung language of the Italians combines with their nature to produce a *sensible* music, just as the mellifluous voice of the female sex is united with a more refined feeling for music. Nature herself has labored on behalf of such peoples. For those who dwelled in a more favorable climate, she has woven finer organs of speech and hearing and created, as it were, a natural string music of sensation. They speak and hear and feel silvery tones, whereas coarser peoples who utter only sounds can also hear only sounds.

They hear only sounds when the former heard tones—is it any wonder, then, that ultimately they also turn their art of listening to and making music into an art of sounds? Accustomed since youth to hear, as it were, heavy masses, which, composed of the most dissimilar parts, only murmur, only produce a din that the ear cannot purify, which therefore also appears as sound before the soul—they will also naturally prefer such heavy masses of tones in their music. They will make every effort to reinforce the effect of a tone they think too weak by playing another simultaneously or rather by destroying the delicate single moment of its essence in the most brutal harmonic fashion. Their music will become the art of feeling all ten tones at once, and therefore none shall be experienced in its primordial musical power. These peoples, who are exceedingly thorough in harmony and composition, very capable in accompaniment and execution, very learned in the science of their art, will make a loud noise in the world and, as they grow used to hearing everything at once, will reach the stage where they no longer hear anything of the single tone that they should have heard only in isolation. They are thus well suited to studying music as a practical art; to measuring mathematically the string that they did not appreciate musically; to counting the vibrations whose initial tone they did not feel; to turning this art into a miracle of musical science, composition, and finger work which they could never experience as a miracle of individual energy. They hear not tones but only sounds; they feel not accents, so they imagine ponderous, Gothic harmonies and theoretical relations.

> Wen aber, o Lycidas
> wen seine Mutter unter den göttlichen
> Gesängen froher Nachtigallchör' empfing,
> wer ihr in sanften Götterfreuden
> nächtlich als Schwan sich vom Busen loswand—
> Ununterwiesen wird der als Knabe schon
> Toneinfalt lieben.

And he will feel that simplicity of tone [*Toneinfalt*] even in the unharmonic melodies of the nightingale and all the singers of the skies; and in the unharmonic accents of Nature's every passion, with each new and lovely twist and variety, he will, like a delicate string tuned to the same pitch, inwardly recognize it and sympathetically repeat it and let it tremble within him forever. And with each tone he will become a more sensitive creature and

> ——froh bestürzt
> sich einen Sänger grüßen hören

and be a monarch of our sensations. Did this son of Nature avail himself of two foreign tones so that he might feel the fundamental? To hear the skyborne singer Aedone did he imagine a fundamental bass accompanying her song? Did he become familiar with the internal power of tones by transforming them into sounds and combining them with all that are both possible and impossible? Did he discover the wonders of imitating Nature and the expression of the heart in a sequence of chords and an interval scale? And did Apelles become a magician of living colors by painting scales of colors and training his eye with such clavichords? And yet that was only more frigid painting and not by a long way music, inward and vital music. O you great harmonists! And then *sound* is *not tone*! And an *art of sounds no art of tones*!

8

Sound is not tone but an aggregate of tones, a bundle of silver darts. In one way or another these must be separated, the air more narrowly enclosed, the string tightened, until one of the tones is fixed. Then it is a dart distinct from the large bundle; what was once body has now become the finest line of contact; then it is musical. Let me use this observation to explain the great *inwardness* of hearing. Nature has made coarse touch the perimeter, so to speak, of our bodily existence; like soft wax it is poured over the surface of our being. The other senses may come closer to our interior, yet my sensation still takes place in the organ itself. The visual image may be present to my soul, but the object of that image hovers clearly outside me. The ear is closest to the soul precisely because it is an *inner* feeling. Viewed as a body, sound affects only the external organs of hearing, where it is still only an outer, general feeling. The filtered simple tone, the mathematical line of sound, as it were—it alone operates on *that* fine auditory nerve which is the neighbor of the mind, and so how inward is it? The tools that Nature employs here in her workshop are the finest, and the tissue that enfolds them so intimately is the most sensitive. It is related to the outer feeling as the line to the body, whereas the inner feeling of the eye seems to relate to the outer feeling only as surface does to body.

Hence the vast, incomparable difference between sound and sensible tone: the former affects only hearing as an outer feeling, the latter affects the soul through an inner feeling. The gentle rustling that I feel so vividly in the "Song to Kleist" by Gleim:

> Freund, welch ein liebliches Geschwätze
> hier dieser Quelle! laß dich nieder!
> So schwätzete des Tejers Quelle
> wenn er im Schatten seines Baumes
> den Rausch der Blätter und die Lispel
> des Zephyrs hörte—

—this gentle, physical feeling is of a quite different nature from a single, spiritual tone, which Gleim subsequently invites us to hear just as vividly:

> —laß dich nieder
> und sitze neben mir und höre
> die Muse meines Tejers, höre
> die Harmonien seiner Leier
> und sieh den Bacchus und den Amor
> ihm horchen: sieh den offnen Busen
> Cytherens wallen; sieh die Nymphen
> der Brunnen ihre Wasserkrüge
> verlassen und zu dieser Quelle
> herfliegen, alle schon im Fluge
> den Sänger horchend—alle wollen
> ihn hören——

A tone sung by this singer and the whispering of the leaves mentioned in the foregoing lines—do they strike the same area of the auditory sense? No more than the thunderclap that convulses me to the core and tears asunder my hearing is the same thing as the single disagreeable tone that also convulses me to the core and threatens to tear asunder my hearing.

This explains the supremacy of hearing over the other senses. The eye, the external watchman of the soul, remains ever a cold observer; it sees a multitude of objects clearly, distinctly, yet also coldly and from the outside. Touch, a strong and thorough natural philosopher among the senses, furnishes the most correct, certain, and as it were complete ideas; it is very powerful so that it can excite the passions, but, united with these, it becomes excessive; yet its feeling always remains external. The imagination must, as it were, take the place of touch in order to make it eloquent; for all the imagination's power, it cannot draw touch into its domain. Hearing alone is the most inward, most profound of the senses. Though it is not as distinct as the eye, neither is it as cold; though it is not as thorough as touch, neither is it as coarse; yet it is closest to sensation as the eye is closest to ideas and touch to the imagination. Nature herself has acknowledged this proximity, for she knew no better path to the soul than through the ear and through language.

Here there would be great scope for the pragmatic historian of music to engage with those arts whereby some ancient peoples sought to make this so very spiritual art even more spiritual and to incorporate it deep into the soul. We are familiar with all the effects that they ascribed to music: in education on the way of thinking and the cultivation of the soul; in politics on the manners of the people; in philosophy on the improvement and pacification of the mind. These historical data would furnish the theorist of the aesthetics of hearing with various phenomena to study which here can only divert me from my path; but what poetic language did they use when they wished to intimate the *inwardness of music as such*? The inner shudder, the all-powerful feeling that seized them they were unable to explain; they knew of nothing in all of visible Nature that could affect them so inwardly and profoundly. So they believed that spirits, spirits of heaven and earth, had been drawn toward them by the chains of music, had descended from celestial spheres and risen from tombs, and floated all about them, invisibly, to be sure, yet all the more sensibly. To feel the presence of these beings would be the inner shudder, the deep feeling that took hold of them when they heard the tones ring out!———Here I wish the philosopher of melody had the magic power to transform into real phenomena all these apparitions conjured to explain the inwardness of music, and when he has investigated *the potency of individual accents and passions and tones and musical elements*, he will be able to!

The aggregate of harmonious tones is still sound as well, though it is the most regular sound; *hence harmony can no more be the fundamental concept of music than composition can be the essence of a body*. The chord consists of three tones, which because they are harmonious are more readily heard together than others; which precisely by dint of being heard together raise a concept of proportion and hence of pleasure. But can this pleasure be the fundamental pleasure of music? It is the result of a composition and thus an arid concept of the mind; the three tones that are prone to being heard together are essential only in their individual elements; their combination as such is nothing but a state—and what shall this state explain? So even if Rameau's observation were as true in itself as it perhaps now appears to be untruth, the philosopher of melody will find it an arid, one-sided, and unfruitful observation. The chord is only sound, and all harmonies of chords are only sounds; sound is only a composition, from which can follow only more composition and its abstraction, relation. Students of melody: Does this give you even the slightest idea of the inner moment of a single tone? Of the power of a single accent on the soul? Of a single succession of accents, which sustains and reinforces that power? Of every succession of every accent in all its different languages of sensation, its emotions and irregularities and disproportions? Of the whole expression of music? No! You know only a combination of many tones to form a sound, where each individual tone forfeits its effect and is nothing in itself; where the blending of the parts into a whole produces a sensation that is distinct from its individual components, which, though beautiful and regular to the mind, is crude and frigid to the ear. You know only a lifeless composition, faced with which you cannot even explain, and perhaps in time will not even be able to feel, what a vastly different effect the mere inversion of the chords would have and how more effective each primordial tone would therefore be if its delicate power were not choked by regular noise. You know only a lifeless regularity, so you imagine nothing but a lifeless succession of lifeless regularities—you hear only sound, not tone; you conceive of mathematical relations because you no longer feel the pleasure of tones.

If there is another sensitive youth who can perceive tones as such, let him become a philosopher in the aesthetics of hearing. Nothing but simple, effective musical moments, individual tone accents of passion—those are the first things that he feels and gathers, which evolve into a *musical monadology*, a philosophy of the *elements of music*. Then he links them by *the bond of succession*, in their agreeableness to the ear, in their effect on the soul; this becomes *melody*, and melody and all that it entails constitute the main area of his investigations. *Harmonics* as such, as we moderns understand the word, is to his aesthetics what logic is to poetry; and what fool would seek the poet's main purpose in logic? From the division I have made, it is apparent that the science I long for scarcely exists as yet. Because *harmonics* is for us northern peoples in particular the preferred and almost exclusive object of the theory of music—fine where its mathematical and practical aspects are concerned, but as far as aesthetics goes harmonics is good for nothing save perhaps for leading us astray into false and dead systems of relations, where the essence of music is lost. If tone is not sound, then a *theory of tone* and not a *theory of sound*, *melody* and not *harmony* constitute the main body of *aesthetic music*.

I cannot lay down rules; my aim is to present a history of individual experiences. As language, music does not of course come as naturally to human beings as song to birds—this is demonstrated by our earliest needs, by our organs of speech that express those needs, by our similarities with other unmusical animals, and by the history of every nation. If the earliest needs are painful sensations, then the earliest language is a shrieking of unarticulated tones; and if the satisfaction of these needs brings pleasure, then their language is likewise a language of sensation, of unarticulated tones. Both are high-pitched, resound loudly, pierce the ear and the soul, and become powerful accents of the emotions—they are the first foundation of language. And if it can now be proved that human beings arrived at musical art by way of language, then it follows that the accents of individual powerful tones were the origin of music.

So human beings formed for themselves a language that was but a succession of rough, high-pitched, strong, and drawn-out accents, insofar as these could express needs, feelings, and sensuous ideas. And, as will be readily apparent to everyone, precisely from these materials did primitive song develop; for how else do song and speech differ than that the former produces not mixed sounds but rather more determinate, more drawn-out tones and accents of sensation? Men thus sang as they spoke but this singing speech was not the music of birds. It lacked *agreeable tones*; for these tones, formed harshly and with difficulty by the earliest, still un-practiced organs of speech, were vented strenuously and ungently, partic-ularly in northern regions. It lacked an *agreeable succession* of these tones; for since they were ejaculated by need and disorderly, violent emotion, they were intended only to pierce and convulse the heart and soul but not to flatter the ear. So if birdsong furnishes us with our first ideas of music in Nature, if the latter's fundamental properties are sweet tones and har-monious sequences meant only for the ear, then the first human language was not music but merely a spoken shrieking.

But is birdsong the earliest natural music? Does a single bird sing merely on account of the physical agreeableness of the tones that it produces, whether for its own benefit or that of other creatures? Does the nightin-gale sing to please its own or another's ear with mere tones and melodies? No, its song is language, the language of passion and of need, like the lion's roar or the wolf's howl and man's first crude singing speech. The latter lies somewhere between the howl of the wolf and birdsong—man has this in common with both: he desires not to sing but to *speak*, as do the bird, wolf, and lion, each in its own way.

But the human race, as the sum of its successive generations, has a dif-ferent character and, as it were, one facet more than the bird, wolf, and lion. For these creatures, their language is a natural instinct and artistic impulse, one that develops at an early age and that they take with them to the grave. The human race, though, is brought together by the long line of its individual members, and thus also by every individual invention, and thus also by language. Language is hereditary; each link in the chain learns it from its predecessor; it is carried forward, constantly changed, and thus often improved, often degraded; it marches onward and lasts for-ever, like the prerogative of humanity, reason. So let us assume as many epochs as are necessary to lend enough perfection to this crude singing speech so that a species of the human race might, from its point of view, think it ideal. That means the development of a more refined song of sweeter-sounding tones and melodies, the essence of which, however, is still to express thought, sensation, need; tone as tone, melody as melody are still only of secondary importance. Song is still *language*. And it is lan-guage that human beings must first forget; for a few moments they must forget to express thought, sensation, need, so that they may cultivate tone as tone and melody as such. In that moment they take the decisive step in the direction of musical art.

Now, nothing in the world is more unnatural and more contrary to the progress of the human spirit than deriving this first step from the imita-tion of birds and so forth. If man wished to emulate the birds, he would of course have found his organs of speech too ungainly to produce *tones agreeable to the ear*; the act of imitation thus seemed to him arduous and unsatisfying. The more we attribute to him a feeling for the agreeableness of bird tones, the more he must have perceived the disagreeableness of his own voice and the less likely we are to find the origin of music in such imitation. Moreover, what does primitive man hear in the nightingale's song that is for him? Does he hear the accents of passion that the nightingale feels, which only its mate hears sympathetically? Does he therefore understand the thread that links its tones? What passions and emotions pass through every twist and turn, rising and falling, growing louder and softer? No! So what can he imitate? Only the *external euphony of the voice* as such, the purity, clarity, firmness, pitch, delicacy, and quickness of its tones. And can he do this? Must not every one of these qualities confound him and, as long as he cannot become a nightingale, deter him from imitation?

That such a frigid, childish whistling after birdsong was not the origin of music is shown by its most ancient forms and the whole stature of the human race as it then was. Passion and emotion were the first perfections that were imparted to music, which the human mind both demanded and loved but to which the imitation of birds alone could not directly lead. Who knows the true inner expression of the bird? Who recognizes therein anything more than the physical melodiousness of the tones? For otherwise, of course, if the earliest music were based on the imitation of birds, this ought to have been the first fully formed part and the expression of human passion the very last. But all the records and documents we have of the oldest music suggest it was the other way around. The mechanically most perfect part of music—roulades, runs, harmonies, artistries for the ear—was the very thing that in those days was wholly unknown, or at least known only very late. In the expression of passion, in the irregular, bold, violent accents of emotion, however, men, by an early stage, had become inimitably and wondrously accomplished. Did they learn even an iota of this from birds? On the contrary, birds might well have led them astray from this path forever!

You men of a later, quite different race! Return to the feeling of your ancestors, and you will find a far closer, more natural source of music: singing speech. What did your forebears desire to express with the earliest music? Passion, emotion—and these were to be found not in birdsong, which for humanity lacks life, but in the singing tones of its own tongue. Here accents of every passion, modulations of every emotion were already present, which were felt powerfully, to which ear, tongue, and soul had been accustomed from infancy, which therefore made it easy to raise, to order, to modulate, to amplify them just that little bit more. And so there developed a wonderful music of all emotions, a new magic language of sensation. Here the first inspired musician discovered a thousandfold means to express all the passions that the human tongue could perhaps have uttered over the centuries, that the human soul could have experienced; a thousandfold means to express what since childhood was peculiar, natural, and familiar to him and to his brothers; which with each passion entered his breast and tripped off his tongue; which others understood just as naturally and powerfully as he. All this expressiveness he discovered before him in a thousand accents, tones, rhythms, and modulations inherent in speech; should he not set it to his account? And then some embellishments were added—and what do we have if not the first music?

Thus music arose from *language*; and when language, as has been sufficiently shown, was originally nothing but *natural poetry*, poetry and music were also inseparable sisters. The latter served the former, the former gave the latter expression, life, sensation, and so together both produced those effects we think so fabulous in ancient history and yet are no fables. The music of the ancients was nothing like ours; it was a living, more mellifluous language. Thus, its principal components as they were then—*rhythmics, metrics, poetics,* and *harmonics*—are by no means present in our music, and of some we can scarcely form a clear idea. The music of the ancients was *vocal music* in the loftiest, noblest sense; *instrumental music* was invented later, only gradually, and among the ancients it was perhaps never quite as elaborate as it is now. How much in the *history of music and poetry* this explains! The great exactitude of prosody, the splendid euphony, the emotion-laden language of poetry supported by music; and from the other side the history of the inventors of instrumentalism, the component parts of their music, its difference from ours, its application, its effects, the respect in which it was held—all this is explained by one principle, which is all too often mistaken and whose consequences will hence naturally be thought equally strange.

Like the restoration of the formative arts, the rebirth of music in Italy is analogous to this first origin. After the theater had degenerated into mere declamation during all the centuries of barbarism, the first attempts at melodrama from the end of the fifteenth to the end of the sixteenth centuries still consisted wholly in melodic poetry. Poetry, tragedies, and pastorals were sung from start to finish; poetry and language ruled absolutely. A wholly novel and late development saw music become the dominant art. Now the expression of passion was sought in unarticulated tones, something that earlier had been the domain solely of the articulated forms of speech, and efforts were made to give to music as such the whole picturesque attitude that as an ancillary art it could not have possessed previously. It was instrumental musicians, of course, who were responsible for this departure whereby language and music were quite transformed—the former by becoming more prosaic, philosophical, and unpoetic; the latter by developing, as a principal art, increasingly in the direction of harmony. Hence all the recent changes in our world. Just as the modern music of all European nations is derived from Italy, so they have all inherited nonpoetic music, and each has modified it after its own manner. The colder, more thorough Germans have raised it to a science and brought harmony, in the modern sense, to such a height of sophistication that I can scarcely conceive of two more conflicting extremes in one discipline than Greek and modern northern music.

In Greek music the science of harmonics was nothing and living expression everything. Born of the language of passion, it remained forever true to its origins: a very simple melody; a uniformity that we would find intolerable in what is for us merely the art of relations and academicism: perhaps very irregular and bold runs, but on the other hand, strong accents, a very rich and fine diversity of keys, great variety in modulation— such were the characteristics of the music of the passions, just as ours is a music of relations and of reason. As the Greek language is related to French, so might the musical art of both nations also be related, we might discover, if only we had as clear a notion of the music of the ancients as we do of their language. Let the dispute over rank finally be resolved, for the world, the times, man himself, his ear, his language, and his music have all changed. Let us start to inquire with a cooler head.

Now, perhaps the praise would be less than impartial if a German were to recommend German music as the ideal object of investigation because it combined melody and harmony to the highest degree. But since, in our theories as in our practice, we incline far more toward harmony and cold, artificial relations, so the aesthetician has, as it were, no fatherland. He is at home wherever he finds musical energy and melody, in Italy and Greece, even in absurd China. And since this emotion-rich essence of music has since time immemorial been so close to language, so *musical poetry*—a theory of which has scarcely been attempted, though we do possess practical examples—represents the great forecourt leading to the gate of a general musical aesthetics.

9

The *dance* of the ancients is nothing but *their music made visible*; hence by explaining one we describe the other. Their music was the language of passion, and so was their dance; the former expressed its energy in the succession of tones, and their dance in the succession of movements; the mere relation of tones was as alien to their music as the relation of lines of movement was to their dance. Therein lies the entire history and genesis of ancient and modern dance.

It is a *music made visible*. For as passions have their tones, so through the expression of Nature they have their gestures and movements also—

the former are for the ear what the latter are for the eye. They are inseparable, and any further quarrel about their rank is pointless. When natural man thus discharges accents of emotions from the innermost folds of
his heart, they are manifested also in his countenance and on his body as
a whole. All these things are so interconnected that as experience has long
taught us, we are plunged into a certain, sometimes violent, tone of the
soul if we physically perform the gestures that typically accompany it; and
that if we see certain gestures imitated in art, no statement is more familiar than this: I hear him say this and that! His countenance is so eloquent
that———the art of gesture is language made visible.

Dance is visible music in a *second way: in the time and modulation of
the movement itself.* Each passion has its own movement: sadness descends slowly, joy rises swiftly, jubilation spins and leaps, disquietude
trembles, totters, and reels. Hence the rhythm of *speech*, hence that of
music, and hence that of *dance*. Where poetry expresses tones in words,
dance does so through gesture and movement, and the praise bestowed
on painting, namely that it is *a mute poetry*, is infinitely truer of dance.
Why dream of a *color clavichord* when dance is living music and, moreover, a unified expression of all the arts of the beautiful? From sculpture
it borrows beautiful bodies, from painting beautiful postures, from music
inward expression and modulation; and to these it adds living Nature and
movement. Dance is the union of all that is beautiful as art, just as poetry
is the union of all that is beautiful as literature. It is living sculpture, painting, music, and, all in all, mute poetry.

We no longer possess this dance, then, no more than we still have the
music of the ancients. Just as the latter is no longer an immediate servant
of passion but has become, rather, a splendid, sovereign art, so too has
the former. It draws with artistic lines of movement and postures, just like
modern music draws with tones and chords—both transformations are
inseparable from each other. A traveler of our century has gone to the
trouble of searching for the remnants of Greek dance in that homeland of
the beautiful, much as ten men before him have sought the relics of the
formative arts. I cannot say whether his work has already appeared, but
it will certainly shed much light on their ancient manners, on their whole
character, on many passages of their writers, and, finally, on the theory of
an art that we know only through extravagant praise—and who, if ever
he were to set eyes on it, could a give a cool description thereof! Lucian's
dialogue on the subject is written with the fire of its living presence;
Plutarch's testimony is more certain; meanwhile, Cahusac demonstrates
that no history of dance can yet be written if one knows not how to become a Greek. Since so many analogies between the ancient Egyptians and
the archaic Chinese have been uncovered in recent times, the manners of
this latter people in general and hence their dance in particular must also

throw a little light on Egyptian art; and perhaps this would make comprehensible those finer qualities of the ancient Greeks which for us have become extinct.

Noverre wished to revive the dance of the passions, but it will stir itself and reawaken to the wonders of its origin only when, after a barbarous age toward which we are perhaps now hastening, human nature once more renews itself and its more undissembled passions speak, as they did at the beginning, through tone and gesture, language and movement. Then in this regenerate age, poetry and music and every fine art of sensation will raise themselves anew; the genius will be enraptured and come to life again, where for us there is only dead, frigid taste. Today the capacious imagination of a Wieland, which, suckled in the embrace of Plato and Lucian, desired also to resuscitate Greek dance in his *Agathon*, must resort to invention; and the aesthetician in general is also obliged to speculate if he wishes to investigate dance; then he will see it and there, as at the meeting place of the arts, perfect the philosophy of the beautiful. Reluctantly, however, I found that Sonnenfels, in his dramaturgy, which is as much a work of the finest taste as Lessing's is of philosophical and dramatic genius; that he, as I say, who in the expression of his style of writing also possesses all the flourishes and graces of dance, fails to fulfill his promise with respect to it, even though he lives where it prospers.

There are two further arts reckoned among the arts of beauty that I have not so far mentioned: *architecture* and *landscape gardening*. A glance at them shows that they are not properly fountains of a new beauty but only beautified mechanical arts, and can therefore have no new sense proper to them. They are only adopted children of the eye; and the eye, drunk on beauty in Nature and art, beautified what it could, and what worthy objects were buildings!

Architecture, therefore, a foster child of other arts, possesses certain abstracted qualities of the beautiful that are manifested therein more distinctly and simply than in these other arts, and in this respect it ought very much to be studied by the philosopher of beauty. Since architecture is a mechanical art, merely clothed in concepts of the beautiful, so with its ideas, too, it is closest to the certainty of truth and stands, by virtue of the characteristics of the beautiful that it originally delivers, as a model, as it were, of solidity and simplicity for other arts. I therefore counsel the investigator of beauty to begin with architecture; let the first impression that it makes on him, with its sublime magnitude, with its precise regularity, with its noble order be, as it were, a plastic logic and mathematics to accompany him on his further travels.

And perhaps no art has been as fortunate as architecture to have had so many master practitioners apply themselves to its theory. From Vitruvius onward and especially beginning with the age when beauty was created anew, what great names appear on textbooks of architecture, the likes of which we do not have in painting and sculpture, at least not in such numbers. The greatest architects, particularly those of Italy, have built and written, and in both ways informed posterity and immortalized, in their buildings as in their writings, the great ideas of their soul.

For that reason I believe the theories of architecture to have a merit that I wish was shared by the general theory of all the arts, namely a noble simplicity even in style and expression. Because master builders were accustomed to endowing their works of stone with a firm, eternal solidity and noble simplicity even in their ornaments, so too they often caused quiet astonishment by realizing the same qualities in their works of instruction. The ideas, the individual parts of Winckelmann's writings are also constructed like statues and their overall arrangement and style like a building.

Would it not be better, for all these reasons, to impart to the soul of the young a few first notions of the beautiful through contemplation of this art, wherein such ideas reveal themselves so grandly and solidly and simply, than through many a more confused theory of poetics or rhetoric? Might it not at least be advantageous not to exclude architecture from a liberal education? Yet I am concerned for the young; might it not at least be necessary for a theorist of the fine arts—what a grand name!—to study a building thoroughly before he ventured near the ideas of *magnitude* and *sublimity*, *unity* and *diversity*, *simplicity* and *regularity*? Our man Riedel has treated of these concepts as if he had never seen a building, and our Klotz, who is ever alert to the shortcomings of others, is adamant that Winckelmann's *Notes on the Architecture of the Ancients* "would admit of still greater enlargement!" As if anyone, even if he had only glanced at Winckelmann's work, could demand that it require a structure. And as if such a demand, which a hundred intelligent men could not satisfy, did not completely expose this fellow.

Landscape gardening delivers the smallest contribution to the universally beautiful. Here in summary are the ideas of a recent French author, who compares gardening with architecture.

> The view of a large and beautiful garden gives us a pleasure that is very similar to the sight of a large and regular building. In both we admire proportion and symmetry, which, as it were, facilitate the ordering in our memory of the ideas we thereby received. The greenery of the garden also gratifies us—green is a color that always pleases the eye, that reminds us of the promises of spring, and that in the heat advertises coolness and shade. The garden also furnishes us with a favorable idea of the man who could rule over Nature in such a

manner———but to a lesser and more imperfect degree than architecture, even the most imperfect architecture. Here the mass of the buildings excites our admiration. It holds vision in a strong tension, and the sensation is enhanced because it is protracted, and without the interference of foreign sensations. The Egyptian pyramids draw the glances of the traveler and instill in him a kind of religious awe. When he has contemplated them for a time with uninterrupted feeling, he says to himself: "And this was made by human hand!", immediately adding: "And it will last forever!" Gothic buildings impress with their mass and lightness, which are combined with the greatest boldness. They furnish the mind with gloomy ideas, but these gloomy ideas are pleasant. The multiplicity of their ornaments and of their proportions produces a succession of sensations rather than a single continuous sensation, thereby detracting from the power of the impression. The regular architecture of a building initially surprises us by its extension, by a succession of identical ornaments, by a kind of uniformity that multiplies the same vibrations in the eye. It reminds us of the power and genius of man; like Gothic architecture, it unites lightness and boldness; it displays smooth surfaces and curves; it positions the angles so as to raise the concept of the pyramids, with which the idea of solidity is associated; it raises the concepts of utility and comfort; and furthermore its symmetry gives us hope that a true picture of all that we admire will be preserved in us. The very symmetry of symmetrical gardens sees to it that they do not delight us for long. As soon as this quality impresses the gardens on our memory, they no longer possess novelty, and the other pleasures besides symmetry that they gave us are neither great nor numerous enough not to be quickly exhausted. Then we experience nothing but tedium in those places where at first sight we were enchanted!

How limited a domain, then, is the proper aesthetics of the garden!

10

We examined the senses of the beautiful in order to assign to each its principal fine art and to analyze the essence of the latter on the basis of the physiology of the former. We then proceeded to the arts of beauty themselves so as to inspect the original and characteristic ideas associated with their respective natures. The paths we traveled were mostly untrodden, and we were obliged to sketch what ought to be done rather than what has already been accomplished. A proper *aesthetics of beautiful feeling*! A *philosophy of beautiful semblance*! An *aesthetic science of music*! These three endeavors we found to be necessary before anyone could contemplate *a theory of the beautiful in all the arts*. We provided outlines, perspectives on obscurities in the history of art, explanations of many a paradox and confusion in the arts, encouragement—in short, our materials carried us away, and I am certain that many readers who are not at home in this or that art reluctantly followed me through such a convoluted labyrinth.

For all that aesthetics has been elaborated from the point of view of psychology, and thus subjectively, it has still not been much developed from the point of view of the objects of art and their beautiful sensuousness: yet without such a treatment a fruitful "Theory of the Beautiful in All the Arts" can never arise. Every art has its original concepts, and every concept its home, so to speak, in one sense. Just as these cannot be equated, just as eye and ear and touch are not one and the same, so the question of where I obtain and analyze every concept cannot be a matter of indifference; each becomes distinct only in its principal sense, in its principal art. And so every theory of the beautiful as such must degenerate into chaos if it does not begin by picking its path through the arts, by putting each idea in its place, by investigating beauty in every sense and in every major phenomenon of every sense, by never inferring deductively from indistinct and complex concepts, but always by following rigorous analysis. But in our age, why dream of a philosophy of the beautiful such as this? In our age? Where nothing is more confused than *textbooks of the beaux arts and belles lettres*; where *poetics* erected on the foundations of *painting* and *reflections on painting* erected on the foundations of *poetry* are revered; where *aesthetics* are filled with Vossius's *Rhetoric* and the *Commentaries on Aesthetics* with Baumgartian *psychology*? Where portions of Home's *Criticism* and Gerard's *Essay on Taste* are taken, combined with other authors and fashioned into something that these two men had no intention of producing at all: a *theory of the beaux arts and belles lettres*? And finally, our journalists? Our German librarians? They mix heaven in earth and earth in heaven. They throw jargon around like the simian artists of Africa; by aping everything that they set eyes on they become as celebrated as those who monkey about with sand and nutshells in perfect harmony. They condemn what they do not understand and speak whereof they know nothing, they dogmatize in metaphors and metaphorize in clichés. A Klotz writes whole books on arts where an artist like Michelangelo would say: "My maid could have explained it better!" And a Riedel writes a theory of the arts without understanding the essence of a single one of them—this is a time of Babelish confusion! If one wished to demonstrate the abuse and estrangement of every concept and restore each to its proper art, then one would have to write a *Laocoön* devoted to every chapter of Riedel's theory. And how many *Laocoön*s would then be needed! *Beauty, unity* and *diversity, magnitude, importance, harmony, nature, naïveté, simplicity, similitude, contrast, truth, probability, rotundity, imitation, illusion, design, coloring, comparisons*—but why reproduce the loathsome blather of his book?

That the fellow has no more an idea of the arts about which he writes than a blind man of color is shown by the *definitions* that he so sagely distills, as if they were some exquisite spirit, from his cobbled-together claptrap about "the constitution of the beautiful work as a whole" and "the constitution of the beautiful ideas and the signs, viewed apart from, and with respect to, its meaning," and so on. I wouldn't need to add or change a thing—these remarks attest to Riedel's explanatory gifts and knowledge of art; nevertheless, I shall take the trouble to analyze several of them. The apprentice will learn more this way than by studying the chapter on the rules of definition in logic, and the thinker himself shall see in Mr. Riedel our century's model of a philosophical mind and in his book our century's model of a philosophical theory. Just please be brave and patient!

Poetry is the art and science of representing perfectly sensuous, beautiful, imaginative, and successive products by means of perfectly harmonious language. It is thus an *art*. And what is an art? According to Mr. R. a few lines earlier, an art is "a regular skill that has its ultimate seat merely in the lower faculty of cognition," and so, following this superlative definition, poetry is fundamentally not an *art*. The regular skill of creating poetic works is called *poetic art*, but never have I heard anyone other than Riedel say "That young man has a lot of *poetry*" instead of "He can write good poems." Conversely, I have never heard "Is that *poetry*, is that what is entailed by the *essence of poetry?*" interpreted as "Is that the skill of creating poetic works?" So let us remove *art* from the definition. So is poetry *science*? The word has many meanings. The science of poetic art signifies—how could it otherwise?—nothing more than *poetic science, poetics, poetic philosophy*; not poetry. A person may master poetry as *science*, but that does not make him a poet. We can see that the word *poetry* has many meanings, and thus it is precisely the first task of any elucidator to resolve this ambiguity, where it can be resolved through words. And where is this not possible? For *poetic art* we Germans have the suggestive word *Dichtkunst*, for poetic *science Poetik*. *Poetry* or *poesy*, as the Opitzes have said, is the essence of the works that poetic art produces and that poetics then defines in rules. *Poems* or *verses* is the name we give to the works themselves—why need there be confusion here? *Poetic art* [*Dichtkunst*] is therefore more definite. *Poetic art* is (let us repeat with all due respect that profound definition!) *the art of representing perfectly sensuous, beautiful, imaginative, and successive products by means of perfectly harmonious language*. Does that not sound lovely? Long, abstract, splendid, and expressed in the latest neologisms. Such a definition compels closer scrutiny.

So: an art of *representing perfectly sensuous products*. *Representing* is a metaphorical term that has no proper place in a definition; *products* is a foolish word, which is even less appropriate in a definition; and then finally to want to *represent products* in a definition of *poetic art* is a manifest error. *Poetic art* does not *represent* products; it is not one of the formative arts that *represent* works to be enjoyed in an eternal glance. It operates energetically, continuously. The poem, as a completed work, as a codex that one has finished reading or writing, is nothing; the succession of sensations experienced during its operation is everything. It is thus not an art of *representing products*.

But onward! What kind of products? *Perfectly sensuous, beautiful, imaginative, and successive* products. Mark it well, apprentice! *Perfectly sensuous, beautiful, imaginative, and successive* products. Mr. Riedel has read Baumgarten; that is why his products of poetry are *perfectly sensuous*. But he did not understand him; that is why his *perfectly sensuous* products are furthermore *beautiful*. Mr. R. has read Darjes; that is why his *perfectly sensuous, beautiful* products are also *imaginative*. But he has also read Lessing; that is why his *perfectly sensuous, beautiful, imaginative* products are also *successive*. And that is the litany in its entirety.

So: *perfectly sensuous, beautiful* products. Are *beautiful* products not *perfectly sensuous*? So why the chatter of such extraneous words? But are all *perfectly sensuous* works of poetry also *beautiful* works? No, and nor may they be. The ugly and the terrible may be ingredients of poetic art that help it to achieve perfect sensuousness, and poetic art will still remain poetic art, for with the phrase "*beautiful* products" poetry is made an ape of fine art. The first phrase suffices, then; now we are left with "*perfectly sensuous, imaginative*, and *successive products by means of language*." Imaginative and successive works by means of language? And how does a language operate other than *successively*? And to whom does it deliver perfectly sensuous ideas if not to the lower faculties of the soul, and thus in the broad sense *imaginatively*? Why does ruminative barbarism require the armor plating of such words when it can think more easily by itself? Indeed, it causes real confusion here, for poetry does not work for the *imagination* alone in the proper sense of the word; it also works for other faculties of the soul—but all that we need is contained in the words *perfectly sensuous*, and the neologisms may be omitted.

We are left, then, with sensuously perfect products *by means of perfectly harmonious language*. That bureaucratic phrase "*by means of*" is wooden and, when applied to poetry, which operates like music, far too lifeless. What about the more powerful word *through*: through *perfectly harmonious language*. As if perfect language were not of necessity also *harmonious*, and more than *harmonious*, more than harmonious even in the way it sounds: *melodic* and God knows what else. And what is harmonious language, anyway? Does it sound harmonious? Is it harmonious with the thoughts it expresses? We can sooner dispense with the epithet before it signifies anything; and what are we now left with after ruthlessly ridding ourselves of this dross? *Sensuously perfect products through per-*

fect language. But *products through the utterance of language* means, in human and rational terms, *ideas,* and *language* that effects a *succession of ideas* is discourse; and *discourse that excites perfectly sensuous ideas in a perfectly sensuous manner* is *perfectly sensuous discourse.* Poetry is thus *perfectly sensuous discourse.* The verbiage of Riedel's definition has been thrown away with the chaff; and we have arrived unnoticed at Baumgarten's definition.

In all the languages in which I have encountered a definition of poetry, I find no pithier and richer words than those used by Baumgarten to fix poetry like a gemstone in the finest setting. Even in Germany, however, despite all the applause that Baumgarten's definition has won among some people, at the hands of others it has met with much opposition and, worse, been so misused by a third group that we might be astonished at three so different responses were there not reasons for all of them. We Germans dispute words as other nations dispute causes; we are as blessed with definitions as others are with inventions, and in his definition Baumgarten has moreover used a word that is rich and pregnant enough to conceal multiple meanings, thus leaving itself open to dispute and misuse: the word *sensuous.* How many concepts German philosophy associates with this word! *Sensuous* leads us back to the source and medium of certain representations, and these are the *senses;* it signifies those faculties of the soul that form such representations, and these are the so-called *lower* faculties of the soul; it characterizes *the species* of representation, confused and pleasant precisely in this rich, engaging confusion; that is, *sensuous;* finally, it refers also to the intensity with which the representations enrapture us and excite *sensuous* passions—on all four conceptual paths the multifaceted words *sensuous, sensitive* are in keeping with the definition of Wolff, Baumgarten, and Mendelssohn. As we can see, the original excellence of this definition lies simply in a linguistic convenience: an expression with all its beautiful frailties and complex indeterminacy seized and in it a whole host of concepts deposited. This explains the fate of Baumgarten's definition. To those incognizant of the energy of the key term, it is an algebraic formula beyond their comprehension, and the French, for example, will find their Batteux ten times better, more distinct and meaningful. Others, who understand the word *sensuous* according to its common usage, half in shadow, will also use it in shadow and misapply it. I can think of more than one example of this in Germany. Only the third party, which analyzes the ideas inherent in the word distinctly and with such rigor as Wolffian philosophy has taught them, will find the definition more distinct, concise, brief, and perfect than any other that we possess.

And that is the value of philosophical definitions in general. If they are perfect, then the elucidator has performed the services of an interpreter of the soul and a master of philosophical language, even if *in doing so* he has not yet immediately become a discoverer of truths. He has distilled an entire science into a few main propositions, these main propositions into a few words, and then these words into a distinct, complete idea, from which the main propositions can once again be inferred and the entire science surveyed—this single idea is his definition. It is a perspective on all of science and the point from which all the chains of axioms, propositions, proofs, and conclusions start; if this point is fixed, if the perspective is general and unrestricted, then the definition is perfect and its author a logical artist inasmuch as he presents us with a large number of concepts contained in a single box of words. We open the first box and within it lies a smaller one, and so on, until we come to the smallest and then, moving back up again, to the biggest, to the whole. He condenses an entire science into a metaphysical formula, in whose brevity, determinacy, and completeness his entire achievement lies. His apish imitator, though, the shallow elucidator who piles up words that signify nothing, that are contradictory, that lie higgledy-piggledy, that are not essential to the whole, that even lead us away from the essence of the whole—what is he good for? For turning the head of one who is not yet familiar with the science in question, or for benumbing and confusing the ear of one who is? And throughout all his definitions that is all my author is good for.

Listen to his definition of *painting*. It is *the art of representing sensuous things as coexisting, for the eye, on a flat surface, through figures, as natural signs, and for pleasure*. If that is the smallest seed to hold within it the entire fruit, if that is the briefest metaphysical formula to deliver the most distinct and complete concept of painting—then, oh dear, how my ear hurts! I hear a formula with eight or nine long terms lacking unity, relation, or connection; I see a seed's knobby form with nine dreadful humps. Let us analyze them.

Painting is the art of *representing* things; I do not know whether the word *represent* belongs more to sculpture than to painting, which only *projects* an image *on a surface*, that is, only *depicts*. Be that as it may, what does painting depict? *Sensuous things*! Oh what a novel idea that is, what an indispensable, essential concept! Painting depicts *sensuous* things and only sensuous things for the eye, on a surface, through figures—a novel, indispensable idea. But this stitched-together humpback is wrong, for painting can also depict *unsensuous* things, even ideas, even passions, even the entire soul. Does it depict *sensuous* things, then? It depicts them sensuously, but does painting *sensuous things* and painting *things sensuously* mean the same? Let us be rid of the word *sensuous*! *To represent things, as coexisting, for the eye, on a flat surface, through figures*: little more than that remains of the definition. *Things as coexisting*? That is self-evident; but if it is self-evident, does it need to be indicated in the definition? Must every quality that the author of *Laocoön* infers from the concept of painting in order to realize his aim of differentiating painting from poetry be included in the fundamental concept, in the definition? Not without everything becoming confused, both the fundamental concept and the consequence. So we are left with representing *things on a surface* and representing them as coexisting. But on a *flat* surface? As if an *uneven* surface were not still a painting? As if a raised surface or a depression depicting objects through colors were not still a painting? And then *to represent for the eye on a surface, through figures, as natural signs*—is there a single abecedarian who can bear to hear our author spelling out this point? A painter depicts objects on a surface, yes, but how else than *through figures* and not through fleshy, voluminous bodies and blocks? Through *figures* as *natural signs*, and which sensible person thinks of figures as zeros and digits? And figures on a surface for the *eye*? And not indeed for smell, not for taste? And to represent *for pleasure*? Why not to arouse emotion, to edify, to tell a story, to communicate a message, to instruct? *For pleasure*? And is it not self-evident that if painting is a *fine art*, it must, to excite sensuous pleasure, depict objects perfectly sensuously? Once again we have thrown away all the dross; and what remains? Well, I look and I look but find nothing! Not a single one of Mr. Riedel's words stands up to scrutiny; here is the old definition: painting is the *fine art* (I shall not explain what these words mean because I take it as read!), the *fine art of depicting on surfaces*. Now look back and consider: What is *art*? What is *fine art*? What can be depicted *on surfaces*? What does it *mean* to *depict*? How does *fine art depict*? And there we have all the treasures of the theory of painting.

If our theorist has not succeeded in defining *painting*, then its sister, sculpture, must surely share the same fate. And this is indeed the case. It is *the art of portraying sensuous things as coexisting on uneven surfaces through natural signs of raised figures and forms, and for pleasure*. Here we see the same allusion to *sensuous* things, *natural signs*, and *pleasure* which I discussed in connection with painting; but what he says about the peculiarities of sculpture is even more confused. Sculpture portrays sensuous things *as coexisting*; nothing could be further from the truth! A single thing fashioned by the sculptor—is that not complete art? Can a single *Apollo* as such not become an ideal sculpture without its forming a group together with other statues? With what must it coexist to become an image? Riedel cannot wriggle out of this by claiming that its limbs are the coexistents—for are they coexisting *things*? Is not the single *Apollo* the *thing*, the *object* of the art? And with whom does it coexist? With its limbs? It is clear that this nonsense is derived from painting, which represents its objects in a continuum, on a two-dimensional surface; the idea of coexistence is thus inseparable from the space on a surface. On the tableau that is painting even a single figure coexists to a certain extent with others, with the air, with the space that surrounds it, with the landscape that looms behind it; with everything together the figure constitutes one surface. But where are the coexistents in sculpture, which presents one tangible body? There are none. There are tangible, whole entities, but each stands alone, each is a quite independent being. The center of a statue's efficacy lies deep within it, not between coexisting objects; hence it does not lie in coexistence, which precisely destroys its essence.

But that is as nothing compared with the following: *it portrays things as coexisting through raised figures and forms on uneven surfaces.* What concept is entailed by *this* definition, no matter how much he might qualify it, other than that of *relief*? And is relief sculpture? Is it the essence, the ideal of sculpture? Sculpture is supposed *to portray things on uneven surfaces through raised figures and forms*; so there must already be *uneven surfaces* that then become the basis of the sculpture, with the raised figures and forms then placed *onto these surfaces.* In no other way can I make sense of the words: to fashion figures and forms *on* uneven surfaces. Indeed, no one will understand the words in any other way. And now imagine the sculptor who fashions *forms on uneven surfaces,* who can fashion *figures,* which otherwise manifest themselves, as other eyes can see, only *on surfaces* and *raise* them. Imagine the wondrous man from another world, and his theorist, who does not know what *surface, figure,* and *form* are, does not know what it means to fashion *forms on surfaces,* and allows his artist to fashion *raised figures* on *uneven surfaces*—imagine the wondrous theorist and his wondrous artist! Finally, he even portrays things *on uneven surfaces* through *natural signs of raised figures and forms.* Not through forms *as natural signs,* as Mendelssohn says, but in the words of Mr. Riedel, who plagiarizes him inconsistently, through natural signs *of raised figures and forms.* And whose head is not spinning after this definition? Does a single intelligent word remain? Not even the last, *to portray,* for does this art do no more than paint a portrait? Apprentice, cross out every word and write the following: "The *fine art of forming bodies*—that is *sculpture.*"

I looked forward more eagerly to Riedel's definition of *music* than to any of his others, because this art has enjoyed the least sustained treatment. But it was here that he disappointed me most. According to Mr. Riedel, music is *the art of rendering actions sensuous for the pleasure of the ear, through measured tones.* The expression *"measured tones"* is figurative and thus not the most fitting for a definition. Who can measure tones? Who can hear colors? However, even if we approved this technical term as a *word,* as a *concept* it signifies nothing, for anyone who knows even a little of music recognizes that the mere *measuring* of tones is the least important aspect of musical theory. The harmony and *melody* of the tones presuppose far more than *modulation*. And if the latter is but one of many means to produce these, then how much less is it the end, the fundamental concept of music? But one fault due to ignorance is compounded by a second, even greater one: *music renders actions sensuous through measured tones*. With an expression like that, it is as if Riedel had dropped from the sky. *To render actions sensuous*—music should or could do this? *To render actions sensuous through tones*, as if there were a single action in the world that could be made sensuous through tones? Finally, *to render something sensuous through tones*—has anyone ever talked like that? Does anyone want to? *To render tones sensuous for the ear*? Does anyone ever render tones sensuous for the foot or the back? And to render sensuous *tones for pleasure*? And not also for something more than cold pleasure: to *bewitch*, to *arouse emotion*, to create an *illusion*? As if music were not already, as the finest art, compelled to work toward pleasure? And as if it ever occurred to music *to render actions sensuous to the ear* or to furnish the scent of a rose for it to taste? Oh, what a definition, what a definition! It has apparently created a deaf, unmusical creature that knows tones only as bodies that are *measured*, that make something *quite sensuous* to the ear, that could make *actions* sensuous; a creature surrounded by nothing but coarse concepts derived from touch, which therefore makes a nonsense of all music. For anyone blessed with the gift of hearing, music is infinitely different. He knows that it can express *sensation, emotion, passion*, but certainly not *action* as such. He knows that in accordance with its essence, music never even means to express *action*, for otherwise it shall become a merely ancillary or even false art. He knows that music does not desire, through tones, to *render* anything *sensuous* to the external drum *of the ear*, but rather that it wishes to *affect the soul, to be expressive*. He knows that it does not count relations or calculate chords for the sake of cold *pleasure* but rather *works toward the innermost energy*. He knows, then, that music is, in short, the *fine art of affecting the soul through harmonious and melodic tones*; or, if we want to describe the constitution of the tones and the energy of their effect using the words *sweet sound* [*Wohllaut*], then music is *the fine art of sweet sound*.

We can readily assume that a person who discourses on music without having an ear for it will also betray his complete lack of eye or ear when speaking of *pantomime, music made visible*. Our elucidator is a case in point. *Pantomime* is supposed to be the *art of imitating the actions that music paints for the ear, through measured and beautifully regular, intricate postures*. How the tongue must toil with every word to express such thoughtlessness to the understanding! Pantomime is the art of *imitating* actions; why precisely *imitating* here, since Mr. R. allows every other art to do more than imitate, namely *to render sensuous*? I already know that all fine arts *imitate*; that is what they do as *arts*: the idea is already contained in the word. If it is reiterated over and above that, it can become misleading. *Pantomime*, the dance of the ancients, was no merely apish imitator; it *was expressive, and in a lively fashion* it *operated* with *all the force* of *illusion*—that is what it did. And with what did it do this? Mr. Riedel says with *actions that music painted for the ear*, and here I see once more the same Riedel we have just encountered. The man who knew things about music that passeth the understanding has similar ideas about music made visible, about dance; his music *paints*, it paints for the *ear*, it paints *actions*, it paints *the actions* that the pantomime is supposed to *imitate*. Listen, just listen! Riedel's music *paints*, and any ear with feeling knows that it cannot properly paint. And if music desires to adopt this as its main purpose, if it leaves its proper domain—that is, sensations—and emulates the painting eye, then it is no longer music, just an empty chime. Riedel's music paints *actions*; yet we have seen that it *never can and never wishes* to paint *these*, that actions can never be painted by unarticulated tones, and that music is even less able *to paint them* for pantomime to follow. And does Riedel's *pantomime* imitate *from there*? From where it cannot be, cannot wish to be, without ruining everything? Where the most wretched imitation in the world would arise? Oh, the things a careless goose quill can write! Sevenfold nonsense in three words—with three words that confound music, confound pantomime, and set the servant above the master and the master above the servant. The things a goose quill can write!

And how does pantomime imitate these novel, hitherto-unheard-of *tone actions*? *Through measured and beautifully regular, intricate postures*; why not through a measured and beautifully regular, intricate train of words, such as Riedel's definitions are? As if *beautiful* postures were not also *regular*, and *regular* postures not also *measured*, and *measured and regular, intricate postures* not also *beautiful*? And as if pantomime demanded nothing but *beautiful* postures, nothing but *regularities*; as if individual, irregular disagreeablenesses were often not also part of the living whole. And as if the *intricacy* of the postures were an essential quality of pantomime. As if, finally, it even imitated *through postures*. What a tangled forest of confusion and falsehoods! Can a pose, as such, imitate an action? Can postures, as such, imitate actions? No more than a single side of a body can ever represent a body in its totality, as a solid. The composition of its sides, and hence here *the succession* of postures, the *variation* in the succession, the actuation of these variations in the succession—these alone constitute the *imitative character* of an action; these alone, therefore, constitute what is *expressive* in pantomime: these alone, therefore, constitute the fundamental concept underlying this particular art, a concept that no word does less to encapsulate than *posture* or *postures*.

And what do we call this *variation in the postures*—what am I doing repeating that doltish word *postures*? I mean, this *actuation of alternating states*—what is it called? *Action*! *Action*, therefore, cannot but be expressed through *action*; that goes without saying. And if music does not have action for its essence, then it cannot have action for its object and therefore cannot express action; that goes without saying. And if music cannot express action, then it cannot paint it for pantomime to follow, and therefore the latter cannot imitate any action by starting out from music; that goes without saying. And if pantomime does indeed express actions, then by virtue of this expression it is not an imitative, ancillary art but an original and a major art—that goes without saying. And so it goes without saying that once again there is not a single intelligent or correct word in all of Riedel's definition, that anything but the spirit of *pantomime* dwells therein.

Pantomime is, so to speak, *visible music in action*, and if we acknowledge the former, then we will also readily acknowledge the latter. Pantomime therefore expresses actions, external and internal actions, just as music expresses sensations, external and internal emotions. It expresses itself through the actions of the body, just as music does through emotion, through tones. Each art remains within its sphere; music does not paint and pantomime does not sit as model, the former through sweet sound, the latter through its postures and lines—all merely work *together*. That which action expresses, the human soul, operates—operates through *everything* at its disposal: facial expressions, gestures, movements, actions; just not through tones, because here music takes its place. This lively effect is therefore the essence of this art, and so *pantomime is the fine art of expressing actions in a lively fashion*. If it also expresses these through tones, then it is natural pantomime; but if music takes it upon itself to express them and to give aural accompaniment to the visible expression of actions; if music clings as closely as possible to pantomime, so that the former speaks as much in the language of emotions as pantomime speaks in the expression of actions, and one does not dominate the other—then we have the *dance of the ancients*.

So that I omit nothing, I shall take up arms against the most beautiful of Riedel's definitions, *the art of building*. *Architecture* is the art *of making* the *products answering the requirements of life* beautiful, *without injury to their perfection* and according to a ground plan of sensuously distinct ideas. Let Crispin enter and explain this Crispinian twaddle! The *products answering the requirements of life*—why not just say buildings? The word is drawn from everyday life just as much as the concept to which it belongs, *the art of building*, and is broad enough to be used in connection with all the species of this art. *Building* is also to a large degree a *mechanical art*; only a part of it can be treated philosophically. So how improper is it to give it anything other than a mechanical name? Furthermore, what are *products answering the requirements of life*? Surely a good deal more than just buildings. And even if I add that concept to the definition, what are, properly speaking, *products of the art of building answering the requirements of life*? Were I not writing about an author *of such good form, so graceful, so decent*——but who wishes to stop at such ambiguities? Architecture is an *art of making buildings beautiful, without injury to their perfection and according to a ground plan of sensuously distinct ideas—makes* buildings *beautiful*! What a loose and feeble expression! The dauber, too, who stands on a scaffold to paint columns where there are none wants *to make* buildings *beautiful*, to make them beautiful according to a *ground plan of sensuously distinct ideas*, to make them beautiful *without injury to their perfection*; and is the dauber, or anyone who tacks decoration onto a building, an artist of architecture? What a difference there is between "*to make buildings beautiful*" and "*to make beautiful buildings, to erect buildings according to the rules of beauty.*" What a difference for anyone familiar with architecture and the German language! Let us continue: to make beautiful buildings, *without injury to their perfection*—so beauty impairs perfection; so these two concepts are antithetical? Nothing of the sort! Only an abuse of the rules of beauty can be contrary to the perfection of a building. A beautiful building without perfection is no longer beautiful as a building; the beauty of the building is precisely its intuitive perfection. The wise words *without injury to* thus cross over into other realms, into the mathematics and economy of building, which have no place here. So beautiful buildings according to a *ground plan of sensuously distinct ideas. Sensuously distinct ideas* are a nonsense. Precisely because they are sensuous they are not distinct, and a *ground plan of sensuously distinct ideas* is truly not Hamannian, but rather Jakob-Böhmian. And are these sensuously distinct ideas supposed to inhere only in the ground plan and not the building itself? Are they not the essence of the intuition? And is the ground plan anything other than a means to aid construction? And must every means, every scaffold, be included in the definition? Moreover, the *ground plan*, then, is supposed to contain sensuously distinct ideas but not the *elevation*? And not every intuitive aspect of architecture? O philosopher of definitions, like the architect you should place no word gratuitously, omit none, and erect none flimsily and crookedly and inadequately, for what would otherwise become of the definition you are building? To the extent that architecture is a *fine art, it erects buildings according to the rules of sensuous perfection*; where it is not, it will have a different definition.

I am weary of corrections and shall leave two equally humpbacked definitions—of *rhetoric* and *landscape gardening*—as they are. There is just one thing I wish to ask not only the impartial judge, who is neither friend nor foe, but also the author's closest ally: whether a mind possessed of such misshapen, contorted, wretched ideas relating to the arts and letters can furnish a theory of them. But look! That is what he does! Theories and Philosophical Libraries and German Libraries and Critical-Philosophical Journals and————oh, this is philosophy's Day of Judgment in Germany!

11

Nevertheless, Riedel's *Theory* might have some worth as an *extract of the works of various authors*, even if our writer was not able to deliver anything of value himself. How as an *extract*? And in no work by superior writers can the extractor find superior *definitions* of the arts? And if not definitions, what about scattered remarks? How will he present them, arrange them, use them—he, a man capable of such appalling *definitions*? And might there already exist works from which a theory of the fine arts could be extracted, without head, only with hands and eyes? Let us take a look at several excellent writers; in doing so we at least lose sight of a woeful one.

In Germany Sulzer's *Theory of Sensations* (which Mr. Riedel has not read or understood, otherwise he could never have stacked up his three fundamental feelings!) is, notwithstanding some embellishment and the all-too-easy gait of the academic lecture, a small monument that stands among much aesthetic rubble, worthy of the hand of a Leibniz or a Wolff. Everything in this theory flows from a simple and manifold, ever active, ever effective principle of the human soul—and thus we read it with precisely the same feeling that we have when we contemplate a gentle spring, which is always the same spring that rises and gushes forth in new streams from a single source. As our lowered eye runs over it in a gentle torpidity and our soul loses itself in thoughts about the music of the ever-renewed streams, we experience those moments of philosophical pleasure when we see so much succession and diversity in our sensations reduced to a unity, and thus always have before us the image of the beauty and perfection of a human soul. Setting aside several points—for example, the weighing up of the feelings, the definition of the differences, and so on—the entire formal portion of this little work is, right down to its smallest part, the metaphysical basis for a future aesthetics.

I say purposely, however, that its *formal* portion is a *metaphysical* basis, for Sulzer's little work is not a theory derived from the *objects* of beauty. Throughout, it considers the sensation of pleasure only metaphysically; it calculates the agreeable strumming on the nerves by the quantity rather than the quality of the impression that the sensations make. The materials are thus too scanty or too one-sided to explain even the effect of the agreeable; and the object as such—art, literature, and the way in which they produce individual, diverse, agreeable sensations—was never its end in view.

But it is the aim of another long-promised work, and Sulzer has given the German public advance notice of the path he means to take and on which he shall seek after beauty in its species and forms and similarities and differences—in all its originality. I am speaking of his *Dictionary of the Beaux Arts and Belles Lettres*, in the announcement of which he also justified his choice of a dictionary. He doubts not that he has thereby won the right to appear before the eyes of posterity; now he has an illustrious predecessor in Rousseau and his dictionary of music, without counting Bayle and the great Encyclopedists. But why, I still ask, and I ask this not simply out of fashionable disapproval, why a *dictionary*? So although his chief aim is to seek out the species and forms of beauty, he means to conceal from us the path he takes, the very thing that is most instructive? To explain the similarities and differences between all the arts and never show the intercommunion of those arts and their concepts other than by bothersomely declaring: "Behold! Behold!?" So throughout all the arts he means to seek out the origins of each concept, without determining the limits of what is proper to each and what is borrowed, and, moreover, without following up the way in which this borrowing has progressed? To withhold from us the entire ground plan of its domain? Too much, too much do we and posterity thereby lose. Precisely this pursuit of concepts through each art is very nearly the main object here; it must be the guiding thread and path for our author, even in the method of his thinking. And though his own discoveries were made by a methodical route, he subsequently wished—"for the sake of readers who desire to look up a concept half heard and misunderstood in polite society"—to cut his whole into pieces, where precisely the structure, where being able to find the concept in the right place was *everything*? Perhaps, even if I were to fathom our author's idea and persuade him of his error, my opinion will come too late to take from his hands the work of Penelope, who at night unstitched the fine fabric she had woven during the day; just as there the magic of art is lost, so here the main energy of the philosophical method.

And I do not know whether for that reason his aesthetics might be an airy castle of abstractions deficient in content, as most of our systems—unfortunately!—are. The greater part of the materials that Mr. Sulzer has collected from the beaux arts and belles lettres serves as the basis for the analysis of each concept; and it would thus become the first factual system in Germany that combined the order and method of analysis with the abundance and richness of a dictionary. The other portion of the materials, scattered historical accounts, are in a dictionary only ever piecework:

they send us from the Orient to the Occident and yet ultimately tell us nothing. But if all accounts were arranged in their proper place, each according to the way in which it has contributed to the growth or expansion or decline of art, or of all fine arts—that is really the only goal of Sulzer's efforts. And this whole toward which he is working, this historical whole—"an edifice of aesthetics built according to epochs, nations, and varieties of taste in all the beaux arts and belles lettres in general!"— this he wanted subsequently to dismember? How will the father know his Apsyrtus again? If a dictionary is not arranged so that all its articles taken together constitute a complete historical and dogmatic whole of the art whereof it treats, then it is imperfect, deceptive, and useless. But if a dictionary is indeed composed in such a manner, if its methodical route leads us to uncover the whole in its interrelations—then what an effort is required to dismember it. I am certain that Rousseau, too, would not have condescended to this work if it had not been so easy for him to pull out and expand his articles from the *Encyclopédie*, merely to earn some pocket money. I am certain that the Diderots and d'Alemberts would not have chosen a dictionary if they had felt strong enough to take on an encyclopedia without the assistance of a thousand different hands and minds. If there should one day be a single man equal to his object, who works freely and as a philosopher—why would such a man alight on this sport with initial letters and hence on a lexicon? The dictionary will give rise to a theory and a philosophical history, and with Sulzer— some promise!—a philosophical theory and history of the beautiful in all arts! How different this work is from Riedel's! And if the latter has any feeling at all, there is nothing better for him to do than either thoroughly improve his own work or, because it cannot be improved without palingenesis, consign it to the benevolent flames. But every word of Riedel's work confirms that Sulzer's dictionary had not yet appeared and that the author was not even acquainted with its outline.

In his *Letters on Sensations*, Moses Mendelssohn distinguishes between beauty and perfection; between obscure, clear, and distinct pleasure; and between the contributions of both body and soul to agreeable sensations. He does this more finely than Sulzer, and he supplements his theory by making that which is not beautiful into a thing of beauty with discernment and an air of the most amiable enthusiasm. The *Letters* and the *Rhapsody on Sensations*, which followed, comprehend man in the totality of his mixed nature and would furnish, if determined more exactly in terms of quantity, an exceedingly philosophical *theory of mixed feelings*. To look for a system of aesthetics in these two works, however, is like Swift's lunar explorer asking for gold among the blessed Selenites; and evidently Mr. R. could find nothing of use here either, for if he had thought it over, he would not have written his introductory chapter on beauty in general, and so forth, and still less his *Letters to the Public*, which is a veritable disgrace to the German public.

The author's treatise *Main Principles of the Beaux Arts and Belles Lettres* is a general map, valuable for him who wishes to survey the area as a whole but too lacking in materials and somewhat underanalyzed for one who might want to travel there, or even to measure the limits of the beautiful proper to each art. Mr. M. did not intend to determine these limits precisely or to furnish each art with its peculiar, original concept; he demonstrated and educed only one *main principle from the top down*. And Mr. R., who does not see this, has allowed himself, by uncomprehendingly plagiarizing this work, to be seduced chiefly by it and by Lessing's *Laocoön* into the worst errors that bedevil his definitions of the fine arts.

Where I have learned most from Mr. M. is in his individual judgments, where he also, following the eulogy of the Athenians in Thucydides, "cultivates refinement without extravagance and knowledge without effeminacy." And how easy it is to recognize him in the *Library of Belles Lettres* and in the *Letters Concerning Recent Literature*. Certain people may say what they please; the work for which Lessing, Mendelssohn, and Abbt were chiefly responsible will remain among the best writing of our century, and the reviews penned by the middle, most impartial, and fairest philosopher could single-handedly lead an apprentice along the path of true philosophy, which has grown dusty in Germany since the Wolffs, Baumgartens, Kästners, Reimaruses, Sulzers, and Mendelssohns no longer walk on it.

Diderot's article "Beau" in the *Encyclopédie* is a short critical summary of what French writers have contributed to this concept. He discusses first of all the dogmas of Plato, Augustine, Crousaz, Hutcheson, and André relating to the beautiful, passes judgment on the Father of the Church to the effect that in his investigation he got lost in the one quality of perfection, that Crousaz chose too many and too unwieldy elements of beauty, and that Hutcheson demonstrated not so much his sixth sense as his perplexity by having to assume a sixth sense, since he himself seeks the beautiful as an intellectual, geometric entity. Diderot then analyzes the inquiry of André and adds a series of philosophical reflections on the formation of the concept of beauty within us, on the differing viewpoints expressed in a number of languages on this concept, on its diversity, and so on, all of which betrays a discerning philosopher who stands out so much from the rest of his nation. The article as a whole is deserving of translation and elucidation, particularly as it would provide a perspective on the theories of beauty developed by Crousaz, André, and Hutcheson. Mr. R. has not deigned to make use of Crousaz or André or Diderot, and I wish he possessed the fundamental sensibility of the Britons, Hutcheson and Home.

Most of the French inquirers into the beautiful, however, have devoted themselves to an investigation not so much of the beautiful as revealed in objects as of the obscure feeling of the same, which this nation, using its favorite word, labels "taste," a word that abounds in all the writings of their bels esprits. Montesquieu, the teacher of kings, is at their head, followed by the St. Evremonds and St. Mards, Fontenelles and Marmontels, Bernis, Voltaires, and even the mathematical d'Alemberts. In all such inquiries into taste one expects nothing but taste itself, swift conviction in a judgment without precise differentiation—fair meadows full of flowers and fruits that are waiting to be gathered, enjoyed, and reaped, but not crops and bundles of flowers that have already been harvested. It would be an immense task to go through them, particularly where they subsequently address the taste of individual arts and the de Piles and Watelets begin to speak. We have the so-called French *theory of the beaux arts and belles lettres* in general—by which I mean the works of Batteux—in two German translations, and I am not the first to complain that Ramler has not improved his author at all and Schlegel only superficially. I now pass from a nation that has such little affection for arid systematicity but loses itself in flowers to another, which, though it has no fondness for it either, gives itself up to serious and thorough observations: the *British*!

Perhaps Home's *Principles of Criticism* in its psychological aspect is already well known in Germany; perhaps I was right when I thought, as I read the work, that I might find every one of those principles in the writings of our philosophers, only expressed differently. Home's book has another side, a world of observations, of individual phenomena and facts, which other thinkers had not brought so closely within the field of study. Mr. R. drew heavily on this excellent book, but two quick glances shall suffice to characterize Home's thought and to show that Riedel certainly did not use it as he ought to have done.

First, Home presents a forest of experiences, observations, and phenomena relating to the soul; but in keeping with his intention, it remains a forest. He divides these data only according to certain *major headings*, such as *novelty*, *beauty*, *sublimity*, and so on, without combining these categories to form a whole. He places his wealth in compartments that are ready to hand and leaves it to his apprentices to classify and arrange them. His book has therefore no system; the fundamental concepts are not progressively elaborated; there is, strictly speaking, no order in its plan. And behold! This very disarray is what must have appealed most to Mr. R. because he imitates it. He leaves untouched the intrinsic value of the materials on which Home bases his observations; what he happily borrows from him is only incidental and assuredly does not betray Home's profundity. But what he learns from him first is the method of allowing the chapters to follow one another in the commendable disorder in which he and Gerard scattered them.

Home has a contrary perfection in the detail of his style, which perhaps keeps in balance the flaws of the whole but which perhaps will be noticed only by his worthy translator and one who studies the book in extracts that do it justice. This is the economy in the particulars of his exposition, the definite, firm outline that states each idea precisely and beautifully, the combination of every word, every metaphor in its place—all this his compiler either did not notice or did not think worth imitating. Rather, since all his writings are as incoherent in their presentation as they are in their ideas, he stands as the best imaginable counterpart to the Briton.

Second, Home wished to deliver *principles* or rather *observations of criticism*; nothing was further from his mind than a *theory of the beaux arts and belles lettres,* and whoever employs his book as such is looking at things quite wrongly. First, it is plain that he does not esteem all arts and branches of letters equally. Nature and poetry provide him with the most material, and look how in the third part he hurries through a discussion of the categories and characteristics of the fine arts proper. The charge leveled at Baumgarten, Meier, and others might also be directed at him—namely, that he has not selected a sufficiently broad range of data and objects for criticism. Since he has such a predilection for poetry and for Shakespeare; since he sacrifices the fine arts, the true children of the original beauty of Nature and the most faithful likenesses of their mother, to her late-born grandchild, to poetry; and since he therefore studies only the obscure copy of many copies, it is surely undeniable that this gives rise to the greatest imbalance in the Englishman's sphere of inquiry as a whole and hence does not yield the *theory of the fine arts* that Mr. R. took it for and plagiarized so conscientiously. Second, it is plain that Home wishes to analyze our sensitive nature rather than beauty in objects; that his book is consequently the most estimable contribution to one aspect of aesthetics, the subjective aspect; that the objective, though, is treated only in scattered remarks or imperfect observations ranged at the end, as in the third section. Can an attentive reader view the principal aim of the book as a *theory of the arts*?

Third, in accordance with his plan, Home infers deductively throughout, starting from above with the emotions and passions and working his way down, and only then does he look for examples. So it goes without saying that these examples, and often Lord Kames's criticism of other examples as well, are not, as Mr. Klotz assures us with puffed-out chest, the most felicitous part of Home's work, for it is truly not his main object. What are examples ripped from their context? Faded, wilted flowers, which perhaps may yet show traces of their former color and beauty but are pale, withered, dying, for they have been removed from their soil, from their roots, from their sap, and lie isolated and alone. Perhaps there really was that phenomenon in Shakespeare, in the whole tone of his play, in the continuous stream of sensation, which the critic observes and wishes to prove at this point; but perhaps he deceives himself with his proof—fine! The mental phenomenon still stands firm, even if his example begins to totter. And if the former is observed correctly—well then, Mr. Klotz, Home did not desire to write a booklet of examples, a commentary on poets, a primer of borrowed beautiful passages, for his observations on sensation were his main end in view. How different are things in a *theory of the fine arts*, where I must not dreamily deduce sensation and then for a good while search for examples in my dreams, but rather draw conclusions only from individual experiences and phenomena in the objects of beauty. Mr. R. has therefore put Home's head on the wrong way round: what should be at the back is at the front; the foremost at the back—what a lovely likeness! A second Home.

Finally, there is Gerard's *Essay on Taste*. The word *taste* already reveals that Gerard is another subjective analyzer of our sensation of beauty and one of the foremost representatives of a philosophy that, if not always profound, is nevertheless fruitful, diverse, and rich in examples. But always it is taste that is his business, and not a theory of the fine arts. Has he done it justice? Has he, in the distribution of the different sides and main stations of his argument, in the arrangement of his themes and chapters, gotten to the bottom of each principal idea or not? Does he not often completely lose the thread of his ideas and, instead of allowing imagination and reason to go their way, judge and Frenchify dishes and roots of taste that lie scattered before him? This I cannot decide; I shall leave that to the Academy that awarded the work a prize. But even in that excellent section of his book where he comes closest to criticism; where he adds and heaps a large sum of sensations without reducing it to first principles; where he is instructive for all those who desire to learn judgment and a model for all those who wish to give an account of their taste; where he might be able to render many parts of Baumgarten's aesthetics productive—in all this Gerard's book is no *theory of the arts*, and I have shown with Home how much Riedel has erred in imitating its method, structure, material, and plan.

And why should I list all the writers, even the best ones, whom Mr. R. has either not used or misused in relation to specific topics? What has become of his concepts of the *beautiful and the sublime*, of *grace*, of *genius*, of *taste*? How battered and bruised are Mendelssohn, Winckelmann, and God knows who else? And where are Burke, Kant, Watelet, Zanotti, and so on? Where are the many excellent discourses on specific topics which can be found already in English philosophies, textbooks on art, weekly and monthly periodicals; which almost every poet and artist, particularly in Italy, has scattered in his works; and which finally editors and critics have given us? As an extract this book is one-sided and founded on abuse, and as a treatise in its own right it amounts to nothing.

12

"But what if Mr. R. made amends in the second part of his book? What if it contained, as he promised it would, an application of the earlier principles to the various kinds of arts and letters? What if the first part were related to the second like applied mathematics to pure mathematics?" Anyone who believes that, who can think it possible—well, until now I have written in vain for him; in vain have I shown that a theory of the beaux arts and belles lettres must pick its way through precisely these matters in order to arrive at principles; in vain have I shown that no principles are possible without data and phenomena, and that these must be drawn from individual species of art; in vain have I shown that words, spoken from the top down, are complex delusions and that all of Riedel's chapters are precisely half understood, borrowed, and parroted delusions of this sort. In vain have I shown that since no ideas were inferred immediately and vividly from works of art, they cannot therefore be applied to these same works. And what do we have left over for an applied aesthetics? The same nonsense as the so-called pure aesthetics of the first part; the most impure in its concepts, treatment, and structure that I know anywhere in the world. What ignoramus would dare even to compare it with mathematics, that most definite, thorough, and exact science?

Here are my ideas for—my outline of—the great path that leads through all the beaux arts and belles lettres to a *theory of the beautiful*. We shall see that the main thing is the path itself: with it everything stands or falls. I will abandon myself, then, to my dreams.

I think that the fine art in which *unity* and *diversity* are manifested most plainly and forcefully is *architecture*. The construction of its parts is very simple; their relation to the proportion of the whole, their reciprocal symmetrical correspondence, their rules of richness and power, of fullness and delicacy, the impression of beauty and propriety that they make, and their magnitude and awesomeness are still very simple—all this is solid and grand and regular, just like an actual building. Of all the arts, architecture is therefore the first vast phenomenon I shall contemplate, and just as all philosophy arose from wonder, as Plato and Aristotle say, so the great, tranquil, unconfused, and eternal awe that this art inspires in us is the first state to attune the philosophical tone of the soul to aesthetics. Young man, in whose soul the philosophy of beauty slumbers, the genius of the arts will awaken you with these powerful and grand ideas, and as he leads you to his inner sanctum, you will see a *building* first and learn to feel and gaze in wonder. I see you sunk in deep contemplation as you compose yourself after the initial impression of *magnitude* and *power* and *sublimity*, as you study in the building, an eternal monument that will outlast centuries and entire races of men, the lineaments of *unity* and *diversity* in the greatest *simplicity, in the most sublime order*, in the most regular *symmetry* and simple *propriety* of taste. All these phenomena appear here unconfusedly, delineated in the firmest contours of certainty. Their effect on the soul is prolonged, and they stand forever before the eye. Gazing at them in wonderment, you will thus develop these phenomena within you, from the elementary and simplest column to the richest diversity of its parts, its whole, its structure; then you will ascend from the symmetry of two columns to their arch and from there to the palace in its entirety; then glide down facades and rows of columns; then return to take the building apart, to seek its ground plan, and to find in every measurement ideas of perfection that are manifested in the simplest contour. Then your imagination will expand until you see in this hollowed-out mountain of marble nothing but an ideal of *intuitive perfection* and lose yourself in wonder. Now go, and do not just take with you this image and the simple ideas that you discovered therein; let it also impress itself on you so that it arranges *your very soul*, so that it endows your soul forever with grandeur and power and simplicity and richness and order and propriety, so that it edifies your soul as if it were a beautiful building. If *that* impression never leaves you, if the organization of its perfections has become integral to you, young man, then you have been initiated into the mysteries of beauty, and the genius of the arts will open its inner sanctum to you. *Architecture* was your logic of beauty; now shall follow its metaphysics.

As yet you have seen no image of Nature, no true ideal of beauty. For whatever one may say about elements of architecture resembling trees, human beings, and plants; whatever Scamozzi may say about giant, Herculean and feminine, heroic and virginal columns—these are all inessential or forced resemblances. The perfection of architecture is clear only in contours and surfaces and bodies; it is entirely fabricated, arbitrarily abstracted, and artistically assembled. It was thus only a preparation before the gates of true art—now the gates open, and behold! An image of Nature, the true ideal of a living beauty: the statue.

Here is *Nature*; here is real *resemblance* and thus *imitation* and thus *truth* in art, which is truth to the degree of feeling, of touching bodies, the surest means of art.

Here is *beauty*, or whatever name one wishes to give to the agreeableness that does not reveal itself solely through imperfect waving and serpentine lines, beautiful oval shapes, and ellipses, all of which manifest themselves only on a surface and will therefore leave behind a never-ending dispute; the agreeableness that reveals itself through *rotundity* and a *tangible shapeliness that is both always the same and ever new*. That is *beauty*!

Here is the *original of expression*, here is the *vitality*, here is the soul that speaks through the body, and thus *illusion* and *living appeal* and *interest*.

Here there is more than the dead *propriety* of architecture; here there is *proportion* in the structure of the limbs and *decency* in the posture and *grace* in the movement and an insatiable wealth of ideas in the *action*.

All these feelings the artist's hand invested tangibly in the dead marble; tangible and incarnate, so to speak, they inhabit, as if in bodily plenitude, the temple of the artistic image. With each word, young man, a new world of fine sensations opens to you. Hear me: step before the works of Phidias and Lysippus, close your eyes, and feel in this sacred darkness the first ideas of *natural beauty* and of *shapeliness* and of *expression* and of *action* and all the innumerable concepts that are dependent on them. Feel them, and you will find that when the authors of language originally spoke of *feeling* and *sensations of beauty*, they gave voice not to some empty silhouette but to truth; you will find that *touch* is just as much the first, faithful, true sense of experience in the world of sensuous beauty as it is in the world of sensuous truth; you will find that the rich abundance of concepts, which here are experienced and not merely lifelessly acknowledged, is the basis of all beauty and has been given bodily form to *cultivate* and *mold* the soul *to the concept of beauty*. Do this, *cultivate* and *mold* yourself, walk among statues as in a *world of original ideas of beauty rendered sensuous*: that shall be your first academy.

In this world of corporeal beauty, however, each figure still appears individually. What can be represented in and through that figure is tangible, but that which is meant to be external to and only distantly connected with it must appear quite separately. So even where there is a fable, a single drama of images native to this art, we cannot really speak of an indivisible whole arising from a single ground; each stands alone, for the continuum that holds them together—the air, the day, the night, the surface that is the domain of sight—cannot be given bodily form. Hence there must be another art that emulates this great enchanted tableau of Nature and, like Nature, uses light and color to project objects onto a surface, where they appear in their continuum, all resting on a single ground, as a unity. And that art, apprentice of beauty, is *painting*! The great forecourt of *the corporeally beautiful* was dark; in sacred, unscattered darkness you walked among works fashioned by and for human hands. Your genius guided you through them toward the dawn and eventually to the light. Now the light is revealed to you: behold! The *magic art practiced by human hands for human eyes* creates a world of the visibly beautiful on a surface, as if the image were more than merely superficial.

Behold: *multiplicity on a single ground*, in a single continuum, in a single patch of light and shadow. So here you shall study the concept of *unity* and *diversity* as *ordonnance*, as *juxtaposition* and *composition*. Here you will find these concepts smooth and perfect, in the *whole* and *in its effect*, in its *groups* and *figures*, *arrangements* and *contrasts*, *light* and *colors*; everywhere there is one fable and one world of *visible diversity* and *unity*: everything down to the smallest nuance combines to illumine these ideas pertaining to the invention, the creation of an interconnected series of beings. Give yourself over to them, for of course the effect of each painted figure on your soul is infinitely weaker than that of a statue, as if it were the latter's shadow. But then this is not the principal efficacy of this art. Its effect resides not in an individual figure as such but rather in a totality of figures and light and colors and spaces. Gather them all within you so that they form a single impression, just as you see from a single point of view, and move out once more from this impression to embrace the whole composition—now you see in a painterly fashion; now you are worthy of surveying one world with one glance and of delighting in its perfection.

Mark you, then: the farther you travel, the more artifice there is in the arts, and with this, painting abounds. You cannot touch and grasp the principal impression which it conveys; the eye must acquire the important habit of assembling it from all its component parts, and thus the study of art develops with each step. Do not fly over its surfaces with a single glance born of ignorance or raw enthusiasm, for that would be to gape and to tarnish the palette. Look! Contemplate! Compare! Gather!

Behold *drawing*! With sculpture this was only an inessential aid that provided the sense of touch with form and thus vanished once it had done so: the servant, who was necessary only because of weakness and for the sake of convenience, retreated as her mistress, form, was due to make her impression. In painting drawing was essential to the artistic effect and therefore had to remain. For *illusion* is the essence of this art, which creates mere illusory images of bodies on a surface, and every helper that participates in the illusion must remain visible: drawing is the foremost such assistant. It sketches the appearance of bodies and produces a beautiful illusion on a surface. And what else does it give up to study? The original idea of *verisimilitude* and with it all the *exactitude* and *correctness* of the lines; the original idea of *intuitive beauty* and with it every *agreeableness* of wavy and serpentine lines, *beautiful oval shapes* and *ellipses*; *elegance* and *taste* in the design.——All this floats in a continuum and thus . . .

Behold the *modeling* of the whole: in *figures*, the *intuitive illusion of substantiality* and therefore the *anatomy of the body and soul*, which reveals *character*; in *landscapes*, the intuitive illusion of existence and thus *expanses* and *distances*, *brightness* and *darkness*, *light* and *shadow*. Finally, the *magic* of color overflows everything, and so . . .

Behold *painterly illusion*, an illusion that is as different from the tangible illusion of sculpture as sight is from touch. There the body came to life and here the whole surface of the picture was enlivened with *figures, light,* and *color;* sculpture became the illusion of *touch* just as painting became that of the *eyes.* Everywhere, then, there arose a *new ideal* that inheres in the totality of an intuitive world full of artifices arrayed on a single surface: the *finest, clearest,* and *most distinct* aesthetics of sight; *a tableau of the wisdom of beauty.* That, young man, is *painting!*

A tableau of the wisdom of beauty: and on a tableau, on a surface, there is not yet properly any succession. Everything is a single moment of a single idea, just as it is only a single tableau, a single surface. Here the appearance of continuous action is just that: appearance, an illusion of the imagination; therefore it is still only the art of a single moment, a single instant. Is there no other art that might achieve its effect over several moments in time? Whose energy would last longer? Which would take possession of duration, time, succession, in the same way that sculpture has annexed corporeality and painting two-dimensional space? If there is indeed such an art, it will be entirely new and distinct, scarcely commensurable with the others, for its perceptions of grace will be as different from theirs as succession is from space, as coexistence is from consecutiveness. Here a new sense will awaken, of which mere eye and touch could form no notion; let us here prepare ourselves for a new world of pleasure in art: *music* rings out.

Here a new sense opens up, a new gateway of the soul, and perceives *tones: tones,* whose every simple moment the ear absorbs with pleasure; *tones,* whose every simple moment touches the soul in a thousand new ways and produces a thousand new and different, yet inward and immediate, sensations; *tones,* the instrument that most directly affects the soul. Whereas the expression of visual art was nothing but surface, music is inner essence; that is, *energetic force, pathos*—how else shall I name it? That which penetrates deep into the soul: the world of a new feeling. All our sensations are here a string music seized by what we call tone in all the intensity of its individual moments and beautiful variations and recurring delicacies of feeling.

So here is *Nature in the language of passion* and of all sensation, here are their accents, and thus here is *imitation* and sympathetic *truth* in tones, utterances of emotion, and *expression.*

Here there is *grace,* or however one wishes to call the primitive sensation that independently of the relations and proportions of the simple moments moves the soul agreeably.

Here there is *beautiful succession* in its first, simple original form; the *melody* of the tones, in their variation, their measure, and their timbre.

Finally, to bind everything together there are *audible relations*: accord, harmony. Partial tones are brought into consonance, and with a single sensation the ear, as it were, divides the indivisible nature of a single moment in time, which nevertheless remains but one moment. Those are the feelings of this new sense. *Impression* and *tone directly affecting the soul, accent of sensation, harmony,* and *beautiful succession*—wherever we find these, whether in thoughts and images, language and colors, they are musical in nature; they have been borrowed from music. But wherever music speaks of symmetry and contrasts, of arrangement, of light and shade in tones, it borrows these concepts from the other arts wherein they are at home; there it is debtor.

Music as such imitates human passions; it excites a succession of inward sensations that are true but not distinct, not intuitive, only obscure in the extreme. Young man, you stood in music's dark auditorium. Music lamented; it sighed, it raged, it exulted; you felt everything, you responded sympathetically as each string was struck,—but over what did you and music lament, sigh, exult, and rage? There was nary a hint of contemplation; everything stirred only in the darkest abyss of your soul, as a living wind disturbs the depths of the ocean. What if there intervened a more distinct human expression *of that* passion which music uttered only indistinctly? What of speech? It may be more distinct, but it is too distinct. Because language has only an arbitrary and hence not as profound a connection to the nature of sensations, it may enlighten but not strengthen. It will sooner deflect and weaken. So is there no natural human expression of passion that is as immediate and necessary as accent, as tone itself? Of course there is! In the body, in the face, in posture, in movement, in action—how naturally and completely the soul expresses itself in these. What an expression! What an effect! And if music now added its tones—but wait! Not added, but enlivened each of these forms of physical expression as naturally as passion produces them, and then impressed them more deeply into our soul with every tone? And what if no part predominated over any other: not music over the intuitive, except only to enliven it, to supply it with energy; not the intuitive over music, except to make its expression clearer through visible movement and action? And if each of these movements and actions now combined all the lines and shapes and postures of the beautiful that were combinable—and in each visibly expressed all the power of passion and melody that was expressible? And if the tones of music now omnipotently accompanied and reinforced them all, bringing everything to realization? And no part prevails over the others, and it all becomes one—well, my sensitive young man, what an impression! The art of beautiful forms and painterly postures and graceful movements and musical energy and human sentiment—all the arts of the beautiful and the delightful work in unison, and the human soul enlivens them: visibly and audibly it enlivens them; through eye and ear, from all sides is the soul assailed—that was the dance of the ancients!

I am too timid to bestow on my little analysis the grand title "The Resolution of Beauty into Its Component Parts;" I am giving only suggestions and hints. A philosophical theory of beauty in all the arts must furnish rather more: elucidation, a coherent, complete system. In his *Theory of the Beaux Arts*, Mr. R. has included a section with the splendid title "The Resolution of Beauty into Its Component Parts;" but his vague and nonsensical gabbling about the αρριτον of beauty and perfect sensuousness and disinterested pleasure is abhorrent and worth less than nothing, as is his grand design to decry every superior analysis of beauty as sterile, arid, and insignificant. But why should we let the barbarous Muse of this theorist trouble us? Let us continue on our path.

The sensations of beauty flow from every sense into the imagination and thus from all fine arts into poetry. Just as the fancy knows nothing without the senses, so poetry knows nothing without the fine arts; the majority of its primitive ideas of beauty originate in them, and if everything is a confluent ocean of agreeable forms and images and tones and emotions, how should I begin draining such a sea without becoming confused, without sinking therein?

Every idea or representation in the fancy is already, as the word suggests, *representation*, that is, *image*, and it is from the visual arts, the arts of representation, of formation, that poetry, the only fine art intended immediately for the soul, must therefore obtain its primitive notions. And whence comes a thought's *grandeur* and *beauty* as an image? And its *resemblance* to Nature? And its *selection* and hence also its beautification? Its beautiful *appearance* in a *composition* and thus its *design*, its *character*, its *coloring*? In which arts are these concepts intuitively and originally known? In the arts of *touch and of the visual appearance of the beautiful*. It is here that these concepts come alive; it is here, therefore, that they can be studied in relation to poetry, which without this instruction remains merely a parrot of the fine arts. It is here, then, that the ideas and laws of *beauty* and *resemblance* and *selection* and *design* and *character* and *color* of the thoughts are to be sought; and just as in metaphysics we abstract and separate a concept, so here we *form* a representation individually, so we *draw* and *depict* it in combination with others. Everywhere poetry becomes an imitator and its theory a pupil of the fine arts. Or else it is idle talk, like almost all the theories of poetry that we possess.

Two ideas shall be combined in a single sentence, contrast, example, simile; the simplest juxtaposition according to the rules of the beautiful is architectural. The firmness of both ideas, their dimensions, their proportion and symmetry, the relation of the essential and purely decorative aspects of their parts to one another—where does all this have a visible model in art? In architecture; and just as architecture is contiguous to mechanics and mathematics, so poetics is adjacent to philosophy and logic.

These two ideas stand in the sentence, contrast, example, and simile like two columns facing each other; do they possess firmness and order? If they consist of parts, are these also constructed so regularly and manifoldly and freely that the whole has a great effect? And are these smaller parts formed as it were from Nature, perfect in themselves and in relation to one another? Are the small and large parts congruent and differentiated—does none carry too heavy a load, are all free of repetition? Are they varied and without confusion? Are their projections and recesses appropriate for the point of view? Are their ornaments judicious and consistent with their arrangement? The model of the arts reaches all the way down to such fundamental relations of the parts of speech, and that model, when it comes to the most frigid relation of composition, is architecture—from the short sentence, contrast, and example to the grand speech, to the simple plan of the great poem—insofar as the latter still depends on mere relations.

But mere relations are not poetry's only love; they are too cold, too dry, too uniform to constitute its main object; and so the more vital art becomes its teacher and Muse. Sculpture departed in its design from the firm, straight outlines of architecture, which aimed to please only with its simplicity and a few gentle slopes and declivities but otherwise loved the hard line of truth; sculpture sought its own line of beauty in Nature, studied and beautified resemblances, learned tangible expression and simple action. If previously unity and symmetry prevailed, then already there began to emerge a beautiful unsymmetry, a charm in the movement and fruitfulness in the action of the individual creature fashioned by this art. Finally, the large-scale arrangement, unity and diverse opposition, the distribution of the groups, and beautiful disorder in the figures, in the light and shade, in the tone of the colors—all this became visible in painting. Poetry borrows from all three arts, but what it borrows from each can be difficult to determine. Where and to what extent must the symmetry of architecture, the simple action of sculpture, and the complex diversity of painting prevail or not prevail? Which structures and forms and manners and colors has each of the most peculiar epochs, nations, and poets loved most? What should be imitated and avoided in each of the arts? And how do we explain each singularity and form and manner? All these questions should be elucidated and determined by the theory of poetry; I leave it to the reader to decide whether we currently have one that is capable of this. Poetry has long been called a kind of mute painting, and for just as long has it been compared with sculpture; but to compare and abstract it philosophically—that has not yet been done.

Poetry is more than mute painting and sculpture, as well as something quite distinct from both. It is speech, it is the music of the soul. The train of thoughts, of images, of words, of tones, is the essence of its expression;

in this it is similar to music, not only insofar as I hear image and tone in a word, and thus a certain harmony that fits together like a chord and constitutes the essence of prosody. In the *succession of words* itself there unfolds first and foremost a melody of ideas and tones; with every word and tone the energy affects the soul more deeply, and everything works toward the whole. Ode and idyll, fable and passionate speech—these are a melody of thoughts, where each tone moves us as it is struck and makes way for the next and, through the sweet trace, the beautiful echo that it leaves behind, dissolves and melts into another. In the very chain of such dissolutions and transitions, which convey the impression ever more deeply into the soul, the efficacy of music has its origin; and through language arises the whole of the ode, the idyll, the fable, the drama, the epic, where each individual moment is nothing by itself and the effect of the whole is everything. Accordingly, a theory of poetry that shows how the whole is formed by the succession and force of its ideas now becomes possible.

Ultimately, poetry ought to render those lively emotions and feelings sensuous which all of these dead arts merely expressed lifelessly and music alone obscurely. What a magnificent example the *dance of the ancients* would be for us, if only it could still be our model. The most vital expression of passion and of every passion through mien, gesture, and posture heaped on, ranged alongside, and following from one another; whatever is called *life* and *charm* and *action*—this, poetry has absorbed; this, poetry has intellectually transplanted into its essence, into its expression, and into the delivery of its expression, the lofty declamation. Divine poetry! Intellectual art of beauty! Queen of all the ideas raised in all the senses! Meeting place of the magic of all the arts!

The remaining characteristics of poetry and the other arts are of secondary importance; they belong to the more specialized practical rules governing a particular art, not to the philosophical theory of beauty in general. Thus each art has a mechanical and craftsmanlike aspect and also a foreign scientific aspect that shares only a distant border with it. One part of the visual arts rests on optics and perspective, music rests on mathematical acoustics, and architecture on God knows how many handicrafts! A large part of poetry is based on grammar, another on logic—at least on the logic of common sense—and a third even on metaphysics. But these are all foundations, means to ends. Whoever introduces them as ends, as the finished theoretical edifice, into his art and even into the aesthetics of beauty is laboring on a trifle as if it were a major work. Might this be one of the reasons why aesthetics proper has not yet advanced very far? Baumgarten's is wholly a secondary structure, and that of Riedel a patchwork of outhouses and chicken coops lacking purpose, plan, and order.

The path that I have sketched is, I believe, the only method of tidying and untangling a science that still remains confused. Such an aesthetics would teach a lesson to our aesthetic prattlers who blather figuratively and floridly about all the arts, or at least expose these fools. Such an aesthetics would lure the young to a science that does not hurl abstract ideas in their faces, in which, passing through all the arts, they enjoy nothing but beautiful appearances; at every step along the way they will be enriched with new phenomena and experiences, ultimately approaching the idea of beauty that stands naked before them. Such an aesthetics would give rise to a science that would form taste in all the arts, in all the objects of sensuous beauty, and thus to a guide to a charming and cultivated manner of thinking. Such an aesthetics would perhaps breathe new life into the old method of educating the young, for the delicate soul would be nourished not with vague and abstract ideas but with firm, substantial notions of beauty, led ever onward, so that finally it becomes a soul full of Greek feeling and Greek philosophy. Infinitely many misapprehended half-ideas, which currently bring aesthetics into disrepute as a frivolous, unphilosophical science, would thereby be corrected or eradicated; in aesthetics would be born the younger, more cheerful sister of logic and the most agreeable daughter of psychology. How useful it would be if the young began with it in school and brought it to completion in the academy. It would be more instructive than logic, for aesthetics is the logic of those faculties which are the first to awaken in the young and of which the untutored child has most need. It would charm more than petty academic histories, for it is as broad and rich and fruitful as boundless, beautiful Nature; it would never be wearying, for it leads us ever onward, from appearance to appearance, from visual art to the ear and from there to the soul itself; it would not, as the sciences often do, dull genius with abstractions. Rather, it would always remain rooted in experience, cultivate the eye, ear, hand, and fancy unobtrusively, and furnish the soul with the abundance of ideas, the taste in beauty, the soundness of judgment and of the senses, which alone make for the beautiful spirit—he who sees and feels and worships beauty wherever he finds it, whether in art or in the lap of infinite Nature; he who seeks beauty among all nations and ages, and even when he finds only the merest trace thereof, inscribes it with fire within himself; he who thus gathers a mind that is great and rich like bountiful Nature and fine and correct like every art; immeasurable like peoples and centuries and yet exact and certain like the age of the best taste. O human soul, you daughter of divine talents, why are you not often and always cultivated in this manner? O science, you who can cultivate us in this way, why do you not yet exist in all your light, order, comprehensibility, abundance, and beauty? *Theory of the beaux arts and belles lettres!*

And now I read that Sulzer's *Dictionary* will soon appear—a welcome arrival despite its format and perhaps the last preliminary contribution to the theory that I desire and seek! My *Critical Forests*, at least my solicitude in the elaboration of the concepts of beauty, which others are so fond of confusing—let this work testify as to whether I deserve to be a reader of that same theory or at least would be an impartial reader. The conclusion of Klopstock's *Messiah*, and a pragmatic translation of the writings of the Orient by Michaelis, and a history of the literature, especially poetry, of antiquity by a second Winckelmann, and new revelations of Wieland's Muse, and Gleim's ancient German ballads, *bards* and *skaldic songs*, and Ramler's Horace, and Meinhardian translations of the greatest poets of every nation, and Heyne's editions of the Greeks and Romans, and Romeos and Saras for our theaters, and Addisons and Sonnenfelses in German prose, and new *Letters Concerning Literature* to scourge our micrologists of antiquity and to renew true philosophy, and Hagedorns in every fine art, and then *a philosophical theory and history of the beaux arts and belles lettres*—some of these wishes of mine are even now being fulfilled; our time is once more raising itself to a new age of German distinction. If it be in your power, O divine Muse, let me live to see the others realized also!

CONCLUSION

In Greece it was patriotism when the hand that elevated the great men of the nation also tore down the statues of the tyrants, and in a degenerate age it is just as patriotic to ennoble a corrupt philosophy and to unmask flagrant ignorance—what harm does it do if this ignorance, which has raised its voice against so many, barks at my shadow also? I say my *shadow*, but what a pity that the name of a quite different writer has thereby been taken in vain and his character, office, and rank maliciously abused by malicious men! What can I, who have unwittingly presented the occasion for such abuses, do to compensate this innocent?

My forests have no order, no method; and since when was this a beauty possessed by forests? According to certain newspapers and libraries, their author has not uttered a single intelligent word therein; and according to certain literary letters, he can write neither Greek nor Latin; the next installment and a second pressing will prove otherwise. Some misunderstandings, repetitions, errors, and overhasty features shall be erased; others, strengthened, supplemented, enlarged; and I hope that my forests will not be unfruitful or disagreeable collections for the lover of the philosophy of the beautiful. That shall be my reply, my triumph! Then shall posterity, that impartial arbiter, read and judge me.

For all that, I cannot suppress a sigh as I reach the end of my labors!

How belittling it is to have to condescend to the work and even more often to the tone of petty people! How humbling to accommodate yourself to a corrupt micrological age, so that you can clear the way for a better one! What have I delivered that will endure, that will still remain after this time has turned to dust? And much more would I have left to do and to deliver! O Muse! Let that be the career of my works! To add something to the chain of ideas linking human souls, or to be silent, to be celebrated during my lifetime, and to die. Italy, France, England, have made their centuries great and gleaming; Germany began to surpass them, yet now it means to sink once more into antiquarian and scholastic micrology. And am I to sink with them?

Shakespeare

IF ANY MAN BRINGS to mind that tremendous image of one "seated high atop some craggy eminence, whirlwinds, tempest, and the roaring sea at his feet, but with the flashing skies about his head," that man is Shakespeare! Only we might add that below him, at the very base of his rocky throne, murmur the multitudes who explain, defend, condemn, excuse, worship, slander, translate, and traduce him—and all of whom he cannot hear!

What a library has already been written about for and against him! And I have no mind to add to it in any way. It is my wish instead that no one in the small circle of those who read these pages would ever again think to write about for or against him, either to excuse or to slander him, but that they explain him, feel him as he is, use him, and—where possible—bring him to life for us Germans. If only this essay can help in some small way to realize this goal!

Shakespeare's boldest enemies—in how many different guises—have accused and mocked him, claiming that though he may be a great poet, he is not a good dramatist; or if he is a good dramatist, then he is not a classical tragedian equal in rank to men such as Sophocles, Euripides, Corneille, and Voltaire, who raised this art to the highest pinnacle of perfection. And Shakespeare's boldest friends have mostly been content to *excuse*, to *defend* him from such attacks; to weigh his beauties against his transgressions of the rules and see the former as compensation for the latter; to utter the *absolvo* over the accused; and then to deify his greatness all the more immoderately, the more they were compelled to shrug their shoulders at his faults. That is how things stand even with the most recent editors and commentators. My hope is that these pages can change the prevailing point of view so that our image of him may emerge into a fuller light.

But is this hope not too bold? Too presumptuous, when so many great men have already written about him? I think not. If I can show that both sides have built their case merely on *prejudice*, on an illusion that does not really exist; if, therefore, I merely have to dispel a cloud from their eyes or at most adjust the image without in the least altering anything in eye or image, then perhaps it is down to my time or even to chance that I should have discovered the spot where I now detain the reader: "Stand here, otherwise you will see nothing but caricature!" If all we ever did was wind and unwind the tangled threads of learning without ever getting any further, then what an unhappy fate we would weave!

From Greece we have inherited the words *drama*, *tragedy*, and *comedy*; and just as the lettered culture of the human race has, on a narrow strip of the earth's surface, made its way only through *tradition*, so a certain stock of rules, which seemed inseparable from its teaching, has naturally accompanied it everywhere in its womb and its language. Since a child cannot be and is not educated by means of reason but by means of authority, impression, and the divinity of example and of habit, so entire nations are to an even greater extent children in everything that they learn. The kernel would not grow without the husk, and they will never get the kernel without the shell, even if they could find no use for the latter. That is the case with Greek and northern drama.

In Greece the drama developed in a way that it could not in the north. In Greece it was what it can never be in the north. In the north it is not and cannot be what it was in Greece. Thus Sophocles' drama and Shakespeare's drama are two things that in a certain respect have scarcely their name in common. I believe I can demonstrate these propositions from Greece itself and in doing so decipher a great deal of the nature of the northern drama and of the greatest northern dramatist, Shakespeare. We shall observe the genesis of the one by means of the other, but at the same time see it transformed, so that it does not remain the same thing at all.

Greek tragedy developed, as it were, out of a single scene, out of the impromptu dithyramb, the mimed dance, the *chorus*. This was enlarged, recast: Aeschylus put two actors on to the stage instead of one, invented the concept of the protagonist, and reduced the choral part. Sophocles added a third actor and introduced scene painting. From such origins, though belatedly, Greek tragedy rose to greatness, became a masterpiece of the human spirit, the summit of poetry, which Aristotle esteems so highly and we, in Sophocles and Euripides, cannot admire deeply enough.

At the same time, however, we see that certain things can be explained in terms of these origins, which, were we to regard them as dead rules, we would be bound to misconstrue dreadfully. That *simplicity of the Greek plot*, that *sobriety of Greek manners*, that sustained, buskined style *of expression, song making, spectacle, unity of time and place*—all these things lay so naturally and inherently, without any artifice and magic, in the origins of Greek tragedy that it was made possible only as a consequence of their refinement. They were the husk in which the fruit grew.

Step back into the infancy of that age: *simplicity of plot* really was so steeped in what was called the *deeds of olden times*, in *republican, patriotic, religious, heroic action*, that the poet had more trouble distinguishing parts in this simple whole, introducing a dramatic beginning, middle, and end, than in forcibly separating them, truncating them, or kneading them into a whole out of many discrete events. This ought to be perfectly understandable to anyone who has read Aeschylus or Sophocles. In Aeschylus, what is tragedy but often *an allegorical, mythological, semi-epic painting*, almost without a succession of scenes, story, or sensations? Or is it even, as the ancients said, nothing but *chorus* into which a certain amount of story has been squeezed? Did the simplicity of Aeschylus's plots demand the least effort and art? And was it any different in the majority of Sophocles' plays? His *Philoctetes, Ajax, Oedipus Coloneus,* and so on, are still very close to the uniformity of their origin, the *dramatic picture framed by the chorus.* No doubt about it! This is the genesis of Greek drama!

Now let us see how much follows from this simple observation. Nothing less than this: "The artificiality of the rules of Greek drama was—not artifice at all! It was Nature!" Unity of plot—was the unity of the action that lay before the *Greeks*; which according to the circumstances of their time, country, religion, and manners could be nothing but this oneness. *Unity of place* was just that, unity of place, for the one brief, solemn action occurred only in a single locality, in the temple, in the palace, as it were in the market square of the nation; to begin with, this action was only mimed and narrated and inserted between the chorus; then finally the entrances of the characters, the scenes were added—but of course it was still but one scene, where the chorus bound everything together, where in the nature of things the stage could never remain empty, and so on. And even a child could see that unity of time now ensued from and naturally accompanied all this. In those days all these things lay in *Nature*, so that the poet, for all his art, could achieve nothing without them!

It is also evident that the art of the Greek poets took the very opposite path to the one that we nowadays ascribe to them. They did not *simplify*, it seems to me, but rather *elaborated*: Aeschylus expanded the *chorus* and Sophocles enlarged upon Aeschylus, and we need only compare the most sophisticated plays of Sophocles and his great masterpiece *Oedipus in Thebes* with *Prometheus* or with accounts of the ancient *dithyramb* to see the astonishing artistry with which he successfully endowed his works. But his was never an art of making a simple plot out of a complex one, but rather of making a complex plot out of a simple one, a beautiful labyrinth of scenes. His greatest concern remained, at the most intricate point in the labyrinth, to foster in his audience the illusion of the earlier simplicity, to unwind the knot of their feelings so gently and gradually as to make them believe they had never lost it, the previous dithyrambic feeling. To this end he expanded each scene, retained the choruses, and turned them into staging-posts for the action; their every word ensured that his audience never lost sight of the whole, kept them in expectation, in the illusion of development, of *familiarity with the action* (all of which the didactic Euripides, when the drama had scarcely reached maturity, promptly neglected to do!). In short, Sophocles gave action *grandeur* (something that has been terribly misunderstood).

It ought to be clear to anyone who reads him without prejudice and from the standpoint of his own time that this is the art which Aristotle values in Sophocles, that in everything he took almost the opposite view to the spin that modern times have chosen to put on him. The very fact that he let Thespis and Aeschylus alone and stuck to the *variety* of Sophocles' poetry; that he took precisely Sophocles' *innovation* as his point of departure and viewed it as the *essence* of this new poetic genre; that it became his dearest wish to develop a new Homer and to compare him favorably with the original; that he did not neglect even the slightest detail that could in performance lend support to his conception of the action possessing *magnitude and grandeur*—all this shows that the great man also philosophized in the grand style of his age, and that he bears no blame at all for the restrictive and infantile follies that have turned him into the paper scaffolding of our stage. In his excellent chapter on the nature of plot, he evidently "knew and recognized no other rules than the gaze of the spectator, soul, illusion!" and expressly stated that *limitations* of length, still less of kind or time or place of the structure, cannot be determined by any other rules. Oh, if Aristotle were alive today and could witness the false, preposterous application of his rules in dramas of a quite different kind! But let us keep to calm and dispassionate inquiry.

As everything in the world changes, so Nature, the true creator of Greek drama, was bound to change also. *The Greek worldview, manners, the state of the republics, the tradition of the heroic age, religion*, even *music, expression*, and *the degrees of illusion* changed. And so naturally enough the material for plots disappeared, too, as well as the opportunity to adapt it and the motive for doing so. To be sure, the poets could draw on older or foreign material and dress it up in the tried-and-tested manner, but that had no effect. Consequently it was devoid of soul. Consequently (why should we mince our words?) it was no longer the thing it once was. It was effigy, imitation, ape, statue, in which only the most devoted lover could still detect the demon that had once brought the statue to life. Let us immediately turn to the new Athenians of Europe (for the Romans were too stupid or too clever or too wild and immoderate to establish a completely Hellenizing theater), and the matter becomes, I think, quite clear.

There is no doubt that this effigy of Greek theater can scarcely be more perfectly conceived and realized than it has been in France. I am not only thinking of the so-called dramatic rules that have been attributed to dear old Aristotle: *the unity of time, place,* and *action, the connection of the scenes, the verisimilitude of the scenery,* and so on. The question I really want to ask is whether anything in the world possibly surpasses the sleek, classical thing that the Corneilles, Racines, and Voltaires have produced, the series of beautiful *scenes, dialogues, verses,* and *rhymes* with their *measure, decorum,* and *brilliance.* Not only does the author of the present essay doubt it, but all the admirers of Voltaire and the French, particularly those noble Athenians themselves, will positively *deny* it—indeed, they have done so often enough already, they are still doing it, and they will continue to do so: "There is nothing better! It cannot be surpassed!" And from the point of view of this outward conformity, with this effigy treading the boards, they are right and must daily be more so, the more every country in Europe is besotted with this slick superficiality and continues to ape it.

But for all that, there is still the oppressive, inescapable feeling that "this is no Greek tragedy! This is no Greek drama in its purpose, effect, kind, and nature!" And that even the most partisan admirer of the French cannot deny, once he has experienced the Greeks. I do not even propose to inquire "whether they observe their Aristotelian rules as scrupulously as they claim to, for Lessing has recently raised serious doubts about the pretensions they trumpet most loudly." But even if we admit that they do keep to these rules, French drama is still not the same thing as Greek drama. Why? Because nothing in their inner essence is the same—not action, manners, language, purpose, nothing. So what is the good of carefully preserved outward similarities? Does anyone really believe that a single one of the great Corneille's heroes is a Roman or French hero? They are Spanish-Senecan heroes! Gallant heroes; adventurous, brave, magnanimous, love-struck, cruel heroes, and therefore dramatic fictions who outside the theater would be branded fools and who even in those days, at least in France, were almost as outlandish as they are in most modern plays. Racine speaks the language of sentiment—granted, in this single instance of agreement he is unsurpassed, but then again—I would not know where sentiment ever spoke in such a way. They are thirdhand pictures of sentiment; they are never or only rarely the immediate, original, unadorned emotions searching for words and finding them at last. Voltaire's beautiful verse, its arrangement, content, economy of images, polish, wit, philosophy—is it not beautiful verse? Indeed it is! The most beautiful that one can imagine, and if I were a Frenchman, I would despair at writing poetry after Voltaire—but beautiful or not, it is not theatrical verse appropriate to the action, language, manners, passions, and purpose of a drama (other than the French kind); it is never-ending rhetoric, lies, and galimatias! And the ultimate *aim* of it all? It is certainly not a Greek aim, a tragic purpose! To stage a beautiful play, as long as it is also a beautiful

action! To let a series of respectable, well-dressed ladies and gentlemen recite beautiful speeches and the most beautiful and useful philosophy in
beautiful verse! And then to put them all in a story that produces the illusion of reality and thus captivates our attention! Finally, to have it all
performed by a number of well-rehearsed ladies and gentlemen, who do
their very best to win our applause and approbation through declamation, stilted delivery of the sentential speeches, and the outward expression of emotions—all this might serve excellently as a living manual, an
exercise in correct expression, in conduct and decorum, as a painting of
good or even heroic manners, and even as a complete academy of national
wisdom and decency in matters of life and death (without taking into account all its subsidiary aims). Beautiful, formative, instructive, and excellent all this may be, but it shows neither hide nor hair of the purpose of
Greek theater.

And what was this purpose? Aristotle declared it to be—and there has
been enough dispute about it ever since—no more nor less than a *certain*
convulsion of the heart, the agitation of the soul to a *certain degree* and
in *certain aspects*; in short, a *species of illusion* that surely no French play
has ever achieved or ever will achieve. And consequently (no matter how
lovely and useful the name that we give it) it is not Greek drama. It is not
Sophoclean tragedy. It is an effigy outwardly resembling Greek drama, but
the effigy lacks spirit, life, nature, truth—that is, all the elements that
move us; that is, the tragic purpose and the accomplishment of that purpose. So can it still be the same thing?

This does not yet decide the value or otherwise of French drama but
only raises the question of difference, which I believe my foregoing remarks have put beyond doubt. I shall leave it to the reader to determine
for himself "whether a half-truthful copying of foreign ages, manners, and
actions, with the exquisite aim of adapting it to a two-hour performance
on our stage, can be thought the equal or indeed the superior of an *imitation* that in a certain respect was the highest expression of a people's national character." I shall leave it to the reader to determine (and here every
Frenchman will have to wriggle out of this difficulty or sing so tunelessly
that he drowns out the reproaches of his critics) whether a poetic work
that properly speaking has *no purpose at all* as a whole—for according
to the testimony of the best philosophers its virtue lies only in the selection of detail—whether such a copy can be equal in value to a *national
institution* whose every little particular produces an effect and betokens
the highest, richest culture. Whether, finally, a time may come when, just
as the greater part and most artificial of Corneille's plays are already forgotten today, Crébillon and Voltaire will be regarded with the same admiration that we now reserve for the *Astrea* of d'Urfé and all the *Clélies*
and *Aspasias* from the age of chivalry: "How clever, wise, inventive, and

well crafted they are! There would be so much to learn from them, but what a pity it is to be found in the *Astrea* and *Clélie*." Their whole art is unnatural, fanciful, dainty! How fortunate if this time had already dawned on our taste for truth! All of French drama would have transformed itself into a collection of beautiful verses, sententiousness, and sentiments—but the great Sophocles *will still stand where he is today*!

So let us now suppose a nation, which due to particular circumstances that will not detain us here, did not care to ape the Greeks and settle for the mere walnut shell but preferred instead to *invent its own drama*. Then, it seems to me, our first questions must once again be: *When? Where? Under what conditions? Out of which materials should it do so?* And no proof is needed that this invention can and will be the result of these questions. If this people does not develop its drama out of the chorus and dithyramb, then it can have no choral or dithyrambic parts. If its *history, tradition,* and *domestic, political, and religious relations* have no such simple character, then naturally its drama cannot partake of this quality either. Where possible, it will *create* its drama out of its history, out of the spirit of the age, manners, opinions, language, national prejudices, traditions, and pastimes, even out of carnival plays and puppet plays (just as the noble Greeks did from the chorus). And what it creates will be drama if it achieves its dramatic purpose among this people. As the reader will see, we have arrived among the *toto divisis ab orbe Britannis* and their great Shakespeare.

That this was not Greece, neither in Shakespeare's day nor earlier, no *pullulus Aristotelis* will deny, and therefore to demand that Greek drama arise then, and in England, to demand that it develop *naturally* (we are not speaking here of mere apery) is worse than asking a sheep to give birth to lion cubs. Our first and last question is simply this: "what is the soil like? How has it been prepared? What has been sown in it? What should it be able to produce?" And heavens, how far we are from Greece! History, tradition, manners, religion, the spirit of the age, of the people, of emotion, and of language—how far all these things are from Greece! Whether the reader knows both ages well or only slightly, he will not for one moment confuse two things that bear no likeness to each other. And if now in this changed time, changed for good or ill, there arose an age, a genius who created dramatic works from this raw material as naturally, sublimely, and originally as the Greeks did from theirs; and if these works reached the same goal by very different paths; and if they were essentially a far more multiformly simple and uniformly complex entity, and thus (according to all metaphysical definitions) a perfect whole—what manner of fool would now compare and even condemn the two things because the latter was not the former? Indeed, the very essence of the latter, its virtue and perfection, resides in the fact that it is not the former, that from the soil of the age a different plant grew.

Shakespeare was confronted with nothing like the simplicity of national manners, deeds, inclinations, and historical traditions that formed the Greek drama. And since, according to the first principle of metaphysics, nothing comes from nothing, then, if it were left to philosophers, not only would there have been no Greek drama, but if nothing else existed besides, no drama at all anywhere in the world would subsequently have developed or could ever develop. But since it is known that genius is more than philosophy and a creator wholly distinct from an analyzer, so a mortal was endowed with divine powers to summon from completely different material and by quite different means precisely the same effect, *fear* and *pity*, and to a degree of which the earlier treatment and material were scarcely capable. Oh, happy was this son of the gods in his undertaking! The very innovativeness, originality, and variety of his work demonstrate the primal power of his vocation.

Shakespeare had no chorus before him, but he did have historical dramas and puppet plays—well then! So from these historical dramas and puppet plays, from this inferior clay, he fashioned the glorious creation that stands before us and lives! He found nothing comparable to the simple character of the Greek people and their polity, but rather a rich variety of different estates, ways of life, convictions, peoples, and idioms—any nostalgia for the simplicity of former times would have been in vain. He therefore brought together the estates and individuals, the peoples and idioms, the kings and fools, fools and kings, to form one glorious whole! He found no such simple spirit of history, plot, and action; he took history as he found it, and with his creative spirit he combined the most diverse material into a wondrous whole, which, if we cannot call *plot* as the Greeks understood the word, we shall describe as *action* in the medieval sense, or what in the modern age is termed *event* (*événement*), great *occurrence*. O Aristotle, if you were alive today, what comparisons you would draw between the modern Sophocles and Homer! You would devise a theory that would do justice to him, the like of which even his own countrymen Home and Hurd, Pope and Johnson have yet to come up with! You would be glad to trace the trajectory of *plot, character, thought, language, song making,* and *spectacle* from each of your plays, as though you were drawing lines from two points at the base of a triangle so that they converge at the point where they complete the figure, the point of *perfection*! You would say to Sophocles: "Paint the sacred panels of this altar! And you, O northern bard, cover every side and every wall of this temple with your immortal fresco!"

Let me continue as interpreter and rhapsodist, for I am closer to Shakespeare than to the Greek. If in Sophocles a single *action* prevails, then

Shakespeare aims at the totality of an *event*, an *occurrence*. If in Sophocles' characters a *single tone* predominates, then Shakespeare assembles all the characters, estates, and ways of life that are necessary to produce the main melody of his symphony. If in Sophocles *a single* refined and musical language resounds as if in some ethereal realm, then Shakespeare speaks the language of all ages, peoples, and races of men; he is the interpreter of Nature in all her tongues—and can both, though they travel so very different paths, be familiars of a single Divinity? And if Sophocles represents and teaches and moves and cultivates *Greeks*, then Shakespeare teaches, moves, and cultivates northern *men*! When I read him, it seems to me that the theater, actors, and scenery disappear! I see only separate leaves from the book of events, of Providence, of the world, blown by the storm of history; individual impressions of peoples, estates, souls, all the most various and independently acting machines, all the unwitting, blind instruments—which is precisely what we are in the hands of the Creator of the world—which come together to form a single, whole dramatic image, an event of singular grandeur that only the poet can survey. Who can conceive of a greater poet of northern man and of his age?

Step before his stage as before an ocean of events, where wave crashes into wave. Scenes from nature come and go, each affecting the other, however disparate they appear to be; they are mutually creative and destructive, so that the intention of the creator, who seems to have combined them all according to a wanton and disordered plan, may be realized—dark little symbols forming the silhouette of a divine theodicy. Lear, the impetuous, fiery dotard, noble yet feeble as he stands before his map, giving away crowns and dividing up his country—the first scene already carries within it the seeds of his later fate, which shall be brought to harvest in the darkest future. Behold! We shall soon see the good-hearted squanderer, the rash and merciless ruler, the childish father even in the antechambers of his daughters, pleading, praying, begging, cursing, ranting, blessing, and—dear Lord!—foreknowing his own madness. Then we shall see him abroad with uncovered head in thunder and lightning, fallen among the lowest class of men, with a fool for company and squatting in the cave of a crazed beggar, almost calling down madness from the heavens. And now we see him as he is, in all the simple majesty of his wretched and abandoned state, and now with his wits restored, illuminated by the last ray of hope, only for it to be extinguished forever, forever! Finally, imprisoned, with the child, the daughter who had comforted and forgiven him dead in his arms, he dies over her body, and the old servant follows the old king into death—my God! What vicissitudes of times, circumstances, storms, weather, and ages. And all of it not merely a single story—a political drama, if you will—moving from a single beginning to a single conclusion, in accordance with the strictest rule of your Aristotle;

rather, come closer, and feel the *human spirit* that also arranged each person and age and character and secondary thing in the picture. Two aged fathers and all their very different children! The son of the one suffers misfortune yet is grateful to his deceived father, the other enjoys abominably good fortune yet is terribly ungrateful to his good-hearted father. One father against his daughters and they against him, their husbands, suitors, and all their accomplices in fortune and misfortune. Blind Gloucester on the arm of the son he fails to recognize, and mad Lear at the feet of his exiled daughter! And now the moment at the crossroads of fortune, when Gloucester dies beneath his tree and the trumpet sounds, all the minor details, motives, characters, and situations condensed into the work—everything is in play, developing into a whole, arranged together to form a *whole* comprising *fathers, children, kings, fools, beggars,* and *misery,* yet throughout which the soul of the event breathes in even the most disparate scenes, in which places, times, circumstances, even, I would say, the heathen *fatalism* and *astrology* that prevail throughout, are so much a part of this whole that I could not change or move a thing or introduce into it elements from other plays or vice versa. And this is not a drama? And Shakespeare is not a dramatic poet? He who embraces a hundred scenes of a world event in his arms, orders them with his gaze, and breathes into them the one soul that suffuses and animates everything; he who captivates our attention, our heart, our every passion, our entire soul from beginning to end—if not more, then let Father Aristotle bear witness: "Creatures and other organic structures must have magnitude and yet be easily taken in by the eye;" and here—good heavens!—how Shakespeare feels the whole course of events in the depths of his soul and brings it to its conclusion! A world of dramatic history, as vast and profound as Nature; but it is the creator who gives us the eyes and the vantage point we need to see so widely and deeply!

In *Othello,* the Moor, what a world! What a whole! A *living history of the genesis, development, eruption, and sad end to the passion of this noble and unfortunate man*! And what complexity! All these different cogs turning within a single mechanism! How this Iago, the Devil in human form, must look on the world and toy with everyone around him! And how *this* particular grouping of *these* particular characters, Cassio and Roderigo, Othello and Desdemona, with their susceptibilities like tinder to his infernal flames, must stand around him; each of them is caught in his net, used by him, and everything hastens to its sad conclusion. If an angel of Providence were to weigh human passions against one another and assemble souls and characters accordingly, and gave them occasions for each to act in the illusion of free will, when all along he led them by this illusion as if tugging at the chain of fate—this is how the human mind devised, conceived, sketched, and guided the events of this work.

There should be no need to remind anyone that time and place always accompany action just as the husk always surrounds the kernel, and yet precisely this point has raised the loudest outcry. If Shakespeare had the divine knack of comprehending an entire world of the most disparate scenes as a single great event, then naturally it was part of the truth of his events to represent time and place ideally in each instance so that they also contributed to the illusion. Is there indeed anyone in the world who is indifferent to the time and place of even the most trifling incidents of his life? And are they not especially important in those situations where the entire soul is agitated, formed, and transformed—in youth, in scenes of passion, in all the actions that shape our lives? Is it not precisely time and place and the fullness of external circumstances that necessarily lend the whole story *substance*, *duration*, and *existence*? And can a child, a youth, a lover, a man in the field of action, ever suffer the amputation of a single detail of his locality, of the how, where, and when, without injury to the larger mental picture we have formed of his soul? In this, Shakespeare is the greatest master, precisely because he is only and always the servant of Nature. When he conceived the events of his drama and revolved them in his mind, he also revolved times and places for each instance! Out of all the possible conjunctions of time and place, Shakespeare selected, as though by some law of fatality, the very ones that were the most powerful, the most appropriate for the feeling of the action; in which the strangest, boldest circumstances best supported the illusion of truth; where the changes of time and place, over which the poet is master, cried out the loudest: "This is no poet, but a creator! This is a history of the world!"

For instance, when the poet turned over in his mind as a fact of creation the terrible regicide, the tragedy called *Macbeth*—if then, my dear reader, you were too timid to give yourself over to the feeling of setting and place in any scene, then woe betide Shakespeare and the withered page in your hand. For you felt nothing of the opening scene with the witches on the heath amid thunder and lightning, nothing when the bloody man brings news of Macbeth's deeds to the king, who sends word that he shall be rewarded with another title, not to mention when the scene abruptly shifts and Macbeth receives the witches' prophetic greeting, is then apprised of Duncan's intentions, and these tidings mingle in his mind! You did not see his wife stride through the castle clutching that fateful letter, who will later wander in a so very different and terrible manner! You did not enjoy with the unsuspecting king the sweet evening air for one last time, in this house where the martlet makes its pendant bed so safely, but you, O king—for unseen forces are at work—you are nearing your murderous grave. The house is in commotion, the servants making ready for guests, and Macbeth for murder! Banquo's preparatory night scene with torch and sword! The dagger, the terrible vision of the dagger! The bell—the deed has scarcely been done and now there is knocking at the door! The discovery, the assembled household—consider every possible time and place, and you will see that the dramatic intention of this work could not have been realized other than *here* and *in this manner*. The scene of Banquo's murder in the wood; the evening banquet and Banquo's ghost—then once again the blasted heath (for Macbeth's terrible, fateful deed has been done!). Now the witches' cavern, the necromancy, the prophecy, the rage and despair! The slaying of Macduff's children, with only their mother to protect them under her wing! And the two fugitives beneath the tree, and then the terrifying sleepwalker roaming through the castle, and the marvelous fulfillment of the prophecy—Birnam Wood drawing near—Macbeth's death by the sword of one not of woman born—I would have to list each and every scene if I wanted to give a name to the setting that is so perfectly in keeping with the spirit of this unnameable whole, *this world of fate, regicide, and magic* that is the soul of the play and breathes life into it right down to the smallest detail of time, place, and even the apparently haphazard episodes in between; I would have to list each and every scene in order to imagine them all as a single dreadful, indivisible whole—and yet for all that I would have said nothing.

The *individual quality* of each drama, each separate universe, accompanies time and place and composition throughout the plays. Lessing compared several features of *Hamlet* with the theatrical queen Semiramis—how the spirit of the place pervades the entire drama from beginning to end! The castle platform and the biting cold, the watch relieved and stories swapped in the night, disbelief and credulity, the star in the sky, and now the ghost appears! Is there anyone who does not sense art and Nature in every word and detail? And so it continues. All ghostly and human guises are exhausted! The cock crows and the drum sounds, the silent beckoning and the nearby hill, words natural and supernatural—what a setting! How deeply truth is embedded in it! And how the terrified king kneels, and Hamlet strays past his father's picture in his mother's chamber! And now the other scene! Hamlet at Ophelia's grave! The pathetic good fellow in all his dealings with Horatio, Ophelia, Laertes, Fortinbras! Hamlet's youthful toying with action, which runs throughout the play and does not become full action almost until the end—if there is anyone who for one moment feels and looks for the boards of the stage and a series of versified and elegant speeches on it, neither Shakespeare nor Sophocles nor indeed any true poet in the world has written for him.

If only I had the words to describe the one main feeling that prevails in each drama and courses through it like a world soul. As it does in *Othello*, where it is truly an essential element of the drama, as it does in the nocturnal search for Desdemona, their fabulous love, the voyage, the tempest, as it does in Othello's volatile passion, in the much-mocked manner of her death, disrobing as she sings her song of willow and the wind knocking; as in the nature of the sin and passion itself—Othello's entrance, his address to the candle, and so on—if only it were possible to capture all this in words, how it is all a vital and profound part of a single world, a single tragic event. But it is not possible. Words cannot even describe or render the most wretched painted picture, so it is assuredly beyond their power to deliver the feeling of a single living world in all the scenes, circumstances, and enchantments of Nature. Examine whichever play you wish, dear reader, whether *Lear* or the *Richard*s, *Julius Caesar* or the *Henry*s, even the supernatural plays and the *divertissements*, especially *Romeo and Juliet*, that sweet drama of love, a romance even in every detail of time and place and dream and poetry—examine the drama you have chosen and try to subtract something from its nature, to exchange it, or even to simplify it for the French stage—a living world in all the authenticity of its truth transformed into this wooden skeleton—a fair exchange, a fine transformation that would be! Deprive this flower of its soil, its sap and vital force, and plant it in the air; deprive this person of place, time, individuality, and you have robbed him of breath and soul, leaving him nothing more than a *simulacrum of a living being*.

So Shakespeare is Sophocles' brother precisely where he seems so dissimilar, only to be inwardly wholly like *him*. Since all illusion is accomplished by means of this authenticity, truth, and creativity of history, then were they absent, not only would illusion be impossible but not a single element of Shakespeare's drama and dramatic spirit would remain (or else I have written in vain). Thus, we see that the whole world is merely the body belonging to this great spirit: all the scenes of Nature are the limbs of this body, just as every character and way of thinking is a feature of this spirit—and we might call the whole by the name of Spinoza's vast God: "Pan! Universum!" Sophocles remained true to Nature when he adapted a single action in a single time and place; Shakespeare could remain true to Nature only if he tossed his world events and human destinies through all the times and places in which—well, in which they occurred. And may God have mercy on the sportive Frenchman who arrives during Shakespeare's fifth act, thinking he will thereby be able to gulp down the quintessence of the play's feeling. That may be possible with some French dramas, because everything is versified and trotted out in scenes merely for theatrical effect; but with Shakespeare he would come away empty-handed. The world event would have already reached its conclusion; he would catch only its last and least consequence—that is, people dropping like flies—quit the playhouse, and sneer: Shakespeare is unto him a stumbling block and his drama the most half-witted foolishness.

The whole knot of questions concerning time and place would have been untangled long ago if a philosophical mind had taken the trouble to ask of the drama, "What do we do mean by *time* and *place* anyway?" If the place is the stage and time the duration of a *divertissement au théâtre*, then the only people in the world to insist on the unities of place and time are the French. The Greeks, with a degree of illusion almost beyond our conception, whose stage was a public institution and was rightly regarded with religious devotion, never gave the unities a single thought. What manner of illusion is it when a person looks at his watch after every scene to ascertain whether such an action could have taken place in such and such a time, and whose heart's delight it then is that the poet has not swindled him of a single moment but has shown just as much on the stage as the spectator would see unfolding in the same time in the snail's pace of his own life—what kind of creature would derive from this his highest pleasure? And what kind of poet would view this as his main object and then pride himself on this nonsense of rules, saying, "How many pretty trifles I have nicely crammed and fitted into the narrow space of this stage called *théâtre Français*, and all in the prescribed time of a social visit; how I have threaded and spun the scenes! How carefully I have patched and stitched it all together!" What a wretched master of ceremonies! A Savoyard of the theater, not a creator, poet, or god of the drama! For if you are a true artist, no clock strikes on tower or temple for you, because you create your own space and time; and if you are able to create a world that cannot but exist in the categories of space and time, behold, your measure of space and duration is there within you, and you must enchant all your spectators so that they believe in it, you must obtrude it on them— or else you are, as I have said, anything but a dramatic poet.

Is there anyone in the world who requires proof that space and time in themselves are nothing, that in their connection to existence, action, passion, train of thought, and degree of attention within and without the soul, they are entirely relative? Were there never occasions in your life, good timekeeper of the drama, when hours seemed like moments and days like hours? Or conversely, when hours stretched into days and the night watch into years? Have you never known situations in your life when your soul sometimes dwelled wholly outside you? Here, in your beloved's romantic chamber; there, staring at that stiff corpse; here, in the oppression of external and humiliating distress—and then your soul took wing and soared beyond world and time, overleaping the spaces and regions of the earth, oblivious to everything around it, to reside in heaven, or in the soul, the heart of the one whose existence you now feel? And if that is possible in your sluggish and somnolent, wormish and vegetable life, where there are roots enough to hold you fast to the dead ground, and every circuit that you creep is measure enough for your snail's pace, then imagine yourself for a moment transported to another, poetic world, to a dream. Have you never felt how in dreams space and time disappear? How insubstantial they must be, mere shadows compared with *action*, with the working of the soul? How it is up to the soul to create its own space, world, and time, however and wherever it wishes? And if you had felt that only once in your life, if you had awoken after a mere quarter of an hour and the obscure remnants of your actions in the dream led you to swear that you had slept, dreamed, and acted for nights at a time, then Mahomet's dream would not for one moment seem absurd to you. And is it not the first and only duty of every genius, of every poet, and of the dramatic poet in particular, to remove you to such a dream? And now think what worlds you would confound if you were to show the poet your pocket watch or your drawing room so that he might teach you to dream according to their dictates.

The poet's space and time lie in the unfolding of his event, in the *ordine successivorum et simultaneorum* of *his* world. How and where does he transport you? As long as he transports you, you are in his world. However quickly or slowly he makes time pass, it is he who makes it pass; it is he who impresses its sequence on you: that is his measure of time—and what a master Shakespeare is in this respect, too! The events in his world begin as slowly and ponderously as they do in Nature, for it is Nature that he represents, only on a reduced scale. How laborious is the preparation before the machinery is set in motion; but once it gets going, how the scenes hurry past, how fleeting the speeches, how winged the souls, the passion, the action, and how powerful then this swift movement, the scattered delivery of individual words when time has run out for everyone. Finally, when the reader is entirely caught up in the illusion he has created and is lost in the abyss of his world and his passion, how bold he becomes, what events he has succeed one another! Lear dies after Cordelia, and Kent after Lear! It is the end of his world, as it were, as if the Day of Judgment had come, when everything, the Heavens included, collides and crashes, and the mountains fall; the measure of time is no more. But not for the merry *Cacklogallinian*, of course, who would arrive unharmed for the fifth act to measure with his watch how many died and how long it took. But dear God, if that is supposed to be criticism, theater, illusion— what might constitute criticism? or illusion? or theater? What do all these empty words signify?

At this point the heart of my inquiry might begin: "How, by what art and manner of creation, was Shakespeare able to transform some worthless romance, tale, or fabulous history into such a living whole? What laws of *historical*, *philosophical*, or *dramatic art* are revealed in every step he takes, in every device he employs?" What an inquiry that would be! How it would profit our historiography, our philosophy of the human soul, our drama. But I am not a member of all our academies of history and philosophy and the fine arts, where of course they devote their thoughts to anything but such a question! Even Shakespeare's countrymen do not consider it. What historical errors his commentators have often rebuked him for; what historical beauties have been censured—for example, in that hefty edition by Warburton! And did the author of the most recent essay on Shakespeare hit on my pet idea and ask, "how did Shakespeare compose drama from romances and tales?" It scarcely occurred to him, no more than it did to the Aristotle of this British Sophocles, Lord Home.

So just a nod in the direction of the usual classification of his plays. Just recently a writer who certainly has a deep feeling for Shakespeare had the idea of making that honest fishmonger of a courtier, with his gray beard and wrinkled face, his eyes purging thick amber and his *plentiful lack of wit together with weak hams*, of making the childish Polonius the poet's Aristotle, and proposed that the series of "-als" and "-cals" that this blatherer spouts should be taken seriously as the basis of classification for all of Shakespeare's plays.[1] I have my doubts. Shakespeare was admittedly cunning enough to put into the mouths of his characters, especially children and fools, the empty *locos communes*, morals, and classifications, which, when applied to a hundred cases, are appropriate to all and to none; and a new Stobaeus and *Florilegium*, or cornucopia of Shakespeare's wisdom, such as the English already possess and we Germans— may God be praised—are supposed to have had recently, would bring the greatest cheer to a Polonius, Lancelot, the *clowns* and *jesters*, poor Richard or the puffed-up *king of knights*, because every character of sound mind in Shakespeare never speaks more than is necessary for the action. But even here I still have my doubts. Polonius is here meant to be the great baby who takes clouds for camels and camels for bass viols, who in his youth once played Julius Caesar, was accounted a good actor, was killed by Brutus, and knows very well "why day is day, night night and time is time"—that is, here too he is spinning a top of theatrical words. But who would wish to erect a theory on such foundations? And what do we gain from the classifications Tragedy, Comedy, History, Pastoral, Tragical-Historical, Historical-Pastoral, Pastoral-Comical, and Comical-Historical-Pastoral? And even were we to shuffle those "-cals" a hundred times, what would we be left with in the end? Not a single one of Shakespeare's play would be a Greek Tragedy, a Comedy, a Pastoral; nor should it be. Each

---

[1] *Briefe über Merkwürdigkeiten der Litteratur. Dritte Sammlung.*

play is History in the broadest sense, which is of course tinged to a greater or lesser degree with tragedy, comedy, and so on, but the colors are so infinitely varied that in the end each play remains and must remain *what it is: History! A history play bringing to life the fortunes of the nation during the Middle Ages!* Or (with the exception of a few interludes and plays proper) a complete *enactment of a world event, of a human destiny possessed of grandeur.*

Sadder and more important is the thought that even this great creator of history and the world soul grows older every day, that the words and customs and categories of the age wither and fall like autumnal leaves, that we are already so far removed from these great ruins of the age of chivalry that even Garrick, who has brought new life to Shakespeare and been the guardian angel of his grave, is obliged to amend, cut, and mutilate much of his work. And soon perhaps, as everything is obliterated and tends in different directions, even his drama will become quite incapable of living performance, will become the dilapidated remains of a colossus, of a pyramid, which all gaze upon with wonder and none understands. I count myself lucky that I still live in the last days of an age when I can understand him; and when you, my friend, who feel and recognize yourself when you read him, and whom I have embraced more than once before his sacred image, when you can still nurture the sweet dream worthy of your gifts, a dream that you will erect a monument to him in our degenerate land, *drawn from our own age of chivalry* and written in our language. I envy you that dream; may your noble German powers not let up until the wreath is hanging aloft. And should you later see how the ground quakes beneath your edifice, and around it the vulgar masses stand still and gape or scoff, and the everlasting pyramids cannot reawaken the spirit of ancient Egypt—your work will endure; and a faithful successor will seek out your grave and write with devoted hand the words that describe the lives of almost all the men of merit in the world: "Voluit! quiescit!"

The Causes of Sunken Taste among the Different Peoples in Whom It Once Blossomed

Multa renascentur, quae iam cecidire.

IT IS A SIGHT WONDROUS to behold that taste, the beautiful gift that heaven seems to have bestowed on the human spirit only when it puts forth its finest flowers, not only appears exclusively within a narrow region of the earth's surface but also holds sway there for only short periods. No sooner has it made itself at home in some fortunate locality than it gathers kindling for its own funeral pyre, until elsewhere another phoenix rises belatedly from its ashes, only to share the same fate as its father.

Whence come these waves on the great ocean of time? Do they arise from internal or external causes? Who teaches us the *great law of Nature governing the changes in taste* as it is revealed in history? And if we knew this law, would it seem to us that we might forestall the causes of the unfortunate decline in taste, that we might seize hold of good taste when it means to take flight? Or, when signs herald its imminent arrival, how can we encourage good taste? How can we ourselves use the seeds of its destruction to restore it to new life? Or, if all this is beyond our power, what effect *does this decline have*? Does it not bring about any other good? Not the happiness of mankind?

Truly this is a philosophical and humane question, one that even contributes to the blossoming of the external constitutions of men! And the path we shall choose to investigate it, the *book of history*, which yields such noteworthy and various cases for our consideration, is certainly the richest, most certain, and agreeable road. Here free truth is its own confirmation and charm.

I shall *first* examine the question on the basis of psychology, mostly *denying* the usefulness of this approach, and clear away the prejudices that would obstruct our passage through history. *Then* I wish to trace the *history of every great age* back to the *profound, universal causes* without which it cannot be put to use at a later date. The *consequences* and their resulting applications shall form the third part of our inquiry.

I

FUNDAMENTAL PRINCIPLES FOR THE CONSIDERATION OF THE QUESTION FROM THE POINT OF VIEW OF PSYCHOLOGY

One is apt to derive the corruptions of taste now from certain powers of *genius*, now from *reason*, now from moral or immoral *impulses*, and then to set whichever of these viewpoints one favors before all the events of history. It is therefore necessary in consideration of our question to begin by marking out the territory that these powers hold within the dominion of the human soul: To what extent must they, can they corrupt taste? Or perhaps they never will?

I. Regardless of how far the ideas of *taste* and *genius* might admit of yet finer analysis, it is widely known that *genius* is generally a *mass* of intensively and extensively striving faculties of the soul; *taste* is *order* in this mass, *proportion*, and therefore the beautiful *quality* of those striving powers. So in themselves taste and genius are never opposed: through Nature alone they can never corrupt each other. This thought merits closer scrutiny, for it is the basis on which all future historical phenomena rest.

α. Genius is an aggregation of natural forces; it therefore issues from Nature's hands and precedes the formation of taste. The Orient, the fatherland of human civilization, was the land of rude, robust, sublime genius long before Greece arrived and roused beauty from its slumber. In Greece itself many uncouth names, monstrous experiments, the rise and fall of exaggerated and waning powers, led the way before these same powers put themselves in order and produced taste. A child initially succumbs to the thousand-form, deep, immeasurable cosmos before the images leave his eyes, separate from one another, and become ideas; only through many improprieties in the crude application of his powers does the wrestler learn to fight and prevail with harmony.

So *with a people that is still rude we must speak not of the decline of taste but of the gradual cultivation of taste, of proportion.* Mayhap here and there a people has happily or apparently aped another and heaps the most extravagant praise on itself for the refinement of its taste. But no one cries out "I can do it! I can do it!" more than a child putting its powers to the test. And if he really could do it, then he would have no need to cry out in that way. In such cases we must be sure neither to disturb nor dishearten, but rather to guide and encourage. All precepts that are imposed on the child prematurely, before he has learned to view the rule as indispensable and hits upon it by himself, as it were, are detrimental and remain detrimental forever, as can be seen with the fixed and prescribed taste that held sway in Egypt and China. The Creator Himself allowed the ferment of chaos to run its course and developed the world toward harmony, order, and beauty only through the inner laws of Nature. A fly violently and unnaturally awoken from its hibernation revives only for a few minutes before dying forever.

β. So if taste can arise only through geniuses—that is, through natural powers that operate quickly and vivaciously—then taste must also *desire to persist* in them; otherwise it is nothing but a reverberation in the air, an echo. An abundance of trees, plants, and meadows makes a garden; and once the garden exists, then order, taste, and landscaping can develop. But without a garden we cultivate the air. We are wont to make a distinction between genius and taste, "as if genius had no need of taste, as if genius were its own compensation for taste, were greater than it, as if only the mind deficient in genius were obliged to console itself with taste, and so on." Dispensing with all such speculation, however, we must ask, If taste does not exist for geniuses in the widest sense, then for whom does it exist? The nobody, the dunderhead can neither use nor comprehend it; taste is only order in the application of powers of genius, and hence taste without genius is an absurdity. Conversely, the more powers a genius possesses, the quicker the powers operate, then the more necessary is the mentor of good taste, so that the powers do not overwhelm and destroy one another and, should they achieve supremacy within the soul, lay waste to other benign powers also.

So when in an age of voluptuousness and general corruption the powers of genius have already squandered themselves, how wretchedly fares the taste that mourns their demise! But if it is something more than mere taste, if it can help, instruct, turn things back *by its deeds*, then let it do so gladly, and its deeds shall have effect. Taste can be truly formed and re-formed only through examples; the precept must have assumed spirit and power, must have been put into practice and become virtue; then it will be recognized, felt, attempted, followed. But if taste is none of these things, then a mere voice cannot help. If a school is so degenerate that there is no power, desire, example, or emulation left either in teacher or pupils, then even the best rules cannot help. And if a body is dying, then even the best diet or exercise cannot help. *This is shown by every lone voice raised in the centuries of barbarism and corrupt taste.* If they were merely voices, they remained ineffectual. *But if these voices were joined with creative powers*, if they roused the genius and stirred others, *then a better age dawned.* The solitary swallow awoken by the first breath of spring prophesied more, and these did not fail to appear. *Taste in one art roused taste in every other art*; there was, so to speak, a harmonious atmosphere in which the similarly tuned strings of all the different instruments vibrated and resonated at a single touch.

Thus only geniuses can and must form and re-form geniuses toward the order, beauty, and proportion of their cognitive or sensuous or practical powers, for here, too, truth and beauty operate only through sympathy and imitation. The more homogeneous the strings, the more they resonate with one another, but rules can never tune a discordant string or produce a sound. As Plato says in his allegory of the magnets and the Corybantes, the poet's powers work most profoundly through direct inspiration and a kind of miracle. Geniuses, who are therefore formed and form others, are the images of the Divinity in their order, beauty, and invisible creative powers; they are the treasures of their age, stars in the night sky that by their very nature illumine the world around them, shining as much light as the darkness can absorb.

γ. And now *the extent to which geniuses alone ruin taste* is as clear as day, namely, *because taste does not exist without them, and geniuses can ruin taste only* if they misuse their powers. There are two ways in which this can happen, through *false ends* and through *false means*. If a vessel is already full and yet more water is poured in, then it flows over. If the mind that is full of power and has already attained its goal wishes to continue, then, in passing beyond the goal, it enters the land of unnaturalness and false taste *in ends*. If it then chooses a will-o'-the-wisp for its goal or desires to soar up to the sun with the wings of Icarus, it will lend its name to swamp and sea: it has chosen false ends and therefore succumbed on the way. Or a genius had a noble and true goal before him but *had no guide to take him there*. In the initial heat of ecstasy he took the wrong path, realized too late that he had gone astray, knew that he was a genius, had yet achieved some good on this wrong path, looked behind him, and did not possess the greatness necessary to give it all up and follow a different road. Rather, objects on his way glittered with charms; he thought himself capable, even on this wrong path, of reaching the destination that no other man had arrived at by such a route; he continued on his journey and with his noble powers became the archetype of false taste, a *seductive and negative greatness*. That is the sad *theory of corrupt taste in all ages, seen from the point of view of genius*.

δ. And at the same time that is, without any declamation, *the genuine eulogy to taste's influence on genius*; taste is namely the rudder steering the powers of genius on the desolate sea of chance. That every man can choose a path and strive on it with fervor is the work of Nature; that he chooses the right path and on it strives toward noble, attainable, useful ends is the work of trial and experience. Happy the man before whom, like Hercules, the goddess appeared to show him the way, to inspire him with courage, and to accompany him to his goal! Such a man will spare himself ten fruitless journeys, from which he would either return, regretful and exhausted from futile effort, or not come back at all. *When the fountainhead of good taste dries up, who shall refill it and enliven it once more?* Newcomers take the place of old, genuine, simple experience, and they attribute the voice of its instruction to envy and inability, which finds fault with them because it cannot surpass them. "He who lies there whimpering in his bed," they say, "is a sick old man, and we climb on craggy and precipitous cliffs!" So divine a spark is the genius that *even on the wrong path, in bad taste,* he can be lured elsewhere only by powers of genius and not by rules. Every seed of Creation is redeemed only by itself.

II. Like genius, *reason* is often *set against taste,* and some think they know well *how the former has contributed to the decline of the latter.* This is just as false and confused.

If taste is nothing more than the order and nimbleness of the powers productive of beauty, then no matter how swiftly taste operates and is felt, it can *operate only through reason, judgment, reflection,* which alone create order. Even the bee's cell (if genius may be compared with the instinct of animals, which are perhaps at bottom all the same) requires the most excellent apian understanding if it shall be brought to perfection. And the nobler a genius, the more worthy the sphere toward which he strives; and the more worthily he consummates his striving, the more he must show *accurate, comprehensive reason* in the most rapid firestorm of activity and sensation. The creator, who surveyed all and found it good, enjoyed, intellectually, the moment of utmost reason and, sensuously, the moment of the most rapturous taste.

When Greek *tragedy* raised itself from the cart of Thespis to Aeschylus and then to the taste of the great Sophocles, what impelled it onward? Genius coupled with reason, reflection combined with the perceptive faculties, *taste*—that is what *bestowed taste on Greek drama.* Its coarseness, solemnity, emptiness, and frigidity were discarded; its efficacy, its action were bent apart and rendered more complex: unity and diversity, *taste, beauty!* If Euripides later turned his back on this established goal of reflecting the oneness, the action—even if he did so with the finest Socratic speeches—then Aristotle shows that the theater did not profit thereby. What created the *art* of the Greeks? *Reflection abounding in genius and deeds.* The ancient Egyptian style was hard, dry, and destitute of posture and action; the Greeks thought, felt, endowed the marble with a beautiful rotundity, melodiousness, action, and thus the taste of Greek art developed. Thus Homer emerged from the many legends, dross, and poets of the Trojan War before him; thus rhetoric developed amid the conflict and ratiocination of civic affairs; thus the other forms of poetry arose out of Homer. Reflection, the assessor of heavenly counsel, guided the Greeks at every step; that is why they climbed to such heights even though they followed a simple path. Conversely, the more they deviated from reason, the more art, science, indeed everything, declined. Understanding is the soul, genius the body, and the manifestation of each in the other is called good taste. So how should they be opposed?

So when *reason is supposed to have promoted false taste*, then one really means *unreason, subtilizing, sophistry*. For otherwise it would mean either that one weaned oneself *from sensuous objects* for the sake of pure reason—and our true reason never does that, for we are not given to float above the stars—or that one has *misapplied one's reason* to sensuous objects, deliberated where one should have felt, separated the distinguishing marks of an object where one should have connected them, laid down rules where one should have acted. And once again that could not be reason, for its first business is to know where it belongs and then to keep its distance, or stay away entirely, from where it does not. On no account could false taste arise through reason.

This is so true that even *productions of false taste* subsequently could not help but *cultivate new reason* and *thereby bring about their own destruction*. Though in the initial ecstasy reason always seemed bewitched and beguiled, as soon as taste, having grown weary in the gardens of illusion, glimpsed itself in the mirror of truth, it took heart and now looked upon the infelicities as maxims of prudence. So sacred and pure is this noble ray of light that like the sun it may be veiled and obscured by clouds, yet its nature cannot be altered and transformed into darkness. It shines and projects its image wherever it works.

It was precisely *through taste* that *the Greeks gained in reason, and it was through their light and easy reason that they gained in taste*. What a *world of occasions* taste delivers to reason for it to practice on! And here everything hovers before us *sensuously*, both means and ends. The judgment arising from such phenomena strikes swiftly, like lightning, and continues to operate just as quickly. In productions of this kind one works with fire and judges and feels with passion: even this judgment and this feeling were a contest among the Greeks. Where everything is still genius, raw power, and tempestuous action, there philosophy is not at home; where a people first awakens and composes itself after the powerful dream, there taste is born and with its swift, correct judgment becomes the forerunner of reflection about even the most unsensuous concepts.

But here too one must be sure not to confer any false privileges on reason, whereby one would ruin everything. Without sense organs and drives, reason is but an idle spectator, and *if these are opposed to it, then discord ensues and taste will never reach maturity. The influence of reason is obscured, deceived, outweighed*; it calls out in vain. One must therefore seek the causes of the corruption of taste elsewhere.

III. These causes have been sought in the *moral powers*, and it is claimed that now devoutness must entail good taste, now corrupt taste brings with it godlessness. With what justification?

1. *Taste and virtue are not identical.* Taste is only the order and harmony of *certain sensuous powers harnessed toward or inhering in a work of art*; virtue is supposed to be the order and harmony of *all our powers harnessed toward the great work of life*—that is a considerable difference! The work of art can be *limited* as follows: (a) The faculties of the soul can be *confined* to it just as the bee's instinct is to the cell; *the majority of the higher and active powers therefore remain disordered and lifeless.* (b) *The work of art can draw people to it in such a way* that precisely this passion *discomposes* the other powers and inclinations, and thus the rage of taste becomes just like any other rage: a trap. (c) Finally, certain works can indeed demand a *passion* of the kind that is *artistically* but not *morally good.* They want a tempest but not the clear light of day. Brutus was no Cicero, and Socrates no Pericles, no Demosthenes. The states in which the finest taste flourished were not the most virtuous, and for all its taste Athens was no match even for Sparta when it came to civic virtue.

True, the poet, the painter, the sculptor, or the musician can use his artistic taste as the *occasion*, the *form*, the *memory*, and the *model* to cultivate his entire soul, his whole life to taste, and that would indeed be virtue. He can do so, but does he want to? Would he want to carry it even to the point of action, knack, and daily habit? That is a quite different question! From an infinitesimally small particle an immeasurable mountain shall spring up—through nothing! All at once!

2. It is undeniable that *where manners are most profoundly corrupt, taste must also be corrupt*, and that is perfectly natural. Taste is only a *phenomenon of reason, of genius, of the sensuous powers and desires.* If the worm now gnaws at these from within, then their external appearance will also be shameful and ugly, and that means *bad taste* in the widest sense. Where there is extravagance, weakness, bondage, and lustfulness, not one faculty of the soul will still have noble ends or noble means. Men place abominable gods on the altar and make abominable offerings to them. The order of the powers is destroyed, and the powers themselves diminish because they are not used, or they are used only discordantly and unworthily. Taste should be the image and garb of virtue; where no trace of virtue remains, its image and garb must vanish also.

This much is therefore certain: *taste assists in maintaining good manners*, though not as good manners but as *beautiful propriety*, as orderliness. And good manners in a certain degree promote taste, insofar as they furnish it with the *materials, examples, and mainsprings with which it works*. Should the beautiful raiment fall away completely, then everything is lost. Taste was the organ of common agreement about concepts of orderliness, and hence at least a seeming mask.

So none of these concepts brings us very far. We must answer the question of how *taste*, the phenomenon of powers of genius, of the understanding, and of moral impulses, strayed from its course not by speculating according to such and such a hypothesis but rather by examining it carefully *from the point of view of history*. In every age this phenomenon must be examined *on its own terms* as if there had existed *no other taste save this one*. And how can we proceed more certainly and deeply than by simply asking of every period, *What are the origins of good taste here? Why did it last for so long?* Then we shall see at once that the very causes of taste led it to forfeit *its good nature*, that other *circumstances* now arose, which destroyed the beautiful phenomenon. On this path it also becomes evident why taste has been *so rare* throughout history, why it has never returned to a place *in the same form* it had previously assumed, and so forth. Finally, this way of viewing the matter gives rise to *the richest and deepest* applications; so let us try it!

II

THE CAUSES OF SUNKEN TASTE AMONG THE DIFFERENT PEOPLES IN WHOM IT ONCE BLOSSOMED

I. If we get to the bottom of *the causes* that gave rise to *Greek* taste and brought it to such florescence, then we are on the way to understanding the *history of declining taste*. Like all things sublunary, these conditions did not last *forever*: different and *deleterious circumstances* soon supervened, and taste sank into corruption, even among the people in whom it was *most natural*.

1. Homer emerged in fair Ionia at a time when he could witness the first steps being taken toward a *more refined civilization* and hear stories of the *robust manners of a former age* passed down in still-vital oral traditions. In those days the heroic myths lived on in the mouths of the Greeks, and at a time when writing and prose had yet to be invented, they naturally assumed poetic form. The heroic exploits of the Greeks at the gates of Troy were an object of national concern, like the voyage of the Argonauts, only brighter, sharper, closer in time; in those great images of their kings before Troy lay the germs of the independent, heroic, and free city-states: ten poets had already sung of the campaign.

Homer, too, sang of it just as naturally, in a manner that his age found most agreeable and mild. In those days the Greek language was blossoming in the air of the Orient; mythology was growing more beautiful and rounded; the passions and the souls of men were open; Homer sang as he saw and heard them, and his songs endured in the ears and on the lips of the Greeks. Finally, Lycurgus collected them, just as the age of Greek civic culture was dawning, and so they became the codex of morals, laws, and aesthetics in the cities: Homer became the father of Greek taste *in the most natural way*. A series of *favorable conditions* formed him and formed Greece for him.

2. *Greek drama* arose just as naturally in the full bloom of its taste. The theater, in which Aeschylus, Sophocles, and Euripides worked wonders, grew out of heroic myths, games, music, entertainments, religious rites (all experienced, combined, and adapted after the Greek fashion). All the elements of tragedy that Aristotle enumerates—*plot, character, thought, song making, language, spectacle*—were contained in the seeds of its origin and were no school secret. The essence of the poem—*action, imitation*—was the touchstone, and anything not fitted to that end was deemed a fault. Every noble man of Greek culture was a judge, as we can see from the dramatic contests, and in its content and influence, too, the stage was a *vital concern of a public* such as Athens was. Aristotle's entire rule book is taken from the *mouth of the people*, just as in northern courts elected arbitrators of the community passed judgment according to the nature of the case. The Greek drama was a *natural flower of the time*, *of the causes* of the *taste* then prevailing, just as were the fables and rhapsodies of the *aoidoi* centuries before. Sophocles emerged in the same way as Homer, and Pindar like them both.

3. Greek *rhetoric* was no different. In the republics it was a *civic institution* and *mainspring*; public spirit, open consultation, commerce, and freedom were its element. There were *men born* to oratory, just as there were men born to liberty and commerce; philosophy, education, and training were directed toward it, to the *life of the republic*, and to the activity of the citizen. The Greek language had attained its *most beautiful, vital form*; all external institutions endeavored to rouse, cultivate, enliven. And so came forward Pericles, Alcibiades, and Demosthenes before the flame was extinguished. The *natural spirit of the Greek republic* and *Greek instruction* pervaded their discourses.

4. Finally, *art*, which was subject to the *widest range of determinants*, followed the very same path. The *culture* of the Greeks, their *feeling* for *fine form*, *easy action*, *mirth and joy*, *mythology*, *religion*, their *love of freedom*, which rewarded their brave men and noble youths—these and so many other causes that Winckelmann has elaborated so

excellently shaped and developed their art into a flower of beauty. Greek art, like all the previous productions of taste, was *living, ennobled Greek nature*.

What follows from all this? A very simple premise, one that we are always only too glad to think artificial and complex: namely, *among the Greeks in their heyday good taste was as much a product of Nature as they themselves were, as was their culture, their climate, their way of life, and their constitution.* It existed, like everything else, *in its particular time and place, without constraint, born of the simplest causes, with contemporary means serving contemporary ends.* And when this beautiful conjunction of time and place was dissolved, its result also perished: Greek taste.

a. If among the *Greeks* someone had fancied himself Homer under circumstances in which no Homer could possibly exist, then it is certain that he could have become only a false Homer. Here Apollonios, who lived in the age of the Ptolemies, shall be my witness. He set sail in the ship of the Argonauts, but how did he arrive there? Had he been there himself? Could anyone climb aboard after him? Did anyone wish to? For this task his age gave him *neither manners nor language, neither content nor ear, nor purpose, nor feeling*; hence he became a frigid imitator; *he sang outside his element*. If in an earlier age the Greeks had aspired to be what they were not, if they had sung what they were not fitted to sing, then good taste would never have flourished among them for so long. However, their tutelary god kept them from striking out along this path of vain, impotent envy. The Greeks sang whereof they were masters: poetry moved with the times; they followed Homer by departing from him.

b. As soon as the time had passed when the *mainsprings of good dramatic taste* worked in harmony, then taste declined. The *subjects for the stage* drawn from Greek myth, which they called the Epic cycle, had been *exhausted*; inferior themes were chosen, or the old ones treated in a novel—which is to say, inferior—fashion. The *original and felicitous spectacle was created* by masters of drama; the models stood there and put their successors in the shade. These imitated instead of adapting the material freely, and a soul torn between freedom and servility never works concertedly and nobly. As taste dwells only in the undivided genius who operates without constraint, so naturally the Greeks strayed ever farther from taste the more they aspired to it through frigid rules and prejudices. The *circumstances of the people* altered. What before was a public concern became a pastime pursued without moderation. Dramatic contests were staged for days on end, with the result that through the sheer quantity of food, the palate became jaded and lost its relish, and the insatiable hunger bred disease. As *the people's spirit of enterprise and freedom* disappeared, the stage lost *its element*; good taste lived on in remnants from the olden days but was unable to bring forth any new productions—the seeds of which we see already in Aristotle's *Poetics*.

c. It was the same with *rhetoric*. Its fire was extinguished as *Greek freedom* declined; in Demosthenes eloquence was a flame blazing forth in the final hour of need. It crept into schools and narrow courtrooms, curled up in the dust, and fell silent. Already Longinus described this in plain and stark terms.

d. *Art*—which was subject to a greater range of determinants and whose domain, moreover, was not wide but very sensuous, vivid, and almost mechanical—*was able to sustain itself longer* and even did so in the forecourt of monarchy—just as long as it either was not a slave or served under a benevolent yoke. Good taste in art was fixed, as it were, and since everything in art *rests* on *practice* and *imitation*, these could not harm but rather preserved it. Many *applications of art*—such as the veneration of gods and the fashioning of idealized statues—*survived*, and the *standing of artists increased* at the courts of connoisseurs, just as victories and riches furnished painting and sculpture with more materials. *Art*, then, along with *comedy*, endured *beyond the age of Greek liberty and activity*; but as we can clearly see, they grew *from the seeds of former ages*. If these seeds had not been planted and nurtured long before, they would not have taken shape. Art, too, had its best days behind it, the days when, more than at any time since, it was the *flower of the nation and living Greek nature*, in the age of good taste, of fame, of activity and liberty, between the Persian and Peloponnesian Wars. Later it flared up in fits and starts, lit by the sparks of earlier ages. That was the fate of *Greek taste right down to its smallest productions*.

Thus, as much as the age of Alexander seemed to those who lived then to be a time of prosperity, it deeply undermined the *original sources of Greek taste*. When the *freedom of the Greeks*, their *public spirit*, and their *easy manner* of acting with joy and mirth were gone, what could bloom then? *Poetry*, when there remained none of the morals and passions of the unbound Muse? Or the *rhetoric* of the brave, enterprising heart, when there was no longer any scope for independent action, no liberty? Even *history* was clapped in chains, and Alexander found no Xenophon or Thucydides, precisely because both could exist only in the absence of an Alexander. *Art* flourished here and there, now and then in royal courts, but these were hothouses and no longer Nature's garden. *Comedy* grew more refined with Menander, precisely because there was nothing left for it to do, and so it could content itself with providing elegant amusement. At the court of Ptolemy there was a Pleiad of poets, but they were a Pleiad in their greatness, too. Only Theocritus, who strayed back into the shepherd's life, which always retains remnants of ancient innocence and truth, found his true sphere; other poets clearly lacked *content*, the inspiration of the *Muse, and an open, vital space in which to work*. Poetry waited in service in the antechamber, carving goblets and flowers in an attempt to find favor, or sought to compensate its deficiencies with artifice, compulsion, flattery, and learning; that is, it spoiled everything. Even the *Greek language* became corrupt when it migrated to other lands, to Asia and Egypt, where so much enthusiasm and sweet poison sprouted forth. Greeks were scattered as far afield as deepest Persia and India. The intellectual, overwrought ideas of Persian philosophy and the new Hellenism were thus in ferment from the Caucasus to Libya; Greek taste lost its intuitiveness, its beautiful sensuality, and its purity; indeed, it would have become a monster if something else had not soon displaced it. However, the *natural character of the Greeks* was not destined to be reduced to the monstrous; even *in its decline* it retained *traces of its former beauty*. Even today the Greeks are *born men of taste*; their ease, their refined organization, their joy, and their mirth guard them against unnaturalness, the bane of good taste. From all accounts it is clear that only the *genius of a beautiful age*, an age perhaps unique in the history of the world, has abandoned them and will never return, certainly not with the *happy concourse of circumstances* then prevailing. Greek taste was the *beautiful national flowering of their free activity, their genius drunk with beauty, their bright, keen understanding*. When this beautiful flower lacked *soil, sap, nourishment, and ether*, and *ill winds began to blow*, it died.

II. The Romans followed hard on the heels of the Greeks, *but for them taste was never what it was for the Greeks*; that is, a *national affair* and the *basis of culture*. It is known how long they managed, indeed even became great and powerful, without taste, so that the old, true Romans resisted its introduction as a foreign and poisonous plant, whereas the Greeks had cultivated themselves as if to the strains of Amphion and Homer. *So even those productions of taste* which were the foundation of the entire culture of the Greeks, *art* and *poetry, never became effective mainsprings* for the *Romans*. Poetry sprang up only belatedly; that is, it was planted from a Greek seed in an emperor's garden, where it blossomed into a beautiful but idle flower. The *theater* (according to Aristotle the *focal point of effective poetry!*) *never had much of an influence among the Romans*, no more than did *art*; and the best poets were versifiers, that is, philosophers or orators or even flatterers in verse. *After Roman poetry's finest period had passed, false taste was able to take root* in the blink of an eye, which could never have happened if poetry, art, and good taste had been a *medium for the nation's way of thinking*. But that the spirit of

Horace and Virgil was not at all the taste of the public is clearly shown by the former's epistle on the art of poetry; despite all the flattery of the poets, Augustus could not for a single moment transform his golden Rome into an Athens of taste and fine feeling.

Rhetoric and *history were the national products of the Roman spirit* through which their taste was formed and through which it imitated the Greeks so excellently and vigorously. The oldest names of the practitioners of their language belong to *historians*; even Ennius worked in this direction, and the old *tragedians* brought more history than poetry to the stage. Cato soon appeared and gave a strong impetus to civic rhetoric and history, until Livy, Cicero, Sallust, and Caesar perfected the taste that might be called Roman spirit. Poetry blossomed only afterward, in the state's first hours of leisure, and certainly contributed much to the development of the language and philosophy of the Romans, but it did so only as an exotic growth and thus did not really shoot forth from, or enrich, the depths of Roman soil. *Roman taste* lay in *history, earnest legal eloquence, deeds*, just as with the Greeks it had been carefree activity, a beautiful sensuality and harmony in everything they did.

Thus, as long as there were conditions in Rome to rouse the genuine spirit of enterprise, eloquence, and history, the firm Roman taste developed. The first *orators* were simple, respectful elders, high priests, generals, censors; their eloquence issued from the heart; their words were deeds and courage. The first *historians* of Rome were chroniclers full of feeling for their city, state, and family, full of unadorned achievements and naked truth. The majesty of their forefathers and the memory of their ancestors enlivened everything they wrote. It was out of this spirit that Rome grew. It was in this spirit that the Gracchi could rage, Cato thunder, Anthony carry his listeners away, until finally Cicero decked himself out with all the euphony of the Greeks. *Oratory* was the rudder that steered their ship with its many achievements and oars, and *history* the chart full of wisdom by which they plotted their course. The Scipios, Catos, Sylla, Crassus, Lucullus, Brutus, Anthony, Pompey, and Caesar were all *orators, historians*, or *friends of the same*: such was the *spirit of old Rome*.

When this spirit receded and republican Rome sank beneath the yoke of monarchy, then for all the high praise lavished on the flowers and laurels that adorned this yoke, there was *just as little* an elegant Augustus and a trifling Maecenas could do with all their patronage *to replace that from which the Roman spirit had sprung*. This is immediately evident after the death of Augustus. One suspicious, envious fox, one monster after another were now beautiful Augustuses, and history has recorded with blood and tears what became of the *true taste, the offspring of the Roman spirit*. Taste was regarded as a rebel and traitor; one tyrant put to death those who answered him in Aeolian dialect, another wished to banish Homer, a third wanted to naturalize new words and letters of the alphabet, a fourth imposed his rhymes and a wretched history written by his own hand as a model to be imitated: this is what prevailed *in place of the Roman spirit and Roman taste.* Everything sank into a slavish fear of the tyrants and their favorites; true *history* held its tongue and was obliged to do so, for where a superior genius shone forth and did not, like Persius, wrap himself in unintelligible obscurity, he was forced to pay for his superior taste and truth with his life. O you assassins of human liberty, you oppressors of the laws of the land and the rights of your fellow citizens: what atrocities against posterity you are guilty of! If but a single Augustus ever thinks to govern with calm, taste, and clemency, if he then makes way for the Tiberiuses, Caligulas, Claudiuses, and Neros of his dynasty—then what a catalog of misdeeds and irreparable crimes rests on his shoulders!

Where was the old *Roman education* now? The venerable *images of their ancestors*? The *freedom* to punish even the censor and the dictator? *The life spent in commerce, the cultivation of the individual for the republic, the honor and self-worth a man derived from the prosperity of the nation,* his right to talk, deliberate, persuade, and act in its name—where was all this now? Sunk in voluptuousness, disgrace, fear, and misery! Eloquence was left to dusty pedants, education to slaves, history to sycophants, the welfare of all to the whims of the tyrant and the fury of his favorites—here let the excellent discourse *on the decline of Roman eloquence* speak in my stead as both judge and witness.

One should not think that *the age had no sense of its own sickness,* which is the accusation often made against it. The aforementioned discourse *on the decline of eloquence, Quintilian, and a few others expose the sources of the degeneracy with bitter feeling.* Who has written more lines and more powerfully on the bad taste then taking root than Petronius? Pliny himself admits frankly that the most unaffected passages in his panegyric, those which cost him the least effort, also had the greatest effect. Even in Seneca there are many references to declining taste, and for Persius, Martial, Juvenal, it was the very object of their biting censure—through which they themselves were corrupted. But how different it is to *observe* and to *eliminate* an evil, to feel the plague and to deliver an entire country from it.

Still less should one think that the *men of taste* (as the term is understood in a chattering age) wanted for food and drink, a roof over their heads, and a place to sleep. After all, Tiberius maintained his academy of grammarians, of whom one morning he demanded that they include in their writings some barbarism he had uttered, and therefore inspired great confidence. Claudius wrote books, among them even a defense of Cicero, and was therefore assuredly a gentleman of taste. He spoke in verse, invented new letters of the alphabet, expanded the museum at Alexandria, and was therefore a great patron of the sciences. Nero robbed Greece of all the beauties he could carry away; he was therefore a great lover of Beauty and enriched Rome with the finest monuments of art. The thrifty Vespasian gave stipends to the Greek and Latin rhetors. Domitian honored Quintilian by even entrusting to him the education of his princes. Trajan wrote to Pliny as a friend to a friend and had statues raised to young men of promise after their deaths. The much-traveled Hadrian was connoisseur, poet, scholar, and artist; at his court there were Atellan games, comedies, rhetors, poets, geometers, philosophers, whose epitaphs he wrote himself, and so on.——Far be it from us to disparage the mote of gold dust scattered from the throne on the poet's harp and the savant's writings, but the gold dust is not everything; rather, it can muffle the sound of the harp and drain color, life, and power from the writing. *Nothing in the world can become what it should become without occasions, impulses, truth, and crying need*, least of all the noblest gifts of God, *taste and genius*. If you remove this tree from its native climate and soil and its open, vaulting, and wild skies and plant it in the confined atmosphere of the hothouse, it will die, even if it seems only sickly. If you vainly feed this precious, foreign cattle outside its element, in public buildings, then, despite the food and water, it will perish; or it will grow fat and degenerate. It does not bear young at all, or does so only with extreme difficulty and rots away in a long, living death. That is how it was with Roman taste, for it too had to be fed.

It is a sad observation but no less true that *as soon as taste has lost its vital element it cannot be restored by individual rules and good intentions*; Quintilian preached in vain, and Pliny and Tacitus, even in the brief, better interlude during which they were active, were still far removed from the old power and simplicity of Roman taste. The reasons for this can be seen in their works. True Roman eloquence can no more manifest itself in a panegyric addressed so narrowly, even if it is dedicated to a Trajan, than the true epistolary spirit, as it were the *spiritus familiaris* of our lives, can do so in *letters* written and collected for public consumption. The profound, overornate brevity of Tacitus is obviously merely a cover for his own deficiencies and those of his age. If history had still been as open, communal, and republican an affair as it was in the time of Sallust and Livy, then Tacitus would not have written so refinedly. In a republic where each man participated in the whole and such subterfuges were unknown, he would have drawn opprobrium and ridicule on his novel with its great malice and state secrets; but then again, in a republic he would never have written it. But now, since he wrote of distant times of tyranny, cunning, and scandal, his *history unknowingly took on the features of his own age*; he flees open simplicity and is fond of the whispering of Harpocrates, who presses his finger to his lips; that is, he loves the utmost ambiguous, mysterious, and complex character. About black, suspicious times he writes suspiciously, blackly, and with philosophical spleen. Good Quintilian wrote his *Institutio* for his own son from the bottom of his heart; but he could not set sail without wind; he was a spouter and cause-monger rather than a Roman and an orator. Seneca wished to overcome his age and overcame it with subtle discernment and sweet faults. His sage was a man who willingly adopted poverty yet dwelled in palaces; his morality soared high in the skies, for down on earth it had little effect. Thus it was with those works still closely bound up with the spirit of the age; the others that followed as ornaments were even more apt to go astray. Just as Seneca the tragedian falls victim to flatulent verbosity because he is unable to achieve onstage what Sophocles had done in Athens, so Lucian's Muse has dropsy, for this was no heroic age. Juvenal's satyr became a robust faun, armed with bloody scourge, because the small, light satyr of Horace was no longer good for anything. Persius's satyr was full of genius, what Tacitus's history might have been, and Silius worshiped Virgil's statue, though without his demon. Finally, Martial picked flowers at the foot of Parnassus, albeit from mires and bogs—the best and easiest he could do for his witty, wanton age. The summit, where the storms rage, would have been too far and too dangerous. About all this there is little to be said except to utter a curse on the tyrants, who, when they shackle *the powers of human endeavor, shackle also every noble flight of the human spirit.*

And that is how the times dragged themselves down until the barbarians advanced and already *languages, manners,* and *mentalities* were gradually *mingling together.* Everywhere within the great Roman Empire there were outlandish warrior tribes; the provinces surged into wanton Rome as citizens but without civic spirit, into exhausted, abandoned Italy; there was a *confusion of tongues.* The emperors were enamored of *barbarian dress* and *barbarian taste;* weary of Greek simplicity, Roman luxury had long loved *Egyptian monstrosity;* and under the thirty tyrants *Asiatic* taste poured into Rome also. Thus arose a cup of trembling in manners, mentalities, as well as peoples. Under Commodus, the Greeks no longer understood Homer, and the Latin tongue inclined toward *rustica Romana;* finally, everything went under in the great barbarian flood. From the times of Hadrian and the Antonine the *Christian religion unwittingly did much to assist* in this devastation. Since the models of taste were associated with the system of idolatry, the Christians, when they fought against the latter, had to appear to wreck or retreat from the former. They destroyed and altered heathen temples as well as beautiful buildings, heathen images as well as beautiful statues, and it seemed to them that the poison of idolatry flowed in the honeyed words of poetry. Their religion would purify the world and raise it to a higher, supersensible system, and so for the time being much of the beautiful sensuality of the ancients was destroyed, until finally the barbarian form embraced everything.

The *decline of Roman taste* has therefore a *simple history*. Roman taste originated in Greece and sojourned in Rome for as long as similar soil, for as long as the climate and good husbandry, permitted. In the course of time it assumed a harder, firmer Roman appearance. Soon storm winds ripped this plant, like everything else, from the earth. For a while, under fortuitously favorable circumstances, it clung to the sod and in particular to *the remnants of the truly great form of Rome* and *its excellent language*; yet it did so with even less power and efficacy. Roman taste was but *a brief flowering*, when *Rome first became aware of its spirit of enterprise with a confident serenity and majesty; partisanship, extravagance, and servility soon eradicated the beautiful, less essential blossom.* Woe betide us, then, if the wish of our grammarians should be granted, who know no *models of the history of taste* save those ages of Rome that are usually figured: the Golden, Silver, Bronze, and so on. They must pass over in silence that which is completely fortuitous, which can never recur, and therewith prophesy our rapid descent into ruin, pestilence, and death, which would matter not a jot to them if only we all spoke Latin.

III. *In modern Europe* we are apt to credit Leo X and the Medici with the restoration of good taste, and nothing could be more true, if only we make sure to distinguish between *genius* and *taste*. The *geniuses who formed the Italian language in poetry and prose* had not waited for the Medici but rather had done their appointed work in a less happy age; and even in Leo's time it was not Ariosto but rather the buffoons and Latin imitators who were rewarded. Since, as is well known, the restorers of the arts and sciences, Lorenzo di Medici, Politian, Bembo, Casa, even the great Michelangelo, da Vinci, and so on, were *Petrarchists* to a man and mingled among the mediocre cinquecentists, we see that the *restoration of good taste had long been secretly at work*. Petrarch, Dante, Boccaccio, Cimabue, and Giotto had been active long before, and *in every benighted age beauty and art have never disappeared so completely from the face of the earth* as people often fancy; but the *mixture of barbarian ideas was spread too deeply and widely*. The current flowed behind a bulwark so deep beneath the earth that only after many futile minor eruptions could it break forth as one, when fate willed it so. And *at the very moment when Greece returned to Italy, the Medici rose to prominence* and reaped what had been sown in the dark centuries.

Do we know, then, what the *taste of the age* was? *What formed it? And transformed it? What it aspired to?* If we do, then we know also the *causes of its decline.* For these were already contained in the *imperfect genesis* itself.

The ancients were rediscovered, and, *following their example*, the Italian language was purified and *smoothed over, their delivery and their art imitated*—what a beautiful, enviable period! Only the refined, discerning, and profound genius of the Italians, still tranquil beneath so much passion, could imitate its forebears and their teachers in this way. But if all these efforts were mere *imitation*, how long could they last? *Until the ancients had been imitated* and *one neither could nor wished to imitate any longer.* Once the tool had been burnished, it was hung up or broken into pieces or allowed to rust over, so that one could polish it all over again—that, it seems to me, is the *history of Italian taste.*

Among the Greeks, taste had been *nature, need*, an *affair* to which *at certain times* and *under certain circumstances everyone* was *invited; it was just the same among the Romans*, though for a shorter time and in a more limited and imperfect manner. This was now even more true of Italy than it was of Rome. *To imitate the ancients simply because they could be imitated* and *because it might be a fine thing to do* is too frigid and timorous a purpose. *To seek reward by a refined and generous connoisseur of art* is a yet more frigid one. *To vie with the ancients*, indeed *to surpass them in their works*, would be a more worthy end, but it was sought by the merest few, indeed could not be sought because the *same vital impulses* did not exist, and anyway modern art was destined to be only another feather in the cap of the ancients. What purpose did, say, the imitated statues of Greek gods and heroes now serve? To represent allegories, virtues, popes, biblical personages? Was this in the least comparable with *Greek art*? The artist, then, was not inspired; the *course of art* was not impelled onward by *living history* and the *noble needs of the people*; nor was it *determined* and *curbed* by them; and behold: therein lay the *decline of art*. If art was merely a matter of *imitation*, then one could equally choose *not* to imitate, or at least to do so only *to a degree*; that is, one could take wing wherever one wished. Neither religion nor history, nor the state, nor the vital taste of the people gave art a *narrow, powerful impetus and kept it within bounds*; art therefore really did float in the air or was only carried on a breath of wind; that is, the goodwill of the artist and his patrons.

Even those *arts* which found a *deeper vocation*, painting and architecture, bear out what I am saying. It is true that they found more *subject matter, need*, and *application* in the state and in religion than did sculpture; but still they could not match the *assured nature* of the Greeks. After all, they were based merely on imitation, not *original, urgent need*. Thus for as long as the prevailing models still had seasoning enough to rouse men to passion and emulation, they were imitated and the first daring attempts felicitous. When the *imitations grew too numerous* and even the successful imitations were disheartening, it was less of an incentive to see oneself exhibited after a hundred other imitators, perhaps as the hundredth-and-first merely *passable imitator*, so artists sought to set themselves apart by their *audacity*. Art had no *new, vital ends to spur it on to good and better things*, and the very qualities that had helped the first painters—*daring*, the *luster of novelty*—now deterred artists or led them astray. Even the striking contours of the beautiful were no longer noticed because they were all too familiar; the sated hen ignored the seed and pecked after colors. What *ruined good taste* was nothing other than the *absence of the need for good taste*.

The *beautiful Latin and Greek languages* were great instruments:,but what are instruments when they become ends in themselves? When Bembo wrote his history of Venice in the Roman language but did not conceive and execute it in the Roman manner; when the cardinal shied away from reading his church's Vulgate in order not to spoil his style and had his Heavenly Father write like a Roman grammarian, into whose form, however, he was unable to pour the content, then one sees the *sport*, the *disproportion between end and means*, the *fanciful compulsion*. And all sport, all *compulsion* and *fancifulness* must come to an end and melt away. Beyond such beautiful though *thoughtless and unmannered imitation of the ancients* nothing was now possible save *dead learning, literalism, acrostics*, and *anagrams*. And that is indeed what came next. The seventeenth century followed the sixteenth, and still Italy was in large part in thrall to this confusion. The seeds of good taste were scattered among the Italians, but they could not take root.

The *decline of poetry* followed the same path. Since poetry was wholly *ideal* and *had as little connection as possible to contemporary needs and ends*, its next step was always going to carry it off to the land of fantasy and exaggeration. That is why the century of the finest Greek taste, which yet pointed everywhere to Nature, correctness, and truth, could also, alongside all the originals and imitations, be teeming with wretched Petrarchists, and those Petrarchists themselves be the imitators of the ancients—clear proof of how *shallow was their taste to cultivate their nature in everything they did*. Ariosto arrived and built an enchanted castle with a hundred gates in the air, for he was unable to build a national temple on firm ground; and what lay above the earth could be only caricature and fiction. Tasso imitated frigidly in the land of fantasy; Marino exaggerated—nothing else could come into being. An English critic is of the opinion that nothing corrupts taste more readily than Italian poets, especially their erotic and bucolic poets; and I am not entirely sure that he is wrong. The most effective and natural genre of poetry, tragedy, has therefore never flourished among them; with music, art, and even—after a fashion—comedy they float in the air, *in an ideal* that never allows them to set foot on terra firma. The reason they can go no further is this: *they have come as far as they can*, and *nothing compels them to become anything else*.

As sad as that may seem from one point of view, seen from the other it is an *excellent instrument of destiny*. Precisely because the Italians only *found*, *reworked*, and *copied* the ancients, and in a way that no one else could, they idealized and imitated, not narrowly and deeply for themselves alone, but *for all of Europe*. They cultivated all their neighbors and scattered the seeds of taste among them: Ariosto cultivated Spenser, the Italian satyr Rabelais, the novellas Shakespeare; the new *political philosophy* arrived with bitter consequences in France and from there moved elsewhere. In matters of art and taste, Charles and Francis vied both with Italy and with each other. The imitators of the Latin language sprouted forth in every land; Italy's location and the vicissitudes of fate determined that it should become a *storehouse of the materials of good taste*, and that is what it has become.

IV. Under Louis XIV a new age of taste returned, to which our foregoing observations also apply, despite the so very different circumstances. It too had long been anticipated by geniuses: Rabelais and Montaigne did not wait for Louis; Corneille had Richelieu and the Academy against him; even the *mightiest* geniuses under Louis did not belong to the courtly circle: Pascal, Fénelon, Rousseau, La Fontaine; and Racine ought not to have been so much a part of it. Thus Louis could rouse not genius but rather *taste*, for he came upon and after an age of geniuses. He was surrounded by *propriety*, *activity*, *splendor*, and *dignity*. In addition, *the language* acquired polish; Louis conducted himself with the same refinement, and every member of *his circle* followed suit; this is the *form that taste assumed*. Though it was no longer capable of flight, *eloquence* at least stirred its wings *with propriety*; though it could no longer produce an effect, the *theater staged the semblance of manners, propriety, philosophy*, and *heroism*. The arts, which could no longer provoke, served Louis' pride and his exploits. Those who could not *compose poetry* wrought *beautiful verses*, and those who could not write *history declaimed* beautifully and drew *pictures*. The *language*, whose strength, richness, and exuberance were long since lost, developed into the *tone of good society*, of *correctness*, and of *decorum*. This was the *color that characterized the age of Louis* and that lay deep in its source.

But soon the corruptions were bound to flow from this very same source. If the roots of taste did not lie deep *in the nation's need*, in the *character* of its manners; if Louis evidently neither had nor could have a *historian of his realm*, such as Xenophon and Livy had been; if his *theater* could not be to *the nation* what the theater had been in Athens; if his

Bourdaloue did not have to speak for or against him, like Demosthenes against Philip and for Athens; and if, as is likely, no Greek would have burst into tears at Bossuet's sublime "Madame est morte! Madame est morte!" then it is clear that the *glittering taste of society and the court* that ruled absolutely *were soon bound to become corrupt*. The same public, the same enlightened and witty circles, which had once endowed the language with *lightness, purity*, and *propriety*, soon gave it *trivial wit, subtleness*, and the *dazzling turn of phrase*. One thus abandoned—as Fénelon, St. Mard, Racine, and who knows how many others have complained—*simple* grandeur, *undismembered and unforced Nature*, and *noble simplicity* and dissected the idea so finely, politely, neologically, and decorously that there was no idea left. What Seneca had been to the Romans Fontenelle was to the French, and La Motte became another Petronius; with his inexhaustible invention, the younger Crébillon brought forth from his polite societies a Chinese figurine, whose heart is fine and small; Marivaux carved up Molière's great character sketches into miniatures of individual sentiments. The academy of good taste delivered what it was supposed to deliver: compliments. The field of courtly taste could produce nothing else. The *fortunes of the state*, on which everything depended, also took a turn for the worse and naturally caused much disruption. Since everything merely floated on the bark of the public, that dreadful monster, *intrigue*, had to confine, arrest, and corrupt taste here more than anywhere. Since *everything rested on fashionable taste*, the *wanton education* and *way of life of the capital* spread even to judges and judgesses, and hence also to writers and artists, not to mention many other shoots sprouting from the same root. *Taste is in a bad way as soon as it can be and is allowed to be merely the taste of society or the court*; it grows feeble, and when it ought to march at the head of the public it brings up the rear instead.

The greatest men of the time, as we see, had to break free in order to breathe clearer air. Rousseau cried out *as if from the wilderness*, and he would not have needed to had it not been so much greener on the other side. Montesquieu, like Horace's Marcellus, grew up like a noble tree, alone in his plot of land; and yet he would not have needed to compensate so much with *esprit* had he been able to embrace his great subject more determinately. Finally, Voltaire, like Columbus, achieved greatness because he believed in another world beyond the age of Louis. He sailed to England, the land of the enemies of his nation's taste, and stole their fire; he cultivated himself outside the elegant circles of Paris, *inter discrimina rerum*, and became Voltaire. The country that spread *lightness, propriety, correctness*,[1] and *clarity* over all of Europe has *for a time per-*

---

[1] Précision.

haps made profound genius and original sentiment difficult for itself. The light is diffused in a warm glow round about and so does not flare up in a bright flame. One stands too close to the statues of former times and merely raises them on pedestals. *Thus the causes of taste in France also carried within them the seeds of its decline.*

Out of modesty I shall not continue. We have seen enough in the *four different periods of taste* to identify the *observations* arising from them, which were the very reason why we passed through them. Namely:

The *age of taste*, as we can see, is in each of its manifestations a *consequence of the powers of genius ordering and regulating themselves.* So though *the sphere of taste* must be as various as the ages themselves, the same rules are always in force. Only the materials and the ends are different.

If no man can bring forth a genius (they shoot up from higher and several causes and often under very precarious circumstances), then, we can see, neither are the *golden ages of taste ever wholly the product of one man's will.* Rather, they follow upon and take their direction from geniuses. In the history of the human race they are like the *consonant intervals on a string*; in between must lie the dissonances from which they stand out.

Consequently, we have solved the puzzle as to why *great men always live together*, which was explained only extremely imperfectly by mechanical *emulation, patronage, climate,* and so on; taken together, all such men are *consonant intervals on a single string.* The dissonances are exhausted; past are the ages of semi- or total barbarism, of empty experiments, of colossal works that have now collapsed on top of one another; *one begins naturally to order and to look about with the former impulses and powers: the human soul is brought into harmony.* Then all arts are united, follow swiftly and promptly upon one another, and at bottom are but a single art. Then there shall be many a Maecenas, many a Maro; and even among such very different activities there is consonance.

The *decline of taste* is therefore just as *natural a phenomenon* as *its emergence*, and in the latter lies already the *disposition to the former.* All that is sublunary is transient; should the *favorable conditions* abate, they will be *replaced* by *detrimental* ones, and *taste sinks into corruption.*

Whoever wishes to influence the *history of taste* must therefore influence its *causes*; let him nurture not the top of the tree or its blossom, but rather *its roots.* Whoever wishes to create a golden age must first create *the conditions for golden ages*; these then arise of their own accord. Whoever wishes to *improve or preserve taste* must remove the *source of the mud* that makes it grow cloudy or *secure the supports that sustain it.* Otherwise his labor is lost.

The *deeper the causes of good taste* lie, the *truer* is its *nature* and the *longer* and more *tenaciously* does it *endure*. That is how things were in Greece, where taste was the *flowering of the nation*, and at certain times among the noble men of Rome also. Greece has never returned, and therefore taste too has *never taken root as deeply or lasted as long*. With us taste is spread only over the surface of the nation.

In Nature, however, *nothing is idle*; forces are never squandered; *all destruction is only apparent*. And the same is true of taste; it is only a *phenomenon* and can *suffer* only as a phenomenon. The clockwork of Nature continues to work toward the good; only what is imperfect and limited (as this whole historical treatise shows) destroys itself; that which *has been brought to perfection* remains, becomes ever more *unsensuous*, and *continues to operate on other planes*. Even *newly made errors* ultimately bring about a *higher good*; they are dissonances that produce a higher harmony.

So we must never stand still and despair at what has been done in the past. As long as Nature rouses geniuses, it also prepares the way for *periods of taste*, and that occurs in *varying intervals from land to land*. If a nation's Spensers, Shakespeares, and Miltons are already in place, then we can be certain that Steele, Pope, and Addison will follow. Perhaps today Germany is working beneath rubble and crumbling monumental edifices toward an age of *exalted philosophical taste, to which everything now existing shall contribute*: fault and virtue, theory and practice, which as yet still blindly collide with one another.

But taste is only a phenomenon, and just as Nature *has subordinated it to higher ends*, so also shall men, her servants and viceroys. Whoever nails a man to a cross to see him die for the sake of art is an evildoer, and whoever sets Rome ablaze to watch Troy burn is a Nero—who, indeed, like a foolish and desperate wretch, must ultimately cry out *qualis artifex pereo!* and be despised, or ridiculed. We are born to create human happiness; God alone creates geniuses, and from geniuses *taste develops by itself*. Like physicians or midwives (after the analogy of Socrates), we need *follow* only *Nature, which always creates, forms, orders*, and then *destroys once more*.

III

CONSEQUENCES

Though at every step history is full of practical lessons, it would be unfortunate, having reached our own age, if we now took our leave of this theme without looking again at its applications. Even if we cannot turn up anything new, such an examination is still necessary and useful.

I. If whoever wishes to be most sure of nurturing taste must nurture genius, those forces of Nature, then we see that *education is the first mainspring of good taste*. But education *with taste, to taste* has all too often
been misconstrued and foolishly applied.

To educate to taste does not mean (or everything I have written has been
in vain) to preach taste, to grouse about good taste, but rather *to demonstrate taste*, to surround the soul with it, to *teach* taste *melodiously and
practically* from childhood; or, in other words, to *bring order* to *a pupil's
powers*, not overhastily but with gentle, continuous, unceasing verve, to
give the soul a bright, unimpeded, and light prospect, to instill in the heart
the gentle feeling of the beautiful and the good accompanied by reason
and choice: that, more than anything else, is *pedagogy, wordless deed, and
guidance*. Through its faculties and the exercise of those faculties, the soul
shall be harmoniously attuned, like the lyre of Apollo. Taste must prevail
in sensations, manners, and actions no less than in cognitions of the fancy
or understanding; in books and written exercises we discern the silhouette of the horse, but not the horse itself in all its strength and power. If
the *foundation* is not laid *more deeply*, then inclination will afterward
carry away the learned fancy and the artistic memory; but if the entire soul
is cultivated, then *taste* must surely follow in every art in which it is
practiced.

But there are no words to express how difficult the *cultivation of taste*
becomes in a *corrupt age*. The pupil is presented with nothing but objects
that always spoil the judicious suggestions and inducements of his tutor;
the sapling grows on the path where every roughshod foot must step over
it—this is also why, with all our theory, we can never reawaken Greek
taste. Our *climate, manners, customs*, even our *intellectual ends*, are in
conflict and bent on the *destruction* of *beautiful sensuality*, from whose
boundaries even our noblest virtue seems to retreat. For us, therefore,
taste must always remain a *matter of secondary importance*, something
that can be sacrificed for the sake of higher motives, whereas among the
Greeks it was the *natural garb* and *embodiment of virtue*.

So every effort applied to the *unification of taste with understanding,
with one's mode of life, and with habit* is invaluable, and here the previous principle—namely, that nothing in Nature occurs in vain—lends us
sterling support. Quintilian, the teacher of taste, strives beyond his time;
the ancient models of taste even more so: the beauty of truth and virtue
is like sunlight, immutable, efficacious, and warming. If in every age there
were three great and good men who combined their strength, they could
work wonders, or like those three righteous men defend a city against the
complete decline of taste and virtue.

It seems to me that in this respect we are *on the threshold of a bright and cloudless future.* If reason also penetrates into those regions where otherwise one only *felt* and created *mechanically*; and if one day reason *recovers from its overtaxing* and (an even greater wish!) joins with *inclination and habit* to form a *universal taste of life*—oh, blessed is the name of the preceding age that contributed hereto, and namely in the deepest springs of habit, mentality, and inclination; that is, in *education.* A better-educated prince; a more firmly established, purer school; a repository of good taste built on wordless deeds—these are a temple sacred to the better humanity of the future!

II. In traditional education the so-called *works of taste*—the exemplary models of the ancients—can become, even when viewed only in the sphere of learning, the *worst occasions of bad taste, disgust, and seduction.* And what replaces them often has an even worse outcome.

If for many years I teach an artistic apprentice to carve only by showing him how to use his tools, so that he never comes face to face with Nature herself, then instead of a sculptor he becomes the most terrible idler, and on top of that he blunts his tool and ruins it forever. It is the same with schoolmasters and cliché-mongers with respect to Cicero and Homer. It is not just that they do not cultivate any Homers or Ciceros (a great deal more would be required to achieve that goal!); their poor captives have never even seen Cicero and Homer, indeed are so disgusted by them that they never want to set eyes on them. Their tutors have cultivated moths who nibble away at Homer and Cicero, reducing them to mere phrases; they have cultivated boys who instead of painting scrape the pigment from the picture or use the banners of good taste as sticks to disturb birds' nests. Surrounded by the beauties of the ancients, the feeling for beauty grows callous, and taste is coerced with the result that it goes to ruin and chases after low, childish, senseless ends.

The antidote supposed to counteract this deplorable bad taste has succeeded only in making things worse. It is claimed that the young ought to be showered with real facts like a corn loft, but then of course they can never become a flower garden in bloom. Already Bacon complained how nothing can become of knowledge when we seek in it only what is useful, immediately useful, and when this happens in education an entire human life is forfeit. Not what, but how the young learn is the *chief concern of education. Taste—that is, order, moderation, and harmony among all the powers*—is the lyre of Amphion or Orpheus, animating the stones so that they build the whole by themselves. Whoever takes the works of the ancients from the hands of the young, no matter what his pretext, no matter what he gives them to read in their stead, whether it be an encyclopedia, a textbook, a rule, a fact, can do nothing to repair the damage. That was the trick played by Julian, but he wanted to inflict the deepest wound on his enemies.

"But genius! The genius will develop by himself; indeed, taste and the works of the ancients can even corrupt him!" That principle, which is the wickedest untruth, is the work of an evil demon. A genius who can be corrupted by taste—let him be so! Better that he be ruined than ruin others. Whoever is worse than he was before after reading the ancients honestly (which is not of course how they are usually read), let him be worse! He was a hopeless case! "Shakespeare! Shakespeare!" they always cry—and what of Shakespeare? Did Shakespeare have no taste, no rules? More than some people, but it was the taste of *his own* time; his own rules governed what *he could accomplish*. Do you think if this genius had lived in the time of the ancients he would have resisted taste with tooth and nail? Or through taste have become worse than he is now? But of course *taste* is a lamentable word when it is parroted after a compendium or crib on natural beauty. True taste works *through geniuses*, and a noble genius is like a star in the darkness. Light reflects only light, the sun only sun.

III. But ultimately, of course, the greatest, the *best school of good taste* is *life* itself. If here poisonous, oppressive shadows loom, then woe betide the delicate sapling! If here venereal distempers ravage good taste, so that clean air becomes all too scarce, woe betide you, impetuous, covetous youth!

How servility oppresses the soul; how the *desire to acquire riches* poisons taste; how, finally, the *hunger for bread* tramples and crushes all that is noble into the dust: here Longinus may speak instead of me.

How *voluptuousness, slavery*, and a *dread of truth, effort, excellence, and honor* are an abyss out of which nothing good grows; the author *of the discourse on the decline of eloquence* laments this with his noble Roman heart. Why echo his complaint?

If *in many estates and professions the word* taste is still a reproach, then hasten thither and remove the thorns even with bloodied hands, and taste will hold sway over new dominions.

If *old habits, envy, and intrigue* join forces holding torches dipped in brimstone, then let the good also come together! Sunlight is stronger than the glow of brimstone torches.

If the prevailing *models of taste are corrupting*, then speak out against them, warn precisely of their faults; or rather, if you can, speak with the compelling eloquence that belongs to the serene and better model.

Finally, since *freedom* and the *feeling of humanity alone* are *the heavenly ether* in which all that is beautiful and good takes seed, without which it must die and decay, let us strive *after these sources of taste* rather than after taste itself. Taste is at last nothing but *truth and goodness* in a *beautiful and sensuous form, understanding* and *virtue in an immaculate garb fit for humanity.* The more we summon humanity on the earth, therefore, the more deeply do we work at realizing the *conditions* so that taste is no longer mere *imitation, fashion,* and *courtly taste,* no longer even a *Greek* and *Roman national medium* that soon destroys itself, but becomes rather, *united with philosophy and virtue,* a *lasting organon of humanity!* *Multa tum, altiora renascentur, quae iam cecidere!*

On the Influence of the Belles Lettres
on the Higher Sciences

Ut hominis decus ingenium,
sic ingenii ipsius eloquentia.
—Cicero

What Influence Do the Belles Lettres Have
on the Higher Sciences?

First we must determine what we mean by "belles lettres" and "higher sciences." If the former are nothing more than what young, idle minds like to understand by the term—that is, a trifling and wanton reading of verses and novels, reviews and witty journals—then we cannot really speak of their having a *good* influence. And since such abuse of the term is nowadays pretty universal, and the Electoral Academy doubtless intends that the answer to the question it has set be on all sides practical and useful, then this treatise must unfortunately begin by addressing the abuse of the matter in hand and the *bad influence* to which it gives rise, so that we may consequently turn to the *better application* of the belles lettres and to their utility.

There is nothing to which the young are more inclined than leaping from the weighty to the frivolous, especially when it is pleasant and possessed of a beautiful surface. The young, then, are prone to setting aside the ancient authors, who are the true exemplars of the beautiful, to neglect philosophy, theology, and a thorough grounding in other departments of knowledge, so that they may take recreation in the witty writings of their own language and therewith fill their imaginations. That is how matters stand in schools and academies, and since it is the early years of life that determine taste, things will carry on in the same vein as they began. We now see, even in ages and professions where we would not suspect them, belletrists and beaux artistes, and of the kind that we would gladly do without: aesthetic-poetic preachers, witty lawyers, painter-philosophers, versifying historians, hypothesizing surveyors and physicians. The frivolous has triumphed over the weighty, the imagination has usurped the understanding; and the more external stimuli and inducements there are to promote these excrescences of the human mind and of belles lettres, the more they flourish, choking what is dry and serious with their exuberant growth.

The considerable harm that ensues from all this, often irreparable for a long while after, is partly done to those individuals who have struck out on the wrong path and partly to the sciences they cultivate or are supposed to cultivate. We become everything that we are meant to be only through effort and practice. Regardless of the pretext under which we neglect these exertions, particularly in younger years, we are always disadvantaged by the fact that our nerves remained untrained, our powers undeveloped; no matter how rich our booty may outwardly seem, therefore, we remain impoverished and feeble within. A youth educated exclusively in the belles lettres is like a milksop bewitched in the garden of Armida or the grotto of Calypso; he will never become a hero or a man of merit if a weightier truth does not appear to him. The beautiful in the sciences after which he chases is mere coloring, mere surface; he pecks at it like the bird does at color, he grasps after it as after a beautiful cloud. The beautiful vision fades, and he is left holding nothing.

What is more, all that glitters is not gold, and not everything is beautiful that appears so to an inexperienced youth or a pampered woman. The fashionable literature of our age is often a garden filled with apples of Sodom: outwardly beautiful, but inwardly full of dust and ashes. A youth who greedily devours the so-called beautiful, with no regard for what it is and how it appears in print, surely does not eat healthily; both good and bad are thrown together in his meal, and most of it is sweet and sumptuous. Taste is corrupted, the soul left uncertain or spoiled. The realm of his knowledge, as narrow as his times, cannot enjoy better fruits than those which the age yields, and he cannot prepare more wholesome sauces. If, moreover, the youth nourished in this manner becomes a judge in the belles lettres before he has become a student, a master before he has become an apprentice, then God forgive him for the havoc he shall wreak! What the Sophists were in the time of Socrates such critics are in our age: they know everything, they pass judgment on everything; they have learned the art of prattling; and is there a topic about which these people cannot prattle? Most of all about matters whereof they know nothing: here they wish were better what they have not understood and there they flaunt their wit and coxcombry.

Every science that such a mind enters is polluted by a foul exhalation and enervated and vitiated by wanton practice. Is not the modern variety of elegant theologian an undignified creature? He preaches not God's Word, but rather fine phrases, Klopstockian hexameters, or Crébillonian morals. He does not expound God's Word, but rather uses it to translate ancient history, letters, and poetry into the most elegant modern form and writes commentaries on Moses, David, and John as if they were Ariosto,

Milton, and La Fontaine. His doctrine is a liberal philosophy of theological opinions, and his pastoral cleverness an aesthetic delight in all prevailing errors and useful vices. What is lacking here is man who desires and seeks both dignity in his office and sharply defined contours in his thinking, for whom the superficially gaudy colors of the belles lettres are nothing but rouge and powder or a fool's coat.

I shall pass over lawyers and physicians, to deliver instead a thumbnail sketch of the milksop who flirts as a bel esprit in philosophy, history, or even mathematics. When he furnishes us with fine words, portraits, pictures, analogies, witty conceits, and anecdotes about all these things; when he does not tell us what has happened but rather paints what ought to have happened, does not show us what exists but instead garlands it with flowers of speech so that it must be guessed at; oh, the fine philosopher, the poetic historian, the witty mathematician, the glorious critic! All these sciences, all higher sciences are corrupted when such apes are the models and serve as exemplars. A Bible is no longer a Bible when it is an illuminated and elegant art book, a precept no longer a precept when it is a hodgepodge of painted opinions, a philosophy no longer a philosophy when it trifles instead of giving instruction and chases after colors and fool's gold instead of seeking truth. What is a history without truth? What is a science without certainty and sharply defined contours? What is a moral philosophy without morals and training? What is wisdom that is full of trifles and elegant foolishness? These butterflies of the belles lettres pilfer from and discredit every profession and estate. They suck from them the useless sap and leave behind a plague of caterpillars to spread havoc.

The highest science of all is undoubtedly the art of living; and how many people the belles lettres have robbed of this one and only, this divine art! Love, which brings happiness, is seldom taught or cultivated by novels: the greatest heroes and heroines in romances find not what they are looking for but often something quite different from that whereof they dreamed. Their overtaxed imagination grows weary and is unable to enjoy what it has, what it is given to savor; enervated, soft, and sensual hands cannot grasp, cannot provide the artistic image that must first be furnished. A fickle youth hastening after pleasure—how can he become a man, a worthy husband and father; a hardworking, untiring guardian of the common weal; an inquiring, fair judge; a meticulous, supportive physician; an industrious sage; a seeker of truth; and a benefactor of the human race in his sphere of activity? All this requires cultivation, education, art, effort, a true heart, sound understanding, an honorable goal, and the will and strength to achieve that goal. If all these things are lacking, if in everything we do we strive only for the fool's gold of that which is agreeable, light, pleasurable, and beautiful and despise that which demands effort and necessitates examination—the gods give us nothing without effort; all their gifts they sell dearly, and dearest of all is their most precious gift, the laurels that reward a clear conscience. The conviction that we have done what we ought to have done, what no one else could do on our behalf is not achieved by the *elogia* of foreign tongues and pens, not through superficial brilliance, not through prattle or affectation in the fine arts. But this conviction is the finest, as well as the highest, science and art of life. Whatever does not lead us thither is vanity, humbug, a finely colored yet bedazzling and perhaps even noxious vapor. Many of the flaws and infelicities that bedevil our governments, estates, offices, sciences, and commerce may be traced back to the unfortunate wantonness of belletristic learning, which manifests itself frequently in our classrooms, schools, churches, palaces, markets, and houses; if we could only dam its springs, then the sewers would soon dry up.

Here, too, the best that we can do is this: to show what is better only as it is, in better concepts and examples; this is the meaning of the question, *What influence do the belles lettres, properly understood and properly practiced, have on higher forms of knowledge?*

The belles lettres are those which *cultivate* the so-called *lower faculties of the soul, sensuous cognition, the wit, the imagination, the sensuous appetites, enjoyment, the passions and inclinations.* Is not this very definition sufficient proof that they therefore *exert* the *finest* and *best influence* on the higher sciences, which concern themselves with judgment and understanding, the will and convictions?

All the powers of our soul are only one power, just as our soul is only one soul. What we call superior and inferior, high and low is only comparatively and relatively so. On the whole, however, a sound understanding is impossible without sound and well-ordered senses, a decisive judgment is impossible without an imagination tamed and heedful of its duty, a good will and character are impossible without passions and inclinations in good order. Hence it is both wrong and foolish to *cultivate the higher sciences without the belles lettres*, to plow the air when the soil lies fallow.

Who has ever known a man of sound understanding to be constantly misled by his sensuous judgment? Who has ever seen aright with his understanding who did not see aright with his eyes and fancy? Who was ever master of his will whose passions did not obey him, who was in thrall to his fancy, who in every one of his secret inclinations felt seven ropes, a thousand ropes binding him, this Samson, without another faculty freeing him? Hence the belles lettres are, or ought to be, orderers of our senses, our imagination, our inclinations and desires; they are the lens reflecting truth, which is revealed to us mortals only as appearance; they are the artisans who order the ground of our souls, so that truth and virtue may be made manifest to us. There is scarcely more that can be said in their *favor*; there is no higher *endorsement*.

Our senses and sensuous knowledge, as well as our secret inclinations and desires, are moreover *the first things that awaken in our soul*; understanding is a latecomer, and virtue, if it is not implanted in the former, generally arrives even later. With the young, therefore, we must begin at an early age to treat and cultivate their sensuous powers sensuously, through simple rules and—even better—through good examples. The belles lettres are compatible and concerned with both, and therefore *to make use of them early and profitably in conformity with the nature and disposition of the human soul* is more than recommended for every other branch of learning, too.

He whose memory, senses, wits, fancy, desire, and inclination grew crooked and dull in his youth—what raw materials shall his understanding have to work with in later years? And in accordance with which forms and formulas? What can his volition do when his powers to imagine, to will, and to act correctly are ruined? He writes on a spoiled, crumpled, and torn scrap of paper; he means to fight with blunt weapons and execute the soul's greatest work of art with clumsy, rusty tools.

As dawn precedes the morning sun, and spring and the seeding of the land are followed by the harvest, *so the belles lettres come before the higher sciences*. They sow what the latter reap: where they furnish us with beautiful semblance, the latter warm and illumine us with all their truth.

The senses and passions, the fancy and inclinations can become in a certain sense the greatest enemies of the good and of truth. Once they have been overcome and reconstituted as sound allies, the matter is settled: the higher sciences are raised in triumph on their shields. True philosophy categorically not only does not contradict the senses but rather corrects, orders, and affirms them. In the finest exposition of history, the action merely chooses the manner of its own expression and inhabits it, just as the soul dwells in the body. True law applies only to *this particular* case and lives therein. The finest theology affects human hearts with the dignity, truth, and simplicity of God. All the higher sciences are thus the fruits produced by the healthy, beautiful, and natural blossoming of other sciences.

I am well aware of the extent of what I have claimed and that one might ask me *where* the belles lettres exist. Without allowing myself thereby to be deflected from my path, I simply say in reply that if there are belles lettres, they *ought* to be precisely that—beautiful—and yet have a proper purpose and use. It is no beautiful science but rather an ugly one that agitates the imagination and misleads it, instead of ordering it and putting it on the right track; that abuses wit instead of using it to clothe truth; that childishly titillates and arouses the passions instead of calming them and directing them toward worthy ends. I am certain that in this respect the ancients possessed *more* belles lettres than we do, and *belles lettres* in their *rightful* place. Their poetry and eloquence, their education and culture contained far more *wisdom* and had more *immediate application to life* than most of our literature and scholastic phrases. Hence, from this point of view also the study of the ancients, practiced properly and in a disciplined fashion, is the *true science of the beautiful that leads us on to higher knowledge*.

For where is so-called fine language so exactly and naturally the image and garb of truth than among the Greeks and Romans? Where does one who wishes to learn the language of Nature learn it better than from her earliest poets? Where does one who wishes to see plain and simple wisdom see it more clearly than in their eloquence and history? Homer was the first philosopher and Plato his pupil; Xenophon and Polybius, Livy and Tacitus are great observers of human nature and of the state, from whom Machiavelli and Grotius acquired their wisdom. Demosthenes and Cicero are jurists from whom one can learn rather more than the number of their periods. Has a great mind of modern times *ever become a reformer in the higher science he practices* by not *studying the ancients*?

For the *theologian*, for example, knowledge and exegesis of the Bible are indispensable, but what theologian has ever pursued this knowledge with distinction and success without a more detailed knowledge of the ancients and without cultivating the belles lettres? For as long as the belles lettres languished, the study and more learned application of the Bible also languished; when the former revived, so too did the latter, and then on they went, almost in step with each other. One part of the Bible is poetry; has anyone ever successfully interpreted it without a feeling for the truth and beauty of poetic art? How many herds and hordes of commentators have dismembered and misinterpreted the prophets and psalms in a wretchedly dogmatic and grammarian manner because the spirit of their exalted poetic language never inspired them? Even the historical and hortatory parts of the Bible are full of pictures and sensuous representation; no one who neglects and fails to appreciate the latter can understand and apply the former.

The *preacher* is supposed to speak to the people. But how shall he speak if he does not know them, if he knows not how to appeal to either their ear or their heart, because he himself is lacking in heart and desires? He is meant to bring home to his flock the history and moral philosophy of another age; how can he do so if he sees neither the former nor the latter in the right light and does not match them with the right sense? I might adduce abundant examples of the errors and false steps arising from this ignorance and want of practice throughout the fields of theology, if only space and my purpose would allow it.

Others have amply demonstrated that it would not be detrimental but rather of the greatest benefit to *jurisprudence* if in it sound understanding and the delicate feeling for truth that is essential to inquiry and expression were given freer rein. No one will doubt that *history* and *statecraft* make good companions of more refined culture and humanity. What could be more humanely conceived and written than a history of mankind? And where might a greater knowledge of mankind and humanity prevail than in the *science that governs men*? So at an age of greater maturity and experience, most deep souls cast aside the toys and rattles of the Muses and move toward this *humane quality* of poetry and history. A human life as pursued by Homer; a reversal of fortune as described by Aeschylus and Sophocles; a character as studied by Sallust and Tacitus; events and passions as unraveled, even in their most hidden threads, by Shakespeare; errors and follies as sketched by Aristophanes and Lucian, Hudibras and Swift; a quiet, homely life as depicted by Horace and Addison—if we failed to acquire from all these writers a knowledge of humanity, a domestic and political wisdom, then where else might we obtain such things? The most celebrated conqueror of all time read Homer as a manual of war, and more than one statesman has learned the tricks of his trade from the ancient historians and orators.

The entire course of history testifies to the connection between the belles lettres and *philosophy*. They both flourished for as long and as often as they remained friends; once they became estranged and inimical to each other, they both went to their grave. Plato was the bee hovering above Homer's flowers, and Aristotle was no enemy of the Muses. But when in the Middle Ages the scholastics retreated from the light of the sun and the day and, in the abyss of their barbarism, spun words and picked apart mere echoes, what became of their logic and metaphysics? Only when the fine arts returned did a light dawn on the abstract sciences; not only did they begin to live in companionship with one another, but often a single mind was an inventor in both. All the brightest minds in philosophy from Bacon to Leibniz were also friends of the delightful and the beautiful; their language was clear, like their spirit, and even their amusements became monuments to truth.

If I were to name all the great names who successfully combined the belles lettres with the higher science that they pursued, indeed even with more than one, then what a list of names I would have before me! It seems almost to be a hallmark of *all* noble minds that they did not mechanically confine themselves to a single art or science but rather enlivened the one with the other and were not, so to speak, complete strangers to any that cultivates the spirit. For all its provinces, the realm of the sciences seems yet one, like the faculties of the human soul; some may lie closer to one another, others may be more distant, but none is cut off and like an island, and entry may be gained to all. In the history of the human spirit, as in the history of human science, there arise the most unusual combinations, and they appear to exist only so that from each a separate new good proceeds. When poet and orator, philosopher and statesman practice theology, they observe and treat it *differently*; but each can find a use for his version which the other could not. The same goes for every other field of the sciences; the flower of the beautiful can flourish in all of them, depending on the species to which it belongs and the locality that now nourishes it. In general, the belles lettres impart *light, life, sensuous truth,* and *richness* to the higher sciences, as all the classes and examples I have mentioned show. They impart these qualities to the *content* as well as to the *form*, to the *thought* as well as to the *expression*; indeed, if they are of the right sort, they should impart these qualities to the *whole spirit* and *character*, the *heart* and *life* of the practitioner. A person who thinks beautifully and acts badly is as malformed and imperfect a creature as one who thinks correctly and expresses himself crookedly and wretchedly. *Unity* is perfection, in the sciences as well as in the faculties of the human soul, in content as in form, in thought as in expression.

I could go into yet more detail and demonstrate how individual branches of learning, both among the belles lettres and the higher sciences, support and elevate one another, but I think it unsuited to my purpose and to the Society for which I am writing. Rather, I will discuss the *order* and *method* that in my opinion and experience might best be employed from childhood so that *both kinds of knowledge* succor and assist each other in the best manner possible.

1. *The belles lettres must precede the higher sciences, but in such a way that truth underpins the former also.*

The order in which the times of day and year, the human lifespan, and the powers of our soul develop point us in this direction. As dawn precedes noon and spring summer, so the blossoms of the soul—the senses and sensuous knowledge—first stir in youth, the springtime of life; therefore the first task of education, which should follow Nature, is to order them. The beautiful and agreeable *history of Nature*, which is, as it were, the image of God's creation, must indubitably precede abstract physics; likewise the light and agreeable *history of mankind* should come before abstract metaphysics and moral philosophy. The branch of logic concerned only with distinct knowledge, with concepts, propositions, and scholarly deductions, ought to be anticipated by another kind of logic, which guides *sound understanding* and the fancy; and since this is achieved more effectively by examples than by precepts, we find ourselves once more on the *beautiful path of the ancient authors*. If they are snatched from the hands of the young, who are then overburdened with so-called higher knowledge, then I cannot say whether the damage could be undone, even if they retain everything they learn. They learn it too early and hence do not learn it properly; a metaphysical child and systematic boy without materials and blossoming knowledge is a young graybeard, who grows old and withered before his time. But if children are furnished with a *wealth of impressions* and sundry instances of *sensuous certainty*, then the distinctness of scholarly concepts will issue forth from them like fruit from the blossom.

In so doing, it goes without saying that when studying either the ancients or the moderns one should not separate the words from the thoughts, the expression from the things expressed, or else the blossom will wilt. He who merely snatches after fine phrases in the ancients has caught not butterflies but only their colors; he who merely hunts for formulas and expressions in the moderns fills the heads of his apprentices with cobwebs. But to show them *good things*, and to do so eloquently, to unfold *beautiful examples* before them, *beautifully presented*, to impress on them *regular images and fancies in beautiful language*—that is instructive and will be of benefit throughout their lives. They are bees in a field of flowers who do not idly flit about but return to the hive laden with nectar; and once they have acquired such booty, the time has come to layer and order it. A youth who has neglected these powers and sciences can, with effort, make good his loss later, but the higher erects itself only on their foundations.

But, I say, the belles lettres must also be founded on truth and utility. A teacher who is experienced in the higher sciences will have, even if he does not formally practice them, the belles lettres in mind and in reserve when he assigns his preparatory exercises. From the time when he learns to spell and read, a person must know what he is reading, and if afterward he must go on to practice composition, he must know what he is writing. It would be the most terrible shame to waste one's labor here, since literature as a whole bears such beautiful fruits and flowers. If this crop is put before a boy and chosen only on the basis of whether it makes a *wholesome* or *unwholesome* meal, if he has practiced with worthy and beautiful examples so that he can feel his own power, then he will never lack for words or subject matter. With the content, the form will impress itself on him, and unconsciously he will continue to think, to write, and, if fortune wills it thus, to act in accordance with that form. Read to him well and, without being aware of it and almost without wanting to, he will learn to read well; let him practice with good examples, and, until he has made these his own, do not let him acquaint himself with the bad; and then he will think well in the higher sciences and hence also express himself well, for the finest garb in which our thoughts can be dressed is always the tightest-fitting clothing of truth. The youth passes unawares into more serious and weighty learning, and no longer does he find it heavy-going; he has, as it were, studied with only *that purpose in mind*.

2. The belles lettres, correctly understood, have the merit *that they are meant for all estates and professions*, whereas every higher science constitutes a separate domain; therefore they must *be universally pursued*, and especially by the young.

In earlier years no man truly knows to what end he is studying; our vocation and affairs do not always depend on our inclination and free choice. So if a person has been prepared too exclusively and narrowly for one of the higher sciences or for a position in life and fortune does not smile on him, he is lost. He cannot be what he wants to be, and there is nothing else he could be.

What is more, no profession or science is really a sphere so completely fenced off that it has nothing at all to do with any others; the wholly one-sided pursuit of a discipline therefore engenders nothing but hatred, envy, unreasonable contempt, and deaf impropriety against every other discipline most closely bordering on our own. The *pure pute* lawyer despises the theologian as unjustly as the theologian, in retaliation, hates and abuses the lawyer. The metaphysician brands the poet a heretic just as the poet mocks the metaphysician—none of this redounds to the credit of science or is of any benefit to the common weal, which has need of every discipline and values each in its own way. The belles lettres and sound understanding are as it were a common pasture where every branch of higher knowledge gathers and recreates itself, where each forgets its particular office and recalls mankind's universal purpose. All those who have visited and tilled this spot since they were young, are, so to speak, childhood friends: they have learned one and the same philosophy of life, prepared in one and the same school.

And since public institutions in particular are places of assembly, which the apprentices leave to enter every profession and take up every office, these common pastures and preparatory exercises cannot be cultivated carefully enough. It is no good if schools are meant only for theologians and the preparatory exercises are assigned as if only theologians were expected to graduate from them, but it would be just as bad if some other science or faculty appointed itself the sole end of education. The belles lettres are called *humaniora*; they serve *mankind* and ought to serve it in *all its professions and forms*. The belles lettres exist for a greater purpose than preaching aesthetically or versifying Anacreontically; the statesman, too, shall find delight and nourishment in them; the philosopher and the surveyor, too, shall use them to develop their soundness of feeling. We are all human beings and should love *humanity*, and in all ages and in all professions it has been the ornaments of mankind who did so.

3. But from this it also follows *what belles lettres actually are*, what merits this name, and with that I return to the beginning of my discourse: they are *humaniora, sciences and exercises that develop the feeling of humanity within us*. Those which develop this feeling are belles lettres; those which do not are not belles lettres, no matter how many glittering titles they may boast.

Languages and *poetry*, *rhetoric* and *history* are reckoned among them, but there always remains the question of how languages and poetry, rhetoric and history are practiced, otherwise they too can become ugly, useless sciences. The feeling of humanity (*sensus humanitatis*) makes them what they are or ought to be. And then *philosophy*, too, is no stranger or enemy to them; rather, they must all be practiced with a kind of philosophy and thereby awakened to *humanity*. Philosophy is hence truly *doctrina humanitatis*. It is undeniable that those ancient theorists, Aristotle and Quintilian, imbued their teaching with this sense of humanity more than most of their modern counterparts. The unfinished poetics of Aristotle acutely analyzes Greek tragedy and even declares the purging of the passions to be its purpose; the teacher of the sciences who elucidated Homer and Sophocles according to this principle would find a large following. Aristotle's *Rhetoric* abounds with knowledge of the human soul and an analysis of the passions, as well as with knowledge of the civic ends and business that oratory should serve. The writings of Plutarch, both his *Essays* and his *Lives*, brim with this feeling of humanity, and herein he is unsurpassed even by Cicero. Quintilian is a threshing floor strewn with purified grains of wisdom. Among modern theorists, Rollin in particular has modeled himself on the taste of the ancients, and in Germany Sulzer especially has theorized about the true and the good in keeping with this taste. On the basis of these authors and others, some among the aforementioned nations and some among others, it is possible to advance a theory of the belles lettres, of which one can say that it serves the higher sciences with spirit and vitality.

But just as theory alone cannot do everything, so we are mostly reliant on *examples* of those who have written and practiced in the *higher* sciences with a true feeling of humanity, and in the *belles lettres* with a sense and foretaste of the higher sciences. I do not care to repeat myself and celebrate once more the ancient poets, orators, historians, and philosophers, *for whom all the branches of science were happily still one*. Among the moderns, too, each *higher* science has possessed *fine* geniuses, who have pursued it in the true spirit of humanity, just as there has been no shortage of poets who were more than poets and impressed this extra dimension on their works. Of the latter, I need mention only the names of a Dante, Petrarch, Tasso, of a Milton, Swift, Pope, of a Haller, Withof, Lichtwer, Lessing, and Kästner; just as among the former I need recall only a Thou and Montaigne, Sidney and Shaftesbury, Machiavelli and Sarpi, Erasmus and Grotius, to renew the memory of so many other geniuses in other higher sciences. A teacher of humanity who teaches in the spirit of these men will teach for all, even if we found ourselves in Trotzendorf's school and were hordes of youths belonging to all manner of estates and offices. He will not throw out *mellitus verborum globules, dictaque papauere et sesamo sparsa: qui inter haec nutriuntur, non magis sapere possunt, quam bene olere, qui in culina habitant,* but rather furnish form and content, so that the *spirit of his pupils shall become bright,* their *fancy and senses well ordered,* their *expression* made *beautiful* by *truth* and *adorned with simplicity,* but mostly so that there develops in them *the feeling of loving humanity everywhere* and *of promoting its true good*—that is the best influence in the higher sciences as well as the great art of life. Happy, then, the land that nurtures the belles lettres! Happy the land where they exercise such an influence on the higher regions of human science!

Does Painting or Music Have a Greater Effect?

A DIVINE COLLOQUY

THERE WERE OCCASIONS when the Muses were at a loss as to what they should talk about, and so from time to time they quarreled over their respective merits, over the value of their arts. One such confabulation between the Muses of *Painting* and of *Music*, whereof word has reached me through secret reports, I wish to relate here, for Father Apollo was presiding. The god, in the eternal bloom of youth, sat beneath his beloved laurel tree, with the youngest and dearest of his daughters, Poetry, in his lap. Her two older sisters sat to the right and left before her and were arguing over the question, *Which of their arts, painting or music, has the greater effect on human souls?*

"Without doubt mine," said the Muse of Painting, "for my domain is as wide and all-encompassing as heaven and earth. All the objects of the world are mine. I can terrify the soul with a flash of lightning in the sky and gladden it with the finest views of earth. I can convulse the soul with menacing rock cliffs and expand it with the sight of the endless ocean. All the passions do I represent: I give them eloquent form and engrave their expression into the soul—is there a wider and greater effect than this?"

"Whether there is a wider and more extensive effect I do not know," replied Music, "but that there is a deeper, more inward, more powerful one, my own art, I believe, bears witness. Your territory is vast, sister, but within this vast territory you have little power, for everywhere you are spread only over the surfaces of things. That you have many objects is undeniable, but you can convey only their external aspect, the image reflected in the mirror. Even of the deepest, most unfathomable objects you deliver no more than this, and hence you achieve, with all your many materials, a very modest effect. I, by contrast (if you will permit me to celebrate my poverty and take pride in my shortcomings), with my paltry seven tones, which nowhere attract attention, which everywhere lie quietly concealed, with these I move every heart capable of feeling; indeed, with them I once built and still sustain the world. At the sound of my lyre all things set themselves in order, even your most beautiful forms: only the relation of my tones made them what they are; only the relation of my tones made them effective. With but a little I accomplish much; through a few invisible waves I encircle the heart *immediately*, pierce it, and carry it away, for all the strings of sensation are my strings; it is *them* that I pluck, not the quivering threads of this poor instrument. Does our Father Apollo wield the paintbrush? No, but he does play the kithara, for music is the art of all arts."

Father Apollo requested that they leave him out of the argument, "For," he said, "you are both my daughters; and in addition to the kithara I wield the arrow of the sun, wherein lie all the colors of light and beauty. Therefore defend yourself better, Painting, my daughter; you seem already defeated. At issue was not the extent but the effect of art."

So Painting made a second sally. "Precisely my effect, Father, is beyond dispute the purest and clearest, the most sublime and enduring effect. My sister had occasion to say that her tones lie inconspicuously, that is, obscurely, in one another; both they and their effect are indeed very opaque. After all, can anyone say what tones mean to express? Do they not speak the most confused tongue of half-sensations, which seem always to draw near our soul and yet never take hold of it; which always, like sand or the ocean waves, wash around us, roar around us, and do not nearly complete their effect in us? They are gone, like the brook, like the breath of wind; and where now is their image, where their voice and language? I, by contrast, may proudly reiterate that I produce the most definite, clear, and enduring effect. My forms have a purity; one *knows* and *retains* what one sees of my work. One retains it not only in one's memory, but in one's gaze, before the eyes of the fancy and before the latest recollection. I write and draw with the ray of sunshine; like the light of the sun my effect is eternal. If anyone has seen one of the heavenly visions of Raphael and his fellows, even for a few moments, the forms, the shapes remain with him. He has visited our heavenly realm, has glimpsed gods and goddesses, has tasted and enjoyed the ambrosia of their lips, the fragrance of their veils, the luster of their countenances; the images, the impressions, and ideas never leave him. Look at you, on the other hand, a poor Muse wandering hither and thither between three strings."

"My sister," interrupted modest Music, nimbly striking a few notes on her instrument, "my sister is once again painting a broad canvas when instead she ought to be deeply and stirringly describing her effect (which is the issue here). No one denies that line is line and color color, that one can see them with one's eyes and see them for as long as one wishes to see them. But to see is not to be moved, and the clearest and most enduring cognition is not sensation. Rather, it is known that the former always hinders the latter to a certain degree, for it is precisely the *coolness* with which one observes that gives rise to a clear concept. You write with the ray of sunshine, but you do so only on frigid memory. Even the enthusiasm with which you, radiant sister, spoke of gods and goddesses, of fragrance and ambrosia, is the fire of the fancy, not of the heart and feeling. None of your favorites has been among us in heaven; he painted only mortals, and it is inconceivable that there have not lived or shall yet live on earth a thousand more beautiful people than those depicted by one of your painters. They copied one another ceaselessly, often placing, when they strove hardest to portray the ideal, monster upon monster, and the range of their so-called divine and heroic forms ultimately became so narrow and impoverished that what you reproach me for was rather true of them: they strummed on an instrument fitted with one and a half broken strings, which they called *antiquity*, a time when the full string music of all the forms and souls of Nature was supposed to have been in their mortal hands. Do you really think, sister, that the dollop of colors lying on the palette can compete with Nature, let alone surpass her all-powerful abundance and truth? The fire kindled and lit on this little wooden panel will not easily warm through a human heart, still less reduce Creation to ashes so that one would need to seek new forms in heaven."

"Your tone grows too harsh, my daughter," said the president of the assembly, interrupting her speech. "You blame the art for the failings of the artist or even of its foolish eulogist. Enough of this; defend your cause. Painting alleged that your effect was obscure and confused, and moreover always incomplete, transient, and brief. Answer her charge."

"I think," she said, "that the charge is easily answered. Who knows this better than you, the father of eternal Music? My sister desires that my tones be shapes and colors, and that is not possible. She desires that I hang my tones on the wall so that they ring out, like Memnon's statue when the sun shines on it, and ring out like a peal of bells forever; this too is impossible and would quickly become very disagreeable indeed. My effect is therefore brief and transient, but for whom is it so? For those poor mortals who succumb so quickly to every sensation. And for them my effect must be as it is precisely because it would be so intense, so powerfully rousing, so overwhelming for them, were it sustained for even a little while longer. No, men are not yet ready for the eternal harmony of the gods; they sink, they drown in the ocean of my art. For that reason they had only a few tones of an infinite string music, in a few keys and in very simple modulations, meted out, counted out, doled out to them. On their strings I merely lisp and float past them like a harmonious breeze. Hence my effect seems to them always incomplete, for it cannot be completed in their nature, or they would themselves become harmony and melody. The obscurity and confusion of their sensations is owing to their organ, not to my tones, for these are pure and bright, the supreme example of harmonious order. They are, as a mortal sage inspired by me once said, the most agreeable, light, and effective of all the symbols representing the relationships and numbers of the cosmos. When you censured me, sister, you in fact offered me praise. When you showed how even so noble a nature as human nature can grasp so little of my all-powerful effect, can bear it only for so brief a time and in such simple forms and series, you really extolled the infinitude of my art and its innermost effect. In the tumult of your colors and forms, by contrast, human nature is never confused and even, as you yourself have said, requires something else that *surpasses* all earthly forms as some measure of protection against their empty recurrence. Man does not require this of me; every earthly being lags endlessly far behind my sensations, and for a long time will a mortal climb, step by step, before he can experience even a little of the tonal edifice of universal perfection, before he can experience even a brief moment of its eternally ascending melody."

As Music uttered these words and the glow of enthusiasm manifested itself in her face and gestures, the Muse Urania sat down next to her and embraced her. The eyes of young Poetry, too, were fixed on her. And Music's very words might almost have carried into song, the better to show all Olympus the effect of her art; but Father Apollo interrupted her at just the right moment and gave her to understand that only earthly music and the effect of music on *human* hearts were at issue in this discussion. "You have vindicated yourself enough, my daughter; indeed, you have praised your art to Olympus. It is time that your sister spoke."

"She has indeed praised her art to Olympus," said Painting, "she who found it so strange that my favorites cherished only the dream of a few divine forms."

"Leave Olympus out of this, my daughter," said Apollo. "You are both celestial beings, and your arts needs must also be heavenly if they shall have effect down on earth. The human soul, too, is our sister, and everything that is supposed to affect it must contain something immeasurable and thus be of heavenly provenance. That is what mortals call it, and they are right. All forms and shapes, no matter how pure and accomplished they may be, remain ineffectual with you, Painting, if no soul, no heavenly spirit animates them. This spirit must also be breathed into every one of your compositions, so that the whole becomes one. Otherwise, no matter how faithful and artful the imitation, everything remains impoverished and lifeless. In you also, Music, the emotion of the soul must link and accompany every tone, otherwise it not only becomes what you claimed the frigid imitations of painting become but potentially is even more disagreeable, since your art lives from the afflatus of this heavenly spirit alone. So desist from this dispute over words and keep to the particular effects of your arts. If you so wish, I shall send for old Aristotle; he is said to be an exceptional master of distinctions and exact definitions. I am sure he will put you right without too much trouble."

Both ladies ruled out the proposed referee and decided, if Apollo did not wish to inconvenience himself, to elect their younger sister, *Poetry*, to this role. "She has learned from us both," they said, "and she loves us both. She is a woman and therefore best placed to judge the arts and effects of women; moreover, she is our sister." They said to Poetry: "Come away from Apollo's lap, where you only confound him with your beautiful locks, and move closer to us." Poetry did so gladly, and the dispute resumed for the third and final time.

"I think, my sisters," said Poetry, "if you desire to reach some kind of understanding, you must, as Father Apollo just said, distinguish more finely the effects toward which you work; you must therefore determine with greater precision the department of the soul that you operate on. You, Painting, affect the fancy more than the heart; but the fancy can also approach the heart, and if it does not reach all the way, then it is usually all the nearer to the understanding. Hence, all your representations are clearer, but—as Music says—colder. There is no shame in that, Painting; it may even work to your advantage, for correctness and truth are the principal means of your effect which you merely clothe with beauty and agreeableness. Every painter would offend greatly if he left this stronghold for the outer fortifications, and threw himself into the lesser task of producing an immediate effect on the heart without correctness and rigorous truth. For you, Painting, a draft and a spirit of the draft that animates the whole is always the main thing; from this I too have long learned and still learn daily. The moving quality of individual facial features, the illusoriness of the carnation and the colors, as well as profound thoughts summoned from afar, are all good and excellent if the main work speaks to the soul—speaks as it can through these means; that is, brightly, clearly, richly, distinctly. The less Painting wishes to operate according to appearance and the more she avoids the hideous representation, the more efficacious she will be, the more she will rise from a mere imitator to become a pure and humble portrayer of the unfathomably deep, ever new and beautiful truth. You, in contrast, Music, you are more to me than Painting can ever be, for, as you rightly said, you are the harmonic foundation and melodic companion of all beauty, even picturesque beauty. But you must admit that without my words, without song, dance, and other actions, the sensations you awaken in men will always be obscure. You speak to the heart but how little to the understanding! And even when you speak to the heart, the emotion you impart is often really nothing but sensual arousal! Are there not also certain beasts who are gladdened or upset by certain tones or a sequence of tones? Indeed, a cruel experiment was once performed in which the brain of living creatures was opened up and now pain, now joy excited in them by the application of certain pressures; were these sensations, crudely effected, anything different from what you bring about, though in an infinitely finer manner? It is true that the whole human heart is your lyre, but do you look to what end you play it? And now, my sisters, I ask you to compare particular cases wherein your art expresses itself and the ends to which it does so."

Painting began, describing the exalted impressions she had sometimes made through pictorial representation. She spoke of the wife of Brutus, who could not be brought to tears until suddenly she caught sight of the image of Andromache, which broke the stoic dam of her feelings. She cited a number of other pictures, which had provoked sudden conversions, had brought consolation and encouragement, and, as if by means of visions from another world, had turned the soul upside down and transformed it.

"Forgive me, sister," said Poetry, "but here too I would like you to attend to which of these effects properly pertain only to you. Most of those you have mentioned lie in the very objects you imitated, and you cannot deny that if Andromache or other noble figures had appeared in the flesh instead of in a picture, whose presence you or I could depict only feebly, the effect they produced would probably have been still greater. Think of the appearance of the Mother of God (as the mortals call her) or of Magdalene, both clothed in every ideal charm that we bestowed on them. You must concede that in this regard you and I were only distant and weak imitators. And where effect is concerned, often a bad and exceedingly unideal appearance of Nature, precisely because of its individual truth and reality, has been infinitely richer in great and good consequences than its most artful imitation through the medium of colors would be. By contrast, you, Music, are always creator, for your art possesses no actual model as such, neither in heaven nor on earth."

"For that very reason," spoke Music, picking up the thread, "my effect is always new, original, and glorious. I am a creator and never imitate; I call forth tones, as the soul calls forth thoughts, as Jupiter called forth worlds out of the void, out of the invisible; and thus do tones enter the soul, like an enchanted language from another world, so that the soul, caught up in the current of the song, forgets itself, loses itself. You have all heard tell of the effects of music in ancient and modern times, though one can never hear these tales enough. There is no need for me to repeat the old stories of Amphion, Orpheus, Linus, Timotheus, Phemius, and so on; on earth on the feast day of Saint Cecilia they are still celebrated and extolled in song."

"But are these effects still equaled?" interrupted Poetry, "and does not the very fact that they are no longer equaled show that even in the age of the ancients they were not entirely yours, were not always the product of the art that particularly in later times you mean to practice wholly without me? In those days I helped you. I lent support to your tones, and you served only to enliven my song. Conversely, I illuminated your language, reinforced it with the power of all the feelings and states of the soul; in this way we produced the effect together. Since we have gone our separate ways, our arts have grown a thousand times more refined; the boundaries between them have been drawn more exactly; the rules have been determined and stand there like Scylla and Charybdis or like the Pillars of Hercules, beyond which no man could sail: yet where now upon the earth do we have an effect such as that acclaimed by the ancients? I am read; you are heard; with me they criticize and yawn, with you they play or chatter; and finally with both of us they nod off."

"That is due not to us," replied Harmony, undaunted, "but to the abuse of our name. I have never recognized the fiddlers and pipers, the tormentors and dalliers of the strings as sons of my art; for what effect do their tones achieve? Have you ever been in the workshop of Vulcan and there mistaken the turnspit for the beautiful Hebe, who mixes the nectar and ambrosial food of the gods? And what are so many quartets and sonatas, trios and symphonies, and especially that wretched multitude of monotonous song melodies, other than the living turnspit of club-footed Vulcan? They say an art has been invented by virtue of which, and by following eternal rules, one can, indeed must, turn out a melody, just like that kitchen utensil rotates in line with its weights. I think we three sisters need not reproach ourselves with the armies of bunglers and suitors."

"And yet," said Poetry, interrupting her, "recall the time of your simple origin and recall the effect you had in those days; even if only half the myths were true which our mother Mnemosyne recounted to us, where do your Orpheus and Amphion create their music now, where are they now at work?"

"It is true," replied Music, "that in many lands the years of my youth have passed; but it is not I, but rather they—the so-called polite world— who have grown old and gray and now instead of enjoying tones wish in part to build or funambulate or play with them. They also construct quite wonderfully tall harmonic edifices, which promptly strive to reach up to heaven, to the understanding, since they are no longer admitted to the inner sanctum, the heart. The simple thing is for them too simple; with the impossibilities they have overcome they seek to surprise, to shine, to dazzle. Sisters, do you think it pleases me when, in order to establish a new music, no tone is allowed to produce its effect but is instead used to paint and poeticize? This is so alien to my art that it is as if someone had the idea of inventing a color clavichord and was puzzled that this sport for children did not provide as much pleasure as the real pianoforte. However, the true effects of my art have certainly not died out on earth completely. Among all peoples, even among the Turks and barbarians, music lives on, and in music each nation enjoys what it is given to enjoy, depending on how far and in which direction its organ has developed. The more refined peoples require a more refined fare; among them, therefore, my effects express themselves more spiritually, and they would think it an unfortunate consequence of my art if it ever caused a person to lose his reason or sink into the lap of a Lais or set Persepolis ablaze. The ultimate ends and pleasures toward which I work are finer, but do not think that I must therefore also act more feebly or uncertainly. How often has the tone of a song, the simple passage of a few heavenly notes lifted a man from the deepest abyss of sorrow into heaven! How often it happens that a simple melody occasions tender, melancholy tears, that a melody suddenly transports people back to the old sentiments and haunts of their youth or to the unfamiliar pastures of a blissful paradise, and equals the enchanted tones of the first age, only in a more refined manner. Certainly, my sisters, a virtuoso of my art can induce a person to experience the most wonderful things, as soon as he studies only the tones that arouse this person most, namely, the passages of the melody, which moves his entire system of sensation. Were he then to keep strictly to melody and seek its greatest effect, he would have the hearts of men in his power, even were they made of steel and iron."

"And could one not reproduce this ancient and *great* effect, dear sister, if your art were joined more closely to mine?" asked Poetry. "I sketch out feelings for you; you may only follow and keep to these."

Music smiled and said: "That would be good; it is also occasionally necessary but hardly sufficient. How often do your poets lead me astray instead of guiding me? Indeed, perhaps they have done most to corrupt my art among men. Moreover, remember, sister, what you yourself said: the musician creates out of himself; each time he must form anew the language of his sensations. If he cannot now do this, if he does not feel the sensations that after all the poet only designates, only imperfectly describes, how shall he then express them? How could the poet impart them to him with words? To impart tones to someone with words, and especially a tonal edifice of sensations that he does not have within him, is impossible; therefore the blame lies with the abuse of music itself and must be rectified from within. Incidentally, we are agreed, sister, that we two, Poetry and Music, belong together, and also produce the greatest effect when we work in concert; however, I would not admit to being merely your handmaiden, for I have been your teacher and possess my own sphere of action. I am served by dance as well as words, gestures and movements as well as your verses; and in reality my essence incorporates all of this: modulation, dance, rhythm. The musician writes poetry when he plays, just like the true poet sings when he composes poetry."

During this discourse time hung heavy with Painting as well as with Father Apollo. For a while the former had been engrossed in sketching a beautiful, tranquil landscape and had forgotten all about the argument. "That," she said, "is the greatest effect of my art: it disposes the soul to peace and serenity. A person who loves painting enjoys every ray of sunshine with good cheer; where others see nothing, he sees the ray's thousandfold play. Everywhere in the lap of Nature he studies her most tranquil and congenial effects and enjoys them without end."

"That may be true of nature and landscape artists," replied Poetry, "but I hear that among your historical painters you also have passionate men such as Music and I scarcely possess. We are reproached for often gifting our favorites with whims instead of enthusiasm; and I believe that if one desires to study and express passions one must indeed feel this passion oneself."

Here Apollo cut Poetry short and gave her to understand that this was all beside the point and if she would pardon him for saying so, in part untrue. "To depict a man raging," he said, "one need not rage oneself; to write of a man raving, one need not rave oneself. Precisely this is the prerogative of heaven-born art: it knows, by virtue of a kind of omniscience and secret presentiment, even the nooks and crannies of the human heart which the artist need not have felt himself but now sees through the light of his Muse and shows others as if by reflecting these rays. Believe me, the drunk is not the finest singer of drunkenness; the poet who depicts every passion, who often depicts them at the same time in the sharpest contrast, cannot indeed possess them all as his personal property; it is enough if, like a placid mirror, he faithfully takes them in and then reflects them. It is the same with painting and music. The greatest artists of every description have always been the most dispassionate and serene characters; they were youths as I am and lived in the splendor of my sun. But see to it that this quarrel is brought to a close."

"You, Painting, produce with your art the brightest, most beautiful, clearest, most enduring representation; through your forms you speak to the fancy and through the fancy to the understanding and to the heart; you refine the gaze, open the gates of Creation, and impart calmness and serenity to your favorites. Are you satisfied? You, Music, however, possess the magic wand of real and direct influence on the human heart; you stir the feelings and passions, though in an obscure manner, and require a guide, an elucidator, who will at least enable you to have a more determinate effect on man's understanding and delight not only his physical but also his moral sense. Are you also satisfied? You both quarrel over the word "effect," which, according to linguistic usage, pertains more to music than to painting, because with the notion of effect we are accustomed only to looking at the intensity of the impression without considering that in the affairs of the intellect and human soul, this quality is occasionally compensated with extent, clarity, and duration. Hence you always argue about whether the ear ought to be the eye and the eye the ear. Calm yourselves. The more different the ways in which you operate, the more characteristically and better you do so. You move one and the same human soul, though in a quite incommensurable manner. If you desire to see the effects of your art at their purest and without descending into a dispute over words, then observe a blind man and a deaf man, and consider what both lack. The deaf man's sight and discernment may be infinitely more refined, but to society he is always dumb and inwardly a man without joy; he lacks the sense and the art that speak directly to his heart. The blind man is a poor man; perhaps he is also wanting certain fine distinctions, forms, and dimensions, which are granted only by the sense and art of sight. Nevertheless, he has the string music of all sensations and passions within him; he can let it ring out when it pleases him and in his dark solitude create for himself a world full of harmony and joys. Blind men were often great musicians and great poets; but has the deaf man, no matter how exact his imitation, ever been as brilliant a draftsman? You will know the answer to that question yourselves. It is enough that you are both my daughters: you, Painting, the draftswoman for the understanding, and you, Music, the speaker to the heart; and you, my dear, youthful Poetry, the pupil and teacher of both."

They embraced one another. Apollo crowned them with his immortal laurels, and for their lengthy discussion Hebe offered them a goblet of refreshing nectar.

On Image, Poetry, and Fable

MAN IS SUCH A COMPLEX, artificial being that despite every effort he can never achieve a wholly simple state. At the very moment that he sees, he also hears and unconsciously enjoys, through all the organs of his manifold machine, external influences that remain largely obscure sensations but nevertheless secretly cooperate on the sum of his whole condition at all times. He floats in a sea of impressions of objects, in which one wave laps against him softly, another more perceptibly, but where sundry changes in the outside world excite his inner being. In this respect also he is a *microcosm*, just as Protagoras, in another context, called him the *measure of all things*.

Of his senses, *sight* and *hearing* are the ones that most intimately and clearly bring before his soul objects drawn from the ocean of obscure sensations; and since he possesses the art of retaining and denominating these objects by means of words, a world of human perceptions and ideas, especially those drawn from sight and hearing, has taken shape in his language, a world that reveals traces of its origin even in the most distant derivation. For this reason, even the most refined operations of the soul have been given names native to sight and hearing, as is shown by the terms *intuitions* and *ideas*, *fancies* and *images*, *representations* and *objects*, and a hundred others besides. After the eye, it is the ear and then the sense of touch, especially the feeling hand, that have furnished the soul with the most ideas; taste and smell have contributed fewer, especially in the northern regions of the world.

For all the objections raised against the name *aesthetics* as the *philosophy of the beautiful*, we must not allow it to perish now, for already a host of the most excellent observations is associated with this term, especially from the philosophers of our nation. Nor is it an inappropriate appellation, if we take it to mean a *philosophy of sensuous feelings*, of which the *philosophy of the agreeable*, of *the sensuously perfect and beautiful*, is indeed a part but certainly not the basest part. Every sensation, like every object of the same, possesses, its own rules of perfection, which the philosopher must seek out in order to find the point of its utmost efficacy and from it derive the rules of art. To this end, he must of necessity compare the sensations belonging to more than one sense, observe what is original and derivative in each, and above all be alert to how one sense supports, corrects, and enlightens the others. Is there a better name for this beautiful branch of philosophy than *aesthetics*? For this name perfectly describes both the scope of its objects and the subject of their effect. A philosophy of *taste*, of the *beautiful*, and so on, that started from but a single sense would necessarily deliver only incomplete fragments to a philosophy concerned with the totality of sensations.

So if sight is the richest, finest, and clearest sense to furnish the soul with a world of sensations and to designate them, then it is above all with vision that the philosophy of sensuous objects must practice before turning to the study of the other senses. In mathematics, optics has not only developed into an independent discipline but was able to become the basis of almost every other science, precisely because Nature presented us, in the structure of the eye and the laws of light, with the most beautiful model of fine exactitude. For the philosophy of sensations a *theory of light and of the image* is of equally manifold utility as soon as we strive to look for that theory in the appearances of various works of art and raise it to the most general rules.

I. On Image

1. I call *image* every representation of an object that is associated with some degree of consciousness of the perception. If it lies before my eye, then it is a bodily, visible image. If it is represented to my imagination, then it is a *fancy* (φαντασμα), which nevertheless borrows its laws from visible objects. In the first instance I am awake, in the second I am dreaming; and we see that man's fancy continues to dream without interruption even while he is in a wakeful state.

All the objects of our senses become ours only to the extent that we *become aware* of them; that is, we designate them, in a more or less clear and vivid fashion, with the stamp *of our consciousness*. In the forest of sensible objects that surrounds me, I find my way to becoming master of the chaos of the sensations assailing me only by separating objects from others, by giving them outline, dimensions, and form; in short, by creating unity in diversity and vividly and confidently designating these objects with the stamp of my *inner sense*, as if this were a seal of truth. Our whole life, then, is to a certain extent *poetics*: we do not see images but rather create them. The Divinity has sketched them for us on a great panel of light, from which we trace their outlines and paint the images in the soul using a finer brush than that of the rays of light. For the image that is projected on the retina of your eye is not the idea that you derive from its object; it is merely a product of your inner sense, a work of art created by your soul's faculty of perception.

2. Hence it follows *that our soul, like our language, allegorizes constantly*. When the soul sees objects as images, or rather when it transforms them into mental images, according to rules that are imprinted on it, what is it doing but translating, *metaschematizing*? And if the soul now strives to illuminate these mental images—which are its work alone—through words, through signs for the sense of hearing, and thereby to express them to others, what is it doing once again but translating, *alloisizing*? The object has so little in common with the image, the image with the thought, the thought with the expression, the visual perception with the name, that they, as it were, touch one another only by virtue of the sensibility of our complex organization, which perceives *several things* through several senses *at the same time*. Only the *communicability* among our several senses and the *harmony prevailing between them*, whereupon this communication rests—only this constitutes the inner form or the so-called perfectibility of man. If we had but one sense and were connected with Creation only by a single aspect of the world, as it were, there would be no possibility of converting objects into images and images into words or other signs. Then we should have to bid farewell to human reason! If a being's power of intuition were multiplied tenfold but remained merely one-sided and unsupported by any other senses, he would be a far more imperfect creature than he is now, when he can convert his meager wealth so frequently and in doing so must always make the effort to adapt it anew, to give it fresh form. This wealth passes through the gates of a different sense and is given a different stamp, in keeping with the different customs prevalent there and the different use to which it is put.

3. Notwithstanding the various names we use to denote the faculties of cognition that deal with images and their expression, all these faculties are subject to *the same laws governing the perfection of an image*: namely, *truth*, *vividness*, and *clarity*. Though every sense and every faculty of cognition has its own character and possesses the aforementioned qualities to a different degree; though one sense can and must limit the others, and the particular purposes to which the presentation of each image is put must also each time alter its point of view, and hence its entire design also, the internal rules of its perfection always remain the same. If our organization and the harmonious attunement of the faculties of the soul made it possible for truth, vividness, and clarity to combine in a single object to the same degree, why should they not be permitted to combine in the same way with one another? In God the highest truth, vividness, and clarity coexist without one of these qualities weakening the others, without Him needing to feel ashamed of any one of them. It is therefore only beggar's pride when the so-called *higher* faculties of the soul are embarrassed by their sisters, whom they contemptuously call *lower*, thinking them not their true siblings but rather their serving girls. Human cognition starts

from the senses and from experience, and everything comes back to them; without limbs and organs, without fancy and memory, the understanding has nothing with which it can occupy itself, reason has nothing whereupon it can reflect, the power of symbolic thought has nothing that it might express through signs. The very truth and vividness of the images therefore contribute to their clarity and distinctness, so that without them all abstraction would be mere illusion. The supreme law of perfection in all arts and sciences must hence be: that in conformity with the purpose of the representation, one quality cannot impair another; for example, clarity impair vividness, vividness impair truth; but rather, each must come to the other's aid and encourage it to realize its goal.

4. Hence we see that the modeler here is really only man's inner sense, which, through the eye and every other organ, creates forms according to internal rules and, as far as it is able, communicates the findings of one particular sense to the others. We also see that this *inner* sense—that is, *the rule of the understanding and consciousness—can be the only yardstick* by which to measure how, in every work in every system of art or of discourse, *an image may be positioned, adjusted, and finished*; in brief, *what degree of truth, vividness, and clarity may be attained by every feature*. General mechanical laws are of no help here, for, as I have said, what we see in external objects does not lie merely in the things themselves but is primarily dependent on the organ that perceives them and the inner sense that becomes conscious of them. The fly sees a different world from that seen by the snail; the fish a different world from that seen by man; and yet they all see one and the same Creation according to the same rules of truth, vividness, and clarity. Discrepancies of this kind are caused by every change in point of view and intensity of light and from time to time by every alteration in the disposition of our body and soul. Nevertheless, the rules governing the representation and the sensation remain the same; indeed, every such instance of change confirms their inner truth. It is therefore foolish to prescribe to the soul how it should make use of some image of Nature; following the internal rules of the understanding and consciousness, the soul must learn to use an image in the manner demanded by this particular work of art, for this particular purpose, at this particular time, in this particular place, according to this particular type of feeling characteristic of the artist and the connoisseur.

Let us take, for example, one and the same allegory, one and the same simile, and apply it in a book treating mathematics and philosophy, in a speech, in a didactic poem, in a song, in an ode, in an epic poem, in a tragedy or a comedy, or whatnot. Does not our inner sense tell us that the image cannot be realized in the same way in these different contexts? An allegory in a drinking song or in one of Plato's philosophical dialogues, in

Aeschylus's choruses or in Aristophanes' sketches, in a statue by Lysippus or in a painting by Apelles will be quite a different matter, even if the same object were depicted in each instance. If we now pursue this variety through all the situations represented by the poem and work of art, through all the passions of the poet and artist, through every change in the national mentality, in the times, in the language, in all the circumstances that determine such productions, and so on, then I do not see what general rules would remain that were applicable to each particular case save those that are given, by an inner necessity, in *the concept of allegory itself and in the nature of the image-making understanding*, namely *truth, vividness, clarity*. Every meter even, every note of a song shades the images of the fancy in its own characteristic way; a picture will seldom allow itself to be wholly translated into another unless animated by a new spirit and re-created, as it were. So things look bad for slavish imitation, every learned theft of allegories and images not one's own, and, finally, for those poetic anthologies and storehouses in which foreign scraps are collected for future use. An unhappy training for the young, who become accustomed to such a mercenary way with images! Let them learn to love, esteem, and admire every beautiful image, every apt simile in its proper place, without even a thought of purloining a single feature of the same to cover their privy parts. The truer and more perfect the image appears to them there and then, the less will they wish to lay their thieving hands on it; instead, they will burn with a desire to draft an image themselves, one equally natural and based on the perceptions of their own sense.

5. So there is no justification in the complaint *that the storehouse of Nature is exhausted* and that we were born too late to depict the lion or the sun better than they have often been described before. To speak of depicting better is beside the point here, for in every age truth has been the same. But that every perceiving person can depict an object *distinctively*, as if it had never before been depicted, it seems to me, no doubter can deny. Homer cannot be surpassed in any of his similes; but no one should wish to surpass him and describe Homer's lions and asses, cranes and flies, better than he has done. If you must include these images in your discourse or poetry, then depict them after your own manner, as you perceived them, as the spirit of your poetry demands. Do so, and you will never find yourself in embarrassment and forced to pilfer one of the ancient poet's similes; indeed, you would scarcely be able to use them unchanged, even had they all been gifted to you. The spirit poeticizes; the inner sense creates images. It creates new images for itself, even though the objects themselves might have been seen and sung a thousand times before, for it sees them with its own eyes, and the more it remains true to itself, the more original will its compositions and descriptions be.

That is also why retouching foreign works is always a difficult task. Let us assume that you add a beautiful feature to another painter's image, that you add a new and apt meaning to the allegory, but in doing so you destroyed the peculiar harmony of the picture as a whole. Was it worth forfeiting the charm of the entire work for the sake of the dazzling streak of color that you smeared over it? The material properties of the image are never really of concern here; what always matters, however, is the creative spirit that invented the whole and that still preserves and animates it.

6. So *no general laws concerning the degree of vividness in the images can properly be inferred* here either. Every work of art has its own tone, its sustained melody, in which nothing must be too shrill or fall silent; a waxing or waning sensation determines this modulation from beginning to end. The same goes for the labors of every poet, writer, and artist; he breathes his genius into the work so that *his* tone rings out. Nowhere is the vividness of the images in conflict with either their truth or their clarity; if it is the right kind of vividness, then it must be supported by the former and in turn promote the latter. Even the so-called confusion of the ode is a confusion governed by rules; that is, a higher order.

Since in the nature of things none of our senses works for itself alone, and we remain an Aeolian harp, stirred by all manner of breezes and elements, *so the vividness of the representation is due precisely to the diversity of that which we felt all at once when we took pleasure in an object.* Our inner poetic sense is able to bind together the manifold features of the sensation so faithfully and accurately that in its artificial world we feel once more the whole living world, for it is precisely the minor details—which the frigid understanding might not have noticed and which the even more frigid vulgar understanding omits as superfluous—that are the truest lineaments of the peculiar feeling and that precisely because of this truth, therefore, possess the most decided efficacy. The so-called redundancy of Homer's similes is the very thing that brings them to life in the first place; he sets them in motion, and so the living creature must of necessity stir its limbs. If these limbs were severed, the lifeless trunk could neither stand nor walk.

Anything further that I might have to say on this topic I shall save for an analysis of the *allegory,* inasmuch as the allegory is used by the *philosopher,* the *poet,* and the *artist,* each adapting it to different ends in different kinds of work. Here it shall suffice to call attention to the unassailable axiom that the whole world would be a dead mass to a creature incapable of feeling; a chaos of colors to a confused spirit; and for a flat vessel an equally flat tableau, devoid of inner certainty and truth. However, the more accurately we perceive truth and the more vividly and deeply we feel it, then the more we depict truth regardless of whether we observe it in pictures or in sensations and musical tones. All these things flow together and are ultimately determined by the object that the picture of Nature represents, by the standpoint from which one sees it, by the organ or tone of the sensation with which one drafts and perceives it. We shall discuss this when we consider more closely the most beautiful picture of human language, *lyric poetry*, and in particular the *ode*.

II. On Poetry

Let us now continue on our way and observe how *poetry* arises from the perceived image. And the transition to this topic lies already in our hands. If, namely, what we call image resides not in the object itself but in our soul, in the nature of our organ and inner sense, which forever creates unity from diversity, and hence, whether consciously or unconsciously, dreams and poeticizes without end, then we need attend only to the *inner form* and *singularity*, or, as it were, the *disposition of the image-making faculty of our soul*, and the nature and favored manner of all human poetry will come to light. We *compose poetry* out of nothing but what we feel within us; just as with individual images we transfer *our sense*, so with whole series of images we project *our manner of feeling and thinking* onto external objects. If this stamp of analogy becomes art, we call it *poetry*. We shall distinguish three main features belonging to this disposition of our sensibility; the remainder will follow quite naturally from these.

1. We see everything in the world produce an effect, and we rightly infer *that an operative force, and consequently a subject, lies behind it*; and since we are persons ourselves, we attribute the efficacy of all natural forces to *personal beings*. Hence the belief that all of Nature is animate, hence those conversations with the things surrounding us, hence the worship and representation of these things as if they operated on us, those prosopopoeia and personifications that we find among all the peoples of the earth. Personifications are for the most part put down to ignorance; but if ignorance is their mother, then the perceiving faculty of understanding is their father. We know no more about the inner forces of Nature than does a tribe of Negroes. We may be acquainted with the effects of sundry forces; we may have attempted not only to reproduce or to harness them but also to bring better order to bear on these forces; nevertheless, even for us all of physics remains a kind of *poetics* for our senses, arranged on the basis of our experiences. And if our mind were to apprehend Nature with different organs, it would necessarily classify it according to different principles. The sensuous man cannot but order the world sensuously, and when he transfers his agency to the efficacy of nat-

ural forces, it seems to him that gods inhabit every element. In the roaring waterfall, in the sea, in the storm, in the thunder and lightning, in the whispering wind, in all the motions of Nature, there are living, operative, acting beings. We know from travel accounts that this belief is common to all sensuous nations; indeed, how could it be otherwise, since we also find it widespread among our own sensuous people, children, women, those in the grip of passion, of ecstasy, those sunk in reverie, or even whenever they are not on their guard? Fear—especially fear of the dark—sorrow, love, yearning, despair, and every other passion—turn every one of us unexpectedly into savages, for whom now this object, now that object seems to be alive and affecting us through strange impressions. During our childhood we perceive the world in this way for many years, and such personifications from our childhood revisit us in our dreams. *Our state of cool reflection is an artificial state, one that is gradually achieved through experience, instruction, and habit* and that we find difficult to maintain when we are confronted with wholly unforeseen situations.

That every nation on the earth fashions these personifications after its own manner requires no proof; every travel account, every mythology is full of such things, and I wish we possessed a *nympheum* of these fancies of our race, collected without adornment and arranged according to climate. It would be the *history of a rational madness*, in which, as Polonius says of Hamlet, there is everywhere *method*; a very diverse anthology, a specimen of the wealth and poverty of human invention.

2. As obvious as it may seem to man that anything that has the power of producing an effect is a person, he cannot conceive any other mode of operation save that which lies in his own nature: *activity* and *passivity*, *giving* and *receiving*, *love* and *hate*, and ultimately nothing but the *two sexes* into which Nature has divided its most animate beings. We see these same categories among humans, among animals, indeed, even among plants and trees; why should they stop here and not also obtain among the higher elemental beings, among the forces of Nature themselves, for after all does not everything in Creation give or take, act or suffer action, hate or love? And in this way heaven was filled with gods and goddesses, and the elements with spirits, all of which flee or attract, sustain or destroy one another. Nature became a battleground of all manner of reciprocal forces either constraining or assisting one another; and what else is she, indeed? Even the philosophy of natural history must order the world in terms of affinities, resemblances, and the two sexes; it can do nothing else. So this offshoot of poetry, too, is given to us in the analogy of Nature; the human mind observed, and the fancy completed the picture. From here immediately flowed another fountain of poetry, namely:

3. *The productions and offspring of all natural phenomena, their al-*

ternating state of life and death. New beings were seen to issue from the unifying power of love, and other forms vanish in depredatory struggles. What, then, was more natural than those theogonies, cosmogonies, and genealogies of emerging and disappearing natural forms, with which all mythologies of the world abound?

These are the three simple ideas from which all poetry of the human spirit has been spun; indeed, I doubt whether there is a fourth. They are

1. *the personification of operative forces;*
2. *love and hate, giving and receiving, activity and rest, union and separation;* in brief, *the two sexes;* and
3. *from the union of two entities the birth of a third; in the conflict between two beings the destruction of one of them.* In this way becoming could be explained through being, death through life.

The oldest mythology and poetics is therefore a *philosophy about the laws of Nature,* an attempt to explain the vicissitudes of the universe in its becoming, persistence, and destruction. This is the role it played among the dullest Negroes and among the cleverest Greeks; beyond this, the human mind cannot, may not, and has no wish to invent. For what could *invention* otherwise mean? Perhaps to lie *ex professo,* like Satan? I fail to comprehend this word when it is used with respect to a human soul, except insofar as it might combine complete absurdities and thereby itself become absurd. Man invents only out of poverty, because he is lacking; he imagines and poeticizes because he does not know. And even then the imaginings of his poetry are really nothing but *sensuous intuition,* designated by his inner sense with the *stamp of analogy.* In real and absolute terms, the human being can neither poeticize nor invent, for otherwise in doing so he would become the creator of another world. What he can do is conjoin images and ideas, designate them with the stamp of *analogy,* thus leaving his own mark on them. This he can and may do. For everything that we call image in Nature becomes such only through the reception and operation of his perceiving, separating, composing, and designating soul.

It is self-evident that for as long as this poetry was for a nation merely *saga,* oral tradition, it remained in some respects unminted gold and in others was quickly bound to become counterfeit. It had to become counterfeit because almost every sayer added to or subtracted from it, even without his knowing and intending to. A few clear, bold, and lively spirits had invented the saga and recounted it; feebler minds understood half of it or nothing at all, but nevertheless they passed it on. In this way the sagas ultimately lost their meaning, and images lost sense and significance. Over the generations historical details found their way into the tale and were bound to, precisely because it was a family saga, a tradition of childhood. No mythology in the world has thus been able to preserve its purity, or it would not have been mythology. Fancies about Nature and the affairs of the race, of the nation, of life, were woven together; and the former were no more pure physics than the latter were pure history. In neither case, however, did the human spirit mean deliberately to invent or to lie; it watched and took note; it expressed itself, as well as it was able, in a language unconnected to the object, an imperfect, symbolic language, and, what was even more difficult, it *told a story*. The saga was passed on from child to child, and the poetic fictions [*Dichtungen*] based on it expanded like a snowball, with good and bad rolled into one. Thus did the saga continue on its way as a daughter of memory, until it became *art*, and this art was called *poetry* [*Dichtkunst*]. The unrefined gold was minted, and the saga itself gave rise to this artistry.

Every storyteller wants to tell his story well and since he makes the wiser teacher, he also wishes to impress his lesson on the mind agreeably, lastingly, vividly; in brief, in the most perfect way. And with that the art of poetry was born. One storyteller invented new, stronger, more vivid, and lovely images and words for the ideas he had inherited or acquired; another devised more exact meters and delightful tones for his words. The language of signs and gestures brought the accent, the modulation of dance brought exquisite rhythms into speech, and suddenly poetic art had come into being, almost without anyone's knowing who was responsible. Every nation that did not bring the art of poetry with it from its ancestral home invented its own; and image, saga, and poetry assumed a new, more beautiful guise with each new form. Mythology has thus remained a crude chaos among every people who has not refined it through hymns and songs, through performance, art, dance, and finally through the written word, as, for instance, most Negro tribes and many American nations show. But as soon as the Peruvian introduced his rain goddess and her brother, the god of thunder, into a song, his poetry took shape. The crude dross of the old saga was thrown away, and this image and that allegory were wound more finely, arranged more carefully through every hymn, through every new meter of the song, every new system of an epic tale, of a dramatic performance, and finally even of a moral and philosophical application. In brief, depending on whether a people was poetic or unpoetic, its mythology and speculation grew polished or remained coarse, as is demonstrated by the great marketplace of nations at every stage of their culture.

We would digress too far if after adducing the origin of poetic art we then embarked on an inquiry into the evolution of every genre of poetry. In our textbooks these genres are classified not according to philosophical principles but rather to historical ones. They have followed history, observing how, here and there, particularly among the Greeks and Romans, one genre or another was designated with a particular name so that in keeping with the purpose of a textbook, rules could be deduced from their examples or rules demonstrated by examples. I do not doubt, therefore, that beyond these genres and appellations, others might be possible and indeed actually exist, if, namely, one were to distinguish them philosophically, for the Greeks and Romans have not exhausted the realm of poetry. Conversely, some of these categories can be brought together under one genre, and perhaps all of them might be comprehended under three or four terms: *epic, lyric, dramatic*, and *simple didactic* poetry. Epic poetry recounts the saga of an action, of an event or history, whether performed by gods or heroes, men or animals, citizens or shepherds. Dramatic poetry represents this action as real, whether sad or joyful, innocent or vicious, as if it were taking place directly before us. Lyric poetry sings, whether of joy or sorrow, hatred or love, whether the lesson is meant for oneself or for others; it suffices to say that it modulates a single feeling. If this modulation is absent and what remains is merely a precept adorned with poetic ornament, then we have dogmatic poetry, which nevertheless always has a share in one or more of the foregoing genres and from which it would need to borrow its embellishments if it were to be worthy of its name. Let us leave these categories of poetry as they are for the time being in order to devote more careful consideration to one of them, one that is closely related to the oldest sagas and poetry: the so-called *Aesopian fable*. We are all familiar with this through common concepts and examples; therefore we must not begin with a definition but rather seek the latter out by investigating the origin of the genre as a whole, for here, too, the genesis of the thing reveals its essence.

III. On the Aesopian Fable

If it is a characteristic, unceasing occupation of the human soul to create images, to separate them from the chaos of natural forms, to observe their mode of operation, and to designate them with a name furnished by the intuiting sense, then it was only a matter of time before the Aesopian fable was born. Man sees only as a human being can; he transfers the sensations and passions in his breast to other creatures, and hence also the intentions and actions typical of his manner of thinking and acting; he sees everything in terms of his own person, according to his measure. This we called *poetry*; and if he now ranges and orders these intuitions in such a way that he recognizes in them a principle founded on experience or a practical lesson and isolates it, then we have the Aesopian fable. Regardless of whether the beings acting in the fable are gods, animals, trees, or men, the main thing is that the intuitive faculty of the soul can imagine them as actors and the power of abstraction deduce from their conduct a lesson applicable to human life. Consequently, the Aesopian fable is nothing but *moralized poetry*.

This position allows us at once to extricate the theory of the fable from the tangle of questions and contradictions in which, perhaps unnecessarily, it has become ensnared. For example:

1. *Why do animals act in the fable? Because they thereby arouse wonder, or because of the constancy of their characters?*

Animals act in the fable because *it seems to sensuous man that everything efficient in Nature acts*; and what beings with the power to produce an effect could be closer to us than animals? A child never doubts that the living creatures with which he associates are in a certain measure his equals and thus they desire, will, and act in the same way that he does. Even when he torments them, he does not think them lifeless Cartesian machines. It is the same with all sensuous peoples. The Arab talks with his horse, the shepherd with his sheep, the hunter with his hound, the Negro with his serpent, the wretched prisoner with the spider and mouse that share his cell. The more man becomes acquainted with a species of animal and converses familiarly with it, the more both grow accustomed to each other and impart to each other their respective qualities. He believes he can understand them and fancies that they also understand him; so the basis of even the boldest Aesopian fable is, according to this fancy of men, given almost as experience, as *historical truth*. To be sure, the various species of animals are very dissimilar in their abilities; they seem to us ever more inscrutable and incomprehensible the less they resemble us or the more distantly they live from us. But metaphysics, that prideful ignoramus, ought to give up the arrogant delusion that the humblest animal is *wholly* unlike man in its activities and aptitudes, for this notion has been amply disproven by natural history. In their whole *disposition of life* animals are organizations just like man is; they merely lack human organization and the prodigious instrument of our abstract, symbolic memories: speech.

Thus talking animals are not really an arbitrary contrivance to arouse wonder[1] but an ancient belief rooted in the delusions of sensuous man, which, strengthened by the authority of the saga, was passed down from the oldest times. No one objected if every animal spoke, as long as it could do so in a manner in keeping with its character and known habits of life. And to the wiseacre, who had his doubts, one needed simply to say: "Once upon a time! There once was a time when animals could talk, when the fox and the snake, too, could talk; now they speak to you only in fictitious fairy tales." Such doubts did not occur to the child or the in-

---

[1] This is the view of *Breitinger* in his instructive *Critical Poetry*, section 7.

tuitive and sensuous man, and all the less the more familiar he was with them and the more he could observe their manners with his own eyes. And it was for children and the common folk that the fable was actually intended.

So if we cannot say that the animal fable was invented merely to arouse *wonder*, might it have been contrived because of the *universally known constancy of animal characters*?[2] I do not think this is the whole answer, either, for the constancy of animal characters was surely one, but not the only, quality that man observed in the animal kingdom and from which he endeavored to draw lessons from the fable.

He found many other attributes of the animal character instructive, for indeed the whole *disposition* of animals, though each species after its own fashion, was very similar to man's mode of life, particularly in his primitive state, and therefore also accessible to human intuition. This similarity, this thorough *analogon rationis humanae*, which even the most stubborn philosopher is obliged to concede, suggested itself to man, and so Nature herself marked out the lineaments of fabular poetry for her intuitive child. Whether we call it truth or probability, this *analogical truth*, with its attendant *vividness* and *clarity*, was the first cause of the fable, for in just this way it acquired all three qualities that an image or an allegory must have to recommend itself to the human soul. To this truth, vividness, and clarity was now added the *constancy* of animal characters, as well as their *diversity*, and consequently the *wealth*, the alternating *novelty*, the *unexpectedness of the instruction*, the most intuitive *simplicity*—indeed, everything else for which we are apt to celebrate the animal fable; yet most of these might be traced back to *intuitive similarity*. The Aesopian fable stood, as it were, on the border between poetry and morality. It flew through all the spaces of Nature, indeed through a "they say" back to primeval times, and drew forth the sap of a lesson from everything that had once been the intuition of the senses. We must never, I believe, remove the fable from its seat, for it was not invented by abstract philosophers for abstract philosophers. Hence the second question will readily answer itself also.

2. *How must animals act in the fable? As animals or as men?*

I would say *as animals but like men*. The intuitive truth and sensuous conviction rests indeed on the very idea that the fox talks and acts as a fox, the lion talks and acts as a lion. If I break through these limits of intuition and elevate the character of the animals so far beyond their usual sphere that the illusion vanishes, then, as Lessing so astutely remarks, the witty ass will become the moralist, and the fabulist, who metamorphosed him

---

[2] This is the view of Lessing in his *Treatises on the Fable*; see pp. 181f.

so preposterously, the ass. The following claim must therefore necessarily admit of qualification:[3] "That once we concede freedom and speech to animals, we must at the same time concede to them *all* modifications of the will and *all* knowledge that follows from those qualities on which our superiority over them solely rests." For this statement could do nothing but rob a fable elevated in such a way of all sensuous intuition and felt truth. If everywhere it is man in disguise, the clever and witty moralist who speaks in the semblance of an animal, then this masquerade may amuse, it is true, and there may well be many good things to learn and hear, but the Aesopian fable as such is thereby destroyed. In the Aesopian fable every animal speaks precisely only in *its* sphere, in keeping with *its* character;[4] not as a man, but like man. The human soul is, as it were, dispersed among all the animal characters, and the fable seeks only here and there to fashion this scattered reason into a whole. Its sweetest charm is precisely this faithful simplicity, this authenticity based on minor details drawn from Nature and the entire sphere of animal life. The more accurately the ass talks—so that, if its mouth were opened, like that of Balaam's ass, it could speak in no other way—then the more truthful and more delightful is the fable. Hence that inimitable charm possessed by so many ancient fables from the Orient, from Greece, and from every other nation that lived closer to the animals than we do. They grasped the *disposition* of the animals through sensuous intuition and could not help, as it were, but poeticize in their sphere. As crude as the lesson sometimes is that they have the creature express, the more powerfully does it penetrate to our heart, as if the spirit of Nature herself were speaking through this being. The more refined fable, where the animal reasons like a philosopher, may be intended for us more refined men, whose palate must be tickled by stronger spices if it shall acquire a taste for this milk diet; but simpler nations would have difficulty in recognizing their old Aesop in a host of fabulists of this ilk and would often wonder why the masks of animals were needed to present these unbestial, polished maxims.

3. *How far does the territory of the fable extend both within and beyond the animal kingdom?*

In my view, as far *as the fabulist dares to give his fictitious action truth, vividness, and clarity; in short, to render his intended lesson intuitively clear.* The borders cannot be drawn more broadly in this respect. To a nation that lives among trees, those trees will speak; it does not find offen-

---

[3] Lessing, *Treatises*, pp. 208, 209f.

[4] Through this determination, Lessing qualifies the claim he has just made; see pp. 208, 209. In Bodmer's examination of Lessing's theory, this qualification has been omitted (p. 201).

sive the idea that one tree should desire to be king before another, for how different is the prestige, the use, and the rank of different trees to the sensuous human being! A nation such as this is not astonished to hear one tree demanding the daughter of another for his bride, for it knows the families of trees and has itself ennobled trees by engrafting. Its language is fashioned in such a way that expressions of this kind—for example, the daughter of the tree, the king of the trees—are not the least bit striking because they have long been used in other poetic fictions, and more boldly. Thus Jotham recounted a bold fable about trees,[5] and Jehoash had a messenger deliver one to the petitioning king,[6] and in neither case did the audience find the fable's meaning strange. In just the same way, mountains, rivers, springs, the sun and moon, stars, the wind, and the clouds are thought by all sensuous peoples to be ensouled, and therefore it does not lie outside the sphere of their intuition when spirits of the mountains, of the streams, of springs, of stars, of wind and the clouds speak to and act in conflict with one another. As we can see, everything depends here on the intuitive sense of the author, on the manner in which he juxtaposes the operative beings and from them invents a world, and, finally, on both the national and individual mentality of the audience to whom he recites his fable. If a fable is written for *readers*, then this is already a twofold art, or a table of the fable, for the purpose of the original invention rested properly on the living situation of the audience who listened and the speaker who addressed them. When Menenius Agrippa delivered his fable about the stomach and the body parts to the assembled people of Rome, he surely did not stop to think whether some members of his audience might entertain philosophical scruples and insist that neither stomach nor hand nor foot possesses the power of speech or is a Roman citizen. He recited his fable, and it met with success: for its meaning was intuitively obvious and convincing to the enraged mob. The same applies to all fabulous creatures, regardless of whether, in the great chain of being, we place them above or below the animal kingdom. If through the intuition that the poet thought to grant me he has not been able to convince me sensuously that these beings are acting, that they are communicating to me a lesson that is necessarily connected with their nature, then I despise the fabulist, no matter if he puts gods or saucepans, intelligent beings or, like Triller, unthinking shirts on the fable's stage. At the very beginning of this treatise I remarked that even with what we call *image* everything depends on the soul that conceives the image; so whoever knows how to build me, in the realm of the fable, a palace fit for habitation from total ruins or ramshackle materials—he is for me the poet and creator of this palace.

[5] Judges 9:7.
[6] 2 Kings 14:9.

Hence I cannot conceal the fact that I think the ingenious authors of the various classifications of the fable into the *mythical* and *hyperphysical*, the *mythical* and *hyperphysical moral*, the *mythical* and *hyperphysical rational*, the *plausible* and *wondrous*, the *wondrous-divine* and *wondrous-bestial*, the *cosmic* and *heterocosmic*, and so on, have labored in vain. The question as to whether the beings who render the action of the fables present to us are gods, men, or animals is neither here nor there for the audience; it is enough if, in the didactic substance of their action, they belong to the *audience's* world, since after all it is to them that the fable is being recounted. Creatures beyond our world we do not know at all, still less a morality outside the circle of humanity. And from which branch of the Linnaean system of Nature the creatures are taken ceases to be of interest to us as soon as we see them fulfill the supreme law of poetry. Even the gods of Aesop are a part of our world, namely the world of the saga, and part of a lesson appropriate and useful to man. The greater or lesser extent to which they are an analogue of our reason alters nothing of the substance of the fable if it remains in keeping with their character.

However, one class of actors merits a more detailed discussion: the *allegorical beings of the fable*. May the *Understanding*, can *Fancy*, *Envy*, *Happiness*, *Fate*, and so forth appear in the fable or not? It seems to me, yes. Let each appear, if it *can* appear, if the poet dares to furnish it with intuitive clarity and agency. If he can do that, then the personified being is a god, a genius, or a demon; if he cannot, then it remains in his poetry but a formless word, an abstraction, a name; as such it is a fault in his work, not because it is allegory but because it is not a being whom he was able to endow with speech and action. So here, too, everything depends on the art of the poet and on the context in which he places his figment. No one reproaches a fabulist if he introduces as actors Death, Sleep, the guardian spirit of man, or a fairy, a nymph, a naiad; it is enough if they were to act in keeping with their character and present themselves in conformity with their reality. For if the ancients ventured to bring gods and Death, or Shakespearean ghosts and shades, to the dramatic stage, why should it not be possible for the fabulist to conjure a spirit or a fictitious abstraction in the far narrower showplace of his poetry and give it such striking intuitiveness that no one can doubt its existence at that very moment? Of course he must be certain of his magical arts, for otherwise every such apparition will be ridiculous, tasteless, or at least ineffectual, particularly if neither Nature nor the saga anticipates, supports, and sustains the illusion that he seeks to cast over us. Beings of this sort cannot appear cautiously enough, and moreover only in the proper place and with decency and dignity; or else they dissolve like soap bubbles; they whistle past our ears like a vacuous torrent of words, and the poet's effort is in vain.

4. *What is it that is made intuitively obvious to us in the fable? Is it a mere rule of thumb or a moral lesson?*

Citing the solitary example of a fable by Holberg, from which it is evident that "no creature is less suited to domestication than a goat," Lessing has demonstrated convincingly enough that not every rule of thumb,[7] not every empty moral lesson is worth the effort of inventing a fable. And what might be the reason for a large portion of the so very insignificant fables with which the world has been inundated unless it was precisely their making this empty goal the very end of their efforts? As soon as I desire to trace every general principle back to a particular case, give it reality in a fictitious or true story, and afterward deduce the principle from that story by means of a simple chymical trick: well, there is nothing simpler but then again nothing more impoverished than the fable.

Therefore, it is commonly said, the fable contains a general *moral* principle.

A general *moral* principle? But when I go through the best fables by the best fabulists, in a fair number of them I do not exactly recognize a *moral* principle, unless the word is taken in a special sense. Often we find the poet really intended to insert only interesting *rules of thumb*, maxims of prudence, and so on, in exceedingly beautiful works of poetry. Moreover, the phrase "*moral* principle" is in itself indeterminate and indistinct. Is it a real moral duty that animals are teaching me? How can I learn such an obligation from an animal, a being that is itself amoral, that acts and must act only in keeping with its character? The fox will ever be a fox, the wolf a wolf, the lion a lion; and I would run the risk of abstracting the most unjust and, for us, the most improper general principles if I were blindly to follow the instinctive conduct of these animals. There would be no act of violence, no cunning, and no bloodthirsty insolence that could not be excused by the example of some animal in a fable, so that precisely from the general *constancy of their character* ultimately nothing but this general principle would follow: "let each man follow his instinct with the consistency of a beast; for the fox must be a fox to the end of its life." That is a moral that would abolish all morality.

"Aesop," says Lessing, "wrote most of his fables to illustrate real incidents. He had therefore to make comprehensible the resemblance between his tale and the actual incident and show that both already give rise to the very same truth, or will certainly do so in the future."[8] If this is true (and the circumstance is as well known as it is undeniable), then it was evidently neither an abstract truth nor a universal moral principle toward

---

[7] Lessing, p. 131.
[8] P. 114.

which the fabulist was working; it was a *particular practical principle*, a *rule of thumb for a specific situation in life* that he wanted to make intuitively obvious in a similar, fictitious situation and applicable to the actual specific incident. And with that we have as clear an answer as possible to our question.

Now, there are those who distinguish between *simple* and *complex* fables; "the former," it is said, "is the kind of fable that contains only a lesson; in addition to this, the latter contains the case in which it applies." But what is a lesson without its application? If I am to comprehend the fable, must I not, when I recognize its abstract principle, immediately picture a particular case in which the principle appears before me again? And once more, what might explain the tediousness and uselessness of many of our books of fables, if not, among other things, those tottering, withered skeletons of general, indefinite, perhaps inapplicable precepts, to acknowledge which the reader would scarcely need to go to the effort of trudging through a fable? The beautiful and engaging quality of the fables of Aesop and other ancient poets springs precisely from the fact that their fable presented a fictitious case that was eminently appropriate to an *actual* case that might be encountered in real life, in which no detail that had not just lent light and life to the actual situation was gratuitous. The fable containing only an abstract lesson lacks this alluring soul; a naked body hangs on the cross, and beneath it the inscription stating its intended meaning. Every teacher who wishes to render a fable of this kind useful in some measure to his pupil must invent for it, as well as he can, a second half, which it is presently wanting, namely the case in which it applies. Otherwise he must crown the child's head with a withered general principle and reap mere husks.

Properly speaking, then, there is no such thing as a simple fable; all fables are composed of the real case to which it should be applied and the fictitious case devised by the fabulist to illustrate the former. That the editors of Aesop's fables often omitted the true and real situation was due to the fact that they either did not know better or were trying to make their task easier. They replaced it with a naked, occasionally even false and distorted, lesson and left it to each reader to determine how best it might be applied; or else they thought they had already concealed the case in which it applied in the lesson itself, as in fact happened on occasion. The older, true fables, however, about whose origin we know a little, were always written down together with this counterpart to their poetic aspect, as is demonstrated by the fables of Jotham and Jehoash, the parable of Nathan, the works of Stesichorus, of Menenius Agrippa, and a great many fables found in the stories and other writings of the Orientals, indeed the whole collection of *Kalila and Dimna*. It is the fault of the editors only that we see the fables of Lockmann and Aesop before us in so abridged a fashion, enthymemes of fabular composition, so to speak; in the same way they also put together the gnomes, the maxims, and the proverbs without their being able to know or say why and wherefore each maxim was originally devised. Derivative fabulists who wrote their works for inclusion in books found this abbreviation very amenable because it spared them the effort of thinking up a case in which a lesson might apply. And why would they have wanted to bother the reader with such a thing, since they wrote to while away the time or to provide moral instruction for an uncertain future? Hence the unbearable tedium when, one after another, we read a number of fables *without application to concrete cases in life*. It is as if a sack full of moral lessons and intuitions had been emptied over our heads, for if only each of these fables appeared in a story in the proper place, it would be indisputably effective. But that is ultimately the fate of *all* anthologies, whether they contain fables, songs, epigrams, maxims, and whatnot: they are scattered leaves, flowers torn from their roots which, wilting, grieve as if on their deathbed. And yet how agreeable it is to read, here and there, a complex fable in Aesop or Phaedrus, Lessing, Hagedorn, Gleim, Gellert, Lichtwer, et al. We feel more satisfied, as it were, and become aware that every fable ought properly to be invented or applied in this way. Lessing in particular is very felicitous in his complex fables.

Far be it from me to banish the simple fable from our modern world of letters or to invite idle minds to append a second half to every work of every master. Nevertheless, no teacher should be ashamed to make this effort with his pupil. Instead of explaining the moral of the story at length and moralizing about it anew,[9] he should insert it in a case to which it applies, and the more this accords with the invented one, the more forceful, vivid, and beautiful the story of the fable will seem to the pupil. Just as Lessing proposed a heuristic use for this kind of poetry in schools with the aim of *cultivating genius* "by now interrupting the narrative, now continuing, now altering this or that circumstance so that another moral may be recognized in it,"[10] and has given some fine examples of this game of invention, so I wish to propose another use for the fable in *cultivating prudence*, which would draw attention to the application of the fable as well as to the invention of similar cases for use in real life. This would involve giving a *straightforward* account of the situation *that the fiction fits* and, more, an exact account that does justice to all the details of the fable. Here not only would the youth learn how to find a general principle in a tale and to abstract a new one from a modified story (the utility of which ex-

---

[9] Unfortunately this is the case with most editions of Aesop intended for children, of whom none reads the so-called moral explanations that lie behind every fable. I do not yet know of a proper *Aesop for Children*.

[10] P. 233.

ercise I do not mean to deny), but he would also grow used to distinguishing the essential from the inessential in the fable itself, to view the whole situation practically, and to exercise the most useful of his faculties of cognition: the *analogical power of invention*. This is indispensable to us in every walk of life. Unceasingly, the soul asks itself in every new situation that it encounters: "Have you been in this situation or a similar one before? Have you observed others in this predicament; if so, how did they behave?" It was to cultivate such practical wisdom that Aesop invented his fables—and not to aid the abstraction of a universal moral truth. He taught men how to orient themselves in life by recalling similar cases, and in his fictions he presented them with cases appropriate to their situation. He left it to them to abstract the meaning of his fables and apply it to their present circumstances. In this way not only did they find a solution to their conundrum, but also their soul grew accustomed to thinking along these lines in other instances, to recollecting similar incidents, and to deriving from them instruction, counsel, and consolation. I know of no more useful way of cultivating the faculties of the human soul than this exercise in *analogical thinking*, whereby one contrives similar cases and describes their similarities in an appropriate manner. Not only is the inherent possibility of a given case thereby made intuitively obvious and the path haphazardly cleared for its application as practical experience, but at the same time we also take the safer course of inventing universal and binding laws for new situations, and in doing so we leave the land of poetry behind and arrive in the realm of certainest truth. In every science the greatest discoveries have always been made by means of *analogies*: a number of similar cases were thought up and experiments made; the results of these experiments were compared, traced back to general concepts, and ultimately to a leading principle; and if this principle was consistent with every one of the posited analogous cases, *then that is how science was invented*. It is the same with the exceptional minds whom we cannot esteem highly enough in everyday life. They know how to help themselves; that is, they have actually experienced similar cases or can invent them with the greatest celerity and hit upon the solution. To cultivate this practical wisdom for science as well as for life is the task of education, and here Aesop's method of instruction provides a good schooling—the elder Aesop's method of instruction, I meant to say; and should you follow it, you would see very well that the point of the fable is not simply to abstract the lesson, that is, to halt midway in your journey, but rather that *you should invent for the whole situation described by the fable, together with its lesson, a congruent case in which it might be applied*. Only then is the whole edifice of the fable complete. From this follows the fifth question.

5. *How must the action of the fable be composed? Is it enough that the whole which it recounts is merely a succession of changes, each of which contributes toward rendering the fable's moral proposition intuitively obvious? Or must the fable's action also be real; that is, a voluntary and intentional transformation of the soul that occurs by choice and intention?*[11]

It is easy to see both whence the difference in these views comes and the only way in which that difference can be abolished. If Aesop and his brethren invented their fables for a situation in real life that demanded *action*, then the fable could not but depict an *analogous action* that gave instruction to the man in despair. Obviously, it was necessary here to imagine a *soul similarly determined with choice and volition*, and in a similar situation. Notwithstanding their simplicity, most fables of the ancients are therefore seldom without a *real action*, since this very quality was supposed to serve as a mirror to a similar determination of the soul. In the interest of brevity, we shall call these *practical fables* or, to retain the classification of Aphthonius, *moral fables*.

Yet it is also undeniable that even among the ancients there are many fables that merely render a *rule of thumb* intuitively obvious. Their function, therefore, is only to invent a situation in which such a rule of thumb is shown in its causes and effects. And what prevents us from calling these fables *theoretical*—or, as Apthonius put it, *rational* or *logical fables*? In these, too, an action takes place, but in a broader sense. More than one acting being can participate in that action, since at bottom it need be nothing more than an *incident*, an *event (événement)* that presents the *rule of thumb* to us clearly and in its entirety.

The modern fabulists have extended the realm of the fable even further. Since they did not compose their work to exemplify situations in real life and therefore wished to make intuitively obvious neither a practical lesson nor an immediate rule of thumb, they were often satisfied with speculation, with an aesthetic judgment, a fine observation, to which they added a few circumstances giving rise to it and finally put these in the mouth of one of the characters in the fable. I have nothing against calling this genre of fable *philosophical* or *conversational* fables; they may contain much that is fine and useful. But even in the fictitious situation, a fine observation of this sort will seldom have been rendered completely intuitable so that it follows by a kind of inner necessity. Here a series of motivating circumstances, often only a succession of ideas, has been assem-

---

[11] The first view is that of Lessing, and the second that of Breitinger, Bodmer, and other theorists.

bled, merely to accommodate the observation. I doubt whether Aristotle would recognize these situations as Aesopian fables, but he certainly would not deny them the name *witty forms of poetry*. Would they lose anything if we were to call them by this name?

Hence it will be easy to judge to what extent one can ascribe *allegory* to the fable or say that a general principle has been *clothed* in its poetry.[12] If every fable is properly a *complex* fable, where for a given case drawn from real life another case, congruent to it, is invented, then this congruence can certainly, in the language of the ancients, be called *allegory*. In both cases the rule of thumb or the practical lesson is intuitable; consequently, one action or event is actually invented as allegory so that it can be applied in place of another. If insignificant rules of thumb are given poetic clothing or foolish fairy tales allegorized into useful lessons, then foolish allegories must doubtless also arise; but the blame for this fault lies with the artisan who chose such poor materials and not with the essence of the art in which he is working. In the same way, the term *clothing* is not actually offensive to the fable; nor does it stand in the way of *intuitive cognition*. Since ancient times men have been fond of saying that Truth, who seldom ventures to show herself naked, prefers to *conceal* herself for greater comfort and the sake of decency. The best fabulists have made this idea their object and were glad when they had procured for the bare exile some dress or other in which she appeared unexpectedly or incognito,[13] and was hence all the more alluring. It was only unskilled hands that rendered Truth wholly unrecognizable in this attire, which cut out this heavy gothic drapery and caused her beautiful limbs to grow crooked under the weight of a thousand folds, of a long train of morals, and of a whole emporium of ornaments. It is impossible for this court dress of Truth, as Gleim calls it, to derogate that diaphanous, modest gown that shows her limbs and her whole figure in the most beautiful proportions. Even the harsher word *disguise* is not inappropriate for a certain class of fables, whose very purpose it was to suspend and conceal the meaning of the fiction for a while, so that at the end of the tale its effect would be all the greater. Often this disguise was so well adapted to its purpose that the poet even had to help his listeners undress it and call to them, as Nathan called out to David:

---

[12] Lessing objected to both, to the *allegory* of fable as well as the *clothing* of the lesson, for which he chose the indisputably more appropriate term *intuition* or *intuitive cognition*. See Lessing, pp. 118–44. In his *Unaesopian Fables* (p. 231), Bodmer rejects Lessing's theory, but few of its arguments seem to me to have been refuted, even where they suggest their own refutation.

[13] See the first fables of Gleim and Lichtwer, among others.

—mutato nomine de te
fabular narratur—

And although I cannot defend this concealment unconditionally, there may yet arise circumstances where it wins more hearts through its illusion than the nakeder truth would ever have won. *Hoc amat obscurum; amat hoc sub luce videri*——

Finally, I am puzzled that the most discerning investigators of the theory of the fable have failed to address what seems to me to be the most substantial question relating to this form of poetry.

6. *Example, comparison, and fable: How do they differ from one another? And on what does the greater power of the fable rest?*

Does not the example also have its own reality, and does it not also represent a rule of thumb or a lesson as intuitively obvious? Is not the comparison also recounted as a real case?

Certainly; and yet the historical example can *bear witness only to the possibility of a thing*, no matter how instructive and encouraging it may otherwise be. But the doubt always remains as to whether among a thousand cases drawn from history the situation then prevailing was identical to the one we now face and whether we may safely follow it. Two speakers who cite historical cases will rarely find it difficult to adduce *conflicting* examples and if not nullify the force of the one with the other, then at least weaken and diminish it, for when the full urn of historical contingencies is poured out anything is possible at any given time.

The comparison marches at the side of the example, for it is only an invented case from *human* history and therefore stands halfway between poetry and truth. So what do both the example and the comparison lack in terms of the convincingness of the Aesopian fable? They lack its main component, *the inner necessity of the thing itself*, which distinguishes the fable from the comparison and all other forms of poetry. An example elucidates, but it does not compel, does not convince. A comparison confers probability, but it lacks the point of inner certainty that is decisive here. Other forms of poetry can recommend a course of action; only the fable is insistent and unavoidable because it shows us intuitively the inner necessity of the action to be taken or the rule of thumb.

And how does it show this? Through the very character of the beings who act in it, be they gods, demons, trees, animals, plants, or anything else that is part of Nature; for the fable introduces them as actors or speakers, so that it avoids the deceptiveness of the example, the deficiencies of the comparison, and shows, through the actions of these creatures, the *moral laws of Creation* in their inner necessity. The character of these beings and their relationship to one another is determined by Nature; they act and must act in keeping with this character, not arbitrarily, but out of necessity (αναγκης). It endures throughout their lifetime, and no species can alter it. Since it is sharply drawn and not, as with men, indeterminate, mutable, and concealed; since everyone, even a child, recognizes it and from youth on associates with the name and outward form of the god, the tree, and the animal its inner character also, indeed its history with its immutable destiny, then it is precisely the fable that presents to us as *necessary* now a lesson, now a rule of thumb drawn from this history, and consequently, indelibly impresses on our mind a word or syllable from the eternal statutes of Nature. A fable that does not achieve this aim (and many stray far from it) may have some worth as an elucidatory example, as a persuasive comparison, as an amusing tale, but it falls short of the lofty goal of its genre. Otherwise why go to the trouble of invention? Why have this whole apparatus of refashioned beings and their relationships to one another if through them something might not be taught and made intuitively obvious with a power the like of which neither history nor comparison is capable?

As proof of my claim, the entire field of the choicest fables lies before me, and I have difficulty in selecting but one. If it were here a matter of arbitrary, petty human morality, then could not every good be opposed with a bad, every duty set against another conflicting obligation that might be manifested just as clearly in the realm of acting beings? Thus, through the example of the hawk, the pike, and other regal murderers one might flatter the cutthroats of the human world in a fine and Aesopian manner; through the example of the sparrow one could advocate lust and even—as the philosopher did—recommend through the example of the swine the wise man's unchanging peace of mind. This is possible only once we reduce the fable to nothing more than *examples* of bestial actions *torn from their context*, which all immediately invalidate themselves because man is not and ought not to be either pike or hawk, swine or sparrow. Therefore it is a question here of *higher, universal laws of Nature, of the immutable union of all beings in the realm of Creation*, where no link in the chain is able to escape but where each must do what it can in its rightful place. That the stronger subdues and devours the weaker, for example, is a sad observation recorded by natural history. But that the weaker can also protect itself against the strong, that understanding, diligence, shrewdness, and ability often count more than blind power, that every creature has its deficiencies and excellencies, its fortune and misfortune, that each must therefore be satisfied with its nature and not covet that of another, and that all shall be for the good if they remain true to their lot on earth—what beautiful poetry on these themes the fable has given us! Poetry that may be considered as *intuitions of Nature, as proofs of the highest, of inner necessity*, and that have been painted as such by poets. The child learns these poetic works and commits them to memory; with this simple intuition he receives into his soul a divine law of Nature, in conformity with which he shall act in his own sphere. How many fine fables there are that show that he who fails to use his reason will inevitably meet his downfall; that he who strives for excellencies alien to his character shamefully sacrifices his own; that he who digs a pit for others often falls in it himself; that throughout Nature a law of requital prevails, so that he who hates is hated, he who persecutes is persecuted; that falsity, deceit, and malice are everywhere despicable, but that truth, love, sociableness, loyalty and order, the observance of the duties to one's father, mother, friends, family, and society are a universal, salutary law of Nature, and so on. On this subject animals are in many respects the most impartial teachers of man, for they speak and act without caprice and only as instruments of the Creator, as it were. If *they* therefore encourage man to be satisfied with his station, to work hard, and to develop every facet of his being to its full potential; if they promote prudence, fairness, loyalty, sociableness, generosity, then it is as if the Creator Himself had issued this decree through the many voices of Nature. That is why the fable likes to linger so much in the animal kingdom, for further down the chain of being we find that the laws of Nature grow more obscure, our similarity and sympathy with these lower forms of life diminish, and higher up the laws of Nature vanish into the clouds. In Aesop's fables, therefore, the gods appear in the main only as arbiters of fate, in instances where without them vexatious cases could not be resolved quickly and intuitively. That is how man also appears in them, now as a lowlier, now as a higher being compared with the animals, but always, in keeping with his disposition as a whole, as a mere creature of Nature. It is such laws governing the eternal order of things that the fable renders intuitively obvious to us, and it is precisely among these that it feels most at home. All that is arbitrary in the world—whether in the social or political world, in the world of the family, of learning, or of manners—is not, for this tutor of *immaculate relationships*, the fabulizing Muse of Nature; such things she leaves to her younger sister, to the conversational tale, and does so gladly.

How I wish that we might collect, from every nation and tongue that has produced them, these pure fables of Nature, which render intuitively obvious to us their rule of thumb or their practical lesson by an inner necessity. I am convinced, too, that this source has not nearly run dry, this field not nearly been harvested completely. Often beautiful poetry is recited badly, often the worst private incidents are recounted to the world in the most ornate and beautiful fashion. But for now it suffices to have elaborated the pure concept of the Aesopian fable, according to which it

is a form of poetry
which exemplifies a general rule of thumb or a practical lesson
for a given case arising in human life
through another, congruent case,
and which makes that lesson so intuitively obvious
in its inner necessity
that the soul is not only persuaded,
but sensuously convinced
by virtue of the represented truth itself.

Editor's Notes

Is the Beauty of the Body a Herald of the Beauty of the Soul?

This essay was first published anonymously in the *Gelehrte Beiträgen zu den Rigischen Anzeigen aufs Jahr 1766*. The text is based on *Ist die Schönheit des Körpers ein Bote von der Schönheit der Seele?* in *Frühe Schriften, 1764–1772*, ed. Ulrich Gaier, vol. 1 of Johann Gottfried Herder, *Werke* (Frankfurt am Main: Deutscher Klassiker Verlag, 1985), pp. 131–48.

our body, the dwelling place of the soul: According to Plato (*Phaedrus* 246c), the soul takes up residence in an earthly body.

Spartans: according to Plutarch's biography of Lycurgus.

Charon: the ferryman who transported dead souls across the river Styx to the Underworld.

Gellert: Christian Fürchtegott Gellert (1715–1769), professor of poetry and morals at the University of Leipzig; after his poem "Die schlauen Mädchen": "Denn überhaupt sagt man, / Daß es kein Mädchen gibt, / Die nicht den Schlaf und ihr Gesichte liebt" (For in general it is said / That there is not a single maid / Who loves not her sleep and her face).

our souls . . . reflected: an extremely loose paraphrase of Plato *Phaedrus* 246a–250c.

Montesquieu, Montaigne, and Beaumelle: Montesquieu, *On the Spirit of the Laws*, vol. 14, chap. 2ff; Montaigne, *Essays*, vol. 3, chap. 12, "On Physiognomy"; in his *Mes pensées* (1755), Laurent Angliviel de la Beaumelle (1726–1773) wrote: "The character of the peoples is invariable" (p. 175).

Wegelin: Jakob Daniel Wegelin (1721–1791); German scholar, author of *Politische und moralische Betrachtungen über die spartanische Gesetz-Gebung des Lykurgus* (1753). Like Rousseau, Wegelin presents the Spartan constitution as the most natural and moral system of government and offers it as a model to imitate in the modern world.

"feeble bodies produce feeble souls": an allusion to Rousseau's *Émile*: "a frail body weakens the soul" (bk. 1).

Hume: cf. Hume: "I am apt to suspect the Negroes . . . to be naturally inferior to the whites. There scarcely ever was a civilized nation of that complexion, nor even any individual eminent either in action or speculation. No ingenious manufacturers amongst them, no arts, no sciences" ("Of National Characters," in *The Philosophical Works*, ed. T. H. Green and T. H. Grose, 4 vols. [London: Longman, 1874–75], 3:252).

"when from crude loam . . . scarce yet done": Ulrich Gaier has suggested that these lines are not a quotation but Herder's own invention (*Werke*, vol. 1, *Frühe Schriften* [Frankfurt am Main: Deutscher Klassiker Verlag, 1985], 998).

Winckelmann . . . most beautiful faces: "For this reason, we seldom find in the fairest portions of Italy the features of the face unfinished, vague, and inex-pressive, as it is frequently the case on the other side of the Alps; but they have partly an air of nobleness, partly of acuteness and intelligence; and the form of the face is generally large and full, and the parts of it in harmony with each other" (*History of Ancient Art*, trans. G. Henry Lodge [Boston: Osgood, 1880], bk. 1, chap. 3, p. 159; repr. in *Essays on the Philosophy and History of Art*, ed. Curtis Bowman, vol. 2 [Bristol: Thoemmes, 2001]).

the aforementioned abbé: In 1754 Winckelmann converted to Catholicism; he be-came an abbé by virtue of his employment in the service of the pope.

talapoins: Buddhist monks or priests in Pegu (Burma).

marabouts: Muslim holy men or mystics in northwestern Africa.

lisping: Alcibiades, according to Aristophanes *Wasps* 44–46.

beautiful maid and ruddy-cheeked maid: In Russian the word for "red" (*krasnyi*) is connected with the word for "beautiful" (*krasivyi*).

nut brown: an allusion to the English ballad "Nut-brown Mayde," which Herder included in his collection of folk songs (*Volkslieder* 2, bk. 2, p. 11; *SWS* 25:415–20).

fraîcheur: freshness, coloring, complexion.

they toil not . . . Solomon: Matthew 6:28.

a statuesque beauty: Francis Bacon, *De Dignitate*, bk. 2, chap. 3.

Julius Caesar: He claimed to be descended from Aeneas, the son of Anchises and Aphrodite; according to Dio Cassius 43.43.2, he always carried with him a pic-ture of Venus.

grace: Winckelmann defines *grace* as "the harmony of agent and action . . . what-ever reasonably pleases in things and actions is gracious. Grace is a gift of heaven; though not like beauty, which must be born with the possessor: whereas nature gives only the dawn, the capability of this" (*On Grace in Works of Art*, trans. Henry Fusseli [London, 1765], p. 273; repr. in *Essays on the Philosophy and History of Art*, ed. Curtis Bowman, vol. 1 [Bristol: Thoemmes, 2001]).

physiognomist: See Cicero: "Zopyrus, who claimed to discern every man's nature from his appearance, accused Socrates in company of a number of vices which he enumerated, and when he was ridiculed by the rest who said they failed to recognize such vices in Socrates, Socrates himself came to his rescue by saying that he was naturally inclined to the vices named, but had cast them out of him by the help of reason" (*Tusculan Disputations* 4.37). The translation is by J. E. King (London: Heinemann, 1927).

air . . . folâtre: a somber, gloomy, forced, awkward, anxious air; a wan, forbid-ding, sour, callous, sullen face; a prude, swell, poseur, coquette, hypocrite, sim-perer; a fusspot, an idler, a prattler, a joker.

Winckelmann: See his *Description of the Torso in the Belvedere in Rome*.

A MONUMENT TO BAUMGARTEN

This fragment, written in 1767, is based on the text *Von Baumgartens Denkmal*, in *Frühe Schriften, 1764–1772*, ed. Ulrich Gaier, vol. 1 of Johann Gottfried

Herder, *Werke* (Frankfurt am Main: Deutscher Klassiker Verlag, 1985), pp. 681–94.

philologist: The philologist in question is Baumgarten's teacher, Martin Christgau. In the preface of his *Meditationes philosophicae*, Baumgarten writes: "Since the time when the worthy co-rector of the gymnasium which flourishes at Berlin, the celebrated Christgau, whom I cannot name without a sense of the deepest gratitude, adroitly guided my first steps in the study of the humanities, scarcely a day has passed for me without verse." (*Reflections on Poetry: Alexander Gottlieb Baumgarten's* Meditationes philosophicae de nonnullis ad poema pertinentibus, trans. Karl Aschenbrenner and William B. Holther [Berkeley: University of California Press, 1954], p. 35).

his biographer: Thomas Abbt (1738–1766), who wrote *Alexander Baumgartens Leben und Charakter* (1765). The quotation is drawn from p. 8.

Wolff's philosophy . . . heresy: Wolff's rationalism, which was seen as implying determinism and the denial of divine revelation, was opposed by the Pietist theological faculty at the University of Halle. When Wolff was succeeded as rector of the university by the theologian Joachim Lange, Lange called on his colleagues to censure Wolff for heresy. Though Wolff escaped this charge, he soon fell foul of King Friedrich Wilhelm I of Prussia, who was told that Wolff's theory of determinism absolved deserters from the army from moral responsibility for their dereliction of duty. Enraged, the king dismissed Wolff in 1723 and ordered him to leave Prussian territory within forty-eight hours or be hanged. Wolffian philosophers in Prussian universities were purged, and in 1729 the use of Wolff's textbooks was forbidden. Wolff did not return to his post until 1740, when he was recalled by Frederick the Great, one of his first acts upon ascending to the throne. Baumgarten studied in Halle from 1730, and in 1735 submitted his dissertation *Meditationes philosophicae*, written and conceived within the Wolffian tradition.

orphanage: The five schools in Halle that had been established by August Hermann Francke since 1695 (the school for the poor, the Pädagogium, the Bürgerschule, the Lateinschule, and the Lehrerseminar) were grouped around the orphanage, with whose name and educational method they were linked. Among the pedagogical innovations developed in Halle was the tabular method devised by Johann Friedrich Hähn (1710–1789), a system aiding the memorization of knowledge (facts) and the arrangement and division of written work. The method was taken up by Wolff in philosophy. Baumgarten originally enjoyed private tuition with Christgau, then moved with his teacher to the Berlin high school Greyfriars in 1727, and in autumn of the same year to the orphanage in Halle, where his eldest brother, Sigmund Jakob, taught (cf. Abbt, *Baumgartens Leben*, p. 9f).

metapoetics: the discipline containing principles that govern poetics. The expression was coined by Abbt (*Baumgartens Leben*, p. 11).

Dido's royal city: Fleeing the kingdom of Tyre, Dido set down in North Africa and bought as much land as could be covered by a bull's hide (*Aeneid* 1.367). Here she founded the city of Carthage.

cognitions that contribute to the poetic: See the end of the preface of *Meditationes*: "To this end, through § 11 I shall be occupied in developing the notion of a poem and the appropriate terminology. From § 13 to § 65 I shall try to work out some view of poetic cognition. From § 65 to § 77 I shall set forth that lucid method of a poem which is common to all poems. Finally, from § 77 to § 107 I shall subject poetic language to a rather careful investigation." See also § 11: "By *poetic* we shall mean whatever can contribute to the perfection of a poem."

oratio sensitiva perfecta: Cf. Baumgarten: "By *poem* we mean a perfect sensate discourse, by *poetics* the body of rules to which a poem conforms, by *philosophical poetics* the science of poetics, by *poetry* the state of composing a poem, and by *poet* the man who enjoys that state" (*Meditationes*, § 9).

1

barbarous terminology: In 1739 Baumgarten published *System of Metaphysics* and endured all the criticisms of obscurity and barbaric expression that he had foreseen and had resolved to endure, for the sake of philosophical exactitude. "'A long time ago,' he was wont to say, 'I had tried to see whether it was possible to give our modern concepts accurate expression in pure Latin: it did not work. I felt as if I were now called to show exactly the connection of all the sinews, muscles and veins of the metaphysical body; I could not impose the old Latin expression so that every piece properly shone through; so I threw away the finery'" (Abbt, *Baumgartens Leben*, pp. 14–15).

extensively clear concepts: an extensively clear representation is one that is clear but confused—that is, a poetic idea. Intensively clear concepts are clear and distinct.

principles of Aristotle, Batteux: In *Poetics* (1447a), Aristotle asserts that imitation is the common property of all forms of poetry; Batteux's principle is the "imitation of beautiful nature" (*belle nature*). Thus, both see the object depicted or imitated by the poem as the focus of poetics and criticism. Conversely, Baumgarten, following Addison and Hutcheson, was interested in the aesthetics of production and reception.

like an enormous ocean . . . that are lifted up to heaven: Aeneid 1.103.

Moses Mendelssohn's eulogium: from *Hauptgrundsätze der schönen Künste und Wissenschaften*. Mendelssohn's essay begins with the words (which Herder paraphrases before quoting him): "For the virtuoso, beaux arts and belles lettres are a preoccupation, for the amateur a source of pleasure, and for the philosopher a school of instruction. The profoundest secrets of our soul lie hidden in the rules of beauty, which the artist's genius feels and the critic reduces to rational inferences. Each rule of beauty is at the same time a psychological discovery."

2

Basedow: Johann Bernhard Basedow (1723–1790), German pedagogue.

Schlegel: Johann Adolf Schlegel (1721–1793), who translated Batteux into German and added elucidatory appendices to his translation.

Meier: Georg Friedrich Meier (1747–1810), pupil and popularizer of Baumgarten.

quasimodogenita: newborn babes, after 1 Peter 2:2. Quasimodogeniti is the first Sunday after Easter.

exsulant: exile.

the altar of Isis: according to Plutarch *De Isis et Osiris* 354, an inscription on the pedestal of the statue of Minerva/Isis in the temple at Sais: "I am all that has been, and is, and shall be; and my robe no mortal has yet uncovered" (trans. Frank Cole Babbitt [London: Heinemann, 1936]).

voluptas: pleasure, desire.

ratio artis, quam docti intelligent: the rule of art that the scholars understand; Quintilian *Institutio oratoria* 4.1.49.

the well-known proverb: after Horace *Epistles* 1.2.69–70 ("Quo semel est inbuta recens, servabit odorem / testa diu").

painting of Apelles: Pliny *Natural History* 35.36. Baumgarten published the first volume of his *Aesthetica* in 1750 and the second in 1758, but the work remained unfinished at the time of his death in 1769.

Lessing: preface to *Laocoön*. Herder also quotes the remark in his conclusion to the *First Grove*.

Socrates: Cicero *Tusculan Disputations* 5.4.10. Herder's appeal to the Greeks as the critical yardstick by which to judge modern aesthetics is based on their sensuality, pragmatism, and refusal to indulge in airy speculation.

Homer's Titaressus: *The Iliad*, trans. A. T. Murray and rev. William F. Wyatt Cambridge, MA. Harvard University Press, 1999), 2.751–55.

St. Mard: Toussaint Rémond de St. Mard (1682–1757), author of *Examen philosophique de la poésie en général*.

CRITICAL FORESTS, OR REFLECTIONS ON THE ART AND SCIENCE OF THE BEAUTIFUL: FIRST GROVE, DEDICATED TO MR. LESSING'S *LAOCOÖN*

This work was first published anonymously in 1769 by Hartknoch in Riga. The text is based on *Kritische Wälder: Erstes Wäldchen*, in *Schriften zur Ästhetik und Literatur, 1767–1781*, ed. Günter E. Grimm, vol. 2 of Johann Gottfried Herder, *Werke* (Frankfurt am Main: Deutscher Klassiker Verlag, 1993), pp. 57–245.

Because this essay is intended as a supplement to Lessing's *Laocoön*, it is best read with a translation of that work to hand; it would be cumbersome here to rehearse every detail of Lessing's argument with which Herder engages. Hence I have highlighted only the most obvious allusions. Quotations from Lessing in the text are drawn from Edward Allen McCormick's translation of *Laocoön* (Baltimore: Johns Hopkins University Press, 1984), chiefly because this is the most widely available edition that also includes the long, discursive footnotes, which Herder will sometimes discuss. Two older translations also retain these footnotes: those by E. C. Beasley (London: Longman, 1893) and Robert Phillimore (London: Routledge, 1910). Where Herder cites Lessing in his own references, I have included the chapter followed by the page number (of the McCormick edition) in square brackets. There are also frequent references to *The Iliad*. Throughout, I have quoted from the translation by A. T.

Murray and revised by William F. Wyatt (Cambridge, MA: Harvard University Press, 1999).

Logau: "Reader, how do I please you? / Reader, how do you please me?" Even the epigraph is a nod in the direction of Lessing, who, together with Karl Wilhelm Ramler, had edited a collection of Friedrich von Logau's (1604–1655) poems entitled *Sinngedichte* (1759). Later pressings of the first edition appeared with a different motto, adapted from Quintilian's *Institutio oratoria* (10.3): "Qui primo decurrere per materiam volunt et sequentes calorem atque impetum ex tempore scribunt,—sylvas vocant" (Those who wish first to run through their matter and, according to zeal and impulse, write on the spur of the moment—they call these writings forests).

1

the three Graces: sister goddesses regarded as the bestowers of beauty and charm and portrayed as women of exquisite beauty; usually spoken of (after Hesiod in *Theogony* 907) as three in number, Aglaia, Thalia, and Euphrosyne.

propitious phantoms that Democritus: Plutarch *Timoleon* 2.

the statue from which it takes its name: A statue of the Trojan priest Laocoön and his sons wrestling with a serpent was discovered in Rome in 1506. The work is described by Pliny in *Natural History* (36.37), where it is attributed to Hagesandrus, Polydorus, and Athenodorus of Rhodes. Though it is now thought to be a Roman copy of a Greek original, the statue came to be regarded as one of the greatest achievements of antique art. Following Winckelmann's description in *Reflections on the Painting and Sculpture of the Greeks*, it became a cult object for German Hellenists and was also discussed by Goethe, Schiller, Heinse, Hegel, and others. See H. B. Nisbet, "Laocoön in Germany: The Reception of the Group since Winckelmann," *Oxford German Studies* 10 (1979): 22–63.

the authorial ἐποίησε: made it (added to the name of the artist on certain antique works). In his *History of Ancient Art*, Winckelmann noted the inscription on the base of the Laocoön statue ("Athanodorus, son of Agesander, of Rhodes, made it"); Lessing quotes the relevant passage and discusses it in *Laocoön* 27.

a collection of materials, an assemblage of unordered notes: In the preface to *Laocoön*, Lessing claims his book was "written as chance dictated," was not structured according to "any systematic development of general principles," and hence was rather "unordered notes for a book than a book itself."

Apollo Smintheus: epithet of Apollo as a god of agriculture, the destroyer of verminous field mice.

at Winckelmann's expense: a reference to Christian Adolf Klotz's review of *Laocoön* (cited by Herder in note 1) and to Friedrich Just Riedel's remarks in his *Theorie der schönen Künste und Wissenschaften* (1767). Klotz (1738–1771) was an antiquarian, a man of letters, and the leader of a literary clique who is the chief villain throughout the *Critical Forests*. Riedel (1742–1785), a writer and aesthetician, was his disciple.

study of Homer . . . morning prayer: In a letter to Christian Ludwig Hagedorn dated 13 January 1759, Winckelmann wrote that "Homer still always comes after my morning prayers" (*Briefe*, 4 vols. [Berlin: de Gruyter, 1952–57],

1:445). The letter was printed in 1759 in the *Bibliothek der schönen Wissenschaften und der freien Künste* (vol. 5).

Academy: a grove sacred to Apollo lying northwest of Athens; the Ilissos was a river to the south of Athens (where Plato's dialogue *Phaedrus* takes place).

deaf and imbecilic like Claudius: Claudius, Roman emperor from 41 to 54 AD, was portrayed as feeble-minded in Seneca's *Apocolocynthosis*. However, it was Caligula, not Claudius, who wanted to ban Homer's poems and remove the statues of Virgil and Livy from libraries (Suetonius *Caligula* 34).

"Reddiderunt forte . . . fiduciam!" (note 1): "The learned man has been made too complacent by the lavish praise with which his first works, which were far superior to his compilation on allegory, have been greeted by many; even by me, as I confess without astonishment or vexation. If only Winckelmann did not sometimes demonstrate through his example that the idle talk of the heralds of his talent as well as of his friends are often ruinous to the author; that applause and praise cause his diligence to diminish and his obscurities and self-assurance to increase."

frogs: Aristophanes *Frogs* 221–68.

song of the sirens: Odyssey 12.165–200. The allusion is not quite accurate, however, because Odysseus stopped up the ears of his companions only and had himself tied to the mast of his ship.

L.'s criticisms of W.: Compare the polemical exchanges in *Laocoön* 1, 25, and esp. 29.

Sophocles' Philoctetes: Lessing's comparison of the conduct of Philoctetes in Sophocles' drama of the same name with the statue of Laocoön is one of the means by which he teases out the fundamental differences between visual art and poetry.

How Virgil, Petronius, and Sadolet depict Laocoön: Aeneid 2.199–224; *Satyricon* 89; Jacopo Sadoleto (1477–1547), Italian humanist and cardinal; wrote the poem "De Laocoontis Statua" (On the Statue of Laocoön) in 1506, immediately after its rediscovery.

Chateaubrun's Philoctetes: Jean-Baptiste Chateaubrun (1688–1775), French playwright; author of a drama entitled *Philoctète* (1755).

shows Spence and Caylus their errors: Joseph Spence (1699–1768), professor of poetry and history at Oxford University. Lessing frequently criticizes Spence's *Polymetis*, which argues that an object ineffective as a painting or statue is not appropriate for poetic description either. Anne Claude Philippe de Tubière, Comte de Caylus (1692–1765), drew up a long list of episodes from *The Iliad*, *The Odyssey*, and *The Aeneid* which he recommended to artists as subject matter for paintings (*Tableaux tirés de l'Iliade, de l'Odyssée d Homère et de l'Eneide de Virgile*, 1757).

before whom . . . Beauty herself appeared: Aphrodite appeared before Praxiteles or Apelles; see *Greek Anthology* 16.159–70, 178–82.

like Kleist's Amynt of his beloved Lalage: "Amynt" is a poem by Ewald Christian von Kleist (1715–1759), first published in 1751.

accompanied by a Greek Grace: In his *History of Ancient Art*, Winckelmann distinguishes the lofty (heavenly) Grace and the pleasing or lovely (earthly) Grace (bk. 8, chap. 2); Herder ascribes to him the former Grace and Lessing the latter. The comparison of the respective styles of Winckelmann and Lessing in the following paragraphs foreshadows Herder's later distinction between work and energy in section 9. Their critical writings embody the characteristics of the very arts they treat.

the shield of Achilles: Iliad 18.474–608.

τεταγμένον: order, disposition.

2

the Philoctetes of Sophocles: Philoctetes, friend of Hercules and heir to his bow and arrows, is bitten by a snake on the way to Troy and marooned on the island Lemnos on account of the fetid stench of his wound. Because a later prophecy declares that Troy can be sacked only with the aid of his bow (with which Paris is slain), Odysseus and Neoptolemus (the son of Achilles) are sent either to persuade him to surrender it or to take it by deceitful means.

the howling cry of a Mars: Iliad 5.859–63.

"What ails thee?": Philoctetes 733–36 (trans. F. Storr [London: Heinemann, 1913]).

I beseech the Gods: Philoctetes 779–81.

Garrick: David Garrick (1717–1779), the most celebrated English actor of his age, renowned for his Shakespearean roles. Lessing himself mentions Garrick (*Laocoön*, 4:32).

Νεοπτόλεμος . . . κνον (note 5): "*Neoptolemus*: Be moving if it please thee. Why, what means this sudden silence, this amazedness? *Philoctetes*: Ah me! Ah me! *Neoptolemus*: What is it? *Philoctetes*: A mere nothing boy; go on" (*Philoctetes* 730–34).

ὦ θεοί: "Ah! Oh God" (*Philoctetes* 737).

ἀπόλωλα . . . παπαππαπαππαπαππαπαῖ: "I am lost, undone! It stabs, stabs me through and through and through. Ah me! Ah me! Ah me!" (*Philoctetes* 743–46).

ἰυγὴν καὶ στόνον: Philoctetes 751.

He regains his senses: Philoctetes 757–820.

Aeschylus: Euripides and Aeschylus both wrote a *Philoctetes*; both are lost and only fragments remain.

Eumenides . . . she miscarried: The Eumenides (kindly ones) was a euphemistic name for the Furies, three daughters of Mother Earth conceived from the blood of Uranus when Kronos castrated him. They were powerful divinities who personified conscience and punished crimes against kindred blood. In Aeschylus's trilogy *The Oresteia*, they pursue Orestes after he kills his mother, Clytemnestra. According to tradition, the appearance of the Furies during the performance of the drama caused men to faint and a pregnant woman to miscarry.

Hudemann's Cain: Ludwig Friedrich Hudemann (1703–1770), German poet; his tragedy *Der Brudermord des Kain* was published in 1765.

ἀᾶ: Woe is me!

twilit chorus: Philoctetes 827–38, 843–64.

dark night enfolded his eyes: for example, Iliad 4.461, 503; 5.310; 11.356.

"suffering nature must have her due": Laocoön 1:9.

ichor: the blood of the Greek gods; see, for example, Iliad 5.340.

Pallas mock her . . . Jupiter, smile at her: Iliad 5.418–29.

Hannibal: The Carthaginian general is supposed to have laughed ironically at the extortionate payment demands made by the Romans (Livy 30.44).

like Mars or Lady Venus: Iliad 5.859 and 343.

Diomedes "stood . . . *enemy*": Notwithstanding the quotation marks, this is a paraphrase rather than a direct quotation.

Sarpedon: son of Zeus and Europa, an ally of Troy; he falls in combat against Patroclus; *Iliad* 16.419–21.

iron-eating Trojan Mars: In *The Iliad* Ares fights on the side of Troy.

an army of weeping heroes: Laocoön 1:8–9: "Homer's heroes not infrequently fall to the ground with a cry." Lessing refers to *Iliad* 7.421–49 and *Odyssey* 4.195–98.

3

Greeks and Trojans . . . forbids the Trojans to weep: Iliad 7.417–29.

Dacier: Anne Lefebvre Dacier (1647–1720), translator of *The Iliad* and *The Odyssey*, wrote a defense of Homer (1716); mentioned by Lessing, *Laocoön* 1:10.

"But why," asks Mr. Lessing, . . . "human feeling": Laocoön 1:10. Herder omits the following sentence from his quotation: "Why does Agamemnon not issue the same command to the Greeks?"

Klotz . . . "clamor et eiulatus . . . tamen" (note 29): "According to the Greeks, cries and loud howling did not diminish the extent of one's courage. Homer's heroes fall with a cry. These very heroes of Homer are more than mere mortals."

thief: that is, Paris; *Iliad* 3.46–51.

"the poet's meaning": Laocoön 1:10. Lessing's next sentence reveals what Herder alludes to as "mere allegory": "He wants to tell us that only the civilized Greek can weep and yet be brave at the same time, while the uncivilized Trojan, to be brave, must first stifle all human feeling."

solely by meter: The elegiac meter is a distich composed of a hexameter and a pentameter.

versus querimoniae: verses of lamentation; after Horace *De arte poetica* 75.

King Regner Lodbrog: mythical Danish king, whose death song is contained in the late twelfth-century Norse epic *Krákumál*. This passage was also cited in Hugh Blair's *Critical Dissertation on the Poems of Ossian* (1763), from where this English translation has been drawn. Paul Heinrich Mallet (1730–1807) wrote several works on ancient Danish and Scandinavian history. His *History of Denmark* was published in 1758, and Herder reviewed its translation from the French in August 1765; see *SWS* 1:73–77.

Ella: a king in England who defeated Regner.

Assbiøn Prude: Herder printed the "Song of the Captured Assbiøn Prude" in the first part of his *Volkslieder* in 1778 (*SWS* 25:257–63).

the Esquimaux at the stake: Herder bases his description on the chapter "On the Manner of Death of the Slaves in Northern America," in Johann Friedrich Schröter's *Allgemeine Geschichte der Länder und Völker von Amerika* (1752–53).

"In their deeds . . . true men": Laocoön 1:9.

semones: demigods; Herder adopts the etymology of Martianus Capella (first half of the fifth century AD): *semis* as if from *semidei*. The semones were Italic deities.

the ancient Scots . . . their originality is a proven fact: The Fragments of Ancient Poetry (1760), *Fingal* (1762), and *Temora* (1763), published by James Macpherson and purported to be translations of the songs of an ancient Scottish bard, Ossian, though they were in fact written by Macpherson himself. The poems, collected together as *The Works of Ossian* in 1765, aroused enormous enthusiasm and considerable controversy throughout Europe in the late eighteenth and early nineteenth centuries. Despite the Edinburgh professor Hugh Blair's stamp of approval in his influential *Critical Dissertation on the Poems of Ossian*, doubts about their authenticity were raised early on. Herder refused to believe the Ossianic songs were fakes and often used them as an example of the creative genius of "barbarous" peoples.

Shilric . . . Vinvela: Shilric is a Fingalian hero, "chief of high Carmora," and lover of Vinvela.

I shall lift from Lessing . . . the Greeks: Laocoön 1:9.

"Comála": Comála is the daughter of King Sarno of Inistore who dies of grief at the false news of Fingal's death.

"like an ancient oak . . . in my place": fragment 7.

Armin and gray-hair'd Carryl: In fragment 11 and the *Songs of Selma*, Armin laments the death of his children and that he is now the last of his race. Carryl's lamentation can be found in fragment 3.

4

"ein Silberton . . . Gefühl": from Klopstock's *Ode auf das Jubelfest der Souveränität in Dänemark* (later retitled *Das neue Jahrhundert*), lines 9–11. The verse begins "O freedom, thou art a silvery tone to the ear / a beacon to the understanding and lofty flight to thought / to the heart great feeling."

patriotic laments: Here Herder is thinking of the patriotic poetry of his contemporaries, such as *Lieder der Deutschen* by Karl Wilhelm Ramler (1725–1798) and *Preußische Kriegslieder* (1758) by Johann Wilhelm Ludwig Gleim.

Ovid: In his *Tristia* and *Epistulae ex Ponto*, written while in exile on the Black Sea, Ovid (43–17 BC) lamented having to live among uncivilized peoples in a raw climate.

Bussy-Rabutin: Roger de Rabutin, Comte de Bussy (1618–1693), author of *Histoire amoureuse des Gaules* (1665), a satire about Louis XIV's relationship with Louise de La Vallière. It earned him the reputation as the Petronius of his age and a thirteen-month stay in the Bastille, followed by a period of exile lasting sixteen years. Herder is here referring to his *Discours du comte de Bussy Rabutin à ses enfants, sur le bon usage des adversitez* (1694).

Priam's heroic laments: Iliad 22.408–29.

Astyanax: Iliad 6.466–81.

Electra: Aeschylus *Choephorae* 124–51; Sophocles *Elektra* 86–120, 130–36, 145–52, and so on.

poignant passing of the Orientals to their fathers: Here Herder is drawing on Johann Jacob Reiske's *Proben der Arabischen Dichtkunst in verliebten und traurigen Gedichten aus dem Motanabbi* (1765).

Haller, Klopstock, Canitz, or Öder: Albrecht von Haller, in *Trauerode beim Absterben seiner geliebten Marianne* (1736) and *Über den Tod seiner zweiten Gemahlin Elisabeth Bücher* (1741); Klopstock, in his *Hinterlaßne Schriften* (1759), pp. viii–x; Friedrich Rudolf Ludwig Freiherr von Canitz (1654–1699), in his *Klagenode über den Tod seiner ersten Gemahlin*; Georg Wilhelm Öder (died 1751) or Georg Christian Öder (1728–1791), a student of Haller.

Ioláüs: Ioláüs was Hercules' nephew and charioteer.

Achates: a faithful comrade of the Trojan hero Aeneas.

Pylades: the son of King Strophios and friend of Orestes.

Pirithoüs: the son of Ixion, king of the Lapiths, husband of Hippodamia. After the latter's death, he descended into the Underworld with Theseus in order to abduct Persephone, but he was captured and enchained.

Achilles: Iliad 18.22–27, 78–93; 19.4–6, 23–27, 305–37; 23.15–23.

Pylades: Euripides *Iphigenia* 716–22; *Orestes* 729–31.

Jonathan: 2 Samuel 1:11–12, 117–19.

a Boeotian ιερος λοχος: an allusion to the sacred band, the three hundred Theban warriors who fought against the Spartans.

Polyphemus: Theocritus (ca. 310–250 BC) treats the love of the cyclops Polyphemus for the Nereid Galatea in Idyll 11.

in letters exchanged between men: *Briefe von den Herren Gleim und Jacobi* (1768).

parenthyrsus: false sentiment, affectation of style.

beautiful poplar tree: Iliad 4.473–89.

Protesilaus: Iliad 2.698–700.

who has acquired aptitudes . . . Pallas to fight: Scamandrius in *Iliad* 5.49–51.

"we more refined Europeans": Laocoön 1:9.

Priam over his slain son: Iliad 22.408, 412–29.

5

the author of the Dramaturgy: Lessing's *Hamburg Dramaturgy* appeared between 1767 and 1769, while Lessing was director at the National Theater. The work consists of critical notes written for the printed programs of the theater's productions.

an untrod shore: Philoctetes 16–47.

Here, we are told, is Philoctetes, the famous son of Poeas: Philoctetes 4–11.

the scene of betrayal: Philoctetes 50–134.

the sly, crafty Ulysses of Homer: Iliad 1.311, 440; 2.173.

a Pythagorean maxim: the *Chrysa epé* (Golden Words), seventy-one hexameters containing the principal ethical maxims of Pythagoras.

a groaning is heard: Philoctetes 201–9.

Peter Quince: The words are spoken by Bottom in Shakespeare's *Midsummer Night's Dream* (1.2.68–69).

How he hopes: Philoctetes 223–31.

he tells Neoptolemus his story: Philoctetes 254–316.

Penia: the personification of poverty.

to fallen Achilles: Philoctetes 332–38.

perhaps already walks among the shades: Philoctetes 492–99.

if only Philoctetes pleaded with him: *Philoctetes* 485–505.

the entreaty of the chorus: *Philoctetes* 506–18.

We grow annoyed: *Philoctetes* 523–38.

"Gods! This wretch": a paraphrase of *Philoctetes* 622–25.

The chorus anticipates it with a song: *Philoctetes* 676–729.

Brumoy: Pierre Brumoy (1688–1742), French Jesuit and scholar; Lessing refers to his work *Théâtre des Grecs* (1730) in support of the claim that "the ancients were little concerned with having acts of equal length" (*Laocoön* 1:8).

principal idea of the play: Lessing writes: "How marvelously the poet has strengthened and enlarged the idea of physical pain!" (*Laocoön* 1:25).

Only the soul of a gladiator: a paraphrase of a passage in Winckelmann's *Reflections on the Painting and Sculpture of the Greeks*: "In the most happy time of their freedom, the humanity of the Greeks abhorred bloody games, which even in Ionick Asia had ceased long before. . . . Antiochus Epiphanes, by ordering shews of Roman gladiators, first prescribed them with such unhappy victims; and custom and time, weakening the pangs of sympathizing humanity, changed even these games into schools of art. There Ctesilaus studied his dying gladiator, in whom you might descry 'how much life was still left in him'" (trans. Henry Fusseli [London, 1765], 10–11; repr. in *Essays on the Philosophy and History of Art*, ed. Curtis Bowman, vol. 1 [Bristol: Thoemmes, 2001]). The statue of the dying gladiator is the so-called Borghese gladiator, now in the Louvre. See also *Laocoön* 28.

Only a monster . . . Michelangelo: a legend spread by the Belgian Jesuit André Schott in the early seventeenth century, which probably has its origins in a classical legend surrounding the Greek painter Parrhasius.

σκευοποιια: the preparing of masks and other stage properties.

Letters Concerning Recent Literature: written by Moses Mendelssohn, Lessing, Friedrich Nicolai, Thomas Abbt, and Friedrich Gabriel Resewitz. Mendelssohn is the "foremost writer" to whom Herder refers, one of whose pseudonyms in the *Letters* was D.

"why the imitation of disgust . . . mixture of pleasure": a not entirely exact quotation from letter 82 of the *Letters Concerning Recent Literature*.

"partly because illusion": letter 84.

the Englishman Smith: Adam Smith (1723–1790), author of *The Theory of Moral Sentiments* (1761), which Lessing cites in *Laocoön* 4:27–28. Like Herder, Lessing describes Smith as an Englishman; in fact Smith was a Scot.

a Robinson Crusoe: a reference to Daniel Defoe's novel *The Life and Strange Surprising Adventures of Robinson Crusoe* (1719), based on the true story of a shipwreck on a desert island. Lessing also likens Philoctetes to Defoe's character in the passage to which Herder subsequently refers as embodying Lessing's "customary strength" (*Laocoön* 1:26).

a new blow: *Philoctetes* 1–134.

hears Ulysses' new betrayal: *Philoctetes* 927–62.

entrust his arrows and his life to Neoptolemus: *Philoctetes* 763–73.

and now the fit comes: *Philoctetes* 782–826.

series of poetic pictures of action: *Laocoön* 4.

6

"*among the ancients beauty . . . plastic arts*": after Winckelmann in *Reflections on the Painting and Sculpture of the Greeks*.

"*The Greeks never depicted a Fury*": Lessing himself qualifies this statement in a footnote in *Laocoön* 9:193–94. The Furies were usually represented as winged maidens with serpents twined in their hair and blood dripping from their eyes.

Mr. Klotz: In *Über den Nutzen und Gebrauch der alten geschnittenen Steine und ihrer Abdrücke* (1768), Klotz reproduces a depiction of a Fury's head.

Pauson, Pyreicus, and other Rhyparographers: A Rhyparographer is a "painter of filth." Pauson was an Athenian painter of the second half of the fifth century BC; he is mentioned by Aristotle in *Poetics* (1448a) for painting people less noble than they were in reality. Pyreicus or Piraeicus was a painter active in the fourth century BC and known for his interiors and scenes of low life.

a political philosopher: Aristotle in *Politics* 8.5; cited by Lessing in the first footnote of chapter 2 of *Laocoön*.

The law of the Thebans εις το χειρον (note 74): to the worst. Aelian recounts that "in Thebes a law was in force which instructed artists—both painters and sculptors—to make their portraits flattering. As punishment for those who produced a sculpture or painting less attractive than the original, the law threatened a fine of a thousand drachmas" (*Varia Historica* 4.4). The law is mentioned by both Lessing and Winckelmann (in *Reflections*).

cacozelia: bad imitation.

Graeculis: little Greeks.

qualitas occulta: hidden quality.

of this L. gives the best example: "'Who would want to paint you when no one even wants to look at you?' an old epigrammatist [Antiochus] asks of an exceedingly deformed man" (*Laocoön* 2:12).

Banier (note 77): Antoine Banier (1673–1741), French archaeologist and author of *La mythologie et les fables expliquées par l'histoire* (1738–40); cited by Lessing.

the Egyptian gods, allegorical monsters: those gods represented with the head of an animal, for example, Anubis (jackal), Apis (bull), or Horus (falcon). They are monsters because they are theriomorphic (having animal form) rather than anthropomorphic. Cf. Winckelmann, *History of Ancient Art*, bk. 2, chap. 2.

like the Persian and Indian gods: Cf. Winckelmann: "Another cause of the slight progress of art among the Persians is their religious service, which was by no means favorable to art; for they believed that the gods could not or must not be figured in human form; the visible heavens and fire were the highest objects of their adoration" (*History of Ancient Art*, trans. G. Henry Lodge [Boston: Osgood, 1880], bk. 2, chap. 5, p. 215; repr. in *Essays on the Philosophy and History of Art*, ed. Curtis Bowman, vol. 2 [Bristol: Thoemmes, 2001]).

like the Etruscan gods, sad and unseemly figures: Winckelmann: "The disposition of the Etruscans appears to have been more tinged with melancholy than was the case with the Greek race—as we may infer from their religious services and their customs" (*History of Ancient Art*, bk. 3, chap. 1, p. 226).

Greek conceptions of the gods were determined by poets: that is, by Hesiod in his *Theogony* and Homer in *The Iliad* and *The Odyssey*.

μειλίχιος: mild, gracious. Zeus μειλίχιος is the protector of those who invoke him with propitiatory offerings.

Moschos: In fact this was in Bion. Both Moschos and Bion were pastoral poets active in the beginning of the third century BC.

Juno, too, can quarrel like a queen: Iliad 4.20–29, 50–67.

Apollo be consumed by brave fury: Iliad 1.43–52.

Gorgons: According to Hesiod, there were three Gorgons (Sthenno, Euryale, and Medusa), winged virgins with serpents for hair whose glance could turn men to stone. Medusa was decapitated by Perseus and her head given to Athena, who then decorated her shield with it.

Bacchantae: The Bacchantae or Maenads were worshipers of Dionysos, who, consumed by frenzy, roamed the woods at night and tore apart animals.

transformed by the virginal Minerva: see Ovid *Metamorphoses* 4.791–803.

the Furies: The Furies were known by two euphemistic names, the Eumenides (kindly ones) and the Semnai (venerable ones).

διεστραμμένους (note 84): Lessing: "In fact, the ancient artists depicted Death and Sleep with a resemblance that we naturally expect to find in twins. They were shown on a chest of cedar in the temple of Juno at Elis as two boys, sleeping in the arms of Night. Only one was white and the other black; the one slept while the other appeared to be sleeping; both had their feet crossed. I prefer to translate Pausanias's words . . . this way rather than by 'with crooked feet.' . . . What could 'crooked feet' mean here?" (*Laocoön* 11:n1).

religious colonies: that is, the appropriation of Greek religion by those peoples colonized or influenced by them, for example, the Romans.

Cerberus: the three-headed hound who guards the gates of the underworld.

Timanthes: a Greek painter who flourished about 400 BC.

idoneus auctor: a reliable witness.

"Timanthes cum moestos . . . ostendere": "After he had painted them all with melancholy expressions, and especially the uncle, and had exhausted every possible picture of sadness, he concealed the face of the father, being unable to depict it in a worthy manner" (Pliny *Natural History* 35.36; also cited by Lessing in *Laocoön* 2:16).

Valerius Maximus: a Roman historian of the first century AD and author of *Factorum ac dictorum memorabilium libri IX*, a collection of famous deeds and sayings. Lessing cites him in *Laocoön* 2:16.

But if the gods demand the sacrifice: At the behest of the high priest Calchas, Agamemnon sacrificed his daughter Iphigenia to appease the goddess Artemis.

More than one poet had already veiled Agamemnon: See Euripides *Iphigenia in Aulis* 1547–1550; Aeschylus and Sophocles also wrote Iphigenia dramas, of which only fragments remain.

Clytemnestra: Cf. Euripides *Iphigenia in Aulis* 899–917, 977–97, 1146–1208.

Hecuba: Euripides *Troiades* 98–152, 466–510, 1156–1250.

its screaming Ajax: that is, as depicted by Timanthes in his painting.

the raving Ajax, the terrible Medea: Herder is referring (following Lessing [*Laocoön* 3:20]) to two paintings by the artist Timomachus, the *Ajax* and the *Medea*, mentioned by Pliny (*Natural History* 7.38.126). After Achilles, Ajax was the mightiest hero of the Greek army. When Ajax attempted to murder the leaders of the Greek army to avenge a perceived slight to his honor, Athena caused him to go insane and to attack herds of sheep instead. Medea was the wife of Jason and murdered her children after her husband betrayed her.

the suffering Hercules: Cf. *Laocoön* 2:18 (in Sophocles' *Trachiniae*; discussed by Lessing in *Laocoön* 4:31–32).

"how much Greek artists avoided the ugly . . . cases": This follows the argument in *Laocoön* 3:19–20 that according to modern theories, "truth and expression" (that is, verisimilitude) are "art's first law," whereas Greek artists saw beauty as the supreme law in imitation.

in which the Greeks, with their Pauson and Pyreicus, were not lacking either: Cf. Lessing: "To be sure, the propensity to this wanton boasting of mere skills, not ennobled by the intrinsic worth of their subjects, is too natural for even the Greeks not to have had their Pauson and Pyreicus. They had them, but they treated them with stern justice" (*Laocoön* 2:13).

Mr. L. is free to believe Valerius (note 91): Lessing: "Nor do I believe Valerius when he says that Ajax was represented as screaming in the above-mentioned picture of Timanthes" (*Laocoön* 2:17).

7

"Indeed, such natural horns . . . man and animal": *Laocoön* 9:n2.

"tibi . . . caput est": "Virginal is thy head when thou appearest without horns"; Ovid *Metamorphoses* 4.19–20; quoted in *Laocoön* 8:51.

the pirates of Homer: *Homeric Hymns* 7.3–5 (hymn to Dionysos).

μυριομορφος: of countless forms.

Orpheus, the epigrammatists, Nonnus: In the *Orphic Hymns* (a collection of eighty-seven hymns attributed to Orpheus), Dionysos is referred to as Zagreus (the hunter), Bassareus (the fox god), Liknites (god of the winnowing fan), Perikionios (of the column), Lenaios (of the winepress), and Eiraphiotes (insewn). The "epigrammists" refers to the anonymous authors of the *Greek Anthology*; Herder presumably has in mind 9.524. Nonnus was a Hellenistic poet (around 400 AD) who portrayed the entire cycle of the Bacchic myth in his *Dionysiaca*.

διμορφος, πολυμορφος, μυριομορφος: having two forms, having many forms, thousand-formed.

κεραος . . . κερασφορος: κεραος = the horned one; δικεραος = having two horns; ξρυσοκεραος = having golden horns; ταυρωρος = having a bull's face; ταυρομετωπος = having a bull's brow; ταυροκεραος = having a bull's horns; κερασφορος = the bearer of horns.

since none are extant today: Lessing assumed that statues of Bacchus with horns were cultic objects, and therefore "it is highly probable that the wrath of pious iconoclasts during the first centuries of Christianity" fell on them. (*Laocoön* 9:55).

Jupiter . . . either sex: Jupiter assumed female form when he seduced Callisto (*Metamorphoses* 2.401–38).

labrys: a double-headed ax; the attribute of Carian Zeus (Zeus Labrandeus, Zeus of the Double Ax) and symbol of the supreme Minoan deity.

Homer, the son of a heavenly genius: Pseudo-Plutarch (2.2) claims Homer's father was the river god Meles; in Antipater his parents are Uranos and Calliope, in Suidas Apollo and Calliope.

8

Pisander: a Greek epic poet (sixth century BC).

Servius: Latin grammarian and commentator (flourished fourth century AD), author of a commentary on Virgil.

Euphormio: Herder means Euphorion, son of Aeschylus, who won a prize in the Great Dionysia of 431 BC.

Quintus Calaber: He was also called Quintus Smyrnaeus; a Greek poet who flourished toward the end of the fourth century AD; author of a sequel to Homer's *Iliad*, which dealt with the Trojan War from the death of Hector until the return of the Greeks.

In his treatment of Laocoön: Here Herder closely follows Lessing's description of bk. 12 of Quintus Calaber's epic (which describes the episode with the Trojan horse).

"Hic aliud . . . Laocoön": "Hereon another, weightier, and by far / More dread occurrence meets us in our woe, / And spreads dismay in unexpectant breasts. Laocoön"; quoted by Lessing, in note 6 of chap. 5.

ενθ' εφανη μενα σημα: then appeared a great portent; *Iliad* 2.308.

attending to the Greek traitor: Sinon, who pretends to be a deserter and persuades the Trojans to bring the wooden horse into the city.

"two serpents . . . tongues": a free translation of *Aeneid* 2.203–11.

which Homer furnished with a single word: Homer describes his serpent as simply "blood-red, terrible" (*Iliad* 2.308–9).

"clamores . . . tollit": "He lifted up his voice in horrible cries to the heavens"; *Aeneid* 2.222; cf. *Laocoön* 4:23.

Petronius: Titus Petronius Arbiter (ca. 27–66 BC), Roman satirist. The passage in question is from *Satyricon* 89; quoted in *Laocoön*, in note 6 of chap. 5.

need the whole . . . his imagination: Petronius has his narrator visit a gallery in Naples, where he sees a painting depicting the fall of Troy. It is uncertain, Herder is saying, whether Petronius (as a historian) is referring to an actual collection of paintings or (as a poet) to a fictitious one. Lessing doubts the painting's existence.

Abbé Terrasson: Jean Terrasson (1670–1750) translated the historian Diodorus Siculus (ca. 90–21 BC) and wrote *Séthos, histoire ou vie: Tirée des monuments anecdotes de l'ancienne Egypte* (1731), a historical novel about Egypt based in part on Diodorus's descriptions of ancient Egypt in his *Bibliotheca historica*.

"The pain . . . great man does": the passage from Winckelmann quoted in chap. 2.

9

all critics who have reflected . . . this idea: Diderot in *Essai sur la peinture* (1765); James Harris in *Discourse on Music, Painting and Poetry* (1744); Abbé Dubos in *Réflexions critiques sur la poésie, la peinture et la musique* (1719); Hagedorn in *Betrachtungen über die Malerei* (1762); and Mendelssohn in *Betrachtungen über die Quellen der schönen Wissenschaften und Künste* (1757).

"assumes such an unnatural appearance . . . disgust or horror": a free quotation from *Laocoön* 3.

a laughing La Mettrie: an allusion to *Laocoön* 3, where a portrait of the French philosopher (1707–1751) is cited as an example of the problematic depiction of the climax of an emotion.

Myron's cow: This is the best-known work of the sculptor Myron (flourished about 450 BC), famous for its verisimilitude.

Huysum: Jan van Huysum (1682–1749), Dutch painter, noted for his pictures of flowers.

the more often we look at it: Lessing writes: "They make a weaker impression the more often we look at them, until finally they fill us with disgust or horror" (*Laocoön* 3:20).

"La Mettrie . . . a grin": *Laocoön* 3:20. Democritus was known as the "laughing philosopher."

Sulzer: Johann Georg Sulzer (1720–1779), Swiss aesthetician; he had announced he was working on *Allgemeine Theorie der schönen Künste*, which eventually appeared between 1771 and 1774.

the classification of Aristotle: in *Nicomachean Ethics* 1094a. Though he does not mention him by name until section 19, Herder's direct source for the application of Aristotle's distinction between "work" and "energy" to art was James Harris's *Discourse on Music, Painting and Poetry* (1744).

aliquid immensum infinitumque: something immeasurable and infinite.

But the tranquil repose . . . expression swell: an allusion to Winckelmann's notion of the "noble simplicity and tranquil grandeur" of Greek art.

10

I believe that the distinction . . . kinds of imitation: Lessing writes at the beginning of *Laocoön* 7: "When we say that the artist imitates the poet or the poet the artist, we can mean one of two things: either that the one takes the other's work as his model, or that both work from the same model and one borrows his manner of presentation from the other."

Juvenal speaks of a soldier's helmet: Satires 11.100–107: "In those days a soldier was a simple man with no appreciation of Greek art. If there were goblets made by great craftsmen in his share of the booty from a sacked city, he would break them up, just so his horse could delight in trappings and his helmet be embossed with images for his enemy to see at the moment of death: Romulus' beast commanded by order of fate to grow tame, or the twin Quirini under the rock, or the image of the god swooping down stripped of shield and spear" (trans. Susanna Morton Braund [Cambridge, MA: Harvard University Press, 2004]).

Addison: Herder has in mind Joseph Addison's *Dialogues upon the Usefulness of Ancient Medals* (1702).

dei pendentis: the hovering or descending god (translated in the note above as "the god swooping down").

the explanation of Addison and Spence: Lessing discusses Addison's and Spence's interpretation of the passage from Juvenal in detail in note 3 of *Laocoön* 7.

Hysteron proteron: a figure of speech in which the word or phrase that should properly come second is put first (for example, "He was bred and born in Yorkshire"), or, more generally, the position or arrangement of things in the reverse of their natural or rational order.

"In the earliest days of the Republic . . . his helmet": a free quotation from *Laocoön* 7:n3.

"It is harsh . . . trifling matter": *Laocoön* 7:n3.

Shakespeare's fine phrase about Mercury: Presumably Herder is thinking of the following lines from *Hamlet*: "A station like the herald Mercury / New lighted on a heaven-kissing hill" (3.4).

the Farnese frescoes by Carracci: Annibale Carracci (1560–1609), Italian painter whose major work consists of the mythological frescoes in the Palazzo Farnese in Rome.

Homer's divine horses . . . ocean: Iliad 5.768–72.

Cacklogallinians: a race of giant fowl endowed with the power of speech and reason in Samuel Brunt's satire *A Voyage to Cacklogallinia with a Description of the Religion, Policy, Customs and Manners of That Country* (1727). Like many in his day, Herder erroneously attributes the work to Jonathan Swift. In the second part of the voyage, the hero and the Cacklogallinians journey to the moon; Herder is referring to the passage in which the lunar explorers rested a while on a cloud to acclimatize themselves to the thin air.

Lessing's amended reading of this passage: Lessing interprets the Latin word *pendentis* in its figurative meaning as "uncertain" or "unresolved" (*Laocoön* 7:n3).

11

within and without the walls of Troy all goes wrong: Horace Epistles 1.2, line 16: "Iliacos intra muros peccatur et extra."

historical mythology takes the place of emblematic mythology: This distinction is from Winckelmann: "The allegory of the ancients might be divided . . . into two classes, viz. the *sublime* [that is, emblematic], and the *more vulgar* [historical]. Symbols of the one might be those by which some mythological or philosophical allusion, or even some unknown or mysterious rite, is expressed. Such as are more commonly understood, viz. personified virtues, vices, etc. might be referred to the other" (*An Answer to the Foregoing Letter*, trans. Henry Fusseli [London, 1765]), 201–2; repr. in *Essays on the Philosophy and History of Art*, ed. Curtis Bowman, vol. 1 [Bristol: Thoemmes, 2001]).

Venus, Juno, and Minerva . . . beauty: Cf. Lessing: "To the sculptor Venus is simply Love; hence he must give her all the modest beauty and all the graceful charm that delight us in an object we love and that we therefore associate with our abstract conception of love. The slightest deviation from this ideal makes its form unrecognizable to us. Give it beauty, but with more majesty than modesty, and we have not a Venus but a Juno. Give it charms, but those which are more commanding and masculine than graceful, and we have not a Venus but a Minerva. Worst of all, a wrathful Venus, a Venus driven by fury and the desire for revenge, is, to the sculptor, a complete contradiction in terms, for love as such is never wrathful or vengeful" (*Laocoön* 8:52–53).

υγρον: the moistness.

poets . . . invented and defined mythology: Hesiod's *Theogony* is the first extant and systematic account of Greek religious beliefs.

Damm's teaching: Christian Tobias Damm (1699–1778), theologian and philosopher, author of *Einleitung in die Götterlehre und Fabelgeschichte der ältesten griechischen und römischen Welt* (1763).

"Sleep no more . . . Adonis lies dying": from Bion, *The Lament for Adonis* (*Idylls* 1.2–11); adapted from the translation by J. M. Edmonds (London: Heinemann, 1928). Cypris is an epithet of Aphrodite.

the idea of love in masquerade?: Cf. Lessing: "Just as this rule is confirmed by the practice of the ancients, so is its intentional violation the favorite fault of modern poets. All of their imaginary beings are masked, and those who understand such masquerades best are usually the ones who least comprehend the main task: how to let their beings act, and reveal their characters through their actions" (*Laocoön* 10:60).

Cupid . . . Psyche: Cf. the story of Amor and Psyche in Apuleius's *Metamorphoses*. A marble group depicting Amor and Psyche is in the Capitoline Museum.

Jupiter . . . Ganymede: A marble copy of a group by Leochares (fourth century AD) is in the Vatican. It represents an eagle bearing away Ganymede. There is another statue of Ganymede in the museum in Olympia. See also Ovid *Metamorphoses* 10.155–61.

Diana . . . Endymion: See Apollodorus 1.56; Cicero *Tusculan Disputations* 1.38.1116b.

Venus . . . skin: *Iliad* 5.334–80.

idol of our modern mythologists: Herder's target here is once again Damm.

"When the poet personifies abstractions . . . attributes": a free quotation from *Laocoön* 10.

like puppets: Cf. Lessing: "If the poet employs these artistic trimmings, he turns that higher being into a puppet" (*Laocoön* 10:60).

"To me the figures of mythology . . . recognized": a paraphrase of *Laocoön* 8:52.

12

"Erycina . . . Cupido": "blithe goddess of Eryx, about whom hover Mirth and Desire" (Horace *Odes* 1.2.33–34). Quotations from Horace in this chapter are drawn from the translation by C. E. Bennett (London: Heinemann, 1964).

When Fear *and* Care: Horace 3.1.37–40.

also flit at night: Horace 2.16.9–12.

when Death: Horace 1.4.13–14.

Fortune, Necessity, Hope, Fidelity: in 1.35.7–22: "Te semper anteit saeva Necessitas, / clavos trabales et cuneos manu / gestans aena, nec severus / uncus abest liquidumque plumbum. / te Spes et albo rara Fides colit / velata panno" (Before thee ever stalks Necessity, grim goddess, with spikes and wedges in her brazen hand; the stout clamp and molten lead are also there. Thee, Hope cherishes and rare Fidelity, her hand bound with cloth of white). Lessing discusses the passage in *Laocoön* 10:n5.

Baxter: William Baxter (1650–1723) produced an edition and commentary of

Horace (1701). Herder ridicules Baxter's method of taking everything in a symbolical sense. A *dilogia* is repetition or ambiguity; that is, words or expressions that lend themselves to allegorical interpretation.

Gesner: Johann Matthias Gesner (1691–1761), rector of the Leipzig Thomasschule and later professor of rhetoric in Göttingen.

Antium: Antium (Anzio) did indeed possess a famous temple to Fortuna. Horace begins his ode with the words "O diva, gratum quae regis Antium" (O goddess that rulest pleasant Antium).

"She can raise us up or humble us": "praesens vel imo tollere de gradu / mortale corpus vel superbos / vertere funeribus triumphos" (mighty to raise our mortal clay from low estate or change proud triumphs into funeral trains) (1.35.2–4).

African Jupiter: the Zeus worshiped in Africa, for example, by the Ptolemists in Egypt.

Madonna in Loretto . . . Madonna in Parma: According to legend, the Virgin Mary's house was located in the Italian town of Loretto. In the Parma Cathedral there is a famous painting by Correggio of Mary's ascension to heaven.

"Thee the poor . . . Carpathian sea": "te pauper ambit sollicita prece / ruris colonus, te dominam aequoris / quicumque Bithyna lacessit / Carpathium pelagus carina" (thee the poor peasant entreats with anxious prayer; thee, as sovereign of the deep, whoever braves the Carpathian sea in Bithnyian bark) (1.35.5–8).

Baxter journeys as far as the moon . . . Gesner's explanation: Gesner takes issue with Baxter's claim that the moon itself is a *sortem fortunae*, that is, part of the domain of the goddess of fortune, but suggests that storms and so forth are, because their causes are inscrutable.

"Thee the wild . . . purple": 1.35.9–12.

"iniuriosio . . . frangat": "fearing lest with wanton foot thou overturn the standing pillar of the State, and lest the thronging mob arouse the peaceable 'to arms! to arms' and thus wreck the ruling power" (1.35.13–16).

"te semper . . . plumbum": 1.35.17–20; see the translation above. Some manuscripts have "serva" (servile) for "saeva" (grim, furious), and this is the reading that Baxter prefers.

Sanadon: Noël Etienne Sanadon (1676–1733), French philologist and translator of Horace (1728). The passage in question is quoted by Lessing in *Laocoön* 10:n5: "I daresay that this picture, taken in detail, would be more beautiful on canvas than in a heroic ode. I cannot bear such a hangman's kit of spikes, wedges, hooks, and molten lead. I have felt in duty bound to lighten this ballast by substituting in the translation general for particular ideas. It is to be regretted that the poet needs this corrective."

"Quod haec imago . . . venustulus!": "That this image was not to the good Sanadon's liking is due to the fact that he is a man of peculiar taste, fastidious and dainty!"

"Neque enim . . . uncus": "He does not seem to have understood how divine are the 'brazen hand' and 'stout clamps.'"

attirail patibulare: hangman's kit, Sanadon used the phrase earlier.

nec abest: nor are they wanting; translated on p. 401 as "are also there."

"te Spes . . . panno": "Thee, Hope cherishes and rare Fidelity, her hand bound with cloth of white" (1.35.21–22).

Spence is wrong: Spence writes: "The next figure here, is that of Honesty, or Fidelity. The Romans called her, Fides. . . . She is represented with an erect open air; and with nothing but a thin robe on, so fine that one might see through it. Horace therefore calls her thin-dressed, in one of his odes" (*Polymetis*, dialogue 10, p. 145). Lessing criticizes Spence in note 5 of *Laocoön* 10.

Bentley: Richard Bentley (1662–1742), philologist and editor of Horace (1711).

"Thus will they ever accompany . . . not like that": a paraphrase of 1.35.22–28.

whose name is ambiguous: "fortune" can mean both "luck" and "fate."

machines: The concept of machine as allegory can be found in Spence's *Polymetis* (dialogue 19, p. 302).

the labor of the Danaides: the fifty daughters of Danaos, all but one of whom murdered their husbands and were condemned to spend the afterlife filling a leaking bucket with water (Ovid *Metamorphoses* 4.462–63).

"she first rears her crest . . . on the earth": Iliad 4.442–43.

Winckelmann's work on allegory: *Versuch einer Allegorie besonders für die Kunst* (1766).

13

When Achilles . . . Hector: Iliad 20.445–46.

"in the language of poetry . . . before him"?: Laocoön 12:69.

gradus ad Parnassum: the steps to Parnassus, the mountain sacred to the Muses and Apollo. Here it refers to a dictionary or handbook for poets containing information on meter, synonyms, etc.

μυθος: mythology, legend, fable.

as long as his Minerva . . . wounded gods: Iliad 5.127–28.

"Achilles did not see . . . invisible": The passage refers to an episode in *The Iliad* (20.443–45) when Apollo rescues Hector from danger by concealing him in mist and bearing him away.

amphibolia: double meanings.

"Neptune blinded": Laocoön 12:69.

"Invisibility . . . fellow gods": Laocoön 12:70. The final sentence in the passage is drawn from note 3 of chap. 12.

Pallas . . . power of prophecy: an apocryphal variation of the cause of Tiresias's blindness; after Callimachus, hymn 5. For the more familiar version of the story, see Ovid *Metamorphoses* 3.317–38.

Calydon: the son of Ares and Astynome; after Pseudo-Plutarch De fluviis 22.4.

Jupiter . . . Heliacmon: after *De fluviis* 18.1. Heliacmon was a Macedonian river god.

"wie . . . beschleichet": "as all maidens do, / likes to steal up to lovers." The lines are from Johann Peter Uz's "Der Morgen." The "sister of Amor" is there identified with Aurora or Dawn.

Why must he steal past . . . divine form: Herder's interpretation of this passage is dubious; there is no suggestion in the text that Apollo's coming "like the night" can be taken to mean "wrapped in darkness"; furthermore, there is no mention whatsoever of him "stealing past" or of assuming divine form.

Thetis . . . to Olympus: The text makes no mention of a cloud.
"That man endures . . . immortals": *Iliad* 5.407.
Jamblichus: the author (ca. 250–325 AD), of a *Life of Pythagorus* and *On the Egyptian Mysteries*.

14

"Nor can the painter . . . gods!": a paraphrase of *Laocoön* 12:67.
the Clarke-Ernesti edition of Homer: Samuel Clarke's edition of Homer (1735–40) was reprinted by Johann August Ernesti in Leipzig (1759–64).
Eustathius: a twelfth-century editor of Homer.
Micromegas: an allusion to Voltaire's story "Micromégas," which concerns a visitor to Earth from Sirius who is "eight leagues tall."
as with that angel in the Koran: Herder's allusion is obscure.
"It was a large, black, rough stone . . . times past": *Laocoön* 12:67.
ἑκατὸν πολείων πρυλέεσσ᾽ ἀραρυῖαν: fitted with the foot soldiers of a hundred cities.
μωρον: simplicity.
This question . . . an Indian: an allusion to Diderot's *Lettre sur les aveugles à l'usage de ceux qui voient* (Letter on the Blind for the Use of Those Who See, 1749), where he has the blind mathematician Nicholas Saunderson say: "Ask an Indian why the world is suspended in the air and he will reply that it is carried on the back of an elephant; and what does the elephant rest on? On a tortoise. And what supports the tortoise?" (*Œvres complètes de Diderot*, ed. J. Assézat ([Paris: Garnier, 1875], 1:308).

15

Several pictures that Mr L. . . . translated: The pictures referred to are episodes from *The Iliad* which Lessing uses to illustrate the weakness of Caylus's argument in his *Tableaux tirés de l'Iliade*. Caylus suggests as a criterion for the quality of poetic works their usefulness for the painter. Lessing imagines that Homer's works had been completely lost and asks if we could ever form a notion of them from paintings based on them. The first translation of *The Iliad* into German was published in 1540 by Eobanus Hessus; Johann Heinrich Voß's influential versions of *The Iliad* and *The Odyssey* did not appear until 1781 and 1793, respectively, that is, after Herder is writing.
Meinhard: Johann Nicolaus Meinhard (1727–1767), a translator whose plan to render the masterpieces of every national literature into German failed because of a lack of public interest.
it is patriotism: a sideswipe aimed at Friedrich Just Riedel, who expressed his skepticism vis-à-vis Meinhard's scheme in his *Denkmahl des Herrn J. N. Meinhard* (1768). In the passages cited by Herder in footnote 200, Riedel writes: "As desirous as I would have been of Meinhard's translation, I freely admit that I would have continued to study my Homer in the original. It is not envy of my countrymen if I do not wish them to have a German Homer: it is patriotism. They should read him in the Greek."
the English Homer: Alexander Pope produced verse translations of both *The Iliad* (1715–20) and *The Odyssey* (1725–26).

"*'round wheels, brazen, eight-spoked'*": Lessing is discussing the description of Hera's chariot (*Iliad* 5.722–23).

Homer's image of Apollo descending: Iliad 1.44–52.

"It is impossible": *Laoöcon* 13:72.

Eupolis . . . Pericles: Eupolis (446–411 BC), one of the leading exponents of Old Comedy. The quotation is from Pliny *Epistles* 1.20.

the speech of Ulysses: Iliad 3.221–23.

erebre, assidue, large: full, uninterrupted, copious.

Menelaus catches sight . . . his bride: Iliad 3.21–29.

16

"*Painting produces its effect . . . the latter*": This is not a direct quotation, but a summary of Lessing's position, as set forth in chaps. 15–18 of *Laocoön*.

Painting produces its effect entirely in space: In the *Fourth Grove* Herder will go further and distinguish between two- and three-dimensional space, and hence between painting and sculpture.

color clavichord: The Jesuit mathematician Louis-Bertrand Castel (1688–1757) spent the best part of thirty years attempting to construct a harpsichord that played music in the medium of light and color rather than sound. Underpinning his various prototypes (the earliest, in around 1730, used colored slips of paper, whereas later models employed a hundred candles illuminating glass filters) was his theory that light is a product of vibration, like sound, and that therefore color and musical tone are analogous in nature. Attempting to relate the spectrum of colors to the overtone series in music and extending this relationship to "shade" in both, he devised a chromatic scale of twelve notes, each step of which is analogous to a specific color. Herder is frequently contemptuous of Castel's invention.

sensuously perfect discourse: Baumgarten's definition of poetry (*Meditationes*, § 7).

another species of discourse: that is, rhetoric. According to Baumgarten, rhetoric is the science of the imperfect or unperfected presentation of sensuous representations, and poetics of the perfected presentation of sensuous representations (*Meditationes*, § 117).

waving or serpentine lines: an allusion to William Hogarth's (1687–1764) ideal of the "waving line" as the "line of beauty" in *Analysis of Beauty* (1753); translated into German in 1754.

that "in the verbal . . . form of language": a paraphrase of *Laocoön* 17:88.

Haller: Albrecht von Haller (1708–1777); quoted by Lessing in *Laocoön* 17:86–87.

17

nexus: Baumgarten's term for the interrelationships of the sensuous representations presented in words and articulated sounds, the framework that connects the individual successive sensuous images into action or plot (*Meditationes*, § 6).

When he has Hebe . . . Juno's chariot: Lessing uses the example in *Laocoön* 16:80.

"*what trouble and effort . . . the whole*": Laocoön 17:86.

Brockes: Barthold Heinrich Brockes (1680–1747), descriptive poet and author of *Irdisches Verngügen in Gott* (1721–48).

the bow of Pandarus: *Iliad* 4.105–26.

the shield of Achilles: *Iliad* 18.468–608.

rightly contrasted with Virgil: Lessing contrasts Homer's description of the shield of Achilles with Virgil's description of the shield of Aeneas (*Aeneid* 8.447–53 and 625–731); see *Laocoön* 18:95.

Perhaps there are ten pictures on the shield: In chap. 19, Lessing refutes claims that the figures Homer describes could not all have found space on the shield by suggesting that "Homer does not have more than ten different pictures on the entire shield" (p. 100). The rest of the sentence is a paraphrase of 18:95.

the scepter of Agamemnon: This is another example of an object described by Homer (*Iliad* 2.100–108), which Lessing uses to illustrate his argument (*Laocoön* 16:82–83).

the Menelaus whom such an arrow will strike: *Iliad* 4.32–147.

Mr. L. is wrong to say . . . picture: *Laocoön* 16:83.

Thetis implores Vulcan . . . work: *Iliad* 18.429–613.

Vulcan . . . lame cupbearer of the gods: *Iliad* 1.584–600.

Achilles has lost his armor . . . slain: *Iliad* 16.786–857, 18.125.

Thersites: the ugliest of the Greeks at Troy; see *Iliad* 2.212–19 and section 20 here.

18

Anacreon: Greek lyric poet (sixth century BC) whose songs mostly celebrate wine and love.

Pindar: Greek odist (ca. 520–445 BC).

Ossian . . . Milton . . . Klopstock: here representatives of northern epic poetry.

Mr. L. should not have confessed . . . conclusions: Lessing writes: "I should put little faith in this dry chain of reasoning did I not find it completely confirmed by the procedure of Homer, or rather if it had not been just this procedure that led me to my conclusions" (*Laocoön* 16:79).

Horace, Pope, Kleist, and Marmontel: Lessing quotes from Horace's *De arte poetica*, Pope's Prologue to *Satires*, Christian Ewald von Kleist's *Der Frühling*, and Marmontel's *Poétique française* (*Laocoön* 17).

"Inceptis . . . locus": Horace *Ars poetica* 14–19 (with the omission of line 17). "Works with noble beginnings and grand promises often have one or two purple patches so stitched on as to glitter far and wide, when Diana's grove and altar . . . or the river Rhine, or the rainbow is being described. For such things there is a place, but not just now."

Pope . . . a banquet of nothing but sauces: Lessing quotes not Pope but William Warburton, the editor of Pope's works (1751); see *Laocoön* 17:n5.

Kleist: Lessing mentions Kleist in the final lines of chap. 17. The title of the critical work on Kleist to which Herder refers is possibly Friedrich Nicolai's *Ehrengedächtnis Herrn E. Chr. v. Kleist* (1760).

Marmontel: Lessing quotes Marmontel in note 6 of chap. 17.

19

Shaftesbury: Anthony Ashley Cooper, third Earl of Shaftesbury (1671–1713), moral philosopher and uncle of James Harris.

It is a pity . . . superior *to the others*: Harris writes: "The Design of this Discourse is to treat Music, Painting and Poetry; to consider in what they agree, and in what they differ; and *which upon the whole is more excellent than the other two*" (*Discourse on Music, Painting and Poetry* 1:2:55).

master of philosophy: Wolfgang Ludwig Gräfenhahn (1718–1767), subrector of the grammar school at Bayreuth. He wrote four speeches, each representing one of the four arts mentioned by Herder, which were read out by pupils of the school (hence "schoolboyish contest").

Painting . . . arbitrary means: Harris, *Three Treatises*, pp. 55–58.

the author of Philosophical Writings: Moses Mendelssohn; Herder is thinking in particular of *On the Main Principles of the Beaux Arts and Belles Lettres*, which was reprinted in Mendelssohn's *Philosophical Writings*.

The fittest subjects of painting . . . *known to but a few*: Harris, *Three Treatises*, pp. 61–65.

The subjects of music . . . sounds, and so on: Harris, *Three Treatises*, pp. 65–67.

The subjects of poetry . . . natural sounds: Harris, *Three Treatises*, pp. 70–74.

the proper subjects of painting . . . tedious or obscure: Harris, *Three Treatises*, pp. 76–79.

There are also subjects . . . brooks no comparison: Harris, *Three Treatises*, pp. 83–93.

20

Constantinus Manasses: the author (1130–1187) of a history of the world; mentioned by Lessing in *Laocoön* 20:104.

Ariosto: Ludovico Ariosto (1474–1533), Italian poet and author of *Orlando Furioso*. Lessing quotes the description of Alcina, the main female character of the poem, from canto 7, stanzas 11–15.

Helen appears, the elders see her: Iliad 3.141–60. Lessing also quotes this passage (chap. 21).

"to show us Helen's beauty by its effect": a paraphrase of Lessing's argument in 21:111.

"white-elbowed Juno": Cf. *Iliad* 1.55 or 195, where Hera is described as "white-armed."

fair-kneed Briseis: Briseis is usually described as "fair-cheeked" (*Iliad* 1.184).

flashing-eyed Pallas: Iliad 1.206.

broad-shouldered Ajax: Iliad 3.227.

swift-footed Achilles: Iliad 23.249.

fair-haired Helen: Iliad 3.328.

Mr. L. asks what a nose . . . to improve: The line is from *Orlando Furioso* 7:12.

And if poetic art . . . Thersites . . . arise: Lessing: "According to this, then, ugliness by its very nature could not be a subject of poetry; and yet Homer has depicted Thersites as being extremely ugly, and this ugliness is described according to its contiguous parts. Why was he able to do with ugliness what he so wisely abstained from attempting to do with beauty?" (*Laocoön* 23:121).

21

en canaille: "like a scoundrel."

"He was so vile," says Homer . . . "among the Greeks": a paraphrase of *Iliad* 2.212–16.

γελοιον: the ridiculous.

Tobias Shandy: Lawrence Sterne, *Tristram Shandy*, vol. 2, chap. 12.

the harmless . . . that Aristotle considers indispensable to the ridiculous: *Poetics* 1449a; see *Laocoön* 23:122.

salva venia: with permission.

Riccius: Angelus Maria Riccius, author of *Dissertationes Homericae* (1740–41).

Mr. Klotz's design: Klotz argues that the exchange between Odysseus and Thersites was more at home in a satire than in a Homeric epic.

Homer himself at times slumbers: an allusion to Horace's *Ars poetica*: "Whenever the good Homer nods" (359).

Sorbonist . . . Moon is full: Sorbonist, a scholar of the Sorbonne, the oldest institution of higher education in Paris; Herder is quoting from Samuel Butler's (1616–1680) comic epic *Hudibras*: "For he a Rope of sand cou'd twist / As tough as learned a Sorbonist; / And weave fine Cobwebs, fit for Scull, / That's empty when the Moon is full" (1.1.157–62).

Claudius Belurgerius: Claude Belurger, French Hellenist, who according to Klotz's authorities had a picture of Thersites painted after the description in book 2 of the *Iliad*.

"Quintilian's words": *Institutio oratoria* 1.2.2.

"Just as . . . unfortunately laugh": *Epistolae Homericae*, pp. 30–31.

"If, on the contrary, we , , , who shriek": *Epistolae Homericae*, pp. 31–44.

Medea were to rejuvenate him: Using her witchcraft, Medea rejuvenates Aeson at the behest of his son, Jason (Ovid *Metamorphoses* 7.159–78).

his temporibus: of the times.

copiam vocabulorum: a rich supply of words.

Hortabur vero . . . copiam (note 266): "This man (Baumeister) encouraged me to study Greek literature in particular, the reading of which came easily to me. Since that time I undertook not so much to read as to devour the divine epics of Homer with Neumann, my roommate, so that we could get through them in their entirety in around 24 days. In those days we only intended to obtain for ourselves a rough impression of the shape and form of a great work of art and to acquire a wide vocabulary."

I can give more instances . . . future time: Herder does so in the *Second Grove*, which is devoted to Klotz.

reconciles him with Agamemnon by means of a subsidiary feature: "Then he sat down, and fear came on him and, stung by pain, he wiped the tear away with a helpless look" (*Iliad* 2.269–70).

the Latin translation: the Clarke-Ernesti edition.

22

mixed feeling: "Mixed feeling," or sensations consisting of both pleasure and displeasure, is a term borrowed from Moses Mendelssohn, who elaborates the concept in the conclusion to his *Letters on Sensations* and also in his *Rhapsody, or Additions to the Letters on Sensations*.

Mr. L. is correct . . . monk's silly whim: *Laocoön* 23:122.

Edmund: the bastard son of Gloucester in *King Lear*, who asks: "Wherefore 'base,' / when my dimensions are as well compact, / My mind as generous, and my shape as true / As honest madam's issue?" (1.2.6–9)

excessive sweetness: In the passage cited by Herder, Mendelssohn writes: "Let us see how this unpleasant feeling is apt to arise naturally. Which senses are most prone to it? In my view they are taste, smell, and touch. The first two *through an excessive sweetness* and the last through an oversoftness of bodies that do not offer sufficient resistance to the nerves that touch them. These objects consequently become unbearable to sight also, simply through the association of ideas when we recall the disgust that they cause taste, smell, or touch."

23

Hogarth's most ingenious composition: Hogarth was noted for his satirical engravings, acute and grotesque caricatures, and exposure of vice and folly.

here I disagree with Mr. L. entirely: See *Laocoön* 25.

lizard . . . Socrates: Lessing (*Laocoön* 25:132) refers to Aristophanes' comedy *The Clouds* (169–74). The lizard is disgusting because it interrupts Socrates' open-mouthed observation of the moon by defecating on him.

All Hottentot tales: Lessing quotes from one such tale ("Tquassouw and Knonmquaiha"), which appeared in the weekly journal *The Connoisseur*.

Hesiod's depiction of Sadness: This is mentioned by Lessing, (*Laocoön* 25:133. Pseudo-Longinus in *On the Sublime* (9.5) criticizes the line "from their noses a discharge flowed" in *Scutum Hercules*, a work falsely attributed to Hesiod.

"Although my reasoning . . . more of the source": a quotation from Lessing's own preface to *Laocoön*, substituting Lessing's name for that of Baumgarten.

24

Since I have had the good fortune . . . nod of approval: Herder notes Winckelmann's applause for the "Pindaric author of the *Fragments*" in a letter to Hamann dated the end of April 1768.

torn . . . murderer's hand: Winckelmann was stabbed to death by an acquaintance, Arcangeli, on 8 June 1768.

tears of melancholy . . . death: See Herder's "Hymn of Praise to My Countryman, J. Winckelmann," written in June 1768 and printed in *SWS* 28:296–98.

should have died in his place: Herder should have been careful what he wished for: Klotz died at the age of thirty-two on 31 December 1771.

Conclusion

They were written as chance dictated . . . disorder: Again, Herder is quoting the preface to *Laocoön*, using the same language to describe the *Critical Forests* as Lessing does to characterize his own work.

the title of my book . . . quibbles: Inevitably, Klotz's disciples did precisely that in an anonymous review of the *First Grove* in *Bibliothek der schönen Wissenschaften*, no. 10 (1769): "He [Herder] will recall a certain Gryphius who also wrote Forests in the last century, not Critical Forests, to be sure, but Forests all the same, which have withered, just as Herder's will soon wither. . . . Truly I have wandered lost through these forests for several days; I fancy I have heard the hooting of night owls and eagle owls. But otherwise I have seen nothing but gnarly pines, caterpillars and cobwebs, and withered branches. If I am not mistaken, the weather has taken a turn for the worse, and I fear, I fear that it will do so again today."

CRITICAL FORESTS: FOURTH GROVE, ON RIEDEL'S *THEORY OF THE BEAUX ARTS*

Written in 1769, this essay was first published in *Johann Gottfried Herders Lebensbild*, ed. Emil Gottfried Herder (Erlangen, 1846), 1:217–520. The text is based on *Kritische Wälder: Viertes Wäldchen*, in *Schriften zur Ästhetik und Literatur, 1767–1781*, ed. Günter E. Grimm, vol. 2 of Johann Gottfried Herder, *Werke* (Frankfurt am Main: Deutscher Klassiker Verlag, 1993), 247–442.

"Unus erat . . . dixere Chaos!": "In all the world one only face of Nature did abide / which men call Chaos" (Ovid *Metamorphoses* 1.6–7). The motto represents Herder's first dig at Friedrich Just Riedel, who is the target of Herder's polemics in the *Fourth Grove*. In Herder's view, Ovid's depiction of Chaos corresponds to Riedel's entire theory of aesthetics.

I

1

our new fashionable philosophy: that is, Riedel's aesthetics.

"Man . . . wherever it is found": The quotation is in fact a paraphrase of Riedel's *Theorie der schönen Künste und Wissenschaften* (Theory of the Beaux Arts and Belles Lettres) (Jena: Cuno, 1767), 7.

the contrary error: that is, the pure sensualism advocated by Riedel.

the soul of a Newton: This passage alludes to Mendelssohn's *Briefe über die Empfindungen* (Letters on Sensations, 1755); see the "Twelfth Letter."

fundamental faculties: Riedel actually uses the term "fundamental drive" (*Grundtrieb*) rather than *Grundkraft*.

Leibniz's pupils: Wolff, Baumgarten, and G. F. Meier.

Mendelssohn and Sulzer: Herder is thinking of Mendelssohn's *Letters on Sensations* and *Phädon, oder Über die Unsterblichkeit der Seele* (Phaedon, or On the Immortality of the Soul, 1767); and Sulzer's *Moralische Betrachtungen über die Werke der Natur* (Moral Reflections on the Works of Nature, 1741) and *Unter-*

suchung über den Ursprung der angenehmen und unangenehmen Empfindungen (Inquiry into the Origin of Agreeable and Disagreeable Sensations, 1762).

Crusian: Christian August Crusius (1715–1775), professor of philosophy in Leipzig; his major work was *Weg zur Gewißheit und Zuverlässigkeit der menschlichen Erkenntnisse* (1747).

the philosophy of the mind, of the heart, of taste: the names that Riedel gives to the three branches of philosophy that he distinguishes (that is, psychology, ethics, and aesthetics).

2

"The sensus communis . . . the good": an indirect quotation from Riedel.

Riedel's Letters on the Public: *Über das Publikum. Briefe an einige Glieder desselben* (1768). Herder has the first letter in mind here.

Plato's dark cave: Plato's famous simile of the cave in *Republic* 514–21b. Herder is comparing Riedel's theory to those captives in the cave who are bound in such a way that they can see only the shadows cast on the walls and not the bodies that throw them.

qualitas occulta: an obscure or indistinct property, a vague feeling.

C.: Christian August Crusius.

Plato barred the corrupting poets: *Republic* 377b–98b.

our great anti-Wolffian thinkers: presumably figures such as Crusius, Joachim Georg Darjes (1714–1791), and Riedel.

Baumgarten's psychology: as developed in the third part of his *Metaphysica* (1739), where he distinguishes between *psychologia empirica* and *psychologia rationalis*.

Klopstock: Friedrich Gottlieb Klopstock (1724–1803), sentimental poet and author of the religious epic *The Messiah*.

Montaigne: Michel Eyquem de Montaigne (1533–1592). The goal of the self-analysis practiced in his *Essays* (1580) was the liberation of the subject from self-deception.

Home's observations: Henry Home, Lord Kames (1696–1782), British philosopher whose major work *Elements of Criticism* (1763–65), in the tradition of Hutcheson, Burke, and Gerard, was enthusiastically received in Germany.

unfeeling demonstrator: that is, as a representative of the Wolffian method.

as the Spartan asked the eulogist of Hercules: The Spartan is Antalcidas; "When a lecturer was about to read a laudatory essay on Hercules, he said, 'Why, who says anything against him?'" (Plutarch *Moralia*, Apophth. lac. Antalc. 5). The translation is by Frank Cole Babbitt (London: Heinemann, 1931).

the magic lantern of the Theosophists: The Theosophists sought knowledge of God through intuition and introspection, a method Herder thinks comparable to the *laterna magica* invented by the Jesuit Athanasius Kircher (1602–1680) which projected images painted on a lens.

3

He distinguishes three paths of aesthetics: in the first letter of *On the Public*.

where the Greek . . . the master: a paraphrase of Riedel; the master is Sophocles, whose dramas Aristotle uses as the basis of his theory of tragedy.

Winckelmann . . . Diderot: Winckelmann devoted an entire essay to the *Apollo Belvedere*. Anton Raphael Mengs (1728–1779), a painter who put Winckelmann's ideals into practice; Herder is referring to Mengs's *Gedanken über die Schönheit und den Geschmack in der Malerei* (1762). Christian Ludwig Hagedorn (1713–1780), landscape painter and author of *Betrachtungen über die Malerei* (1762). William Hogarth (1697–1764), painter and caricaturist, author of *Analysis of Beauty* (1755). Joseph Addison (1672–1719), critic and editor of *The Spectator*, in successive numbers of which appeared his discussion of *Paradise Lost* (1712). Home discusses Shakespeare in *Elements of Criticism*. Melchiore Cesarotti (1730–1808), Italian poet and translator of Ossian (1763). Georg Christoph Meier, pupil and popularizer of Baumgarten, author of *Beurtheilung des Heldengedichts, der Messias* (1749). Vincenzo Scamozzi (1552–1616), architect and author of *L'Idea dell'architettura universale* (1615). Giacomo Barozzi da Vignola (1507–1573), Michelangelo's successor as chief architect on Saint Peter's Cathedral in Rome and author of *Regole degli cinque ordini d'architettura* (1563) and *Regole della perspettiva pratica* (1583). Jean-Philippe Rameau (1683–1764), composer and musicologist, author of *Traité de l'harmonie réduite à des principes naturels* (1722). Christoph Nichelmann (1717–1762), composer and author of *Die Melodie nach ihrem Wesen, sowohl als nach ihren Eigenschaften* (1755). Jean-Georges Noverre (1727–1810), dancer, choreographer, and author of *Lettres sur la danse et sur les ballets* (1760). Herder is thinking of Diderot's *Essai sur la peinture* (1765) and *Discours sur la poésie dramatique* (1758).

"This rule," says Mr. R.: "The first lawgiver of art [that is, Aristotle] observed a single work, which was rightly admired by all of Greece. He analyzed the play's structure, disposition, and economy, and finally its individual parts; each observation he made becomes for him a rule, which the poet perhaps had in mind and perhaps did not, and thus arose a rulebook for the epic and the drama" (*On the Public*, p. 7, first letter).

"The rules that the art theorist": a paraphrase of Riedel: "When the theorist discovers the rules according to which Homer composes by turning the pages of *The Iliad*, for whom else should these rules be meant? For Milton, for Klopstock, for Camoens, for Voltaire? No then!" (*On the Public*, p. 9; first letter).

Schönaich: Christoph Otto von Schönaich (1725–1807), poet and follower of Gottsched; he also wrote a satire directed at Klopstock.

Butler: Samuel Butler (1612–1680), author of the satirical heroic epic *Hudibras* (1663–78), cited by Riedel.

for any genius . . . flown before: Riedel: "Another poet who is genius enough to open up a new path thereby becomes his own lawgiver and effortlessly shakes off the fetters with which Aristotle, Le Bossu, and Curtius would like to enchain him" (*On the Public*, pp. 9–10; first letter). The same point of view for which Herder here reproaches Riedel he will later praise when it is espoused by Young.

"But such rules go into too much detail!": Herder paraphrases the first of the reasons adduced by Riedel for his rejection of the Aristotelian path in aesthetics (*On the Public*, p. 9; first letter).

"How easy it is . . . rules": a paraphrase of the second reason advanced by Riedel (*On the Public*, p. 9; first letter).

in an example: The example is Homer's similes, which were often criticized in the eighteenth century for holding up the natural development of the action. Breitinger had defended Homer's practice in his *Critische Abhandlung von der Natur* (1740). Herder discusses the issue in the *First Grove*.

"As if . . . beauty . . . truth!": Riedel: "It would be a fine thing indeed if it were possible to define beauty like truth, to treat an ode like a *sorites*, the epic like a disputation, and to deduce a series of irrefutable conclusions from the prescribed rules of an artwork" (*On the Public*, p. 12; first letter). *Sorites* is a term denoting a form of connecting several logical propositions.

"Beauty is an αρριτον that is felt rather than taught": a quotation from Riedel, *On the Public*, p. 15. An αρριτον is something that is indefinable or inexpressible.

"But the idea that this inexpressible moment . . . think": "A sensitive soul will find beauty more beautiful and judge more correctly and artlessly than an apprentice who has studied every book from Aristotle onward—all the way to Baumgarten" (Riedel, *Theory of the Beaux Arts and Belles Lettres*, p. 34).

"arbitrary concepts . . . arbitrary rules": "Strictly speaking, arbitrary concepts entail only arbitrary rules, which have binding force only for one who takes these concepts to be true" (*On the Public*, p. 15; first letter).

"But perhaps . . . works of art?": "But perhaps these definitions, in order not to be arbitrary, are formed all too slavishly and abstracted merely from such works of art as are already to hand" (*On the Public*, p.15; first letter).

the Homean manner of thinking: Of the three aestheticians whom Riedel discusses, Home receives the most praise because he "studies the human heart with its manifold turns and changes" and "opens up sensation and follows its trail to the innermost recesses" (*On the Public*, p. 16; first letter).

4

as Mendelssohn and Sulzer have shown: Herder means Mendelssohn's work *Hauptgrundsätze der schönen Künste und Wissenschaften* (On the Main Principles of the Beaux Arts and Belles Lettres, 1757) and Sulzer's *Kurzer Begriff aller Wissenschaften* (A Brief Compendium of all Sciences, 1745).

Baumgarten . . . the art of thinking beautifully: Aesthetica, § 1.

scientia de pulcro et pulcris philosophice cogitans: the science of the beautiful and of thinking philosophically about the beautiful.

if Meier adds . . . sensuous cognition: In his *Anfangsgründe aller schönen Wissenschaften* (Fundamentals of All Belles Lettres, 1748–50), Meier speaks of the "improvement of the lower faculties of the soul" as one of the aims of that branch of aesthetics which treats of sensuous cognition (§ 10).

a natural and an artificial aesthetics: Baumgarten distinguishes between *aesthetica naturalis* (the human soul's inborn ability to think beautifully) and *aesthetica artificialis* (the science of the beautiful) in §§ 2 and 3 of *Aesthetica*.

"Is . . . the scope of the philosopher?": Baumgarten does indeed consider a number of criticisms that might be leveled at his conception of aesthetics (*Aesthetica*, §§ 5–12). This one, and Baumgarten's reply, can be found in *Aesthetica*, § 6.

"But confusion is the mother of error": This and Baumgarten's replies, which Herder paraphrases, are from *Aesthetica*, § 7.

"*Distinct cognition is better!*": *Aesthetica*, § 8.

"*if the analogue of reason . . . itself*": *Aesthetica*, § 9. Herder is referring to the criticism that Baumgarten's definition of the sensuous implies a devaluing of reason.

aesthetics is . . . not science but art: *Aesthetica*, § 11.

"*aims to accommodate . . . comprehension*": *Aesthetica*, § 3.

captus: the power of comprehension.

"*that it affords . . . the boundaries of the distinct*": *Aesthetica*, § 3.

its observations . . . practical rules of thumb: *Aesthetica*, § 3.

"*it gives us an advantage . . . daily business*": *Aesthetica*, § 3.

Meier's tautologies: the following quotations refer to *Fundamentals*, §§ 10, 14, 17, 13, and 14.

5

fundamental feeling: Riedel, *Theory*, p. 10. That is, for Riedel beauty is a quality inhering not in an object itself but only in the subjective sensation of the observer.

man . . . a thinking and perceiving vegetable: This and the subsequent paragraphs are inspired by Locke's *Essay Concerning Human Understanding*: "He . . . will, perhaps, find Reason to imagine, That a *Foetus in the Mother's Womb*, *differs not much from the State of a Vegetable*; but passes the greatest part of its time without perception or thought. . . . Follow a *Child* from its birth, and observe the alterations that time makes, and you shall find, as the Mind by the Senses comes more and more to be furnished with *Ideas*, it comes to be more and more awake; thinks more, the more it has matter to think on" (2:i, 21–22). Herder follows Locke in assuming that there are no innate ideas or "immediate feelings" in the human mind; judgments are formed on the basis of sensory experience; but because the first and most necessary such judgments take place at an early stage in our mental development, they are erroneously taken by us to be inborn.

obscure idea of his ego . . . truth outside us: that is, the "original *sensus communis*," which Herder described in section 1: an awareness of self and the external world.

Sulzer has explained: in his *Theory of the Agreeable and Disagreeable Sensations*.

"*habitual ability to judge . . . immediately*": after Meier, *Fundamentals*, vol. 2, § 467.

our sentimental philosophers: that is, sensualists and empiricists.

6

Mr. R. has therefore fallen prey to opinions: The subjectivist and relativist views attributed to Riedel in this paragraph are expressed in the third letter of *On the Public*, which is addressed to Mendelssohn (hence the reference to the latter's reaction). Here is a typical example: "One object can be now *beautiful*, now *ugly*, depending on the different subjects who experience it, just as pumpernickel is *good* for a Westphalian stomach and *bad* for a maid of honor."

polygraph: someone who writes a great deal.

Unity . . . diversity: the prerequisites of aesthetic pleasure for Baumgarten, who makes the condition of sensuous cognition the extensive clarity (multiplicity of an object's characteristics) and the confused cognition that apprehends the object in its complexity.

"*The* sensus communis . . . *in order to live*": Riedel, *Theory*, p. 7.

Pythians: seers, named after Pythia, the priestess of Apollo at the Delphic oracle.

tripod: Sitting on a tripod and inhaling intoxicating fumes, Pythia would enter a trance.

thyrsus staffs: staffs tipped with an ornament such as a pinecone, carried by Dionysos and his votaries.

the music of a rude, warlike people: that is, of the Dorians and Spartans. In *The Republic* (398c–99d) Plato prefers such music to the effect of flutes and elegies.

the songs of Tyrtaeus: Greek elegist (ca. 680–600 BC), composed war songs for the Spartans.

Phryne: fourth-century BC Athenian courtesan, lover, and model of Praxiteles and Apelles.

harmonically frigid tactics among the tones: contrapuntal, polyphonic music.

Klotz, whose visit he honors as if it were Apollo dropping by: Riedel dedicates the sixth letter of *On the Public* to Klotz, which begins with the words "A visit from Apollo with all his Muses would not have been as dear to me as was yours."

guild philosopher: an allusion to the academic clique around Klotz.

7

epitomator: a writer of extracts and summaries.

in his investigation of beauty . . . sublime: Riedel, *Theory*, chaps. 3 and 4.

Shaftesbury's and Harris's inquiries: Anthony Ashley Cooper, third Earl of Shaftesbury (1671–1713), author of *A Letter Concerning Enthusiasm* (1708) and *An Inquiry Concerning Virtue and Merit* (1709); James Harris (1709–1780), nephew of Shaftesbury; Herder is alluding to his *Three Treatises* (1744).

Lessing's essays on the fable and on painting: Lessing's *Fabeln* (1759) and *Laocoön*.

Sisyphus and the Danaides: Sisyphus was doomed forever to roll a boulder up a hill; the Danaides, forty-nine sisters who murdered their husbands on their wedding night, were condemned to draw water with a leaky bucket for all eternity.

Dusch: Johann Jakob Dusch (1725–1787), author of comic epics and didactic poems.

II

1

Mr. R. has used this occasion . . . Home and Mendelssohn (footnote): Home writes: "The term *beauty*, in its native signification, is appropriated to objects of sight" (*Elements of Criticism*, chap. 3, "Beauty"), to which Riedel replies: "Home is right in terms of the *native signification*; but we must choose the most apt meanings here, those which the words actually possess, and not those which they ought to have" (*Theory*, pp. 9–10). He goes on to say of Mendelssohn's claim that beauty "is the self-empowered mistress of all our sensations, the basis of all our natural drives" (in *Main Principles of the Beaux Arts and Belles Lettres*): "I cannot imagine that beauty is the basis of hunger and thirst; it is the basis of the drives of pleasure, but not of the drives of mere interest."

our vulgar critics and librarians: By "librarians" Herder means the authors of various literary journals of the time, for example, the *Deutsche Bibliothek der schönen Wissenschaften* and the *Philosophische Bibliothek* (both associated with the Klotz circle).

music, which for the Greeks had a wider range of signification: For the ancient Greeks, "music" was an umbrella term encompassing all the arts practiced by the Muses, including poetry and dance; furthermore, it possessed a political, ethical, and educational dimension, in addition to a merely aesthetic importance.

one that we lack even more than the first: As Herder complains in a later section of the *Fourth Grove*, contemporary musicological treatises such as Rameau's *Traité de l'harmonie réduite à ses principes naturels* (1722) and d'Alembert's *Éléments de musique théorique et pratique* (1752) are mainly concerned with the physical and mathematical aspects of music (length of strings, overtones, measurable vibrations, and so on), rather than the philosophical investigation of the nature of music as such.

the most philosophical treatise: an allusion to Mendelssohn's *On the Main Principles of the Beaux Arts and Belles Lettres*.

The man blind from birth whom Diderot observed: in *Lettre sur les aveugles à l'usage de ceux qui voient* (Letter on the Blind for the Use of Those Who See, 1749).

blind Saunderson: Nicholas Saunderson (1682–1739), mathematician and author of *Elements of Algebra* (1740), in the preface of which his "palpable arithmetic" was explained; mentioned by Diderot.

even the rays of the sun had to be transformed into a body: Diderot: "The blind man therefore takes the presuppositions as they are given to him; he holds a ray of light to be a thin elastic thread or a succession of particles that strike our eyes with an unbelievable speed; and he calculates accordingly" (*Lettre sur les aveugles à l'usage de ceux qui voient*, in *Œvres complètes de Diderot*, ed. J. Assézat [Paris: Garnier, 1875], 1:302).

the man born blind . . . Cheselden: William Cheselden (1688–1752), English surgeon, performed an operation to restore the sight of a young man in 1729. The famous case is discussed by Voltaire in *Éléments de la philosophie de Newton* (1758); Cheselden later described the procedure in his *Account of Observations made by a young Gentleman who was born blind or lost his sight so early that he had no remembrance of ever having seen, and was couch'd between thirteen and fourteen years of age*. Herder made excerpts from it in his papers (*Nachlaß*, 5:15), which are reprinted in *Werke*, ed. Wolfgang Pross, vol. 2 (Munich: Hanser, 1987), 1224–1225: "When he first saw, he was so far from making any judgments about distances that he thought all objects whatever touch'd his eyes (as he express'd it). . . . He knew not the shape of any thing, nor any one thing from another, however different in shape or magnitude; but upon being told what things were, whose form he knew before from feeling, he would carefully observe that he might know them again; but having too many objects to learn at once, he forgot many of them. . . . He was very much surprised, that those things which he had liked best, did not appear most agreeable to his eyes, expecting those persons would appear most beautiful that he loved most, and such things to be most agreeable to his sight, that were so to his taste. We thought he soon knew what pictures represented . . . but we found afterwards we were mistaken; for about two months after he was couch'd; he discovered at once they represented solid bodies, when to that time he consider'd them only as party-color'd planes and surfaces diversified with variety of paint; but even then he was no less surprized, expecting the pictures would feel like the things they represented, and was amaz'd when he found those parts, which by their light and shadow appear'd now round and uneven, felt only like the flat rest, and ask'd which was the lying sense, feeling or seeing."

I could demonstrate . . . optics and logic: Herder is referring to George Berkeley's *Essay towards a New Theory of Vision* (1709), §§ 40–53.

Rousseau: Jean-Jacques Rousseau in *Émile*.

"Now I understand . . . a trumpet": after Locke: "A studious blind man, who had mightily beat his head about visible objects, and made use of the explication of his books and friends, to understand those names of light and colours which often came in his way, bragged one day, That he now understood what scarlet signified. Upon which, his friend demanding what scarlet was? The blind man answered, It was like the sound of a trumpet" (*Essay Concerning Human Understanding*, 3:iv, 11).

a philosophy of feeling that is no mere metaphor: Baumgarten's work remains metaphorical because it is an abstract discussion and definition of the term *aesthetics* and not, as Herder desires, an aesthetics of the individual senses and the arts pertaining to them.

gusto . . . *the Spanish*: The shift in the meaning of "taste" from referring exclusively to one of the five senses to an ethical and aesthetic concept begins with the Spanish writer Baltasar Gracián (1601–1658). Important interventions in the subsequent debate about taste include (in France) Dominique Bouhours' *La manière de bien penser dans les ouvrages de l'esprit* (1687), Jean de la Bruyère's *Caractères* (1688), and Jean-Baptiste Dubos' *Réflexions critiques sur la poésie et la peinture* (1719); (in Britain) David Hume's *On the Standard of Taste* (1757) and Alexander Gerard's *Essay on Taste* (1759); (in Germany) Christian Thomasius's *Von Nachahmung der Franzosen* (1687) and Johann Ulrich von König's *Untersuchung von dem guten Geschmack* (1727).

translated back into Latin: in Baumgarten's *Aesthetica*, where taste is defined as *cognitio sensitiva* (sensuous cognition) and *analogon rationis* (analogue of reason).

2

"the object that is pleasing . . . that is satisfying": an accurate paraphrase of Riedel, *Theory*, pp. 20–21.

a device emblazoned on your title page: as in Riedel's *Theory*.

his αρριτον of a Quaker feeling: a feeling that causes one to "quake" or tremble, like the members of the Religious Society of Friends when they receive the "inner light" of God; that is, a source of immediate, unreflective conviction.

Gerard . . . Home: Alexander Gerard (1728–1795), Scottish theologian and author of *An Essay on Taste* (1759). Home (Lord Kames) is Riedel's main authority.

Where there is beauty . . . invention: Herder is referring to Riedel's discussion of beauty at the end of chap. 3 of *Theory*.

ad captum: for the purpose of comprehension, that is, the accommodation to the intellectual level of the public; *ad captum ipsorum*—according to its own powers of comprehension; *ad captum nostrum*—according to our own state of knowledge.

Montesquieu: Charles de Secondat, Baron de La Brède et de Montesquieu (1689–1755), French writer and philosopher. Herder is referring here to his main work, *De l'esprit des loix* (1748), which views political and legal structures as influenced by the climatic and social conditions of particular peoples.

the citizens of Abdera: According to Lucian (*How to Write History* 1), the inhabitants of the Thracian city were overcome by a fever that saw them "going mad with tragedies, shouting iambics, and creating a din . . . hour after hour, day after day, until winter and a severe cold spell stopped their noise" (trans. A. M. Harmon [London: Heinemann, 1969]).

Pernety: Antoine-Joseph Pernety (1716–1796), Benedictine monk and librarian of Frederick the Great, author of *Dictionnaire portratif de peinture* (translated into German as *Des Herrn Pernety Handlexicon der bildenden Künste* in 1764).

Meusel: Johann Georg Meusel (1743–1820), literary historian and follower of Klotz.

Correggio: Antonio Allegri (ca. 1489–1534), Italian painter.

3

the painter . . . closed door: Herder's reference is obscure.

the . . . Webbs: theorists like Daniel Webb (1719–1798), author of *An Inquiry into the Beauties of Painting* (1760).

the viewer sunk . . . Apollo Belvedere: presumably Winckelmann, whose description of the *Apollo* Belvedere influenced this passage. The statue, named for its location in the Cortile del Belvedere in Rome, is a Roman marble copy of a Greek bronze original, made some time in the second half of the fourth century BC.

"das alter Griechen . . . verband": "which ancient Grecian hand, / by Graces led, joined with solid stone"; source unknown.

Belvedere Torso . . . Niobe: The *Belvedere Torso* is a statue of a male nude in the Vatican museum. The work, signed by Apollonius of Athens (active first century BC), was long thought to be of Hercules. Apollonius probably copied a second-century BC original. The statue of Niobe stands in the Uffizi in Florence. It is likely a Roman imitation of the group mentioned by Pliny (*Natural History* 36.4) and attributed either to Praxiteles or Scopas.

it feels . . . Eternal Youth: This passage is closely modeled on Winckelmann's words in *Description of the Torso in the Belvedere in Rome*. Achelous: Hercules fought and defeated the river god Achelous in a battle over Deianeira, a princess who later became his wife; Geryon: a three-headed giant and grandson of Medusa, vanquished by Hercules as his tenth labor; edge of the earth: the

Straits of Gibraltar, known to the Greeks as the Pillars of Hercules and supposedly erected by him to mark the limits of the world; Nemean lion: Hercules'
first labor was to kill this supernatural beast; immortality and Eternal Youth:
after his apotheosis, Hercules was married to Hebe, goddess of youth.

André Bardon: Michel François André Bardon (1700–1783), French painter,
poet, and composer, author of *Éléments de peinture pratique* (1766).

quantité . . . bien desordre: quantity of the beautiful figures, superabundance of
the objects, picturesque arrangement, poetic thoughts, beautiful disorder.

whether art ought to express only beautiful bodies: Cf. *Laocoön*, 2 and 24.

Saint Bartholomew: one of the first disciples of Christ, who is supposed to have
proselytized in Armenia, where he was flayed.

non me Praxiteles sed Marcus finxit Agrati: "Praxiteles did not make me, but
Marco d'Agrate"; inscription on the base of a statue of Bartholomew in Milan
Cathedral. Praxiteles was an Athenian sculptor (active fourth century AD).
Herder means to oppose the beauty of Praxiteles' works (for example, his *Kni-
dian Aphrodite*) with the repulsive sculpture by Marco d'Agrate (ca. 1504–
1574), which depicts Bartholomew with his flayed skin draped over his shoulder.

In one passage in his confused book: chap. 9 ("Similarity and Contrast") of Riedel's *Theory*.

why a marble statue . . . colors: Riedel: "If a marble statue is clothed with color,
like a painting, the similarity becomes too complete and it no longer affects us.
From a distance we can mistake it for a real person. Although we discover our
error when we approach it, no other response is awakened in us than astonishment at what has deceived us" (*Theory*, pp. 133–34). Riedel then adds: "The
idea of similarity descends into an idea of identity" (p. 134). He then uses the
same argument in conjunction with Myron's cow.

Phidias: Greek sculptor (active fifth century BC).

Myron: Greek sculptor (active fifth century BC), famous for his lifelike depictions
of animals.

"Why would the artist Myron's cow . . . hair?": Riedel: "We take pleasure in looking at an animal carved out of stone. But if the artist Myron had covered his
cow in hair, it would have looked too much like the original to give us pleasure,
and it would always lose out by comparison" (*Theory*, p. 142).

a partly mosaic work . . . golden eyes: that is, the practice of inserting eyes into
the sockets of statues.

wet drapery: Cf. Winckelmann: "By Drapery is to be understood all that the art
teaches of covering the nudities, and folding the garments. . . . The Greek Drapery, in order to help the Contour, was, for the most part, taken from thin and
wet garments, which of course clasped the body, and discovered the shape" (*Reflections on the Painting and Sculpture of the Greeks*, trans. Henry Fusseli [Lon-
don, 1765], 28–29; repr. in *Essays on the Philosophy and History of Art*, ed.
Curtis Bowman, vol. 1 [Bristol: Thoemmes, 2001]).

Descartes . . . optics: Descartes' work *Dioptrique, météores, géométrie* (1637),
which contains a treatise on the nature of light and the law of refraction.

Albani: Cf. Winckelmann's *Essay on the Capacity for the Sentiment for the Beautiful in Art* (1763): "Cardinal Alessandro Albani is able, merely by touching and

feeling, to say of many coins which emperor they represent" (in *Essays on the Philosophy and History of Art*, 1:xxviii). Winckelmann worked as a librarian for Albani, one of the greatest collectors of antiquities in the eighteenth century.

4

"wenn Zephyrs . . . Duft": from Ewald Christian Kleist's "Milon und Iris", in *Neue Gedichte* (1758). "When Zepyhr's wings thereupon /waft the blossoms of the trees, / the silvery stream, proud of her cover, / murmurs gaily past and exhales a sweet odor."

The tree . . . Petrarch's Laura: Francesco Petrarca (1304–1374), Italian poet and humanist, whose poetry celebrates Laura de Noves as the embodiment of love.

color clavichord: See note to *First Grove*, section 16.

Van Loo: Charles-André Vanloo (1705–1765), court painter of Louis XV of France, to whose portrait Herder is alluding.

Third: the third criterion by which painting and sculpture can be differentiated, after (1) the coexistence of objects in painting, and (2) the impossibility of uniting coexistence and succession.

dispute over whether the ancients . . . perspective: See, for example, *Laocoön* 19.

the Jupiter *of Phidias*: the huge figure of Zeus created by Phidias for the temple in Olympia, made of wood and decorated with ivory and gold.

counterpart in Homer: See *First Grove*, section 14.

Hogarth: In his *Analysis of Beauty*, Hogarth observes that the legs and thighs of the *Apollo Belvedere* are "too long and too large for the upper parts," but this nevertheless contributes to the statue's "remarkable beauty" (chap. 11).

5

the Egyptians . . . their misshapen figures: Herder is subscribing to the view set forth by Winckelmann that the Egyptians aspired not to beauty but to sublimity, which supposedly explains why their representation of the human form does not match that of the Greeks.

the Egyptians . . . the human spirit: In *Yet Another Philosophy of History*, Herder describes Egyptian civilization as the "boyhood" of the human spirit; the Egyptians thus play the same role in the history of the human race as a child or Cheselden's blind man plays in a human life.

like Swift's moon: an allusion to the satire *A Voyage to Cacklogallinia* (1727) by Samuel Brunt, though often attributed to Jonathan Swift in the eighteenth century. In the second part of the voyage, "A Journey to the Moon," the travelers encounter the two species of Selenites mentioned by Herder: the souls or spirits of dead inhabitants of the earth, and gigantic apparitions, which are the thoughts of vicious earth dwellers, cut loose from the body while the soul dreams.

our second education: In *Journal of My Voyage*, Herder distinguishes between an external education by others and an inner education, practiced by oneself.

this hard and lawful people . . . experiments: Cf. Winckelmann: "As their physicians durst prescribe no other remedies than those recorded in the sacred books, so their artists were not permitted to deviate from the ancient style; for their laws allowed no further scope to the mind than mere imitation of their forefathers, and prohibited all innovations" (*History of Ancient Art*, trans. G. Henry Lodge [Boston: Osgood, 1880]), bk. 2, chap. 1, p. 171; repr. in *Essays on the Philosophy and History of Art*, ed. Curtis Bowman, vol. 2 (Bristol: Thoemmes, 2001]).

becomes canon too soon . . . infallible: Cf. Winckelmann: "In their usages and religious forms, the Egyptians insisted upon a strict observance of the primitive ordinances, even under the Roman emperors" (*History of Ancient Art*, bk. 2, chap. 1, p. 170).

have arrived directly at the perspectival relief: the relief as part of the *skene*, or backdrop of the Greek theater.

Morelly: Abbé Morelly (1716–1781), French philosopher. Herder is referring to his *Physique de la beauté ou pouvoir naturel de ses charmes* (1748).

Baumgarten and Boden: See Baumgarten, *Aesthetica* §§ 451, 614–87; *Metaphysica*, §§ 514, 518. Benjamin Gottlieb Lorenz Boden (1737–1782), *De umbra poetica* (1764).

Lambert: Johann Heinrich Lambert (1728–1777), natural philosopher and mathematician; here Herder is alluding to the fourth part of Lambert's *Neues Organon* (New Organon, 1764).

as Winckelmann has claimed: in *Von der Fähigkeit der Empfindung des Schönen in der Kunst* (Essay on the Capacity for the Sentiment for the Beautiful in Art, 1763).

Mengs . . . Hagedorn: Herder is referring to Mengs's *Gedanken über die Schönheit und den Geschmack in der Malerei* (Thoughts on Beauty and Taste in Painting, 1762) and Hagedorn's *Betrachtungen über die Malerei* (Reflections on Painting, 1762).

the poetic theory of painting: the principle of *ut pictura poesis*, of painterly description, attacked by Lessing in *Laocoön*.

de Piles: Roger de Piles (1635–1709), French painter and author of several works on art, for example, *Conversations sur la connaissance de la peinture* (Conversations on the Appreciation of Painting, 1677) and *Cours de peinture par principes* (The Principles of Painting, 1708).

Félibien: André Félibien (1619–1695), French architect and author of many works on art, such as *Entretiens sur les vies et sur les ouvrages des plus excellens peintres anciens et modernes* (Conversations on the Lives and Works of the Most Excellent Ancient and Modern Painters, 1666–88) and *Des principes de l'architecture, de la sculpture, de la peinture et des autres arts qui en dépendent* (On the Principles of Architecture, Sculpture, Painting and Other Dependent Arts, 1699).

Lairesse: Gerard van Lairesse (1640–1711), Dutch painter and writer on art.

Klotz . . . citations: in Klotz's writings on coins and gemstones, which Herder criticizes in the *Third Grove*.

6

Euler: Leonhard Euler (1707–1783), Swiss mathematician who in his *Tentamen novae theoriae musicae* (Attempt at a New Theory of Music, 1738) sought to quantify dissonance.

d'Alembert: Jean Le Rond d'Alembert (1717–1783), French mathematician and philosopher who investigated the differential equations of vibrating strings; author of *Éléments de musique théorique et pratique, suivant les principes de M. Rameau* (1752) and *Réflexions sur la théorie de la musique* (1777).

Mersenne: Martin Mersenne (1588–1648), mathematician and musicologist, author of *Harmonie universelle* (1636).

Gravesande: Willem Jakob's Gravesande (1688–1742), lawyer, mathematician, and physicist. Herder is referring to his *Physices elementa mathematica experimentis confirmata* (1720–21), in which he sees the theory of music as part of the science of Nature.

Sauveur: Joseph Sauveur (1653–1716), French mathematician and physicist who investigated acoustics. He was the first to suggest that a vibrating string produced its primary or fundamental tone and harmonics (overtones) at the same time.

Quantz: Johann Joachim Quantz (1687–1773), flute teacher of Frederick the Great, author of *Instruction pour le jouer de la flûte traversière* (1752).

Bach: Carl Philipp Emanuel Bach (1714–1788), harpsichordist at the court of Frederick the Great, author of *Versuch über die wahre Art, das Clavier zu spielen* (Essay on the True Art of Playing the Keyboard Instruments, 1753–62).

Mozart: Leopold Mozart (1719–1787), court composer of the archbishop of Salzburg, author of *Versuch einer gründlichen Violinschule* (A Treatise on the Fundamental Principles of Violin Playing, 1756).

Agricola: Johann Friedrich Agricola (1720–1774), singing master at the Berlin court; Herder is referring to his 1757 translation of Pietro Francesco Tosi's *Opinioni di cantori antichi e moderni* (1723).

Newton . . . equations: An allusion to Newton's *Analysis per aequationes numero terminorum infinitas* (Of Analysis by Equations of an Infinite Number of Terms, written in 1669, not published until 1711).

musical accent: the means by which the fundamental tone is emphasized in a group of notes, by dynamic, rhythmic, melodic, or harmonic means.

A relation of the overtones, *says Rameau*: Jean-Philippe Rameau (1683–1764), composer and musicologist, author of *Traité de l'harmonie* (1722). For Rameau, harmony—not melody—was the basis of musical expression. He argued that harmony derives from the overtones generated by a vibrating string or tube. He also introduced the important and influential theory of chord inversion.

Sulzer's theory . . . negatively: In his *Inquiry into the Origin of Agreeable and Disagreeable Sensations* (1762), Sulzer explains the variety in the nature of sensation as the product of the physiological differences in the nerves of the respective sense organs: the nerves of the sense of touch are the coarsest, those of sight the finest. Herder sees a parallel between Rameau's argument (based on strings) and Sulzer's theory (based on nerves), and he regards the latter as insufficient as the former's physical-mathematical model of explanation.

the string is still . . . fundamental tone: Herder wrongly assumes that it is simply the thickness or coarseness of the string that produces the aftertones or overtones; but in reality every tone has overtones, even though the number may vary from instrument to instrument.

Rameau's fundamental harmony: The harmonic chord comprising the fundamental tone and overtones.

7

as Euler has enumerated them: in his *Tentamen novae theoriae musicae* (1738).

Either a homogeneous . . . the feeling of the beautiful, *or pleasure*: Herder is referring to Burke's *Philosophical Enquiry into the Origin of Our Ideas of the Sublime and the Beautiful* (1757), pt. 4, §§ 5 and 19.

main division in music between hard *and* soft: that is, into flat and sharp.

the analogy between the entire general sensibility of body and soul: See Sulzer: "Every such sensation [in the soul] is produced by an emotion of the nerves of the body, and presupposes as a principle that the soul can have no sensations from the senses without an *analogous emotion* in the nerves of the senses" (*Vermischte philosophische Schriften* [Miscellaneous Philosophical Writings; Leipzig, 1773–81], 1:54).

Mendelssohn . . . Lessing: Mendelssohn in *Über das Erhabene und Naïve in den schönen Wissenschaften* (1758); Lessing did indeed plan a translation of Burke's *Philosophical Enquiry* but never completed it.

self-preservation and the social passions: Burke connects the beautiful with the instinct for self-preservation and the sublime with the social drives.

It is a pity . . . feelings: pt. 3 of the *Philosophical Enquiry*, where Burke treats the feeling of the beautiful, the individual senses, and the sensations experienced by them.

darkness and brightness . . . cries of animals: On darkness, see *Philosophical Enquiry*, pt. 4, §§ 14–16; power and privation: pt. 2, §§ 5–6; smallness: pt. 3, § 13; vastness: pt. 2, § 7; infinity: pt. 2, § 8; light: pt. 2, § 14; color: pt. 2, § 16, and pt. 3, § 17; bitterness and smell: pt. 2, § 21; sound and loudness: pt. 2, § 17; cries of animals: pt. 2, § 20.

Burke confessed . . . beautiful in music: in pt. 3, § 25.

Dryden's Timotheus: Timotheus is a kithara player in John Dryden's (1631–1700) drama *Alexander's Feast; or, The Power of Musique* (1697), whose playing and singing has a remarkable effect on Alexander. He conjures up the whole gamut of human emotion: pride, ecstasy, love, fear, grief, and so on (hence "all the labyrinths of sensation").

peoples who associated their tones . . . vice: The Greek modes were associated with particular characteristics: thus the Doric mode was warlike and the Lydian one soft and elegiac.

a Benda violin: a violin owned by either Franz Benda (1709–1786), the founder of a violin school, or his son Georg Anton Benda (1722–1795).

"den Himmel . . . und Vergnügen singt": "opens up the heavens to him and sings / peace and pleasure into his whole heart." After Kleist's "Milon und Iris."

"Wen aber, o Lycidas": after Ramler's "To Lycidas" (1767), as is the quotation immediately following. "But, O Lycidas, he whom / his mother received among the heavenly / songs of glad nightingale choirs, / who as a swan loosed himself / nightly from her bosom in joy divine— / even as a boy and untutored / will he love the simplicity of tone."

"froh bestürzt . . . hören": "glad and amazed / hear himself greet a singer."

Aedone: In Klopstock's "Bardale" the nightingale is originally called Aedon and its mother Aedone.

fundamental bass: or *basse fondamentale*, a term introduced by Rameau to describe the root note of a chord.

Apelles: Greek painter (ca. 352–308 BC); after Ramler's ode "To the King" (1766).

8

"Freund . . . hörte": In fact, the poem is Gleim's "An Uz" (To Uz): "Friend, how pleasantly does / this spring here babble! Sit thee down! / So did Anacreon's spring babble / when, in the shadow of his tree, / he heard the rustle of leaves / and the whisper of the zephyr."

"laß dich nieder . . . ihn hören": "sit thee down beside me / and hear the Muse of Anacreon, / hear the strains of his lyre / and see Bacchus and Amor / lend him their ears: / see the open bosom of Cythera flush and heave; / see the nymphs abandon their jugs and fly hither / all listening to the singer as they fly— / all desire to hear him."

We are familiar . . . ascribed to music: See for example, Plato *Republic* 398d–400b.

Rameau's observation: that is, his mathematical proof of the relation between the length of the string and pitch.

chord is only sound: that is, not a simple tone, and hence it does not directly affect the soul or the lower cognitive faculties but instead is the product of the understanding.

lifeless composition: that is, a mathematical product arranged according to rules rather than feeling.

the imitation of birds: Bernard le Bovier de Fontenelle (1657–1757) argued that language arose out of the imitation of birdsong.

the rebirth of music in Italy: Herder means the development of opera, in which the unity of word and music that characterized Greek tragedy was reestablished.

A wholly novel and late development: In early opera, music was indeed subordinate to the text. In the mid-seventeenth century, however, the aria—which, as Herder suggests, performs a function analogous to monologue in conventional drama—became increasingly important.

9

music made visible: The phrase is from John Brown's *Dissertation on Poetry and Music* (1763).

a mute poetry: Cf. Lessing's preface to his *Laocoön*.

traveler of our century: Pierre Augustin Guys in his *Voyage littéraire de la Grèce* (1783).

Lucian's dialogue: Lucian (120–190 AD), Greek author of the dialogue *The Dance*.

Plutarch's testimony: See, for example, Pseudo-Plutarch's *Peri musikes*.

Cahusac: Louis de Cahusac (1700–1789), *Traité historique de la dance ancienne et moderne* (Historical Treatise on Ancient and Modern Dance, 1753).

ancient Egyptians . . . Chinese: an allusion to Joseph de Guignes, *Mémoire dans lequel on prouve que les chinois sont une colonie égyptienne* (Dissertation in which It Is Proven That the Chinese are an Egyptian Colony, 1759).

Noverre: Herder is thinking of his *Lettres sur la danse et sur les ballets* (Letters on Dancing and Ballets, 1760).

Agathon: *The History of Agathon*, a novel by Christoph Martin Wieland (1733–1813); the reference is to bk. 4, chaps. 5 and 6.

Sonnenfels . . . Lessing's: Josef von Sonnenfels (1733–1817), author of *Briefe über die Wienerische Schaubühne* (Letters on the Viennese Stage, 1768); Lessing's *Hamburg Dramaturgy* (1767–69).

Vitruvius: Marcus Vitruvius (late first century BC), Roman architect and engineer, author of *De architectura*.

age when beauty was created anew: that is, the Renaissance.

great names . . . textbooks of architecture: for example, Leon Battista Alberti (1404–1472), Vincenzo Scamozzi (1522–1616), and Giacomo da Vignola (1507–1573).

a theorist of the fine arts: that is, Riedel.

magnitude and sublimity . . . regularity: Herder is referring to specific chapters in Riedel's *Theory*: "On Magnitude and the Sublime" (chap. 4), "Unity and Diversity" (chap. 5), "Nature, Simplicity and Naïveté" (chap. 6).

Klotz: Klotz reviewed Winckelmann's work (published in 1762) in the *Bibliothek der schönen Wissenschaften und Künste* (Library of Beaux Arts and Belles Lettres).

the ideas of a recent French author: Herder quotes from an anonymous work entitled *Architecture des jardins* (1757).

10

Vossius's Rhetoric: Gerardus Johannes Vossius (1577–1649), Dutch polymath and theologian, author of the influential textbook *Ars rhetorica* (1623).

than a blind man of color: Herder is turning Riedel's own words against him: "If Nature had withheld from a man the fine organs necessary for delicate sensation, then one could no more give him a notion of beauty than a blind man of color" (*Theory*, p. 34).

"the constitution . . . meaning": after Riedel, *Theory*, p. 25.

Poetry is the art . . . language: a direct quotation from Riedel, *Theory*, p. 31.

"a regular skill . . . lower faculty of cognition": a direct quotation from Riedel, *Theory*, p. 31.

Opitzes: Martin Optiz (1597–1639), author of an influential treatise on poetics entitled *Buch von der deutschen Poeterey* (1624), and his successors.

Mr. Riedel has read Baumgarten: Riedel echoes Baumgarten's declaration: "The aim of aesthetics is the perfection of sensuous cognition. By that I mean beauty" (*Aesthetica*, § 14). Riedel writes: "The more perfect the sensuous cognition, the greater its beauty" (*Theory*, p. 34).

Darjes: Joachim Georg Darjes (1714–1791), professor of philosophy in Jena and Frankfurt an der Oder, opponent of Wolffianism and Riedel's teacher. According to Darjes, sensory perception must pertain either to the intellect or to the imagination (*facultas imaginandi*). Riedel: "The inner feeling of beauty either pertains to the mere imagination or is based on higher ideas of order, magnitude, sublimity, virtue, nobility, and morality. The former we call *imaginative* and the latter *intellectual* beauty" (*Theory*, 14).

Baumgarten's definition: that is, that a poem is "perfect sensate discourse" (*Meditationes*, § 9).

all the applause: from Kant and Mendelssohn, for example.

the definition of Wolff, Baumgarten, and Mendelssohn: In Wolff's *Vernünftige Gedanken von den Kräften des menschlichen Verstandes* (Rational Thoughts on the Powers of the Human Understanding, 1712) and *Psychologia empirica* (1732); Baumgarten's *Meditationes* and *Metaphysica* (1739); Mendelssohn's *Letters on Sensations* (1755).

Batteux: Charles Batteux (1713–1780), author of *Traité des beaux-arts réduits à un seul principe* (1747); he defines the task of art as the imitation of *belle nature*, by means of which the intellect can raise itself above empirical reality.

his definition of painting: Herder supplies a direct quotation of Riedel's definition (*Theory*, p. 31).

natural signs, *as Mendelssohn says*: Cf. the short essay *On the Main Principles of the Beaux Arts and Belles Lettres*: "The visible natural signs that appear alongside one another must be represented by lines and figures. This can occur either by means of surfaces or by means of bodies."

Riedel's definition of music: Riedel, *Theory*, pp. 31–32.

Pantomime is supposed to be the art: Riedel, *Theory*, p. 32.

the art of building: Riedel, *Theory*, p. 32.

Crispin: a comedy character, a fool.

Sensuously distinct ideas *are a nonsense*: that is, the two terms are mutually exclusive, since sensuousness pertains to the lower and distinctness to the higher faculties of the soul.

Hamannian: Herder is turning Riedel's own joke against him: Riedel criticizes the allusive and obscure quality of Hamann's style, which Herder himself admired. Jakob Böhme (1575–1624) was a mystic and therefore the epitome of an obscurantist thinker; Herder cites him as a negative counterpart to Hamann.

two equally humpbacked definitions: Riedel: "Rhetoric is the science of rendering sensuous and sometimes distinct thoughts sensuous by way of harmonious discourse and appropriate gestures for the purpose of persuasion, instruction, and agitation" (*Theory*, p. 31). "Gardening is the art of refining the layout and order of vegetation and of beautifying real Nature after the model of ideal Nature" (*Theory*, p. 32).

Philosophical Libraries and German Libraries: Riedel was editor of the *Philosophische Bibliothek* and was a contributor to Klotz's *Deutsche Bibliothek der schönen Wissenschaften*.

11

extract of works of various authors: the subtitle of Riedel's book.

Dictionary of the Beaux Arts and Belles Lettres: Sulzer's *Allgemeine Theorie der schönen Künste in einzeln, nach alphabetischer Ordnung der Kunstwörter auf einander folgenden Artikeln abgehandelt* (General Theory of the Fine Arts, in Separate Articles, Arranged in the Alphabetical Order of the Technical Terms,

1771–74). Herder had hoped this would render Riedel's work obsolete, but he was disappointed with the final product.

in the announcement: in the seventy-eighth letter in *Letters Concerning Recent Literature*, 17 January 1760; Sulzer claims to have chosen the dictionary form because "an alphabetic work attracts more connoisseurs than a system." It was, he added, the work by which he wanted posterity to judge his reputation.

Rousseau: Rousseau's *Dictionnaire de musique* (1757).

Bayle: Pierre Bayle (1647–1706), French philosopher and author of *Dictionnaire historique et critique* (1695–97). The "great Encyclopedists" are the contributors to Diderot's and d'Alembert's *Encyclopédie ou Dictionnaire raisonné, des arts et des métiers* (1751–80).

his chief aim is to seek out the species and forms of beauty: "My first concern is to examine carefully the proper nature and constitution of that which in art is beautiful, agreeable, pleasing, and charming—or the nature of the aesthetic in general—and to make it recognizable in its various forms to my readers. To this end I was obliged, in all works of taste from architecture to poetry, to distinguish everything that connoisseurs have deemed beautiful or aesthetically good. From the comparison of this *beauty* as it is manifested in these works of such variety, I had to learn to discern its essence and its true constitution and hence to render distinct to the understanding that which taste feels indistinctly" (Sulzer, *Letters Concerning Recent Literature*, 78th letter).

"for the sake . . . polite society": Sulzer, in *Letters Concerning Recent Literature*.

Penelope: *Odyssey* 2.93–110.

"an edifice of aesthetics . . . in general!": a free rendering of Sulzer's announcement of his project in *Letters Concerning Recent Literature*.

Apsyrtus: a brother of Medea, whom she killed, dismembered, and threw into a river to hold up her pursuers.

Moses Mendelssohn . . . sensations: in the fifth and tenth letters in *Letters on Sensations*.

Rhapsody: *Rhapsody, or Additions to the Letters on Sensations* (1761).

Swift's lunar explorer: in *Voyage to Cacklogallinia* (a work falsely attributed to Swift), the character Probusomo, who is sent to bring back gold from the moon. But one of the Selenites (as the inhabitants of the moon are called) tells him that gold and other precious metals are deemed worthless there.

Thucydides: *The History of the Peloponnesian War* 2.40.

Kästner: Abraham Gotthelf Kästner (1719–1800), mathematician and author of moral and aesthetic treatises.

Reimarus: Hermann Samuel Reimarus (1694–1768), theologian and disciple of Wolff.

Crousaz: Jean Pierre de Crousaz (1663–1750), author of *Traité du beau* (1712).

André: Yves-Marie André (1693–1764), author of *Essais sur le beau* (1741).

sixth sense: an allusion to Hutcheson's "moral sense," the organ of judgment, in *Illustrations upon the Moral Sense* (1728).

Montesquieu: Montesquieu wrote the article "Taste" for the *Encyclopédie*.

St. Evremond: Charles de Marguetel de Saint-Denis, Seigneur de Saint-Evremond (1613–1703), *Oeuvres* (1709).

St. Mard: Toussaint Rémond de Saint-Mard (1682–1757), author of *Examen philosophique de la poésie en général.*

Marmontel: Jean-François Marmontel (1723–1799), author of *Poétique française* (1763).

Bernis: François-Joachim de Pierre, cardinal of Bernis (1715–1794), *Oeuvres* (1752).

Watelet: Claude-Henri Watelet (1718–1786), author of *Dictionnaire des arts de peinture, sculpture et gravure.*

the works of Batteux: *Les Beaux-arts réduit à un même principe* (1743) was translated by Johann Adolf Schlegel in 1751 and again by C. W. Ramler in 1756–58.

Mr. Riedel drew heavily . . . book: in the first letter of *On the Public.*

his worthy translator: Johann Nicolaus Meinhard's (1727–1767) translation of Home's work appeared between 1763 and 1766.

as Mr. Klotz assures us: in his *Über den Nutzen und Gebrauch der alten geschnittenen Steine und ihrer Abdrücke* (1768).

Gerard's Essay On Taste: In his *Essay on Taste* (1759), Gerard defines taste as consisting "in the improvement of those principles which are commonly called the powers of the imagination."

the Academy . . . prize: In 1756 Gerard's essay won the prize awarded by the Philosophical Society of Edinburgh for the best submission on the subject of taste.

Zanotti: Francesco Maria Zanotti (1692–1777), author of *La filosofia morale* (1754).

12

the second part of his book: Riedel planned but never completed a second part of his *Theory.*

all philosophy arose from wonder: See Plato *Theatetus* 155d; Aristotle *Metaphysics* 982b.

Lysippus: Lysippus of Sikyon (fourth century BC), Greek sculptor.

ordonnance: order.

"The Resolution of Beauty . . . Parts": the title of Riedel's third chapter.

perfect sensuousness: Riedel: "Inquire after the common rule to which the productions of the beaux arts and belles lettres are subject, and it will turn out to be beauty, or perfect sensuousness itself" (*Theory*, p. 34).

disinterested pleasure: Riedel: "Inquire after the touchstone of beauty, and it will turn out to be pleasure that issues from beauty and is without interest" (*Theory*, pp. 34–35).

every superior analysis of beauty as sterile: Riedel: "And so we might have blithely wandered through a topic that in the manner in which it is generally treated by our aestheticians, is just as sterile and insignificant as the logical controversy over the supreme principle of all human knowledge" (*Theory*, p. 35).

Two ideas . . . sentence: an allusion to Baumgarten's *Meditationes*, where philosophy and poetics are portrayed as being linked.

conclusion of Klopstock's Messiah: The final cantos of the religious epic, begun in 1745, did not appear until 1773.

Michaelis: Johann David Michaelis (1717–1791), orientalist and theologian. Herder hopes to find in a translation of Hebrew literature a similar experience to that offered by his reading of Ossian.

Gleim's ancient German ballads: Johann Wilhelm Ludwig Gleim (1719–1803), Anacreontic poet, whose poems in *Preußische Kriegslieder* (1758) were inspired by the ballads collected in Percy's *Reliques of Ancient English Poetry*.

Ramler's Horace: Karl Wilhelm Ramler (1725–1798), author of a book of Horatian odes (1769).

Heyne: Christian Gottlob Heyne, editor of Epictetus, Virgil, and Pindar.

Romeos and Saras: an allusion to Christian Felix Weiße's *Romeo und Julia* (1767) and to Lessing's drama *Miß Sara Sampson* (1755).

Addisons and Sonnenfelses: In 1765 Sonnenfels established the weekly journal *Der Vertraute*, based on Addison's *Spectator* and *Tatler*. Herder is arguing for the proliferation of moral weeklies after the British model.

CONCLUSION

the name of a quite different writer: Like the *Fragments*, the *Critical Forests* had appeared anonymously (a by no means uncommon literary practice of the time). Despite being unmasked by Klotz, Herder continued—unconvincingly—to deny he was the author of the *Critical Forests*, even to Hamann.

he can write neither Greek nor Latin: One of the criticisms leveled at the author of the *Critical Forests* was his inadequate grasp of Greek and Latin.

Shakespeare

This essay was first published in *Von deutscher Art und Kunst* (Hamburg, 1773). The text is based on *Shakespeare*, in *Schriften zur Ästhetik und Literatur, 1767–1781*, ed. Günter E. Grimm, vol. 2 of Johann Gottfried Herder, *Werke* (Frankfurt am Main: Deutscher Klassiker Verlag, 1993), pp. 498–521.

If any man . . . image: an allusion to Mark Akenside, *The Pleasures of the Imagination* (1744), 3:550–59:

> Hence when lightning fires
> The arch of heav'n, and thunders rock the ground,
> When furious whirlwinds rend the howling air,
> And ocean, groaning from his lowest bed,
> Heaves his tempest'ous billows to the sky;
> Amid the mighty uproar, while below
> The nations tremble, Shakespeare looks abroad
> From some high cliff superior, and enjoys
> The elemental war. . . .

What a library: for example, John Dryden's *Essay of Dramatick Poesie* (1668), Pope's preface to his edition of *The Works of Shakespeare* (1726), Edward Young's *Conjectures on Original Composition* (1759), Henry Home's *Elements of Criticism* (1762–65), Samuel Johnson's preface to his edition of *The Plays of William Shakespeare* (1747), and Elizabeth Montagu's *Essay on the Writings and Genius of Shakespear* (1769); and in France: Voltaire's remarks in his *Let-*

tres écrites de Londres sur les Anglois et autres sujets (1734); in Germany: Johann Elias Schlegel's *Vergleichung Shakespeares und Andreas Grpyhs* (1741), Wilhelm Heinrich von Gerstenberg's *Briefe über Merkwürdigkeiten der Litteratur*, nos. 14–18 (1766), Lessing in *Letters Concerning Recent Literature* (1759) and in *Hamburg Dramaturgy* (1767); Johann Joachim Eschenburg, who translated Hurd and Montagu (1771).

Shakespeare's boldest friends: for example, Pope, Johnson, and Gerstenberg.

his transgressions of the rules: the three classical unities of time, place, and action.

dithyramb: According to Aristotle, tragedy originated in an introductory tale improvised by the leader of the chorus, the purpose of which was to state the theme that the dithyramb would elaborate (*Poetics* 4.1449a14–15). Herder's account of the development of Greek tragedy follows that of Aristotle.

simplicity of the Greek plot: Aristotle distinguishes between simple and complex plots and states that the "successful plot" of a tragedy must have "a single and not . . . a double issue" (trans. W. Hamilton Pye [London: Heinemann, 1956], 13.1453a6).

buskined: Buskins were high, thick-soled boots worn by actors in ancient Athenian tragedy; hence *buskined* means "dignified, elevated, lofty."

the artificiality of the rules . . . Nature!: The theory (as embodied in Aristotle) and practice of art (Sophocles) in Greece together constitute a unity, emerging naturally as the consequence of historical conditions. Aristotle did not "invent" his theory but merely discovered certain organic laws.

the art of the Greek poets . . . ascribe to them: Herder's target here is Lessing, who in section 46 of his *Hamburg Dramaturgy* had argued that the Greek tragedians simplified originally complex plots for the sake of the unities of time and place.

the previous dithyrambic feeling: that is, the idea of a simple, single scene.

Thespis: a Greek poet of the sixth century BC, traditionally credited with the invention of tragedy. He introduced an actor separated from the chorus and the dialogue between the leader of the chorus and this actor.

excellent chapter on the nature of plot: *Poetics* 7. Aristotle writes that "the proper limit" of plot length is "the magnitude which admits of a change from good fortune to bad, in a sequence of events which follow one another either inevitably or according to probability" (*Poetics* 7.1451a12).

the so-called dramatic rules . . . Aristotle: by Corneille (*Discours des trois unités*, 1660), Boileau (*Ars poétique*, 1674), and René Le Bossu (*Traité du poème épique*, 1674), but also by German imitators such as Johann Christoph Gottsched in his *Critische Dichtkunst* (1740).

Lessing: Hamburg Dramaturgy, §§ 36–50 (1767).

Spanish-Senecan heroes: an allusion to the sources of the French tragedians Corneille (his *Cid* was based on the drama *The Youthful Deeds of Cid* by Guillen de Castro and Seneca's *Cinna*) and Racine (his *Phédre* was inspired by Seneca's *Phaedra*). Corneille and Racine saw themselves as continuing the later Euripidean and Senecan tradition of tragedy, whereas Herder views Sophocles as the apotheosis of tragic drama.

galimatias: confused language, meaningless talk, nonsense.

Aristole has declared it to be: Aristotle's theory of the cathartic effect of tragedy, which consists in arousing the purgative emotions of fear and pity (*Poetics* 6.1449b2–3).

"two-hour performance": as demanded by Corneille in his *Discours des trois unités*. Lessing, like Herder, also criticizes the Frenchman for following the letter of Aristotle's rules but not the spirit of drama (*Hamburg Dramaturgy*, § 45).

national institution: an allusion to the fact that Greek tragedies were performed as religious celebrations in Athens.

Crébillon: Prosper Jolyot de Crébillon (1674–1762), a rival of Voltaire who wrote tragedies based on classical and mythological sources such as *Idoménée* (1705) and *Rhadamiste et Zénobie* (1711).

Astrea: *L'Astrée* was a pastoral romance by Honoré d'Urfé (1567–1625) which appeared between 1607 and 1627.

Clélies *and* Aspasias: Clélie is the eponymous heroine of Mademoiselle de Scudéry's *Clélie*, a ten-volume, pseudohistorical romance that appeared between 1654 and 1660. Aspasia, originally a Greek courtesan and later the wife of Pericles, was the title of several eighteenth-century French novels, as well as of a tale by Wieland sending up the French literature of love and society.

toto divisis ab orbe Britannis: the Britons, divided from the rest of the world; after Virgil *Ecologues* 1.66.

pullulus Aristotelis: pupil of Aristotle (literally, "chicken").

since . . . genius is more than philosophy . . . analyzer: Cf. Young, *Thoughts*: "§ 138 By the praise of Genius we detract not from Learning. . . . § 141 Learning we thank, Genius we revere; That gives us pleasure, This gives us rapture; That informs, This inspires; and is itself inspired; for Genius is from Heaven, Learning from man. . . . § 142 Learning is borrowed knowledge; Genius is knowlege innate, and quite our own. § 143 Therefore, as *Bacon* observes, it may take a nobler name, and be called Wisdom; in which sense of wisdom, some are born wise."

Home . . . Johnson: Henry Home (1696–1782), author of *Elements of Criticism* (1762); Richard Hurd (1720–1808), whose translation of Horace's *Ars poetica* (1749) contained a commentary in which the different kinds of drama were analyzed; Alexander Pope's 1725 edition of Shakespeare defended the poet against charges of having misapplied the Aristotelian rules; in the foreword to his own edition of Shakespeare in 1765, Samuel Johnson characterized Shakespeare as a natural genius who is permitted to ignore all rules.

plot, character, thought, language, song making, *and* spectacle: the six elements of tragedy, as outlined by Aristotle in *Poetics* 6.1450b19–28.

interpreter of Nature: an allusion to Bacon's notion of the *homo minister et interpres naturae*, the human being as the servant and interpreter of Nature.

Lear: *King Lear*, 1.1.

the strictest rule of your Aristotle: Aristole demands that tragedy represent a single, whole action (*Poetics* 8).

two aged fathers: Lear and Gloucester. The structure of *King Lear* defies Aristotle's ban on plots with a double issue (*Poetics* 13).

Blind Gloucester: *King Lear*, 4.6.

Father Aristotle: *Poetics* 7.

Lessing compared: in *Hamburg Dramaturgy*, § 11–12, where Lessing compares Voltaire's use of the ghost in his *Semiramis* with Shakespeare's in *Hamlet*.

Shakespeare is Sophocles' brother: Cf. Young: "§ 295 *Shakespeare* mingled no water with his wine, lower'd his Genius by no vapid Imitation. § 296 *Shakespeare* gave us a *Shakespeare*, nor could the first in antient fame have given us more. § 297 *Shakespeare* is not their Son, but Brother; their Equal, and that, in spite of all his faults."

Spinoza's vast God: Together with Lessing and Goethe, Herder helped stimulate the enormous interest in Spinoza's pantheism in Germany. Spinoza's God, who is identical to nature, also moves in Shakespeare's plays.

sportive Frenchman: Voltaire, who criticized Shakespeare in *Essai sur la poésie épique* (1728) and *Lettres sur les Anglais* (1734).

Shakespeare . . . foolishness: an allusion to 1 Corinthians 1:23.

What do we mean by time and place anyway?: Here Herder's criticisms are directed at Corneille's arguments in *Discours sur les trois unités* 3, where he demands that the length of the performance exactly match that of the action represented on the stage.

Savoyard of the theater: a posturer, mountebank.

Mahomet's dream: Mohammed's vision of the beauties of Paradise.

ordine successivorum et simultaneorum: order of succession and simultaneity.

Cacklogallinian: a race of giant fowl in Samuel Brunt's satire *A Voyage to Cacklogallinia with a Description of the Religion, Policy, Customs and Manners of That Country* (1727). Hamann and Herder identified this land of learned poultry as France (not least due to the similarity of the word with "Gaul," "Gallic"). Like many in his day, Herder mistakenly thinks this voyage is one of the travels undertaken by Swift's Gulliver.

Warburton: William Warburton's (1698–1779) eight-volume edition of Shakespeare (1747).

author of the . . . essay: The author in question is actually a woman: Elizabeth Montagu (1720–1800), founder of the Blue-stocking Club. Herder reviewed the German translation of her anonymous *Essay on the Writings and Genius of Shakespear* (1769) in 1771.

a writer . . . feeling for Shakespeare: Heinrich Wilhelm von Gerstenberg's (1737–1823) *Versuch über Shakespeares Werke und Genie* (Essay on Shakespeare's Works and Genius) appeared in his *Briefe über Merkwürdigkeiten der Litteratur*, second collection (not third, as in Herder's footnote), pp. 14–18 (Letters on the Curiosities of Literature, 1766). Gerstenberg's attempt to classify Shakespeare's dramas according to the categories of Polonius in *Hamlet*, 2.2, can be found in letter 17.

honest fishmonger . . . gray beard . . . weak hams: Polonius in *Hamlet*, 2.2.176 and 201–4.

the series of "-als" and "-cals": Polonius speaks of "tragedy, comedy, history, pastoral, pastoral-comical, historical-pastoral-tragical-historical, tragical-comical-historical-pastoral" (2.2.398–401).

locos communes: commonplaces.

Stobaeus: Johannes Stobaeus (fifth century AD) compiled various series of extracts of Greek authors, one of which is known as *Florilegium* and served as a model for later cornucopias. The "new" Stobaeus is William Dodd's anthology *The Beauties of Shakespeare* (1752), which was widely read in Germany also (by

Goethe, among others). J. J. Eschenburg (1743–1820), one of Shakespeare's German translators, planned a similar anthology in German.

fools in Shakespeare's plays: "Lancelot" is Lancelot Gobbo, Shylock's servant in *The Merchant of Venice*; "clowns and jesters" refers to figures such as Feste in *Twelfth Night* and Touchstone in *As You Like It*; "poor Richard" is the inept king in *Richard II*; the "king of knights" is the buffoonish Sir John Falstaff in *Henry IV, Parts I and II*.

the great baby . . . "time is time": "great baby": *Hamlet*, 2.2.384; "clouds for camels": 3.2.365; "played Julius Caesar": 3.2.95–100; "why day is day": 2.2.89.

Garrick: David Garrick (1717–1779) created a more naturalistic method of acting and went back to the original, uncut Shakespearean texts. In 1769, he organized a Shakespeare festival in Stratford, which awakened new interest in Shakespeare.

you, my friend: that is, Goethe. His "monument" is *Götz von Berlichingen*, a drama set in Germany's own "age of chivalry," which Goethe sent to Herder at the end of 1771. Herder looks to Goethe to take up the challenge of Shakespeare at this turning point in the development of German dramatic literature. "*Voluit! quiescit!*": He has striven! Now he rests!"

The Causes of Sunken Taste among the Different Peoples in Whom It Once Blossomed

This essay was first published in 1775 by Christian Friedrich Voß on behalf of the Royal Academy of Sciences. The text is based on *Ursachen des gesunkenen Geschmacks bei den Völkern, da er geblühet*, in *Schriften zu Philosophie, Literatur, Kunst und Altertum, 1774–1787*, ed. Jürgen Brummack and Martin Bollacher, vol. 4 of Johann Gottfried Herder, *Werke* (Frankfurt am Main: Deutscher Klassiker Verlag, 1994), pp. 109–48.

"Multa renascentur, quae iam cecidire": "Many things that have fallen out of use shall be born again"; from Horace *De arte poetica* 70.

I

intensively and extensively: an allusion to Johann Kaspar Lavater (1741–1801), in the fourth volume of his *Physiognomische Fragmente* (Leipzig, 1775–78).

aggregation of natural forces: another allusion to Lavater.

Plato says in his allegory: Herder is referring to *Ion* (533de). Socrates compares poetic inspiration both to the magnetization of iron rings, which then form a chain ("In like manner the Muse first of all inspires men herself; and from these inspired persons a chain of other persons is suspended, who take the inspiration" [trans. Jowett]), and the ecstatic revelry of the Corybantes, the attendants of the Greek nature goddess Cybele.

images of the Divinity: yet another allusion to Lavater.

he will lend his name to swamp and sea: Icarus, who flew too close to the sun with his wax wings, gave his name to the Icarian Sea (in which he drowned) and the island of Icaria (where he was buried) (Ovid *Metamorphoses* 8.230, 235). Here Herder seems to be conflating the image with that of a victim of a will-o'-the-wisp falling into a swamp.

Hercules: Xenophon *Memorabilia* 2.1.21–34. Vice and Virtue appear before Hercules at a crossroads and attempt to persuade him to follow their respective paths.

firestorm: Another allusion to Lavater.

When Greek tragedy . . . *cart of Thespis*: Horace *De arte poetica* 275–80: "Thespis is said to have discovered the Tragic Muse, a type unknown before, and to have carried his pieces in wagons to be sung and acted by players with faces smeared with wine-lees" (trans. H. Rushton Fairclough [London: Heinemann, 1929]).

Aristotle: Here Herder is thinking of chap. 6 of the *Poetics*, as well as the criticism of the Euripidean chorus in chap. 18.

gardens of illusion: the garden of the enchantress Armida in Torquato Tasso's *Jerusalem Delivered* (1581), an image often used by Herder (bk. 14, canto 76, and bk. 16, cantos 1–19); the mirror of truth in which Rinaldo looks (bk. 16, canto 29).

II

Homer emerged in fair Ionia: This paragraph draws on Thomas Blackwell's *Enquiry into the Life and Writings of Homer* (1735).

Lycurgus: after Plutarch *Lycurgus* 4.

All the elements of tragedy that Aristotle enumerates: *Poetics* 6.

aoidoi: singers.

that Winckelmann has elaborated so excellently: in his *History of Ancient Art*, bk. 4, chap. 1.

Apollonios: Even Callimachus, a contemporary of Apollonios Rhodios (active third century BC), dismissed as flawed his attempt, in *Argonautica*, to write a Homeric epic in Hellenistic times.

Ptolemies: the Macedonian Greek rulers of Egypt from the death of Alexander the Great to Cleopatra.

tutelary god: that is, one of the Lares, the Roman guardian spirits of house and fields.

the Epic cycle: the series of epic poems written by later poets (Cyclic poets) to complete Homer and presenting (with *The Iliad* and *The Odyssey*) a continuous history of the Trojan war and of all the heroes engaged in it.

the seeds . . . in Aristotle's Poetics: Aristotle views the tragedy as a genre that has already reached its *telos* (chap. 4), and the great examples that he cites are more than one hundred years old at the time of his writing.

Longinus: See Pseudo-Longinus *On the Sublime* 44.

Pleiad: The Pleiades were the seven daughters of Atlas and Pleione and gave their name to a cluster of small stars in the constellation Taurus, commonly spoken of as seven, though only six are visible to the naked eye. By extension, the term is applied to a brilliant group of seven people such as the group of poets of the French Renaissance, called in French *La Pléiade* and including Ronsard and Du

Bellay. Here, Herder is using the term contemptuously: this Pleiad achieved only a seventh of the greatness of its predecessors.

carving goblets and flowers: Herder is thinking of *technopaignia*, a highly stylized presentation of a poem in which its layout matches its subject and which emerged in the fourth century AD.

the old, true Romans . . . taste: Cato the Elder (234–149 BC), stout defender of native Roman traditions and literature against the increasing influence of Greek culture. See Plutarch *Cato* 22.5–7.

Amphion: Horace *De arte poetica* 394–96.

an emperor's garden: that is, Augustus Octavian.

according to Aristotle . . . effective poetry: Aristotle justifies the precedence of tragedy over epic precisely in terms of effect (*Poetics* 26).

Ennius: Quintus Ennius (239–169 BC), author of the historical epic *Annales*.

Anthony: Marcus Antonius was one of the most significant orators of his age.

one tyrant . . . model: Herder draws his anecdotes from Suetonius's *Lives of the Caesars*. The first emperor is Tiberius ("Aeolian dialect"; or rather, Doric: *Tiberius* 56); the second is Caligula ("banish Homer": *Caligula* 34); the third is Claudius ("naturalize new words": *Claudius* 41); the final emperor is Nero (*Nero* 12), whom Herder conflates with Claudius, the real amateur historian.

Persius: Aulus Persius (34–62 AD), satirical poet whose writings were notoriously obscure.

discourse on the decline of Roman eloquence: The *Dialogus de oratoribus* is commonly attributed to Tacitus, but in Herder's time it was presumed to be the work of Quintilian, who wrote *De causis corruptae eloquentiae*, now lost.

Petronius: *Satyricon* 1–5 (on eloquence) and 88 (on sculpture and painting).

Pliny: The work in question is the *Panegyricus* of Pliny the Younger, dedicated to the emperor Trajan.

Tiberius . . . epitaphs he wrote himself: Many of these details are also drawn from Suetonius: *Tiberius* 56; *Claudius* 41–42; *Vespasian* 18. Quintilian mentions his employment as tutor at the court of Domitian in *Institutio oratoria* 4.Pro2. For the correspondence between Trajan and Pliny the Younger, see *Epistles* 10. On Hadrian, see *Historia Augusta* 14.8–9 and 16.10; on his love of Atellan games (a native Italic form of comedy), see 26.4.

panegyric: the *Panegyricus* of Pliny the Younger.

spiritus familiarus: the prevailing spirit of Cicero's private letters, who here is Herder's opposing ideal.

Harpocrates: a god of silence, often depicted as a small boy with a finger pressed to his lips.

Good Quintilian . . . his heart: In the preface to *Institutio oratoria* 6, Quintilian writes that his book shall compensate for the death of his son.

Seneca . . . palaces: Herder is thinking of the tension between Seneca's wealth and power and his ideal of the wise man; see, for example, *De vita beata* 17–19; on his wealth, see Tacitus *Annales* 13.42, 14.52–56.

thirty tyrants: rebel leaders of various provinces in the Roman Empire at the time of Gallienus (reigned 253–68 AD).

cup of trembling: Isaiah 51:17, 22.

Under Commodus, the Greeks: This anecdote is drawn from Winckelmann, *History of Ancient Art*, bk. 12, chap. 2.

rustica Romana: the transition to Vulgar Latin and the early development of the Romance vernaculars.

Antonine: the Roman emperors Antoninus Pius (r. 138–161) and Marcus Aurelius Antoninus (r. 161–180).

if only we . . . distinguish between genius *and* taste: Here Herder is taking issue with Voltaire, who in his *Essai sur les moeurs* argues that papal patronage roused the geniuses of the Renaissance.

Politian: Angiolo Poliziano (1454–1494), Italian scholar and poet.

Bembo: Pietro Bembo (1470–1547), Italian cardinal and humanist scholar.

Casa: Giovanni della Casa (1503–1556), archbishop of Benevento, poet, and author of a treatise on good manners.

Cimabue: Benciviene di Pepo (ca. 1240–1302), Italian painter and mosaicist.

Bembo: Bembo consciously imitated the style of classical Latin prose (and Cicero in particular) in his *Historia veneta* (History of Venice). The identity of the cardinal is uncertain.

enchanted castle: The image that Herder uses to describe Ariosto's *Orlando furioso* (1516) is drawn from the work itself: the castle of the magician Atlante high up in the Pyrenees (canto 2, 41–44).

Marino: Giambattista Marino (1569–1625), influential Italian poet.

An English critic: He is unknown.

Italian satyr: Teofilo Folengo's (1491–1544) *Baldus*, which, like *Don Quixote*, is a burlesque of the chivalric romance.

"Madame est morte!": from Bossuet's eulogy to Henrietta Anna of England, duchess of Orléans (held on 21 August 1670).

Fénelon: François de Fénelon (1615–1715), in *Dialogues sur l'éloquence en général et sur celle de la chaire en particulier* (published posthumously in 1718).

St. Mard: Rémond de Saint-Mard (1682–1757), in *Sur la poésie en général* (1734).

Racine: Louis Racine (1692–1763), poet and son of Jean Racine, in his *Réflexions sur la poésie* (1747).

Horace's Marcellus: *Odes* 1.12.45–46.

Voltaire . . . sailed to England: Exiled from France, Voltaire lived in Britain between 1726 and 1729 and was impressed by the political freedoms and scientific preeminence that the British enjoyed.

inter discrimina rerum: The phrase is borrowed from Virgil's *Aeneid* 1.204 (where it reads "per tot discrimina rerum," that is, "through so many grave dangers").

many a Maecenas, many a Maro: an allusion to Martial 8.65.

qualis artifex pereo: what an artist is now about to perish! (after Suetonius *Nero* 49).

III

the analogy of Socrates: Plato *Theaetetus* 148d–151d.

three righteous men: a possible allusion to Genesis 18:23–32, but as the original manuscript shows, here Herder is thinking of the contemporaries Pliny, Tacitus, and Quintilian, whose combined effort after the end of tyranny brings about a revival in Roman culture (*SWS* 5:650).

antidote: The target here is Johann Bernhard Basedow (1723–1790), a pedagogue who emphasized realistic teaching and introduced nature study, physical education, and manual training into the curriculum of the Philanthropium, the school at Dessau that he established.

Bacon: Francis Bacon, *Advancement of Learning*, 1:5, 11.

Longinus: Pseudo-Longinus *Peri Hypsous* 9.3.

the author . . . eloquence: *Tacitus Dialogus* 28–29.

ON THE INFLUENCE OF THE BELLES LETTRES ON THE HIGHER SCIENCES

The essay was published in the first and only volume of the *Abhandlungen der baierischen Akademie über Gegenstände der schönen Wissenschaften* in 1781. The text is based on *Über den Einfluss der schönen in die höhern Wissenschaften*, in *Schriften zu Philosophie, Literatur, Kunst und Altertum, 1774–1787*, ed. Jürgen Brummack and Martin Bollacher, vol. 4 of Johann Gottfried Herder, *Werke* (Frankfurt am Main: Deutscher Klassiker Verlag, 1994), pp. 215–32.

"*Ut hominis . . . eloquentia*": after Cicero *Brutus* 15.59–60, where it reads: "ut enim hominis decus ingenium, sic ingeni ipsius lumen est eloquentia" (for as reason is the glory of a man, so the lamp of reason is eloquence).

the garden of Armida . . . Calypso: The enchantress Armida in Tasso's *Jerusalem Delivered* bewitches the hero Rinaldo. With Calypso, Herder is thinking not only of *The Odyssey* (bk. 5) but also of Fénelon's *Télémaque*, who stays with Calypso (despite the disapproval of Minerva) throughout the first seven books of *Suite du quatrième livre de l'Odyssée d'Homère, ou les avantures de Télémaque, fils d'Ulysse* (1699).

apples of Sodom: Josephus described these as of fair appearance externally but dissolving, when grasped, into smoke and ashes; they were assumed to refer to *Calotropis procera*. The term is often used figuratively to denote any hollow or specious thing.

Crébillonian morals: Herder often uses Claude-Prosper Jolyot de Crébillon as a typical example of an excessively rococo style.

the gods: an allusion to Epicharmus: "The gods sell to us all the goods they give us" (fragment B15).

elogia: eulogies.

Samson: Judges 16:6–8.

Machiavelli: Machiavelli's *Discourses* alludes to Livius even in the title: *Discorsi sopra la prima deca di Tito Livio* (1517).

Grotius: Hugo Grotius's (1583–1645) major work *De jure belli ac pacis* (Concerning War and Peace, 1625), usually considered the first definitive text on international law, draws heavily on ancient writers.

Hudibras: Herder means Samuel Butler, the author of the mock epic *Hudibras*.

The most celebrated conqueror . . . manual of war: Alexander's view that *The Iliad* was "a perfect portable treasure of all military virtue and knowledge" is recorded in Plutarch *Alexander* 8.

pure pute: mere, pure.

Plutarch's essays: Herder is thinking chiefly of the *Moralia* and *On the Education of Children*.

Quintilian . . . grains of wisdom: Herder has in mind Quintilian's *Institutio oratoria*, a textbook on rhetoric.

Rollin: Charles Rollin (1661–1741), French historian and educator; Herder is presumably thinking of his *Traité des études, ou La manière d'étudier et d'enseigner les belles lettres* (1726–31).

Sulzer: Herder means Sulzer's pedagogical works: *Versuch von der Erziehung und Unterrichtung der Kinder* (Essay on the Education and Instruction of Children, 1748) and the *Vorübungen zur Erweckung der Aufmerksamkeit und des Nachdenkens* (Preliminary Exercises Designed to Awaken Attention and Reflection, 1768).

Haller: Albrecht von Haller (1708–1777), Swiss physiologist, botanist, and poet.

Withof: Johann Philipp Lorenz Withof (1725–1789), professor of rhetoric and didactic poet.

Lichtwer: Magnus Gottfried Lichtwer (1719–1783), German writer best known for his *Vier Bücher Äsopischer Fabeln* (Four Books of Aesopian Fables, 1748).

Kästner: Abraham Gotthelf Kästner (1719–1800), mathematician and author of ethical and aesthetic treatises.

Thou: Jacques-Auguste de Thou (1553–1617), French historian and magistrate.

Sarpi: Paolo Sarpi (1552–1623), Italian historian.

Trotzendorf's school: Valentin Trotzendorf (1490–1556) was, from 1531, the rector of a school in Goldberg, which he reformed along humanist lines. The running of the school was inspired by the model of the Roman state: as "consuls" and "censors," pupils played an active role in maintaining discipline.

mellitus . . . habitant: from Petronius: "Honey-balls of phrases, every word and act besprinkled with poppy-seed and sesame. . . . People who are fed on this diet can no more be sensible than people who live in the kitchen can be savoury" (*Satyricon* 1–2). The translation is by Michael Heseltine (London: Heinemann, 1961).

DOES PAINTING OR MUSIC HAVE A GREATER EFFECT? A DIVINE COLLOQUY

This essay was originally published in the first collection of the *Zerstreute Blätter* (Gotha, 1785). The text is based on *Ob Malerei oder Tonkunst eine größere Wirkung gewähre?* in *Sämtliche Werke*, ed. Bernhard Suphan (Berlin: Weidmann, 1877–1913), 15:222–40.

the Muses: According to Hesiod, the Muses were the nine daughters of Zeus and the titan Mnemosyne and goddesses of the arts and sciences who gave human artists their inspiration. They were Calliope (epic poetry), Clio (history), Euterpe (flute music), Terpsichore (dance and choral song), Erato (love poetry), Melpomene (tragedy), Thalia (comedy), Polyhymnia (sacred song), and Urania (astronomy). The Muses were linked with Apollo, who as the god of music and prophecy was their leader.

three strings: the early lyre had only three strings.

Memnon's statue: two colossal statues that are all that remain of a temple built by the pharaoh Amenhotep III in the fourteenth century BC. After the temple collapsed in an earthquake in the first century BC, one of the statues began to produce a musical sound at sunrise, presumably caused by dew heated by rapid changes in the morning-air temperature and escaping as steam through the narrow holes of the statue's broken surface. The Greeks believed the singing statue depicted Memnon, a king of Ethiopia and son of the dawn goddess Eos, who died at the hands of Achilles in the Trojan War. The sound was supposedly Memnon greeting his mother, Eos, who wept for the tragic death of her son. The statue was repaired by the Roman emperor Septimus Severus and ceased singing.

a mortal sage: the Greek philosopher and religious teacher Pythagoras, who believed in the importance of numbers as a guide to the interpretation of the world. He may have been led to this view by the discovery, attributed to him, of the musical relations corresponding to the principal intervals of the musical scale. Another doctrine associated with the Pythagorean school is the harmony of the spheres. It was believed that each planet, revolving around its ring or sphere, produced a musical note determined by its velocity and that these notes formed a scale, or *harmonia*.

carnation: flesh tones.

the wife of Brutus: Porcia, wife of Marcus Junius Brutus, consul of Rome and one of the conspirators against Julius Caesar. Cf. Plutarch's *Life of Brutus*: "As Porcia was about to return thence to Rome, she tried to conceal her distress, but a certain painting betrayed her, in spite of her noble spirit hitherto. Its subject was Greek—Andromache bidding farewell to Hector; she was taking from his arms their little son, while her eyes were fixed upon her husband. When Porcia saw this, the image of her own sorrow presented by it caused her to burst into tears, and she would visit it many times a day and weep before it" (23.2) (*Plutarch's Lives*, trans. Bernadotte Perrin, vol. 6 [London: Heinemann; New York: Putnam, 1918]).

Amphion: a son of Zeus and the nymph Antiope, the queen of Thebes. He was taught music by Hermes, who gifted him a beautiful golden lyre. When Amphion became king of Thebes, after exacting a terrible revenge on the usurping king Lycus, he fortified the city with a wall. When he played his lyre, the magic of his music caused the stones to move into place of their own accord.

Orpheus: son of Apollo and Calliope, the Muse of Epic Poetry, the greatest musician and singer of Greek mythology, whose songs charmed wild animals. Even stones and trees came to hear him play.

Linus: son of Amphimarus and the Muse Urania, a famous musician who was said to have been slain by Apollo because he had challenged him to a contest (Pausanias 9.29.6). A later story makes him the teacher of Heracles, by whom he was killed because he had rebuked his pupil for stupidity (Apollodorus 2.4.9).

Timotheus: Greek poet and musician (ca. 450–ca. 360 BC), who claimed to have introduced the use of eleven strings or notes on the kithara. His innovations met with sharp attacks in Athens and Sparta.

Phemius: singer in the household of Odysseus in Ithaca; he was forced to sing for the suitors and was pardoned by Odysseus.

Saint Cecilia: patron saint of music, whose feast day falls on November 22.

Scylla and Charbydis: Scylla was a sea monster who lived beneath a dangerous rock on one side of the Strait of Messina, opposite the whirlpool Charbydis. She threatened passing ships and in *The Odyssey* ate six of Odysseus's companions.

Pillars of Hercules: the ancient name for promontories flanking the east entrance to the Straits of Gibraltar; they were thought to mark the boundary of the navigable world.

Mnemosyne: daughter of Uranus and Gaea, the goddess of memory whose nine daughters fathered by Zeus became the Muses.

Lais: a beautiful and very expensive courtesan thought to have come from Corinth.

set Persepolis ablaze: According to the account of Curtius, Persepolis, the capital of the Persian Empire, was drunkenly destroyed by Alexander the Great at the instigation of Thais, a courtesan (*History of Alexander* 5.7.3–6).

ON IMAGE, POETRY, AND FABLE

This essay was first published in the third collection of *Zerstreute Blätter* (Gotha, 1787), pp. 87–190. The text is based on *Über Bild, Dichtung und Fabel*, in *Schriften zu Philosophie, Literatur, Kunst und Altertum, 1774–1787*, ed. Jürgen Brummack and Martin Bollacher, vol. 4 of Johann Gottfried Herder, *Werke* (Frankfurt am Main: Deutscher Klassiker Verlag, 1994), pp. 631–77. The appendix discussing Aristotle has been omitted here.

Protagoras: According to Plato in *Theaetetus*, Protagoras began his work *Truth* with the sentence "Man is the measure of all things" (161c).

intuitions *and* ideas, fancies *and* images, representations *and* objects: "intuition": in German, *Anschauungen*, from *schauen*, "to look or see"; "idea" is derived from the Greek εἶδος, "that which is seen," "form"; "fancy" or "fantasy" is derived from φαντασία, "a making visible," φαντάρζειν, "to make visible"; an "image" or "picture" (*Bild*) is obviously something seen; "representation" (*Vorstellung*) and "object" (*Gegenstand*) involve the sense of something placed before the eyes.

1. On Image

allegorizes: in the original sense of allegory (ἀλληγοραί): "Speaking otherwise than one seems to speak."

alloisizing: from αλλοιόω ("to change, alter").

the so-called confusion of the ode: a reference to Boileau's notion of the *beau désordre* of the ode expressed in his *Art poétique*. Mendelssohn had spoken in the *Letters Concerning Recent Literature* (275th letter) of the "higher order" of the ode "which may be concealed but never neglected."

I shall save for an analysis of the allegory: Herder returns to the topic in *Adrastea* (*SWS* 23:309–29).

2. On Poetry

prosopopoeia: a rhetorical figure by which an inanimate or abstract thing is represented as a person; a personification.

Personifications are . . . ignorance: for example, by Bernard Le Bovier de Fontenelle in *De l'origine des fables* (1727) and Antoine Banier in *Mythologie et les fables expliquées par l'histoire* (1738–40).

nympheum: Properly speaking, a *nympheum* is a grotto or shrine dedicated to a nymph. Herder is using the term in the sense of "museum" or "anthology."

Polonius: *Hamlet*, 2.2.207.

The oldest mythology . . . laws of Nature: Here Herder is indebted to the ideas of Christian Gottlob Heyne, who in his commentary on Apollodorus (*Ad Apollodori Atheniensis Bibliothecam*, 1783) distinguishes two kinds of primitive mythology: the philosophical, which seeks to explain nature, and the historical, which serves as a record of ancient history. Herder is concerned almost exclusively with the first kind.

Man invents . . . *poverty*: Both William Warburton (*The Divine Legation of Moses*, 1738–41) and Heyne cite the early poverty of human language as the prerequisite for mythology and fabular poetry. The fable developed after an initial phase in which human beings communicated by means of symbolic actions and gestures.

the Peruvian: Cf. the Peruvian poem "An die Regensgöttin" (To the Goddess of Rain), in *Volkslieder* (Folk Songs), *SWS* 25:469–70.

3. On the Aesopian Fable

analogon rationis humanae: the "analogue of human reason"; the form of cognition based on perception and memory which Leibniz attributed to the animals.

on the border between poetry and morality: An allusion to Lessing's preface to his *Fables*: "Es gefiel mir auf diesem gemeinschaftlichen Raine der Poesie und Moral" (This common border of poetry and morality pleased me) (*Sämtliche Schriften*, ed. Karl Lachmann, 23 vols. [Stuttgart: Göschen, 1886–1924], 7: 415).

"they say": "The ancients . . . liked to begin their fables with φασι ['they say']" (Lessing, *Fables*, in *Sämtliche Schriften*, 7:449).

the witty ass will become the moralist: in Lessing's fable "Aesop and the Ass": "The ass said to Aesop: 'If you bring out another little story about me, then at least let me say something quite sensible and witty.' 'You say something witty!' said Aesop. 'How would that be proper? Would people not say that you are the moralist and I the ass?'"

The human soul . . . dispersed . . . fashion . . . whole: Herder is reinterpreting a motif that was prevalent in poetry and the theory of the fable since La Fontaine. See Breitinger: "The ancients wrote that when Prometheus wanted to create man, he took from each animal its predominant inclination and from such diverse elements assembled our human race; that is how the work arose that one calls the microcosm. Thus the fables are a canvas upon which everyone can find his likeness" (*Critische Dichtkunst*, 1:205).

Menenius Agrippa: The apologue is recounted in Livy 2.32.8–12.

Triller: The fable in question is not in fact by Daniel Wilhelm Triller (1695–1782), author of *Neue äsopische Fabeln* (New Aesopian Fables, 1737); instead, it appears in the anonymous *Neue Fabeln und Erzählungen* (New Fables and Tales, 1749), p. 18.

the various classifications of the fable: Herder criticizes not typologies of the fable as such but those which are based on the nature or treatment of the characters. This mode of analysis goes back to Aphthonius, who distinguishes between rational (human), moral (animal), and mixed fables. Christian Wolff, in his *Philosophia practica universalis*, modified this classification, as did Lessing, in whose third essay on the fable ("On the Classification of Fables") the first six types mentioned here can be found. This is one of the rare occasions when Herder allows himself a gibe at Lessing's expense. Breitinger discusses Aphthonius, Wolff, and Lessing in section 7 of *Lessingische unäsopische Fabeln* (Lessing's Un-Aesopian Fables). The division according to the degrees of the wondrous is made by Breitinger in *Critische Dichtkunst*. *Figmenta vera* and *figmenta heterocosmica* ("tales from the real" and "tales from a possible world") are Baumgarten's terms, which Breitinger applied to the fable.

the allegorical beings of the fable: that is, the personifications.

the parable of Nathan: 2 Samuel 12:1–10.

Stesichorus: See Aristotle *Rhetoric* 2.20.5.

Kalila and Dimna: an Indian collection of fables.

enthymemes: imperfect or contracted syllogisms.

scattered leaves: the title of Herder's collection in which this essay originally appeared (*Zerstreute Blätter*).

Just as Lessing . . . schools: in his fifth essay, "On a Particular Use of Fables in Schools."

The elder Aesop's method: as opposed to that of the younger Aesop, that is, Lessing.

to what extent one can ascribe allegory *to the fable*: Lessing discusses this question in the essay "On the Essence of the Fable."

the term clothing: Lessing had criticized the idea that the moral of the fable was *déguisée* or *caché* in favor of the notion that it should be susceptible to "intuitive cognition."

Since ancient times men: Herder is alluding to the story of how the fable arose as recounted by Lichtwer in the first edition of his *Vier Bücher Aesopischer Fablen* (Four Books of Aesopian Fables, 1748). Since the loss of primordial Wisdom and Candor, naked Truth no longer has a place in the world and must hence clothe herself in the dress of Lie (that is, fictional allegory).

court dress of Truth: after Gleim's poem "Die reisende Fabel" (The Journey of the Fable). The Fable receives new clothes as she travels from Greece (Aesop) to Rome (Phaedrus) and finally to Paris, where La Fontaine dresses her in the most splendid gown yet at the court of Louis XIV.

"mutato nomine . . . narratur": "Change but the name, and the tale is told of you" (Horace *Satires* 1.1.69–70).

Hoc amat obscurum; amat hoc sub luce videri: adapted from Horace's *Ars poetica*: "This loves the shade, that loves to be seen in the light" (363).

Example, comparison, and fable: as discussed by Aristotle in *Rhetoric* 2.20.

as the philosopher did: Pyrrho, according to Diogenes Laertius 9.68: "When his fellow-passengers on board a ship were all unnerved by a storm, he kept calm and confident, pointing to a little pig in the ship that went on eating, and telling them that such was the unperturbed state in which the wise man should keep himself" (trans. R. D. Hicks [London: Heinemann, 1927]).

Bibliography

Adler, Hans. 1990. *Die Prägnanz des Dunklen: Gnoseologie-Ästhetik-Geschichtsphilosophie bei Johann Gottfried Herder*. Hamburg: Felix Meiner.

Baumgarten, Alexander. 1954. *Reflections on Poetry: Meditationes philosophicae de nonnullis ad poema pertinentibus*. Translated by Karl Aschenbrenner and William B. Holther. Berkeley: University of California Press.

———. 1983. *Theoretische Ästhetik: Die grundlegenden Abschnitte aus der "Aesthetica" (1750/1758)*. Hamburg: Felix Meiner.

Beck, Lewis White. 1969. *Early German Philosophy: Kant and His Predecessors*. Cambridge, MA: Harvard University Press.

Begenau, Heinz. 1956. *Grundzüge der Ästhetik Herders*. Weimar: Hermann Böhlaus Nachfolger.

Berlin, Isaiah. 1976. *Vico and Herder*. London: Hogarth Press.

Brummack, Jürgen. 1987. "Herders Theorie der Fabel." In *Johann Gottfried Herder, 1744–1803*, ed. Gerhard Sauer, 251–66. Hamburg: Felix Meiner.

Cassirer, Ernst. 1951. *The Philosophy of the Enlightenment*. Boston: Beacon Press.

Clark, Robert T., Jr. 1946. "Hamann's Opinion of Herder's *Ursachen des gesunkenen Geschmacks*." *MLN* 61: 94–99.

———. 1955. *Herder: His Life and Thought*. Berkeley: University of California Press.

Eagleton, Terry. 1990. *The Ideology of the Aesthetic*. Oxford: Blackwell.

Fugate, Joe K. 1966. *The Psychological Basis of Herder's Aesthetics*. The Hague: Mouton.

Gabler, Hans-Jürgen. 1982. *Geschmack und Gesellschaft: Rhetorische und sozialgeschichtliche Aspekte der frühaufklärerischen Geschmackskategorie*. Frankfurt am Main: Peter Lang.

Gessinger, Joachim. 1996. "'Das Gefühl liegt dem Gehör so nahe': The Physiological Foundations of Herder's Theory of Cognition." In *Johann Gottfried Herder: Academic Disciplines and the Pursuit of Knowledge*, ed. Wulf Koepke 32–52. Columbia, SC: Camden House.

Gross, Steffen W. 2002. "The Neglected Programme of Aesthetics." *British Journal of Aesthetics* 42:403–14.

Günther, Hans. 1903. "Johann Gottfried Herders Stellung zur Musik." Diss., University of Leipzig.

Hammermeister, Kai. 2002. *The German Aesthetic Tradition*. Cambridge: Cambridge University Press.

Haym, Rudolf. 1877–85. *Herder nach seinem Leben und seinen Werken*. 2 vols. Berlin: Gärtner.

Heinz, Marion. 1994. *Sensualistischer Idealismus: Untersuchungen zur Erkenntnistheorie des jungen Herder (1763–1778)*. Hamburg: Felix Meiner.

Henry, Harald. 1941. *Herder und Lessing: Umrisse ihrer Beziehung*. Würzburg: Triltsch.

Huber, Kurt. 1936. "Herders Begründung der Musikästhetik." *Archiv für Musikforschung* 1:103–22.

Irmscher, Hans-Dietrich. 1987. "Zur Ästhetik des jungen Herder." In *Johann Gottfried Herder, 1744–1803*, ed. Gerhard Sauder, 43–76. Hamburg: Felix Meiner.

Jacoby, Günther. 1907. *Herders und Kants Ästhetik.* Leipzig: Dürrsche Buchhandlung.

Koepke, Wulf, ed. 1996. *Johann Gottfried Herder: Academic Disciplines and the Pursuit of Knowledge.* Columbia, SC: Camden House.

Lippman, Edward. 1992. *A History of Western Musical Aesthetics.* Lincoln: University of Nebraska Press.

Markwardt, Bruno. 1925. *Herders Kritische Wälder: Ein Beitrag zur Kunst- und Weltanschauung des jungen Herder.* Leipzig: Quelle und Meyer.

May, Kurt. 1923. *Lessings und Herders kunsttheoretische Gedanken in ihrem Zusammenhang.* Berlin: Ebering.

Mendelssohn, Moses. 1997. *Philosophical Writings.* Translated by Daniel O. Dahlstrom. Cambridge: Cambridge University Press.

Murray, Penelope, ed. 1989. *Genius: The History of an Idea.* Oxford: Blackwell.

Nisbet, H. B. 1970. *Herder and the Philosophy and History of Science.* Cambridge: Modern Humanities Research Association.

———. 1979. "Laocoon in Germany: The Reception of the Group since Winckelmann." *Oxford German Studies* 19:22–63.

Nisbet, H. B., and Claude Rawson, eds. 1997. *The Cambridge History of Literary Criticism.* Vol. 4, *The Eighteenth Century.* Cambridge: Cambridge University Press.

Noel, Thomas. 1975. *Theories of the Fable in the Eighteenth Century.* New York: Columbia University Press.

Norton, Robert E. 1991. *Herder's Aesthetics and the European Enlightenment.* Ithaca, NY: Cornell University Press.

Nufer, Wolfgang. 1929. *Herders Ideen zur Verbindung von Poesie, Musik und Tanz.* Berlin. Reprint, Nendeln: Kraus, 1967.

Reiss, Hans. 1994. "The 'Naturalization' of the Term 'Ästhetik' in Eighteenth-Century German: Alexander Gottlieb Baumgarten and His Impact." *Modern Language Review* 89:645–58.

Richter, Simon. 1992. *Laocoon's Body and the Aesthetics of Pain: Winckelmann, Lessing, Herder, Moritz, Goethe.* Detroit, MI: Wayne State University Press.

Riedel, Friedrich Just. 1767. *Theorie der schönen Künste und Wissenschaften: Ein Auszug aus den Werken verschiedener Schriftsteller.* Jena: Cuno.

———. 1973. *Briefe über das Publikum.* Vienna: Österreichischer Bundesverlag für Unterricht, Wissenschaft und Kunst.

Sauder, Gerhard, ed. 1987. *Johann Gottfried Herder, 1744–1803.* Hamburg: Felix Meiner.

Schings, Hans-Jürgen, ed. 1994. *Der ganze Mensch: Anthropologie und Literatur im 18. Jahrhundert.* Stuttgart: Metzler.

Schneider, Helmut J. 1996. "The Cold Eye: Herder's Critique of Enlightenment Visualism." In *Johann Gottfried Herder: Academic Disciplines and the Pursuit of Knowledge*, ed. Wulf Koepke, 53–60. Columbia, SC: Camden House.

Schümmer, Franz. 1955. "Die Entwicklung des Geschmackbegriffs in der Philosophie des 17. und 18. Jahrhunderts." *Archiv für Begriffsgeschichte* 1:120–41.

Schütze, Martin. 1926. "Herder's Conception of 'Bild.'" *Germanic Review* 1:21–35.

Shaw, Leroy R. 1960. "Henry Home of Kames: Precursor of Herder." *Germanic Review* 35:16–27.

Solms, Friedhelm. 1990. *Disciplina aesthetica: Zur Frühgeschichte der ästhetischen Theorie bei Baumgarten und Herder*. Stuttgart: Klett-Cotta.

Terras, Rita. 1972. "Friedrich Justus Riedel: The Aesthetic Theory of a German Sensualist." *Lessing Yearbook* 4:157–82.

Van Der Laan, James. 1990. "Herder's Essayistic Style." In *Johann Gottfried Herder: Language, History, and the Enlightenment*, ed. Wulf Koepke, 108–23. Columbia, SC: Camden House.

Wellbery, David E. 1984. *Lessing's Laocoon: Semiotics and Aesthetics in the Age of Reason*. Cambridge: Cambridge University Press.

Wilhelm, Richard. 1933. *Friedrich Justus Riedel und die Ästhetik der Aufklärung*. Heidelberg: Winters.

Wolf, Hermann. 1925. "Die Genielehre des jungen Herder." *Deutsche Vierteljahrsschrift für Literaturwissenschaft und Geistesgeschichte* 3:401–30.

Zammito, John. 2001. *Kant, Herder, and the Birth of Anthropology*. Chicago: University of Chicago Press.

Index